Foundations for Teaching

English Language Learners

Foundations for Teaching

English Language Learners

Research, Theory, Policy, and Practice

Third Edition

WAYNE E. WRIGHT

CASLON

Philadelphia

Caslon, Inc.
825 N. 27th St.
Philadelphia, PA 19130

caslonpublishing.com

9 8 7 6 5 4

Library of Congress Cataloging-in-Publication Data

Names: Wright, Wayne E. author
Title: Foundations for teaching English language learners : research, theory, policy, and practice / Wayne E. Wright.
Description: Third edition. | Philadelphia : Caslon, [2019] | Includes bibliographical references and index.
Identifiers: LCCN 2019002641 (print) | LCCN 2019006831 (ebook) | ISBN 9781934000373 (electronic book) | ISBN 9781934000366 (alk. paper)
Subjects: LCSH: English language—Study and teaching—Foreign speakers. | English language—Study and teaching—Technological innovations. | English language—Computer-assisted instruction. | Web-based instruction.
Classification: LCC PE1128.A2 (ebook) | LCC PE1128.A2 W75 2019 (print) | DDC 428.0071—dc23
LC record available at https://lccn.loc.gov/2019002641

Cover photograph: Rick Reinhard

Background graphic from popov48/stock.adobe.com

Printed in the United States of America.

Preface

Teaching English language learners (ELLs) is an integral part of K–12 education today in the United States. According to the National Center for Education Statistics, approximately 10% of the total U.S. student population is labeled ELL, with considerable variation across rural, suburban, urban, geographic, and socioeconomic contexts. Although states, teacher education programs, and districts require different coursework and competencies in ELL education, all educators—including general education and content-area teachers as well as literacy, special education, and English language development (ELD) specialists—share responsibility for ELLs. The third edition of *Foundations for Teaching English Language Learners: Research, Theory, Policy, and Practice* by Wayne E. Wright prepares all teachers to integrate ELLs into their classes, engage all students with rigorous standards-aligned curriculum and texts, promote the development of oral and written English for academic purposes, and get students to graduation. At the same time, this text shows teachers how to create enriching linguistically and culturally responsive classrooms and schools that benefit all students.

Educators need to remember that all ELLs are, in fact, multilingual learners who draw on all of the languages in their linguistic repertoires as resources for learning (García et al, 2016). However, not all multilingual learners are officially designated ELL. In many districts, the academic mainstream includes a large population of "English speakers" who also speak languages other than English at home. Today, we find more multilingual learners—from more diverse backgrounds, enrolled in more classrooms, more schools, and more districts throughout the United States—than ever before. Approximately 22% of children in the United States speak a language other than English at home (Annie C. Casey Foundation, 2016), and more than 350 different languages are represented, including many indigenous languages (U.S. Census Bureau, 2015). Critics argue that defining "ELLs" or "English speakers" simply in terms of English renders the home languages of these students invisible in the general education classroom. The third edition of *Foundations for Teaching English Language Learners* encourages a strong language-as-resource orientation, not only for ELLs, but for all students.

New to the Third Edition

Much has changed in demographics, research, theory, policy, and practice since the second edition of this book was published. The third edition updates, reviews, synthesizes, and critiques each of these areas as they relate to ELLs.

A greater focus in the field on sociocultural and bilingual approaches to teaching ELLs is continuing to challenge traditional beliefs and assumptions and has resulted in new research and emerging theories to guide practice. Readers familiar with the second edition will find in this third edition an even greater focus on viewing students, learning, and teaching through a bilingual lens. Awareness of and attention to translanguaging, the everyday language practices of bilinguals, (García, 2009) has been growing rapidly. New research has informed attempts to build frameworks that use translanguaging as a pedagogical tool to enable students to draw on all of their linguistic resources during new academic content-area instruction (García et al, 2016). Thus, translanguaging is interwoven throughout all chapters, with special attention in a renamed and revised Chapter 11 to dive deeper into what constitutes a translanguaging pedagogy, the research supporting it, and specific translanguaging strategies teachers can leverage in the classroom.

The transition from No Child Left Behind (NCLB) to the Every Student Succeeds Act (ESSA) of 2015 has led to important changes in policy and accountability requirements, which are reflected in significant revisions to Chapters 4 and 6. For example, ESSA grants states greater flexibility in assessing ELLs. The accountability systems are more sophisticated and afford states the opportunity to set more reasonable achievement goals for ELLs that take into consideration their continuing growth. Most important, ELLs' progress in learning and attaining English language proficiency is now a central component of school accountability determinations. Now, more than ever before, schools must be attuned to the linguistic and academic needs of their ELLs. Other chapters have also been revised to reflect the new requirements, expectations, and practices of ESSA.

Other revisions reflect the current challenges school districts are facing with the implementation of the Common Core State Standards (CCSS) in English language arts and mathematics, the Next Generation Science Standards, or their states' own college- and career-readiness standards. Most states have abandoned multi-state consortia (such as PARCC and Smarter Balanced) to develop their own computer-based "next generation" assessments of the CCSS. In contrast, all but a few of the largest states are now members of one of the multi-state consortia that share common English language proficiency (ELP) standards and assessments (WIDA and ELPA21). This third edition includes examples of ELP standards and language progressions from WIDA and ELPA21, and from non-consortia states such as California, New York, and Texas.

We have also seen a great increase in bilingual education, particularly in dual language bilingual education programs that promote (1) bilingualism and biliteracy; (2) academic achievement in two languages; and (3) sociocultural competence for students from minority language homes, English-speaking homes, or both. California's Proposition 227 was overturned by Proposition 58, and Massachusetts's Question 2 was overturned by the LOOK Act, thus removing restrictions on bilingual education in those states. Dual language programs are growing in popularity across the country, with 1,703 dual language programs registered at the time of this writing (duallanguageschools.org, 2019). Furthermore, over 70% of the states now offer some form of the Seal of Biliteracy to recognize graduating seniors with demonstrated bilingual and biliteracy skills, and most remaining states are in various stages of seeking approval for the seal. New sections have been added throughout the book to address these developments.

Other new theories, concepts, and items of research are interwoven throughout the book. Chapters focused on language and content-area instruction (Chapters 7–10) are grounded in the findings of the latest research synthesis conducted by the National Academies of Sciences, Engineering, and Medicine in their 2017 report Promoting the Educational Success of Children and Youth Learning English: Promising Futures. The review of effective instruction in Chapter 11 includes and expands on the Teachers of English to Speakers of Other Languages (2018) set of six principles for the exemplary teaching of ELLs. Other new concepts, theories, and practices in this edition include ePortfolios, growth models, superdiversity, universal design, raciolinguistics, microaggressions, productive talk moves, bilingual assessments, translingual practice, language progressions, morphological awareness, evidenced-based writing, conversational discourse, challenges with online testing, culturally sustaining pedagogies, targeted support and improvement plans, intercultural communicative competence, theory of language as a human cultural invention and tool, one-way versus two-way models of dual language education, interdisciplinary and integrated views of the science of language, and many others.

Throughout the text, older references have been removed and hundreds of new references have been added to reflect the latest research and thinking in the field. Several boxes, tables, and figures have been revised or added. Recent books and articles have been added to the Recommended Reading at the end of each chapter. Several changes have been made to the Discussion Questions and Research Activities, many of which are integrated with new videos and other online resources. Also, the links to online resources in the text of each chapter have been updated and are fully accessible through a new companion website for this edition. Several chapter links and activities are integrated with the Purdue English Language Learner Language Portraits (Purdue ELLLPs), a new, free online resource developed by the author that was inspired by and developed to complement this book. The Purdue ELLLPs features over two dozen virtual ELL student portraits containing sociolinguistic profiles, video samples of oral language and reading, and samples of unedited writing, along with easy online access to the formative assessment tools highlighted in this book that can be used to assess the students' language proficiency. A QR code at the beginning of each chapter now makes it even easier for readers to quickly access a chapter's online resources (these appear in a second color) through the companion website on their smart phone or other mobile device.

Comprehensive, Learner-Centered Approach

Foundations for Teaching English Language Learners provides current and future educators with a solid foundation from which to make informed decisions regarding ELLs. The book takes a comprehensive, learner-centered approach to research, theory, policy, and practice. The special features of the book and the companion website facilitate prospective and practicing teachers' and administrators' learning about how to educate ELLs in their classes, schools, and communities. These features also support professors, instructors, and professional development providers who are responsible for ensuring that their students (i.e., teacher education candidates or participants in on-site professional learning configurations) develop the competencies they need in educating linguistically and culturally diverse learners.

The book begins by looking closely at who the students are, emphasizing the diversity represented by the English language learner designation. Prospective teachers are introduced to the challenges these learners face in school, as well as what they need to know and be able to do to address each learner's needs. Concrete examples of classroom practice illustrate key points. Samples of student work are included for discussion and analysis to give readers practical experience making the kinds of instructional decisions they will make as teachers.

Research

The practices, strategies, and techniques discussed throughout this book are firmly grounded in research. Each chapter provides a survey of what we know from scientific research related to the chapter content. These surveys include, for example, the findings of major national reviews of the literature on language and literacy instruction for ELLs.

Students are asked to look critically at the research, review the current controversies in the field, and identify gaps to be addressed. Activities at the end of chapters and on the companion website provide students with opportunities to make research-based decisions about what constitutes effective policies, programs, and practices.

Theory

Foundations for Teaching English Language Learners reviews theories of second language acquisition, language learning and teaching, literacy development, bilingualism, and sociocultural perspectives. Language and literacy development for academic purposes are important concerns, and the spectrum of second language and literacy approaches and methods are included. Readers see how the sociocultural context shapes learning and teaching as they analyze how different theories of language and literacy development are reflected in policies, programs, and practices. Readers are encouraged to develop their own approaches to providing effective instruction for ELLs based on the theories and research reviewed and synthesized in the text and in relation to the contexts of their own classrooms, schools, and communities.

Policy

Foundations for Teaching English Language Learners skillfully links macro language and education policy debates to the decision-making power that educators have within their local domains of authority. Chapters analyze the evolution of federal and state language education policy, review the range of program models that we find in schools, outline the essential components of effective programs, and introduce readers to the fundamentals of assessment and accountability. Special features in the book and on the companion website encourage readers to review and respond to these policies and to make decisions about appropriate policies, programs, and accountability systems for ELLs at the local district, school, and community levels.

Practice

Foundations for Teaching English Language Learners makes explicit connections among theory, research, policy, and practice. Chapters on oral language, reading, writing, content-area instruction, translanguaging, effective instruction, and advocacy begin by reviewing the research, theories of language and literacy learning, and policy debates surrounding the topic. Then, each chapter describes a range of research-based practices (i.e., approaches, methods, strategies, and techniques) that teachers can implement. This comprehensive, balanced approach equips prospective teachers with the knowledge and skills they need to provide equal educational opportunities for ELLs.

Special Features

Foundations for Teaching English Language Learners uses special features to structure student learning, teaching, and research. These features also facilitate course preparation for professors.

Guiding Questions

Each chapter opens with a series of questions that preview the concepts and practical focus of the chapter. Guiding Questions encourage users to read with a specific purpose in mind and to summarize and synthesize major concepts. These questions also prepare readers to apply what they learn in the chapter to ELL teaching and learning situations.

Key Terms

Key Terms listed at the beginning of each chapter offer a powerful way to approach the concepts discussed in the chapter. These terms are boldfaced and defined in the text. These terms also appear in the Glossary and on the companion website.

Figures, Tables, and Boxes

Every chapter is supplemented with summaries, photographs, illustrations, samples of student work, or resources for additional research and practice. This material is presented in figures, tables, and boxes that enhance the chapter content.

Discussion Questions

Five end-of-chapter Discussion Questions provide opportunities for students to reinforce their understanding of the material covered in the chapter, and to reflect on and apply chapter content to their own learning and teaching contexts. These include traditional questions, questions based on online videos, and questions based on analyzing an online document, such as a lesson plan or policy statement. Discussion Questions may be used for individual reflection or group discussions in traditional class sessions, in hybrid or online classes, or as homework assignments.

Research Activities

Research Activities offer students the opportunity to conduct short classroom-based, school-based, and online research projects on topics and issues discussed in the chapter. Professors can also ask students to expand any of these activities into larger culminating projects and incorporate them into their learning and teaching portfolios.

The Research Activities for each chapter are short and focused. These activities include an ELL Student Interview or Assessment, an ELL Teacher Interview, an ELL Classroom Observation, and an Online Research Activity. This design ensures that students in all types of learning situations (e.g., traditional classes with field observation components; brief summer courses with limited access to ELL students, teachers, and classes; online or hybrid courses) can easily complete at least one research activity.

Recommended Reading

The list of Recommended Reading at the end of each chapter, which includes books and journal articles, has been updated to reflect recent developments in the field. The readings are annotated with suggestions for the further study of topics presented in the chapter.

QR Codes for Easy Access

A QR code at the beginning of each chapter may be scanned by a smartphone or other mobile device to provide quick access to all online resources indicated in the book in a second color.

Companion Website

Foundations for Teaching English Language Learners includes an extensive companion website, which adds value by providing a space for professors and students to interact and collaborate beyond the traditional university class.

Students can use the companion website to participate in discussions about course topics with classmates and with other student communities around the country. Professors can give assignments and track students' activities on the site for evaluation purposes, saving the time of setting up assignments and discussion boards on other course management systems.

The companion website is organized into sections aligned with chapters of the book, and each includes resources that enrich student learning and facilitate professors' class preparation. Companion website users will find the following:

Links, highlighted in the book, to additional readings, professional organizations, useful teaching and learning resources, videos of instructional practices, and expert commentary

Downloads, including forms, templates, and review activities that students can complete and use to enhance learning

Discussion Questions that invite students to: share their thoughts, ideas, and experiences relevant to the chapter content; view and analyze related videos and documents; and read and comment on postings from other students

Research Activities are enriched on the companion website; students can upload and share their findings in multimedia formats through the incorporation of text, images, video, hyperlinks, and uploaded documents

Review Questions that students can complete online in a selected-response format, with results made available to students and course instructors

Professors' Resource Room

This feature is for professors only. The Resource Room provides professors with (1) tools for setting up class sections so students can self-register; (2) a control panel to quickly locate, assess, and comment on students' discussions, research postings, and activities; (3) slide presentations for each chapter for the professor's use in class; and (4) the Professor Café, where professors can interact and share resources.

Access to the Companion Website

Access to the companion website is included with every new copy of *Foundations for Teaching English Language Learners*. Professors and students can go to http://wright3ed .caslonpublishing.com and use the access code found with the book to register as a companion website user. Those with a used copy may purchase access to the companion website with this link.

Acknowledgments

First, I must acknowledge my former ELLs, who taught me about their strengths and unique language, academic, and cultural needs. Working in the Long Beach Unified School District afforded me numerous opportunities to learn from many outstanding administrators and teachers dedicated to providing high-quality instruction for ELLs: too many to list here, but you know who you are. Thank you!

This book is also a reflection of what I learned during my graduate training with many exceptional professors. In particular, I wish to thank my advisor, mentor, and friend, Terrence G. Wiley. Previous editions of this book were also made possible with the support of former students at the University of Texas at San Antonio (UTSA): James Knaack, Mariana Kuhl, Hsiao-Ping Wu, Pei-Yu Shih, Sun-Yun Yang, Elizabeth Hubbs, and Octavio Castro. My former UTSA colleagues gave helpful feedback and other assistance: Juliet Langman, Peter Sayer, Bertha Perez, Shannon Sauro, Francis Hult, Howard Smith, Patricia Sanchez, Becky Huang, Robert Milk, Belinda Flores, and Betty Merchant. At Purdue University I've also been blessed with strong support from colleagues, including: Phillip VanFossen, Janet Alsup, Maryann Santos, Trish Morita-Mullaney, Virak Chan, and Susan Britsch. Purdue students and staff provided valuable assistance with updates to the text and the companion website: Alsu Gilmetdinova, Chen Li, Marie Cinatl, Haiyan Li, and Emily Strudeman. The following students helped develop the Purdue ELL Language Portraits website, which was inspired by and now provides additional resources for this book: Marquetta Strait, Rudy Rico, Jieun Lim, Fang Gao, Samantha Miller, and Jeffrey Wright.

I am deeply indebted to my Purdue colleague Trish Morita-Mullaney, who led our effort to secure two large grants from the U.S. Department of Education to focus on ELL literacy and dual language bilingual education. Our work with ELL and bilingual teachers and families has led to many new insights and resources featured in this edition. I wish to thank the members of our research team: Ming Ming Chiu, Jennifer Renn, Anne Garcia, Susan King, Claudia Krogmeir, Alejandro Rodriguez de Jesús, Haiyan Li, Rong Zhang, Woongsik Choi, Annamarie King, and Breeah Carey. Thank you also to Star Watanaphol for the photos which appear in this edition, and to teacher Luzelena Ortiz-Lopez and students Catherine, Brennen, Emma, Jeffrey, and Thomas for appearing in the photos. And a big thanks to teacher Tiffany Jenkins and her ESL students for their help making videos for the SOLOM-R practice.

I owe a great deal of gratitude to my editor, Rebecca Field, for her enduring enthusiasm for this book and helpful feedback. Charles Field has been a constant source of encouragement and guidance. Debby Smith, with her amazing eye for detail, was instrumental in helping proofread the final drafts of the first, second, and third editions. Nancy Lombardi, Lisa Green, and others associated with Caslon have contributed in many unseen ways to the production of this book.

Finally, I wish to thank my dear wife, Phal Mao Wright, and our three amazing children, Jeffrey Sovan, Michael Sopat, and Catherine Sophaline Wright. Their experiences as students and learners have given me new perspectives on education. I appreciate their love and patience, their role as unpaid consultants, and their willingness to be neglected as I spent many late nights writing and revising.

Contents

One **Who Are English Language Learners?** 1

Key Terms
Guiding Questions

Who Are English Language Learner Teachers? 2
Defining and Identifying English Language Learners 3
Labeling English Language Learners 4
Historical and Current Demographic Trends 6
Diversity of English Language Learners 10
Home Languages 11
Levels of English Language Proficiency 13
Socioeconomic Status 13
Educational Achievement 13
Special Education Considerations 17
Culture and Identity 18
Understanding Diversity Informs Effective Practice 23
Promoting Bilingualism on the Individual and Societal Levels 23
Learning More about Your English Language Learners 25

Summary 26
Discussion Questions 27
Research Activities 27
Recommended Reading 28

Two **Language** 29

Key Terms
Guiding Questions

What Is Language? 30
Why Teachers Need to Know about Language 30
Language Standards for All Students 31
What Teachers Need to Know about Language 33
Phonology 33
Morphology 33
Syntax 34
Semantics 35
Pragmatics 36
Lexicon 37
Spelling 37

What Does It Mean to "Know" a Language?   38
   Communicative Competence   38
   Register and Genre   39
   Social Practice and Discourse   39
   Language Variation   40
   Bilingualism and Translanguaging   41
Language for Academic Purposes   42
   Language for Academic Success in Language Arts, Mathematics, Science, and Social Studies   43
   Academic and Language Demands   45

Summary   47
Discussion Questions   47
Research Activities   48
Recommended Reading   48

Three Language Learning and Teaching   50
Key Terms
Guiding Questions

First Language Acquisition Theories   51
Second Language Acquisition Theories   51
   Cognitive Approaches to Second Language Acquisition   52
   Sociocultural Perspectives on Language Learning and Teaching   57
All Teachers Are Language Teachers   61
Traditional Second Language Teaching Approaches and Methods   62
   Grammar-Translation Method   62
   Audiolingual Method   62
   Natural Approach   63
   Communicative Language Teaching   63
   Content-Based Instruction   64
   Whole Language, Multiple Intelligences, and Cooperative Learning   64
   Critical Pedagogy   65
   Beyond Approaches and Methods   65

Summary   66
Discussion Questions   67
Research Activities   67
Recommended Reading   68

Four Language and Education Policy   69
Key Terms
Guiding Questions

Historical Perspective   70
Evolution of Federal Policy for English Language Learners   74
   Title VII Bilingual Education Act (1968–2002)   74
   No Child Left Behind (2002–2016)   75
   Obama Administration and Federal Education Policy   76
   Every Student Succeeds Act (2015–Present)   77

State-Led Initiatives and Consortia   82
  Common Core State Standards Initiative   82
  Common Core State Standards Assessment Consortia   84
  English Language Proficiency Assessment Consortia   85
State Policies for English Language Learners   85
Important Court Decisions and Legislation   87
Language Policy at the Local Level   88

Summary   90
Discussion Questions   90
Research Activities   91
Recommended Reading   91

Five
Instructional Models and Programs   92
  Key Terms
  Guiding Questions

Evolving Perspectives   94
Essential Components of Instructional Programs for English Language
  Learners   94
  English as a Second Language   94
  Content-Area Instruction   96
  Bilingual Strategies   98
  Difference between English as a Second Language and Sheltered Instruction   99
  Relationship between English as a Second Language and English Language Arts   101
Program Models for English Language Learners and Other Multilingual
  Learners   101
  Bilingual Models   102
  English-Medium Models   112
Typology of Program Models for English Language Learners   118
Collaboration among English as a Second Language, Bilingual, Sheltered English
  Immersion, and Mainstream Teachers   121
Determining the Most Appropriate Instructional Programs for Your School   121

Summary   123
Discussion Questions   123
Research Activities   123
Recommended Reading   124

Six
Assessment   125
  Key Terms
  Guiding Questions

Assessment Basics   126
  Summative and Formative Assessments   127
  Norm-Referenced and Criterion-Referenced Tests   127
  Reliability   129
  Validity   130
  Bias   132

Critical Look at Testing Requirements for English Language Learners   134
    Joint Standards for Educational Testing   134
    Content-Area Testing   135
    Language Proficiency Testing   141
    Consequential Validity   146
Alternative Authentic Assessments for English Language Learners   147
    Observation   148
    Performance Assessment   149
    Self-Assessment and Peer Assessment   149
    Portfolio Assessment   151
Need for Multiple Measures   152

Summary   153
Discussion Questions   154
Research Activities   154
Recommended Reading   155

Seven Listening and Speaking   156

Key Terms
Guiding Questions

What We Know from Research about Oral Language and English Language
    Learners   158
    Center for Research on Education, Diversity, and Excellence Report   158
    National Literacy Panel Report   160
    National Academies Report   161
Using Theory to Guide Decision Making   162
    Silent Period and Wait Time   162
    Teacher Talk in the Classroom   163
    Correcting Student Speech Errors   164
    Productive Talk Moves   165
    Vocabulary Development   167
Using Standards to Focus Instruction   170
    Common Core State Standards for Speaking and Listening   170
    English Language Proficiency Standards for Listening and Speaking   171
Promoting Oral Language Development in the Classroom   173
    Listening   173
    Speaking   178
    Strategies for Classroom Interaction   180
Assessing Listening and Speaking   186

Summary   191
Discussion Questions   191
Research Activities   192
Recommended Reading   192

Eight **Reading**   193

Key Terms
Guiding Questions

Balanced Approach to Literacy Instruction   194
How Reading Promotes English Language Development   194
What We Know from Research about Reading Instruction for English Language
  Learners   196
Common Core State Standards for Reading   200
  Major Shifts for English Language Arts and Literacy   200
  Text Complexity   202
Promoting Reading Development for English Language Learners   203
  Vocabulary Development through Reading   203
  Using English Language Development Standards to Guide Reading Instruction   206
  Selecting Texts   207
  Structuring Activities   207
  Reading to, with, *and by English Language Learners*   207
  Reader's Workshop   219
  Postreading Activities   219
  Strategies for Reading across the Curriculum   222
  Reading Digital Texts   222
Assessing Reading   224
  Concepts of Print Checklists   224
  Running Records   224
  Reading Self-Assessments   230
Summary   230
Discussion Questions   231
Research Activities   232
Recommended Reading   232

Nine **Writing**   233

Key Terms
Guiding Questions

What We Know from Research on Writing Instruction for English Language
  Learners   234
Theoretical Frameworks for Second Language Writing and Translingual
  Practices   236
Relationship between Reading and Writing   237
Stages in English Language Learner Writing Development   238
Common Core State Standards for Writing   241
Promoting Writing Development for English Language Learners in the
  Classroom   243
  Using English Language Proficiency Standards to Guide Writing Instruction   243
  Writing to, with, *and by English Language Learners*   243
Writing across the Curriculum   257

Writing with Technology   258
   Word Processing   259
   Online Message Boards   260
   Key Pals (E-mail and Instant Messaging)   260
   Multimedia Presentations   260
   Blogs, Tweets, and Wikis   261
   Digital Storytelling   261
   Txtng Language Use   262
Home-School Writing Connection   263
Assessing Writing   264
   Standardized High-Stakes Writing Exams   264
   Classroom-Based Writing Assessment   265

Summary   270
Discussion Questions   270
Research Activities   271
Recommended Reading   271

Ten Content-Area Instruction   272

Key Terms
Guiding Questions

Principled Approach to Teaching Content to English Language Leaners   273
   Differentiated Instruction for English Language Learners in Content-Area Classes   273
   Language and Content-Area Objectives   274
   Using English Language Proficiency Standards to Guide Content-Area Instruction   275
   Strategies for Modifying Textbooks and Instructional Materials   276
   Thematic Teaching and Lesson Planning   276
   Use of Literature across the Content Areas   278
   Multicultural Perspectives   278
Sheltered Instruction in the Content Areas   278
   Mathematics   279
   Science   283
   Social Studies   291
   Art, Music, and Physical Education   297
Assessing the Content Areas   299

Summary   299
Discussion Questions   300
Research Activities   301
Recommended Reading   301

Eleven Translanguaging, Effective Instruction, and Advocacy for English Language Learners   302

Key Terms
Guiding Questions

Support for a Translanguaging Pedagogy   303
   Translanguaging Strategies   306

Effective Programs and Advocacy for English Language Learners   313
    Providing Effective English Language Learner Programs   313
    Advocating for English Language Learners   316
    Increasing Opportunities for Parental Engagement   319
Action Research   321

Summary   323
Discussion Questions   323
Research Activities   324
Recommended Reading   325

    Glossary   327
    Youth and Children's Literature   334
    References   335
    Index   347

Foundations for Teaching

English Language Learners

One

Who Are English Language Learners?

English learners fully and meaningfully access and participate in a twenty-first century education from early childhood through grade twelve that results in their attaining high levels of English proficiency, mastery of grade-level standards, and opportunities to develop proficiency in multiple languages.

—CALIFORNIA ENGLISH LEARNER ROADMAP

KEY TERMS

- additive bilingualism
- assimilationist discourses
- culturally sustaining pedagogies
- dual language learner
- dynamic bilingualism
- emergent bilingual
- English language leaner
- heritage language
- language-as-problem orientation
- language-as-resource orientation
- language majority student
- language minority student
- multilingual learner
- multi-tiered systems of support
- pluralist discourses
- redesignation
- response to intervention
- sequential bilingualism
- simultaneous bilingualism
- special education
- subtractive bilingualism
- superdiversity

GUIDING QUESTIONS

1. What kinds of diversity do we find within the category "English language learners"?
2. What are the pros and cons of different labels for English language learners?
3. Where do we find English language learners in the United States, in the past and today?
4. Why do teachers need to know specific information about their English language learners' home languages and literacies, English language proficiency, educational histories, and sociocultural experiences?
5. How can teachers learn about their English language learners' backgrounds?

An **English language learner (ELL)** is a student who is in the process of attaining proficiency in English as a new, additional language. Despite the unifying label, ELLs are an extremely diverse group. Consider each of the following students, all of whom are officially classified as ELLs by their schools:

Sonia, a kindergarten student, was born in Ukraine. Her family left Ukraine because of the revolution and mounting civil unrest there. They arrived in the United States when Sonia was 4 years old. Her father is a graduate student and speaks English well. Her mother is a maintenance worker and can speak a little English. Her parents prefer to speak Ukrainian and Russian at home. Sonia was exposed to all three languages but speaks mostly English and Russian with her three older brothers.

Zoey, a kindergarten student, was born in Indiana. Her father is from Puerto Rico and manages a local sporting goods store. Her mother is from Mexico and works as a cashier. Both parents speak English well and use both Spanish and English at home.

Brittany, a 1st grade student, was born in Argentina. She arrived in the United States last year with her mother. Though her mother speaks English well, she prefers to speak

1

Spanish with Brittany at home. Brittany attended kindergarten in Argentina but did not fully develop her reading and writing skills in Spanish.

Josue, a 6th grade student, was born in California. After kindergarten, he moved back to Mexico with his family for 2 years. When he was 7 years old, his family came back to the United States. Josue's father works in construction and his mother is a stay-at-home mom. Both parents speak only a little English, and Josue speaks mostly Spanish with them and both Spanish and English with his younger brother.

Pedro, a 10th grade student, was born in Panama and has been in the United States for only 4 months. His parents do not speak any English. Pedro was born deaf but has cochlear implants. He functions well in the hearing world, but his hearing disability affects his pronunciation. Pedro was a strong student at good schools in Panama, where he learned both Spanish and Portuguese at home and at school. He is now making rapid progress in English.

Ziyi, a 10th grade student, was born in China. She came to the United States when she was 5 years old. She never attended school in China and began her schooling in the United States in the 1st grade. Her parents work at a large Chinese buffet restaurant. Ziyi has an older sister and the family speaks mainly Chinese at home.

You can meet these students and view detailed profiles of their oral language and literacy skills in English on the companion website. Their profiles are just a small sample of the great diversity among ELLs. ELLs vary widely by race, ethnicity, home language, level of schooling, socioeconomic status, parents' level of education, parents' proficiency in English, proficiency and literacy in their home language, and proficiency in English. Many ELLs have had limited access to education, and some may have experienced disruptions in their education in their home countries or in refugee camps. Some have experienced war first hand. Others come from stable countries with access to high-quality education. Many ELLs have parents who have had limited or even no opportunities to attend school. Others have highly educated parents who may have some proficiency in English. Most ELLs are born in the United States, but the level of English spoken in their homes varies considerably. Nonetheless, all of these students are classified as ELLs by U.S. schools if it is determined that they are not yet proficient in English.

Who Are English Language Learner Teachers?

In many schools, ELL students are typically assigned to English as a second language (ESL) teachers or specialists who pull students out of their classrooms, go into their classrooms a few hours a week to provide instruction and support, or teach self-contained ESL classes all day or for one or more periods a day. It has become clear, however, that all teachers are ELL teachers, because all share in the responsibility of meeting the language and academic needs of ELLs. ELL students' success is ensured when generalists (mainstream), ESL, bilingual, **special education**, subject-area teachers and specialists, and administrators work together to use sound theory, research-based principles, flexible frameworks, and authentic evidence to inform their decisions about programs, curriculum, instruction, and assessment. Thus, this book aims to help all teachers in various roles gain the foundational knowledge and skills needed to work effectively with ELL students as they collaborate with other colleagues in their schools and districts.

ELLs are entitled to equal access to educational opportunities. This means they are entitled to (1) high-quality language instruction to develop proficiency in English and (2) high-quality academic instruction across the content areas. Both types of instruction are needed for ELLs to be successful in school and in society. Greater opportunities for success are provided when schools also help students develop and maintain proficiency in their home languages.

How educators choose to view their ELLs affects how they organize teaching and learning in their classes and how administrators structure programs in their schools and districts. Ruiz (1984) makes an important distinction between a **language-as-problem orientation** and a **language-as-resource orientation**. de Jong (2011) makes a similar distinction between schools that maintain **assimilationist discourses** and those that maintain **pluralist discourses**. Schools that maintain assimilationist (or monolingual) discourses devalue ELLs' home languages and cultures, seeing them as problems to overcome. More effective schools, in contrast, engage in pluralist (or multilingual) discourses by recognizing ELLs' home languages and cultures as rich resources for helping ELLs learn English and academic content, and they strive to help students develop high levels of proficiency and literacy in both languages. Even where bilingual programs are not feasible, teachers can still value the home languages of their ELLs and draw on them as resources. The approaches, methods, and strategies presented throughout this book are consistent with the pluralist perspective.

Defining and Identifying English Language Learners

In the Every Student Succeeds Act (ESSA), the federal government defines "English learners" as students who were not born in the United States or whose native language is a language other than English, and

> whose difficulties in speaking, reading, writing, or understanding the English language may be sufficient to deny the individual—(i) the ability to meet challenging State academic standards; (ii) the ability to successfully achieve in classrooms where the language of instruction is English; or (iii) the opportunity to participate fully in society.[1]

The actual process of identifying ELLs varies greatly from state to state and even from school district to school district within the same state.

Parents complete a home language survey when they enroll their children in school. The purpose of these surveys, which vary by state and school district, is to determine whether a language other than English is the primary language spoken at home and whether the student speaks that language. If the student does speak a language other than English at home, he or she is given a screening test to assess English language proficiency (ELP). These tests, like the surveys, vary across states and districts and are far from perfect. Because language proficiency is a complex construct, no single test can give a true measure of a student's actual proficiency in English, and different tests may give different results for the same student.

Even more problematic is determining when an ELL has attained enough proficiency in English to be redesignated as fluent English proficient. This **redesignation** means the student no longer requires specialized language and content instruction and is considered ready to participate in mainstream classes. Redesignation procedures also vary widely across school districts and states. Some rely on a single measure (the results of an English proficiency test), some also consider student scores on state standardized tests,

---

[1] Every Student Succeeds Act (ESSA), Pub. L, No, 114–95, 129 Stat. 1802 (2015), Title VIII, SEC. 8101, (20)(D).

and some consider subjective measures such as teachers' recommendations and evidence from formative assessments of student performance.

Because of the limitations of ELP testing, states and school districts have traditionally tried to err on the side of caution to ensure that ELLs receive the ESL instruction and other services to which they are entitled and that are necessary for academic success. In the early 2000s, many states created or adopted new statewide ELP standards, tests, and redesignation procedures to comply with federal requirements to identify ELLs and track their progress in learning and attaining proficiency in English. In some states, these tests underidentified ELLs or redesignated them before they were ready. Thus, many students were forced into mainstream classrooms before they attained the level of English proficiency necessary to succeed in those classrooms.

In the 2010s, states made further changes to ELP standards or tests to address new federal requirements. Currently, nearly all states are members of one of two state consortia with common ELP standards and tests. While state membership varies each year, most states joined the WIDA Consortium, while a much smaller number joined the English Language Proficiency Assessment for the 21st Century (ELPA21) consortium. A few states (e.g., California, Arizona, Texas, and New York) have developed their own ELP standards and assessments.

Although official ELP tests can be helpful, they provide only a snapshot of a student's performance at the date and time the test was given. A more dependable determination of an ELL's proficiency in English is the teacher's informed observations. Teachers who understand second language development and who engage in effective instructional and authentic assessment practices speak to their students and listen to them talk every day. They read with their students and ask them questions about what they read. They read their students' writing and discuss their work with them throughout the school year.

Labeling English Language Learners

One major issue in the field is the lack of consistency and agreement about what to call students who are not yet proficient in English. In this book you will most often see *English language learner* or *ELL*. First used by LaCelle-Peterson and Rivera in 1994, *ELL* has become the most commonly used term in the field. Sometimes shortened to *English learner (EL)*, this term is an improvement over the previous widely used label *limited English proficient (LEP)*. The LEP label was used in federal education policy for over 10 years under No Child Left Behind (NCLB). Most scholars in the field object to the word *limited* because it suggests a deficit in the students themselves or that their lack of proficiency in English is a permanent condition. Nothing in the LEP label indicates that students are actively learning and attaining proficiency in their new language. In recognition of these concerns, federal education policy under ESSA now uses the term *English learner*.

The ELL label has a more positive focus. It portrays students as actively learning English. The term, according to the scholars who introduced it,

> underscores the fact that, in addition to meeting all the academic challenges that face their monolingual peers, these students are mastering another language—something too few monolingual English-speakers are currently asked to do in U.S. schools. The term follows conventional educational usage in that it focuses on what students are accomplishing, rather than on any temporary "limitation" they face prior to having done so, just as we refer to advanced teacher candidates as

"student teachers" rather than "limited teaching proficient individuals," and to college students who concentrate their studies in physics as "physics majors" rather than as "students with limited physics proficiency." (LaCelle-Peterson & Rivera, 1994, p. 55)

Although *ELL* is a much better label than *LEP*, it has its own set of problems. First, aren't "native" English speakers also continuing their English language development? The Common Core State Standards, adopted by most states, include explicit language standards for all students. This inclusion points to the fact that even monolingual English-speaking students must learn new English vocabulary and they must learn how to read and write new genres as they move up in grade level. Furthermore, the category native English speaker includes students who speak a nonstandard variety of English (e.g., Chicano English, African American vernacular English or Ebonics) and who learn standard English at school.

Second, the term *ELL* focuses attention only on English. García (2009b) introduced the alternative term **emergent bilingual**, which is growing in acceptance and use. This term draws attention to the home language or languages in the linguistic repertoires of the students, along with their growing abilities in a new language (e.g., English) and situates them on a continuum of bilingual development. More important, the emergent bilingual label emphasizes that a fundamental goal of language education programs should be to help students attain high levels of proficiency in their home languages and English. García also uses the term **dynamic bilingualism** to emphasize that emergent bilinguals are not simply "double monolinguals" who keep their languages separate for different contexts. Instead, they draw on their range of languages in their linguistic repertoires in complex and dynamic ways with varying degrees of proficiency while engaging in interactions and academic tasks inside and outside of the classroom.

The emergent bilingual label also reflects the reality that many ELLs—the majority of whom are born in the United States—have grown up in homes where varieties of English and one or more other languages are used (Escamilla et al., 2013). Their **simultaneous bilingualism** is in contrast to **sequential bilingualism**, which may apply to newcomer ELLs who already speak the language or languages of their home country but then start to learn English as a new language at school. For example, four of the students introduced at the beginning of this chapter—Sonia from Ukraine, Brittany from Argentina, Pedro from Panama, and Ziyi from China—may be considered sequential bilinguals because they did not start learning English until after they arrived in the United States. In contrast, Zoey and Josue were born in the United States and grew up in homes where both Spanish and English are spoken. Thus, they would be considered simultaneous bilinguals. But the lines between simultaneous and sequential bilingualism can be fuzzy. Ziyi and Brittany came to the United States at very young ages (5 and 6) and thus moved into a more simultaneous bilingual context. Two of the students—Pedro and Sonia—come from trilingual families. Pedro was a simultaneous bilingual of Spanish and Portuguese and sequentially began learning English several years later. Sonia was a simultaneous bilingual of Russian and Ukrainian from ages 0 to 3 and became a simultaneous trilingual at age 4 after coming to the United States.

While many are embracing *emergent bilingual* as a replacement for the ELL label, it should be noted that not all emergent bilinguals are ELLs. The emergent bilingual label may also be used to refer to English-speaking students learning a new language in a bilingual immersion or dual language program, or to English-dominant students in a **heritage language** program. Caution should also be given to equating *bilingual* with *not English-proficient* or to suggesting that students with high levels of bilingual ability are simply "emerging." There is growing use of terms such as **multilingual learner**, which may capture a broader range of students who are bi/multilingual or who are learning, and learning through, more than one language.

The term **dual language learner** is now commonly used to refer to young children between the ages of 0 and 8 who have at least one parent who speaks a language other than English at home (Park, Zong, & Batalova, 2018). Following this definition, the Migration Policy Institute estimates about one third of the nation's children are dual language learners. Other scholars define dual language learners more narrowly as children under the age of 5, especially those participating in early childhood education programs (García & Markos, 2015). Many other labels have been and continue to be used to describe this same population of students. One commonly used term is **language minority student**, which covers all students in the United States who speak languages other than standard English, including nonstandard varieties of English. The term *minoritized* is now often used in place of *minority* to emphasize the effects of unequal power relations and the ways dominant groups marginalize some groups in society (Link, Gallo, & Wortham, 2017).

In contrast, **language majority student** refers to students who speak the dominant societal language, standard English. Although ELLs clearly are language minority students, care should be taken not to use the term *language minority students* when referring exclusively to ELLs. Language minority students may be proficient in English and may not have had opportunities to develop oral proficiency and literacy skills in their home language. Also, in increasing numbers of schools and communities across the United States, the majority of students are speakers of "minority" languages. Some use the term *culturally and linguistically diverse students* to refer to the combination of ethnic and linguistic minority students. Although this term avoids the minority label and calls attention to culture and language, it excludes standard English speakers who are white. Are these students not also part of the cultural and linguistic diversity of our schools?

The label *heritage language* comes from the field of world languages. Students from homes where a language other than English is spoken and who speak or at least understand some of that language may be labeled as heritage language speakers, regardless of whether they are ELLs or proficient English speakers. As a group, heritage language speakers have a wide range of linguistic and cultural expertise on which educators can readily build, and though some may be highly bilingual and biliterate, most have some degree of oral proficiency in their heritage language but cannot read or write it. Despite the positive qualities most people see in the term *heritage language speaker,* some have expressed concern that this label, with its emphasis on heritage, points more to the past than to the future (Wiley, 2014). The terms *community languages* and *community language speakers* may be better alternatives. These terms are used in Australia and in some European countries but have not caught on in the United States.

LEP, unfortunately, is the legal term that was used in federal legislation and in some state legislation for many years. Thus, this book uses *LEP* when discussing these historic policies and *ELL* in all other contexts. Teachers are encouraged to look critically at the ways language learners are described and evaluated in their schools and communities, as well as in the media, and to consider the implications of these labeling practices.

Historical and Current Demographic Trends

The United States has always been a nation of immigrants and continues to have high rates of immigration. According to the U.S. Census Bureau (2016), foreign-born immi-

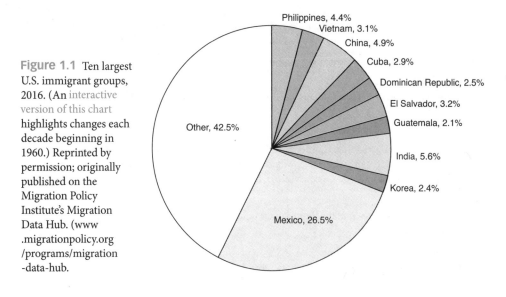

Figure 1.1 Ten largest U.S. immigrant groups, 2016. (An interactive version of this chart highlights changes each decade beginning in 1960.) Reprinted by permission; originally published on the Migration Policy Institute's Migration Data Hub. (www .migrationpolicy.org /programs/migration -data-hub.

grants made up about 13.2% of the U.S. population between 2012 and 2016. Although the absolute number of immigrants coming to the United States is at an all-time high, the percentage of the immigrant population is slightly lower than it was around the turn of the 20th century, when the immigrant population was as high as 14.8%. In the late 1800s and early 1900s, the vast majority of immigrants were from Europe and Canada, but now most immigrants are from Latin America and Asia. In 2013, India and China surpassed Mexico as the top countries of origin for recently arrived immigrants (Zong, Batalova, & Hallock, 2018). Figure 1.1 shows the countries of origin for the 10 largest immigrant groups in the United States.

Table 1.1 States with the Largest English Language Learner Populations, 2015–2016

State	No. of ELLs	Percentage of Total Student Population
California	1,307,804	21.0
Texas	892,082	16.8
Florida	268,189	9.6
New York	216,378	8.0
Illinois	194,040	9.5
Washington	112,763	10.4
Colorado	104,289	11.6
Virginia	109,104	8.5
Georgia	112,006	6.4
North Carolina	102,090	6.6

National Center for Educational Statistics, 2017.

Box 1.1 English Language Learners in U.S. Pre-K–12 Population, by State

Number of English Language Learners, 2014–2015 School Year

Over 80,000
California, Colorado, Florida, Georgia, Illinois, New York, North Carolina, Texas, Virginia, Washington

20,000–80,000
Alabama, Arizona, Arkansas, Connecticut, Indiana, Iowa, Kansas, Kentucky, Maryland, Massachusetts, Michigan, Minnesota, Missouri, Nebraska, Nevada, New Jersey, New Mexico, Ohio, Oklahoma, Oregon, Pennsylvania, South Carolina, Tennessee, Utah, Wisconsin

5,000–19,999
Alaska, Delaware, Hawaii, Idaho, Louisiana, Maine, Mississippi, Rhode Island, South Dakota, Washington, DC

Fewer than 5,000
Montana, New Hampshire, North Dakota, Vermont, West Virginia, Wyoming

According to analysis of U.S. Census and American Community Survey data by the Migration Policy Institute, in 2016 about 18 million children had at least one parent who was born outside the United States (Zong et al., 2018). These children of immigrants make up 26% of the total U.S. population under the age of 18. Thus, a little more than 1 in 4 are children of immigrants. A common misconception is that most children of immigrants are foreign born and that many are "illegal aliens." In reality, 88% of children of immigrants are U.S.-born citizens. Furthermore, between 2000 and 2016, the number of foreign-born children declined 21%, while the number of U.S. native-born children of immigrants increased by 53%. Undocumented immigrant children make up less than 2% of students. The growth in the number of children of immigrants plays an important role in preserving and increasing teaching positions and preventing the closure of many schools.

Another common misconception is that immigrants today are slow to learn English and that most children of immigrants have limited English proficiency. In reality, data from U.S. Census Bureau's 2016 American Community Survey reveals that slightly less than half (49%) of immigrants ages 5 or older have limited English proficiency. Among school-aged children (5–17) who speak Spanish or an Asian/Pacific Islander or Indo-European language at home, between 74% and 81% are proficient English speakers (U.S. Census Bureau, 2018). Only about one third of the children of immigrants are classified as ELLs, and most ELLs are U.S.-born citizens (Capps et al., 2006).

According to the National Center for Educational Statistics (2018), in the 2015–2016 school year, the total ELL enrollment was 4.8 million students. Nationally, ELLs make up about 9.5% of the total student population. About 75% of the ELL population is concentrated in just 10 states with populations ranging from 102,000 to over 1.3 million (Table 1.1). The ELL population is also substantial across the other states, with populations between 3,000 and 80,000 (Box 1.1).

A different picture emerges if we examine the density of the ELL population. In 28 states ELLs make up 6% or more of the total student population (Figure 1.2). Also revealing is the fact that in five states the ELL growth rate from 2009 to 2015 was over 40%, and 27 other states had growth rates between 1% and 39%. Nineteen states, including those with historically large numbers of ELLs, are seeing a decline in their percentage of

Box 1.1 *continued*

Percentage Change in Number of English Language Learners from 2000–2010 to 2014–2015

Increase: over 40%
Louisiana, Mississippi, Rhode Island, West Virginia, Wyoming,

Increase: 20%–40%
Arkansas, Delaware, Georgia, Iowa, Kansas, Kentucky, Maryland, Massachusetts, Michigan, Missouri, New Jersey, Oklahoma, South Carolina

Increase: 1%–19%
Alabama, Connecticut, Illinois, Indiana, Maine, Minnesota, Nevada, Ohio, Pennsylvania, South Dakota, Tennessee, Texas, Virginia, Washington

Decrease: 1%–19.9%
Alaska, California, Colorado, Florida, Hawaii, Montana, Nebraska, New Hampshire, New York, North Carolina, Utah, Vermont, Washington, DC, Wisconsin

Decrease: 20%–38%
Arizona, Idaho, New Mexico, North Dakota, Oregon

ELLs also make up a large percentage of students in the Commonwealths of Puerto Rico and the Northern Mariana Islands; in the U.S. territories of American Samoa, Guam, and the Virgin Islands; and in the Pacific Island nations in free association with the United States—the Federated States of Micronesia, Marshal Islands, and Palau.

Office of English Language Acquisition, 2017.

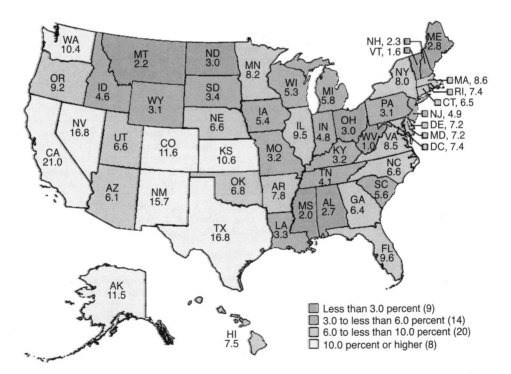

Figure 1.2 Percentage of public school students who were English language learners, by state: school year 2015–2016. U. S. average: 9.5 percent. (National Center for Educational Statistics, 2018.)

ELLs as families move around the country, bringing in new diversity to several states (see Box 1.1).

Because of the growth in the ELL population across the United States, it is imperative that all future and current classroom teachers and specialists receive the necessary training and certification to provide effective language and content instruction. As these numbers indicate, teachers will likely find ELLs in their schools and classrooms regardless of where they teach.

Diversity of English Language Learners

Research on ELLs' academic achievement, language development, and cultural integration highlights a range of sociocultural factors that influence success at school (National Academies, 2017). Although current accountability requirements do not mandate collecting data on students' prior schooling, cultural background, or home language and literacy practices, teachers of ELLs should have this critical information in order to address the needs of this diverse population.

The descriptions of the six ELLs at the beginning of this chapter illustrate why using a singular label to encompass the immense diversity among ELLs is problematic. ELLs

Table 1.2 Types of English Language Learners

Type	Description
Native U.S.-born ELLs	ELLs who are U.S.-born citizens. The majority of ELLs fall into this category.
Foreign-born ELLs	ELLs who were born outside the United States.
Indigenous ELLs	ELLs from Native American tribes.
Transnational ELLs	ELLs who frequently travel between the United States and their home country.
Newcomer ELLs	ELLs who have been in the United States for 1 to 2 years.
Highly schooled newcomer ELLs	ELLs who have been in the United States for 1 to 2 years but who obtained high-quality education prior to migration.
Refugee ELLs	ELLs who entered the United States with refugee status, often as a result of war or political persecution.
Students with interrupted formal education	Students who had limited to no access to schools in their home or previous countries, or whose education was interrupted because of war or civil conflict. Many refugee ELLs fall into this category.
Long-term ELLs	Students who remain classified as ELLs for 5 years or longer.
Special education ELLs	ELLs who are also identified as needing special education services.
Gifted and talented ELLs	ELLs who also qualify to participate in gifted and talented education programs.
Reclassified ELLs	Former ELLs who have met their state's linguistic and academic criteria to be exited from ELL programs and reclassified as fluent English proficient.

These categories are not exhaustive or mutually exclusive. An individual ELL may be in more than one category.

may be in any one of more than a dozen categories (Table 1.2). Of these six students, for example, Sonia, Brittany, and Pedro are foreign-born newcomer ELLs, while Zoey and Josue are U.S.-born ELLs. Josue is also a transnational ELL, and Ziyi may be considered a long-term ELL. Pedro may be considered both a highly schooled newcomer ELL and a special education ELL because of the speech and hearing services he receives at school in addition to ESL. These categories should not be used as additional official labels; rather, they are meant to help teachers understand the diversity of ELLs and implications for instruction.

This section explores the diversity of ELLs that teachers are likely to find in their schools. We begin with home languages, levels of English language proficiency, socio-economic status, and educational achievement. Next we explore special education considerations for ELLs, including the approach that should be followed to determine whether a student is in need of special education services. We then consider the cultural diversity of ELLs and issues that may impact their identity development. We conclude this section with a discussion on how an understanding of the diversity among ELLs is essential to inform effective practice.

Home Languages

The U.S. Census Bureau (2015) estimates approximately 350 different languages are spoken in the United States. Following English, Spanish is the second most common language. Spanish speakers, at over 3.7 million, make up over 80% of the ELL population. The other top nine languages spoken by ELLs have a combined total of 385,450 speakers (Table 1.3). State by state, however, 40 different languages make up the top five languages spoken by ELLs, and in the following five states, a language other than Spanish is most commonly spoken by ELLs: Alaska (Yup'ik), Hawai'i (Ilocano), Maine (Somali), Montana (German), and Vermont (Nepali) (NCELA, 2018).

Table 1.3 Languages Most Frequently Reported Spoken by English Language Learners, 2015–2016

Language	No. of ELLs
Spanish	3,714,066
Arabic	106,917
Chinese*	92,277
Vietnamese	68,221
Somali	27,516
Haitian	24,346
Tagalog	20,552
Hmong	19,422
Portuguese	14,502
Russian	11,697

*Includes Mandarin, Cantonese, and other Chinese languages.
Adapted from the Office of English Language Acquisition, 2018.

Box 1.2 Spanish-Speaking Countries and Territories

Spanish-speaking English language learners come from many different countries, including those listed here. In many of these countries, Spanish is the national language; others have a different official or dominant language but large Spanish-speaking populations. The United States is one of the top five Spanish-speaking countries in the world.

Andorra	Ecuador	Panama
Argentina	El Salvador	Paraguay
Belize	Equatorial Guinea	Peru
Bolivia	France	Philippines
Chile	Gibraltar	Puerto Rico
Colombia	Guatemala	Spain
Costa Rica	Honduras	Trinidad and Tobago
Cuba	Mexico	United States
Curacao	Morocco	Uruguay
Dominican Republic	Nicaragua	Venezuela

Simons & Fennig, 2018.

Even within the large group of Spanish-speaking ELLs, there is great diversity. A large number of ELLs (or their parents) are from Mexico, though many Spanish-speaking students or their families come from other countries. Spanish, like English, is a major international language. Worldwide, Spanish is spoken by over 442 million people as a native language, and an additional 70 million people speak it as a second language (Simons & Fennig, 2018). Spanish is an official language in countries in Europe; the Caribbean; and North, Central, and South America, and it is widely spoken as a second language in many other countries throughout the world (Box 1.2). Spanish, like English, varies from country to country and region to region. Just as English speakers from California, Texas, Boston, Australia, England, and New Zealand may speak a different variety of English, Spanish-speaking ELLs speak different varieties of Spanish, influenced by their or their family's country and region of origin, and the varieties they are exposed to in the United States.

It is important to recognize that though ELLs may come from a Spanish-speaking country, their home language may not be Spanish. A growing number of immigrant students come from indigenous groups within these countries and have their own unique languages and cultures. Educators also need to be aware of the great linguistic diversity masked by the label *Asian*. Hundreds of languages are spoken across 21 Asian countries. Likewise, black immigrant ELLs who come from wide variety of African and Caribbean countries bring considerable linguistic and cultural diversity and speak a wide range of languages (Park et al., 2018). The term **superdiversity** is now commonly used in multilingual contexts to describe diversity between and within immigrant and ethnic minority groups (Park et al., 2018). In other words, *superdiversity* emphasizes the diversity within diversity and considers many factors, including race, culture, language, ethnicity, education level, migration history, and socioeconomic status.

Students may vary widely in oral proficiency and literacy skills in their home languages. Many ELLs may speak a variety of their home language that differs from the standard variety. In addition, ELLs will typically have literacy skills in their home languages only if they have had the opportunity to learn to read and write them in school in their home country, or in the United States in a bilingual program or an afterschool heritage language program. Thus, for example, of the six students introduced at the beginning of the chapter, only Pedro would likely have "grade-level" literacy skills in Spanish. Josue also would have developed some literacy skills in Spanish when he moved to

Mexico and attended grades 1 and 2 before returning to the United States. Ziyi has maintained her Chinese speaking skills but can read and write only a few characters in Chinese after attending a weekend heritage language class for about a year.

Levels of English Language Proficiency

ELLs differ substantially in their level of English proficiency. The ELL label covers students from those who speak little to no English to those who are highly advanced and nearly ready to be redesignated as proficient. WIDA states use the consortium's six levels of English proficiency to describe what ELLs can do at each level (Table 1.4). ELPA21 states and nonconsortium states use different names and definitions for five levels of English proficiency. An understanding of what ELLs can do with oral and written English at these different levels of English proficiency is crucial if teachers are to provide effective language and content area instruction. The six students highlighted at the beginning of this chapter have a range of official (WIDA) overall English proficiency levels: Sonia, Brittany, and Pedro are at Level 2.8 (Emerging), Josue is at Level 3.5 (Developing), Ziyi is at Level 4.8 (Expanding), and Zoey is at Level 5.0 (Bridging). Consideration must be given, however, to domain-specific proficiency. For example, the K–1 students (Sonia, Brittany, and Zoey) have stronger oral language skills in English because their English reading and writing skills are just developing at these grade levels. Ziyi is also stronger in her listening and speaking skills, and it is mainly her reading and writing scores that have kept her classified as an ELL for many years. Some highly schooled newcomers study English as a foreign language before they come to the United States and often have stronger literacy skills in English than oral language skills. As these examples suggest, effective instruction would look quite different for these students because of the variations in their levels of English proficiency.

Socioeconomic Status

Berliner (2013) notes a consistent research finding that high rates of poverty are strongly associated with low levels of educational achievement. "Sadly," he says, compared with "all other wealthy nations, the USA has the largest income gap between its wealthy and its poor citizen" (p. 1). He identifies several out-of-school factors that affect the academic success of students living in poverty. Reardon (2011), in an analysis of decades of income and achievement data trends, found that the income gap between high- and low-income families has widened since the early 1960s and that the academic achievement gap between students from high- and low-income families has also widened. This income/achievement gap has increased, even as the achievement gaps along racial and ethnic lines have decreased. Reardon concludes that "family income is now nearly as strong . . . as parental education in predicting children's achievement" (p. 5). Estimates suggest that over 60% of ELLs come from low-income families (Capps et al., 2006). According to an analysis by the Migration Policy Institute (2016), 45% of limited English-proficient adults (ages 25 and older) lack a high school diploma, compared with 9% of English-proficient adults who lack a high school diploma. About 15% of limited English-proficient adults have a college degree, compared with 32% of English-proficient adults who do.

Educational Achievement

As these demographics reveal, the majority of ELLs are ethnic minorities from low-income families. Historically, the U.S. education system has done an inadequate job in providing equitable educational opportunities to poor and minority students. Today, despite tough talk about high standards and accountability and policies that claim to leave

Table 1.4 WIDA's CAN DO Descriptors for English Language Proficiency Levels, Pre-K–12

For the given level of English language proficiency, with support, English language learners can

Level 1 Entering	Level 2 Emerging	Level 3 Developing	Level 4 Expanding	Level 5 Bridging
Writing				
• Label objects, pictures, diagrams • Draw in response to a prompt • Produce icons, symbols, words, phrases to meaning	• Make lists • Produce drawings, phrases, short sentences, notes • Give information requested from oral or written directions	• Produce bare-bones expository or narrative texts • Compare/contrast information • Describe events, people, processes, procedures	• Summarize information from graphics or notes • Edit and revise writing • Create original ideas or detailed responses	• Apply information to new contexts • React to multiple genres and discourses • Author multiple forms/genres of writing
Reading				
• Match icons and symbols to words, phrases, or environmental print • Identify concepts about print and text features	• Locate and classify information • Identify facts and explicit messages • Select language patterns associated with facts	• Sequence pictures, events, processes • Identify main ideas • Use context clues to determine meaning of words	• Interpret information or data • Find details that support main ideas • Identify word families, figures of speech	• Conduct research to glean information from multiple sources • Draw conclusions from explicit and implicit text
Speaking				
• Name objects, people, pictures • Answer WH (who, what, when, where, which) questions	• Ask WH questions • Describe pictures, events, objects, people • Restate facts	• Formulate hypotheses, make predictions • Describe processes, procedures • Retell stories or events	• Discuss stories, issues, concepts • Give speeches, oral reports • Offer creative solutions to issues, problems	• Engage in debates • Explain phenomena, give examples, and justify responses • Express and defend points of view
Listening				
• Point to stated pictures, words, phrases • Follow one-step directions • Match oral statements to objects, figures, or illustrations	• Sort pictures, objects according to oral instructions • Follow two-step oral directions • Match information from oral descriptions to objects, illustrations	• Locate, select, order information from oral descriptors • Follow multi-step oral directions • Categorize or sequence oral information using pictures, objects	• Compare/contrast functions, relationships from oral information • Analyze and apply oral information • Identify cause and effect from oral discourse	• Draw conclusions from oral information • Construct models based on oral discourse • Make connections from oral discourse

Level 6 Reaching

Variability of students' cognitive development because of age, grade-level spans, diversity of educational experiences, and diagnosed disabilities (if any) are to be considered in using this information.

Courtesy of WIDA Consortium; 2012b, pp. 7–8.

no child behind, make every student succeed, or make all children college and career ready, there continues to be a wide gap in academic achievement between poor, minority, and ELLs and middle- to upper-class white students.

By the time NCLB came to an end, most states failed to meet their achievement targets for ELLs in learning and attaining English and in passing state reading and math tests (American Institutes for Research, 2012). Although these dismal results reflect major issues and flaws in NCLB's accountability system for ELLs, they nonetheless revealed that states were failing to meet the achievement expectations for ELLs.

The National Assessment of Education Progress (NAEP) also reveals low ELL academic achievement. On the 2017 NAEP reading test, 68% of grade 4 and 68% of grade 8 ELLs were below basic; only 9% of grade 4 and 5% of grade 8 ELLs scored at or above proficient; on the 2017 NAEP math test, 47% of grade 4 and 71% of grade 8 ELLs were below basic; only 14% of grade 4 and 6% of grade 8 scored at or above proficient.

In addition, despite some improvement, drop-out rates continue to be substantially higher for Latinx students than for white students. According to the National Center for Educational Statistics (2016), in 2015 the graduation rate for Latinx students was 78%, compared with 88% for white students. Graduation rates were even lower for Native American/Alaska Native students at 72% and African American students at 75%. The graduation rate was the highest for Asian and Pacific Island students at 90%.

Such data, however, can be misleading and feeds into the Asian American model-minority myth, which suggests that all Asian Americans students do well academically and Asian American families do well economically. A closer examination reveals that many Asian American students are struggling in school, many of their families live in poverty, and many continue to face discrimination. The Asian American model-minority myth has been widely criticized for masking the educational and linguistic needs of Asian American students, particularly Asian American students who are ELLs.[2] For example, many Hmong and Khmer (Cambodian) ELLs make slower progress than others in attaining proficiency in English and face academic challenges. Newcomer Karen, Karenii, Chin, and other refugee students from Myanmar (Burma), along with Bhutanese newcomer students arriving from Nepali refugee camps, are adding to the diversity of Asian American ELLs with substantial linguistic and academic needs. While the Asian American model-minority myth persists, scant attention has been paid to the fact that sub-Saharan African immigrants now have the highest rates of educational attainment compared with other immigrant groups (Zong & Batalova, 2017). But as with the myth about Asian American achievement, care must be taken to ensure that the needs of specific African immigrant ELLs are not masked by this broad-brush accolade of "success."

Schools are also seeing an increase in the number of students from Middle Eastern, Asian, and African countries, including refugees from Afghanistan, Bhutan, Burma, Burundi, Democratic Republic of Congo, Eritrea, Ethiopia, Iran, Iraq, Liberia, Rwanda, Somalia, Sudan, and Syria. Many of these Asian, African, and Middle Eastern refugee students have experienced the trauma of war and thus are students with interrupted formal education (Cohan & Honigsfeld, 2017). Many were subject to discrimination and may have been denied access to education in their home countries. Some may be entering school for the first time, while others may have had disruptions in their education because of war and limited schooling opportunities in refugee camps.

In the past, some researchers placed the blame for underachievement on the students and their families with claims of lower IQs and cognitive inferiority. Several scholars

---

[2] See Boun & Wright, 2013; Hartlep, 2017.

have thoroughly refuted these outdated claims.[3] Academic underachievement is better understood through the principle of opportunity to learn. Poor and minority students tend to be segregated in the most overcrowded and underfunded schools. A report from the U.S. Commission on Human Rights (2018) found that "the highest-poverty districts receive an average of $1,200 less per-pupil than the lowest-poverty districts, and districts serving the largest numbers of students of color receive about $2,000 less per-pupil than districts who serve the fewest students of color" (pp. 6–7). The commission laments:

> Although the United States Supreme Court ruled in 1954 that public education is a right that should be available to all on equal terms, the longstanding and persistent reality is that vast funding inequities in our state public education systems is a significant factor in rendering the education available to millions of American public school students profoundly unequal. (p. 105)

ELLs in particular tend to be highly segregated. In California, for example, more than half of the state's ELL students of elementary-school age attended just 21% of the state's public elementary schools, where they constituted more than half of the student body (Rumberger, Gándara, & Merino, 2006). Nationally, 70% of ELLs of elementary-school age attended only 10% of the country's public elementary schools (de Cohen, Deterding, & Clewell, 2005). The American Institutes for Research (2012) found that schools with high concentrations of poor and ELLs were least likely to meet federal academic achievement targets. The U.S. Commission on Human Rights (2018) reports that "low-income students and students of color are often relegated to low-quality school facilities that lack equitable access to [experienced] teachers, instructional materials, technology and technology support, critical facilities, and physical maintenance" (p. 105). These factors impact student academic achievement.

Researchers from Education Trust found that poor and minority children are about two times more likely than all other students to be assigned to a novice teacher, and that at the secondary level, they are more likely to be taught by teachers who lack expertise in the subject they teach, that is, teachers without a major or minor in that subject. In discussing these findings, the researchers note the irony of assigning students with the greatest needs to the least qualified teachers. They conclude:

> Public education cannot fulfill its mission if students growing up in poverty, students of color and low-performing students continue to be disproportionately taught by inexperienced, under-qualified teachers. These manifestly unequal opportunities make a mockery of our commitment to equal opportunity and undermine genuine social mobility. What we have is a caste system of public education that metes out educational opportunity based on wealth and privilege, rather than on student or community needs. (Peske & Haycock, 2006, p. 15)

Additionally, poor and minority students, as noted earlier, tend to have parents with low levels of education who are unable to provide assistance with difficult schoolwork or afford expensive supplemental educational services. Those whose parents do not know English have a further obstacle to learning. Many also live in low-income neighborhoods, where living conditions are crowded, crime rates are high, and access to good school and community libraries is minimal. These conditions can make finding quiet places to study, do homework, and obtain resources to complete school assignments a challenge. Krashen

---

[3] For examples of studies that place the blame for underachievement on students and their families, see Herrnstein & Murray, 1994; Jensen, 1995, 1998; Terman, 1916. For studies that refute these claims, see Fagan & Holland, 2002; Fish, 2002; Gould, 1981; Hakuta, 1986; Hout, 2002; Jencks & Phillips, 1998; Mensh & Mensh, 1991; Nisbett, 1998; Sacks, 1999.

(2014) has found strong correlations between school and community libraries and student reading scores—the better the libraries, the better the test scores. Thus, poor and minority students, who have little access to interesting books and other reading materials from libraries and whose families are less able to purchase books for their children to read for pleasure at home, read less and have lower reading scores than students from wealthier neighborhoods. For many ELLs, all of these factors are compounded by the fact that they are still learning English at the same time they are receiving instruction through this new language.

Although limited resources and the challenges of learning English may impede opportunities to learn, ELLs can learn and reach the highest levels of academic achievement. Teachers, administrators, and political leaders must therefore take these challenges into consideration when creating policies, designing programs, and making instructional decisions. They also should build on the considerable strengths that ELLs bring with them to school, including their home languages and the funds of knowledge they have access to in their homes. *Funds of knowledge*, a concept developed by Luis C. Moll and his colleagues, refers to the body of knowledge, cultural artifacts, and cultural resources that are present in students' homes and communities and can be drawn on as a basis for learning (González, Moll, & Amanti, 2005).

Special Education Considerations

Many educators question how to distinguish between learning disabilities and language difficulties in ELLs. A report commissioned by the U.S. Department of Education concludes, "No single method has proven effective in differentiating between English learner students who have difficulty acquiring language skills and those who have learning disabilities" (Burr, Haas, & Ferriere, 2015, p. i). This is a serious issue. Misidentified students could be placed improperly in special education programs, or students who truly need special education services could be prevented from receiving them. Drawing from an extensive review of the research literature, the report provides the following questions educators can ask to "help determine whether an English learner student's academic difficulties are caused by a learning disability or by struggles with second-language acquisition or some other factor":

- Is the student receiving instruction of sufficient quality to enable him or her to
- make the accepted levels of academic progress?
- How does the student's progress in hearing, speaking, reading, and writing English as a second language compare with the expected rate of progress for his or her age and initial level of English proficiency?
- To what extent are behaviors that might otherwise indicate a learning disability considered to be normal for the child's cultural background or to be part of the process of U.S. acculturation?
- How might additional factors—including socioeconomic status, previous education experience, fluency in his or her first language, attitude toward school, attitude toward learning English, and personality attributes—impact the student's academic progress? (p. 4)

Hamayan, Marler, Sánchez-López, and Damico (2013) also emphasize the need to consider a wide range of factors to determine whether an ELL is also learning disabled. They offer a framework to consider the needs of ELLs through a collaborative model of information gathering and service provision. Teams of special education and ESL/bilingual teachers who collectively have the needed expertise explore factors that influence an ELL's

> ### Box 1.3 Response to Intervention and English Language Learners
>
> Response to intervention (RTI) is a school-wide model focused on close monitoring of student progress and providing interventions in three tiers: tier 1—universal screening and research-based instruction (all students); tier 2—more intensive, targeted, short-term support and supplemental instruction through small-group instruction (20%–30% of students); and tier 3—intensive individualized instruction and interventions (5%–10% of students).
>
> The RTI model originated in special education and is used to identify students in need of special education services or placement (tier 3). The principles and practices in this book provide the foundation needed for effective tier 1 and tier 2 instruction and support for ELLs. But since RTI has gone mainstream and school-wide, concerns have arisen about its appropriateness for ELLs, including the following:
>
> - Screening and monitoring assessments used in tier 1 and tier 2 may be inappropriate for ELLs.
> - Though tier 1 and tier 2 are assumed to represent high-quality, effective instruction for ELLs, the materials, trained teachers, and supportive policy environments needed for effective ELL program models are often missing.
> - ELLs are blamed for not responding to (ineffective) tier 1 and tier 2 interventions, reinforcing a deficit view of students and inappropriate placement into special education (tier 3).
>
> RTI relies heavily on observations of student responses to interventions designed by classroom teachers; thus it is limited by teachers' knowledge and skills in working with ELLs (Burr et al., 2015). In addition, a major problem with the RTI model is the whole notion of "interventions." ELLs do not need *intervention*. They need *instruction*. No temporary "intervention" is going to quickly make them proficient in English. Rather, ELLs need consistent, high-quality language and content-area instruction appropriate to their educational background and level of English proficiency for several years across grade levels. To properly identify ELLs truly in need of special education services, the extensive framework outlined by Hamayan et al (2013) should be followed.

response to instruction and interventions. These factors include (1) the learning environment created for ELLs, (2) personal and family issues, (3) physical and psychological development, (4) previous schooling, (5) social and academic language development in the first and the second language, (6) academic achievement in both languages, and (7) cultural differences. Team members work together to describe the learning difficulties they observe before diagnosing. They outline a continuum of interventions and measure the ELL's response to those interventions. Many schools use the **response to intervention** (RTI) model or other models of **multi-tiered systems of support** (MTSS) to provide differentiated classroom instruction and to identify students in need of more supplemental instruction or intensive individualized support through special education services. While such models sound promising, implementation of RTI has been highly problematic, especially with ELLs (Box 1.3).

Culture and Identity

ELLs represent a wide variety of ethnic and cultural groups. Teachers need to know their students' cultural backgrounds and how culture influences learning at school. But what do we mean by culture? Culture involves much more than the food, dress, art, music, and holidays of an ethnic group. These outward manifestations of culture are what Hamayan (2012) refers to as the tip of the iceberg. Below the surface, the iceberg is massive, and this portion represents the norms and values that consist of the ways people interact with and make sense of their surroundings. Some of these below-the-surface aspects of culture include etiquette involving eye contact, notions of modesty, ways of ordering of time, conversational patterns, approaches to problem solving, preferences for competition or cooperation, and conceptions of beauty and status and mobility. These below-the-surface aspects of the home culture may differ from or even be in conflict with aspects of the dominant culture that are privileged in the schools.

As teachers begin to understand their students' cultural backgrounds, they must be careful to avoid stereotypes and generalizations. For example, in many schools today there is a tendency to generalize the cultures of Mexico and China and assume they apply equally to all Latinx and Asian students, respectively, and to focus on surface manifestations of culture. In my former elementary school, the overwhelming majority of the Asian students (who made up about 45% of the school's population) were Cambodian Americans. Yet the only Asian-related lesson some of the teachers in the school did all year was about Chinese New Year. The red envelopes, worksheets with dragons, and signs that read "Gung Hay Fat Choy" were just as foreign to the Cambodian American students as they were to other non-Chinese students in the school. Likewise, school-wide celebrations for Cinco de Mayo—which is really more of a commercially contrived U.S. holiday than an authentic traditional Mexican holiday—hold little meaning for Spanish-speaking students whose families are not from Mexico. Although there may be similar cultural traits across students labeled as Latinx, Asian, Native American, Middle Eastern, or African, it is important to be aware of the distinct history and culture of each ethnic group.

It is also important to recognize that ELLs may not necessarily come from a singular cultural or linguistic background. I have had Asian students who are fluent in Spanish because they came to the United States after living in South America. I recall one Korean student whose family came to the United States from Peru. She worked in a small local Mexican market, and when customers wondered aloud in Spanish why a "Chinese" girl was working there, she shocked them by responding in fluent Spanish. While visiting a high school ESL class in San Antonio, Texas, I noticed many Middle Eastern students using bilingual Russian-English dictionaries. I learned that they had spent time and attended school in one or more Russian-speaking countries after escaping from war in their own countries. Jaumont (2017) observed that French heritage language programs in New York City are typically dominated by immigrant students from West Africa and the Caribbean. Duran (2017) describes the Burmese, Thai, and English language skills Karenni students picked up on their refugee journey to the United States. She refers to these as their multilingual repertoires and "accumulated literacies." Educators must look beyond static notions of language and culture to consider the ways that students' specific histories and experiences influence their expertise.

Another common misconception is that all ELLs are immigrants (or "foreigners"), born outside of the United States. As noted earlier, most ELLs are U.S.-born citizens. Typically, U.S.-born ELLs represent the second generation, born to immigrant parents who may or may not speak English well. Very few ELLs are members of the third generation, meaning their parents were born in the United States but their grandparents were born in a different country. There are significant differences between U.S.-born and foreign-born ELLs, even among students from the same ethnic group. ELLs in these two groups bring to school a different set of strengths and challenges (Box 1.4).

While ELLs are learning at school, they are also developing their identities. Norton (2013) describes identity as "dynamic" and "multiple" and "a site of struggle," noting that a student's identity is shaped by the economic, historical, political, and cultural contexts

Box 1.4 U.S.- and Foreign-Born English Language Learners

Teachers should consider some of the following differences between U.S.-born and foreign-born ELLs:

- U.S.-born ELLs (who make up the majority of ELLs) receive extensive exposure to English before beginning school from radio, television, movies, video games, the Internet, social media, friends, older siblings, relatives, neighbors, and other community members.
- U.S.-born ELLs, unless they participate in bilingual education programs or heritage language programs outside of school, often do not have opportunities to fully develop their home language, particularly in the area of literacy.
- Foreign-born ELLs who attended school in their home country typically have strong home language skills, including literacy in their home language or languages.
- Foreign-born students with strong home language literacy skills may learn to read and write in English faster and better than U.S.-born ELLs.
- U.S.-born ELLs (unless they are in bilingual programs) face the difficult task of learning to read and write first in their weaker language (English) and thus may need more time to develop their literacy skills in English.
- Some older foreign-born ELLs may have studied English as a foreign language in school. These programs typically place more emphasis on literacy than oral language, and thus these students may initially read and write English better than they can speak it.
- Some foreign-born ELLs have experienced disruptions in their education or never attended school in their home countries (or in refugee camps) because of poverty, oppression, or war.

in which he or she lives and learns. Language also plays a major role in the development of identity because students' identities are socially constructed through their language-mediated interactions and relationships. ELLs often struggle as they learn and adjust to a new language and culture that may be vastly different from the language and culture of their home. ELLs formulate, reformulate, and negotiate their identities as they deal with and attempt to resolve the conflicts between what they encounter at home, in school, and in the dominant society culture. Their academic success depends in large part on how the school and the wider society treat them, their language, their culture, their families, and their communities.

Classic and recent research studies have documented the effect that cultural differences can have on student success in the classroom.[4] English-speaking students from the dominant group generally find that the culture of the school closely matches that of their homes, and thus they have an advantage as they enter school. ELLs, however, may experience a cultural and linguistic mismatch between the culture and language of their home and the school's culture and language. They are disadvantaged when schools do not recognize, value, and incorporate these differences.

Helping ELLs succeed academically requires helping them adjust to the culture of the classroom and the school by giving them access to what McKinney and Norton (2008) call "dominant or privileged ways of knowing and doing" (p. 201). In the United States, education has functioned and continues to function as a tool for assimilation that encourages immigrant children to abandon their home language and culture and become monolingual English-speaking Americans. Studies by Portes and Rumbaut (2014) have shown, however, that students who assimilate quickly often have deep conflicts at home, and these conflicts can lead to academic and social difficulties.

---

[4] The classic studies are Heath, 1983; Philips, 1983. More recent studies include Castagno & McCarty, 2018; Espinoza-Herold & González-Carriedo, 2017; Huffman, 2018.

Assimilation is the ideology behind the great melting pot, a metaphor for the notion that immigrants to the United States willingly abandon their language and culture to become Americans. A serious flaw in the melting pot metaphor is that some immigrants, especially people of color, do not "melt" into the whole as easily as others. Regardless of how "Americanized" they become, many other Americans will nonetheless question their "American-ness." For example, when the U.S. ice-skating champion Michelle Kwan came in second place to fellow U.S. teammate Tara Lipinski in the 1998 Winter Olympics, Asian Americans were dismayed by an MSNBC.com headline announcing, "American Beats Out Kwan!" The network removed the headline and apologized after receiving a flood of complaints. Both skaters are U.S. born and come from immigrant families—Kwan's from Hong Kong and Lipinski's from Poland. But why was Kwan's American identity questioned while Lipinski's was not? Simply put, Lipinski melts better because she is white. The challenge continues. The *Los Angeles Times* reported that when the Team USA snowboarder Chloe Kim won a gold medal in the 2018 Winter Olympics, a journalist from the *Bleacher Report* uploaded a photo of Chloe's family celebrating her win under the caption "An American Family." The post, shared over 13,000 times, garnered some negative comments accusing the reporter of trying to make a "political statement." Some even assumed the journalist, Joon Lee, was a "foreign journalist." He's a native of Boston (Shyong, 2018).

Many third-, fourth-, and fifth-generation Asian and Latinx Americans who have never spoken any language other than English often have encounters with other Americans who assume they do not speak English, or who act with surprise when they hear them talk and ask, "How did you learn to speak English so well?" Worse yet, many have been told, "Go back to your country." Even seemingly innocent questions such as "What are you" (in reference to one's race/ethnicity), "Where are you from," and especially the typical follow-up response, "No, where are you really from?" when asked of U.S.-born people of color are "microaggressions" that send the subtle message, "You don't belong here."

Another problem with the assimilationist melting pot metaphor is the assumption that immigrants must give up their home language and culture to become Americans. An alternative to assimilation, however, is acculturation—immigrants and their children can adapt to the new language and culture without having to sacrifice their own. The melting pot metaphor is inaccurate for describing U.S. society because our nation is made up of many cultural groups distinguished by class, gender, religion, ethnicity, and language (Gollnick & Chin, 2016). A more accurate metaphor is the salad bowl, where each ingredient maintains its unique characteristics but all ingredients together make up a single wonderful whole.

Maintaining or developing a home culture while learning and adjusting to American culture is neither simple nor straightforward. Culture is dynamic and multifaceted. What is "American" culture anyway? And what exactly is the home "culture" of ELLs? Just as my "American" culture is not the same as my parents' "American" culture, the home culture of ELLs may be much different from the culture their parents attempt to bring with them from their home country. Parents often have idealized notions of what their culture is and should be, and they become dismayed when their children who are growing up in the United States do not fully adopt it. Rather than fully adopt "American" culture (whatever that may be) or adopt their parents' idealized notions of the native culture, many children of immigrants forge a style of cultural identity that is neither one nor the other but a hybrid of the two that is uniquely theirs. This hybridization is referred to by some scholars as a "third space."[5] One example of hybridization is hip hop culture, which is

---

[5] See, e.g., Bhabha, 2004; Gee, 2012.

highly influenced by young urban African Americans. Hip hop may be the American culture, and Hip Hop Nation Language (Alim, 2015) the variety of English, that many ELLs and other minority students experience growing up in inner cities.

School programs should encourage ELLs to create new, positive sociocultural identities that can help them negotiate the dynamic new world in which they are living, rather than encourage them to assimilate to mainstream norms. Multicultural education can help prepare all students to live in our multicultural society, with attention to the complex social challenges—including racism, discrimination, and other issues of inequality—that continue to plague our society. In short, educators have a responsibility to help prepare the next generation to continue working to solve important social problems related to diversity that past generations have failed to fully address.

Most educators agree that multicultural education is important, but there are vast differences in how schools address it. Banks (2018), one of the pioneers of multicultural education, looked at how schools provide multicultural education and identified four levels: (1) contributions, (2) additive, (3) transformative, and (4) social action. Level 1 entails briefly mentioning the contributions individual minorities or ethnic groups have made to the United States, for example, by celebrating Martin Luther King Jr. Day or reading a side-bar paragraph in the textbook about Cesar Chavez or the Chinese workers who built the railroads. Level 2 entails making up for gaps in the mainstream curriculum by adding new material, such as a unit about the internment of Japanese Americans during World War II, which typically gets just brief mention in core textbooks. At level 3, teachers move beyond simply informing students of historical or current events and help them develop critical perspectives on issues of justice, equality, and democracy in society. For example, students might discuss continuing problems of school segregation and why schools with large numbers of immigrant and ELLs receive less funding than schools that serve majority students. At level 4, students go beyond discussing these issues and take on action research projects aimed at making positive changes in the name of social equity. For example, students might collect data on per-pupil spending and resources in minority and majority schools and present their findings to the school board and local press. Most teachers and schools appear to be more comfortable with levels 1 and 2. These provide a good start but are not sufficient to prepare students to understand and begin to address the unequal power relationships in our society that may limit the life opportunities of the students, their families, and their communities.

Field (2008) emphasizes that it is important for educators to have an understanding of power relationships among social identity groups in the communities in which they teach in order to develop policies, programs, and practices that can (1) help elevate the status of minority languages and their speakers, (2) provide more access to opportunities for language minority students, and (3) challenge the dominant identity and power relations that exist on the local level. Paris and Alim (2017) address these issues of power and social inequities and go beyond traditional notions of multicultural education by calling for **culturally sustaining pedagogies**. They explain that CSP "seeks to perpetuate and foster—to sustain—linguistic, literate, and cultural pluralism as part of schooling for positive social transformation" (p. 1). They argue:

> For too long we have taught our youth (and our teachers) that Dominant American English (DAE) and other White middle-class normed practices and ways of being alone are the key to power, while denying the languages and other cultural practices that students of color bring to the classroom. Ironically, this outdated philosophy will not grant our young people access to power; rather, it may increasingly deny them that access. (p. 6)

Understanding Diversity Informs Effective Practice

Educators who work with ELLs must be aware of the diversity in their schools and surrounding communities. The following questions can guide teachers' inquiry: What countries are the students or their families from? What languages and language varieties are spoken in their homes? What are their ethnicities and with which cultural groups do they identify? How long have the students (or their families) been in the United States? What prior schooling do the students have, either in their home countries or in the United States? Can they read and write in their home languages? What are the parents' levels of education, and do they have literacy skills in their home languages? What are the students' neighborhoods like? What is each student's socioeconomic status? What birth position does each student hold among his or her siblings, or is he or she an only child?

Teachers must be able to answer these basic questions about the ELLs in their classroom if they are to provide effective instruction for them. Knowing a student's ethnicity and country of origin, for example, allows the teacher to incorporate appropriate multicultural education strategies and techniques into the curriculum. Knowing the student's home language or languages allows the teacher to provide primary language support that can accelerate the student's acquisition of English and comprehension of academic instruction. If the student has literacy skills in his or her home language, the teacher can use bilingual dictionaries and other written materials in that language to provide support and use strategies that facilitate literacy transfer from the home language to English. Likewise, knowing what language and literacy skills the parents have helps the teacher determine in what language to send home notes and other school communications and whether to arrange for an interpreter at parent conferences or other school meetings.

The more the teacher knows about a student's experiences, the more he or she can assume about the expertise that student is likely to have. For example, if the student has attended school in his or her home country, the teacher may assume that the student has some literacy skills in his or her home language and also has learned academic content through that language. If the student has been educated mostly in the United States and has not participated in bilingual programs (or heritage language programs outside of school), the teacher may assume that the student cannot read or write in his or her home language because there have been no opportunities to develop these skills. If the parents have low levels of education, and if the family lives in a low-income neighborhood, the teacher should take into consideration the factors related to poverty discussed earlier and find ways to address these issues in the classroom. If the student is one of the younger children in the family, and the family has been in the United States for several years, it is likely that the older siblings speak English and use it often in the home. But if the student is the oldest or only child, such support may not be present.

Promoting Bilingualism on the Individual and Societal Levels

Subtractive bilingualism occurs when a new language replaces a student's home language. In contrast, **additive bilingualism** occurs when a student develops proficiency in a new language without losing his or her home language. This form of bilingualism should be the goal of all school language programs. Thus, as ELLs diligently strive to learn their new language, English should be viewed as an additional language rather than as a replacement for their home language. Additive bilingualism is encouraged when schools value linguistic diversity, adopt a language-as-resource orientation, engage in

Box 1.5 Potential Consequences of Primary Language Loss

- Children are unable to communicate effectively with their parents.
- Parents have difficulty passing on their values, beliefs, understandings, and wisdom.
- Conflicts arise between children and parents because of a communication breakdown.
- Children lose respect for their parents.
- Children experience difficulty, embarrassment, and shame when trying to communicate with older relatives and community members.
- Children face humiliation and shame when they return to their (or their parents') home country and cannot effectively communicate.
- Children become ashamed of their home language and culture and struggle with identity issues.
- Students have fewer job opportunities than they would have had, had they maintained their home language.
- The society as a whole loses needed linguistic resources to fulfill the language demands of national and international institutions, organizations, and agencies.

Fillmore, 1991; Wright, 2004a.

pluralist discourses, and promote culturally sustaining pedagogies by providing opportunities for ELLs to use and develop their home language skills, alongside English, for academic purposes.

When ESL and content instruction in English pressure students to replace or demote the home language, subtractive bilingualism may occur. Such programs offer ELLs no opportunity to develop and maintain their home language for academic purposes. Schools that take this assimilationist approach fail to take into consideration the needs of the student as a whole, and the needs of the student's family and community, as well as the wider society. Fillmore (1991), in an article titled "When Learning a Second Language Means Losing the First," details the harsh consequences that can befall ELLs when English replaces their home language. Losing proficiency in the home language before attaining proficiency in standard English, for example, often leads to academic difficulties. In particular, learning to read in English is more difficult if students cannot read in their home language. My own research with Cambodian American students who received English-only instruction found similar consequences (Box 1.5).

The concepts of additive and subtractive bilingualism, however, may be somewhat misleading. It suggests simply adding to or subtracting from something that already exists. But as noted earlier, most ELLs are simultaneous bilinguals, that is, they were born in the United States and are growing up in homes and neighborhoods where varieties of home languages and English are used. Furthermore, for students (younger ones in particular) to become highly bilingual and biliterate, they must have opportunities to further develop their home languages at school. Thus, it may be more accurate to describe this phenomenon as dynamic bilingualism (García & Kleyn, 2016). And, also as noted earlier, emergent bilinguals draw on their developing linguistic resources from their home and new languages in dynamic ways to interact with others and engage in collaborative tasks. García (2017) argues, "bilingualism is never just additive, but inherently dinámico" (p. 257).

Encouraging ELLs to maintain and develop their home languages while they develop proficiency in English benefits the individual ELL and his or her family and community, as well as the nation. The United States needs bilingual citizens who can fulfill the myriad jobs in the government, service, business, and education sectors that require bilingual

Box 1.6 Need for Bilingual Citizens

The following is a random sample of headlines that appeared in newspapers around the country in 2017. What do these headlines indicate about the need for bilingual citizens in the United States? How are the educational policies and programs in your community's schools addressing this growing need?

Help Wanted: Bilingual teachers for schools—*Marin Independent Journal* (CA)

Police Department graduates first bilingual community academy—*Muskogee Phoenix* (OK)

CISD to pilot 2-way dual language program—*Cleburne Times-Review* (TX)

Changing demographics: More Hispanic students means bilingual schools—*State Journal Register* (IL)

¿Habla arte? How LA art galleries are reaching out to Spanish speakers—*The Guardian* (CA)

Bilingual yoga energizes downtown Watsonville—*Santa Cruz Sentinel* (CA)

Announcing 2017 bilingual nature hike and campfire schedule—*Chicago Daily Herald* (IL)

CASA Kane County needs bilingual—*Chicago Daily Herald* (IL)

Bilingual education regains foothold in Massachusetts—*Telegram & Gazette* (MA)

Bilingual kindergarten enrollment date nears—*Walla Walla Union Bulletin* (WA)

Ruidoso bilingual classrooms named among best in state—*Ruidoso News* (NM)

Muskogee library offers bilingual story time—*Muskogee Phoenix* (OK)

Rep. Larsen participates in bilingual radio interview—*Skagit Valley Herald* (WA)

County adds full-time bilingual clerk—*Ottumwa Courier* (IA)

Buffalo school district recruits bilingual teachers in Puerto Rico—*Wall Street Journal* (NY)

CNT seeks bilingual call center workers—*Journal Record* (OK)

Austin moms create mobile apps for bilingual home, kids' sports games—*Austin-American Statesman* (TX)

Convergys needs Spanish speakers—*Pueblo Chieftan* (CO)

BCSD woos bilingual ed teachers with bonuses—*Bakersfield Californian* (CA)

Elementary schools begin dual language program—*Tampa Bay Times* (FL)

---

skills to interact with immigrants who have not yet learned English, to communicate with international tourists and other visitors, and to help ensure the country's success in international relations, global business, and national security (Box 1.6).

Learning More about Your English Language Learners

As outlined in the earlier discussion of the language-as-resource orientation, teachers need to know the following about each student: (1) languages and literacies used at home; (2) ELP level; (3) educational history in the home country and in the United States; (4) length of time in the United States; (5) reason for immigration; (6) number of siblings; and (7) parents' educational history, employment, and proficiency in English and other languages. The ELL Student Profile form on the companion website can be used to help gather and analyze this important information.

How can teachers obtain this information, some of which may be considered private and personal? Students' academic files should contain a copy of a home language survey that indicates the languages used at home and the results of any ELP testing (and sometimes home language proficiency testing) conducted at the time of enrollment or at the end of the previous school year. School enrollment papers and the school emergency cards that parents typically fill out each year may list parents' occupations and work phone numbers, as well as the names and grades of school age siblings. A teacher could also obtain much of this information simply by asking the parents, in a sensitive way, at a back-to-school program or during parent conferences. Teachers can also obtain this information from the students in appropriate ways. For example, at the beginning of the school year, students can draw pictures, share photographs, and write and talk about their families as part of an "All about Me" unit.

Once teachers have basic information about the home countries, ethnic and cultural groups, and languages of their students, they can obtain further information by searching the Internet. For example, teachers can learn about the history and educational system of the home country of a student born outside of the United States, as well as any difficulties there that may have caused the student's family to leave their country and come to the United States. Information about the student's ethnicity and culture may help explain some of the student's behaviors in class and suggest things the teacher can do to be sensitive to his or her culture and incorporate aspects of that culture into the classroom. A search for information about the student's language may reveal some important similarities and differences between the home language and English that can help the teacher plan effective ESL instruction (see Funk, 2012).

Another important use of this information is for teachers to identify appropriate supplemental educational materials for use in the classroom, such as bilingual (or bilingual picture) dictionaries and fiction and nonfiction books in the students' home languages, including, if appropriate, bilingual versions with English and another language. Teachers can also identify multicultural literature that may be interesting and motivating to ELLs in learning to read and could help other students learn about and appreciate their ELL classmates' cultures. These ideas and additional suggestions are discussed in more detail in other chapters.

Summary

ELLs are a diverse group, despite the misleading unifying label. ELLs come from a wide range of ethnic, cultural, linguistic, educational, and socioeconomic backgrounds. While many are foreign born, the majority are U.S.-born citizens. Procedures for identifying and redesignating ELLs can vary across schools, districts, and states. Many different labels are used to describe students who are learning English, and each has its own positive and negative aspects. *ELL* is used in this book because it focuses on the students as active learners who are on their way to attaining proficiency in English. But ELLs are also recognized as emergent bilinguals. Immigration to the United States is occurring at rates similar to those of the early 1900s, but today's immigrants come primarily from Latin American and Asian countries rather than European countries. The growth rate of the ELL population far surpasses that of the total student population. ELLs make up about 9.5% of the total U.S. population, and the number of ELLs is growing rapidly. In addition to language and academic learning challenges, ELLs also face cultural adjustment challenges, including pressure to assimilate. The melting pot is an outdated metaphor that never accurately captured the reality of diversity in the United States. Students' acculturation, however, may not necessarily be full acceptance of either the home or the dominant culture, but instead students may develop new hybrid forms of cultural identity. All teachers share the responsibility for ELLs, and teachers and administrators in various roles must collaborate to ensure student success. Teachers must get to know their students by obtaining information about their sociocultural background. This information will help teachers make the best possible decisions for providing effective instruction for their ELLs.

Discussion Questions

1. Review the profiles of the students at the beginning of the chapter, including their extended profiles on the companion website. Which students are likely to face the greatest challenges in learning English and academic content? Which ones might have fewer challenges? Why?

2. Consider the different labels that have been used to describe students who are not yet proficient in English. Which ones have you heard used in your school or program? Which do you prefer? Why?

3. How can poverty affect the teaching and learning of ELLs? What is the danger in attributing students' underachievement to cognitive deficits rather than seeking to understand sociocultural factors that can affect students' opportunities to learn? Describe your own experiences or observations related to this issue.

4. View the news report video clip describing a class for refugee newcomer students in the Indianapolis, Indiana, area. What are some of the challenges these students face in U.S. schools? What are some challenges their teachers face? How would you address these challenges?

5. View the video of the San Antonio, Texas, teacher Kerry Haupert (named Innovator of the Year by her school district for her work with newcomer ELLs). How does she view her students? What are some ways that she advocates for them? Why are these and other similar characteristics important for teachers of ELLs to have?

Research Activities

1. *ELL Student Interview and Assessment* Work with a current ELL and complete the ELL Student Profile form, then answer the following questions:
   a. Which factors may positively influence this student's English language development? Why?
   b. Which factors may be obstacles to this student's English language development? Why?
   c. How easy or difficult do you think it will be for this student to develop literacy skills in English? Why?
   d. What are some particular things the teacher should do to address this student's unique needs as revealed in your answers to (a) through (c)?

2. *ELL Teacher Interview* Interview a current teacher of ELLs. Ask what type of ELLs the teacher has in his or her classroom and what challenges they face. Ask whether the teacher enjoys working with ELLs, and why. What advice does he or she have for other or future teachers of ELLs?

3. *ELL Classroom Observation* Observe a classroom with ELLs. Are most of the ELLs from the same cultural and language background, or do they represent a range of backgrounds? What is the range of English proficiency of the students? How well are they able to engage in classroom instruction and activities? What strategies, techniques, or accommodations, if any, does the teacher appear to make for his or her ELLs?

4. *Online Research Activity* Using the Great Schools website, look up the demographics of one of your local schools to see the percentage of students in each

racial/ethnic category, the percentage of economically disadvantaged students, and the percentage of ELLs. Also, review other factors such as the levels of teacher experience and the ratio of students to teachers. How might these demographic and other factors be interrelated? If possible, contact a staff member from the school to get more detailed information on the ELLs' countries of origin, ethnicities, and languages and their levels of ELP. Discuss the implications of your findings for the school's instructional programs.

Recommended Reading

Custodio, B. K., & O'Loughlin, J. B. (2017). *Students with interrupted formal education: Bridging where they are and what they need.* Thousand Oaks, CA: Corwin.

This book focuses on a subgroup of ELLs with unique and substantial needs—students with interrupted formal education (SIFE). The authors provide insights into the strengths and challenges SIFE students face, with many specific strategies to provide targeted support.

Paris, D., & Alim, S. (Eds.). (2017). *Culturally sustaining pedagogies: Teaching and learning for justice in a changing world.* New York: Teachers College Press.

This book emphasizes schools as sites for fostering the linguistic, literate, and cultural practices of students of color. Chapters are written by leading experts who provide examples of what culturally sustaining pedagogies look like in actual classrooms.

Thorpe, H. (2017). *The newcomers: Finding refuge, friendship, and hope in an American classroom.* New York: Scribner.

The journalist Helen Thorpe spent a year in a Denver, Colorado, high school ESL classroom documenting the work of the teacher and following the lives of his 22 newcomer immigrant and refugee students from many different countries. Their compelling stories provided an intimate look at who are ELLs.

Two

Language

Classrooms are, first and foremost, language environments . . . . Language lies at the very heart of teaching and learning.

—Francis Bailey, Beverley Burkett, and Donald Freeman

KEY TERMS

- academic language proficiency
- communicative competence
- discourse/Discourse
- genre
- lexicon
- morphology

- phonology
- pragmatics
- register
- semantics
- syntax
- translanguaging

GUIDING QUESTIONS

1. What do teachers need to know about language, and why do they need to know it?
2. How can knowledge of language help teachers to "think linguistically" about their students, curriculum, and classroom instruction?
3. What does it mean to "know a language"?
4. What do teachers need to know about language for academic or disciplinary purposes?

As we begin our discussion, consider the following questions teachers might ask about language issues that arise in their classrooms.

1. Vihn has difficulty pronouncing *th* words. Does he have a speech impediment?
2. Chanyoung always leaves off the final *s* when she reads. I've told her a million times that plural words end with an *s*. Why is she refusing to read the words correctly?
3. Rosa always switches words around in the sentence, saying and writing things like "car red" instead of "red car." Is she dyslexic?
4. Suling always mixes up the gender-specific pronouns, calling girls "he" or "him" and boys "she" or "her." I keep correcting her, but she just doesn't get it. And if she calls me "Mrs." Wright one more time I'm going to scream! Can't she tell the difference between boys and girls? Should I refer her to special education?
5. Reading time was over and students were supposed to put their books away and start working on their math worksheets. But Thanawan just kept right on reading. I said to her, "Why are you still reading instead of doing your math?" She smiled and said, "Oh, because I not finish yet," and she just kept on reading. Why did she disobey me so rudely?
6. During student oral presentations on sea mammals, William, one of my African-American students, begins: "I gonna aks you a question. Why whales have blow holes? Whales gotta have blowholes because dey be breathin' oxygen just like all da udder mammals." I just don't understand why William speaks such poor English.
7. My principal just bought us a great software program that drills ELLs in English. If they get 30 drills in a row right they get rewarded with a little animation where a bunny pops out of the tree and does a little dance. The box the software came

in says the students will be speaking English in 3 or 4 weeks. Does this mean our ELLs will be ready for the poetry analysis unit we're starting next month?

8. RoDay quickly finished her math and spelling worksheets. And she seemed to do just fine reading along with the other students when we did a choral reading of a story from our reading basal. But unlike the other students, she has done hardly any work writing an alternative ending to the story. Why is she refusing to do an assignment that should be fun?

An important goal of this chapter is to help you answer questions like these and address similar issues with informed confidence by "thinking linguistically" about your students and your curriculum and classroom instruction. We begin by defining language and then consider why all teachers need to know about language. Next we focus on five major subsystems of language (phonology, morphology, syntax, semantics, and pragmatics) and how knowledge of these subsystems can inform the teaching of pronunciation, grammar, vocabulary, and spelling. Then we discuss what it means to know a language, with attention to the kinds of communicative practices students need for successful interaction in their classrooms and schools. When teachers understand the language demands of school, they can make principled decisions about language learning and teaching that build on the linguistic and cultural resources students bring with them to school. In our discussion, the preceding questions are referred to as "situation 1," "situation 2," and so on.

What Is Language?

One of the characteristics of being human that separates us from other species is the ability to use language. As humans we tend to take this amazing ability for granted. And because language is ubiquitous, we rarely stop to think about what it actually is.

Crystal (2001) defines language as "the systematic, conventional use of sounds, signs, or written symbols in a human society for communication and self-expression" (p. 184). Linguists study the underlying system of language, which includes the properties of words and how words are combined to form sentences and make meaning. Linguists also study language use, or language as an act of speaking (or signing) and writing in different situations. They examine different aspects of communication, including the context, the background of speakers, the interactive nature and purpose of communication, and language variation. Providing effective language and content instruction for ELLs requires a basic understanding of language at these different levels of abstraction.

Why Teachers Need to Know about Language

Fillmore and Snow (2018) identify five functions that teachers perform that have consequences in their work with ELLs. For teachers to perform each of these functions, they must have a thorough understanding of language.

Teacher as communicator. Teachers must know enough about the structure of language to speak and write so their students can understand them, and they must be able to understand what their students are saying. Understanding student talk is essential to teachers' ability to analyze what students know, how they understand, and what teaching methods would be most useful. Effective communication with linguistically and culturally diverse students includes recognizing, valuing, and drawing on their home languages

(languages other than English and nonstandard varieties of English) as resources in teaching and learning.

Teacher as educator. Teachers need to know which language problems will resolve themselves and which problems need attention and intervention. Teachers need to select or modify the language used in instruction (written and oral) to make complex content-area concepts comprehensible to ELLs at different English proficiency levels.

Teacher as evaluator. Teachers frequently make judgments based on language behaviors of students that have enormous consequences for the students' lives. These include everyday judgments and responses that affect students' sense of themselves as learners, as well as decisions about reading group placement, promotion, and referral for evaluation. For example, when educators mistake language differences or English language development issues for cognitive deficiencies, many ELLs and speakers of nonstandard varieties of English are inappropriately placed in special education or provided with inappropriate and ineffective interventions. Teachers must recognize the problems of using assessment instruments designed for monolingual standard English speakers. They must become skilled in the use of authentic assessment tools and procedures to accurately evaluate ELLs' language and literacy abilities in English and in their home languages and know how to use these results to track student progress and plan effective instruction.

Teacher as an educated human being. Teachers should understand the role of language in education and know something about the differences between the structure of English and that of other languages. Public ignorance about language and language issues has resulted in damaging policies (e.g., restrictions on bilingual education programs for ELLs in California, Arizona, and Massachusetts), public debates driven by misinformation and misunderstandings (e.g., about nonstandard varieties of English), and pedagogically unsound decisions in schools (e.g., about methods for teaching English or reading).

Teacher as agent of socialization. Immigrant and minority students may find the culture of the school vastly different from the culture of their home, and the teacher may be their first contact with the social world outside the home and even, among ELLs, their first contact with English. Thus, the ways teachers organize their programs and practices helps students adjust to the everyday practices, the system of values and beliefs, and the means and manners of communication at school and in society. In this role, as in their role as communicators, teachers who respect their students' home languages and cultures can be most effective in helping students make the necessary transitions without undercutting the role that parents and families must continue to play in their education and development.

All classrooms are language environments, and language is at the heart of teaching and learning. To help students succeed in the classroom and in school, teachers need to "think linguistically," that is, teachers need to "understand language as an integral element in the content they teach, the contributions that their students make in the classroom, and how these students participate in lessons and activities" (Bailey, Burkett, & Freeman, 2008, p. 609).

Language Standards for All Students

The recognition that language lies at the heart of teaching and learning, not just for ELLs but for all students, is reflected in the Common Core State Standards (CCSS), which have been widely adopted across the country. These include six language standards related to conventions of standard English, knowledge of language, and vocabulary acquisition and use (Box 2.1). The need for these language standards for all students is explained as follows:

> To build a foundation for college and career readiness in language, students must gain control over many conventions of standard English grammar, usage, and mechanics as well as learn other ways to use language to convey meaning effectively. They must also be able to determine or clarify the meaning of grade-appropriate words encountered through listening, reading, and media use; come to appreciate that words have nonliteral meanings, shadings of meaning, and relationships to other words; and expand their vocabulary in the course of studying content. (ELA Standards, p. 25. © Copyright 2010 National Governors Association Center for Best Practices and Council of Chief State School Officers. All rights reserved.)

This focus on raising the bar of language for all students may be a positive development. Mainstream (generalist/content area) teachers will likely look to their colleagues in English as a second language (ESL) and bilingual education for help. But with monolingual English speakers being held to higher language standards, ELLs will have even further to go to catch up.

Language is more complex than these language standards suggest. To ensure that all students, particularly ELLs, can use oral and written language to meet rigorous content-area standards, all teachers must develop a foundational understanding of language and language use.

Box 2.1 Common Core State Standards: College and Career Readiness Anchor Standards for Language

Conventions of Standard English

1. Demonstrate command of the conventions of standard English grammar and usage when writing or speaking.
2. Demonstrate command of the conventions of standard English capitalization, punctuation, and spelling when writing.

Knowledge of Language

3. Apply knowledge of language to understand how language functions in different contexts, to make effective choices for meaning or style, and to comprehend more fully when reading or listening.

Vocabulary Acquisition and Use

4. Determine or clarify the meaning of unknown and multiple-meaning words and phrases by using context clues, analyzing meaningful word parts, and consulting general and specialized reference materials, as appropriate.
5. Demonstrate understanding of figurative language, word relationships, and nuances in word meanings.
6. Acquire and use accurately a range of general academic and domain-specific words and phrases sufficient for reading, writing, speaking, and listening at the college and career readiness level; demonstrate independence in gathering vocabulary knowledge when encountering an unknown term important to comprehension or expression.

What Teachers Need to Know about Language

In this section we look briefly at five subsystems of language traditionally studied by linguists—phonology, morphology, syntax, semantics, and pragmatics—and we see how teachers can draw on this knowledge when helping ELLs in the areas of vocabulary, grammar, and spelling.

Phonology

Phonology is the study of the sound systems of languages. Segmental phonology focuses on the discrete sounds within a language, called phonemes; suprasegmental phonology focuses on intonation, stress patterns, and other features that occur across phonemes.

Phonemes are the smallest units of sound in a language. A change in phoneme causes a change in meaning; for example, a slight difference in vowel sound changes the word *bit* to *bet*. Allophones are the manifestations of a single phoneme in speech; for example, *peak* and *speak* include the phoneme /p/, but the manifestation of the *p* sound is slightly different. In *peak,* the *p* is aspirated (a small puff of air is released when you say it), whereas in *speak,* the *p* is unaspirated. (Say both words with the back of your hand in front of your mouth to feel the difference.) Thus, the phoneme /p/ is manifested in these words by its allophones [p^H] (aspirated) and [p] (unaspirated). Note that saying *speak* with an aspirated *p* [p^H] does not change the meaning of the word; it just sounds a bit funny. In some languages, however, such as Khmer and Thai, a change in aspiration changes the meaning of the word. In these languages, the aspirated and unaspirated *p* would be two separate phonemes.

Phonology also involves syllable structure and the sequence of sounds in a word. For example, English words use several different patterns of consonants (C) and vowels (V)—V (*I*), VC (*it*), CCV (*spy*), CV (*hi*), CVC (*mat*), CVCC (*best*), CVCCC (*burned*), CVVC (*quit*), and CCVVCCC (*squints*). Our knowledge of phonology and of these patterns helps us recognize words that could be English words even though they are not (e.g., *gub, tricand, subgrased*), and words that could not be English words (e.g., *ntrgn, aeouiv, pmuououeg*). Note that you can read the first set of words but not the second.

Knowledge of phonology helps teachers understand issues related to pronunciation, accents, and regional varieties of English. Student difficulties in pronunciation often have to do with the fact that some English phonemes may not exist (or may vary slightly) in a student's home language, and vice versa. Also, some of the sequences of sounds allowed in English are not allowed in other languages, and vice versa. A foreign-sounding accent is usually a result of small differences in phonology between English and the speaker's home language. For example, in situation 1 at the beginning of the chapter, Vihn may have difficulty pronouncing the *th* sound because this phoneme does not exist in Vietnamese. He does not need to be sent to the speech therapist, and in time he will likely acquire the *th* sound on his own, especially if he is a younger student. If not, and if the teacher or student feels it is necessary, activities such as using minimal pairs (e.g., *thing/ding*) can help him improve his pronunciation.

Morphology

Morphology is the study of the structure of words. Every word is made up of one or more morphemes. Morphemes are the smallest units that carry meaning or have a grammatical function. For example, the word *books* has two morphemes: *book* conveys the content meaning of a bound text that can be read, and *–s* conveys the grammatical meaning of plurality, indicating that there is more than one book. *Book* is a free morpheme, because it can stand as a word by itself; *–s* is a bound morpheme, because it cannot stand on its own and must be bound to a free morpheme.

Linguists divide morphology into two subcategories: inflectional morphology and derivational morphology. Inflectional morphology addresses the way bound morphemes make inflectional changes to a word, such as changes related to number (e.g., *book/books*), tense (e.g., *jump/jumps/jumped/jumping*), and degree (e.g., *fast/faster/fastest*). Derivational (or lexical) morphology addresses word formation, that is, the way words are derived from other words, and includes the use of prefixes (a bound morpheme affixed in front of a free morpheme; e.g., *mis–* in *misrepresent*) and suffixes (a bound morpheme affixed after a free morpheme; e.g., *–ation* in *misrepresentation*). Bound morphemes can change the lexical category (noun, verb, adjective, etc.) of a word. For example, *teach* is a verb, but the addition of the suffix *–er* changes it to a noun—*teacher*. Bound morphemes can also change a noun to a verb (e.g., *idol/idolize*), a noun to an adjective (e.g., *sin/sinful*), an adjective to a verb (*tight/tighten*), or an adjective to an adverb (*quiet/quietly*). New words can also be derived without changing the lexical category, for example, *tie/untie, representation/misrepresentation, test/pretest, wife/ex-wife*.

Morphology also addresses the creation of new vocabulary through techniques such as compounding (e.g., *sunroof*), borrowing from other languages (e.g., *karaoke* from Japanese, *algebra* from Arabic, *patio* from Spanish), shortening (e.g., the *fed*, from *federal government*), and blending (e.g., *smog* from *smoke* and *fog*). New vocabulary is also created through the use of acronyms (abbreviations that can be pronounced as a word, e.g., *NASA*), and initialisms (abbreviations in which each letter name is pronounced, e.g., *ESL*). The proliferation of "net-speak" or the acronyms and initialisms used in online communication (e-mail, chat, text-messaging) also falls within the venue of morphology; acronyms such as LOL (laughing out loud) and BFF (best friends forever), once constrained to these online text environments, are now creeping into oral speech and even students' schoolwork.

Teachers can use their knowledge of how words are structured to help students develop their morphological awareness: understand how to change verb tenses; how to make compound words, plurals and possessives, and comparatives and superlatives; and how to use contractions. Through word study lessons, teachers can help students use morphemes to create new words. For example, if students know the meaning of *record* they can figure out *records, recorded,* and *recording*. They can also learn how new words are formed in English (e.g., *skydive, vlogging, glamping, mansplain, ringtone, supersize*).

One of the challenges of teaching a new language is that the rules of morphology differ across languages. For example, many languages do not use inflectional morphemes to indicate number or tense, such as *–s* or *–ed* in English, but instead use a stand-alone morpheme, a separate word, to indicate number or tense. Thus, Chanyoung's problem reading words with a final *s* in situation 2 may not be a reading problem. Rather, it may be related to morphological differences between how plurality is marked in Korean and English.

Syntax

Syntax is the study of the rules governing the way words are combined to form sentences and the rules governing the arrangement of sentences in sequences. Syntax is what most teachers think of as grammar. Once we understand the basic rules of grammar, we can produce an unlimited number of sentences. Think about how many new phrases or sentences you speak or write every day that you have never uttered before; your knowledge of syntax allows you to do this.

Syntax is about the relationships between words. You can think of syntax as helping us understand who did what to whom when, where, and how. For example, our knowledge of syntactic rules in English helps us understand the difference between *Dad gave my book to Mom* and *Mom gave my book to Dad*. Even if we are not able to articulate the rules, our underlying knowledge of word order in English (which has a relatively strict subject-verb-object word order) tells us that *Dad* is the subject and *Mom* is the object of the first sentence, while *Mom* is the subject and *Dad* is the object of the second sentence. Our knowledge of syntax also tells us that *To book my gave Dad Mom* is not an acceptable English sentence. Knowing the meaning of these individual words is not sufficient to understand the different meanings conveyed by these sentences. Knowledge of the syntactic rules governing word order in English is necessary to comprehend the meaning.

For ELLs, producing grammatically correct phrases and sentences can be a major challenge because the rules for syntax vary across languages. For example, *Tomorrow I go house friend* is acceptable according to syntactic rules governing word order in Khmer, but the syntactic rules in English would require *Tomorrow I am going to my friend's house*. Like Rosa in situation 3, Spanish speakers who are beginning to learn English may produce utterances like "car red," "house big," and "friend good" because, according to the syntactic word order rules in Spanish, the adjective generally follows the noun it modifies. Thus, the teacher can rest assured that Rosa is not dyslexic. Errors like these are normal at the beginning stages of English language development.

Semantics

Semantics is the study of the meaning of words, phrases, and sentences. Individual words have semantic features that indicate various properties or meanings inherent in the word. For example, the word *woman* contains the following semantic features: animate, human, female, adult; the word *girl,* in contrast, has only three of these semantic features: animate, human, female. Our understanding of semantic features helps us recognize the oddity of a sentence such as *My poodle is an excellent cook.* Although the syntax of the sentence is acceptable, the semantic features of *poodle* do not include *human,* and only humans get to cook.

Semantics also helps us understand the relationships between words, using the following terms:

- *Synonyms.* Words that have the same linguistic meaning (*evil/wicked, cold/freezing, large/huge*)
- *Antonyms.* Words that are opposite in meaning (*rich/poor, happy/sad, hot/cold*)
- *Homophones.* Words that sound the same but have different meanings (*bear/bare, to/two/too, meat/meet*)
- *Homonyms.* Words that have two or more different meanings (*chair*: 1. an object to sit on, 2. leader of a committee or a department).
- *Hyponyms.* Words that are included in the meaning of another word (*dog* is a hyponym of *animal; rose* is a hyponym of *flower*). Hyponyms can be arranged in a hierarchical relationship: *pit bull → dog → mammal → animal → creature → living thing.*
- *Converseness.* Refers to a reciprocal semantic relationship between words (husband/wife, child/parent, grandchild/grandparent, buy/sell, give/receive)
- *Polysemy.* Refers to two or more related meanings that a word can have (*plain*: 1. easy, clear (*plain English*), 2. undecorated (*plain white shirt*), 3. not good looking (*plain Jane*).

- *Part/whole relationships.* Refers to the relationship between words in which one or more words are part of another word (*hand → arm; second → minute; hand, elbow, forearm, wrist → arm; second, minute, hour → day*).

Semantics also addresses issues such as modality (mood), which enables us to distinguish between a command (*Bring your homework tomorrow*), a statement (*He will bring his homework tomorrow*), permission (*You may bring your homework tomorrow*), and probability (*He will probably bring his homework tomorrow*). Semantics includes the way we can refer to real-world entities, including the use of personal pronouns (*I, you, her*) and other deictic expressions that provide orientation or points of reference (*here, there, now, then*).

Teachers can use their understanding of semantics to develop vocabulary lessons that are based on lists of semantically related words, which are much easier to learn than lists of semantically unrelated words. An understanding of semantics can also inform the teaching of cognates—words that are similar in English and a student's home language because they come from the same root (e.g., *important* in English and *importante* in Spanish).

Not all cognates, however, are fully equivalent. Some are partial cognates. For example, in English *parents* has a specific meaning (birth mother and father), but in Spanish *parientes* refers to relatives in general. There are also false cognates. For example, *éxito* in Spanish means "success," not "exit," as it might appear. Direct translation can be complicated because the "same" word may not contain the same semantic features across languages. For example, a Khmer speaker may say "open the light" or "open the radio" because the semantic properties of *open* in Khmer include the turning on of electrical items. Suling's confusion with English gender pronouns in situation 4 is a semantic issue. Her teacher can be assured that Suling knows the difference between boys and girls; but because most third-person pronouns are not marked for gender in Khmer, it may take a little time for Suling to figure out the semantic properties of gender in pronouns such as *he/she, him/her,* and *his/hers* in English.

Pragmatics

Pragmatics is the study of language from the point of view of the users, especially in terms of the choices they make, the constraints they encounter in using language in social interaction, and the effects their use of language has on the other participants in an act of communication (Crystal, 2010). Pragmatics includes the study of "invisible" meaning or how we recognize what is meant even when it is not actually stated. A lot more is communicated in conversation than is actually said. Recognizing the invisible, or beneath-the-surface, meaning depends on certain socially constructed assumptions and expectations that the speaker shares with the listener.

Pragmatics can help us understand how language users interpret speech acts, such as requests, commands, questions, and statements. Speech acts can be direct or indirect. For example, my wife asks me (in a harsh tone), "Why did you leave the door open?" My understanding of pragmatics tells me that although this utterance has the surface structure of a question, it is actually an indirect request or command for me to close the door. An understanding of the difference between direct and indirect speech acts can help us explain the miscommunication that arose in situation 5. If Thanawan interpreted the teacher's utterance, "Why are you still reading instead of doing your math?" as a simple question, then her response, "Oh, because I not finish yet" is an appropriate answer. But the teacher's interpretation of Thanawan's response as rude and disobedient suggests that the teacher's utterance was meant not as a question but as an indirect request to stop reading and start doing math.

Pragmatics also helps us understand how we use language to start, maintain, and end conversations, take turns, express opinions, agree and disagree, negotiate social status in relationships, save face, and make excuses. From pragmatics, we understand that it's not just what we say but often how we say it that conveys the intended meaning (or how the listener interprets what was said). Thus, teachers can draw on their understanding of pragmatics to help their ELLs learn the underlying rules of interaction needed for successful communication with English speakers inside and outside of the classroom and school.

Lexicon

The vocabulary of a language is its **lexicon**. To use a word from the lexicon, a speaker needs four kinds of information:

- its sounds and their sequencing (phonological information),
- its meanings (semantic information),
- its category (e.g., noun or verb) and how to use it in a sentence (syntactic information), and
- how related words such as the plural (for nouns) and past tense (for verbs) are formed (morphological information). (Finegan, 2012, p. 39)

Children growing up in English-speaking families acquire English vocabulary very rapidly and usually with little direct assistance. They pick up words in conversation and by reading and being read to. A typical 2nd grade student knows the meaning of 6,000 words by the end of grade 2 (Biemiller, 2010). On average, children between the ages of 1 and 17 add 13 words a day to their growing vocabulary; by the time they are 17, they know about 80,000 words (Fillmore & Snow, 2018). Clearly, there is a large vocabulary gap between ELLs and their English-proficient peers. Folse (2011) notes, however, that "one estimate of ELLs' lexical needs is approximately 2,000 words to maintain conversations, 5,000 to read authentic texts, and perhaps 10,000 to comprehend challenging academic materials" (p. 362). Teachers can help ELLs acquire new words in instructional and natural, noninstructional ways by understanding that vocabulary acquisition happens most easily in context and related to topics that the students care about. Thus, talk about mothers and fathers should include talk about brothers, sisters, grandfathers, grandmothers, aunts, uncles, and cousins; talk about food should include talk about eating, cooking, utensils, and kitchen appliances.

Spelling

Teachers who have some knowledge of the history of the English language can help ELLs understand the often confusing English spelling system. Between the 11th and 15th centuries when Middle English was spoken, spelling and pronunciation were more closely related. In the past 600 years, however, English has changed considerably. Freeman and Freeman (2014) note that modern American English is more logical and systematic than it may seem. The spelling system, they point out, is not based simply on spelling words the way they sound. Two words may be spelled similarly because they are related in meaning rather than sound, and words borrowed from other languages may be spelled in ways that reflect their origin. Thus words such as *know* and *acknowledge* or *sign* and *signify* have spellings that are semantically related, but with roots that are pronounced differently. Words such as *croissant, tamale,* and *jaguar* are spelled the way they are to reflect their origin (French, Spanish, and Guarani, respectively).

What Does It Mean to "Know" a Language?

We frequently hear people ask questions such as, "Do you speak English?" "Do you know Spanish?" or "Are you fluent in Arabic?" But what it means to speak, know, or be fluent in a language depends, first, on how language and language proficiency are conceptualized. Earlier approaches to second language learning viewed language as a set of discrete skills, including reading, writing, listening, and speaking. Knowing a language meant mastering these skills, including memorizing vocabulary words and grammar rules. Such a narrow view of language and language proficiency, however, has proved insufficient for our understanding of how ELLs develop the English they need to participate and achieve across content areas at school and in society. This section reviews developments in and challenges to our understanding of what it means to know a language.

Communicative Competence

From a sociocultural perspective, knowing a language means being able to use it to communicate effectively and appropriately with other speakers of the language. This ability is referred to as **communicative competence**, a term introduced in the late 1960s by Dell Hymes, one of the founders of sociolinguistics (Kern & Kramsch, 2014). Later, Canale and Swain (1980) identified and defined four interrelated components of communicative competence and applied it to language teaching and learning:

1. *Grammatical competence.* The ability to recognize the lexical, morphological, syntactic, and phonological features of a language and use them to interpret and form words and sentences.
2. *Discourse competence.* The ability to connect a series of utterances, written words, or phrases to form a meaningful whole.
3. *Sociolinguistic competence.* The ability to understand the social context in which language is used, including the roles of the participants.
4. *Strategic competence.* The ability to use coping strategies in unfamiliar contexts when imperfect knowledge of rules (or factors that limit their application) may lead to a breakdown in communication.

A fifth competence was later added to address the cultural component of language learning—*intercultural communicative competence* (Byram, 1997). Teachers need to remember that we find cross-cultural differences in the ways people use oral and written language in different speech communities. Thus, what is considered an appropriate way, for example, to agree or disagree, to ask a question, or to say no in one speech community may be considered inappropriate in another. As research on cross-cultural differences in ways of speaking has demonstrated, these differences can lead to miscommunication, stereotyping, and discrimination.

Philips' (1983) classic ethnography of communication at school provides an excellent example of how cultural differences can cause miscommunication. Philips found that students from the Warm Springs Indian Reservation in Oregon tended to pause longer than standard-English-speaking white middle-class students before responding and that the Anglo teacher often interpreted the longer pause as an indication that the child did not know the answer or was being intentionally uncooperative. As a result of this miscommunication, the Anglo teacher called on the Anglo students more often and positioned the Warm Springs Indian students as invisible in the classroom interaction. Philips argues that this ongoing positioning at school socializes the Warm Springs Indian students into seeing themselves as invisible relative to Anglo students and helps explain the subordinate status of Warm Springs Indians in the larger society.

Invisible meaning that is based on certain assumptions and expectations can pose serious challenges to ELLs who do not share the assumptions and expectations of standard-English-speaking students and teachers. Even those who quickly learn vocabulary and grammar may continue to struggle with issues related to pragmatics and sociolinguistics. Thus, it is necessary for teachers to have a strong understanding of this important area of language use so they can make the invisible visible for their students.

Register and Genre

The degree to which one knows a language or is communicatively competent depends on the social setting in which the language is used. Linguists use the term *register* to refer to the variations in language, including the choice of words and grammar that reflect the social setting in which it is used. Think about the difference between the way you speak in a formal setting, such as a class at the university, and in an informal setting, such as a gathering with close friends. Or think about the difference between the writing style you use for an academic paper and the style you use in an e-mail, text message, or social media post. These are examples of formal and informal registers.

Halliday's theory of systemic functional linguistics (SFL) can be useful to teachers in understanding the linguistic challenges ELLs face with advanced language and literacy tasks at school (Halliday & Matthiessen, 2004). In SFL, the notion of linguistic register is employed to understand how language is related to the context in which it is used. What makes a register unique is the range of lexical and grammatical features that create the specific context. In SFL theory, a **genre** is a goal-directed activity, such as the creation of a particular kind of text to achieve a particular cultural purpose. The meaning of a text (either spoken or written) is based on the lexical and grammatical choices that the speaker or writer makes. Thus, through SFL theory, it is possible to identify the lexical and grammatical features that make a particular genre the kind of text it is. In other words, SFL allows teachers to pinpoint what makes a personal narrative a personal narrative, a persuasive essay a persuasive essay, a science lab report a science lab report, a history report a history report, and so on (Brisk & Parra, 2018). Once teachers are able to identify the lexical and grammatical features of these genres, they can make them more explicit to their ELLs and enhance their learning of these genres (de Oliveira & Avalos, 2018).

Social Practice and Discourse

What it means to know a language involves much more than isolated skills and communicative functions. Sociolinguists today view language as holistic, dynamic social practice or discourse, and they look at the ways that people use language to make meaning in context. Language is an integral part of all human action that is inseparable from physical, social, and symbolic action (Walqui, 2015). García (2009a) uses the terms *languaging* or *language practices* to draw attention to this dynamism.

Gee (2012) makes a distinction between **discourse** ("little d") and **Discourse** ("Big D"). "Little d" discourse refers to "language in use or connected stretches of language that make sense, like conversations, stories, reports, arguments, essays, and so forth" (p. 151). These discourses include, for example, the ways that a doctor uses oral and written language within the context of an appointment with a patient, or the ways that a scientist uses oral and written language within the context of a scientific experiment. In contrast, according to Gee, "'Big D' Discourse is always more than just language" (p. 151).

> A Discourse with a capital "D" is composed of distinctive ways of speaking/listening and often, too, writing/reading *coupled* with distinctive ways of acting, interacting, valuing, feeling, dressing, thinking, believing with other people and with various objects, tools, and technologies, so as to enact specific socially recognizable identities engaged in specific socially recognizable activities. These identities might be things like being–doing a Los Angeles Latino street-gang member, a Los Angeles policeman, a field biologist, a first-grade student in a specific classroom and school, a "SPED" student, a certain type of doctor, lawyer, teacher, African-American, worker in a "total quality control" workplace, man, woman, boyfriend, girlfriend, or regular at the local bar, etc. and etc. through a nearly endless list. Discourses are all about how people "get their acts together" to get recognized as a given kind of person at a specific time and place. (p. 152)[1]

A teacher, for example, draws on Discourses of schooling as she participates in student-teacher interactions, which in turn helps construct her identity as a teacher, the student's identity as a student, and the meaningfulness of their student-teacher relationship.

Since the 1990s, sociolinguistic research has highlighted the ideological and sociopolitical dimension of language. The seminal work of Schieffelin, Woolard, and Kroskrity (1998) explores language ideologies, which can be understood as beliefs about languages and speakers of languages that are reflected in what people say, enacted in everyday activities, and structured by power relations. Educators need to understand how local language ideologies, for example, about Spanish, Chinese, Arabic, Navajo—and about speakers of those languages—influence the Discourses of schooling. Of particular importance is how ELLs come to see themselves, their home languages, and their educational opportunities relative to English speakers through discourse practices at school. Because language ideologies are socially constructed through discourse, it is possible for educators to challenge and potentially transform meaning relations in ways that are more equitable for linguistically and culturally diverse learners.

Language Variation

The term *standard American English* is used to refer to the variety of English spoken by members of the dominant society in the United States, and it is the variety taught and assessed in school. Many students, however, in their homes and communities speak regional or nonstandard varieties of English that differ in phonology, morphology, syntax, semantics, pragmatics, and vocabulary. Teachers need to understand that these nonstandard varieties are not "bad English." Rather, they are rule-governed and legitimate varieties of English. But because standard English is the variety spoken by the dominant and powerful group in U.S. society, it is taken for granted as the norm. It is elevated to the role of "proper English," and all other varieties are deemed "substandard."

A controversy, for example, over a proposal by the Oakland Unified School District to recognize African American Vernacular English, or Ebonics, as a legitimate variety of English for instructional purposes at school was based on the stigma attached to Ebonics because it is a nonstandard variety of English. The district's proposal resulted in an emo-

---

[1]Reprinted by permission, Gee, J. P. (2012). *Social linguistics and literacies: Ideology in discourses* (4th ed.). New York: Routledge.

tional national debate and even mockery on late-night television. Lost in the debate, however, was the objective of the proposal: to help African American students, who spoke Ebonics at home and who were doing poorly in school, to learn standard English—the variety needed to succeed academically and in society. In other words, the district planned to use Ebonics to help students learn standard English (Rickford, 2005). Although this approach is grounded in research on language teaching and learning, public outrage over Oakland's efforts to recognize the legitimacy of Ebonics dominated the debate. Discrimination against a person's language or way of speaking is rarely based on the language itself. As the controversy over Ebonics suggests, the discrimination may be less about the language and more about the people who speak it. Raciolinguistics considers the ways that race intertwines with language, including how language can shape our ideas about race (Alim, Rickford, & Ball, 2016).

In situation 6, William's speech is not "poor English"; rather, it is proper African American Vernacular English, a legitimate nonstandard variety of English. Looking past the nonstandard features of his oral language reveals that William's opening of his oral presentation is quite intelligent and effective. Teachers should also be aware that ELLs growing up in areas where nonstandard varieties of English are spoken will likely pick up features of these varieties. These students are sometimes referred to as "standard English language learners" (SELLs). To provide the best education possible for SELLs and other nonstandard-English-speaking students, educators need to learn pedagogically sound and culturally sensitive methods for helping students learn standard English without delegitimizing the variety of their homes and communities.

Bilingualism and Translanguaging

Teachers who work with ELLs also need to understand something about bilingualism—even when they are teaching in English-medium programs. As many socioculturalists remind us, emergent bilinguals draw on all of the languages (including varieties of the "same" language) in their linguistic repertoire to make meaning. When teachers look only at English, or only at standard English, they render the students' other languages invisible and deny the students the opportunity to use their home languages as resources.

We find two different conceptualizations of bilingualism in research and practice. Valdés (2014) notes that early scholarship reflected a narrow notion of bilingualism and considered only people who could use two languages perfectly in all situations with native-like control as bilinguals. In contrast, recent scholarship takes a broader view of bilingualism and considers all individuals who have competence in more than one language (even to a limited degree) as bilinguals. Valdés argues that because bilingual individuals develop and use their languages for different purposes, they do not develop identical strengths in each language. For example, the same individual may speak to a grandmother in Russian, share secrets with a sibling in English, tell jokes with a cousin in English and Russian, and read poetry and pray exclusively in Russian.

Reflecting a holistic, dynamic notion of bilingualism, García (2009a) introduced the term *translanguaging* to the field:

> When describing the language practices of bilinguals from the perspective of the users themselves, and not simply describing bilingual language use or bilingual contact from the perspective of the language itself, the language practices are examples of what we are here calling translanguaging.... For us, translanguagings are multiple discursive practices in which bilinguals engage in order to make sense of their bilingual worlds. (p. 45)

Translanguaging refers to "the complex and fluid language practices of bilinguals" (Lin & He, 2017) and "the ways in which bilinguals use their complex semiotic repertoire to act, know, and to be" (García & Li Wei, 2015, p. 237). Teachers need to remember that the languages in an individual's linguistic repertoire are not separate and compartmentalized. Students always draw on what they know and can do in one language to make new meanings in another. Translanguaging also refers to a range of pedagogical approaches that teachers can use to leverage these complex and fluid language practices of their bilingual students (García, Johnson, & Seltzer, 2016).

Teaching "English" to ELLs includes teaching students how to use language appropriately in classroom interactions. All teachers need to develop an understanding of the phonology, morphology, syntax, semantics, and pragmatics of English, as well as the dominant linguistic and cultural norms or social practices at school. Effective teaching of ELLs also involves understanding language variation, bilingualism, and ways to challenge and potentially transform dominant linguistic and cultural norms so that all students, including ELLs and speakers of nonstandard varieties of English, can succeed.

Language for Academic Purposes

Equipped with this foundational understanding of what we mean by language and what it means to know a language, we turn to a closer look at the language students need for academic purposes at school. We begin with a brief history of the notion of language proficiency for conversational and academic purposes with attention to challenges and developments in the field. Then we turn to a functional, communicative approach to consider what language students need for academic success in the content areas.

Cummins (2008) had a significant influence on ELL education with a distinction he developed in the late 1970s between what he called basic interpersonal communication skills (BICS) and cognitive academic language proficiency (CALP). Cummins (2012) argues that it takes about 1 to 2 years for ELLs to develop conversational fluency in English but that it takes 5 years or longer for ELLs to catch up to proficient English speakers in **academic language proficiency**. Other researchers have backed these claims (Box 2.2). An understanding of how long it takes for ELLs to develop sufficient proficiency in English for academic purposes can inform our response to the claim that accompanies the software in situation 7. No software program, no matter how engaging, will prepare a beginning ELL for participation in a mainstream poetry analysis unit in just a few weeks.

Cummins's work, however, has been subject to substantial criticism, including the charge that the distinction between conversational proficiency and academic language proficiency is an oversimplification of the complex construct of language proficiency, and that the use of these terms leads to misunderstandings about language (Valdés, Poza, & Brooks, 2015; Wiley, 2005). Wiley and Rolstad (2014) note that a major problem with these fuzzy constructs is the confounding of academic language with literacy. They argue that the focus should be on the communicative functions of language and the heavily contextualized language used in the teaching of academic subjects. Wiley and Rolstad point out that language and literacy development always takes place in specific social contexts (e.g., a chemistry classroom), each of which has specific literacy practices (e.g., lab reports), and each student's motivation, involvement, and success depend on the manner in which these literacy practices build on his or her prior knowledge (see also Gee, 2014). Wiley and Rolstad note that much of what falls under academic language proficiency is really just academic socialization to specific school-based literacy prac-

Box 2.2 How Long Does It Take for English Language Learners to Attain Proficiency in English?

Estimates vary, but the quick answer to this question is that it takes about 4 to 7 years for an ELL to attain proficiency in English (Hakuta, Butler, & Witt, 2000). For example, a detailed study in Nevada commissioned by the U.S. Department of Education followed 3 cohorts of ELLs in grades kindergarten, 3, and 6 for 6 years, and found that 65% of the students were reclassified as English proficient within 6 years (Haas, Huang, Tran, & Yu, 2016). But stating it in these simple terms can be misleading. Closer analyses of state assessment and redesignation data reveal that it may take only 2 to 4 years for ELLs to develop oral language skills in English to a level similar to those of native English-speaking peers, but it can take from 5 to 8 years for ELLs to catch up to native speakers in the English language proficiency required for academic purposes, which includes grade-level literacy skills in English (Crawford & Krashen, 2015).

Fillmore (2013), however, whose research in the 1970s helped contribute to these estimates, now suggests that these long periods are the result of inadequate instructional programs. ELLs, she argues, "are going to have to learn the kind of English needed for literacy and learning faster and more successfully than they presently do, say, in 2–3 years, 4 years max!" She is not suggesting that ELLs become "fluent" speakers in this time. Rather, she is arguing that ELLs "can learn complex, challenging materials well before they have learned all the intricacy of the grammar of English." Fillmore (2014) claims that this kind of learning will be possible only if we remove structural and instructional obstacles, and, among other strategies, provide ELLs with appropriate instruction and support to read and comprehend rigorous, grade-level, complex academic texts that contain the linguistic data needed to push them to the highest levels of English proficiency. These strong assertions, however, have yet to be backed by research.

tices. Thus, they argue, the focus should be on understanding what these specific practices are, rather than on achieving a general English proficiency that is not specific to any particular context.

In other words, the construct of academic language proficiency is too general. It is too simplistic, fuzzy, and unhelpful to claim that a single construct called "academic language" exists, and that once students learn it they can master any academic content area. Similarly, Fillmore (2013) argues that the kind of language required for classroom success "is sometimes described as 'academic English,' although it is by no means just one unified type that could be easily characterized, packaged up and taught" (p. 52).

Language for Academic Success in Language Arts, Mathematics, Science, and Social Studies

The oversimplication and inadequacies of the term *academic language* have caused language experts to struggle in their attempts to unpack it. Educators also are unable to define and describe *academic language* with any precision or consistency (Bailey & Huang 2011; DiCerbo, Anstrom, Baker, & Rivera, 2014). Chamot (2009), for example, identifies the following academic language functions: seek information, inform, compare, order, classify, analyze, infer, justify and persuade, solve problems, synthesize, and evaluate. For the academic language function *order,* for example, students use language to sequence objects, ideas, or events by creating a timeline, continuum, cycle, or narrative sequence. Chamot's cognitive academic language learning approach (CALLA) shows teachers how they can structure their classes to help ELLs learn to use English for these academic purposes. Note, however, that Chamot's list of academic language functions is no different from the social language functions a group of students might use as they organize, play, and discuss a soccer match on the playground. Look at each function in Chamot's list and think about how it would be used in this context. You will see that these functions are not unique to academic contexts.

Some efforts to determine what exactly academic language is have focused narrowly on vocabulary. Attempts have been made to produce academic word lists for students to master.[2] A current trend distinguishes three tiers of vocabulary:

- Tier 1: basic words (e.g., *block, baby, happy, walk*)
- Tier 2: more sophisticated words that are of high utility for literate language users (e.g., *coincidence, absurd, industrious, fortunate*)
- Tier 3: words that apply to specific content areas and domains and words that are very rare (e.g., *isotope, lathe, peninsula, refinery*). (Beck, McKeown, & Kucan, 2013)

Advocates for direct vocabulary instruction argue that the greatest focus should be on teaching tier 2 words, because these "high use" academic words are less common in everyday conversations and more characteristic of written texts (Beck et al., 2013). As high-utility words, they are likely to appear in a variety of texts across content areas and thus can yield greater reading comprehension. But ELLs, especially those at lower proficiency levels, will also need ample opportunities and support to learn tier 1 words. Also many tier 1 words have very specialized meanings in different content areas (e.g., *table, face, plate, tissue*). And even more advanced ELLs may need support in mastering content-specific tier 3 vocabulary. While vocabulary development is essential, learning the type of language needed for academic success goes well beyond learning new words.

The WIDA English language development standards and other English language proficiency standards, such as those aligned with the ELPA21 Consortium, reflect national efforts to delineate what academic language proficiency means for ELLs that goes beyond simple lists of vocabulary words. The WIDA standards, for example, emphasize that academic language proficiency includes being able to communicate for social, intercultural, and instructional purposes within the school setting and being able to communicate information, ideas, and concepts necessary for academic success in language arts, mathematics, science, and social studies (Box 2.3). These standards reflect a more current view of language that delineates the different kinds of language demands associated with the different academic content areas.

Rolstad (2004) argues schools need to help students learn many registers or Discourses.

> Students need to learn all the registers of the subjects they study in school, each with its peculiar vocabulary and whatever other linguistic features that inhere. At the same time, they must also learn those registers that are necessary for their social success in school as well as in other areas of their lives. Social, communicative competence requires the acquisition of myriad registers, or Discourses, ways of talking to other students, inside and outside of class, and ways of talking to teachers, each of whom may have his or her own preferences for interaction. (pp. 1997–1998)

Thus, rather than put the focus on *academic language* as a single, unifying construct, the focus should be on how language and literacy are actually used in the classroom for teaching and learning specific academic subjects, and on finding ways to help ELLs learn and use these correctly and appropriately in academic settings.

---

[2] See, for example, Biemiller, 2010; Coxhead, 2000; Marzano & Pickering, 2005.

Box 2.3 WIDA's English Language Development Standards and TESOL's English Language Proficiency Standards

Standard 1: English language learners **communicate** for **social* and instructional** purposes within the school setting.

Standard 2: English language learners **communicate** information, ideas, and concepts necessary for academic success in the content area of **language arts**.

Standard 3: English language learners **communicate** information, ideas, and concepts necessary for academic success in the content area of **mathematics**.

Standard 4: English language learners **communicate** information, ideas, and concepts necessary for academic success in the content area of **science**.

Standard 5: English language learners **communicate** information, ideas, and concepts necessary for academic success in the content area of **social studies**.

*TESOL standards include the word "intercultural."
TESOL, 2006; WIDA Consortium, 2012a.
Courtesy of WIDA Consortium.

Academic and Language Demands

MacSwan and Rolstad (2003) introduced the concept of "second language instructional competence" (SLIC) as an alternative to academic language. Rolstad (2017) explains that "children have developed SLIC once they have learned English well enough to understand school subject matter instruction in the majority language." She emphasizes that SLIC does not ascribe any special linguistic or cognitive status to the language of schooling. She argues, "learning to use and understand language in academic settings is part of learning academic subject matter, just as learning to use and understand language in any out-of-school endeavor (farming, boat building, residential constructions, among many others)" (p. 503). SLIC acknowledges that ELLs "need time and learning experience before they can and should be placed in mainstream classes where specially prepared teachers with language-teaching expertise may not be available" (p. 502).

The concept of SLIC helps us to focus more clearly on the specific subject matter or task at hand. Teachers can ask themselves, What is "the amount and type of linguistic proficiency that is required for that student to engage the subject matter at hand?" or, What level of oral and written language is required for students to "understand the language of instruction sufficiently well at that moment, in that context, to participate in that lesson and learn from it?" (Rolstad, 2004, p. 1998).

The amount of SLIC needed will vary from subject to subject and from task to task, in accordance with the language demands of the specific task within a given content area. For example, in situation 8, RoDay, a Karenni refugee who has attended school in the United States for less than 2 years, is not "refusing" to do her written assignment. Nor is the problem that RoDay lacks "academic English." Rather, the language demands of the assignment to write an alternative ending to a story are far greater than those of the other academic tasks—the worksheets and the choral reading—that she completed with little difficulty. To accomplish the task of writing an alternative ending, RoDay will need adequate instruction, ample scaffolding support, and perhaps even a modified assignment more appropriate to her levels of proficiency in English reading and writing. Thus, by thinking linguistically about specific students and the language demands of specific academic tasks, teachers can make informed instructional decisions about how best to help each student accomplish these tasks.

Box 2.4 Key Common Core State Standard English Language Arts Practice 4: Build and Present Knowledge through Research by Integrating, Comparing, and Synthesizing Ideas from Texts

Analytical Tasks

Tasks that are primarily introduced at the elementary level

Gather evidence from a wide range of sources
Synthesize multiple sources on a subject
Use technology in the creation and production of research

Tasks that are primarily introduced at the secondary level (in addition to elementary)

Narrow or broaden the inquiry when appropriate
Verify the accuracy of sources
Rely on sources that have been vetted for accuracy and credibility
Analyze and compare evidence, selecting the strongest to answer the research question
Assemble evidence into logical sequences to support claims or argument
Interpret evidence to provide deeper insight into research question
Generate additional research questions to further inquiry

Receptive Language Functions

Receptive language functions that are primarily introduced at the elementary school level

Comprehend texts used as sources for research
Comprehend written research products produced by peers
Comprehend oral and written discourse about the research process
Comprehend oral and written discourse about research conducted by others

Receptive language functions that are primarily introduced at the secondary school level (in addition to elementary)

Comprehend oral and written classroom discourse about the task of integrating, comparing, and synthesizing ideas
Comprehend oral and written classroom discourse about critiques of one's research as well as the research of others

Productive Language Functions

Productive language functions that are introduced primarily at the elementary level

Communicate orally and in writing ideas, concepts, and information related to building and presenting knowledge, including
    Demonstrating a coherent understanding of a topic or issue by integrating information presented in different texts or formats
    Producing and interpreting evidence in logical sequences to support claims or thesis
    Describing results of research

Productive language functions that are introduced primarily at the secondary school level (in addition to elementary)

Communicate orally and in writing ideas, concepts, and information related to building and presenting knowledge, including
    Presenting a synthesis of ideas in two or more texts to show a coherent understanding on similar topics or events
    Explaining implications of research
    Explaining own research process
    Asking questions and hypothesizing about others' research

In the context of the CCSS and the Next Generation Science Standards (NGSS), linguists and educators have focused considerable attention on these notions of discipline-specific language demands in the standards. The Council of Chief State School Officers coordinated the development of the English Language Proficiency Development Framework to provide guidance to states on how to use the expectations of the CCSS and NGSS as tools for the creation and evaluation of ELP standards. According to the executive summary of the framework, the CCSS, as well as the NGSS, spell out the sophisticated language competencies that students will need to perform across their respective academic subject areas. These include close reading and constructing effective arguments to support their conclusions, identifying a speaker's key points and elaborating on these ideas in group settings, and constructing and testing models and predictions as well as strategically choosing and efficiently implementing procedures to solve problems. But they also implicitly demand that students acquire ever-increasing command of language in order to acquire and perform the knowledge and skills articulated in the standards (CCSSO, 2012, p. ii).

The framework outlines the underlying English language practices embedded in the CCSS and NGSS so that teachers can clearly articulate the language that ELLs need to accomplish related academic tasks. Box 2.4 provides a concrete example of how the framework can be used to focus on the language demands embedded in the Common Core English language arts standards by considering the receptive (listening and reading) and productive (speaking and writing) functions of language students need to conduct and present research.

Summary

Knowledge of language is relevant to the many roles teachers play as communicators, educators, evaluators, educated human beings, and agents of socialization. Teachers need to know about phonology, morphology, syntax, semantics, pragmatics, and how the lexicon is structured and acquired. They need to know about language variation and bilingualism and be able to recognize and value nonstandard varieties of English as well as languages other than English, while helping students develop standard English. When teachers understand what it means to "know" a language, they can help their students develop the communicative competence needed for social and academic purposes in school and beyond. Using this foundational knowledge to think linguistically about their students, the standards, the curriculum, and their classroom instruction, teachers can identify the specific language demands of different academic tasks, and they can determine how best to help each student meet these demands to ensure his or her English language development and academic success in the classroom.

Discussion Questions

1. Fillmore and Snow identify five functions that teachers perform for which they need to know about language. Are these functions relevant only for teachers of ELLs, or are they important for all teachers? Of the teachers you know, how many do you think have the kind of knowledge Fillmore and Snow deem essential? In what ways might the lack of such knowledge affect instruction?

2. Go back to the situations at the beginning of this chapter. For each one, discuss what misunderstanding the teacher may have, and discuss how an understanding of language can help the teacher pinpoint the issues and address them in an appropriate manner. What other examples have you run across where misunderstandings about language led to problems?

3. Think linguistically about the following academic tasks to identify the specific language skills and levels of English proficiency (or amount of second language instructional competence) that students would need to successfully engage in them: (a) listen and take notes during a high school class lecture on U.S. history, (b) solve 50 2-digit addition and subtraction problems, (c) read a chapter in a 5th grade science book and answer the questions at the end, (d) sing along and do movements to a song, (e) listen to a book read aloud by a 1st grade teacher and draw a picture of your favorite part, (f) practice for an 8th grade reading comprehension test (reading text passages and answering multiple-choice questions), (g) work cooperatively with a group of peers to carry out a science experiment, and (h) write a persuasive essay.

4. View the video of Professors David Freeman and Yvonne Freeman, authors of many books on teaching ELLs, discussing the notion of "academic language." According to the Freemans, how is academic language much more than simply learning new vocabulary? How does the Freemans' view of academic language correspond with scholars who argue that there is no such thing as a single, unified construct of academic English?

5. Review the document "Key Takeaways from the K–12 Common Core State Standards in English Language Arts." What are the specific language areas and skills being targeted for *all* students in the standards? What opportunities and challenges may these standards pose for ELLs?

Research Activities

1. *ELL Student Interview* Ask a current or former ELL student about each of the five subsystems of language discussed in this chapter. Which proved to be the most challenging, and why? What strategies did the student or his or her teacher use to help in these areas?

2. *ELL Teacher Interview* Ask an ELL teacher what he or she knows about linguistics and how this knowledge helps him or her address language-related issues that arise in the classroom. Ask for specific examples.

3. *ELL Classroom Observation* Visit an ELL classroom and make a list of the academic lessons, activities, and tasks you observe. Describe the language skills students needed to participate or complete each one of these successfully. Did each one require the same type of language skills to complete? How did the amount of SLIC students needed to complete each lesson, activity, or task vary?

4. *Online Research Activity* Search online to find an ESL lesson plan; ESL instructional materials; or a video of ESL instruction, games, or activities for children (search "ESL children"). Analyze the language demands of the activity or lesson, and describe the language skills students would need to participate successfully.

Recommended Reading

Adger, C. T., Snow, C. E., & Christian, D. (Eds.). (2018). *What teachers need to know about language* (2nd ed.). Washington, DC: Center for Applied Linguistics.

The contributors to this newly updated edition of this book provide essential knowledge of the nature of language that teachers need to be effective in the classroom.

Freeman, D. E., & Freeman, Y. S. (2014). *Essential linguistics: What you need to know to teach reading, ESL, spelling, phonics, and grammar* (2nd ed.). Portsmouth, NH: Heinemann.

An excellent introduction to linguistics for teachers, with clear teaching examples.

Valdés, G., Menken, K., & Castro, M. (2015). *Common Core, bilingual and English language learners: A resource for educators*. Philadelphia: Caslon.

This edited volume brings together leading experts who answer educators' questions about how ELLs/emergent bilinguals can meet the academic and linguistic demands of CCSS. Chapter 2 is dedicated to fundamental language issues.

Three

Language Learning and Teaching

To transform classrooms into stimulating arenas where ideas are exchanged, problematized, built upon and enhanced, teachers need to revisit how they conceptualize language, and recognize how these conceptualizations influence their behavior in classes.

—Aida Walqui

KEY TERMS
- affective filter
- cognitive approaches
- communicative language teaching
- comprehensible input
- comprehensible output
- content-based instruction
- language socialization
- scaffolding
- sociocultural perspectives
- teaching for transfer
- zone of proximal development

GUIDING QUESTIONS
1. How do students develop proficiency in a new language?
2. How can different theories of language learning inform effective practice?
3. How do you develop your own personal approach to providing effective language and content instruction for English language learners?

To ensure that ELLs receive effective language and content instruction, all teachers must have an understanding of theories and research related to how students develop proficiency in a new language. Philosophers since at least the time of Plato have speculated on this issue, and linguistic theories began emerging in the early 1900s. Modern linguists continue to conduct research and debate exactly how young children are able to acquire their first language and how people acquire or learn a second or additional language. Each of these theories provides important insights for effective practice.

We begin with a brief discussion of Noam Chomsky's revolutionary contributions to the field of first language acquisition. From there we turn to major contributions to the field of second language acquisition that largely reflect a cognitive psychological perspective. Next we discuss sociocultural perspectives on language learning and teaching that challenge traditional cognitive approaches. Although these perspectives come from different theoretical orientations and use different terminology, both provide important insights that have been influential in molding how teachers structure opportunities for students to learn and use language for academic purposes in the classroom environment. Then we discuss the application of these theories by looking at several approaches and methods in language learning and teaching that have been influential in K–12 education. We conclude with a discussion about how teachers can move beyond traditional approaches and develop their own principled approach grounded in an understanding of language and language development.

First Language Acquisition Theories

Newborn babies are unable to speak, but by the time they are 5 years old (assuming no cognitive or developmental disorders), they have a fully developed language system. Two major theories have evolved to explain this amazing achievement. In the behaviorist perspective, the well-known psychologist B. F. Skinner and others hypothesized that children learn their first language through imitation and positive reinforcement. Young children imitate the speech they hear around them, and adults positively reinforce their meaningful utterances, helping them develop habits of correct speech. This view was prominent throughout the 1940s and 1950s but was challenged by Noam Chomsky in 1959.

Chomsky, widely recognized as one of the world's most influential linguists, demonstrated that children are able to produce language and unique utterances that go well beyond what they could reasonably have been exposed to and imitated. He hypothesized that children have an innate ability—they are prewired—to learn language. Chomsky's theories, often referred to as the innatist perspective, suggest the presence of a language acquisition device (LAD) that enables children to figure out the underlying rules of the language on their own because of their exposure to samples of natural language. He refers to these underlying rules as universal grammar. Once the LAD is activated and children internalize the rules for the structure (syntax) of their language or languages, they can generate an infinite number of unique, grammatically correct utterances.

Chomsky's theories were revolutionary and they led to a rejection of the behaviorist perspectives on language acquisition. Although his work remains influential, with most linguists agreeing that children have some form of genetic predisposition for language learning, new research is emerging from within linguistics and other academic fields. Those who accept Chomsky's ideas at some level vigorously debate exactly how they work, while others challenge the core of his ideas (Dor, 2015; Everett, 2008; Frank, Bod, & Christiansen, 2012; Wolfe, 2016). For example, Everett (2017), a linguist who spent 30 years studying the language of a primitive tribe—the Pirahã—deep in the Amazon jungle found that universal grammar could not account for their language, which appears to be unrelated to any other language in the world. Everett argues that language is not innate but rather is a human cultural invention that has evolved since the time of our earliest ancestors (*Homo erectus*) over 1 million years ago: "Language gradually emerged from a culture, formed by people who communicated with one another via human brains. *Language is the handmaiden of culture*" (p. xvii, emphasis in original). Cristiansen and Chater (2017) argue that this alternative emerging paradigm will lead to a more interdisciplinary and integrated view of the science of language, which will lead to new breakthroughs in our understandings of the origin of language and of first and second language acquisition. These breakthroughs will likely have strong implications for language teaching and learning.

Second Language Acquisition Theories

Lightbown and Spada (2013) identify four major perspectives from which theories about second language acquisition (SLA) have emerged: behaviorism, the innatist perspective, the cognitive/developmental perspective (psychological theories), and the sociocultural perspective. Atkinson (2011) makes a simpler distinction between traditional cognitivists approaches to SLA (beginning with Chomsky's challenges to behaviorism) and a range of alternatives to SLA, which includes sociocultural approaches. To keep things simple, in the sections that follow, we first explore cognitive theories and approaches to SLA and then turn to sociocultural perspectives on language learning and teaching. While these various theories present sometimes very different and contrasting ideas, knowledge of both perspectives on language learning and teaching provides teachers with the foundation they need to form their own approach to instructing ELLs.

Cognitive Approaches to Second Language Acquisition

Those who take **cognitive approaches** to SLA are most interested in what is happening inside the brain of the language learner. Because we do not know exactly how people learn their first language, there are many competing theories and much debate over how people learn a second (or third or more) language (Boxes 3.1 and 3.2). Nonetheless, excellent research in the field of SLA has led to the development of several plausible theories that have important implications for second language teaching and learning.

Cognitivist theories of SLA first emerged as a direct challenge to behaviorism. B. F. Skinner's theories of learning as habit formation through stimulus and response with negative and positive reinforcement greatly influenced second language teaching from the 1940s to the 1970s, with classes focused mainly on memorization and language drills. By the end of the 1970s, however, following Chomsky's challenges, most SLA researchers

---

Box 3.1 Critical Period Hypothesis

Do younger students learn a second language better and faster than older students?
The critical period hypothesis holds that language learning must take place during early childhood if an individual is to attain "native-like" proficiency. This hypothesis has supported the popular view that young children have cognitive advantages that enable them to learn languages better and faster than adults. This long-held view has been called into question by more recent research that found this ability may last into the late teenage years (Hartshorne, Tenenbaum, & Pinker, 2018), and casts doubt on whether the advantages are indeed cognitive.

Other research has challenged the critical period hypothesis with evidence that adults can and do learn languages successfully and even attain "native-like" proficiency (Baker & Wright, 2017). Research has shown that younger students do have some advantages over adult learners of a second language. Most of these advantages, however, are social rather than cognitive. Research has also revealed advantages that adults have over younger children in learning a second language.

Advantages of Young Children in Language Learning

- Young school-age children often have greater motivation, pressure, needs, and opportunities to develop second language proficiency than adults.
- Younger students receive a much greater amount of instructional time in the K–12 educational systems to learn a language (e.g., 6 hours a day, 5 days a week) than the typical adult learner, who may receive only a few hours of instruction a week.
- Younger learners may have a lower affective filter than older students; thus, they may feel more comfortable using their new language.

Advantages of Older Students and Adults in Language Learning

- Older learners may be literate in their first language and have other knowledge and skills that can readily transfer to a second language.
- Older learners may have learning strategies they developed in the first language that will help them as they learn a second language.

"If we could combine the maturity and articulated necessity of the older with the impressionability, imitativeness, spontaneity, and unselfconsciousness of the younger, we would surely have a recipe for rapid and proficient bilingual acquisition" (Edwards, 2013, p. 17).

> **Box 3.2 English May Not Be the Second Language**
>
> Although we use the terms *second language acquisition* and *second language teaching* with some ELLs, English may be their third, fourth, or even fifth or higher language. Much of what researchers talk about under the label *second language acquisition* still applies to these students' efforts to learn English. Researchers, however, are beginning to explore the many factors that may be unique to the acquisition of a third language, a fourth language, and so on. To acknowledge that many students have proficiency in more than two languages, several states use the term *new language* instead of *second language* (see, e.g., EngageNY, 2013), as does the National Board for Professional Teaching Standards (1998) in its national teacher certification programs.

had rejected the behaviorist perspective. Nonetheless, methods connected with behaviorism can still be found in many language classrooms and textbooks.

Although Chomsky's work focuses on first language acquisition, his theories have been highly influential on SLA researchers and theories. Many researchers argue that we learn a second language in much the same way we learn our first language, and that second language learners also access universal grammar to form internal rules about the language that are based on the input they receive.

Monitor Model

One of the most influential cognitive models of SLA is known as the monitor model, developed by Krashen in the 1980s (1985, 2004a). This model includes five interrelated hypotheses:

1. *Acquisition-Learning Hypothesis.* Krashen argues that there is a fundamental difference between learning a language and acquiring a language. Language acquisition is a subconscious process. We are not aware that it is happening, and we are not even aware that we possess any new knowledge that is subconsciously stored in our brains. Language learning, in contrast, is a conscious process; it is what we do in school. When we are learning, we know we are learning and the learned knowledge is represented consciously in our brains. Learning results in knowing *about* the language rather than *knowing* the language (i.e., the ability to use it for authentic communicative purposes). Krashen argues that because of the complexity of language, the vast majority is acquired rather than consciously learned.

2. *Natural Order Hypothesis.* Krashen asserts that we acquire the parts of a language in a predictable order. For example, the *–ing* marker in English (the progressive) is acquired fairly early, whereas the third-person singular *–s* is acquired much later or may not be acquired at all by older ELLs. Because the natural order appears to be immune to teaching, drilling a student on a grammatical item before he or she is ready to acquire it will be of little use.

3. *Monitor Hypothesis.* Krashen notes that although most language is acquired, we can use learned language to monitor or inspect what we acquire and then correct errors. Sometimes we make a correction internally before we actually say or write something; other times we self-correct after producing a sentence. The monitor is like a little language teacher in our heads reminding us of the rules. Krashen asserts that the monitor can make a small contribution to accuracy but acquisition is responsible for fluency and most of our accuracy.

4. *Input (Comprehension) Hypothesis.* This is Krashen's most important hypothesis because it directly addresses how language acquisition occurs. He originally called

it the input hypothesis but renamed it the comprehension hypothesis to more accurately reflect what it says (Krashen, 2004a). According to this hypothesis, we
acquire language when we understand messages or obtain **comprehensible input**.
That is, we acquire language when we understand the things we hear or read.
Krashen offers the formula $i + 1$ to explain comprehensible input; i represents a
student's current level of proficiency, and +1 represents input that is just slightly
above that level. He suggests that we move from i to $i + 1$ by understanding input
containing $i + 1$. We are able to do this "with the help of our previously acquired
linguistic competence, as well as extra-linguistic knowledge, which includes our
knowledge of the world and our knowledge of the situation. In other words, we
use context" (Krashen, 1985, p. 5). Thus, $i + 1$ is the key to providing comprehensible input that enables further acquisition to take place. Krashen argues that
we acquire language and develop literacy by understanding messages, not by
consciously learning about language and not by memorizing grammar rules and
vocabulary.

5. *Affective Filter Hypothesis.* Krashen explains that the **affective filter** controls how
   much comprehensible input gets through to the learner. Even though the student
   is exposed to input, anxiety, low self-esteem, or a sense that he or she is not a potential member of the group that speaks the language—the affective filter—will
   keep it out. Thus, a major goal in language teaching and learning is to "lower" the
   affective filter to maximize comprehensible input. This hypothesis has been useful
   in explaining why individual students make different amounts of progress when
   presented with the same input.

Comprehensible input, Krashen (1985) points out, is the essential ingredient for SLA.
He summarizes the five hypotheses with a single claim:

> People acquire second languages only if they obtain comprehensible input and
> if their affective filters are low enough to allow the input "in." When the filter is
> "down" and appropriate comprehensible input is presented (and comprehended),
> acquisition is inevitable. It is, in fact, unavoidable and cannot be prevented. (p. 4)

Although Krashen's hypotheses have been and continue to be highly influential, they
have been criticized for their emphasis on acquisition over learning and, in their application to classroom teaching, what seems to be the lack of direct instruction on grammatical and other language forms. Research shows, however, that despite the considerable
progress students can make through exposure to comprehensible input without direct
instruction, they may reach a point where further progress requires guided instruction
(Lightbown & Spada, 2013).

Krashen does acknowledge a role for some direct teaching, as addressed in the monitor hypothesis, but his theories do not necessarily provide guidance about what should
be directly taught and what students will naturally acquire on their own.

Critics of the natural order hypothesis point out that no one has been able to identify
a strict order in which different grammatical forms and other components of a language
are acquired, nor has anyone been able to account for the tremendous variation we see
in the order in which individuals acquire the different forms. Another criticism is that
the constructs i and +1 from the comprehension hypothesis cannot be operationalized
with any degree of exactness. Because of the complexity of language and the limitations
we have in determining a student's actual language proficiency through language proficiency tests, we cannot obtain a precise measure of a student's i. Assuming we could measure i, exactly how much is +1?

Of greater concern to Krashen's critics, however, is his oversimplification of complex processes in SLA and his downplaying of the importance of production (i.e., speaking and writing) in SLA. It may strike some as counterintuitive that one can acquire a new language without ever having to speak it. But, Krashen (1985) asserts, "speaking is a *result* of acquisition and not its *cause*. Speech cannot be taught directly but 'emerges' on its own as a result of building competence via comprehensible input" (p. 2; emphasis added). He adds, however, that speaking can be an indirect aid to language acquisition. Speaking results in conversation, and what the other person says is an excellent source of comprehensible input. Speaking can also help by making the learner feel more like a user of the second language, and this feeling helps lower the affective filter. Krashen (2017) continues to respond to his critics and maintains that research supports his hypotheses.

Despite the criticisms, Krashen's theories have inspired a considerable amount of research, much of it by scholars in psychology whose work has led to several psychological theories of SLA. Cognitive and developmental psychologists believe that there is no distinction in the brain between learning and acquisition and that, therefore, general theories of learning are sufficient to account for language learning. Among these are the information-processing model, connectionism, and the competition model. VanPatten (2017) argues, however, that language acquisition involves processes and mechanisms that are unique to language. He and other psycholinguists are interested in understanding the processes and mechanisms that enable a learner to comprehend and produce language.

Interaction Hypothesis

Researchers have argued that interaction is essential for SLA to occur, and thus they have studied the ways in which speakers modify their speech and their interaction patterns to help learners participate in conversation (Gass, 2018). Long (2018), who developed the interaction hypothesis, agrees that comprehensible input is needed, but he focuses on how input can be made comprehensible through modified interaction, arguing that learners need opportunities to interact with other speakers and reach mutual comprehension. In modified interaction, particularly interactions between a language learner and a proficient speaker, the speakers may make several modifications as they converse to get their meanings across (Swain & Suzuki, 2008). Some of these modifications may include simplifying the language, reducing the rate of speech, and using gestures. Proficient speakers might repeat or paraphrase what they say and use comprehension checks, asking the learner during the conversation, "Do you understand?" The learner may make clarification requests with questions such as, "Can you repeat that please?" or "I'm sorry, what did you say?" or even a simple, "Huh?" along with a puzzled look. The proficient speaker also provides corrective feedback, which may take the form of direct correction or indirect correction through more subtle means, such as repeating what the learner said but recasting it in the correct form. All these corrections are made within the natural flow of the conversation. For example, if the learner says, "I go to doctor yesterday," the proficient speaker might respond, "You went to the doctor yesterday? Why? Are you sick?"

Comprehensible Output Hypothesis

Swain (2005) brought attention to the importance of output in SLA in the late 1980s with her **comprehensible output** hypothesis. Swain argues that when learners are in conversation, making an effort to produce language that the person with whom they are conversing can understand, they are most likely to see the limits of their second language ability and the need to find better ways to get their meaning across. Knowing they have to speak forces them to pay more attention to what they are saying. Thus, Swain and others argue that comprehensible input alone is insufficient, and creating comprehensible output is also needed to facilitate language acquisition. Krashen (1998, 2017) disagrees. He argues that spoken (and written) output occurs too infrequently to be a major source of language development.

Noticing Hypothesis

Schmidt (2012) points out in his noticing hypothesis that learners cannot acquire specific language features in the input unless they notice them. Learners may notice language features when, for example, their teachers bring these features to their attention in class or when something in the input is different from what they expected. Psycholinguists continue to debate the importance of awareness and attention in SLA, and research on these issues is ongoing.

Processability Theory

Pienemann (2015) argues in his processability theory that the sequence in which learners acquire certain language features depends on how easy they are to process. Part of this ease depends on where features occur within a sentence in the input; those at the beginning or end are easier to process than those in the middle. He also theorizes that learners acquire some linguistic features in the same sequence, even if they progress at different rates, while they acquire other linguistic features in different sequences, according to when they were processed.

Input Processing Model

VanPatten developed the input processing model, which looks at how learners make sense out of input and how they get linguistic data from it (VanPatten & Jegerski, 2010). VanPatten (2017) argues that "communicative input is the essential external ingredient for language acquisition" (p. 35). He defines input as the language learners hear or see in a communicative context, or language that is "embedded in a communicative event that the learner attends to for its meaning" (p. 59). He stresses that to be successful, learners must have access to input and interaction with other speakers of the second language they are learning. In his model, VanPatten (2003) accepts the processability theory and adds the following:

- Learners always process input for meaning first and rely on content words before anything else to get that meaning.
- When a content word and a grammatical form encode the same meaning (e.g., pastness is encoded by both a time reference, such as "yesterday," and a verb inflection, such as *–ed*), learners rely on the content word and "skip" the grammatical form.
- Learners rely on a first-noun strategy to understand "who did what to whom." (p. 41)[1]

VanPatten (2003) also addresses how newly processed input leads to changes in the learner's developing linguistic system. He explains that this system change involves two subprocesses. The first, *accommodation,* describes the process by which learners actually incorporate a grammatical form or structure into the "mental picture" of the language they are creating. The second, *restructuring,* describes the process by which the incorporation of a form or structure makes other things change without the learner's ever know-

---

[1] VanPatten, B. (2003). *From input to output: A teacher's guide to second language acquisition.* Copyright McGraw-Hill Education, reprinted by permission.

ing. Finally, VanPatten addresses *output processing* to explain how learners are able to make use of their acquired implicit knowledge in conversations with others.

To summarize, VanPatten (2003) declares:

> Language acquisition happens in only one way and all learners must undergo it. Learners must have exposure to communicative input and they must process it; the brain must organize data. Learners must acquire output procedures, and they need to interact with other speakers. There is no way around these fundamental aspects of acquisition; they are the basics. (p. 96)[2]

Transfer from First Language to Second Language

From a cognitive psychological perspective we may consider how students draw on what they know in their first language (L1) as they are learning a second language (L2). Students are able to take much of the content-area knowledge and literacy skills they gained in their L1 and transfer them to their L2. This ability to transfer knowledge and skills means that students who have literacy skills in their L1 will likely make rapid progress in learning to read and write in English (National Academies, 2017). Likewise, students who have developed substantial content-area knowledge through their L1 do not need to relearn the same concepts in English. ELLs who have advanced skills in math, for example, do not need to relearn these concepts in English; they just need to learn the language necessary to demonstrate what they already know.

Although linguists and language educators recognize that much of what transfers from one language to another is beneficial (i.e., positive transfer), in some instances, transfer from the L1 may cause interference (i.e., negative transfer). Students may attempt, for example, to apply their knowledge of the syntax of their L1 to English (e.g., a Spanish speaker saying "house of friend" rather than "friend's house"). Although more research is needed to determine precisely what does and does not transfer, teachers can be assured that students' knowledge and literacy skills in their L1 is a strength that will facilitate their academic and English language development. Effective teachers recognize and value the vast store of knowledge students have in their first language and provide instruction that enables students to draw on this knowledge. Cummins (2017) calls this **teaching for transfer**.

Sociocultural Perspectives on Language Learning and Teaching

In general, **sociocultural perspectives** on language learning and teaching stand in contrast to cognitive psychological approaches because the focus is not on what happens inside the brain of the learner but on the sociocultural context surrounding the learner that facilitates the learning process. Sociocultural perspectives have been growing in popularity because they help teachers consider and address the linguistic and cultural diversity of their students, the languages and literacies their students use at home and in the community, and the languages and literacies needed for success in learning English and academic content at school and beyond. In the sections that follow, we first discuss major contributions from the field of sociolinguists that began in the late 1960s. Then we turn to the late Russian social psychologist Lev Vygotsky, whose work has had a great influence on the field since the 1990s. Next we look at recent work on language socialization and conclude with a brief discussion of bilingual perspectives on language teaching and learning.

---

[2] VanPatten, B. (2003). *From input to output: A teacher's guide to second language acquisition.* Copyright McGraw-Hill Education, reprinted by permission.

A note on terminology: socioculturally oriented researchers and practitioners challenge some of the terms that emerged from traditional cognitive approaches and use alternative terms that better reflect the lived experiences of culturally and linguistically diverse students and of how languages are learned and taught. For example, rather than *first language, native language,* or *primary language,* the term *home language* is often preferred to highlight the language or languages students actually use to communicate with family members and others in their homes. Some students may be "simultaneous" bilinguals who grow up using two or more languages at home. As we have seen, some socioculturalists prefer the term *emergent bilingual* to *ELL* because it focuses attention on the ways students draw on all of their resources in their bilingual, multidialectal linguistic repertoires to learn, even when they are enrolled in English-medium programs. To take into account the fact that English might be a student's third or fourth language, many states, educators, and programs use the term *English as an additional language* or *English as a new language* rather than *English as a second language.* The term *new language* may also be used to refer to English-proficient students in dual language or world language programs.

The use of this new terminology, however, is not yet widespread even among those who tend to favor sociocultural approaches, nor is there complete agreement on what these terms mean and how to use them consistently. Also, most state policies and programs continue to use traditional terminology. Thus, throughout this book traditional terms are used alongside newer terms as appropriate.

Sociolinguistic Contributions

Sociolinguistic research began in the late 1960s in an effort to understand the relationship between languages and the societies in which they are used. Though the research was not focused on language teaching and learning in general, the findings of these studies can help teachers make informed decisions in addressing the needs of their ELLs. For example, Hymes's (1972) notion of communicative competence provides the basis for **communicative language teaching (CLT)** and **content-based instruction (CBI)** approaches. Research on nonstandard varieties of language, such as African American Vernacular English (Ebonics) and TexMex (Spanglish) has shown that linguistically these varieties are rule-governed and logical systems, yet they are often unfairly stigmatized by speakers of dominant, standardized varieties of languages, leading to inequities for speakers of these varieties in schools. Sociolinguistic research also can help educators understand the dynamics of the relationship between English and other languages spoken by ELLs, their families, and their communities, and the implications for structuring language and content-area instruction programs best suited to their needs and interests.

Zone of Proximal Development and Scaffolding

Activity theory stems from the pioneering work of Vygotsky (1978), a Russian psychologist who studied child development in the 1920s and 1930s. Vygotsky died in 1934 at the young age of 38 from tuberculosis, and some of his most influential work was published only after his death. English translations of his work did not appear until the late 1960s, but since then they have been highly influential in the West in psychology and education (see, e.g., Moll, 2013). Vygotsky's influence on language learning and teaching began gaining momentum in the 1990s.

According to Vygotsky, learning is a social activity, and knowledge is constructed through interaction and collaboration with others. Children's learning takes place when they interact and collaborate with adults or more skillful peers. Thus, children's language, a form of knowledge in Vygotsky's view, develops primarily from interactions (conversations) in social settings, especially in a supportive interactive environment. Through these "processes of meaning-making in collaborative activity . . . language itself develops as a 'tool' for making meaning" (Mitchell, Myles, & Marsden, 2013, p. 227).

Vygotsky identified the **zone of proximal development** (ZPD) as a domain or metaphoric space where children can reach a higher level of knowledge and performance with the support of an adult or other more knowledgeable person. This assistance within the ZPD is called **scaffolding**, evoking a construction metaphor, where scaffolding is temporarily used to build something and removed once the building is completed. As with the rest of Vygotsky's theory, researchers apply the concepts of ZPD and scaffolding to the process of language learning and teaching (Gibbons, 2014; Walqui & van Lier, 2010). For example, Zwiers and Crawford (2011) identify five core communication skills that ELLs need and can develop within the ZPD through productive academic conversations with their teachers and peers across the content areas: (1) elaborating and clarifying, (2) supporting ideas with evidence, (3) building on or challenging ideas, (4) paraphrasing, and (5) synthesizing.

Teachers often incorrectly view Vygotsky's ZPD as essentially the same principle as the $i + 1$ in Krashen's input hypothesis. Although it is tempting to view them as the same, since both appear to be addressing the issue of providing something just above a learner's current level of proficiency, the two concepts depend on very different ideas about how development occurs. Krashen's theory reflects a cognitive perspective and focuses on the acquisition of a second language and the provision of comprehensible input that contains linguistic forms and structures that are just beyond the student's current level and just beyond what he or she is ready to acquire. Vygotsky's theory is about knowledge development in general, with an emphasis on how learners co-construct knowledge based on their interactions with others in a given sociocultural context. For example, drawing on the input hypothesis, a teacher wishing to help a student use correct forms of the past tense to talk about yesterday's field trip to the museum will facilitate multiple opportunities for students to receive comprehensible input by hearing speech (from the teacher or other students) and reading text that contains examples of correct past-tense use. The hope is that students will acquire the past-tense forms naturally. In contrast, a teacher drawing on ZPD may plan for more deliberate and meaningful instruction of past-tense forms, working with students to co-construct their knowledge and understanding of the past tense. For example, the teacher and students might co-construct a text (shared writing) to talk about the field trip and thus provide opportunities to teach students the correct use of the forms and guide their use of past tense as they write the text together. The teacher might create a word chart listing the past-tense forms they need in their writing. The writing activity might be followed by students working in pairs to talk about the field trip in preparation for writing their own stories. The teacher could monitor students' use of past tense in their speaking and writing and provide assistance as needed, such as referring them back to the chart or adding new words as needed. These activities take place within the students' ZPD, and the teacher provides the scaffolding necessary for students to understand and use the past-tense forms correctly.

Vygotsky's emphasis on interaction seems closely related also to Long's psycholinguistic interaction hypothesis. Long and other psycholinguists, however, are more interested in the cognitive processes initiated by input and output in the conversations, whereas in the sociocultural perspective the focus is on the conversations themselves, with learning occurring through the social interaction.

Sociocultural theory, then, gives much greater emphasis to the role of speaking and collaborating in learning a second language and thus has opened the way for researchers to focus on collaboration and interaction as key to language learning and teaching.

Swain, for example, extends her work on her comprehensible output by focusing on collaborative dialogues through which language use and language learning co-occur (Swain & Suzuki, 2008).

Vygotsky's ideas have also been widely embraced by educators, who appreciate the important role given to teachers and to classroom interaction in sociocultural theory (Mitchell, Myles, & Marsden, 2013). Teachers are elevated from mere facilitators of comprehensible or modified input to knowledgeable, skilled experts who interact and collaborate with students, and who carefully plan and scaffold instruction within the ZPD to co-construct knowledge with their students.

Language Socialization Research

Language socialization research stems from the early work of Ochs and Schieffelin (1984). Language socialization researchers investigate how children are socialized through language in their respective speech communities across a wide range of sociocultural contexts (Ochs & Schieffelin, 2017). **Language socialization** refers to "the process by which individuals acquire the knowledge and practices that enable them to participate effectively in a language community" (Langman, 2008, p. 489). In addition, language and cultural learning are considered inseparable. As students learn the new language, they gain knowledge about how to use the language in sociocultural contexts and construct their social identities through their participation in language-mediated activities. This work helps teachers recognize that when they work with ELLs they are not just teaching them a new language but they are also socializing their students into a community of English language speakers in their classes, programs, and schools.

Bilingual and Multilingual Pluralist Perspectives

Socioculturalists increasingly look at the education of students officially designated as ELL through a bilingual lens. de Jong (2011) presents four guiding principles that educators can use to guide their decision making about policies, programming, curriculum, instruction, assessment, and accountability from a bilingual perspective: (1) striving for equity, (2) affirming linguistic and cultural identities, (3) promoting developmental bilingualism, and (4) structuring for integration. These principles reflect an understanding of relationships between language and power, and they can help teachers act on their holistic bilingual assumptions about language teaching and learning in ways that elevate the status of languages other than English and varieties other than standard English, use these languages as resources for learning, and improve educational opportunities for students who have traditionally been marginalized.

It is important to distinguish between bilingual education programs, which use two languages for instructional purposes, and a bilingual perspective, which can be embraced by teachers who work with bilingual learners in any type of instructional program—including those that use English as the medium of instruction. It is also important to recognize that not all bilingual education programs embrace holistic, dynamic, bilingual perspectives.

Teachers who look at language teaching and learning from a monolingual perspective may feel reluctant to allow students to use any of their home language in the classroom. This approach reflects a language-as-problem orientation. Bilingual teachers who look at bilingual education from a fragmented or compartmentalized perspective may insist on the strict separation of languages, depending on the time or subjects that have been designated for instruction in one language or the other, and may discourage children from translanguaging (Sayer, 2008). This monolingual, compartmentalized perspective has been dominant in U.S. schools for decades.

In contrast, teachers who look at language teaching and learning from a dynamic bilingual perspective see translanguaging as an integral part of the perfectly natural and normal ways bilinguals use their languages in their everyday lives. Sayer (2013), for example, conducted an ethnographic study in a 2nd grade classroom in Texas where students and their teacher moved "fluidly between not just Spanish and English, but also the standard and vernacular varieties" (i.e., TexMex) as students were engaged in making sense of academic content and standard language instruction. Sayer also found that these translanguaging practices provided students "a legitimized means of performing desired identities" as bilingual Latinos. García & Kleyn (2016) offer several case studies of New York teachers making effective use of translanguaging pedagogies across subjects and grade levels.

Bilingual education programs that reflect a holistic bilingual perspective bring the two languages together in intentional and strategic ways. Escamilla et al. (2013) present a holistic biliteracy framework that views (bi)literacy broadly as a system that includes oracy, reading, writing, and metalanguage (not just as reading and writing). According to this framework, teachers place the two languages side by side for instructional and assessment purposes and document students' trajectories toward biliteracy. Beeman and Urow (2013) contribute the notion of the Bridge, the instructional moment when teachers bring the two languages together strategically and intentionally to promote cross-linguistic transfer.

García, Johnson, and Seltzer (2016) have created a translanguaging guide for educators with a wide range of strategies where teachers and students can use their bilingualism as a rich resource for effective teaching and learning of language and academic content in any classroom. For example, teachers may preview a lesson in the home language and then teach it in English or allow groups of students to discuss in their home language a story they read in English. Teachers may make use of bilingual books or encourage students to write their own. Many of these strategies are consistent with the notion of teaching for transfer grounded in traditional cognitive perspectives. But while socioculturally oriented teachers recognize translanguaging as a powerful way to help students transfer knowledge from their home language to English, they do not view it as a one-way process or as a means to an end. Rather, they recognize that positive transfer can also go from English to the home language, and that conversations and activities involving all of students' languages or dialects are in and of themselves legitimate forms of communication that can be effective in maximizing students' comprehension of rigorous academic content. Thus, translanguaging can also refer to pedagogical practices that use bilingualism as a resource rather than ignore it or perceive it as a problem (García, 2017).

All Teachers Are Language Teachers

Depending on how schools structure programs for ELLs, some teachers may get the false impression that English language development is solely the responsibility of the ESL teacher or specialist. But whether you are, or plan to become, a "regular, mainstream" classroom teacher, a content-area teacher or specialist, a special education teacher, a bilingual teacher, or an ESL teacher, you are also a language teacher. As a language teacher, you share responsibility for helping your ELLs develop their proficiency in English and their ability to use oral and written English for academic purposes across content areas. Content teachers, for example, teach lessons with both language and content objectives. In schools with ESL or bilingual teachers/specialists, there are several points of collaboration for language and content teachers, for example, planning lessons that address

English language proficiency standards, providing support to identify the language demands of differentiated content areas, writing appropriate language objectives, differentiating instruction for ELLs based on their current levels of proficiency, strategically using home languages to support learning, and creating and using appropriate formative assessments. As language and content teachers clarify their roles and responsibilities for teaching ELLs, they can collaborate in effective ways to ensure their students' success in meeting language and content standards. In schools where there are no designated language teachers, it is essential that content teachers also provide the types of language instruction typically provided by language teachers and lead discussions with other decision makers at the school.

Traditional Second Language Teaching Approaches and Methods

The approaches and methods used in teaching a second language have evolved along with, and been influenced by, traditional cognitive theories of SLA, and more recently by sociocultural perspectives on language teaching and learning. The term *approaches* refers to an overarching philosophy of second language instruction; *methods* refers to a set of procedures for delivering second language instruction. Richards and Rodgers (2014) have identified and described over a dozen different approaches and methods that have been used since the 19th century. Some have come and gone and some overlap. In reviewing ESL curricular materials or visiting the classrooms of effective ESL teachers, you will most likely see a mixture of approaches and methods in use. Let us briefly look at some of the more common approaches and methods that continue to have an influence today on instruction for K–12 ELLs.

Grammar-Translation Method

The grammar-translation method, based to a large extent on the way Latin was traditionally taught, was predominant from the 1840s to the 1940s. Students were required to analyze and memorize rules of grammar, then translate sentences between the two languages. This approach is not based on any theory and has no advocates, but it continues to be used widely among teachers with little training or experience. When opposition to grammar-translation developed and language educators and researchers began asking why methods for teaching Latin—no longer a spoken language—were being used to teach modern languages, new methods were developed.

Audiolingual Method

The audiolingual method grew out of the need for foreign language proficiency in the U.S. military after the United States entered World War II. Its appearance coincided with other efforts in the late 1930s and early 1940s to apply principles of structural linguistics to language teaching. The audiolingual method was highly influenced by behaviorism, the dominant view of second language learning at the time. Language learning was viewed as mechanical habit formation accomplished through dialogue memorization and drills focused on particular language structures. Audiolingualism fell out of favor by the 1970s following Chomksy's challenge to behaviorist theories of language learning. Also, many language teachers, and students themselves, were frustrated when students had difficulty moving from their memorized dialogues and drills to real-life communication. While audiolingualism is no longer the dominant method, vestiges of it are still apparent in many textbook dialogues and drills, language labs, and even in commercial language learning audio programs, computer software, and mobile apps.

Natural Approach

In the late 1970s, Terrell developed an approach that was later popularized in the 1980s through collaboration with Krashen as the "natural approach" (Krashen & Terrell, 1983). The natural approach essentially applies Krashen's five hypotheses to the communicative language learning classroom. In contrast to audiolingualism and other methods with a focus on grammar, the natural approach emphasizes the use of comprehensible input in the classroom so that students can acquire the language and its structures naturally as they use it for meaningful communication. The teacher's job is to provide comprehensible input in a safe and enjoyable classroom environment. Such an environment helps to lower the affective filter and thus maximize comprehensible input. The teacher uses a wide variety of techniques, such as total physical response (TPR), which involves students' responding physically to a series of commands, ample visuals and realia (real objects), small-group work, and any other activities involving meaningful communication that can facilitate the provision of comprehensible input. Krashen and Terrell also outlined five stages of language acquisition: preproduction, early production, speech emergence, intermediate, and advanced. Using these stages, teachers can identify appropriate activities and expectations for students that facilitate the provision of comprehensible input $(i + 1)$ and enhance SLA. Because students acquire vocabulary and grammar naturally, there is little need for direct instruction and practice through the use of memorized dialogues or drills.

The natural approach, like Krashen's theories on which the approach is based, has been highly criticized for lacking a clear focus, providing too little guidance for teachers, and leaving too much to chance in terms of students' learning needed vocabulary and grammatical forms. Many educators who have seen students succeed in learning languages with the natural approach continue to use it. But criticisms of it have led to increased attention to form in CLT.

Communicative Language Teaching

CLT emerged in the 1980s and remains the approach favored by most experienced language teachers and researchers. CLT grew out of dissatisfaction with audiolingualism, which produced students who could memorize dialogues and respond to drills but who had difficulty actually communicating with other speakers of the target language. CLT draws on Hymes's notion of communicative competence; thus, the focus is on learning language to actually use it to communicate in the target language with other speakers. CLT is not a singular teaching method but a set of core principles that can be applied and interpreted in a variety of ways (Van Patten, 2017). These principles include the following:

- Learners learn a language through using it to communicate.
- Authentic and meaningful communication should be the goal of classroom activities.
- Fluency is an important dimension of communication.
- Communication involves the integration of different language skills.
- Learning is a process of creative construction and involves trial and error. (p. 105)[3]

---

[3]Richards, J. C., & Rodgers, T. S. (2014). *Approaches and methods in language teaching* (3rd ed.). New York: Cambridge University Press.

CLT's emphasis on authentic meaningful communication and learning as creative instruction makes it highly compatible with the sociocultural perspective. In CLT there is an emphasis on providing grammar instruction—a "focus on form"—within the communicative context of a particular academic subject or field. Van Patten (2017) emphasizes that "any focus on form should be input-oriented and meaning-based" (p. 97). The example given earlier of teaching the past tense from a sociocultural perspective illustrates this focus on form in a CLT classroom. The goal of grammar instruction in CLT is not simply to memorize a rule but to develop the ability to effectively comprehend and convey intended meanings when reading books or other texts, making an oral presentation, writing a science or history report, or collaborating with peers to conduct a scientific experiment.

Content-Based Instruction

Content-based instruction (CBI) is an approach to second language teaching in which content-area subjects and topics are used as the basis of instruction. The content area provides a meaningful context for authentic communication as learners collaborate to complete carefully designed academic tasks. Thus, CBI is a specific form of CLT that focuses on teaching students to successfully communicate about the content area. This approach is consistent with the goal of most K–12 ELL programs, which is to prepare students for mainstream content area classrooms.

When CBI was introduced, ESL teachers used content areas such as math, science, and social studies as vehicles for language instruction, though their instructional and assessment focus was on English language development rather than content. Few ESL teachers, however, were properly trained to teach such content areas, and the ELL population was growing rapidly in schools. One solution was to train content-area teachers to help ELLs learn the content area while supporting their English language development. This type of instruction is called sheltered instruction, or specially designed academic instruction in English (SDAIE). CBI can now be thought of as a cover term for a continuum of approaches that integrate content and language instruction. On one end is content-area instruction by ESL teachers who focus on language development; on the other is sheltered instruction by content-area teachers who are trained to make complex content-area concepts comprehensible to ELLs at different English language proficiency levels.

Bilingual, ESL, and content-area teachers with ELLs in their classes receive training in sheltered instruction. The cognitive academic language learning approach (CALLA) developed in the 1980s (Chamot, 2009) and the sheltered instruction observation protocol (SIOP) model developed in the 1990s (Echevarria, Vogt, & Short, 2017) remain popular models for providing CBI for ELLs in K–12.

Whole Language, Multiple Intelligences, and Cooperative Learning

Whole language, multiple intelligences, and cooperative learning were not designed specifically for language teaching and learning, but teachers of ELLs have found them well suited for use in language learning classrooms, especially those following a CLT approach. Whole language is a philosophy of literacy instruction that places emphasis on teaching reading strategies and skills within the meaningful context of whole stories, poems, and other texts (a top-down approach). Although the term *whole language* is now used infrequently because of political controversy over what some perceived to be its rejection of training in basic skills such as phonics, the strategies and practices associated with whole language are still in common use. Multiple intelligences, a theory proposed by Gardner (2011), asserts that intelligence is multidimensional; thus, classroom instruction should be designed to maximize learning according to the particular set of intelligences a child may have. These intelligences include linguistic, logical/mathematical, spatial, musical, kinesthetic, interpersonal, intrapersonal, and naturalistic. Teachers have found that multiple intelligences approaches to teaching help them identify and teach to their ELLs' strengths in both language and content-area instruction. Cooperative learning focuses on the use of small groups within which students collaborate to solve problems or complete academic tasks. Cooperative learning appeals to language teachers because it offers rich opportunities for students to engage in meaningful communication and obtain comprehensible input as they interact to complete academic tasks.

Critical Pedagogy

Paulo Freire, a Brazilian educator, developed critical pedagogy in the 1960s while seeking ways to offer an education to impoverished and illiterate adult students in his country that would help them improve their situation and thus transform their lives and the society in which they lived. Many educators in the field of language education have recognized the importance of critical pedagogy in helping ELLs understand and confront unequal power relations as they attain English proficiency and learn academic content. Thus, critical pedagogy is often a key component of sociocultural approaches to teaching and learning.

Freire (1993) decried what he referred to as the "banking" concept of education, according to which teachers simply make deposits of essential knowledge and skills into the heads of students. The assumption is that "the teacher knows everything and the students know nothing" (p. 54). Freire called for a transformative education that would "liberate" impoverished students from their oppressed status. To accomplish this, Freire developed a process that encourages students to confront the social issues that contribute to their oppression in the dominant society. Critical pedagogy involves "problem posing, reflective thinking, knowledge gathering, and collaborative decision making," and it helps students and teachers "find and express their voice, in oral and written form" (Ovando & Combs, 2018, p. 101). Critical pedagogy requires teachers to take some risks by exploring new knowledge and opening themselves to new ways of perceiving the world, including thinking about ways to transform power relations that exist within and outside of schools. Freire's concepts are central to levels 3 (transformative) and 4 (social action) of James Banks's levels of multicultural education.

Beyond Approaches and Methods

Richards and Rodgers (2014) acknowledge that although it is useful to study and understand different approaches and methods, teachers should keep in mind that adherence to a specific method may restrict a teacher's creativity and professional judgment. Current knowledge is always changing, and no one method or approach is applicable to every language classroom in the world. The context of the classroom and the needs of the students should be the starting point, rather than any given method.

Teachers can use the following questions to guide their decisions about what strategies to use to promote ELLs' content-area learning through English, their English language development, and their cultural integration into the classroom and school community:

- What are the students' strengths and needs?
- What are the instructional goals?

- What is likely to be challenging about these goals for these students?
- What strategies can help address these challenges?
- How will you know whether these strategies are effective?

When teachers know their ELLs' language, literacy, content, and culture strengths and needs, they can compare them to the students' language, literacy, content, and culture instructional goals. Teachers can then determine what is likely to be challenging about a particular activity, lesson, or unit for those students and select appropriate instructional and assessment strategies.

Richards and Rodgers (2014) suggest that teachers try out different methods and approaches. In doing so they should be flexible and creative, drawing on their own beliefs, values, principles, and experiences to adapt the methods and approaches they use to the realities of the classroom. They refer to this process as the development of a "personal approach" to teaching and a set of core principles to draw on when teaching. They offer the following examples:

- Engage all learners in the lesson.
- Make learners the focus of the lesson.
- Provide maximum opportunities for student participation.
- Be tolerant of learners' mistakes.
- Develop learners' confidence.
- Respond to learners' difficulties and build on them.
- Use a maximum amount of student-to-student activities.
- Promote cooperation among learners.
- Address learners' needs and interests. (p. 353)[4]

The methods and approaches highlighted in this book reflect these principles and are grounded in our current understandings of theory, research, and best practices in language learning and teaching. The chapters that follow introduce you to a wide range of strategies and techniques that promote listening, speaking, reading, and writing across the content areas that are consistent with what we know about language teaching and learning. As you draw on these understandings, strategies, and techniques to develop your own personal and principled approach to teaching ELLs, be sure also to apply your understanding of the sociocultural contexts of your classroom, program, school, district, and community.

Summary

While linguists continue to conduct research on exactly how one learns a language, we can focus on the areas of consensus that have important implications for teaching and learning. Whether one takes a cognitive or sociocultural view of language development, researchers and educators seem to agree on the need for students to receive comprehensible input and to engage in meaningful interactions with other speakers of the target language. Thus, teachers need to find ways to make their instruction comprehensible for ELLs, and they need to provide ample opportunities for meaningful interactions in the classroom. Teachers' experiences and classroom-based research have given us a good sense of what does and does not work.

We can look at constructs of comprehensible input and we can consider a student's ZPD. While these concepts may be impossible to operationalize, teachers interact with their students every day—talk with them, listen to them talk, read with them, listen to

---

[4]Richards, J. C., & Rodgers, T. S. (2014). *Approaches and methods in language teaching* (3rd ed.). New York: Cambridge University Press.

them read, write with them, and read what they write. Thus, teachers will have a sense of what is and is not comprehensible for their students, and what type and amount of scaffolding is needed to help them succeed.

When teachers know their students well and understand the sociocultural contexts of their classroom, school, and community, they draw on their knowledge of language teaching and learning theories, methods, and approaches to inform their own principled approach to providing the type of learning environment that builds on their students' strengths and addresses their unique needs. They can provide appropriate instruction, activities, and opportunities for meaningful interaction to help their students continue to make progress in developing proficiency in English and in the content areas.

Discussion Questions

1. Of the language learning theories discussed in this chapter, which do you most agree with? Do you find that cognitive and sociocultural theories are incompatible? If not, discuss some ways drawing on different theories can help inform your instruction.

2. Describe your experiences with the various methods and approaches presented in this chapter, either learning under them or putting them into practice in your own classroom. Which did you find to be the most effective?

3. Why is it important to go beyond methods and approaches and develop your own personal approach to teaching ELLs? What are some of the core principles you would draw on to inform your own personal approach?

4. View the video from the 1980s of Stephen Krashen describing his second language acquisition hypotheses. What does he argue are the most important features of second language acquisition? Compare and contrast his theories with the others described in this chapter.

5. Review the document "Guiding Principles of Language Development" from the WIDA Consortium, which serves as the cornerstone of WIDA's English language development standards. How can these ten principles help you develop your own personal approach to teaching ELLs? What are some ways you would put these principles into practice in your own classroom?

Research Activities

1. *ELL Student Interview* Ask a current or former ELL about the kinds of lessons, activities, strategies, techniques, and materials a teacher used to help him or her learn English. Use this information to determine the methods and approaches the teacher may have been using. Ask how effective the student felt this instruction was, and whether there is anything he or she wishes the teacher had done differently.

2. *ELL Teacher Interview* Ask an ELL teacher what approaches or methods he or she uses in the classroom. Ask why he or she has chosen to use these and how effective they are in helping students learn English.

3. *ELL Classroom Observation* Observe one or more ESL lessons in a classroom, and review any textbooks or other curricular materials used in the lesson. Which approaches or methods do the teacher's instruction and curricular materials seem to align with most closely? How effective did you find the lesson to be? Is there anything you would have done differently?

4. *Online Research Activity* If you are bilingual, or have attempted to learn a new language, write your own language learning story modeled on my "How I Learned My Second Language" story. Tie your experiences to the ideas, theories, and methods discussed in this chapter that helped you understand your experience. What are some lessons you learned from your experience that might influence your instruction in your classroom? Consider making it into a digital story by incorporating photos, audio, or video clips.

Recommended Reading

Lightbown, P. M., & Spada, N. (2013). *How languages are learned* (4th ed.). New York: Oxford University Press.

> An excellent and easy-to-read introduction to second language acquisition theories.

Savile-Troike, M., & Barto, K. (2017). *Introducing second language acquisition* (3rd ed.). Cambridge: Cambridge University Press.

> Comprehensive but accessible introduction to the field of second language acquisition.

VanPatten, B. (2017). *While we're on the topic: BVP on language, acquisition, and classroom practice.* Alexandria, VA: The American Council on the Teaching of Foreign Languages.

> In a highly engaging style, provides language teachers with principles of CLT and discusses how language is acquired, the roles of input and interaction, tasks and activities, and focus on form.

Four

Language and Education Policy

Educators can play significant roles in advocating for their students and mitigating the effects of poorly conceived or inappropriate educational language policies, or where more favorable policies have been implemented, teachers can enhance their students' educational opportunities by building on students' home and community languages while helping them to learn the dominant languages typically required as media of instruction.

—TERRENCE G. WILEY

KEY TERMS

- Bilingual Education Act (Title VII) of 1968
- Common Core State Standards
- comprehensive support and improvement
- Elementary and Secondary Education Act
- English for the Children initiatives
- Equal Educational Opportunities Act
- ESEA Flexibility
- Every Student Succeeds Act
- Lau Remedies
- Look Act
- No Child Left Behind Act
- Proposition 58
- Race to the Top
- targeted support and improvement

GUIDING QUESTIONS

1. How has the policy context surrounding the education of ELLs changed in the United States?
2. How do national state-led consortia and individual state policies and initiatives influence the education of ELLs on the local district and school levels?
3. How have the courts influenced the education of ELLs?
4. How can educators use their understanding of the policy and legislative context surrounding ELL education to enhance their ELLs' access to educational opportunities?

Language and education policy for ELLs in the United States is complicated by the absence of a centralized education system. Policies that outline rules, regulations, and procedures related to educating ELLs may come from the federal government, state governments, voter initiatives, or court decisions. Policies are set by powerful institutions usually controlled by members of the dominant group. Some policies have had a discriminatory impact on minorities. Other policies may have been designed to ensure the protection of minority rights. Sometimes various stakeholders reach compromises through the democratic process to ensure fairness to all involved. Other times, those negatively affected by policies have turned to the courts for assistance; these efforts result in decisions that either uphold or require changes to existing policies. As we see in this chapter, the pendulum swings between discourses of relative tolerance or support for linguistic diversity and discourses of increased language restrictionism and English-only efforts. These discourses have serious implications for the education of ELLs.

Educators who work with ELLs need to understand the history and the current language and education policies and legislation that affect their students and classrooms. We begin with a brief history of bilingual education and the evolution of federal policy regarding the education of ELLs. Then we review national state-led consortia and individual state policies and initiatives regarding ELLs and look at the important role the courts have played in guiding policies for these students. The chapter concludes by emphasizing how educators can draw on their understanding of the larger policy context to develop sound policies on the local district and school levels that ensure equal educational opportunities for their ELLs.

Historical Perspective

Educators in the United States have long faced the challenge of educating ELLs and the need for special programs to address their needs. Many people mistakenly believe that this challenge is a relatively new phenomenon and that in the past immigrants and their children quickly gave up their home languages and cultures to become Americanized monolingual English speakers. The United States is now, always has been, and will continue to be a multilingual and multicultural country (Shin, 2013).

Many people also assume that English is the official language of the United States. But the founding fathers never declared any language as an official language, and the U.S. Constitution has never been amended to declare English as the official language. To the founders, declaring an official language would have been unnecessary. By the time the Constitution was ratified, English was well established as the dominant language. Also, the founders respected diversity among those who had fought for independence and were hesitant to offend them by restricting their languages or in any way implying their inferiority. Throughout U.S. history English has functioned as if it were the official language, and therefore, there has never been a need for an official designation.

Bilingual education has been referred to by some critics as an "experiment" that began with the passage of the federal Bilingual Education Act of 1968. The reality is bilingual education is as old as the country itself. Home language instruction and bilingual education were common in areas where other language groups settled and made up a major portion of the local population (Box 4.1 and Figure 4.1). For example, German bilingual education was offered in the 17th century and continued to be common in German communities throughout the country until World War I (Figure 4.2). Spanish bilingual education programs were common throughout the Southwest in the 19th century. Blanton (2007) documents the history of bilingual education in Texas beginning in 1836. In 1848 the territory of New Mexico, which included modern-day Arizona and parts of Colorado, Utah, and Nevada, had a law calling for Spanish-English bilingual programs. Other schools in the United States offered instruction in Chinese, Japanese, French, Cherokee, Swedish, Danish, Norwegian, Italian, Polish, Dutch, and Czech (Crawford, 2015). In Texas, for example, in the small community of Danevang, founded by settlers from Denmark, students were taught Danish language and history at the Danevang School, which was established in about 1895 (Davis, 2010) (Figure 4.3).

In 1858 the *American Journal of Education* published an article, translated from German, describing the work of the German scholar Wolfgang Ratich, who in 1612 decried the sink-or-swim method and proposed that young students be instructed in their native language first and attain sufficient literacy skills before they are transitioned to other languages. As Ratich stated, "After the mother tongue, then the other languages" (von Raumer, 1858, p. 229). Ratich had many critics at the time who, like present-day critics of

Box 4.1 American Bilingual Tradition: Education

1800s

- French was a compulsory subject in Massachusetts high schools.
- Dutch was taught in the district schools of seven communities in Michigan.
- German was taught in Washington, DC, elementary schools.
- Many midwestern high schools were bilingual German-English.

Early 1900s

- In some towns in Indiana, Minnesota, Missouri, New Jersey, and Texas nearly all elementary school students received German instruction.
- Swedish, Norwegian, and Danish were taught in many high schools and elementary schools in Illinois, Iowa, Minnesota, Nebraska, North Dakota, South Dakota, Washington, and Wisconsin.
- Czech was taught in some schools in Texas and Nebraska and was likely taught in other elementary schools throughout the Midwest.
- Polish was taught in public schools in Milwaukee, and Italian was taught at all grade levels in elementary school.
- Spanish was a compulsory subject in New Mexico public high schools.
- The French, Russian, Hungarian, and Italian governments provided support to public and private schools for the teaching of French in New Orleans, Russian in Alaska, Magyar in Connecticut, and Italian in schools throughout the country.

Mid 1900s

- Spanish was taught in elementary schools in several cities, including Corpus Christi, San Antonio, and El Paso, TX; Los Angeles and San Diego, CA; and Gainesville and Miami, FL.

Kloss, 1998.

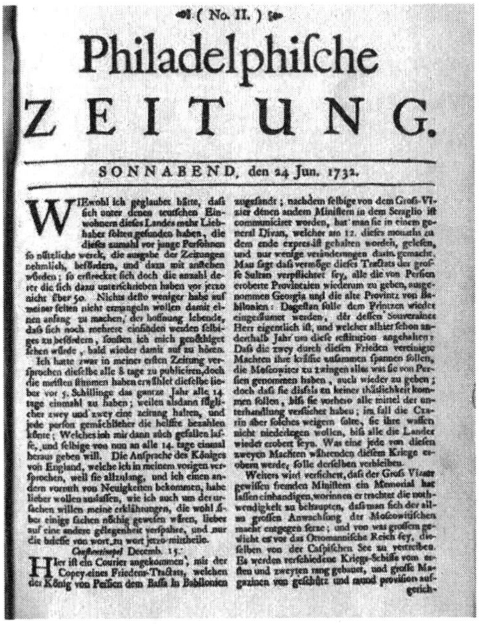

(No. II.)

Philadelphiſche

ZEITUNG.

SONNABEND, den 24 Jun. 1732.

WIEwohl ich geglaubet hätte, daſs ſich unter denen teutſchen Einwohnern dieſes Landes mehr Liebhaber ſolten gefunden haben, die dieſes zumahl vor junge Perſohnen ſo nützliche werck, die ausgabe der Zeitungen nehmlich, beförderen, und dazu mit anſtehen würden; ſo erſtrecket ſich doch die anzahl derer die ſich dazu unterſchrieben haben vor jetzo nicht über 50. Nichts deſto weniger habe auf meiner ſeiten nicht ermangeln wollen damit einen anfang zu machen, der hoffnung lebende, daſs ſich noch mehrere einfinden werden ſelbiges zu beförderen, ſonſten ich mich genöthiget ſehen würde, bald wieder damit auf zu hören.

Ich hatte zwar in meiner erſten Zeitung verſprochen dieſelbe alle 8 tage zu publiciren, doch die meiſten ſtimmen haben erwählet dieſelbe lieber vor 5. Schillinge das gantze Jahr alle 14. tage einmahl zu haben; weilen alsdann füglicher zwey und zwey eine zeitung halten, und jede perſon gemächlicher die helffte bezahlen könte; Welches ich mir dann auch gefallen laſſe, und ſelbige von nun an alle 14. tage einmal heraus geben will. Die Anſprache des Königes von England, welche ich in meinem vorigen verſprochen, weil ſie allzulang, und ich einen andern vorrath von Neuigkeiten bekommen, habe lieber wollen auslaſſen, wie ich auch um der urſachen willen meine erklährungen, die wohl über einige ſachen nöthig geweſen wären, lieber auf eine andere gelegenheit verſpahre, und nur die brieffe von wort zu wort jetzo mittheile.

Conſtantinopel Decemb. 15.

HIer iſt ein Courier angekommen, mit der Copey eines Friedens-Tractats, welchen der König von Perſien dem Baſſa in Babilonien zugeſandt; nachdem ſelbige von dem Groſs-Vizier denen andern Miniſtern in dem Seraglio iſt communiciret worden, hat man ſie in einem general Divan, welcher am 12. dieſes monaths zu dem ende expres iſt gehalten worden, geleſen, und nur wenige veränderungen darin gemacht. Man ſagt daſs vermöge dieſes Tractats der groſſe Sultan verpflichtet ſey, alle die von Perſien eroberte Provintzien wiederum zu geben, ausgenommen Georgia und die alte Provintz von Babilonien: Dageſtan ſolle dem Printzen wieder eingeräumet werden, der deſſen Souveraine Herr eigentlich iſt, und welcher alhier ſchon anderthalb Jahr um dieſe reſtitution angehalten: Daſs die zwey durch dieſen Frieden vereinigte Machten ihre kräffte zuſammen ſpannen ſollen, die Moſcowiter zu zwingen alles was ſie von Perſien genommen haben, auch wieder zu geben; doch daſs ſie diſsfals zu keiner thätlichkeit kommen ſollen, biſs ſie vorhero alle mittel der unterhandlung verſuchet haben; im fall die Czarin aber ſolches weigern ſolte, ſie ihre waffen nicht niederlegen wollen, biſs alle die Lander wieder erobert ſeyn. Was eine jede von dieſen zweyen Machten währenden dieſem Kriege erobern werde, ſolle derſelben verbleiben.

Weiters wird verſichert, daſs der Groſs Vizier gewiſſen fremden Miniſtern ein Memorial hat laſſen einhandigen, worinnen er trachtet die nothwendigkeit zu behaupten, daſs man ſich der allzu groſſen Anwachſung der Moſcowitiſchen macht entgegen ſetze; und von was groſſem gewicht es vor das Ottomanniſche Reich ſey, dieſelben von der Caſpiſchen See zu vertreiben. Es werden verſchiedene Kriegs-Schiffe vom erſten und zweyten rang gebauet, und groſſe Magazinen von geſchütz und mund proviſion aufgerich-

Figure 4.1 Front page of the *Philadelphische Zeitung*, June 24, 1732. This was America's first German-language newspaper, printed by Benjamin Franklin. (Retrieved from Library of Congress, www.loc.gov/rr/european/imde/images/zeitung.jpg)

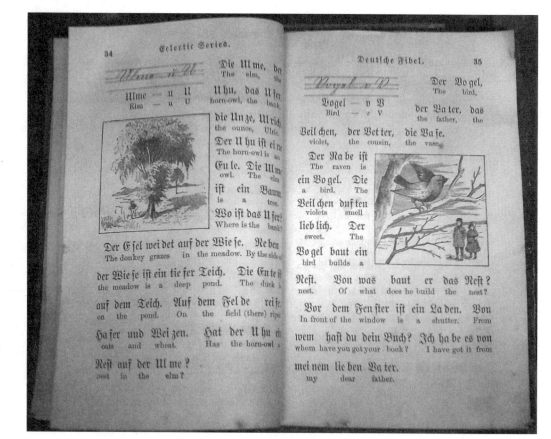

Figure 4.2 Bilingual German primer used in Texas and other German schools in the United States in the early 1900s. Published by the American Book Company, New York. (From University of Texas–San Antonio Libraries Special Collections.)

bilingual education, found his ideas to be radical and scandalous. Ratich died before he was given a fair chance to prove his ideas, but others carried on his work. Among them was a language teacher named Hedwig who put Ratich's methods to work in Germany shortly after his death and "was considered one of the most skillful teachers of his day" (p. 251).

Language minorities have always been a part of the American landscape, but their unique languages and cultural practices have not always been warmly welcomed by the broader society. Although there are many instances in the country's history in which languages other than English were tolerated or even promoted, there also have been waves of linguistic restrictionism, that is, policies and practices that attempted to limit or outlaw the use of languages other than English. Such language restrictions by the dominant group in society against language minority communities were most often imposed for purposes of social control, not to help immigrants (and non-English-speaking native-born Americans) learn English. For example:

- Enslaved Africans were prohibited from using their native tongues for fear their doing so would facilitate resistance or rebellion.
- In the 1740s, southern colonies institutionalized "compulsory ignorance" laws which prohibited enslaved Africans from acquiring English literacy. These slave codes remained in force until the end of the Civil War in 1865.

Figure 4.3 Danevang School, 1908. (Photo no. 072–0724 from University of Texas–San Antonio Libraries Special Collections.)

- English proficiency was made a requirement for naturalization and citizenship at the turn of the 20th century.
- The Americanization movement during and after World War I pushed the belief that to be American means to speak only English.
- Coercive assimilation policies targeted Native Americans through the establishment of English-only Indian boarding schools. These schools were designed to eradicate Indian languages and cultural practices and facilitated the taking of Native American land.
- After World War I, heavy restrictions were placed on German-language instruction in schools.
- After World War II, Japanese-language schools in California and Hawaii were closed. (Wiley & Wright, 2004)[1]

Restrictions on languages other than English tend to come in waves. Before 1900, several states and local school districts had laws or policies that allowed bilingual education, or at least did not restrict schools from offering such programs (see the examples in Box 4.1). By the late 1880s and early 1900s, however, several states implemented laws requiring that English be used as the language of instruction in schools.

Language restrictionism is usually tied to other forms of discrimination. Thus, attempts at language restrictionism are rarely about concerns over the languages themselves but, rather, about the individuals who speak them (Wiley, 2012). The recent calls for language restriction coincide with mounting concerns by the majority about chang-

---

[1] Wiley, T. G., & Wright, W. E. (2004). Against the undertow: The politics of language instruction in the United States. *Educational Policy, 18*(1), 142–168. © Copyright 2004 Sage Publications, reprinted by permission.

ing demographics with a large and growing Latinx population. Debates over bilingual education take place in the context of larger debates over issues of immigration.

Evolution of Federal Policy for English Language Learners

Although the United States has a long history of language diversity, federal involvement in education is a fairly recent endeavor. Education is not addressed in the U.S. Constitution. The United States did not have a Department of Education until 1980. Education is the responsibility of each state.

The federal government has great interest in ensuring the country has well-educated citizens, but because of the lack of jurisdiction, the best it can do is to offer funding to supplement state and local funding for schools. The catch is that if states accept federal funding for education, they must follow federal education policies. Currently, all states accept federal funding, which typically makes up less than 10% of each school's funding. Nonetheless, all states are subject to federal education law.

Before 1968, there were no federal educational language policies for ELLs. Too often, schools ignored the needs of language minority students and simply placed them in regular (often segregated) classrooms, where they were left to "sink or swim." Education for language minority students began to improve during the time of the civil rights movement and President Lyndon B. Johnson's War on Poverty. In 1965 Congress passed the **Elementary and Secondary Education Act (ESEA)**. Some of the key components of the ESEA are funds, policies, and procedures that target students from low-income families.

Title VII Bilingual Education Act (1968–2002)

Within the context of the civil rights movement, educators and policymakers became more sensitive to the needs of the rapidly growing language minority student population. Concerned educators noted a high drop-out rate among Mexican American students. According to the 1960 U.S. Census, white students on average completed 14 years of schooling, while Mexican American students on average completed less than 5 years.

In 1966 a conference on the education of Spanish-speaking children sponsored by the National Education Association resulted in an influential report titled *The Invisible Minority . . . pero no vencibles* [but undefeatable]. The report outlined areas of concern and described innovative education programs in southwestern states that made use of students' home languages. A successful two-way bilingual program for Cuban refugee students at Coral Way Elementary School in Florida also garnered much attention. The report recommended repeal of state English-only instruction laws and declared, "Instruction in pre-school and throughout the early grades should be in both Spanish and English" and "English should be taught as a second language" (National Education Association, 1966, p. 6).

Soon after the report was published, Senator Ralph Yarborough of Texas introduced a bill to provide federal funding for school districts to support bilingual education programs. His bill eventually became the 1968 **Bilingual Education Act** and entered into federal law as Title VII of the ESEA. The Bilingual Education Act provided grants to school districts and other eligible entities through a competitive grant process. Thus, most regulations associated with Title VII applied only to funded programs.

Yarborough's original bill applied only to Spanish-surnamed students, but 37 similar proposals introduced by other legislators were ultimately merged into the final bill, which called for the inclusion of all "children of limited-English speaking ability" (LESA), defined as "children who come from environments where the dominant language is other than English." The LESA label and additional poverty criteria stressed that the population to be served was deficient in English and very poor and thus needed remediation. This deficit view of students is apparent in the findings section of the Bilingual Education Act (§701), which describes the presence of "millions of children of limited English-speaking ability" as "one of the most acute educational problems in the United States" and as a "unique and perplexing educational situation."

The original version of the Bilingual Education Act was vague about solutions and, ironically, did not include a definition of bilingual education. This omission resulted in great confusion and little agreement among educators and policymakers on the purpose and goals of Title VII and how students would benefit from instruction in their home language. Programs receiving Title VII funds were called "bilingual education" programs, yet were not consistent in the use of students' home languages.

The passage of the Bilingual Education Act led to the adoption of similar policies in several states. By the early 2000s, 32 states had statutes allowing home language instruction, and seven states mandated it under certain conditions; seven other states stopped enforcing their laws prohibiting home language instruction (Crawford, 2015).

Since 1968, the ESEA has been reauthorized seven times (1974, 1978, 1984, 1988, 1994, 2001, 2015). By 1994, after five reauthorizations and numerous debates and compromises between advocates and opponents of bilingual education, the goals of Title VII were clarified and definitions of the target population and the programs to serve them were made more explicit. Each reauthorization resulted in greater recognition of the personal and societal benefits of bilingualism and bilingual education. The focus on helping ELLs achieve fluency in English remained constant. Each reauthorization, however, expanded the types of programs eligible for Title VII funding. Transitional bilingual education programs were the most likely to receive funding. And though compromises led to some funding for nonbilingual approaches, the majority of funds were reserved for programs that provided at least some home language instruction. In addition, there was increasing support for developmental and dual language programs. Many saw this support as key to changing the public's view of bilingual education from a compensatory program to an enrichment program. The Bilingual Education Act was reauthorized for the final time in 1994 and remained in effect until 2002. A detailed discussion of the reauthorizations is available on the Companion Website.

No Child Left Behind (2002–2016)

Federal policy for ELLs changed dramatically when the ESEA was reauthorized as the **No Child Left Behind Act (NCLB) of 2001** (Public Law 107–110) under President George W. Bush. Implementation began in 2002. The Title VII Bilingual Education Act was replaced by Title III, "Language Instruction for Limited English Proficient and Immigrant Students." Note that the word *bilingual* was removed, and that NCLB used the limited English proficient (LEP) label depicting students from a deficit view. Bilingual programs were neither encouraged nor restricted.

Title I of NCLB placed heavy emphasis on accountability through high-stakes testing in English language arts/reading and mathematics in grades 3 through 8 and once in high school. Science exams were also required three times between grades 3 and 12. ELLs were required to take state tests regardless of their English proficiency or how long they had been in the country. Two exceptions were eventually added for newcomer ELLs in the United States for less than one year. Beginning in 2002, they could be excluded from reading tests, and beginning in 2006 their math test scores could be excluded from school AYP calculations.

Each state was required to create academic content standards and assessments to measure those standards and use the results to hold schools accountable. All students—including ELLs—were expected to pass these state tests by 2014. Progress was tracked by student subgroups, including "limited English proficient students." If any subgroup failed to make adequate yearly progress (AYP), the entire school was deemed as failing. Consistent failure led to school sanctions. Under Title III, each state was required to establish English language proficiency (ELP) standards and annual ELP tests for ELLs in all grade levels. School districts were expected to have annual increases in the percentage of ELLs (1) making progress in learning English, (2) attaining English proficiency, and (3) passing state English language arts and math tests.

NCLB drove U.S. education policy for 14 years. It had a major impact on ELLs. While it brought some attention to their needs (Haycock, 2006), the heavy focus on high-stakes testing typically resulted in "teach-to-the-test" curricular programs that were inappropriate for ELLs and tended to discourage bilingual education programs (Gandara & Hopkins, 2010; Menken, 2008; Wright, 2007). Despite allowances for testing in the home language, the vast majority of ELLs took state tests in English. Thus, schools were held accountable for test scores of questionable validity.

Widespread evidence shows that NCLB's technical flaws, unrealistic expectations, and overreliance on high-stakes tests ended up causing more harm than good (Baker & Wright, 2017; Menken, 2008; Nichols & Berliner, 2007; Wright, 2005, 2008). Eventually, policymakers from both major parties agreed that NCLB was unrealistic, highly flawed, and failing to produce promised academic gains. NCLB was literally leaving children behind, including many ELLs. Nevertheless, Congress allowed NCLB to continue unchanged for 7 years past the 2008 ESEA reauthorization due date. By 2014, schools were far from meeting NCLB's 100% test-passing rate expectation. But even before NCLB came to an official end, the Obama administration allowed states flexibility in meeting the law's requirements.

Obama Administration and Federal Education Policy

Frustrated by congressional inaction, the Obama administration found ways to work around NCLB by launching other significant school-reform initiatives, which led to substantial changes at the federal level. These reforms set the stage for state-led standards and assessment initiatives and the eventual reauthorization of the ESEA.

Race to the Top (2009–2015)

The American Recovery and Reinvestment Act of 2009 included over $44 billion in stimulus funding for education. Part of this act was **Race to the Top** (RTTT), which provided over $4 billion in competitive grants for states to begin education reform efforts. Nearly half of the states received these grants. To qualify, states had to agree to adopt college-and-career-readiness standards, and they were expected to develop high-quality assessments that were valid and reliable for all students, including ELLs and students with disabilities (U.S. Department of Education 2009a, 2009b). ELL advocates and civil rights groups expressed concern that ELL issues were not being adequately addressed and that RTTT continued the emphasis on high-stakes testing (Sawchuk, 2010; Zehr, 2010a).

Elementary and Secondary Education Act Flexibility (2011–2016)

In 2011, the Obama administration invited states to apply for **ESEA Flexibility**, which essentially provided waivers from NCLB's Title I accountability requirements. Each state had to propose an alternative accountability system addressing key principles similar to those of RTTT. This included developing or adopting college-and-career readiness and corresponding "next generation" assessments. States were required to revise their ELP standards to reflect academic language skills corresponding with the college-and-career-readiness standards. In addition, states were expected to establish interventions focused on improving the performance of ELLs (U.S. Department of Education, 2012). By 2015, 43 states, the District of Columbia, and Puerto Rico had been approved for ESEA Flexibility. Most state flexibility applications provided little detail about how ELL issues would be addressed. In many state plans, ELLs were combined with other "at-risk" students into one large subgroup. Many ELL advocates expressed concerned that such practice would mask the unique linguistic, cultural, and academic needs of ELLs (Morita-Mullaney, 2017).

Every Student Succeeds Act (2015–Present)

At the end of 2015, U.S. Congress reauthorized the ESEA as the **Every Student Succeeds Act** (ESSA). President Obama signed it into law on December 10, 2015. ESSA maintains the standards and testing requirements of NCLB but affords states much greater flexibility in establishing school accountability programs. Most state ESSA implementation plans were reviewed for federal approval during the 2017–2018 school year. Thus, full implementation of ESSA essentially began in the 2018–2019 school year. The basic requirements of ESSA and their implications for ELLs are outlined in the following sections. While many educators and scholars are concerned about the continued reliance on high-stakes testing for school accountability, ESSA appears to be an improvement over NCLB and affords states an opportunity to establish more flexible and reasonable expectations for ELLs and other students and their schools. It is too early to tell how effectively states will implement these policies and how these policies will impact the education of ELLs.

Title I: Improving the Academic Achievement of the Economically Disadvantaged

The purpose of Title I is "to provide all children significant opportunity to receive a fair, equitable, and high-quality education, and to close educational achievement gaps" (ESSA §1001). Title I requires annual assessments in English language arts/reading and mathematics for all students in grades 3 through 8 and in high school, and three assessments of Science between grades 3 and 12. State assessments must be aligned with "challenging state academic standards" that are "aligned with entrance requirements for credit-bearing coursework in the system of public higher education in the State and relevant career and technical education standards" (ESSA §1111(b)(1)(D)(i)). In other words, state assessments must be aligned with "college-and-career-readiness standards." States may also develop or adopt alternative academic achievement standards for "students with the most significant cognitive disabilities" that are aligned with "challenging state academic achievement standards" (ESSA §1111(b)(1)(E)(i)(I)).

States have the right to voluntarily join in partnerships with other states to share common standards and assessments. Most states have adopted the Common Core State Standards but have elected to develop their own state assessments to measure student attainment of these standards. Title I specifies that the U.S. Secretary of Education may not "attempt to influence, incentivize, or coerce" states to adopt the Common Core State Standards or any other common assessments or standards (ESSA §1111(j)(1)).

Progress in meeting academic achievement standards and passing state assessments must be tracked for different student subgroups: (1) economically disadvantaged students, (2) Students from major racial and ethnic groups, (3) Children with disabilities, and (4) English learners. For purposes of accountability, the English learner subgroup may include former ELLs up to 4 years after they have attained English proficiency.

Title I requires that ELLs be included in state achievement assessments, and that they be assessed in a "valid and reliable manner." In addition, states must provide ELLs with "appropriate accommodations" and "to the extent practicable, assessments in the language and form most likely to yield accurate data on what such students know and can do in academic content areas, until such students have achieved English language proficiency" (ESSA §1111(b)(2)(B)(vii)(III)). States are expected to make every effort to provide assessments in languages other than English spoken by a significant number of ELLs. When such assessments are available, they may be used for ELLs for up to 3 years. This period may be extended for 2 additional years case by case for students who have not "not yet reached a level of English proficiency sufficient to yield valid and reliable information on what such students know and can do on tests (written in English) of reading or language arts" (ESSA §1111(b) (2)(B)(ix)).Some states pushed back on the notion of home language assessments in their ESSA plans; some responded positively with plans to develop assessments in Spanish or other languages, while others indicated openness to exploring the possibility. It remains to be seen how many states will actually develop or adopt home language assessments.

Nonetheless, the reality is that the vast majority of ELLs across the country will be assessed only in English. This raises serious concerns about the validity and reliability of ELL assessment scores. In an attempt to address this issue, Title I offers two options. Under option 1, ELLs who have been in the one of the 50 states or the District of Columbia for less than a year may be excluded from the English language arts/reading assessment but would be still be required to take the math assessment. However, their math assessment scores may be excluded from school accountability formulas. Most states, however, have chosen the more flexible option 2:

1st Year

- ELLs are required to take English language arts/reading and math assessments.
- Scores are reported to the public.
- Scores are not included in school accountability formulas.

2nd Year

- A measure of ELLs' growth on English language arts/reading and math assessments are incorporated into school accountability formulas.

3rd Year and Beyond

- ELL scores on English language arts/reading and math assessments are fully included in the school accountability formulas (ESSA §1111(b)(3)(A)(ii)(II)(aa–cc)).

States may use computer-adaptive assessments, that is, computer-based assessments that adjust the difficulty level of the questions based on each student's previous answers. States are also afforded flexibility in designing "innovative assessments." For example, rather than giving a single summative multiple-choice exam at the end of the school year, states could elect to establish a system "administered through multiple statewide interim assessments during the course of the academic year that result in a single summative score that provides valid, reliable, and transparent information on student achievement or growth" (ESSA §1111(b)(2)(B)(viii)(II)). These assessments could include measures of student academic growth and may include portfolios, projects, or extended performance tasks.

States also have the option to simply use the ACT or SAT exams in lieu of their own high school achievement test.

Only a few states, however, have considered the innovative assessment options in their ESSA plans (Gewertz, 2018). Thus, the vast majority of ELLs and other students in the country will continue to be assessed with end-of-year summative high-stakes exams. While many of these assessments will be administered by computer and may involve some use of computer-adaptive assessment or technology-enhanced test questions, in general these assessments will mostly look and function like traditional paper-and-pencil exams. As such, they will continue to pose the same challenges ELLs have traditionally faced on high-stakes tests in a language they are still learning.

Title I also requires states to establish ELP standards and assessments that are aligned with these standards. The ELP standard must address the domains of listening, speaking, reading, and writing; it must address different proficiency levels; and it must be aligned with challenging state academic standards. ELLs in all grades must take the ELP assessment each year.

States have the option of developing their own ELP standards and assessments, or joining a consortium to share common standards and assessments with other states. Most states have joined such consortia (WIDA and ELPA21). These are discussed in the next section. While ELP standards and assessments are important for guiding instruction and tracking student progress in developing proficiency, they have their own unique set of problems. As noted previously, the construct of language proficiency is highly complex and multidimensional, making it nearly impossible to organize language into neat lists of specific knowledge and skills, and very difficult to measure with accuracy.

Under Title I, states must establish school accountability programs that include the following indicators:

1. Student performance on annual state English language arts/reading and math assessments
2. ELL progress in achieving proficiency in English
3. Graduation rate (for high schools)
4. A measure of student growth or other academic indicator (grades K–8)
5. At least one other indicator (e.g., student and teacher engagement, school climate/safety, access to advanced placement courses)

The first four indicators must carry the greater weight in school accountability formulas. While states have flexibility to establish expectations for accountability purposes, most have established long-term goals for 6 or more years to increase the number of students in each subgroup who pass the exams or to close the achievement gap between different student subgroups. States set increasing annual goals towards meeting these long-term goals. For indicator 2, states have established long-term goals to ensure that ELLs make progress in learning English and ultimately attain ELP. Attaining annual and long-term targets toward these goals adds significant weight to a school's accountability formula. For indicator 3, states have established goals to increase graduate rates for ELLs and other subgroups of students. Most states have adopted various measures of student growth to address indicator 4. Indicator 5 is an attempt to include some form of non-test-based indicators of high-quality education in the school accountability formula, and states have proposed a variety of indicators. One concern is how such indicators can be fairly quantified.

Overall, this system of indicators is an attempt to move away from state school accountability systems that simply focus on the number of students who pass or fail state exams to systems that encompass multiple measures of students and school achievement.

While this is a welcomed development, note that three of the four most heavily weighted indicators (1, 2, and 4) rely on state assessments.

In addition to including the five indicators, states are expected to ensure that in each school at least 95% of all students, and 95% of students in each subgroup, participate in state assessments. States may allow parents to opt-out their children from state assessments, but must determine consequences for schools that have less than 95% participation rates.

School districts must intervene and establish **targeted support and improvement** (TSI) plans in schools where ELLs or other subgroups of students are consistently underperforming. Underperforming is defined as performing at or below the performance of all students in the lowest-performing schools. Schools that have one or more chronically low-performing subgroups are identified for **comprehensive support and improvement** (CSI), and the district must develop and implement a CSI plan for the school. Districts must also develop CSI plans for the lowest-performing 5% of all schools, and for any high schools with lower than a 67% graduation rate. In developing TSI and CSI plans for schools, school districts must ensure that the plans (1) are informed by student performance against state-determined long-term goals, (2) include evidence-based interventions, (3) are based on school-level needs assessment, (4) identify resource inequities, and (5) are approved by school, district, and state education leaders. Once implemented, plans must be monitored and periodically reviewed by the state educational agency.

If there is a lack of improvement within 4 years of a CSI plan implementation, schools are subject to "more rigorous State-determined action," which may include "addressing school-level operations." This could involve, for example, state takeover of the school, firing the principal, converting the school to a charter school, or other sanctions.

Title III: Language Instruction for English Learners and Immigrant Students

Title III provides formula grants to state education agencies, which, in turn, make subgrants to eligible local education agencies (i.e., school districts and charter schools). Title III does not make any distinctions between bilingual and nonbilingual programs. It only requires that ELLs be placed in "language instruction education programs," defined as an instructional course:

> (A) in which an English learner is placed for the purpose of developing and attaining English proficiency, while meeting challenging State academic standards; and

> (B) that may make instructional use of both English and a child's native language to enable the child to develop and attain English proficiency, and may include the participation of English proficient children if such course is designed to enable all participating children to become proficient in English and a second language (ESSA §3201(7)(A–B)).

Thus, any program for ELLs must meet only two requirements: teach English and teach academic content, as outlined in state ELP and academic standards. Instruction in home languages is optional. This option, without referring to transitional bilingual education or dual language programs by name, nonetheless makes allowances for these types of programs. Special allowances are made for programs for Native American (including Pacific Islander) children and children in Puerto Rico to learn and study Native American languages and Spanish, but these programs must have explicit outcomes related to "increased English proficiency among such children."

Title III gives ultimate authority to each state to determine what programs it will allow. To receive Title III funds, school districts must submit plans to the state, which in turn must submit plans to the U.S. Department of Education. These plans must describe how each eligible entity will be "given the flexibility to teach English learners using a high-quality, effective language instruction curriculum for teaching English learners in the manner the eligible entity determines to be the most effective" (ESSA §3113(b)(5) (A–B)).

Title III does not include any recognition of the personal and societal benefits of bilingual education and bilingualism. The recognition of the linguistic resources ELLs bring to school and the benefits of bilingualism to society that were so apparent in the 1994 reauthorization of the Title VII Bilingual Education Act were stripped from federal law under NCLB and remain absent under ESSA. Nor is there any acknowledgment of the factors that have negatively affected the education of ELLs, such as segregation, improper placement in special education, underrepresentation of ELLs in gifted and talented education, and shortages of bilingual teachers. Not addressed are issues of cultural differences or the need for multicultural understanding.

The focus of Title III is English. One stated purpose of Title III is to ensure that ELLs "attain English proficiency and develop high levels of academic achievement in English" and "meet the same challenging State academic standards that all children are expected to meet." Title III is designed to assist teachers, principals and other school leaders and state and local education agencies in "establishing, implementing, and sustaining effective language instruction educational programs" that prepare ELLs to "enter all-English instructional settings." Another stated purpose of Title III is "to promote parental, family, and community participation in language educational programs for the parents, families, and communities of English learners" (ESSA §3102(1–5)).

While the text of Title III makes no explicit references to bilingualism and bilingual education, the Non-Regulatory Guidance document for Title III issued by the U.S. Department of Education (2016a) acknowledges the strong research base supporting home language development:

> States and LEAs may wish to incorporate methods of supporting home language development. Research on language use in early childhood programs and in elementary school, and on supporting home language development, including fostering bilingualism, maintaining cultural connections and communication with family members, and the transferability of home language skills to English language acquisition, suggests that systematic and deliberate exposure to English, paired with supporting home language development within high quality educational settings, can result in strong, positive outcomes for children who are non-native English speakers, as well as positive outcomes for native English speakers. (p. 20)

Furthermore, the *English Learner Tool Kit* issued by the U.S. Department of Education (2016b) lists bilingual program models that are "considered educationally sound in theory" (p. 4) and thus acceptable as language education instructional programs under ESSA. The Department of Education has also funded National Teacher Professional Development grants as authorized by ESSA that give some priority to developing dual language bilingual education programs.

Title III requires states to establish and implement "standardized, statewide entrance and exit procedures" for ELLs, with the expectation that any potential ELLs be assessed within 30 days of school enrollment (ESSA §3113(b)(2)). To identify ELLs, most school districts administer a home language survey at the time of initial school enrollment to determine whether students have a home language other than English. Students are then assessed with an ELP test. Those determined to be lower than proficient are identified as ELLs. There is great variability in home language surveys, ELP tests, and procedures used to identify ELLs across states and school districts. These inconsistencies make it difficult to measure the national ELL population accurately.

Most of the other provisions of Title III relate to regulations on the use of Title III funds and state, district, and school monitoring and reporting requirements. These include reporting on the progress of ELLs in learning and attaining English and passing state achievement tests. States must report disaggregated data on ELLs with a disability and ELLs who have not attained proficiency within 5 years of initial classification (i.e., "long-term ELLs"). Title III funds may be used to provide ELL licensure and professional development for teachers and principals, to develop or support ELL programs (including pre-school, dual credit, and early college high schools), and to provide subgrants to schools that have had a recent significant increase in the number of immigrant students.

For ELLs to be successful under the new ESSA federal education policy, it is essential that teachers be familiar with the general requirements described earlier as well as the specifics of their own state's ESSA plan. Teachers much ensure that their ELLs benefit from the flexible and positive aspects of ESSA, while watching for any harmful or unintended consequences and advocate for changes when needed.

State-Led Initiatives and Consortia

With the absence of a national centralized education system, each state and territory of the United States must develop its own standards, curriculum, and assessments. While these must be aligned with federal education policy to be eligible to receive federal school funding, the U.S. government lacks the authority to impose a specific national curriculum and assessments. As states work to comply with federal policy, we potentially could have more than 50 different sets of standards and assessments with varying degrees of rigor and expectations. Such as system makes it difficult to make meaningful comparisons across states, particularly for ELLs as each state defines, identifies, assesses, and redesignates ELLs in different ways. Furthermore, less-populated states often have fewer resources and less expertise to develop sophisticated school accountability systems.

To address these issues, many states have joined together in coalitions to share common standards and assessments. We turn next to these state-led initiatives.

Common Core State Standards Initiative

The **Common Core State Standards (CCSS)** Initiative is a state-led effort initiated by the National Governors Association and the Council of Chief State School Officers. The initiative developed common language arts and mathematics standards for states to voluntarily adopt. The CCSS are described as rigorous, internationally benchmarked college-and-career-ready "next generation" standards that are designed to raise the bar and ensure that all high school graduates are prepared for the academic rigors of college course work and the demands of the workforce.

The CCSS aligned well with the Obama Administration's requirements for RTTT and ESEA Flexibility, which encouraged state adoption. The CCSS also fully meet the requirements of ESSA. Individual states and territories began to voluntarily adopt the CCSS in 2010. By 2018, 41 states, the District of Columbia, four U.S. territories, and the Department of Defense school system had adopted the CCSS, which must make up at least 85% of their state's language arts and mathematics standards. As of 2018 Alaska, Indiana, Florida, Nebraska, Oklahoma, South Carolina, Texas, Virginia, and Puerto Rico had not adopted the CCSS. Minnesota adopted only the English language arts standards. Indiana, Florida, and South Carolina originally adopted the CCSS but later pulled out. Their state standards, however, are "highly influenced" by the CCSS. A separate but related national effort led to the release of the Next Generation Science Standards in 2013, which so far have been adopted by 19 states plus the District of Columbia and will likely be adopted by many more.

The CCSS Initiative stresses that it does not call for or support a "national curriculum"; rather, the CCSS identify the essential knowledge and skills that all students need but do not specify how they are to be taught. Nonetheless, these nearly national standards have opened the way for the development of common textbooks, digital media, and teaching materials that are aligned to CCSS and that can be used across the country. The CCSS Initiative was also designed to enable common comprehensive assessment systems to replace existing state testing programs. The CCSS have generated substantial controversy. Critics have questioned why the CCSS have been adopted so widely without any field testing and whether they are really a federal encroachment on states rather than a true "state-led" effort (Box 4.2).

The CCSS do not specifically address ELLs and do not replace the state ELP standards required by ESSA. But they do include specific language standards and are designed to

---

Box 4.2 Are the Common Core State Standards a "State-Led" Grassroots Effort?

Some critics charge that the CCSS are not a voluntary state-led grassroots effort but rather have been driven by big business and the federal government. Ravitch (2013b) notes that "they were developed by an organization called Achieve and the National Governors Association, both of which were generously funded by the Gates Foundation" and argues that "it was well understood by states that they would not be eligible for Race to the Top funding ($4.35 billion) unless they adopted the Common Core standards" (p. 1). Most states seeking ESEA Flexibility adopted the CCSS also because of pressure to meet federal requirements for "college and career readiness standards," though some states (e.g., Texas, Indiana) elected to develop their own. In 2010, the Obama administration provided $330 million in funding through the RTTT Assessment Grant program to two state consortia (PARCC and Smarter Balanced) to develop a "new generation of tests" aligned with the CCSS. The federal government also provided over $16 million in funding to two consortia of states, WIDA and ELPA21, to develop new generation English language proficiency assessments that are based on standards that correspond with the CCSS.

The business community's staunch support for the CCSS, even in the face of growing bipartisan opposition, suggests they have much to gain (Krashen, 2012; Ravitch, 2013a, 2013b; Strauss, 2013). Indeed, Weiss (2011), who was the chief of staff to U.S. Secretary of Education Arne Duncan, declared in the Harvard Business Review blog that "the adoption of common standards and shared assessments means that education entrepreneurs will enjoy national markets where the best products can be taken to scale" (p. 1). The business community has already provided millions of dollars in grants and other financial support to various entities involved in the CCSS, and the leaders of 73 top business corporations took out a full-page advertisement in the *New York Times* on February 12, 2013, to publish an open letter of support for the CCSS.

Political backlash, mostly from conservative lawmakers who viewed the CCSS as an intrusion into state rights, led to a clause in ESSA that prohibits the U.S. Secretary of Education from encouraging states to adopt the CCSS or join any other standards and assessment state consortiums.

develop the "academic language" skills of all students. The CCSS do not specify the language of instruction and thus are compatible with bilingual education approaches. For example, the New York Bilingual Common Core Initiative has established home and new language arts progressions and other tools to help teachers differentiate language arts instruction according to students' language development levels. Teachers can also use these progressions to support dynamic bilingual and biliteracy development in CCSS classrooms (EngageNY, 2013). At the same time, the Chief Council of State School Officers, the California Department of Education, and the San Diego County Office of Education have created a translated and linguistically augmented version of the CCSS in Spanish titled Common Core en Español.

ELL advocates and experts are divided over the implications of the CCSS for ELLs. Some, as noted earlier, question the real agenda behind the standards and are concerned that raising the bar for all students with rigorous new standards, increasing the use of high-stakes standardized tests, and emphasizing the use of complex informational texts will only leave ELLs even further behind (Crawford, 2012; Krashen, 2012; Ravitch, 2013b).

Other ELL experts, however, view the CCSS as an opportunity to make much-needed instructional and assessment changes that will lead to higher levels of achievement for ELLs (Calderón, 2013; Fillmore, 2014; Hakuta, 2011). Pompa and Hakuta (2012) note the potential benefits for ELLs:

> The current policy environment is inhospitable to the improvement of educational prospects for ELLs. Yet the wave of reform unleashed by the new standards offers opportunities for better policies that would benefit ELLs because of an amplified focus on language. The policy, practice and research communities concerned with ELLs must emerge with a clear and coherent consensus on the aspects of the CCSS that advance educational prospects for ELLs, to help define what is appropriate and well-tailored to the needs of the range of ELL students. (p. 6)

Several ELL experts are working within state consortia related to the CCSS, and a team of prominent national ELL experts has formed the Understanding Language group. The purpose of the Understanding Language national initiative is to develop knowledge and resources to help content-area teachers meet the linguistics needs of ELLs as they address the CCSS.

Common Core State Standards Assessment Consortia

Two state consortia received federal funding to develop "next-generation" English language arts and mathematics assessments designed to measure student achievement of the CCSS: the Partnership for the Assessment of Readiness for College and Careers (PARCC) and the Smarter Balanced Assessment Consortium ("Smarter Balanced" for short). Both consortia developed online end-of-year summative assessments, along with optional online formative assessments for use at different points throughout a school year. In 2016, however, PARCC switched to an end-of-year only summative assessment. Online assessments require schools to have access to a substantial number of sophisticated computers with fast and reliable Internet access. Both consortia collaborate with ELL experts to develop policies, procedures, and accommodations for ELLs. The assessments were first administered in the 2014–2015 school year. The PARCC and Smarter Balanced tests meet the current requirements of ESSA for English language arts and mathematics assessments. Both also claim the ability to measure the progress of individual students' growth, which many states use in their ESSA accountability plans. Initial enthusiasm was high among Common Core states, with well-over half of the states and territories joining one or the other testing consortium. By 2018, however, fewer than half the states and territories remained members due largely to political backlash against the CCSS and the desire of states to have more control over the assessments. Thus, most states and territories now use their own assessments to meet ESSA assessment requirements.

English Language Proficiency Assessment Consortia

The WIDA state consortium, led by Wisconsin, was established in 2002 to develop common ELP standards and assessments to comply with federal policy.[2] WIDA's ELP assessment is called the Assessing Comprehension and Communication in English State-to-State for English Language Learners (ACCESS for ELLs). As of 2018, 39 states and territories were participating in the WIDA Consortium. WIDA has made revisions to its standards to comply with the requirement for member states that received ESEA Flexibility or that had adopted the CCSS to have ELP standards that correspond with college-and-career-readiness standards. WIDA's ELP standards and assessments are now used by member states to meet the requirements of ESSA. With some federal funding, and through collaboration with the Center for Applied Linguistics, WIDA's ELP assessment was converted to an online version—ACCESS 2.0—which was first administered in the 2015–2016 school year.

A much smaller state consortium—the English Language Proficiency Assessment for the 21st Century (ELPA21)—was established in 2012 by a group of states led by Oregon with assistance from the Council of Chief State School Officers and the Center for Research on Evaluation, Standards and Student Testing (CRESST). ELPA21 was awarded a federal grant for the creation of a common online ELP assessment based on ELP standards developed by WestEd that are aligned with the CCSS. The Educational Testing Service (ETS) was contracted to help develop the ELPA21 assessment, which was administered for the first time in the 2016–2017 school year. As of 2018 there were seven state members of ELPA21, Arkansas, Iowa, Nebraska, Ohio, Oregon, Washington, and West Virginia.

Thus, most states (and territories) have joined WIDA, and a handful of others are part of ELPA21. Some of the larger and more populous states—Arizona, California, Texas, and New York—have remained independent and developed their own ELP standards and assessments. As of 2018 only 4 other states remain outside of these consortia—Connecticut, Kansas, Louisiana, and Mississippi—though some of these states were previous members of one of these consortia, and may still be using the shared standards, but not the shared assessments.

State Policies for English Language Learners

Bilingual education, as discussed earlier, was once common in this country, particularly in isolated areas where immigrants from non-English-speaking countries settled and were the dominant groups and in areas of the Southwest where Spanish speakers were long the dominant group. As state governments began assuming more responsibility for public schooling and as pressure built during the Americanization movement, many states passed English-only instruction laws. After the passage of the Bilingual Education Act in

---

[2] WIDA initially stood for the original four members of the consortium: Wisconsin, Illinois, Delaware, and Arkansas. As more states joined, WIDA became "World-class Instructional Design and Assessment." The consortium later dropped this name, and now simply goes by WIDA, which is not an acronym for anything.

1968 and the *Lau v. Nichols* decision by the U.S. Supreme Court in 1974 (discussed in the next section), many state governments repealed these laws and many others also created their own bilingual education mandates.

The policy scene changed dramatically in the late 1990s and early 2000s after voters in California, Arizona, and Massachusetts approved **English for the Children initiatives**, which placed restrictions on bilingual education programs. In 1998 California voters approved Proposition 227, in 2000 Arizona voters approved Proposition 203, and in 2002 Massachusetts voters approved Question 2. An attempt to pass a similar initiative in Colorado (Amendment 31) failed.

The initiatives were authored, funded, and led by a millionaire California software developer, Ron Unz, who ignored the history, purpose, design of, and research on bilingual programs. He claimed that bilingual education programs are a violation of immigrant children's right to learn English and used misleading statistics and data and false claims in making the case for eliminating bilingual education programs. The Companion Website contains a short article with details about these misleading and false claims.

Analyses of the impact of the initiatives have found no evidence that the replacement of bilingual education programs with mandates for structured (or sheltered) English immersion have helped ELLs learn English faster or perform at higher levels on state achievement tests (American Institutes for Research & WestEd, 2006; Hill, 2006; Mahoney, Thompson, & MacSwan, 2005; Wright & Pu, 2005). Arizona education officials attempted to claim that Proposition 203 resulted in more than doubling the number of ELLs attaining English proficiency each year (Zehr, 2010b). An investigation by the federal Office of Civil Rights in 2010, however, revealed that Arizona's ELP test was not providing a valid measure of ELLs' English proficiency, and that the state was forcing students out of ELL programs and into mainstream classroom before they had attained sufficient English proficiency (Office for Civil Rights, 2010).

Despite the opposition, bilingual education continued to thrive, even in the three states that passed the English for the Children initiatives. Several schools in California, Arizona, and Massachusetts used the waiver provisions of the law to continue bilingual programs because they were effective and parents wanted them (Combs, Evans, Fletcher, Para, and Jiménez, 2005; de Jong, Gort, and Cobb, 2005; Wright, 2004b, 2005). The annual conference of the California Association for Bilingual Education continued to draw thousands of educators each year. In 2012, California was the first state in the country to establish the Seal of Biliteracy to officially recognize the bilingual skills of graduating seniors on their high school diplomas.

In recognition of the inappropriate restrictions Proposition 227 placed on bilingual education programs, in 2014 California Senator Ricardo Lara drafted Senate Bill 1174 to create an opportunity for voters to repeal Proposition 227. The bill was approved, and a voter initiative was placed on the November 2016 ballot as **Proposition 58** under the title "English Proficiency. Multilingual Education." Proposition 58 emphasized that schools must ensure that students become proficient in English. But it also authorized school districts to establish dual-language immersion programs for both native and non-native English speakers. It called for parental and community input on language acquisition programs and recognized the rights of parents to select available programs that best meet their children's needs. Proposition 58 easily passed on November 8, 2016, with 72% voter approval. On November 22, 2017 the governor of Massachusetts signed Bill H.4032, "An Act relative to language opportunity for our kids (LOOK)" (Massachusetts Language Opportunity Coalition, 2017). The **LOOK Act** essentially reversed Question 2 and allows school districts flexibility in choosing bilingual education or other "language acquisition programs" (Massachusetts Department of Elementary and Secondary Education, 2018).

Several states still have strong bilingual education policies, and in most other states, bilingual education is neither restricted nor required but remains a viable option. Nearly half of the states in the country have professional organizations for bilingual education, and most states reported that one or more school districts offer bilingual programs (OELA, 2012). Thus, many schools are continuing to provide bilingual programs because they have found them to be effective in meeting the language and academic needs of their ELLs.

Important Court Decisions and Legislation

Historical reluctance by many states throughout the country to provide equitable educational opportunities to ELLs and other minority students and controversies over the use of languages other than English in public schools have sparked a large number of lawsuits. Court decisions in these lawsuits have led to legislative changes that have helped to shape the policy climate of today. Here we briefly look at a few key court rulings that have affected ELL education. A more detailed review of these and other cases is available on the Companion Website.

Brown v. Board of Education (1954) along with other segregation cases have made it clear that ELLs cannot be fully separated from other students throughout their education under the guise of helping them learn English. But *Brown* also made clear that states are responsible for providing students with "equal educational opportunities," opening the way for high-quality bilingual programs. Court rulings in cases such as *Meyer v. Nebraska* (1923) and *Farrington v. Tokushige* (1927) have established states' authority to determine the language of instruction in public schools, but the court protected the right of parents to organize after-school and weekend heritage language classes for their children.

The 1974 Supreme Court case *Lau v. Nichols* resulted in perhaps the most important court decision regarding ELL education. Chinese American students in San Francisco were placed in mainstream classrooms despite their lack of proficiency in English and left to "sink or swim." The district argued that the Chinese American students received treatment equal to that of other students. Justice William Douglass, in writing the court's opinion, strongly disagreed, arguing, "There is no equality of treatment merely by providing students with the same facilities, textbooks, teachers, and curriculum; for students who do not understand English are effectively foreclosed from any meaningful education."

Following the court's decision, the U.S. Department of Education's Office of Civil Rights created the **Lau Remedies** to go after districts that were ignoring the needs of ELLs. The Lau Remedies essentially required districts to implement bilingual education programs for ELLs. The essence of *Lau* was codified into federal law though the **Equal Educational Opportunities Act** of 1974, soon after the case was decided. Section 1703(f) declares: "No state shall deny educational opportunities to an individual on account of his or her race, color, sex, or national origin." This includes "the failure of an educational agency to take appropriate action to overcome language barriers that impede equal participation by its students in its instructional programs." Although other legal actions have since made it clear that the Supreme Court did not mandate bilingual education, the Equal Educational Opportunities Act remains in effect and several subsequent lawsuits have been based on this important legislation.

The right to bilingual education suffered a further blow in 1981 in the Texas case *Castañeda v. Pickard*. Although the federal court found that the Raymondville School District fell far short of meeting the requirements of the EEOA, the court did not support the plaintiff's demands for bilingual education. A major outcome of this case, however, is a three-pronged test to determine whether schools are taking "appropriate action" to address the needs of ELLs as required by the Equal Educational Opportunities Act.

The Castañeda standard mandates that ELL programs be (1) based on a sound educational theory, (2) implemented effectively with sufficient resources and personnel, and (3) evaluated to determine whether they are effective in helping students overcome language barriers (Del Valle, 2003). The Castañeda standard has essentially become the law of the land in determining the adequacy of programs for ELLs. The Castañeda test, however, has shortcomings. Under the first two prongs, nearly any program can be justified by an educational theory, and some approaches require very little in the way of staff or funding (Del Valle, 2003). Under the third prong, a certain amount of time must pass before a determination can be made about the adequacy of the programs. Thus, many students may be harmed before inadequate programs are identified and rectified. Because of the ambiguous reference to "harm," in some cases the Castañeda test has been used successfully to rectify inadequate programs for ELLs (e.g., *Gomez v. Illinois State Board of Education*, 1987), while in other cases, the tests' shortcomings have led to decisions upholding policies and programs of highly questionable quality (e.g., *Flores v. Arizona*, 2000).

These cases, along with many others, demonstrate that courts have been reluctant to mandate a particular educational model or to give language minorities fundamental rights directly related to the use of their home languages. But the courts have made it clear that schools may not ignore the unique needs of ELLs. Any program for ELLs, regardless of the language of instruction or the models used, must do two very important things: teach English and teach academic content. Schools must provide English language development instruction for ELLs because they are not yet proficient in English, and because they need fluency in English to succeed in mainstream classrooms and to be successful in life in general in the United States. At the same time, schools cannot focus just on teaching English. Students must also learn the same academic content their English-proficient peers are learning in such subjects as language arts, math, science, social studies, music, art, and physical education. In the next chapter we review the different program models for ELLs and how these programs address the legal requirements for teaching English and the content areas.

Box 4.3 provides a list of federal legal obligations states and local districts and schools have related to the education of ELLs.

Language Policy at the Local Level

Federal and state policies for ELLs have raised awareness that schools are responsible for meeting the needs of ELLs. An important first step in assuming that responsibility is to articulate a school or district language policy. "A language policy," according to Corson (1999),

> is a document compiled by the staff of a school, who are often assisted by other members of the school community, to which the staff give their assent and commitment. It identifies areas in the school's scope of operations and programs where language problems exist that need the commonly agreed approach offered by a policy. A language policy sets out what the school intends to do about these areas of concern and includes provisions for follow-up, monitoring, and revision of the policy itself in light of changing circumstances. It is a dynamic action statement that changes along with the dynamic context of a school. (p. 1)[3]

---

[3] Corson, D. (1999). *Language policy in schools: A resource for teachers and administrators.* Mahwah, NJ: Lawrence Erlbaum, reprinted with permission.

Box 4.3 School and District State Obligations
for ELLs under Title VI and the EEOA

The following list is adapted from the *Title III Non-Regulatory Guidelines* issued by the U.S. Department of Education (2016, pp. 6–7). To meet their obligations under the Title VI Civil Rights Act and the Equal Education Opportunity Act, schools and districts must:

- identify and assess all potential ELL students in a timely, valid, and reliable manner;
- provide ELL students with a language assistance program that is educationally sound and proven successful, consistent with *Castañeda v. Pickard* and the Supreme Court decision in *Lau v. Nichols*;
- provide sufficiently well prepared and trained staff and support the language assistance programs for ELL students;
- ensure that ELL students have equal opportunities to meaningfully participate in all curricular and extracurricular activities;
- avoid unnecessary segregation of ELL students;
- ensure that ELL students who have or are suspected of having a disability are identified, located, and evaluated in a timely manner and that the language needs of students who need special education and disability related services because of their disability are considered in evaluations and delivery of services;
- meet the needs of ELL students who opt out of language assistance programs;
- monitor and evaluate ELL students in language assistance programs to ensure their progress with respect to acquiring English proficiency and grade-level content knowledge;
- exit ELL students from language assistance programs when they are proficient in English;
- monitor exited ELL students to ensure they were not prematurely exited and that any academic deficits incurred in the language assistance program have been remedied;
- evaluate the effectiveness of a school district's language assistance program(s) to ensure that ELL students in each program acquire English proficiency and that each program is reasonably calculated to allow students to attain parity of participation in the standard instructional program within a reasonable time; and
- ensure meaningful communication with parents of ELLs.

Corson (2001) asserts that in multilingual settings like the United States, three policy principles are necessary:

1. Children have the right to be educated in their home language.
2. If the first principle cannot be met, children have the right to attend a school that respects and values their home language.
3. Children have the right to learn the standard language variety (e.g., standard English in the United States) to the highest level of proficiency possible.

These three principles should be a starting point for schools in developing their own language policies. A school's language policy, along with an accompanying implementation manual or guide, provides the necessary structure for ensuring that ELLs have equal access to educational opportunities on the local level. The programs for ELLs that are based on the policy reflect the mission and vision of the school and the district for all students, including ELLs. The language policy and implementation guide provide a vehicle for creating a coherent vision of ELL education and for the institutionalization of effective programs. When every educator who is responsible for the education of ELLs on the local level shares a common understanding, a common language, and a common practice committed to equal access to educational opportunities for ELLs, programs improve, instruction improves, and ELL performance improves (Field & Menken, 2015).

Summary

The United States has a long history of bilingual education, though direct federal involvement in the education of ELLs which essentially began with the passage of Title VII Bilingual Education Act of 1968. More than 30 years of federal funding and support for bilingual education came to an abrupt end in 2001 with the passage of the NCLB, which focused exclusively on English. While bilingual education was still allowed under NCLB, and continues to be allowed under ESSA, whatever ELL programs districts choose to offer, they must ensure that ELLs learn English as quickly as possible.

The passage of ESSA in 2015 is affording states new opportunities for greater flexibility in teaching and assessing ELLs. States have the ability to establish more reasonable expectations for ELLs in school accountability programs. But concerns remain about the continued focus on accountability through high-stakes testing.

Since 2002, state education policies have been driven largely by federal policy and greatly influenced by state involvement (or lack of involvement) in the various standards and assessment consortia. Bilingual education remains a viable option, despite restrictions resulting from voter initiatives in a few states in the late 1990s and early 2000s. The reversal of these propositions in California and Massachusetts, along with the U.S. Department of Education's recognition of the research base supportive of home language development and acknowledgment that bilingual programs meet ESSA's requirements for effective language instruction educational programs provides further evidence of the viability of bilingual education.

The courts play a significant role in the development of policy for ELLs and have made it clear that language minorities have the right to teach their children their home language through private language classes, that schools cannot ignore the linguistic and academic needs of ELLs, that programs for ELLs must be based on sound educational theory, that ELL programs must be provided with adequate resources and properly trained teachers, and that programs must be evaluated to ensure that they are sufficient in meeting student needs. With a strong understanding of history and the limitations of and potential opportunities provided by current language and education policies, teachers can effectively work with their districts and schools to develop their own language policies and procedures to ensure that their ELL programs comply with all federal and state policies and meet the needs of the students and communities they serve.

Discussion Questions

1. How has federal policy for ELLs changed since 1968? What are the requirements of ESSA and how do they differ from earlier federal policies? Do you feel these are positive or negative changes for ELLs? Why?

2. Is your state a member of a Common Core (PARCC or Smarter Balanced) or ELP (WIDA or ELPA21) state consortia or both? If so, how does membership in these consortia impact the education of your ELLs? If not, what has your state developed in terms of standards and assessments and how do they impact your ELLs?

3. What has been the role of the courts in guiding federal policy for ELLs? What has case law identified as the main responsibilities of schools in meeting their needs? Which case set forth a test for determining the adequacy of an ELL program, and what are the three prongs of this test? What are the shortcomings of this test in ensuring high-quality programs for ELLs?

4. Download and review a copy of your state's approved ESSA Plan from your state department of education website, along with any associated training doc-

uments. What are your state's specific plans for including ELLs in state assessments? How are ELP results used in school accountability formulas? What are the benefits and challenges your state's ESSA plans may pose for your ELLs?

5. View the short video clip, *Take Charge on ESSA!* produced by the National Education Association (NEA). How does the NEA view the changes from NCLB to ESSA? What do they encourage teachers and others to do? Why is this important for students, especially for ELLs?

Research Activities

1. *ELL Student Interview* Interview a current or former ELL student. Ask questions to determine the extent to which the student has or has not benefited from the language and education policies in your state.

2. *ELL Teacher Interview* Interview a teacher of ELLs. Ask what impact ESSA has had on his or her classroom and whether the law's focus on standards and high-stakes testing has been beneficial or harmful to the ELLs. If the teacher is in a state that is in the PARCC, Smarter Balanced, WIDA, or ELPA21 consortium, ask what changes have come as a result, how the teacher feels about the changes, and the impacts so far on ELLs.

3. *ELL Classroom Observation* To understand how policy gets translated into practice, choose one or more of the policies described in this chapter that is applicable to your state (e.g., ESSA, CCSS, bilingual education requirements or restrictions). With an understanding of the requirements of the policy, observe a classroom of ELLs and determine some of the specific ways the policy affects the classroom structure, teacher instruction, and student learning.

4. *Online Research Activity* Obtain detailed school achievement and accountability data for your own school or for a school with which you are familiar. These can typically be obtained in the form of school report cards available from your state's Department of Education website. Compare the achievement of ELLs with state, consortia, or federal expectations, and with other student groups in the school.

Recommended Reading

Heineke, A. J. (2017). *Restrictive language policy in practice: English learners in Arizona*. Bristol, UK: Multilingual Matters.

This book takes a critical look at Arizona's Proposition 203 and the implementation of its mandated sheltered English immersion model, revealing the harm of Arizona's policies and the need for changes to better address the needs of ELLs, as well as the need to prepare and professionalize teachers of English learners.

Teachers of English to Speakers of Other Languages. (2016). *English learners and ESSA: What educators need to know*. Alexandria, VA: TESOL Press.

This resource kit from TESOL helps teachers educate themselves and others on the requirements of ESSA for ELLs to advocate for policies, funding uses, and other priorities at the local and state levels to improve instruction for ELLs so these students can achieve language proficiency and academic success.

U.S. Department of Education (2016a). *English learner tool kit for state and local education agencies*. Washington, DC: Office of English Language Acquisition.

The helpful guide provides clear explanations of the civil rights and other legal obligations to ELLs, tools schools can use as self-monitoring tools, and additional resources that may provide further relevant information and assistance.

Five

Instructional Models and Programs

There is no equality of treatment merely by providing students with the same facilities, textbooks, teachers, and curriculum; for students who do not understand English are effectively foreclosed from any meaningful education.

—Lau v. Nichols

KEY TERMS

- bilingual immersion
- bilingual strategies
- developmental bilingual education
- dual language education
- English as a second language
- English language development
- heritage language program
- heteroglossic perspective
- home language instruction
- monoglossic perspective
- newcomer program

- one-way immersion
- sheltered English immersion
- sheltered instruction
- Sheltered Instruction Observation Protocol
- specially designed academic instruction in English
- submersion
- transitional bilingual education
- translanguaging pedagogy
- two-way immersion

GUIDING QUESTIONS

1. What are the essential components of any instructional models and programs for ELLs?
2. What is the difference between English as a second language and sheltered instruction?
3. What are the pros and cons of various English-medium and bilingual education models and programs?
4. How can educators determine what type of program is appropriate for their context?

Language and education policies for ELLs are realized at the district, school, and classroom levels through a variety of instructional programs. The Every Student Succeeds Act (ESSA) requires schools to provide effective "language instruction educational programs." Box 5.1 provides a list of themes that emerged from a review of the literature on effective ELL programs, as described in a report commissioned by the U.S. Department of Education. As we saw earlier, ESSA holds states accountable for the academic achievement and English language development of ELLs and grants each state the flexibility to identify which program models are eligible for funding. Educators who work with ELLs determine which instructional programs are appropriate for their students and school. Their decisions must be based on a consideration of research, federal and state policies, and the needs, desires, strengths, and characteristics of their students and community. All teachers—including general education, bilingual, and ESL teachers, as well as literacy and special education specialists—are responsible for developing the knowledge and skills they need to educate the ELLs in their classes.

An understanding of the range of instructional programs for linguistically and culturally diverse learners, including ELLs, is an important part of that knowledge base. We begin with a discussion of new perspectives on instructional programs for ELLs and move

Box 5.1 U.S. Department of Education Review of Foundational Literature on Effective English Language Learner Program Models

To help schools implement federal policy requiring effective ELL programs, referred to as "language instructional education programs" under the Every Student Succeeds Act (ESSA), the U.S. Department of Education commissioned a report to review the foundational literature on the topic. The following themes emerged from this review.

1. High standards and challenging content are good for ELLs.
2. Having an ELL program model is important.
3. No one approach or model is appropriate for all ELLs.
4. Instructional practices are important variables in ELL program model design and implementation.
5. Literacy and oral language development in English are critical instructional components for any ELL program model.
6. Academic language seems to be important in ELL instruction.
7. ELLs need instruction that is specifically cognizant of their needs as second-language learners.
8. Teachers need to be prepared to teach ELLs.
9. Newcomer models are a programmatic option that school districts may use to meet the needs of newly identified ELLs at the secondary level.
10. ELLs' scores on academic content assessments should be interpreted with great care.
11. Current assessments may not be sufficient measures of the linguistic proficiency necessary to support success in mainstream content classrooms.
12. Culture and community matter.

Modified from Faulkner-Bond et al., 2012.

on to the essential components of ELL programs: English as a second language, content-area instruction taught in the home language or through sheltered English instruction, and bilingual strategies to strengthen ELLs' opportunities to learn. We then discuss the differences between English as a second language and sheltered English content-area instruction, and the relationship between English as a second language and English language arts. Finally, we examine the different program models for ELLs, looking first at bilingual models and then at English-medium models. Throughout our discussion, we must keep in mind that bilingual and English-medium programs are always evolving in response to changes in student demographics, advances in our understanding of bilingualism and education, and the increasing participation of English speakers in bilingual programs.

There is no one-size-fits-all program appropriate for all students in all schools. But as research related to each model shows, strong forms of bilingual education that aim for bilingualism and biliteracy, academic achievement, and intercultural competence provide students with the best opportunities to draw on all of their linguistic resources while learning challenging academic content. After our review of instructional programs for ELLs, we briefly discuss how district and community leaders can work together to choose what kinds of programs are appropriate for language learners in their schools. We also consider how teachers collaborate in creative ways to ensure ELL success. Collaborations vary according the sociolinguistic situation, the types of instructional programs for ELLs that are implemented in schools, and the role of teachers and administrators.

Evolving Perspectives

Taking a sociocultural view of bilingualism, García (2009a) and others have given us a new way of understanding and challenging the traditional program models described in this chapter, most of which have grown out of cognitive views of second language learning. García makes a distinction between monoglossic and heteroglossic perspectives of bilingualism.

Most bilingual programs are grounded in a **monoglossic perspective,** which views monolingualism as the norm and treats the languages of bilinguals as two separate, distinct systems, as if students are two monolinguals in one (double monolingualism). A **heteroglossic perspective** views bilingualism as the norm and treats the languages of bilinguals as co-existing. Drawing on García's distinction, Flores and Beardsmore (2015) argue that monoglossic perspectives and practices erase the natural, fluid ways bilingual students use their languages in everyday life. Students do not compartmentalize their language practices into neat and discrete languages as is expected in many bilingual programs (García & Lin, 2017). Thus, they argue, effective programs should be grounded in heteroglossic perspectives.

This view is realized through translanguaging practices, by which teachers can help students draw on all of their linguistic resources—including standard and nonstandard forms of home languages and English—as they work to communicate and engage in academic tasks in the classroom. Wright & Baker (2017) note, "We thus seem to be witnesses to a historical change from effective *models* to effective *practices*, although the latter is built upon the former, and space can be made in existing program models for multilingual/heteroglossic perspectives and effective translanguaging practices" (p. 73). Faltis and Ramírez-Marin (2015) argue that such an approach is especially appropriate and needed for ELLs at the secondary level. While these new ideas have yet to be developed into full pedagogical models, they suggest powerful ways that schools can strengthen their bilingual and English-medium program design and implementation.

Essential Components of Instructional Programs for English Language Learners

All effective instructional programs for ELLs have three essential components: English as a second language instruction, content-area instruction, and bilingual strategies. Table 5.1 highlights each of these components with their various options.

English as a Second Language

English language instruction for students who have been identified as ELLs is called **English as a second language** (ESL). In many states it is called **English language development** (ELD). Some states use the term *English for speakers of other languages (ESOL)*, and others use *English as a new language (ENL)* or *English as an additional language (EAL)*. Because there are many students for whom English is a third, fourth, or even higher-number language, these labels may be more accurate. But since these terms are essentially synonymous, for the sake of simplicity, we use the more common terms, *ESL or ELD*, from here on. The purpose of ESL instruction is to enable ELLs to develop their proficiency in English by mastering the skills of listening, speaking, reading, and writing to the extent that they are able to use the English language appropriately and effectively for

Table 5.1 Essential Components of Effective Programs for English Language Learners

Standards-Based English as a Second Language		Standards-Based Content-Area Instruction		Bilingual Strategies
Pull-Out English as a Second Language	**In-Class English as a Second Language**	**Home Language Instruction**	**Sheltered Instruction**	
A teacher trained and certified to work with ELLs pulls students out of the regular classroom for ESL instruction.	The classroom teacher is trained and certified to work with ELLs and provides ESL instruction within the classroom.	One or more content areas are taught in students' home languages	One or more content areas are taught in English using sheltered instruction strategies and techniques.	The classroom teacher employs a variety of bilingual strategies and techniques involving the effective use of students' home languages to increase their comprehension of English during ESL and sheltered-content instruction.

authentic communicative purposes and to achieve academic success in English-language elementary and secondary classrooms.

ESL is a separate content area, like math, science, social studies, and language arts. And like them, it has its own set of curricular materials and must have its own separate time slot within the daily teaching schedule. It also has its own set of standards, as mandated by ESSA. In California and other states, such as those in the WIDA Consortium, these are called ELD standards, while in other states they are called English language proficiency (ELP) standards or simply ESL standards.

Many schools make the mistake of providing daily ESL instruction only for ELLs at the beginning stages of English language development and stop once the students reach the intermediate level. This mistake is based on the false assumption that the students no longer need ESL because they can develop fluency in English through content-area instruction alone. Data collected for the state of California show that beginning-level ELLs move up to the intermediate levels within 2 to 3 years, but then most get stuck at the intermediate and advanced levels, often for several years (American Institutes for Research & WestEd, 2006; Hill, 2006). A study in Nevada revealed that only 65% of ELLs in cohorts of kindergarten and 3rd and 6th grade students attained English proficiency within a 6-year period (Haas, Huang, Tran, & Yu, 2016). This study also found that less than half of the students moved up at the rate of one English proficiency level per year. These studies reveal that all ELLs—including those at the intermediate and advanced levels—need consistent, high-quality ESL instruction to reach the "proficient" level.

ESL instruction at the intermediate and advanced levels should provide more emphasis on increasing vocabulary and developing skills in advanced literacy. Many teachers report that ELLs at these higher levels have good listening and speaking skills (often described as "native-like") and that they sound fluent when they read text aloud. The problem is that ELLs often do not fully comprehend what they read because they are still developing higher-level vocabulary and knowledge of more complex sentence structures.

They may not yet have enough background knowledge to understand cultural references in the text, or an understanding of the more subtle uses of language and of the ways language use differs for social and academic purposes in the various content areas (e.g., the language of English language arts differs from the language of mathematics). These same issues can lead to difficulties for students when they are writing in English. ESL at the intermediate and advanced levels focuses on these areas. ESL instruction is usually delivered through a pull-out program or in class by the classroom teacher at the elementary level, and in stand-alone classes at the secondary level.

Content-Area Instruction

Comprehensible content-area instruction is the second essential component of every program for ELLs. The most effective way to make content comprehensible is to teach it in the students' home languages. When home language instruction is not possible, teachers use sheltered English instruction.

Home Language Content-Area Instruction

Learning new concepts and skills can be challenging, and it's even harder in a language you do not know or are still in the process of learning. Students learn best in the language they understand best. Thus, providing ELLs with content-area instruction in their home language while they are learning English as a new language helps to ensure that they will learn complex academic content and master grade-level content standards. It also ensures that they won't fall farther behind their English-proficient peers in those academic subjects.

The same principle applies to home language literacy instruction. It is much easier for students to learn to read and write in the language they know best. Students need to learn how to read only once. Many of the skills students develop when learning to read and write in their home language easily transfer to English. This ease of transfer is true for all written languages, even those that do not use the same script (letters, alphabet) as English, such as Chinese (Pu, 2008) and Khmer (Zehler & Sapru, 2008). **Home language instruction** is a distinguishing feature of the bilingual education models described in this chapter for ELLs, simultaneous bilinguals, and heritage language speakers.

Effective content-area instruction in ELLs' home language requires a certified bilingual teacher who is fully proficient in that language and in English. It also requires appropriate curricular materials in the students' home language. Home language content-area instruction is aligned with content standards established for proficient English speakers, and we see variation in the ways states address this challenge. Some states, such as Texas and the states and territories in the WIDA Consortium, have adopted separate Spanish language arts standards aligned with state English language arts standards. Spanish language arts standards reflect unique aspects of listening, speaking, reading, and writing in Spanish. The New York State Education Department launched the Bilingual Common Core Initiative in 2013 and created Home and New Language Arts Progressions that teachers can use to differentiate language arts instruction according to students' levels of home and new language development. WIDA has also developed broader Spanish language development standards that parallel the ELD standards for use in programs where students receive content-area instruction in Spanish. In 2013, the Council of Chief State School Officers (CCSSO), the California Department of Education (CDE), and the San Diego County Office of Education (SDCOE) launched the Common Core Translation Project. Also known as the Common Core en Español, this project provides a translation of the Common Core State Standards for English language arts and math from English to Spanish but includes a linguistic augmentation that highlights similarities and differ-ences between English and Spanish and identifies concrete ways that teachers can teach for cross-linguistic transfer. Typically, the amount of home language instruction is grad-ually reduced, and the amount of sheltered instruction is increased each year as students learn more English.

Sheltered Content-Area Instruction

Sheltered instruction refers to grade-level content-area instruction that is provided in English but in a manner that makes it comprehensible to ELLs while promoting their English language development (Echevarria & Graves, 2014). The word *sheltered* is a met-aphor for simplifying the language without watering down the content, while protecting ELLs from language demands that may be beyond their comprehension. Some states, such as California, refer to sheltered instruction as **specially designed academic instruction in English** (SDAIE).

I prefer the term *SDAIE* because it emphasizes that the instruction is different from regular instruction in English but is on grade level and appropriately challenging. *SDAIE* has a positive connotation, suggesting that ELLs can and will learn academic content in English if the instruction is specially designed for them. But because *sheltered instruction* is widely used and recognized, I use that term from here on.

The **Sheltered Instruction Observation Protocol** (SIOP) model offers guidance to teachers who use sheltered instruction by helping them systematically plan, teach, ob-serve, and evaluate effective instruction for ELLs (Echevarria, Vogt, & Short, 2017). The model was developed in the late 1990s by Echevarria, Vogt, and Short, who recognized the importance of sheltered instruction but were concerned that teachers lacked a clear understanding of how to provide it consistently and effectively. The SIOP model identifies eight key components of effective sheltered instruction: *preparation, building background, comprehensible input, strategies, interaction, practice and application, lesson delivery,* and *review and assessment*. Thirty items are organized into these eight components. The SIOP model is field tested, and there is some research evidence of its validity and reliability as an observation protocol, as well as its effectiveness as a pedagogical approach (Echevarria, Short, & Powers, 2006; Short, Fidelman, & Louguit, 2012).

The items under *preparation* include having clear language and content-area objec-tives, appropriate content concepts, and plans for introducing meaningful activities and using supplementary materials. *Building background* items include building on students' prior knowledge and teaching key vocabulary. *Comprehensible input* items include pro-viding clear explanations of academic tasks and teachers' adjusting their speech (vocab-ulary, pace, sentence complexity, etc.) to an appropriate level for their students. *Strategies* include using scaffolding, promoting higher-order thinking skills, and teaching learning strategies. *Interaction* items include using wait time effectively, grouping students, and using primary language support to maximize students' ability to interact with the teacher and each other. *Practice and application* items include hands-on, cooperative learning ac-tivities that integrate the four language skills (listening, speaking, reading, and writing) and allow students to apply their content and language knowledge. *Lesson delivery* items include meeting stated language and content-area objectives, pacing the lesson appropri-ately, and ensuring that students are engaged in the lesson. The *review and assessment* items include reviewing vocabulary and key concepts, providing feedback, and conduct-ing assessments of students' learning.

The SIOP model has become very popular, with school districts encouraging teachers and administrators to receive SIOP training. Some critics express concern that SIOP is too rigid, behavioristic, and lacking in solid theoretical grounding (Crawford & Reyes,

2015). Another concern is that some administrators assume that a few days of SIOP training for teachers is sufficient to address ELLs' needs. Research has shown that SIOP training alone is insufficient to prepare teachers to work effectively with ELLs (McIntyre, Kyle, Chen, Munoz, & Beldon, 2010). Professional development in second language teaching, learning, and assessment, as well as an understanding of the sociocultural, historical, economic, and political factors that can affect students' English language development and academic content learning provide the foundation for effective sheltered instruction in the classroom. Thus, these foundational issues and constructs are emphasized throughout this book and in teacher education programs leading to certification in working with ELLs. Educators also need to understand how sheltered instruction fits into their overall instructional program for ELLs, whether bilingual or English-medium.

In practice, we find considerable variation in how sheltered instruction is implemented at both the elementary and secondary levels. For example, some districts offer sheltered instruction that serve ELLs exclusively and provide most or all of their content-area instruction in separate sheltered classes. Other districts may offer some sheltered content-area classes in, for example, math, science, English language arts, or social studies, and students can select classes from the bilingual, sheltered, and general education programs. The most common approach is for general education teachers to use sheltered instruction strategies with the entire class to ensure that all students—including ELLs—are successful in engaging with complex content and texts appropriate to their grade level.

A key feature of the SIOP model is its inclusion of language objectives within the context of content-area instruction in English. This feature highlights the fact that content-area teachers—in addition to ESL and bilingual teachers/specialists—also have responsibility for helping ELLs develop their proficiency in English, particularly in the discipline-specific ways language is used in the content areas they teach. For example, the content objectives of a SIOP math lesson plan for teaching long division would include the math standards for long division, as well as language objectives for learning the vocabulary associated with long division and the language needed for talking about and completing long division problems. The language objectives are informed by state ELP standards. Again, all teachers share in the responsibility of helping ELLs meet these standards. Note, however, that this combination of language objectives with content objectives does not eliminate the need for separate ESL instruction, whether by an ESL teacher/specialist or the classroom teachers themselves.

Echevarria, one of the creators of the SIOP model, emphasizes that ELLs need ESL instruction in addition to sheltered instruction (Echevarria & Graves, 2014). Sheltered instruction was designed for ELLs with at least intermediate proficiency and basic literacy skills; but because of a nationwide shortage of bilingual teachers, the scarcity of bilingual programs in languages other than Spanish, and policies in some states that discourage bilingual education, many teachers are faced with the challenge of providing sheltered content-area instruction to lower-level ELLs before they are really ready for it. Nonetheless, state/consortia ELD (or ELP) standards can help teachers differentiate their content-area instruction with objectives that are appropriate to the students' levels of English. Specific examples appear in later chapters.

Bilingual Strategies

We refer to the third essential component of instructional programs for ELLs as **bilingual strategies.** The traditional way to look at bilingual strategies is from the perspective of primary language support, which reflects a monoglossic orientation. Primary language support involves the brief use of students' home languages during ESL and sheltered instruction by the teacher, a paraprofessional, or the students themselves. The purpose of is to make content-area instruction in English more comprehensible, especially for ELLs at early stages of English language development. This approach reflects a language-as-resource orientation toward students' home languages, which are understood as important scaffolds and supports in instruction.

New developments in the field of bilingualism and education challenge educators to shift their perspective on the ways multilinguals use languages to learn. From a sociocultural perspective, the dynamic language practices of multilinguals can be referred to as translanguaging (García & Li Wei, 2014). Teachers can use bilingual or translanguaging strategies to leverage students' bilingualism for learning in any context. This perspective on bilingualism and education also sees languages as resources to develop but does not see the home language as a scaffold or support to be removed when ELLs no longer need it. It sees multilingualism holistically, with bilinguals drawing on all of the languages in their linguistic repertoire to make meaning, even when using one language exclusively (e.g., English) rather than another (e.g., Spanish).

García, Johnson, and Seltzer (2016) have put forward a **translanguaging pedagogy** that teachers can use to leverage the language practices of multilingual learners in bilingual and English-medium contexts. They identify four purposes of translanguaging that work together to advance social justice:

1. Supporting students as they engage with and comprehend complex content and texts
2. Providing opportunities for students to develop linguistic practices for academic contexts
3. Making space for students' bilingualism and ways of knowing
4. Supporting students' bilingual identities and socioemotional development (p. 7)

When teachers "make space for translanguaging," they purposefully leverage students' bilingualism for learning. Teachers do not need to speak the home languages of their students to facilitate effective use of translanguaging within different bilingual and English-medium program models. Further discussion and specific examples of translanguaging strategies appear in later chapters.

Difference between English as a Second Language and Sheltered Instruction

Educators are often confused about the difference between ESL and sheltered instruction. Many believe they are the same thing. They are not, and it is imperative that educators understand the difference. The focus of ESL is teaching English; the focus of sheltered instruction is teaching academic content (Table 5.2).

To illustrate the difference, let us return to the earlier example of teaching long division. The sheltered instruction lesson and the ESL lesson both include content and language objectives as the SIOP requires, but the two objectives are weighted differently. The primary instructional and assessment goals of the sheltered instruction lesson involve content. The instructional goal is for ELLs to understand the concept of long division and to be able to solve long division problems on their own. And though the same math standards are addressed for all students, the math instruction and assessments are differentiated for ELLs in accordance with their ELP level. The teacher teaches the language of math (vocabulary, listening, speaking, reading, writing) so that ELLs can participate and achieve during the lesson, but the major concern is the content learning. In other words, with proper language objectives and scaffolding, ELLs can successfully learn long divi-

Table 5.2 English as a Second Language Instruction Compared with Sheltered Instruction

	English as a Second Language Instruction	Sheltered Instruction
Definition	Teaching English to students who are not yet proficient in the language	Making content-area instruction comprehensible to ELLs in English while supporting their English language development
Concepts or areas of focus	Listening, speaking, reading, writing, vocabulary, communicative competence	English language arts, math, science, social studies, art, music, physical education, and other content areas
Standards	English language proficiency standards	Content-area standards
Goal	Communicative competence for social and academic purposes	Content-area knowledge and skills
Assessment	State English language proficiency assessment Classroom-based formative and summative English language proficiency assessments	State academic achievement assessments Classroom-based formative and summative content-area assessments

sion despite their use of "imperfect" English. In contrast, during the ESL lesson, math may be the topic, but language is the primary instructional and assessment goal. The ESL instruction would focus on helping ELLs learn and use specific math vocabulary correctly and appropriately to verbally explain in English the steps and procedures involved in solving a long division problem, and to read and comprehend long division problems. The ESL teacher uses the math lesson as a vehicle to teach language, and language learning is the primary concern. If students are struggling with math concepts and skills, they can learn the language they need in ESL to explain to their math teachers what they do not understand.

The overlap in content and language provide points of collaboration for sheltered instruction and ESL teachers. For example, the sheltered instruction teacher can identify the ways that reading, writing, listening, and speaking are used for academic purposes in the specific content area, and the ESL teacher can provide more focused ESL instruction in these academic language functions across content areas. If the classroom teacher is responsible for teaching both ESL and the content areas, he or she is in an excellent position to ensure that ESL instruction provides the support needed for the ELLs to be successful in sheltered-content lessons.

Again, the inclusion of language objectives alongside content-area objectives in sheltered instruction is an important and effective way to help students develop proficiency in the discipline-specific uses of English within these content areas. These language objectives are not, however, a substitute for ESL instruction. Language learned in ESL lessons supports student learning in sheltered content-area instruction and lays the foundation for further language acquisition to take place through the language objectives of the sheltered content-area lessons. Simply stated, sheltered content-area instruction *supplements* but does not *supplant* effective, systematic, and direct ESL instruction for ELLs. Effective programs for ELLs include both ESL and sheltered instruction.

Relationship between English as a Second Language and English Language Arts

The relationship between ESL and English language arts can also cause confusion. Providing language arts instruction to ELLs in English is not the same as teaching ESL. Even if language arts instruction is provided using sheltered instruction strategies, it cannot substitute for ESL instruction. Recall that ESSA requires states to have separate ELP and English language arts standards in addition to standards in other content areas. ELP standards and English language arts content standards are to be aligned but are nonetheless separate. English language arts standards and instruction are designed for proficient English-speaking students to refine skills in a language they already know. Few high school English teachers would describe themselves as language specialists. To them, English is a *subject* to be mastered, not a *language* to be learned. Thus, ESL teachers are more like world language teachers who teach a language and culture that is new to their students.

English language arts instruction in the United States has traditionally focused on teaching reading and writing. Regular classroom teachers have typically spent little time, if any, on oral language skills because proficient English speakers are already proficient listeners and speakers of the language. The Common Core State Standards for English Language Arts, however, include explicit language standards and listening and speaking standards that are designed to expand the language skills of proficient English speakers. With this raising of the bar, ELLs may be left even farther behind unless they are provided with substantial sheltered English language arts instruction in addition to extensive ESL instruction.

Unfortunately, some schools attempt to combine English language arts and ESL instruction. Some textbook companies produce English language arts series that include peripheral suggestions in the teachers' guides and supplemental materials for meeting the needs of ELLs. These materials are welcome additions insofar as they help teachers shelter their English language arts instruction. But they must not replace direct ESL instruction. A better approach, which other textbook companies have taken, is to provide a comprehensive ESL program combined with a separate but corresponding sheltered English language arts programs.

Program Models for English Language Learners and Other Multilingual Learners

The wide variety of program models currently in use for ELLs and other multilingual learners can be classified as either bilingual or English-medium. A bilingual program is defined here as any program in which one or more content areas is taught in the students' home language. In English-medium programs, all content areas are taught in English using sheltered instruction strategies, but this does not mean these programs are "English only." Effective English-medium programs use bilingual strategies in creative ways to maximize student comprehension and learning.

One major problem we face in the field of language education is inconsistency in how programs are labeled in the literature and in practice (Faulkner-Bond et al., 2012). This brief review of prototypical program models for ELLs and other multilingual learners uses the following guiding questions to clarify the program labels used here:

1. Who are the target populations?
2. What are the goals of the program?

3. How is the program structured?
4. What does the research say about the effectiveness of the program?

Using consistent terms allows us to compare different program types to determine which are the most effective for ELLs and other students and which are the most appropriate for a particular school and community. As you read through these program models, be aware that in practice they are usually not as neat and tidy as described here because of variations and constraints in local contexts, and the role educators play as policymakers as they interpret, negotiate, and implement policy mandates from above (Menken & García, 2010).

Bilingual Models

The following sections examine five bilingual models commonly found in the field today: transitional bilingual education, developmental bilingual education, dual language programs, bilingual immersion programs, and heritage language programs. Changing demographics and evolving perspectives on bilingual education have broadened our understanding of target populations in bilingual education programs. Bilingual programs now serve ELLs and non-ELLs. The variation in the "ELL" category is great and can include students with limited or interrupted formal education, refugees, immigrants, and adopted children. The variation in the "non-ELL" category is also great and can include simultaneous bilinguals (who grow up using two languages in their everyday lives), heritage language speakers (who are often English dominant with varying abilities in their heritage language), and students from monolingual English-speaking homes who want to become bilingual, biliterate, and interculturally competent. We focus on different target populations throughout our discussion in order to see how this variation influences decision making.

Transitional Bilingual Education

Transitional bilingual education (TBE) programs, also called early-exit programs, are the most common type of bilingual program in the United States. TBE programs target ELLs who speak the same home language and are most commonly implemented in the primary grades of elementary school. The goal of TBE programs is to transition ELLs to an English-medium classroom as quickly as possible. By providing content-area instruction in the students' home languages, schools can ensure that students do not fall behind academically while they are learning English.

Most TBE programs begin in kindergarten with about 90% of language arts and other content-area instruction taught in the home language and about 10% taught through sheltered English instruction, in addition to daily ESL instruction. Each year the amount of home language instruction is decreased and the amount of sheltered instruction is increased. Students first learn to read and write in their home language, to ensure that they do not fall behind academically while learning English. After 2 to 3 years, the students are transitioned to English language arts instruction, and the following year they are placed in English-medium classrooms (Figure 5.1). Some weaker versions of this model attempt to transition students to all-English instruction much sooner. Table 5.3 presents a sample of the subjects that a school might offer in kindergarten through 3rd grade, gradually transitioning from mostly home language instruction to mostly sheltered English instruction.

Longitudinal research on the effectiveness of different types of bilingual and English-medium programs demonstrates that TBE programs are more effective than English-medium programs but less effective than other bilingual education models in ensuring that ELLs reach parity with their English-speaking peers by the time they complete the

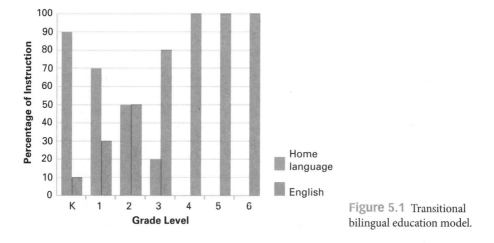

Figure 5.1 Transitional bilingual education model.

program (Thomas & Collier, 2002; Umansky & Reardon, 2014; Valentino & Reardon, 2014).

Researchers and practitioners have identified the following challenges associated with TBE:

- TBE programs tend to have a "language-as-problem" orientation and thus take a deficit view of ELLs. Also, because the goal of TBE programs is quick transition to English, these programs tend to lead to subtractive bilingualism. Many researchers and practitioners see the TBE model as essentially a remedial program (see, e.g., Crawford, 2015; Ovando & Combs, 2018).
- TBE programs reflect an assumption that ELLs can become proficient in English in 2 to 3 years and thus be ready for all-English instruction in mainstream classrooms (i.e., classrooms designed for proficient English speakers that provide little to no supports for ELLs). But few students learn a second language fluently that quickly. Thus, many ELLs are pushed into mainstream classrooms before they are ready.
- ELLs in TBE programs may be segregated from the academic mainstream for most or all of their instructional day, making it difficult for them to find opportunities to interact with and learn alongside their English-proficient peers.
- Many ELLs do not begin school in the United States in kindergarten. They start in the grade level that matches their age at their time of arrival. Since most TBE

Table 5.3 Content-Area and English as a Second Language Instruction in Transitional Bilingual Education Programs

	Kindergarten	1st Grade	2nd Grade	3rd Grade
Home language instruction	Language arts, social studies, science, math	Language arts, social studies, science	Language arts, social studies	Language arts
Sheltered instruction	Art, music, physical education	Math, art, music, physical education	Science, math, art, music, physical education	Language arts, social studies, science, math, art, music, physical education
ESL (daily)	30–60 minutes	30–60 minutes	30 60 minutes	30–60 minutes

programs are in the elementary grades, there may not be a TBE program available for many ELLs who would benefit from home language instruction in one or more content areas.

Despite these concerns, TBE programs are the most common because in the past they received the greatest amount of federal support. Although TBE can be seen as a "weak" model of bilingual education because it leads to monolingualism in English rather than bilingualism and biliteracy (Baker & Wright, 2017), the TBE approach is still much preferred over English-only models. Offering students, particularly young children, an opportunity to develop literacy skills and academic content in their home language while they are developing proficiency in English is much more humane than simply throwing them into an English-only classroom where they may become frustrated and discouraged. Schools with established, effective TBE programs are often able to evolve to one of the stronger models of bilingual education described in the following sections. Box 5.2 provides an overview of the TBE model.

Developmental Bilingual Education

Developmental bilingual education (DBE) is also sometimes called maintenance or late-exit bilingual education, or one-way dual language bilingual education. DBE programs are much less common than TBE programs in the United States in large part because of the lack of federal funding over the years for this model. Like TBE programs, prototypical DBE programs target ELLs who speak the same home language, they are most often found in elementary schools, and they are taught by qualified bilingual teachers. The goals of DBE programs, however, are different. DBE programs aim to help the students develop both English and their home language, so that they become fully bilingual and biliterate, achieving academically through both languages and developing a positive sense of their cultural heritage and ethnolinguistic identities.

Most DBE programs begin in kindergarten and continue through the highest grade level in the school, which might be 5th or 6th grade. Some DBE programs in K–8 schools

---

Box 5.2 Transitional Bilingual Education

Other name	Early-exit bilingual education
Target population	ELLs who speak the same home language
Typical grade span	K–3
Language goal	Learn English as quickly as possible to transition to the academic mainstream
Academic goal	Meet the same grade-level content-area standards as English-fluent peers and enter an English-only mainstream classroom as soon as possible
Culture goals	Acculturation to mainstream school and community; assimilation
ESL instruction	30–60 minutes a day
Content-area instruction	Initially about 90% in the home language and 10% through sheltered English instruction; home language instruction decreases rapidly as students are quickly transitioned to sheltered instruction as they move up in grade level
Bilingual strategies	Used during ESL and sheltered instruction as needed
Effectiveness research	TBE programs are more effective than English-only programs but less effective than other models of bilingual education in ensuring that ELLs achieve parity with their English-speaking peers

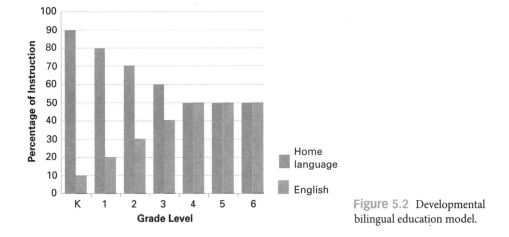

Figure 5.2 Developmental bilingual education model.

last through the middle-school grades. As in TBE programs, ELLs initially receive about 90% of their content-area instruction, including initial literacy instruction, in their home language, in addition to ESL instruction. Sheltered English instruction increases with each grade level until students receive an equal balance of instruction in both languages. Figure 5.2 shows the relationship between the home language and English instruction in DBE programs.

Because of its emphasis on bilingualism and biliteracy, DBE is a much stronger model for ELLs (Baker & Wright, 2017). The home language is viewed as a resource. It is used for instructional purposes and further developed even after ELLs have attained sufficient proficiency in English to handle English-medium instruction. Because a DBE program could constitute half or more of a child's education and in such a program students have the opportunity to develop their home language skills to a higher level than in a TBE program, they are much more likely to be proficient bilinguals by the time they graduate from high school. Thomas and Collier's (2002, 2013) longitudinal research shows that ELLs who graduate from well-implemented DBE programs ultimately achieve educational parity with their English-speaking counterparts. Escamilla, Hopewell, and Butvilofsky (2013) provide longitudinal evidence that emergent bilingual learners in well-implemented DBE programs based on their "Literacy Squared" framework outperform ELLs in English-medium classes on standardized academic achievement tests. DBE programs are also empowering to parents who don't speak English because they are able to be much more involved in their child's education, including being able to help their children with their reading and other homework.

Schools with DBE programs may face political pressure to push English literacy earlier and faster, particularly in states where high-stakes tests are administered only in English (Wright, 2007). School and district administrators may worry that if extensive English literacy and content instruction in English is delayed to the later elementary grades, students will not have the English skills necessary to pass the test. This is not a flaw in the DBE models but a flaw in the testing and accountability systems that do not value and fail to accommodate high-quality education programs for ELLs. Box 5.3 provides an overview of the DBE model.

Dual Language Programs

The term **_dual language education_**, according to Howard et al. (2018), "refers to any program that provides literacy and content instruction to all students through two languages and that promotes bilingualism and biliteracy, grade-level academic achievement,

Box 5.3 Developmental Bilingual Education

Other names	Maintenance bilingual education; late-exit bilingual education
Target population	ELLs who speak the same home language
Typical grade span	K–6
Language goals	Bilingualism and biliteracy
Academic goals	Meet the same grade-level content-area standards as English-fluent peers; be prepared to fulfill societal needs requiring citizens with bilingual skills
Culture goal	Biculturalism
ESL instruction	30–60 minutes a day
Content-area instruction	Initially about 90% in the home language and 10% through sheltered instruction; home language instruction decreases slowly and sheltered instruction increases as students move up in grade level; instruction continues in both languages until the end of the program, even after students attain proficiency in English
Bilingual strategies	Used during ESL and sheltered instruction as needed
Effectiveness research	ELLs achieve parity with English-speaking peers and become bilingual, biliterate, and bicultural

and sociocultural competence for all students" (p. 3). Sociocultural competence includes identity development, cross-cultural competence, and multicultural appreciation. Based on the student population served, dual language programs are **one-way immersion** or **two-way immersion**. One-way immersion programs typically serve students who all speak the same home language. One-way immersion programs for ELLs who speak the target home language are best referred to as DBE programs, as described earlier. One-way immersion programs for English speakers are best referred to as bilingual immersion programs, as we will discuss later.

Traditionally, the term *dual language* referred to two-way immersion programs, which serve both English speakers and ELLs from the same language background. These programs were described by various combinations of these terms, such as dual immersion and dual language immersion. García (2009a) prefers to call them dual language bilingual education programs, to emphasize that dual language programs are a form of bilingual education. Two-way programs were originally designed for even numbers of ELLs and English-proficient students. But as Howard et al. (2018) note, there may be students who have proficiency in both languages at the time of enrollment. Thus, they say, as a rule of thumb, "to be considered a two-way program, no less than one third and no more than two thirds of the student population should be monolingual or dominant in either English or the partner language at the time of enrollment" (p. 3). Dual language programs typically begin in kindergarten (or pre-K) and continue through the elementary school grades, though a growing number of these programs can also be found in middle schools and high schools.

English speakers and ELLs in prototypical two-way dual language programs spend most of the day together in the same classroom, where they receive content-area instruction in both languages from qualified bilingual teachers. Content-area instruction is taught in sheltered English and in a sheltered version of the other language, such as Spanish, to make instruction comprehensible for students new to Spanish. Students learn to read and write in both languages, either simultaneously or first in one language and later in the other. Teachers also provide daily ESL instruction for their ELLs, and instruction in the partner language (e.g., Spanish as an additional language).

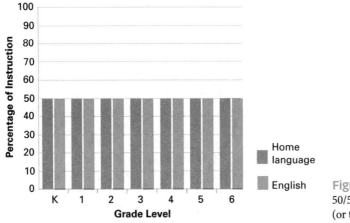

Figure 5.3 Traditional 50/50 dual language model (or two-way immersion).

We find two prototypical two-way models of dual language bilingual education: the 50/50 model and the 90/10 model, referring to the percentage of time allocated to each language for instructional purposes. Thus, in the 50/50 model, 50% of the instruction is in the home language of the ELLs and 50% is in English (Figure 5.3). In the 90/10 model, 90% of instruction is in the home language of the ELLs for the first few years and 10% is in English. As students move up in grade level, the amount of instruction in each language balances out to 50/50 (Figure 5.4). Some schools prefer an 80/20 or 70/30 model, which operate on the same principles but include more English at the beginning. For ELLs, the program functions as a developmental bilingual model and for the English speakers, the program functions as a bilingual immersion model (discussed in the next section).

Traditionally, dual language researchers and practitioners advocated a rigid separation of the two languages for instructional purposes. Some programs go as far as having teachers wear color-coded tags (or articles of clothing) to indicate which language must be used by teachers and students for a particular lesson or activity or for a particular time (e.g., red = English, blue = Spanish). This practice has received more and more criticism, however, because it does not reflect how languages are used in real life, it does not take advantage of the two linguistic systems for social or academic purposes, and it does not affirm students' identities (Beeman & Urow, 2013; Sayer, 2008). Thus, some dual language programs embrace the more natural and flexible ways students translanguage for authentic communication and learning purposes. While translanguaging is becoming more accepted and valued in dual language programs, teachers must ensure that translanguaging

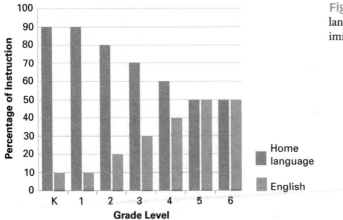

Figure 5.4 90/10 dual language model (or two-way immersion).

strategies are used purposely and effectively in ways that meet the language development goals for both languages.

Dual language programs vary considerably in the amount of time spent on instruction in each language, which language is used for initial literacy instruction, and which subjects are taught in which languages. Most dual language programs in the United States are for Spanish and English speakers, but there are also programs for speakers of Vietnamese, Russian, French, Mandarin Chinese, Korean, Navajo, Arabic, Japanese, Portuguese, and others.

What is exciting about the two-way dual language models is that theoretically their use puts the ELLs on an equal footing with the English-speaking students. When instruction is in the partner language, the English speakers must rely on their ELL peers, just as the ELLs must rely on the English speakers when instruction is in English. The ELLs' home language is viewed as a resource to help the ELLs learn English and academic content and as a valuable asset that the English speakers also want to acquire. Thus, dual language programs have helped change the view of bilingual education so it is seen no longer as a remedial program for ELLs but as an enrichment program for all students. Comparative longitudinal research demonstrates that dual language programs are the most effective programs for ELLs (Alvear, 2015; Lindholm-Leary & Hernández, 2011; Ramirez, 1992; Steele et al., 2017; Thomas & Collier, 2002, 2013; Umansky & Reardon, 2014; Valentino & Reardon, 2014). Dual language programs have grown in popularity with increases in federal support and the growing demand of ELLs' parents and parents of monolingual English speakers who want their children to be bilingual.

Student and community demographics have led to innovative variations in dual language programs. Whereas the traditional dual language model targets equal numbers of ELL and native English speakers, in practice the target populations in these programs are much more diverse and integrated. For example, the English speakers may include simultaneous bilingual and heritage language speakers from bilingual homes, and students from homes where only English is spoken. In other words, a dual language classroom may be made up of all Latinx students, half of whom are ELLs and half of whom are proficient English speakers with varying levels of Spanish language and literacy development. The Gómez and Gómez Dual Language Enrichment Model is designed for schools in regions where the majority of the students are Latinx (e.g., South Texas) and follows a unique 50–50 model that divides language of instruction by content area as well as by time (Gómez, Freeman, & Freeman, 2005). This model does not require an equal distribution of ELLs and English-dominant students as the traditional two-way requires. It has become very popular in Texas and is being adopted in other states as well, though some scholars are concerned about the model and its implementation (see, e.g., Palmer, Zuñiga, & Henderson, 2015). Educators who want to develop dual language programs in their school and community contexts need to begin with a clear understanding of their target populations and design their programs accordingly.

Scholars have identified several issues and challenges related to dual language programs in general. Whereas Spanish programs are relatively easy to develop because of the large number of Latinx ELLs and the availability of Spanish bilingual teachers and materials, it can be quite difficult to develop programs in other languages where there are fewer students, and teachers and materials are in short supply. Also, while native English speakers may be interested in learning high-demand languages such as Spanish, Chinese, Japanese, and Arabic, there may be little interest for languages such as Somali, Karen, or Haitian Creole. This problem can be overcome in programs that follow the model in which all students are from the same language background, but half are ELLs and half are English dominant.

Box 5.4   Dual Language Bilingual Education

Other names	Two-way immersion; dual language immersion
Target population	ELLs who speak the same home language and English speakers who want to learn the home language of the ELLs
Typical grade span	K–6
Language goals	Bilingualism and biliteracy
Academic goals	Meet grade-level content-area standards; be prepared to fulfill societal needs requiring citizens with bilingual skills
Culture goals	Biculturalism; cross-cultural understanding; cultural pluralism
Content-area instruction	50/50 model: 50% in the home language of ELLs and 50% in English
	The 90/10 model: Initially 90% in the ELLs' home language and 10% in English; instruction evens out gradually to 50/50 as students move up in grade level
Bilingual strategies	May be used during English instruction or for non-ELL English speakers during instruction in the ELLs' home language
Effectiveness research	English speakers and ELLs reach or exceed grade-level expectations and become bilingual and biliterate with strong cross-cultural communication skills

Another major issue is the reality that English is the dominant or more powerful language of the United States, which makes it very difficult to value both languages equally within a dual language program and school (Cervantes-Soon et al., 2017). Standard English, and proficient speakers of standard English, will always be more privileged. Valdés (1997) has long warned that dual language educators need to be careful not to address the interests of more vocal middle-class English-speaking constituents over less vocal minority constituents in placement or instruction. Valdés also warned that if dual language educators fail to consider language and power relations among target populations (e.g., English speakers and Spanish speakers) at school and in the community, speakers of minority languages may be exploited for the language resource they provide for white English speakers without actually gaining access to equal educational opportunities at school or job opportunities in society. Cervantes-Soon et al. (2017) argue that dual language programs must develop "critical consciousness" to ensure that ELLs attain the linguistic, academic, and cross-cultural benefits that dual language programs aim to offer.

Despite these challenges, dual language programs have been found to encourage friendships and cross-cultural understanding between English-speaking students and minority-language students, as well as among their families (Howard et al., 2018). Perhaps these graduates of dual language programs will be at the forefront of resolving many of the social inequities our past generations have failed to solve. Box 5.4 provides an overview of the dual language program model.

Bilingual Immersion Programs

Bilingual immersion programs in the United States (not to be confused with English immersion), target English-speaking students exclusively. As noted earlier, these programs are also called one-way dual language programs. Alternatively, program names may simply reflect the focal language, for example, Spanish immersion or French immersion. The goals are for English speakers to become bilingual and biliterate, to achieve academically in both languages, and to develop cross-cultural understanding. This model was developed in Canada, where monolingual English speakers are immersed for lan-

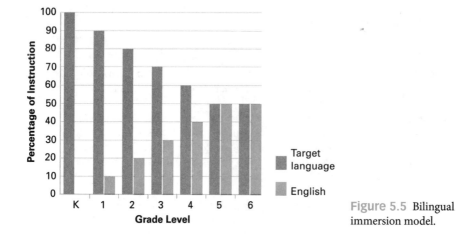

Figure 5.5 Bilingual immersion model.

guage and content-area instruction in French. Extensive research demonstrates the effectiveness of these programs (Lyster & Genesee, 2012). In the United States, the bilingual immersion model is commonly implemented with English speakers wishing to learn a high-demand world language. There are also bilingual immersion programs in the United States to help Hawaiian and Native American students learn their "native" language, which they or their parents may or may not speak at home. Because indigenous languages in the United States are threatened with extinction, educators working with students from these language groups view bilingual immersion programs as a key component for helping to preserve indigenous languages by passing them down to the next generation.

Bilingual immersion instruction begins in the non-English language, which is typically the language in which the students have the least amount of proficiency. Some programs provide up to 100% of instruction in the non-English language for the first year or two of the program. As the students increase their proficiency in the non-English language, English is slowly introduced and eventually both languages are given an equal amount of instructional time. Bilingual immersion programs are most commonly found in elementary schools and last for several years, usually up to 5th or 6th grade (Figure 5.5). Box 5.5 provides an overview of the bilingual immersion model.

One source of confusion is that bilingual immersion programs are often called dual language programs or dual immersion. More confusing is that in some places both one-way and two-way programs are simply called "dual language" programs. For example, Utah has come to be seen as a leader in dual language education with many programs in Spanish and Chinese throughout the state; the majority of Utah's programs, however, are one-way programs that target proficient English speakers and thus exclude many Latinx and Chinese ELL students who would greatly benefit from a two-way dual language program (Freire, Valdez, & Delevan, 2017). Because many states are following Utah's example, this "dual language boom" is benefiting far more native English speakers than ELL students. Schools with bilingual immersion programs, however, can easily convert them into two-way programs and thus provide a more equitable program for the ELLs and a more effective program for the proficient English speakers as well.

Heritage Language Programs

The term ***heritage language program*** is used for a wide range of in-school and after-school or weekend programs that provide opportunities for language minority students to learn or further develop proficiency in their "heritage language." A heritage language student can be either an ELL or a student who is proficient in English and may have little

Box 5.5   Bilingual Immersion

Other names	Immersion program; one-way dual immersion
Target population	Language minority students (ELL or non-ELL) who have little to no proficiency in the target language (e.g., Native American students, Hawaiian students); English speakers who want to learn a world language
Typical grade span	K–6 (some programs may extend to 8th grade or into high school)
Academic goals	Meet grade-level expectations; be prepared to fulfill societal needs requiring citizens with bilingual skills
Culture goals	Biculturalism; cross-cultural understanding and communication skills
ESL instruction	30–60 minutes a day (only if program includes ELLs)
Content-area instruction	Initially 90% to 100% in the non-English language for the first year or two of the program; instruction evens out gradually to 50% in English and 50% in the non-English language as students move up in grade level
Bilingual strategies	May be used as needed
Effectiveness research	Language minority students and language majority students reach or exceed grade-level expectations and become bilingual, biliterate, and cross culturally competent

or no proficiency in his or her heritage language, as is common for second and third generation immigrant students (Valdés, 2014).

In-school heritage language programs at the elementary school could include any of the types of bilingual education programs described earlier for ELLs or could simply be programs that provide an hour or more of heritage language instruction during the week as an additional subject. At the secondary level, heritage language programs are typically world (foreign) language classes geared to students from homes where the language is spoken (Chik & Wright, 2017). These courses have names such as Spanish for Spanish speakers, Korean for heritage speakers, Arabic for heritage learners, and so forth. Educators have found that courses like these are particularly effective because ELLs typically need world language credit to graduate from high school or to get into colleges and universities with world language study requirements. Many universities also offer heritage language courses. Students who take these courses tend to be highly motivated by opportunities to develop greater proficiency and literacy abilities in their home languages, particularly because the vast majority have been in English-only education programs where they have had no opportunities for home language and literacy development (Carreira & Chik, 2018).

These world language courses for heritage language speakers are much more appropriate and effective than regular world language classes. In Spanish classes, for example, world language classes that target English speakers teach the standard Spanish dialect, which may differ substantially from the variety of Spanish spoken by Spanish-speaking ELLs. A good heritage language class recognizes and builds on the strengths of heritage language speakers by recognizing that these students may already have some vocabulary as well as listening, speaking, and perhaps literacy skills in the heritage language. The courses can also be designed to recognize and value the variety of the language spoken by the students, while helping them to develop proficiency in a standard dialect of the language.

Schools that have transitional bilingual programs are well positioned to offer heritage language programs for former ELLs who have exited the bilingual program. Learning in

Box 5.6 Heritage Language Programs

Other names	Community language programs; world language programs for native speakers (e.g., Spanish for Spanish speakers)
Target population	Heritage language speakers (ELL or non-ELL) who have varying levels of proficiency in their heritage languages
Typical grade span	Any grade level: pre-K–12 and college or university
Language goals	Broaden linguistic repertoire in the heritage language, with attention to the standard variety and literacy in that language
Academic goals	Meet the grade-level content-area standards related to world language learning or native language arts standards; be prepared to fulfill societal needs requiring citizens with bilingual skills
Culture goals	Biculturalism; cross-cultural communication skills
Program features	Between 1 and 5 or more hours a week, the heritage language is taught as a separate subject in school; out-of-school programs and foreign language courses designed for native speakers at the college or university level are also offered
Effectiveness research	Heritage language students typically make much faster progress and attain higher levels of proficiency in the target language than traditional (non–heritage language) foreign language students

a heritage language program (e.g., Spanish for Spanish speakers) gives these students opportunities to maintain and develop their home language after they enter English-medium instruction and helps counter the trend toward subtractive bilingualism we see in most TBE programs. Some secondary schools have developed specialized heritage language courses for graduates of DBE and dual language programs. Some double as Advanced Placement (AP) world language courses, meaning students can further develop their language skills and attain valuable college world language credits while still in high school. In states with the Seal of Biliteracy, high school heritage language programs are often key to ensuring that ELLs and former ELLs qualify for the seal and receive recognition of their bilingualism.

Many after-school and weekend heritage language programs are operated by community-based organizations within language minority communities, such as Chinese and Korean schools run on the weekends by Chinese American and Korean American organizations, temples, and churches (Lee & Wright, 2014). Some public schools provide heritage language classes after school. In Fresno, California, for example, the school district, in cooperation with local community organizations, offers the Khmer Emerging Education Program (Project KEEP) 2 days a week at one of its elementary schools (Wright, 2014). Box 5.6 provides an overview of the heritage language program model.

English-Medium Models

Although bilingual education programs are more effective than English-medium programs, they are not always feasible. In a few states, legislation places restrictions on bilingual programs; in some communities, educators, parents, or community members may be opposed to bilingual education because of their ideologies or misunderstandings of the program; schools that want to start bilingual programs may be unable to because of a shortage of bilingual teachers or because they have a large number of language groups and insufficient numbers of speakers of the same home language to make offering a bilingual education program practicable. In these instances, high-quality English-medium programs are the next best option. In English-medium programs all subjects are taught in English. English-medium does not mean English only. Effective programs provide a combination of sheltered content-area instruction, ESL instruction, and bilingual strategies. The following sections describe English-medium programs commonly found in schools today.

Pull-Out English as a Second Language Instruction

The goal of ESL instruction is to enable ELLs to increase their level of English proficiency each year and ultimately to be redesignated as "fluent English proficient" and no longer in need of ESL instruction. Pull-out ESL is a commonly used model, particularly in elementary schools where ELLs make up a small portion of the total school population. In these schools, ELLs are typically spread out across several classrooms. A certified ESL teacher pulls small groups of ELLs out of their regular classrooms to provide ESL instruction, typically for 30 to 60 minutes or more a day. Though students need daily instruction, some schools are able to offer ESL only 2 or 3 days a week because of a shortage of ESL teachers.

The pull-out ESL model has been highly criticized as the least effective model (Ovando & Combs, 2018). The problems are many. First, and perhaps most important, students miss out on instruction in their regular classrooms when they are pulled out. Second, pull-out ESL may lead some general education elementary and secondary classroom teachers to the view that the ELLs are mainly the responsibility of the ESL teacher. Third, many students feel stigmatized about being pulled out day after day in front of their English-only peers. In a study of former ELLs I conducted in California, one of the students described her feelings about being pulled out: "The other kids wouldn't say anything, but I would feel lost. Here I go again. Why do I have to do this? I felt so dumb. I felt like I'm dumb" (Wright, 1998). And finally, ESL instruction provided by the pull-out teacher typically is not coordinated with what the students are learning in their regular classrooms, largely because ESL teachers generally pull students from several different classrooms, making it very difficult to coordinate with every teacher. Furthermore, pull-out ESL teachers sometimes find that mainstream teachers are unwilling to collaborate.

Pull-out ESL may be more expensive than other models because it requires that one or more teachers be hired in addition to the regular classroom teachers. Another difficulty is finding space for the pull-out ESL class in overcrowded schools. In some instances, ESL classes are held in portable classrooms far away from the main buildings where "real" learning is taking place. It can be far worse. I have seen ESL classes taught in cafeterias, auditorium lobbies, auditorium stages, teacher lounges, converted broom closets, basements, storage rooms, and hallways. These poor accommodations may send the signal to the ELLs, and to the teachers, that ESL instruction is a low priority and that ELLs are second-class citizens within the school.

Despite these drawbacks, there are some benefits of pull-out ESL. For example, in my research with former ELLs in California (Wright, 1998, 2004a), I found a number of students who did not receive any pull-out ESL instruction but were simply placed in mainstream English-only classrooms. These students described feeling frustrated and lost during the first few years of their education. One student commented, "I just sat there." Another mentioned that occasionally his teacher would try to call on him but he would simply sit quietly until she called on someone else because he could not understand the questions. Many of the students sought help outside of school. Pull-out ESL would have been a much better alternative for these students who received no help at all. In a study I conducted in Texas of newly arrived Khmer students in the 5th grade who received pull-out ESL instruction (Wright & Li, 2006), I found that although their regular classroom teacher did an excellent job accommodating their needs in her classroom, these students were much more active, engaged, and vocal during their ESL time. The ESL teacher created

Box 5.7 Pull-Out English as a Second Language

Other name	ESL withdrawal classes
Target population	ELLs
Typical grade span	K–6 (In secondary schools ESL is provided as a separate class period)
Language goals	Help students attain proficiency in English
Academic goals	Help students gain the English proficiency needed to understand content-area instruction
Culture goals	Acculturation to mainstream school and society; assimilation common
ESL instruction	30–60 minutes a day
Bilingual strategies	May be used as needed
Effectiveness research	Pull-out ESL in isolation does not enable ELLs to achieve parity with English-speaking peers; it is, however, an integral part of effective sheltered English programs when ESL is not provided in the classroom

a safe environment that effectively lowered the affective filter of her ELLs. The students enjoyed their time in the ESL classroom and developed a wonderful relationship with their ESL teacher. They made much greater progress in both language and academic development than they would have without pull-out ESL instruction, and their experiences in the positive, supportive environment of the pull-out ESL class made their school experience much more enjoyable. Box 5.7 provides an overview of the pull-out ESL model.

In-Class English as a Second Language Instruction

In-class ESL instruction is provided by the regular classroom teacher. This model is preferred over the pull-out ESL model for several reasons: (1) the students do not miss anything in class by being pulled out, (2) classroom teachers can coordinate their ESL instruction to prepare ELLs for specific sheltered content-area lessons, (3) the classroom teachers take full responsibility for the education of all their students, (4) classroom teachers take what they learn about the ELLs through ESL instruction to help tailor their language and content objectives of their sheltered content-area instruction to appropriate levels, and (5) classroom teachers can coordinate interactions between ELLs and non-ELLs in the classroom that will further assist ELLs in learning English. Finally, the school saves money by not having to hire additional teachers.

To provide effective ESL instruction, classroom teachers must be trained and certified to teach ESL. They must also be provided with an ESL curriculum and instructional materials. There are many frustrated ESL teachers who find they need to create their own curriculum and make or buy their own materials because their schools and districts fail to provide them.

Once classroom teachers have been trained to provide ESL instruction, they must do so. It is not enough for a teacher to claim, because there are ELLs in the classroom, "I teach ESL all day." ESL is a separate content area, with its own content standards, curriculum, and teaching materials. Thus, when there is no ESL pull-out program in place, the classroom teacher must provide in class the same type of instruction that a pull-out ESL teacher would provide.

A better alternative to pull-out ESL may be pull-in ESL or push-in ESL, meaning that the ESL teacher goes into the regular classroom to work with the classroom teacher and her ELLs. The danger with this model, however, is that the ESL teacher may end up just working in the back of the room with the ELLs, or worse, just hanging out while the teacher lectures, then simply providing assistance here and there to individual ELLs while they do seat work. In these instances, the ESL teacher is treated more like a paraprofessional rather than a fellow teacher.

For pull-in ESL to be effective, the ESL and classroom teachers need to collaborate in a co-teaching model, working together to address the content and language objectives of sheltered content-area lessons, and planning and delivering effective ESL lessons (Dove & Honigsfeld, 2017). The ESL teacher can serve as a valuable resource to the classroom teacher, helping her recognize the language demands of upcoming lessons and activities, setting appropriate language objectives, and offering advice and demonstrations of how to make modifications and provide effective scaffolding and accommodations. Through such collaboration, both teachers recognize they share in the responsibility for ensuring the success of their ELLs.

In secondary grades, ELLs are typically provided with one or two course periods of ESL. These courses, too, must be taught by a certified ESL teacher who has a curriculum to follow and materials to use. This instruction can be made more effective if the ESL teacher coordinates with the ELLs' general education teachers, though just as in the elementary school, coordination can be particularly challenging because of the large number of teachers in a typical middle or high school. Some secondary schools also make use of the pull-in model where the ESL teacher, in addition to teaching separate ESL courses, will spend one or more periods a day in content-area classrooms co-teaching with and helping the content-area teacher implement effective sheltered instruction.

Sheltered (Structured) English Immersion

Sheltered English immersion (SEI), sometimes called structured English immersion, typically refers to self-contained grade-level classrooms for ELLs with teachers who are trained and certified to provide language and content instruction for ELLs. In SEI classrooms, the classroom teacher provides daily ESL instruction and sheltered content-area instruction. In addition, even though all instruction is in English, teachers should purposefully use bilingual strategies to help students engage with complex content and texts and learn to use oral and written English for academic purposes. SEI is the model that was mandated by the English for the Children initiatives; but even these laws acknowledged the important role of students' home languages, stating that teachers "may use a minimal amount of the child's language when necessary."

When a bilingual program is not viable for policy, ideological, or practical reasons, an SEI program is the next best option. It is helpful to think of effective SEI instruction according to the following formula, where SI stands for sheltered instruction and BLS stands for bilingual strategies:

$$SEI = ESL + SI + BLS.$$

In other words, a high-quality SEI program includes daily direct, systematic ESL instruction, sheltered content-area instruction, and productive use of bilingual strategies. The English for the Children initiatives say that ELLs should be in SEI classrooms only for a period not normally intended to exceed 1 year. But as we saw in an earlier chapter, there is no research that suggests that most ELLs can learn enough English in 1 year to be placed in a mainstream classroom. Furthermore, federal law makes it clear that ELLs are to receive ESL and sheltered instruction until they are redesignated as fluent English proficient and thus no longer in need of special services.

One area of concern is that many SEI classrooms are SEI in name only. If the classroom teacher is not certified to work with ELLs or fails to provide ESL, sheltered instruc-

Box 5.8 Sheltered English Immersion

Other names	Structured English immersion, sheltered classrooms, self-contained ESL classrooms (at the secondary level: sheltered math, ESL science, specially designed academic instruction in English [SDAIE] social studies, etc.)
Target population	ELLs (but class may also contain non-ELLs)
Typical grade span	K–12 (In secondary schools sheltered subject areas are provided as separate class periods)
Language goals	Help students attain proficiency in English
Academic goals	Meet the same grade-level academic standards required for all students
Culture goals	Assimilation or acculturation
ESL instruction	30–60 minutes a day, provided in class by the classroom teacher
Content-area instruction	All subjects taught in English through sheltered instruction
Bilingual strategies	Used as needed during ESL and sheltered instruction
Effectiveness research	More effective than pull-out ESL in isolation but not as effective as bilingual program models

tion, and primary language support, then the classroom is not an SEI classroom at all. It's a mainstream, sink-or-swim, English-only classroom. Box 5.8 provides an overview of the SEI model.

Newcomer Programs

Newcomer ELLs are best served by bilingual programs, but when these are not available, a **newcomer program** may be the best approach. Newcomer programs are "specialized academic environments that serve newly arrived, immigrant English language learners for a limited period of time," typically for 1 to 2 years (Short & Boyson, 2012, p. viii). These programs recognize that newly arrived ELLs with little to no proficiency in English will have a very difficult time learning in a classroom where English is the language of instruction (including SEI classrooms).

Although there is no one set model, a comprehensive review of U.S. newcomer programs at the secondary level found that the main goals of these programs include (1) helping students acquire beginning English skills, (2) providing some instruction in the core content areas, (3) guiding students' acculturation to the school system in the United States, and (4) developing or strengthening students' home language literacy skills (Short & Boyson, 2012, p. viii). Newcomer program classrooms are taught by trained and certified ELL teachers. Bilingual teachers who speak the language of their ELLs are most effective because they can use bilingual strategies with the students and communicate with their parents.

Newcomer programs attempt to provide some sheltered instruction, especially to address literacy and numeracy development when the newcomers have had limited former schooling. The greatest focus, however, is on providing intensive ESL instruction so the students can acquire enough English to participate in an SEI classroom 1 or 2 years later. Some school districts establish separate newcomer schools where district resources and personnel can be concentrated to best meet the students' needs. Students are sometimes bussed to the newcomer center from their neighborhood schools, stay there all day or part of the day, and then return to their home school. Other newcomer programs are

Box 5.9 Newcomer Programs

Other name	Newcomer centers
Target population	ELLs who have recently arrived to the United States and have little to no English proficiency (and sometimes limited former schooling)
Typical grade span	Any grade level, pre-K–12
Number of years	1–2 years
Language goals	Help newcomer ELLs learn enough English to be able to participate in a sheltered English immersion classroom within a year or two
Academic goals	Help newcomer ELLs learn basic reading and writing skills in English and expose them to the content areas, with a focus on developing the vocabulary and language skills needed to learn these subjects through sheltered instruction once they exit the newcomer program
Culture goals	Acculturation to mainstream school and society
ESL instruction	Intensive, for 1 hour or more a day
Content-area instruction	Sheltered instruction uses the content areas for vocabulary and other English language skills development, with a focus on beginning skills in English reading and writing; some programs may also include home language content-area instruction.
Bilingual strategies	Used throughout the day
Effectiveness research	Programs vary widely, but overall research shows they are effective in meeting the unique needs of newcomer ELLs

centers within existing schools where newly arrived ELLs may spend anywhere from a couple of hours to the whole day.

Newcomer programs have been criticized for segregating ELLs into separate classrooms or schools. Many schools, however, are highly diverse with newcomer ELLs from a variety of racial, ethnic, and linguistic backgrounds. Newcomer programs are also sometimes criticized for lacking a focus on content-area instruction and for being expensive to operate. For newcomer programs to be effective, the district must make a real commitment to provide the school with the best teachers, adequate resources, a clear curriculum, and small class sizes. High-stakes testing and school accountability have posed serious challenges to these programs, however, because newcomer students are rarely ready to take and pass state tests in English. A unique challenge for high school newcomer programs is ensuring that students receive adequate support and have pathways to earn sufficient credits to graduate (Sugarman, 2017). Box 5.9 provides an overview of the newcomer program model.

Submersion (Sink or Swim)

One final approach to teaching ELLs is to do nothing at all for them. **Submersion** means placing an ELL in a mainstream classroom where there is no ESL instruction, no sheltered instruction, and no use of bilingual strategies to support student learning. Furthermore, the teachers are not certified to teach ELLs. Thus, as the alternative name implies, these students are left to sink or swim. Unfortunately, submersion is very common, even though it is in violation of federal law.

There are many excellent and experienced mainstream teachers with no training in ESL who regularly have ELLs placed in their classrooms, and who try their best to meet their needs. These teachers should take the initiative to complete ESL certification and other training to better meet the needs of their students. With such training they can transform their mainstream classrooms into sheltered English immersion classrooms fairly quickly. In addition, they should advocate for the creation of one or more of the models described in this chapter and insist their schools and districts provide the materials and support necessary to do so.

Teachers should be aware that many SEI classrooms are SEI in name only. In Box 5.10, the left column provides a list of indicators that can be used to determine whether an SEI classroom is really just a submersion mainstream classroom in disguise. If any of the items on the checklist applies to a program designated as SEI, major changes need to be implemented if ELLs are to make progress in learning English and academic content. Fortunately, with a little effort, a submersion program can be transformed into an effective SEI program. The strategies listed in the right column can help teachers make these important transformations.

Typology of Program Models for English Language Learners

Baker & Wright (2017) have created a typology of programs for ELLs in which they classify program models as (a) monolingual forms of education, (b) weak forms of bilingual education, or (c) strong forms of bilingual education. These classifications relate to the societal aims and language outcomes of different program models. In Table 5.4 I have adapted the typology to classify the programs discussed in this chapter. The strongest forms are those that help ELLs—and in some instances, English speakers—become fully bilingual, biliterate, and bicultural. Monolingual forms of education, in contrast, are the weakest of all of these programs. They make little to no use of ELLs' home languages, they aim for social and cultural assimilation of students, and they frequently result in the loss of students' ability to speak their home language. As this typology illustrates, not all bilingual education programs are strong. The societal aim of TBE programs is the same as the monolingual forms—assimilation.

It is important to emphasize that educators have choices in the ways they organize their programs and practices for bilingual learners, and these choices may have strong implications for students, schools, and communities. For example, schools that offer TBE programs can challenge the subtractive outcomes often associated with these programs by offering exiting students opportunities to take heritage language classes such as Spanish-for-Spanish-speakers. These heritage language programs can build on the linguistic and cultural strengths that Spanish speakers in the local community bring with them to school, and help students learn standard Spanish and literacies in Spanish. An effective Spanish-for-Spanish-speakers program would encourage many more bilingual students to strengthen their Spanish and earn the Seal of Biliteracy.

The accuracy of any system of categorization like this is limited because of variations in programs. For example, I categorize heritage language programs as weak or strong forms of bilingual education. Those that provide a few hours or less of instruction each week are weak forms, and those that provide an hour or more a day are strong forms. The value of such a typology, however, is that it reveals that programs for ELLs are multidimensional. In other words, as Baker and Wright (2017) observe, "Bilingual education is not just about education. There are sociocultural, political, and economic issues ever present in the debate over the provision of bilingual education" (p. 198). This statement applies to English-medium programs as well.

Many so-called sheltered English immersion (SEI) classrooms are nothing more than submersion (sink-or-swim) classrooms. The following chart can help you identify submersion classrooms and transform them into effective SEI classrooms.

Indicators of a Submersion (Sink-or-Swim) Classroom*

Transforming a Submersion Classroom into an Effective Sheltered English Immersion Classroom

Indicators of a Submersion (Sink-or-Swim) Classroom*	Transforming a Submersion Classroom into an Effective Sheltered English Immersion Classroom
Textbooks and materials used are identical to those used in mainstream classrooms.	Obtain textbooks and materials appropriate to ELLs' academic and language proficiency levels or modify those in use.
In-class assignments and homework are identical to those used in mainstream classrooms.	Differentiate assignments and homework according to ELLs' academic and language proficiency levels.
The teacher lacks state certification for teaching ELLs; feels ill-prepared to work with ELLs.	Pursue and complete ELL teacher certification and additional professional development opportunities.
The teacher cannot identify the ELLs or their level of English language proficiency.	Create and become familiar with a list of ELLs and their current levels of English proficiency.
The teacher is unable to identify or describe each ELL's home country, ethnicity, home language, prior schooling, literacy in home language, or length of time in the United States.	Complete and become familiar with ELL profiles for each student.
The teacher knows little about the ELLs' languages and cultures.	Learn more about the languages and cultures of students through Internet searches, articles, books, bilingual colleagues, and conversations with the students and their parents.
The teacher makes little to no effort to modify his or her speech to make it more comprehensible for the ELLs.	Modify the rate and complexity of your speech to make it appropriate to ELLs' language proficiency levels.
There is no regularly scheduled time for daily ESL instruction, or the teacher claims, "I teach ESL all day."	Learn the important difference between ESL and sheltered instruction. Provide regularly scheduled, daily ESL instruction.
The teacher cannot articulate specific sheltering strategies or techniques.	Learn and use effective sheltered instruction strategies and techniques.
Content-area lessons lack language objectives.	Develop both content and language objectives for each content-area lesson.
ELLs do not actively participate in classroom discussions and other activities.	Ensure that class discussions and activities are structured to maximize ELL participation.
The teacher makes little to no use of, or allowance for, the ELLs' home languages in the classroom.	Provide translanguaging or primary language support.
Much of the teaching of the ELLs has been delegated to a paraprofessional.	Ensure that you provide ESL and sheltered instruction and that the paraprofessional provides additional supplemental instruction and support under the teacher's expert guidance.
The teacher uses one-size-fits-all or scripted curricular programs.	Discard or modify any curricular programs that are inappropriate to the linguistic and academic needs of ELLs.
There is a heavy focus on test preparation using test-prep materials and frequent benchmark testing with materials designed for English-proficient students.	Minimize time spent on test preparation and ensure that any test preparation is appropriate to ELLs' levels of academic and language proficiency; ensure that test preparation does not supplant ESL and sheltered instruction.
The teacher claims that the strategies used with ELLs are "just good teaching."	Learn the importance difference between "good teaching" for all students and essential teaching for ELLs, including strategies that specifically address their unique linguistic, academic, and cultural needs.

*Based on findings from Wright & Choi, 2005.

Table 5.4 Typology of Program Models for English Language Learners

Program Model	Students	Language of Instruction	Societal Aim	Language Outcome Aim
Monolingual Forms of Education				
Mainstream (submersion)	ELLs	English	Assimilation	English monolingualism
ESL	ELLs	English	Assimilation	English monolingualism
Sheltered/structured English immersion	ELLs	English	Assimilation	English monolingualism
Newcomer centers	ELLs	English	Assimilation	English monolingualism
Weak Forms of Bilingual Education				
Transitional bilingual education	ELLs	Moves quickly from home language to English	Assimilation	Relative English monolingualism
Heritage language programs (only a few hours or less each week of heritage language instruction)	Heritage language speakers with varying degrees of proficiency in the heritage language	Heritage language	Biculturalism	Broaden linguistic repertoire of heritage language speaker
Strong Forms of Bilingual Education				
Developmental bilingual education	ELLs	Bilingual with initial emphasis on the home language	Biculturalism	Bilingualism and biliteracy
Dual language	ELLs and English-proficient students	English and the home language of the ELLs	Biculturalism	Bilingualism and biliteracy
Bilingual immersion	Native English speakers, or English-dominant language minority students with little proficiency in their home language	Bilingual with initial emphasis on the non-English language	Biculturalism	Bilingualism and biliteracy
Heritage language programs (1 hour or more of daily heritage language instruction)	Heritage language speakers with varying degrees of proficiency in the heritage language	Heritage language	Biculturalism	Bilingualism and biliteracy

Adapted from Baker, C., & Wright, W. E. (2017). *Foundations of bilingual education and bilingualism* (6th ed.), pg 199. Bristol, UK: Multilingual Matters, reprinted with permission.

Collaboration among English as a Second Language, Bilingual, Sheltered English Immersion, and Mainstream Teachers

Often several of the programs described in this chapter are found in a single school. An elementary school may have an ESL specialist who pulls students out of bilingual, sheltered English immersion, or mainstream classrooms for daily ESL instruction or who pushes into those classes to work with ELLs. At the secondary level, ELLs typically have one or two periods of stand-alone ESL in addition to some combination of bilingual, sheltered content-area, and mainstream classes. As emphasized throughout this chapter, to provide the most effective instruction possible, ESL and classroom teachers need to work collaboratively and engage in co-teaching (Dove & Honigsfeld, 2017).

As schools turn to co-teaching, teachers are developing innovative ways to collaborate on content and language objectives, lesson planning, lesson delivery, and assessment. ESL specialists are also taking on leadership roles in terms of curriculum, instruction, and assessment. For example, we now find ESL specialists who are responsible for coordinating ESL throughout a district or region, ESL demonstration teachers, and ESL coaches who work in various ways with general education, bilingual education, and sheltered instruction content-area teachers. While challenging, this collaboration can be accomplished formally through regular meetings before or after school in grade-level or content-area faculty meetings. The ESL teacher could also spend time during planning periods observing content-area instruction in different classrooms with ELLs. Chatting informally in the hallways, visiting each other's classrooms, eating lunch together, or communicating by text messages and e-mails can also help. The purpose is to share what is being taught in the classrooms so that relevant lessons can be provided in ESL and support provided to the classroom teacher.

In schools that have a variety of programs but no ESL specialist, bilingual and SEI classroom teachers can help each other and the mainstream teachers by sharing ideas and resources with members of the same grade-level teams and help look over ELLs' work. I recall a SEI teacher at my former elementary school who was puzzling over the writing of one of her Spanish-speaking beginning ELLs. The full page of writing appeared to be in Spanish but the student insisted it was in English. When the teacher showed it to one of her bilingual teacher colleagues, the bilingual teacher smiled and said, "This is a perfect example of a student with Spanish writing skills using Spanish phonics to write in English. Here, let me read it to you." As she read aloud, it became clear the student had written the paper in English. The SEI teacher was surprised and relieved. She asked the bilingual teacher for suggestions about how to help the student transfer her Spanish literacy skills to English. For successful collaboration such as this to work, teachers need to move beyond the view of "my students/your students" to "our students" and make a shared commitment to ensuring that all students in the school succeed.

Determining the Most Appropriate Instructional Programs for Your School

While strong forms of bilingual education with the goal of helping all students become bilingual/biliterate and master academic content should be available to all ELLs, the reality is that no single model is appropriate for all students in all school contexts. The appropriate models for a school must be determined by teachers and administrators working collaboratively to study the characteristics and needs of the ELLs; the desires of their parents and community; the current and potential resources of the school; and local, state, and federal policies. For example, strong forms of bilingual education may be very feasible in a school with large numbers of Spanish-speaking ELLs and less feasible in a school with dozens of different languages but only a few speakers of each language. Furthermore, bilingual teachers and resources are more readily available in a language such as Spanish, and much more difficult to find in languages such as Somali, Maay, or Karenii. Schools that have a large number of Spanish-speaking ELLs but that also have many other ELLs who speak different languages should not make that an excuse not to provide a bilingual program for the Spanish-speaking students. The argument is often, "If we can't provide a bilingual program for all the languages, then we shouldn't do one just for the Spanish speakers." But this response would be like the school cafeteria saying it doesn't have enough tater tots for all the students so no one gets any tater tots. Schools should provide the strongest ELL program possible for as many students as possible, and the next best program for those students for whom such a program is not feasible.

The lack of teachers and resources in some languages does not mean bilingual programs are impossible. For example, when my former school district in Long Beach started a Khmer (Cambodian) bilingual program, potential bilingual teachers were recruited from the community and provided with training and support to become certified. These teachers worked after school and during the summers to create Khmer-language books and curricular materials for their classrooms. Many books were created by simply printing and pasting translations over the text of existing English books. I've seen similar strategies employed to establish bilingual programs in languages such as Hmong, Vietnamese, and Arabic. The questions in Box 5.11 can be used to begin the conversation among administrators and teachers about the most appropriate models for their context.

Box 5.11 Determining the Most Appropriate English Language Learner Program Model

As teachers and administrators collaborate to develop the most appropriate program models and structures for the ELLs in their schools, the following questions can help start the conversation:

- Who are our ELLs?
- What are our goals for their language and academic achievement?
- What are their prior education experiences? Have the students had prior opportunities to develop literacy skills or receive content instruction in their home language?
- How many students in each grade level are at each state-defined level of English proficiency?
- What languages do the ELLs speak?
- How many ELLs at each grade level speak one or more of these languages?
- Are there enough speakers of one or more languages at each target grade level to be able to offer a bilingual program?
- How many certified bilingual teachers for these languages do we have or are available to be hired? If none, are bilingual individuals available to be trained, certified, and hired as teachers?
- Do the parents want their children to be bilingual and biliterate? Have they been informed of the goals and objectives of different ELL program models and the research supporting bilingual instruction?
- What are the state policies regarding ELL program models?
- What books and instructional materials are available to provide instruction or support in the home language? If few are available, what resources can be used to purchase or create them?

Regardless of the models selected, schools and teachers must fully commit to implementing them to the best of their ability.

Summary

All programs for ELLs must, at a minimum, ensure that ELLs learn both English and academic content. Thus, each program must include ESL instruction and content-area instruction. The teaching of content areas may be provided through home language instruction or sheltered instruction or a combination of the two. Schools should also use bilingual strategies as much as possible, especially in English-medium programs, so students may draw on all of their linguistic resources when learning academic content and a new language. Although dual language and DBE models are considered the strongest for ELLs and other multilingual students, no single approach is appropriate for all contexts. The appropriate models for a school must be determined by teachers and administrators working collaboratively to study the characteristics and needs of the ELLs and other students, the desires of their parents and community, and the resources of the school. Co-teaching models enable mainstream, ESL, SEI, and bilingual teachers and specialists to work collaboratively to address ELL student needs. Regardless of the programs selected, schools and teachers must fully commit to implementing them to the best of their ability to ensure that every ELL student succeeds.

Discussion Questions

1. What factors should a school take into consideration when deciding which programs to offer? Discuss the types of ELL programs offered by a school you are familiar with. Do you feel these programs are appropriate and effective? Why or why not?

2. What minimally should be included in any program for ELLs? Why are these components critical? What can result if one or more of these components are left out of a program for ELLs?

3. In schools that place ELLs in mainstream submersion classes or in classrooms that are SEI in name only, what changes can teachers make to transform their classrooms into effective SEI classrooms?

4. Based on the typology by Baker and Wright (see Table 5.4), what are the criteria that makes an ELL program weak or strong? What changes can be made to monolingual and weak forms of bilingual education to make them stronger? How would ELL students benefit from these changes?

5. View the video of a 3rd-grade SEI classroom. What are the key features that distinguish this classroom from a mainstream classroom? What strategies and techniques does the teacher appear to be using to make the instruction comprehensible? What model does the teacher use to guide her sheltered instruction? Do you feel the instruction is effective? Why or why not?

Research Activities

1. *ELL Student Interview* Interview a current or former ELL student who has participated in one of the programs described in this chapter. Ask the student to provide details about the teacher, the students, the curriculum, and the amount and type of instruction provided in English and the student's home

language. How does the student's description compare with the description of the program in this chapter?

2. *ELL Teacher Interview* Interview a current ELL teacher who teaches in one of the programs described in this chapter. Ask the teacher to describe the program, the rationale, the academic and linguistic goals, the curriculum used, how English and the home language are used, what a typical day is like for students in the classroom, and how effective the teacher feels the program is in meeting the needs of the ELLs. How does the teacher's description compare with the description of the program model in this chapter?

3. *ELL Classroom Observation* Observe a classroom for ELLs following one of the programs described in this chapter. Pay attention to how the classroom and instruction are structured, the curriculum being used, when and how much the teacher and students use English and the home language, and the ELLs' levels of engagement. What appears to be the linguistic and academic goals of the program? How effective do you feel the model is in meeting the needs of the ELL students? How does your observation compare with the description of the program in this chapter?

4. *Online Research Activity* Find a video, description, or news article of one of the ELL programs described in this chapter. What are the characteristics of the program, and how do they compare with the description in this chapter? Describe and critically analyze the content in terms of how the program is portrayed.

Recommended Reading

Baker, C. & Wright, W. E. (2017). *Foundations of bilingual education and bilingualism* (6th ed.). Bristol, UK: Multilingual Matters.

This comprehensive book provides educators with a solid foundation on definitions, development, and measurement of bilingualism at the individual and societal levels, detailed descriptions and examples of a variety of bilingual education programs, research on the effectiveness of various bilingual program models, and much more.

Dove, M. G., & Honigsfeld, A. (2017). *Co-teaching for English learners: A guide to collaborative planning, instruction, assessment, and reflection.* Thousand Oaks, CA: Corwin.

The authors provide several successful collaboration models that bring ESL and mainstream teachers together to provide effective co-teaching for ELLs.

Echevarria, J., Vogt, M., & Short, D. (2017). *Making content comprehensible for English learners: The SIOP model* (5th ed.). Boston, MA: Pearson.

The authors introduce their SIOP model. They provide the theoretical and research background of the 30 items on the SIOP and include vignettes of sheltered instruction for readers to evaluate and discuss using the SIOP.

Six

Assessment

An ELL's English language proficiency level clearly affects her ability to learn academic content in English and to demonstrate academic knowledge and skills on assessment events carried out in English.

—JAMAL ABEDI AND ROBERT LINQUANTI

KEY TERMS

- accommodations
- assessment
- bias
- consequential validity
- criterion-referenced test
- critical language testing
- dynamic assessment
- evaluation
- formative assessment
- growth models
- multiple measures
- next-generation assessments
- norm-referenced test
- performance assessment
- portfolio assessment
- reliability
- standard error of measurement
- summative assessment
- testing
- universal design
- validity
- value-added measures

GUIDING QUESTIONS

1. What are the differences between testing, assessment, and evaluation?
2. Why should ELL educators be wary of overreliance on standardized tests of ELLs' academic achievement and English language proficiency?
3. What are the challenges of measuring achievement, growth, and English language proficiency under the Every Student Succeeds Act (ESSA)?
4. What are the challenges associated with online assessments?
5. How can ELL educators use authentic alternative assessments to provide valid and reliable evidence of ELLs' growth and achievement?
6. Why is there a need for multiple measures?

ELLs are probably the most tested students in our educational system. In addition to taking the same federal and state tests required for all students, ELLs take language proficiency tests every year. ELLs also participate in district-level and school-level tests, and they take classroom-based tests developed by their teachers. In one Texas school district, between March and the end of the school year, 5th grade ELLs were required to take nine different state and district tests.

Educators need to be aware of the heavy testing burden placed on ELLs and the impact test results can have on students' and teachers' lives. Test results are often used to determine whether students are placed in or exited from special programs, allowed to progress to the next grade level, required to attend summer school, or awarded a high school diploma. Test scores are also often used to judge the adequacy and skills of teachers, to determine, for example, which teachers receive monetary rewards, which teachers must obtain additional training, and which teachers may be required to find another job. Shohamy (2001) has outlined specific features of the power inherent in tests (Box 6.1).

Nonetheless, assessment of ELLs is one of most important things teachers do in the classroom, and proper assessment is essential for identifying students' strengths and areas in need of improvement in their language proficiency and academic development. This chapter provides a foundation for fair assessment of ELLs. First we explore basic principles of assessment and then look critically at current testing requirements for ELLs. Finally, we explore alternative and authentic forms of assessment and highlight the need for multiple measures of ELLs' learning.

Assessment Basics

Testing refers to the administration of tests. A test is a single instrument designed to systematically measure a sample of a student's ability at one particular time. A test is like a photographic snapshot. A snapshot can be misleading because it cannot show what took place before or after it was taken, or the context in which it was taken. Likewise, a single test does not provide any information about what a student could do before or after taking the test. Nor can a test possibly measure everything a student knows and can do. A test can collect only a "sample" of a student's knowledge and ability.

Assessment is much broader than testing. Gottlieb (2016) defines assessment as "the planning, collection, analysis, interpretation, and use of data from multiple sources over time that communicate student performance in relation to standards, learning goals, learning targets, or differentiated learning objectives" (p. 241). Assessment involves (1) planning what, how, and when to assess, with attention to the varied purposes of different constituents or stakeholders, including students, parents, teachers, and local and state administrators; (2) collecting appropriate data from a variety of sources, ranging from informal observations of students in class to more formal scoring of student performances on specific tasks using common rubrics; (3) analyzing student performance data, looking for strengths to build on, and identifying areas in need of further instruction and assistance; (4) reporting student strengths and needs in ways that are beneficial to students, teachers, and the school; and (5) using student performance data to identify what a student must learn in order to progress to the next level. Thus, assessment offers a much more comprehensive picture of student growth and achievement than a single test allows. The concept of **dynamic assessment** emphasizes that teaching and learning are "an inherent part of all assessment regardless of purpose or context" (Poehner, Davin, & Lantoff, 2017, p. 243). Gottlieb (2016) distinguishes between assessment *as* learning, assessment *for* learning, and assessment *of* learning. In assessment *as* learning, students regularly self-reflect on their academic progress and language development and plan their future learning. In assessment *for* learning, teachers plan and use evidence from classroom-based assessments to modify their instruction and provide students descriptive and detailed feedback on their learning. In assessment *of* learning, school leaders use assessment data from standardized tests to report on students' progress in their language and academic achievement and inform decision making at the school or district level.

Evaluation refers to the use of the evidence gathered through assessment to make a judgment about the effectiveness of students' learning, of the teacher's teaching, or of the educational programs provided to the students. Final grades are one example of student evaluation. Teachers use assessment data to evaluate the effectiveness of their teaching, and they make adjustments accordingly. Assessment data can help educational leaders evaluate programs to determine whether they are meeting the needs of their students. Assessment data can also help educational leaders identify ways that they can improve their programs and practices to better serve those students.

Summative and Formative Assessments

A **summative assessment** provides a summary of what a student knows and can do. Summative assessments typically are given at the end of a unit or perhaps at the end of a school year. A **formative assessment**, in contrast, provides information to a teacher about how a student is doing and what modifications may be needed in instruction. Think of *form*ative assessments as helping in*form* teachers what to do next instructionally. A formative assessment may be a formal assessment, or it may be as informal as a teacher walking around and observing students' progress while they are working independently at their desks or in small groups. Effective teachers of ELLs make use of both formative and summative assessments, examples of which are given in this and subsequent chapters.

Norm-Referenced and Criterion-Referenced Tests

A **norm-referenced test** is used to compare a student's score to those of other students. Test results are usually reported as percentile rankings. These represent how a student's score compares with the scores of students in the test's norming population, that is, a group of students—the "norming group"—that has already taken the same test. For example, a score at the 71st percentile means that the student scored higher than 71% of the students in the norming population. Norm-referenced tests are also used to compare the performances of classrooms, schools, districts, and even states. Commonly used norm-referenced tests include the Stanford Achievement Test, 10th edition (SAT-10); the TerraNova; the Iowa Test of Basic Skills (ITBS); the Metropolitan Achievement Test (MAT); and the Comprehensive Test of Basic Skills (CTBS). IQ tests, such as the Stanford-Binet and the Wechsler Intelligence Scale for Children, and college-entrance tests, such as the SAT, ACT, and the GRE, are also norm-referenced tests.

A **criterion-referenced test**, in contrast, determines how much a student has learned by tallying how many questions are answered correctly. These tests are designed to determine whether a student meets specific criteria, such as course objectives or state standards. Scores are usually reported as raw scores or converted to percentages. For example, a student who answered 45 out of 50 questions correctly on a math test would receive a score of 90%, indicating the percentage of correct answers. Most of the tests designed by teachers for classroom use are criterion-referenced tests. Many school districts also develop their own criterion-referenced tests to monitor student and school progress. Developers of criterion-referenced tests establish minimum passing scores (called cut-scores). The home page for the National Center for Fair and Open Testing provides more information on different types of tests, as well as information about uses and abuses of high-stakes testing.

Standards-based tests, such as the academic achievement tests required by the ESSA, are criterion-referenced tests. Cut scores are established by states and are often reported at three or four levels. For example, students who do not meet or exceed the passing score may be deemed "below the standard"; those who score at or just above the passing score may be deemed "basic"; and those who score well above the passing score may be deemed "excelling" or noted for "commended performance."

Note the tremendous differences between norm-referenced and criterion-referenced tests. Norm-referenced tests do not actually tell us how well a student did in answering the questions or mastering the content; they tell only how a student performed in comparison with other students. Theoretically, if all students answered every question correctly, all students would be at the 50th percentile, that is, they would all be average. Likewise, if all students got every answer wrong, all students would be at the 50th percentile, because zero would be the average score. Of course, these extremes do not occur because norm-referenced tests are designed to sort and rank students along a bell-curve distribution, and test developers tinker with their tests until they achieve this distribution in the norming population. Thus, tests are also designed so that it is highly unlikely that all students at a given grade level will be able to answer all the questions correctly.

Both norm-referenced and criterion-referenced tests are problematic for ELLs. With norm-referenced tests, ELLs are unlikely to be deemed "above average," because ELLs typically are underrepresented, if included at all, in the norming population, and the purpose of these tests is to rank students along a bell curve. Criterion-referenced tests may be considered fairer for ELLs, because their scores on these tests supposedly reflect their knowledge of the content, rather than how they compare with their English-speaking peers. Both norm-referenced and criterion-referenced tests in English, however, are problematic for ELLs because they lack proficiency in the language of the test. Also, both types of test are subject to test score inflation, particularly when they are part of high-stakes accountability systems and teachers feel pressured to teach to them. The pressure on schools to have high average passing rates to meet the criteria of state and federal accountability programs may tempt them to use questionable strategies that minimize or eliminate the impact of ELL test scores. Thus, many ELLs are made invisible in the very system that claims to be making them visible and addressing their needs.

Efforts to minimize the impact of ELL test scores on district and school averages could also be seen as acknowledgment that there are unresolved issues related to the reliability and validity of test scores for ELLs, and thus it is unfair to schools to include ELL scores for accountability purposes. Let's now look at these issues of reliability and validity.

Reliability

The concept of **reliability** recognizes that no test (or testing situation) is free of error, and that these errors result in misrepresentation of students' knowledge and ability. Reliability, according to Popham (2017, p. 72), "refers to the consistency with which a test measures whatever it's measuring" or "the extent to which students' scores on tests are free from errors of measurement." Think of reliability as consistency, which can be illustrated by the following three types of reliability evidence:

1. *Internal reliability.* How consistently do the test items function?
   You have likely encountered poorly written or simply bad questions on a test that even the most prepared students may not be able to answer correctly. These items lack consistency with other test items. If there are many poorly written or unfair questions, the test will lack internal reliability. It will not be able to properly distinguish between higher-level and lower-level students, or between students who are well prepared and those who are not.
2. *Stability.* How consistent are the results of a test across different testing occasions? Theoretically, if a teacher gives a test on Monday and gives the same test on Tuesday and does not provide any additional teaching on the topic between the two tests, the results should be the same. Many factors, however, can affect test results, as any teacher can attest. Did the students eat breakfast? Is a student feeling ill or concerned about a problem at home? Did the students see something on television covering the same topics on the test after school on Monday? These and other factors can introduce errors of measurement.
3. *Alternative forms.* How consistent are two or more different forms of a test?
   Teachers, or testing companies, may want to have more than one form of their test available to prevent cheating, or, if a test is reused in the future, to ensure that teachers and students don't remember the questions or the answers. These alternative forms are not identical; thus, the possibility of measurement error is introduced.

In instances of more holistic assessment, such as scoring a student essay, reliability refers to the consistency of those who are doing the scoring. If one teacher grades all the essays, how consistent is she in how she grades the papers at the top of the pile compared with how she grades those near the bottom? If two or more people are grading the essays, how consistent are they in applying the same scoring criteria? If they read the same essay, would they give it the same score? This issue is referred to as inter-rater reliability. It is nearly impossible to have 100% inter-rater reliability, because people are different and the grading of essays is highly subjective.

Procedures for determining the reliability of testing instruments are often based on mathematical formulas, resulting in numbers proclaiming just how reliable an instrument is internally, or how consistent it is at different times or in different forms. For large-scale assessments, such as state tests, a **standard error of measurement** (SEM) should be reported. The SEM indicates a range of trustworthiness of an individual student's score. For example, if a test has an SEM of 3, and the student scores 49, then the student's actual score is 49 +/- 3, that is, somewhere between 46 and 52.

The implications of the SEM are enormous. Consider, for example, if the cut score for passing a test is 50 but an ELL scored 49, he would be deemed as failing the test. But if the SEM for the test is 3, his score may have actually been 50, 51, or 52, which are passing scores. Likewise, a student who passes with a score of 50 may actually have obtained a failing score of 47 to 49. Imagine if the student were held back a grade or denied a high school diploma because of his "failing" score. It is possible the student was unfairly penalized, with major social consequences, all because of errors inherent in the test, not in the student's actual performance.

Another problem related to the SEM is the tendency for schools to focus all of their instructional attention on students who "just barely" missed passing the test by a few points. In many schools these students are referred to as the "bubble kids" (Lauen & Gaddis, 2012). Again, the SEM reveals that if these students are given the exact same test again, they may pass it without any instructional interventions, simply because their "failing" score was due to measurement error. Thus, these schools may be wasting tremendous amounts of instructional time that could be put to much better use, such as providing English language development instruction rather than test preparation.

Validity

Validity refers to the accuracy with which a test or assessment measures what it purports to measure. Although people talk about a test being valid, tests themselves do not possess (or lack) validity. The issue is the validity of the inferences that are based on the score (Popham, 2017). Thus, validity refers to how test scores are interpreted and used. For example, if a teacher wants to measure students' English spelling ability, scores from a subtraction test would not allow for any valid inferences about their spelling ability.

Essential to understanding validity is the notion of assessment domains—the broad range of concepts, knowledge, and skills that a teacher wants to assess in a given subject or area. For example, consider the assessment domain of whole-number two-digit multiplication. To make valid score-based inferences, the test must ask students to solve two-digit multiplication problems. Could the teacher give a test with every possible two-digit multiplication problem? Technically it's possible, but a test with thousands of problems would be too much. A more reasonable test would include just a sample of two-digit multiplication problems. A student's performance on this sample would allow the teacher to make an inference about his or her ability to solve this type of problem, including similar problems not on the test.

Samples, however, must be carefully selected to ensure that they are representative of the entire domain. If, for example, the multiplication test had just three problems, or if it consisted solely of numbers multiplied by 10 or did not include problems that require regrouping, the teacher could not make valid score-based inferences about each student's ability to multiply two-digit numbers. Determining an appropriate number of test items and identifying items that are truly representative of the entire domain is a serious challenge in developing tests from which valid score-based inferences may be drawn.

Unlike reliability, validity cannot be easily established though mathematical formulas. Rather, just as a lawyer gathers evidence to make a legal case, a variety of evidence must be gathered to make the case for validity. In the following list we consider three sources of validity evidence as described by Popham (2017, p. 101):

1. *Test content*—The extent to which an assessment procedure adequately represents the content of the curricular aim(s) being measured.
2. *Internal structure*—The extent to which the internal organization of a test confirms an accurate assessment of the construct supposedly being measured.
3. *Relations to other variables*—The degree to which an inferred construct appears to exist and has been accurately measured for the intended use.

The tests described earlier—the subtraction test used to measure spelling and the multiplication test that includes only numbers multiplied by 10—reveal the relevance of *test content*. These tests lack content validity. For *internal structure*, let's consider a test that supposedly measures listening comprehension. If students listen to a recorded conversation, then respond to written multiple-choice questions about the conversation, they are also being assessed on their English reading comprehension. In other words, students might fully comprehend the oral conversation, but if they cannot read and understand the questions and the answer choices, their score will not provide an accurate measure of their listening comprehension. It is very difficult to isolate the construct of listening comprehension from other constructs on a standardized test. Another example is a widely used language proficiency test that attempts to resolve the issue of isolating listening comprehension by having students point to specific items in an illustrated scene in response to oral directions. These directions begin with a simple command, such as, "Point to the dog." But then they get increasingly longer and more complex, ending with something like, "Point to the dog if the girl is holding a red balloon in her left hand, otherwise point to the cat underneath the wing of the airplane." At some point this listening comprehension test becomes a test of working memory, which is a different construct. Also, the language the students are expected to listen to and comprehend on the test is far beyond anything they would ever hear in real life.

To understand *relations to other variables*, let's consider reading comprehension as an example of an inferred construct. How do we define reading comprehension and how do we measure it? Would the ability to follow directions on a medicine bottle be sufficient? Does a student lack reading comprehension skills if he is unable to explain the multiple layers of meaning of the John Keats poem "Ode on a Grecian Urn"? Since there are multiple skills involved in reading comprehension that cannot possibly all be measured, which skills are selected? Most reading comprehension tests involve reading passages, then answering questions. But how are the reading passages selected? How representative are the selected passages of the entire domain of possible texts students might encounter? How representative are the types of questions (e.g., factual recall, main idea, supporting details, inferences, author's purpose) that are selected? Reading comprehension is a complex construct, and measuring it is equally complex.

In addition, *relations to other variables* includes considerations of test-criterion relationships. Popham (2017) explains: "This source of validity evidence is collected only in situations where educators are using an assessment procedure to predict how well students will perform on some subsequent criterion variable" (p. 112). For example, English language proficiency tests are supposed to predict how well a student will perform in a mainstream classroom. Criterion-related evidence for these tests should be gathered with data showing that students who score low on the test struggle with the English language demands of a mainstream classroom, while those who score high on the test are better able to cope. Such data, however, are rarely, if ever, collected

Tests are flawed measuring instruments because test scores can be affected by a wide variety of factors that have nothing to do with what the test is attempting to measure. These factors are sources of what testing experts call "construct-irrelevant variance." Haladyna (2002) offers a more practical term: *test score pollution*. Any factor that interferes with an accurate interpretation can be viewed as polluting the valid interpretation of the test score. Test score pollution that results in threats to validity includes "mismatched tests, cheating on the test, inappropriate test preparation, inappropriate or unfair test administration, and failing to consider the context for a student's or a group of students' performance" (p. 57). Haladyna notes that ELLs' limited English proficiency is a major source of test score pollution that can seriously affect a student's score.

Consider the example of a math test in English that is full of word problems. An ELL may have been a top math student in her home country but would have great difficulty passing this test because she has trouble reading or understanding the questions in En-

---

Box 6.2 Threats to Valid Interpretations of English Language Learner Test Scores

- If the test is timed, the student may not have enough time to finish the test, because the thought process for translation requires extra time.
- The English reading comprehension level of the test may be too difficult, so the test becomes a measure of English reading comprehension rather than a measure of achievement.
- The education program of a transplanted student is not likely to be very strong and therefore can result in lower achievement and lower test scores.
- The teaching quality may be inferior, especially if a bilingual teacher is needed but not available.
- If teaching is done in English and the student's English language proficiency is not good, the student is failing to learn English and not keeping up in other areas of study.
- If these students attend schools in school districts with limited services (e.g., in poverty-stricken areas), they are less likely to receive the special attention that more affluent school districts provide. Underfunded schools tend to have underfunded programs for the neediest students.
- If these students live in social or cultural isolation, they are likely to underachieve.

Haladyna, T. (2002). *Essentials of standardized testing* (pp. 186–187). Boston: Pearson/Allyn & Bacon, reprinted with permission.

glish. The math test becomes instead a test of English reading comprehension—not the construct the math test was designed to measure. Hence, lack of English proficiency is a source of construct irrelevance, the test score is polluted, and we cannot make any valid interpretations about the student's math ability. Haladyna (2002) outlines several threats to the valid interpretation of ELL test scores (Box 6.2).

Bias

Bias in testing and assessment refers to the qualities of an assessment instrument that penalize a group of students because of their gender, religion, ethnicity, socioeconomic status, or any other characteristic that defines them as a group. The issue of bias is really an issue of validity, because bias is one of the threats to valid test score use and interpretation; or as Haladyna would say, bias is a source of test score pollution.

Concerned educators have long pointed out examples of questions on standardized tests that focus heavily on sports and thus may be biased against girls and in favor of boys or that use names common only among white Americans. Bias is harder to find these days because test developers have become more sensitive and strive to eliminate potential bias in their testing instruments. Most companies have developed bias elimination handbooks and guidelines for their internal use that go beyond the superficial sprinkling of ethnic names throughout test questions. Despite these efforts, problems still occur and educators continue to find examples of subtle forms of bias in test questions, for example, items that require familiarity with the cultural norms and practices of white middle-class Americans.

Reducing bias is more complex than using diverse names and avoiding certain topics. The biggest source of bias for ELLs is the language of the test. Simply put, a test written in English is biased in favor of students who are proficient speakers of English and biased against those who are not.

In an effort to understand the extent to which linguistic bias may be present on a state high-stakes test, my colleague Xiaoshi Li and I analyzed a state 5th-grade math test in Texas and compared it with math worksheets that had been completed over the school year by newcomer ELLs from Cambodia (Wright & Li, 2006, 2008). The students, Nitha and Bora, spoke no English when they arrived 2 months into the school year, yet they were expected to pass the state math test—in English—less than 6 months later. Both students were very bright and made great progress in learning English, math, and other subjects during the school year. They had done well in math in Cambodia, but the academic standards in Texas were much higher than those of the Cambodian education system, where impoverished schools do not have enough textbooks and most teachers never attended or graduated from high school. Their school in Texas worked hard to provide as much math instruction as possible in an effort to help them catch up to their grade-level peers. With assistance—including primary language support—the girls were able to complete dozens of worksheets as part of their math instruction throughout the year, most of which contained simple word problems written for students below the 5th-grade level.

When comparing vocabulary, we found that the number of unique words on the worksheets and on the math test was about 300. The math test, however, contained nearly twice as many academic and math-specific vocabulary words as Nitha and Bora had encountered on their math worksheets. Many math-specific academic words, such as *digit, diagram, parallel, congruent, rectangular,* and *transformation,* did not appear once in their worksheets, yet understanding these key words was necessary to solve the problems on the math test. These newcomer ELLs simply did not have the English math-specific vocabulary they needed to read and understand the test questions. We then did a comparison of syntactic complexity and found that the math test had a greater variety of syntactic features than the worksheets and over twice as many of the more complex syntactic features (Figure 6.1). Thus, when the girls attempted to take the state math test, they encountered long sentences that were much more complex than anything they had ever encountered during their regular math instruction.

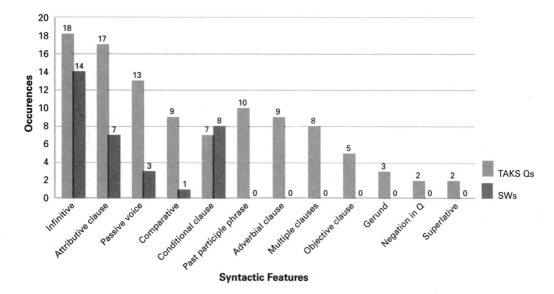

Figure 6.1 Linguistic complexity of students' math worksheets (SWs) compared with that of the 5th-grade math Texas Assessment of Knowledge and Skills (TAKS Qs). (With kind permission from Springer Science+Business Media: Wright, W. E., & Li, X. [2008]. High-stakes math tests: How No Child Left Behind leaves newcomer English language learners behind. *Language Policy,* 7[3], 237–266, fig. 1. © Springer Science+Business Media Dordrecht 2008.)

The following concluding sentences from word problems illustrate the difference between the syntactic complexity of the worksheets and that of the math test:

- *Student worksheet:* How many does he have left?
- *State math test:* What information is needed to find the approximate number of sheets of paper Juan had left after the school year was over?

Note that the student worksheet question is a single clause, whereas the math test question contains multiple clauses of different types. The math test question is much more linguistically complex and would pose a significant challenge to newly arrived ELLs—even those who are really good at math. For proficient speakers of English, however, the linguistic complexity of this sentence would not pose a significant challenge. Thus, this test question exemplifies the type of linguistic bias that is inherent in tests administered to students who are not yet proficient in the language of the test.

Critical Look at Testing Requirements for English Language Learners

Equipped with an understanding of assessment basics, we now review some of the challenges associated with testing requirements for ELLs. We begin with a look at professional standards for test development and use. Then we take a critical look at the content and language testing requirements for ELLs as mandated by federal policy under the ESSA, which includes testing accommodations, online assessments, and the use of growth models for accountability purposes. Finally, we address the importance of considerations of consequential validity.

Joint Standards for Educational Testing

Three major national professional organizations—the American Education Research Association, the American Psychological Association, and the National Council on Measurement in Education (2014)—have developed a set of standards for educational (and psychological) testing. These are commonly referred to as the Joint Standards. Many of the standards in chapter 3, titled "Fairness in Testing," address issues specific to the testing of ELLs.

The Joint Standards recognize that lack of English proficiency is a source of construct irrelevance. That is, any test given to ELLs in English becomes, in effect, a language test, with results that may not accurately reflect the students' competencies in the construct intended to be measured. The Joint Standards declare that test norms based on the scores of "native" speakers of English should not be used with students whose first language is not English. The standards acknowledge the problems of translation, noting that we cannot assume that a translation of a test is equivalent in content, difficulty level, reliability, and validity to the original English version. The standards also recognize that simply testing students in their "native" language alone is problematic because bilingual students may not test well in either language, especially if they haven't received literacy or content-area instruction in their home language.

Key to proper test use, the Joint Standards declare, is an understanding of an individual student's bilingualism. The standards also address issues related to the use of interpreters, modifications of tests (accommodations) for ELLs, the need for validity evidence, and guidance in interpreting test scores. When a test is used to make high-stakes decisions, for example, the standards suggest that the test user review the test itself and consider using additional tests, observational information, or modified forms of the chosen test to ensure that enough adequate information is obtained before making a decision. The attention the Joint Standards brings to issues of testing ELLs is greatly needed. Unfortunately, there are no enforcement mechanisms for the Joint Standards. In other words, there is no accountability system in place by which to hold accountable those whose develop, use, and interpret tests for accountability purposes.

The Joint Standards support the concept of **universal design** in the assessment of culturally and linguistically diverse students:

> Universal design is an approach to test design that seeks to maximize accessibility for all intended examinees. Universal design . . . demands that test developers be clear on the construct(s) to be measured, including the target of the assessment, the purpose for which scores will be used, the inferences that will be made from the scores, and the characteristics of examinees and subgroups of the intended test population that could influence access. Test items and tasks can then be purposively designed and developed from the outset to reflect the intended construct, to minimize construct-irrelevant features that might otherwise impeded the performance of intended examinee groups, and to maximize, to the extent possible, access for as many examinees as possible in the intended population regardless of race, ethnicity, age, gender, socioeconomic, status, disability, or language and cultural background. (p. 50)

The political push over the past two decades with federal mandates for high-stakes state tests that include ELLs has revealed many examples of how the Joint Standards are being ignored and violated, resulting in unfair consequences for ELLs and their schools based on test score interpretations of questionable validity.

Content-Area Testing

The main purpose of content-area testing is to determine how well students are performing in a particular subject area. Teachers often create their own content-area tests throughout the year (e.g., spelling tests, math tests) or use the end-of-chapter or unit tests that come with their curricular programs, for both formative and summative assessment purposes. States also create their own large-scale content-area assessments that are aligned with their state content standards and use the standardized assessment data for summative purposes.

The most commonly tested subject areas on large-scale content-area assessments are English language arts/reading, math, and science, because the ESSA has mandated that each state assess students in these areas. Many states, however, also test students in writing, and some also test students in social studies/history and other content areas. Large-scale standardized content-area tests are used for purposes of accountability for teachers and schools, as well as for students.

Accommodations for English Language Learners
In partial recognition of the problems involved in testing ELLs, the ESSA simply mandates that ELLs be assessed in a "valid and reliable manner" through the use of "appropriate accommodations." According to Abedi (2017):

> Test accommodations refer to changes in the test process, in the test itself, or in the test response format. The goal of accommodations is to provide a fair opportunity for non-native speakers of the assessment language and students with dis-

abilities to demonstrate what they know and can do, to level the playing field, so to speak, without giving them an advantage over students who do not receive the accommodation. (p. 304)

The ESSA specifies that **accommodations** could include, "to the extent practicable, assessments in the language and form most likely to yield accurate data on what such students know and can do in academic content areas, until such students have achieved English language proficiency" (ESSA §1111(b)(2)(B)(vii)(III)).

Providing tests in the ELLs' home language or using other accommodations is not as easy as it might seem. Extensive reviews of the research on testing accommodations for ELLs have found only a limited number of studies, and most of the findings are inconclusive (Rivera & Collum, 2006). As Abedi (2017) concludes: "Unfortunately, research on the validity of accommodations is very limited and the validity of only a handful of accommodation strategies used for ELLs have been experimentally examined" (p. 306). He adds: "Existing research on some forms of accommodations is not conclusive" and "for many forms of accommodations used by different states there is very limited empirical data to support their validity" (p. 308). So far, research can suggest only two kinds of accommodation with the potential to support ELLs' access to test content: testing students in their home language, and simplifying the language used in the test.

Tests in the home language appear to be the best accommodation. If students are tested in the language they know best, they should have a better chance of demonstrating what they know and what they can do. It is not possible, however, to simply translate a test from English to another language. Creating tests in the home language that are truly equivalent to the English versions is difficult, expensive, and time consuming. Only a small number of states have home-language versions of their state tests, and nearly all of them are in Spanish. Thus, the vast majority of ELLs, especially those who speak a language other than Spanish, have no access to this accommodation. Even states that have home-language tests may have them for only certain grade levels and typically place restrictions on how many years students can take them.

Furthermore, home-language tests are not beneficial to all ELLs. Many ELLs are unable to read and write in their home language because they have received literacy instruction only in English. Even if they are literate in their home language, they may not be familiar with discipline-specific vocabulary if most of their instruction has been in English. Thus, home-language tests are appropriate only for ELLs who (1) are literate in their home language, and (2) have received home-language content instruction in the subjects being tested (e.g., students enrolled in bilingual education programs or newcomers with schooling from their home country).

The other accommodation that appears to have potential is to simplify the language so that ELLs have a better chance of understanding the questions. This accommodation is referred to as linguistic simplification. A few states, such as Tennessee, have experimented with linguistically simplified (or "plain English") tests. But it is difficult to create such tests that still cover the same construct as the original versions. Texas, for example, has comprehensive "linguistically accommodated testing" procedures that include detailed instructions for test administrators on allowable ways to simplify test items. These procedures, however, may be provided only when specifically requested by an ELL during the test. More research is needed to determine whether linguistic simplification is beneficial to ELLs, and whether with its use validity can be maintained.

Abedi's (2017) review found that "there is no firm evidence to suggest that the accommodations used widely by school districts are effective, feasible, and valid" (p. 314). This finding reveals that federal policy requires something we really do not yet know how to do—test ELLs in a valid and reliable manner through the use of accommodations. In the absence of a research base to guide practice, states have had to piece together accommodation policies. These practices vary widely and most states use accommodation frameworks that were developed for special education students, most of which are not appropriate for ELLs and fail to address their unique linguistic needs.

In an effort to assist states and schools, Abedi and Ewers (2013) created a research-based decision algorithm "based on which decisions can be made on which accommodations can best fit their students with particular academic backgrounds" (p. 317). This algorithm reveals that not all accommodations are appropriate for all students. For example, an accommodation allowing students to use a bilingual dictionary is of little benefit to Laotian American students who cannot read Lao. Schools must make individualized accommodation decisions based on each student's specific background and needs. While helpful, such algorithms still do not resolve the fact that we know little about how to provide accommodations that are actually beneficial to the ELLs while maintaining the validity of the test. There are problems associated with all of the commonly used testing accommodations for ELLs (Table 6.1). These problems remain unresolved as we enter into the era of ESSA.

Some experimentation has begun with bilingual assessments. For example, a selected-response test may include questions in English in the left column and in the other language in the right column. Students can choose which language to respond in, or they may simply refer to the other language to help them comprehend. A constructed response test item or performance assessment could include prompts in both languages, and students could choose which language to respond in, or even engage in translanguaging by responding using both languages in the same answer. The principle here is that the purpose is to assess content knowledge; thus, it is more effective to allow the student to draw on his or her entire linguistic repertoire to comprehend the questions or task and perform the task or answer the question. As Shohamy and Menken (2015) argue:

> For assessment of emergent bilinguals to be valid and fair, it is essential that they too use language flexibility, creating affordances for home languages as well as practices in the new language. If, for instance, our purpose is to measure a students' understandings of math content, then assessments must be created that allow for this knowledge—rather than language proficiency—to be what is truly measured. (pp. 264–265)

Shohamy (2011) demonstrates this potential in a study that found that bilingual students performed better on a bilingual math test than they did on a monolingual version in their second language. Research on these types of dynamic bilingual assessments is just beginning, but they hold great potential for more valid and fair assessments for ELLs.

Challenges of Measuring Achievement and Growth for the English Language Learner Subgroup under the Every Student Succeeds Act

A major criticism of No Child Left Behind (NCLB) was that it was a proficiency-based accountability system only. In other words, student academic success was defined solely as meeting or exceeding a predetermined bar—a cut score that students must meet or exceed to be deemed as passing. Proficiency-based systems do not account for students' academic growth during the school year. This problem is illustrated in Figure 6.2. Student A, a native English speaker, began 4th grade at about grade level and learned enough to pass the state test at the end of the year. Student B, a bright newcomer ELL who arrived in the United States less than a year before entering 4th grade, began the school year at just above the kindergarten level. She made over 2 years of growth in the 4th grade.

Table 6.1 Rationale and Problems Associated with Testing Accommodations for English Language Learners

Accommodation	Rationale	Problems
Tests administered in the home language	Results will be more accurate if students are tested in the more proficient language.	• Practical only if there are large concentrations of ELLs who speak the same home language. • Effective only if students are literate in their home language and have received home language content instruction in the subject being tested. • Direct translations of English tests may change the tested constructs or difficulty level. • Development of parallel tests in other languages is expensive and time consuming.
Linguistically simplified tests	Removing difficult vocabulary and syntax may help ELLs comprehend questions.	• Requires the creation of a separate test, which can be expensive. • Difficult to create linguistically simplified test items covering the same constructs as the original test. • May not be appropriate for reading tests where comprehension of grade-level text in English is part of the construct being assessed.
Bilingual dictionaries or glossaries provided	Allowing ELLs to look up words they do not know can help them comprehend the questions.	• Feasible only if students can read in their home language and know how to use a (bilingual) dictionary. • Dictionary may provide definitions, explanations, or examples that give away answers. • Students who learn content in English may not be familiar with content words in their home language. • Using a dictionary takes up a lot of time. • Referring to a dictionary in front of their peers may be embarrassing to ELLs.

Nonetheless, under NCLB, Student B was deemed a "failure" (along with her teacher) because she did not meet or exceed the passing standard for the 4th grade test. In contrast, Student A had significantly less growth in the same period but was deemed a "success."

Proficiency-based measures (i.e., passing or failing the test) are also required by ESSA. But the ESSA attempts an improvement over past practice by allowing states the option of including some kind of growth measure or other academic indicator. Most states have elected to adopt a growth measure. Under such a hybrid system, a school would get credit for both Student A's passing the 4th grade test and Student B's impressive 2+ years of academic growth. Depending on how states design their **growth models** and the weighting of proficiency and growth indicators, it is technically possible that a school would get more credit for Student B's growth than for Student A's passing score, or at least get more credit for Student B's growth than for Student's A's growth. This allowance for growth indicators is a positive and welcome development.

Growth models rely, however, on high-stakes standardized test scores and are still in the experimental stage. Experimentation with growth models began in the late 2000s and were used mainly to evaluate teachers rather than whole schools (Doran, 2017). Growth models were widely misunderstood and misused to unfairly sort and rank teachers (Harris, 2011). This abuse of growth models led to warnings by leading test experts and professional organizations that "test scores alone are not sufficiently reliable and valid indicators of teacher effectiveness" and thus should not be used for high-stakes decision

Table 6.1 *(continues)*

Accommodation	Rationale	Problems
Oral interpretation of test directions and/or test items	Oral translation by a bilingual interpreter can make the questions more comprehensible for ELLs.	• Translation of test directions does little to help with understanding the actual test items. • Oral translation of long or complex problems can be difficult to follow and comprehend. • Students taught in English may not know the equivalent key content words in their home language. • Oral interpretation of reading comprehension passages and test questions changes the test construct from English reading to home language oral listening. • Finding qualified interpreters who can fully comprehend and translate questions accurately can be difficult. • Providing accurate interpretation without also providing additional information or explanations that may give away the answer can be difficult.
Test read aloud in English	Hearing the questions can help ELLs who have difficulty reading in English.	• Of little use to ELLs who also have low levels of English speaking and listening ability. • Long complex problems are difficult to follow and comprehend orally. • ELLs may be embarrassed to request or receive this assistance in front of their peers. • Reading aloud on reading comprehension tests changes the construct to listening comprehension.
Extra time provided	ELLs may read more slowly and may be translating in their heads; thus, they need extra time to finish the test.	• Of little benefit to ELLs at the lowest levels of English proficiency. • Of no benefit to ELLs when test is untimed for all students
Test administered individually or in small group	ELLs may feel more comfortable away from their English-proficient peers; they can take the test with a trained teacher who can provide other accommodations.	• Does nothing to address linguistic needs of students unless done to facilitate the provision of direct linguistic accommodations.

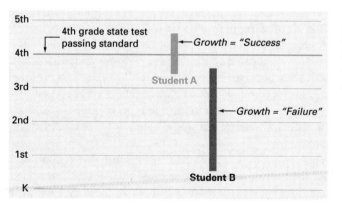

Figure 6.2 Illustration of how proficiency-based-only accountability systems do not account for students' growth.

making (Economic Policy Institute, 2010, p. 2). The use of growth models to measure teacher effectiveness was driven in part by the requirements of Race to the Top and ESEA Flexibility. Fortunately, in some recognition of past abuse, the ESSA does not require teacher evaluations to be tied to their students' test scores.

Thus, the shift is now to use growth models for school-level measures of effectiveness. There are different types of growth models that states may adopt for use under the ESSA (D'Brot, 2017). These models are statistically complex, but essentially, they are based on comparisons of students' current test scores and their scores from previous years. Simpler models calculate gain scores by subtracting the current score from a previous score. Other models use previous test scores to estimate students' growth rates. Some models use student growth percentiles, where a student's growth is compared with that of his or her peers who had similar previous test scores. Thus, for example, a student could be determined to be growing at a rate faster than 47% of her classmates. In **value-added measures** (VAMs), students' actual scores are compared with predicted-scores based on their previous year test performances. VAMs attempt to provide an estimate of the "school effect," that is, the school's contributions to student achievement gains (Harris, 2011).

Some models attempt to consider ELLs' past and current levels of English proficiency, or factors such as poverty, in determining their academic growth. Complex tables may be established to determine how much credit each students' growth contributes to (or detracts from) the overall growth indicator for the school. While complex, teachers should have some idea of what type of growth model their state has adopted, how it works in general, and how it works in particular for their ELLs.

The past abuses of VAMs are based on several myths (Bracey, 2007), some of which apply to other types of growth models as well. First is the *accuracy myth*: growth scores are often too inaccurate to be used to make reasonable judgments about school effectiveness. For example, in models that rely on a bell curve (e.g., VAMs, growth percentiles) to rank teachers, classrooms, or individual students, no matter how high the achievement or growth, half will be below average (Harris, 2011). In an analysis of VAM models, Kane (2017) warns that "random errors in the previous scores will introduce bias into predictions of the current scores" and thereby generate large bias in VAM estimates of school effects (p. 1). Specifically, "the estimated VAM effects would tend to be overestimated for teachers and schools with relatively high-scoring students and they would tend to be underestimated for teachers and schools with relatively low-scoring students" (p. 12).

Also, for VAM measures to be accurate, there needs to be stability in the test and passing standards used in the current and previous years. As past practice has revealed, however, states often find it necessary to make substantial changes to their tests and how they are scored for a variety of educational and political reasons. Furthermore, though effective teaching entails much more than raising test scores, growth models are based only on standardized test scores. Sparking children's curiosity and imagination, helping them develop a love of reading, developing their creativity, building their self-esteem, helping them see themselves as lifelong learners, and preparing them to be good citizens are all part of the magic of teaching that can never be measured by a standardized test. When it comes to ELLs, effective teaching can never be captured by a test scores alone. Growth models also make the assumption that test scores are valid for ELLs. As documented earlier, however, we still do not know how to include ELLs in large-scale, high-stakes standardized tests in a valid and reliable manner (Abedi, 2017; Francis, Rivera, Lesaux, Kieffer, & Rivera, 2006).

Second is the *curriculum-control myth*. Growth measures assume that schools and teachers have full control over the curriculum. Yet schools and their teachers are often forced to use curricular programs or instructional methods in which they have little faith. ELL educators often work in a climate in which the creation of instruction models and state restrictions has been driven by political will rather than sound educational research. For example, many schools provide English-only instruction for ELLs because of state or local restrictions on bilingual education.

Third is the *similar-test myth*. Many growth models assume that previous and current year tests are essentially equivalent in content and level of difficulty. But as Bracey (2007) points out, "What if mathematics in one year is mostly about fractions and decimals, and the next year mostly about geometry and statistics? Does subtracting year one's scores from year two's make sense?" (p. 1). In several states ELLs may be tested in their home language one year and in English the next. How can growth models account for this difference, especially for students who do well on home-language tests but struggle the first time they take the tests in English? A false picture of student regression may be created, with blame placed on the teacher or school.

While the potential for growth models is promising, and the move away from a proficiency-only model of school accountability is welcome, it remains to be seen how well growth indicators in various state ESSA plans will function for accountability purposes. It is important that educators work with their local district leaders, union leaders, and policymakers to ensure that growth indicators are not used in ways that are misleading and harmful to ELLs, their teachers, and their schools. Growth models must be used responsibly, with a full understanding of their limitations, and should be only one of several pieces of information within a system of multiple measures of ELLs. These multiple measures, along with a wide variety of alternative and authentic assessments given throughout the school year, can provide the most accurate (valid) and fair assessment of students' knowledge, abilities, and growth.

Language Proficiency Testing

When parents enroll their children in school, a home-language survey is given to determine whether a language other than English is used in the home, and if so, the extent to which this language is used with and by the children. Different states use different home-language surveys, but the purpose is to identify students with a primary home language other than English (PHLOTE). Each PHLOTE student is then flagged for language-proficiency testing to determine whether he or she is an ELL, and if so, at what level of English language proficiency. Many school districts also assess PHLOTE students' proficiency in the standard variety of their home language (See MacSwan, Rolstad, & Glass, 2002, for a critique of this practice). This practice sometimes results in the false labeling of some young Latinx students as both non-English- and non-Spanish-speaking (Box 6.3).

Once students have been identified and placed in appropriate ELL programs (if available), their language proficiency is assessed annually to determine their progress in learning English, as required under the ESSA. Students should also participate in formative assessments that provide information that can drive effective ESL instruction (MacDonald et al., 2015). Language-testing experts call the influence that language tests and assessments have on teaching the "washback effect." Washback can be positive, meaning it provides useful feedback and drives beneficial instruction. Or washback can be negative, perhaps better referred to as "backwash," such as when high-stakes tests force instructional attention to a narrow set of discrete skills.

At the end of each school year, a summative language proficiency test or assessment is administered to determine the students' progress in learning English over the school year. The results are used to determine or help inform decisions about when each student has reached a level of proficiency high enough to be redesignated as fluent English profi-

Box 6.3 Non-Nons

Are There Students with No Language?

Non-nons is used in some schools to refer to Latinx ELLs officially designated as non-English-speaking and non-Spanish-speaking. This designation results from language proficiency tests administered to students in both Spanish and English. Students who perform poorly on both tests are deemed to lack proficiency in any language. Teachers often buy into this construct, complaining about students who "don't know English or Spanish." Linguistically, this notion is absurd. All normal children (i.e., those without cognitive or speech-related disabilities) naturally acquire and master the language or languages of their speech community, typically by the age of 5.

MacSwan, Rolstad, and Glass (2002) investigated the non-non issue and determined that the problem is not children with no language but rather invalid language tests. They found that the tests gave heavy weight to literacy skills and standard Spanish. Students who spoke vernacular varieties of Spanish daily at home were considered non-Spanish-speaking simply because they never had the opportunity to learn standard Spanish or to read and write in Spanish.

They concluded that language proficiency tests, and the resultant non-non labels, create a false and potentially harmful description of many ELLs. The non-non label draws attention away from the real issues, such as the need to help ELLs further develop their home language at school and thus create a foundation on which to build their new language, and the need to help ELLs learn a standard variety of Spanish without devaluing the variety they speak at home.

cient and thus no longer in need of specialized ELL programs and services. Under the ESSA, the results of English language proficiency (ELP) assessments must be reported to the state and the federal government for accountability purposes. Thus, language tests serve several purposes: identification, program placement, monitoring of progress, reporting for accountability purposes, redesignation, and program evaluation.

Complexity of the Language Proficiency Construct

Mandates for language proficiency testing are pushing practices that are not supported by research. As noted earlier, language proficiency is a complex construct for which there is no simple measure. The ways we use language vary greatly and depend on context, whom we are interacting with, what we are communicating about, and why. Current widely used standards-based ELP assessments for ESSA accountability purposes—ACCESS 2.0 (WIDA) and ELPA21—are vast improvements over past language tests and offer useful and essential information for providing appropriate instruction for ELLs at differing levels of English proficiency. Yet no test can ever fully capture a student's true ability in English or any other language. Language proficiency standards assume a linear development of English proficiency through predefined stages. But as Poza and Valdés (2017) assert, "The state of knowledge about stages of acquisition in L2 learning does not support precise expectations about the sequence of development of English." Thus, they conclude that the ESSA's mandates for constructing ELP assessments with developmental sequences and progressions of English language development "is very much a minefield" (p. 435).

The situation is made more complex for ELLs because they are emergent bilinguals with varying degrees of proficiency in their home languages and English. Language tests, however, are based on the norms of monolingual speakers and therefore treat bilingual students as if they were two monolingual speakers of two different languages in one person. But bilingual individuals' brains are not simply divided in half with the home language on one side and English on the other. Rather, the two languages interact in ways that linguists and cognitive scientists are just beginning to explore. As Valdés and Figueroa (1994) pointed out many years ago:

> When a bilingual individual confronts a monolingual test, developed by monolingual individuals, and standardized and normed on a monolingual population, both the test taker and the test are asked to do something they cannot. The bilingual test taker cannot perform like a monolingual. The monolingual test cannot "measure" in the other language. (p. 87)

Pray (2003) documented another problem with language proficiency tests. She found that when they are given to "native" speakers of English, the test results classify many as limited English proficient. Thus, on one hand, these tests appear to hold ELLs to a higher standard of proficiency than their English-proficient peers. On the other hand, some language proficiency tests may falsely indicate that students have attained proficiency in English when in fact there are many gaps in their language ability. The danger here is that students may be exited from ELL programs before they are ready for mainstream instruction. With federal pressure on school districts to demonstrate progress and redesignate ELLs as quickly as possible, some states may be tempted to make less demanding language proficiency tests or lower the passing standards and thus push students into mainstream classrooms before they are ready. Such was the case in Arizona in 2010 when the U.S. Office of Civil Rights found the state to be in violation of the Equal Educational Opportunities Act.

In the past, language proficiency tests attempted to measure discrete, isolated skills. The notion of communicative competence developed by Hymes (1972) led to attempts to measure students' abilities to actually use language to accomplish authentic and specific communicative tasks. A language test, however, can never truly measure authentic or natural language use. Thus, all language tests are indirect measures of the complex construct of language proficiency, and results of these tests allow for only limited inferences about students' language abilities. Thus, it is essential to also use a wide range of formative authentic English proficiency assessments throughout the year.

Challenges with ESSA Requirements for Language Proficiency

Under ESSA, schools are expected to ensure that ELLs make progress in learning English and ultimately attain proficiency. In many state ESSA plans, this expectation makes up 10% of the annual accountability rating for each school. This is an important expectation, but it creates many challenges. First, there has to be reasonable limit on the percentage of ELLs expected to attain proficiency each year. Also, there is a disconnect between research, which suggests that it takes between 4 and 7 years to obtain fluency in a second language (Crawford & Krashen, 2015), and the structure of ELP assessments, which typically define only four or five levels of English proficiency. Thus, if a state has only four levels of proficiency but it takes a student 6 years to become fluent, and the student is expected to move up one proficiency level each year, there are not enough levels to reflect the student's progress. In California, for example, state reports have documented that ELLs move up quickly at the lower levels but get stuck in the higher levels for several years (Hill, 2006). In Nevada, a longitudinal, 6-year study found that less than half of any group of ELLs met the expected progress of increases in English proficiency at the rate of one level a year (Haas, Huang, Tran, & Yu, 2016).

ESSA affords states flexibility in setting reasonable English language proficiency progress and attainment goals. For example, in many state ESSA plans, long-term goals are set over a period of several years, with annual progress toward these goals along the way.

More important, many states consider factors such as ELLs' starting English proficiency level, or numbers of years they have been in the country, then use these factors to set individualized growth targets for each student (Goldschmidt, 2018). While inclusion of these factors is more complex to track and use to determine progress, it provides ELLs and their teachers with more reasonable goals.

Some of these concepts originated with a report and guidelines commissioned by the U.S. Department of Education a few years before ESSA was passed (Cook, Linquanti, Chinen, & Jung, 2012). The authors of the report stressed that these guidelines are just "the beginning of the discussion" and acknowledged, "We don't think we have all the answers" (Maxwell, 2012, p. 1). One major challenge is that states lacked valid baseline data from previous ELP assessments to establish their ESSA goals. Thus, states will likely need to adjust their long-term and annual goals as they obtain more accurate data from their current ELP assessments. Another issue is inconsistency in how states assess English language proficiency and inconsistency in how states use the results to make decisions about when to exit students from ELL programs (American Institutes for Research, 2012). There is variability even among states using common standards and assessments as part of the WIDA and ELPA21 consortia. A handbook published in 2018 by the Chief Council of State School Officers (CCSSO) attempts to provide further guidance for states in developing and monitoring the required ELP indicator under ESSA (Goldschmidt, 2018). States are continuing to grapple with these issues, and while the flexibility is promising, it is only just beginning. It remains to be seen whether these changes will be sufficient to establish ambitious but realistic expectations for ELLs' progress in learning English and attaining English language proficiency.

Challenges with Online Testing

Many states are now administering their ESSA required English language arts/reading, mathematics, science, and ELP tests in an online format via computers, tablets, or other Internet devices. This group includes states that are part of the Common Core State Standards assessment consortium (PARCC and Smarter Balanced) as well as states that are part of the two English language proficiency assessment consortia (WIDA and ELPA21). Thus, in most states ELLs and other students will likely take one or more state-assessments in an online format. These **"next-generation assessments"** are very different from traditional paper-and-pencil tests. For example, the Smarter Balanced assessments feature the use of computer-adaptive testing, meaning that the difficulty of the test items presented to each student varies in accordance with the student's performance on previous questions. Students who answer one or more questions correctly will be presented with more challenging questions, while those who miss one or more questions will be given simpler questions.

Online tests may take advantage of the technology to include technology-enhanced items that go beyond what can be done with paper-based tests. For example, PARCC performance assessments include computer-based simulations such as a research simulation task that may require students "to conduct electronic searches (within a predefined set of digital sources), evaluate the quality of the sources, and compose an essay or research paper using evidence from them" (Educational Testing Service, 2012, p. 17). Smarter Balanced performance assessments include "real-world scenarios and complex tasks" that involve "student-initiated planning, management of information and ideas, interaction with other materials, and production of an extended response such as an oral presentation, exhibit, product development, or an extended written piece" (p. 25). The comprehensive assessments also go beyond traditional selected-response test items to include constructed responses (i.e., short written answers) and technology-enhanced items. For example, on PARCC English language arts assessments, students may be asked to demonstrate comprehension of a text with tasks that call for dragging and dropping, cutting and pasting, or shading parts of the text; on the mathematics assessments, students may be asked to "create equations, graph functions, draw lines of symmetry, or create bar graphs" (p. 18). Likewise, the ACCESS 2.0 (WIDA) and the ELPA21 assessments take advantage of technology, allowing more promising ways to measure students' listening, speaking, reading, and writing skills in English. For example, students can interact with animations and images to indicate vocabulary knowledge, follow instructions to complete performance tasks that demonstrate listening proficiency, and respond orally to questions in a simulated conversation. Online tests also open up many possibilities for providing built-in accommodations for English language learners. For example, students could click on unknown words to hear them pronounced, to see pictures and written definitions, or to see and hear translations in their home language.

While the concept of online tests is promising, administering such high-stakes tests presents many challenges. First, these types of technology-enhanced items are new, and thus their use must be carefully monitored and researched to ensure that they are valid measures of the content and constructs they intend to measure. One concern, particularly for ELLs who have had limited access to technology, is the degree to which these tests are measuring technology skills rather than language and content knowledge. Second, questions remain regarding the extent to which the device on which the students take the test may impact their performance. For example, does screen size or the type of keyboard, or the use of a mouse or a touchscreen make a difference when students take the assessment on different devices (e.g., a desktop computer, a laptop, Chromebook, Surface Pro, iPad, or iPad mini)? Is the text large enough to read across platforms? Do students have to scroll on some devices to see the entire test item? Or do they need to zoom in to make out smaller images or text? What about the quality and volume of the audio (e.g., for listening tests or accommodations), and the quality and comfort of the headphones, or the quality of the microphone (e.g., for speaking tests)? A third concern is the expense of purchasing and maintaining enough computers or devices for a large number of students, and ensuring that they are set up and working properly at the time of testing. And finally, a major concern is ensuring that the school has strong and fast enough WiFi or wired network, and that the test server is secure and has enough bandwidth to handle the high load of simultaneous users.

The early experiences of statewide online testing revealed numerous problems. Some major issues were reported by *Education Week* for five states during testing in spring 2018:

1. New York—Students across the state had difficulty logging into the test and over 4,700 students were unable to submit their tests responses due to a cyberattack on the testing server.
2. Minnesota—Connectivity and login problems delayed testing for some schools.
3. Mississippi—Over 30% of the school districts experienced connectivity issues, and some students were unable to submit their tests.
4. Ohio—Login problems across the state.
5. Tennessee —Login problems across the state and a cyberattack on the test server prevented thousands of students from submitting their tests. Human error at schools led to over 1,000 students taking the wrong version of the test. (Harold, 2018)

It is important to acknowledge that traditional paper-and-pencil tests have also unfairly penalized thousands of students. While online testing may be improving and has gone smoothly for most states and students, as it use increases educators must remain vigilant to ensure that technology issues do not unfairly penalize their students and their schools. Teachers of ELLs must also ensure that their students are familiar and comfortable with any technology devices used for testing and understand how to complete the test in the online format.

Consequential Validity

Messick (1995) has raised the issue that validity should also be concerned with the consequences associated with the interpretation and use of test scores. He argues, "Any negative impact on individuals or groups should not derive from any source of test invalidity such as construct under-representation or construct-irrelevant variance. . . . Moreover, low scores should not occur because the measurement contains something irrelevant that interferes with the affected students' demonstration of competence" (p. 7). Messick's concerns are often described as **consequential validity**. Mahoney (2017) argues for a unified view of validity that shift the thinking away from validating tests to validating how test scores are actually used, especially scores of ELLs. Shohamy (2017) refers to this "examination and the uses and consequences of tests in education and society" as **critical language testing** (p. 441).

Chief among the many threats to the valid interpretation of test scores for ELLs is that the students' lack of proficiency in the language of the test—English—introduces a major source of construct irrelevance (e.g., a math test becomes an English proficiency test). Yet, despite the validity issues, test scores of ELLs are used to make high-stakes decisions.

Many bad decisions are based on invalid interpretations of test scores, and these decisions can have harmful effects on ELLs, teachers, classrooms, and schools. Research has documented the following:

- Narrowing of the curriculum to only those content areas covered on the test; little instruction in writing, social studies, art, music, physical education, health, or other non-tested subjects; elimination of recess to make more time for instruction and test preparation
- Adoption of curricular programs designed to raise test scores such as one-size-fits-all scripted phonics and reading programs or literacy interventions that are inappropriate for ELLs; frequent benchmark testing using tests similar in format and content to the state test that take time away from instruction; funds used to purchase test preparation materials rather than appropriate ESL materials
- Elimination of bilingual and heritage language programs so that the language of instruction is exclusively in the language of the test (English); replacement of much-needed ESL instruction with test preparation
- Reduction in the use of sheltered instruction strategies that make complex content-area instruction comprehensible for ELLs; reduction in the amount of time to engage students in conversations and other interactive activities that promote English language development; restrictions placed on certain activities or strategies, such as drawing, use of video, and field trips that benefit ELLs' language and academic development but are deemed as wasting instructional time
- Purposeful under-identification of ELLs so the school can avoid being held accountable for an ELL subgroup; encouraging secondary ELLs to drop out; using high school exit exams that often deny ELLs a high school diploma on completion of school and thus restrict their future opportunities
- Creation of a stressful school environment focused on testing, leading to test anxiety for students, less enjoyment, high turnover of teachers and administrators, with ELLs taught by least-experienced teachers

- Poor performance of ELLs on high-stakes tests, leading to lowered self-confidence; inappropriate placement or retention of students; frustrated and demoralized teachers who become reluctant to work with ELLs; parents who complain about the presence of ELLs at school[1]

Consequential validity dictates that these harmful effects must be taken into consideration and changes made. As Mahoney (2017) argues:

Good validity takes into account how a test will be used, the consequences of using it in those ways and for whom the test was intended. It also includes empirical evidence, with external checks, that the intended use of the test does work as it should for emergent bilinguals. (p. 43)

In the past, there were mounting concerns about unrealistic expectations and the harmful effects of NCLB on ELLs, leading to a joint statement issued in 2008 by the National Education Association and 144 other national organizations representing a broad range of educational, ethnic, religious, and professional groups, calling for changes to be made to the law. The changes reflected in ESSA addresses many of the concerns raised. But the principles underlying ESSA still rely heavily on accountability through high-stakes testing. Although changes were made to the ways in which ELLs participate and are accommodated on these tests, the research remains insufficient to show how ELLs can be tested in a valid and reliable manner. Hence, teachers and schools will continue to be held accountable for ELL test scores of questionable validity.

Alternative Authentic Assessments for English Language Learners

Because of the difficulties involved in assessing the learning and progress of ELLs using high-stakes standardized tests, effective teachers of ELLs use their own alternative authentic assessments throughout the school year for both formative and summative purposes. These assessments are alternative because they are unlike the standardized tests and traditional pencil-and-paper classroom-based tests created by teachers or pulled from textbooks. They are authentic because they more closely match instructional practices in the classroom and they reflect the knowledge and skills ELLs need outside of the classroom.

According to Herrera, Cabral, and Murry (2013), authentic assessments:

- Are generally developed directly from classroom instruction, group work, and related classroom activities and provide an alternative to traditional assessments
- Can be considered valid and reliable in that they genuinely and consistently assess a student's classroom performance
- Facilitate the student's participation in the evaluation process
- Include measurements and evaluations relevant to both the teacher and the student
- Emphasize real-world problems, tasks, or applications that are relevant to the student and his or her community (pp. 22–23)[2]

---

[1] For research documenting these and other harmful effects of bad decisions based on the invalid interpretation of ELL test scores, see Amrein & Berliner, 2002; Haney, 2002; Nichols & Berliner, 2007; Wright, 2006a, 2007.

[2] Herrera, Socorro G.; Murry, Kevin G.; Cabral, Robin M. *Assessment accommodations for classroom teachers of culturally and linguistically diverse students* (2nd ed.). © 2013, pp. 22–23. Reprinted by permission of Pearson Education, Inc., New York, New York.

The authors also note that authentic assessments "identify and build on student strengths such as language, prior experiences, interest, and funds of knowledge to facilitate learning" (p. 23).

When a program's goals include bilingualism and biliteracy, authentic assessments need to be used in both languages (see Escamilla, Hopewell, & Butvilofsky, 2013). The use of common assessments ensures that teachers share a language and a practice that is focused on improved student performance. Teachers use this balanced assessment and accountability system to counter the over reliance on high-stakes standardized tests (Gottlieb, 2016).

Some common alternative authentic assessments include observation, performance assessment, self-assessment, peer assessment, and portfolio assessment. We now look briefly at each of these.

Observation

The easiest way to assess ELLs is simply to observe them. Want to know how they are progressing in listening and speaking English? Talk with them. Observe their interactions in the classroom during group and pair work, during informal transition periods in class, and out on the playground or in the hallway. Want to know how well they are reading? Listen to them read. Want to know how well they are writing? Watch them while they are writing and read what they write. Want to know how well they understood the math lesson? Observe them completing independent math work at their desk or in cooperative groups.

Informal observation can be facilitated through the use of anecdotal records. This means jotting down quick notes on things you observe the student doing. I used to carry around a clipboard on which I had an index card for each student. The index cards were taped onto the clipboard in a flip-file fashion to make it easy to quickly find and flip to a student's card (large sticky notes work just as well). I would make notes about the students' linguistic and academic performances during lessons as I observed them working collaboratively and independently, including the date of the observation. Once a student's card was full, I would review it and then drop it in his or her portfolio. The clipboard also enabled to me to quickly figure out which students I had been ignoring and needed to spend more time observing. The anecdotal records helped me focus on the students and their progress and alerted me to students in need of extra assistance. I also shared the records with parents during parent conferences. Today anecdotal records can be easily recorded and organized on a teachers' tablet or other mobile device. These devices would also make it easy to snap quick photos of students' work, or even record short audio or video clips of their language use.

Observations can be conducted more systematically with a checklist. Teachers can create their own checklists or use those provided in a given curriculum program. A checklist to track students' progress during silent reading time, for example, might include some of the following items:

- ☐ Read at least 90% of the time
- ☐ Selected books appropriate to reading level
- ☐ Held the book properly
- ☐ Tracked text with finger while reading
  Read aloud
  - ☐ with great difficulty
  - ☐ with moderate difficulty
  - ☐ with good fluency

Checklists should be reviewed by the teacher, placed in the students' portfolio, and shared with parents and students themselves. When students know the teacher is watching— and, more important, what the teacher is watching for—they are more likely to live up to the teacher's high expectations.

Performance Assessment

A **performance assessment** is also a form of observation but more structured. Students are asked to perform a specific task or create a specific product, and the teacher evaluates the process, the final product, or both, according to a pre-established set of criteria. For example, suppose a teacher wanted to observe students' ability to retell a story they had read or that had been read to them. A checklist for this task could look something like this:

- ☐ Identified the main characters
- ☐ Identified the setting
- ☐ Told what happened at the beginning of the story
- ☐ Told what happened in the middle of the story
- ☐ Told what happened at the end of the story
- ☐ Identified the problem
- ☐ Identified the solution

Such a checklist could be customized for a specific book, listing characters and key plot sequences.

Most performance and other forms of authentic assessments are evaluated according to a rubric, which is a more sophisticated form of observation checklist. Rubrics contain several categories, with the performance for each category scored on a scale (e.g., 1–4)— the higher the number, the better the student did in meeting the teacher's expectation for the given category. Table 6.2 is an example of a rubric a teacher could use for a performance assessment of students given the task to create a bar graph showing their favorite (or what they consider the least disgusting) cafeteria food.

Rubrics are an effective tool for assessing performance because they allow the teacher to establish up-front the expectations for a particular assignment or activity. Unlike a single score or grade, the rubric allows students to see precisely where they met the expectations and where more work is needed. The most effective use of rubrics entails going over the rubric with students before they start working on the task. If students are to meet high expectations, they need to know what those expectations are. Some teachers involve students in the creation of the rubrics.

Self-Assessment and Peer Assessment

Authentic assessments can be made even more effective if students are involved in assessing their own work and performance and that of their classmates. Self-assessment and peer assessment can be facilitated through the use of a checklist or a rubric. A student might use the following checklist to score a report about a field trip:

Field Trip Report Checklist

    Content
- ☐ My report has a title.
- ☐ I wrote at least three paragraphs.
- ☐ My report tells where we went.
- ☐ My report tells when we went.

Table 6.2 Example of a Rubric for Performance Assessment

Bar Graph Evaluation

Student Name:

Category	4	3	2	1
Title	The title is creative and clearly relates to the problem being graphed. It is printed at the top of the graph.	The title clearly relates to the problem being graphed and is printed at the top of the graph.	A title is present at the top of the graph.	A title is not present.
Labeling of X axis	The X axis has a clear, neat label that describes the units used for the independent variable.	The X axis has a clear label that describes the units used for the independent variable.	The X axis has a label.	The X axis is not labeled.
Labeling of Y axis	The Y axis has a clear, neat label that describes the units and the dependent variable.	The Y axis has a clear label that describes the units and the dependent variable.	The Y axis has a label.	The Y axis is not labeled.
Units	All units are described in a key and are appropriately sized for the data set.	Most units are described in a key and are appropriately sized for the data set.	All units are described in a key but are not appropriately sized for the data set.	Units are neither described nor appropriately sized for the data set.
Accuracy of plot	All values are depicted correctly and are easy to see. A ruler was used to make the bars neat.	All values are depicted correctly and are easy to see.	Some values are depicted incorrectly.	All values are depicted incorrectly.
Neatness and attractiveness	Exceptionally well designed, neat, and attractive. Colors that go well together are used to make the graph more readable.	Neat and relatively attractive.	Lines are neatly drawn but the graph appears quite plain.	Appears messy and "thrown together" in a hurry. Lines are visibly crooked.

Created with Rubistar at rubistar.4teachers.org,

☐ My report tells what we did.
☐ My report tells what I liked and didn't like.
☐ My report tells what I learned.

Format and Mechanics

☐ I started each sentence with a capital letter.
☐ I ended each sentence with a "." or "?" or "!"
☐ I indented each paragraph.
☐ I proofread my story and corrected spelling and grammar errors.

A similar checklist could be used for students to assess a report written by another student.

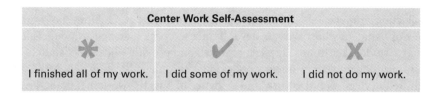

Center Work Self-Assessment		
✳	✔	✘
I finished all of my work.	I did some of my work.	I did not do my work.

Figure 6.3 Example of a self-assessment rubric.

Rubrics can be used in the same manner for self-assessments or peer assessments. For younger students, however, rubrics may need to be simpler than those used by the teacher. For example, the rubric in Figure 6.3 could be used by kindergarten or 1st grade students to self-assess their work at learning centers. Self-assessments can also take the form of prompts students complete to reflect on their learning and work. These reflections can be done through discussions, teacher-student conferences, or daily or weekly reflection logs, with prompts such as these:

- Today I learned . . .
- I am going to use what I learned to . . .
- Today I did a good job in . . .
- Today I had trouble with . . .
- Tomorrow I am going to try harder to . . .
- I need more help with . . .
- I want to learn more about . . .

Reflective self-assessments can be very effective in making students aware of what they have learned and how they are progressing and can prepare them for further learning that can advance them to the next level.

Peer assessment can be very effective, but teachers should keep in mind that students need to be well trained in how to assess their peers. Proper training in peer assessment can help students do higher-quality work themselves because they know exactly what the evaluation criteria are. Training can also help avoid conflicts over fairness and whether one student is evaluating another's work too harshly or incorrectly. Care also must be taken in determining which students assess which other students. A newly arrived ELL at beginning levels of English, for example, should not be expected to assess the writing of a more advanced ELL. Peer assessment, however, does not replace teacher assessment. The purpose of peer assessment is for students to internalize the high expectations and provide assistance to each other in meeting these expectations. It is not a strategy to save the teacher time by having students grade each other's work. In fact, this practice is forbidden in many schools because student privacy laws forbid teachers from making a student's grades known to other students in the class. But even in schools where such rules are strictly enforced, as long as the peer assessments do not result in final scores or grades that get entered into a teacher's grade book, the kinds described here should be allowed because of the valuable feedback peers can provide to each other.

Portfolio Assessment

Portfolio assessment is one of the most effective ways to measure a student's progress. The teacher collects samples of the student's work throughout the year and organizes it in a portfolio. Much like an artist's portfolio, a student portfolio is a collection of work that demonstrates the student's progress and achievement in meeting grade-level standards.

That collection, however, should not be just a hodgepodge resembling the overloaded backpack of a student whose parents never bother to check it and clear it out each day.

Effective student portfolios are well organized and provide evidence of student learning. Most include samples of student work along with some indication of how the student rated himself or herself on the work, and evidence of how the work met grade-level curricular standards (Herrera et al., 2013). Some teachers use working portfolios, which hold samples of students' work in progress. Others use showcase portfolios, which hold samples of the students' best work. With showcase portfolios, many teachers prefer to decide what goes in, but others argue that the students should be allowed to pick their best work for inclusion. I prefer a mixed approach, with some pieces chosen by the teacher and others by the student and teacher together.

A portfolio should be organized by content area (or separate portfolios should be set up for each content area) and should include representative work samples from the beginning, middle, and end of the school year. Students' progress in writing, for example, could be easily observed by comparing writing samples completed by students during the first few weeks of school, those completed just before winter break, and those completed near the end of the school year. If these are accompanied by completed rubrics and student self-assessments, the portfolio will present a clear record of the students' learning and mastery of the writing process and proper use of writing conventions and style.

Teachers will want to ensure that there are samples of different genres of writing in the portfolio. But to allow for useful comparisons of each student's work throughout the year, the portfolio should include at least three samples from the same genre. The writing portfolio might include a first-person narrative written at the beginning of the year, another in the middle of the year, and a third at the end of the year. The math portfolio might include a timed test of addition facts given at the beginning of the year and repeated at the middle and end to document the students' improvement in speed and accuracy.

In many schools, grade-level teams decide what to include in student portfolios to ensure consistency in portfolio assessment for each grade level. In my former school district, we had district-wide standards for math portfolios. Some teachers felt that this rigidity defeated the purpose of a portfolio as an alternative and authentic assessment; others were grateful for the guidance. All agreed, however, that the variety of samples in the portfolio provided a much better indication of their students' progress in learning math than did the state math test given at the end of the school year.

Some schools also use a pivotal portfolio, which is a portfolio that follows the student year to year throughout the program (Gottlieb & Nguyen, 2007). Teams of teachers decide what kinds of summative and formative student data to include in the pivotal portfolio, when to collect it, and what rubrics to use. With increasing access to technology, students can easily build electronic portfolios (e-portfolios). As Fox (2017) notes, "e-portfolios have emerged as an important assessment alternative, which can provide a more flexible, less cumbersome, and longer-term record of a student's development or a program's performance" (p. 135). These portfolios can include photos or scans of traditional paper-based work but can also easily incorporate audio or video recordings of student performance assessments and student-created multimedia projects.

Need for Multiple Measures

Among the many other problems with state high-stakes tests is that they provide just one piece of evidence about what students know and can do. As noted earlier, ESSA attempts to address this issue by requiring states to include in their accountability systems more than just passing rates on state academic achievement tests. States must also include a measure of student growth or other academic indicator, ELL student progress in achieving English language proficiency, and at least one other indicator. While this "other indicator" is to be something non-test-based, all of the other indicators are test based, and these test-based indicators carry the most weight in the school's accountability rating.

As we have seen, test-score-based evidence is a limited single-snapshot in time and is often of questionable validity, especially for ELLs. The reality is that despite the inadequacies of standardized high-stakes tests, they are firmly the center of ESSA and state education policies. Therefore, it is imperative that teachers use several alternative and authentic assessments throughout the year. In other words, teachers need to use **multiple measures** of a student's progress that include, but go beyond, state test scores. Multiple measures of ELLs are important because, as the school year progresses, ELLs learn more and more English. At any point, they likely know more English than they did the last time they took a test or completed an assessment. Thus, along with providing strong evidence of a student's knowledge and skills, multiple measures enable teachers to track the student's progress and growth during the school year.

When I was an elementary school teacher, I was required to administer the state's high-stakes test (SAT-9) in English to my 2nd grade students, all of whom were ELLs. Their scores were not very high. At the end of the school year, I was required to sit down with my principal to go over my students' test scores. I brought along samples from their portfolios. The portfolios provided evidence that when many of my students came to me at the beginning of the school year they were reading at the kindergarten or beginning of 1st grade level but most had made over a year's growth in their reading ability. I showed him writing samples from the beginning of year, which revealed that many students had struggled just to write a full sentence, and then I showed him how these same students by the end of the year were writing full paragraphs and stories. I showed evidence that students who began the year unable to add or subtract were now able to do grade-level math work. In short, the multiple measures of my students gathered in their portfolios throughout the year demonstrated that most of them had made tremendous progress. The state's test made my students—and me as their teacher—look like failures. The authentic assessments, in contrast, provided substantial evidence that my students worked hard and made more progress than most students make in a single school year. They were anything but failures. My principal agreed that these alternative assessments provided a more fair and accurate measure of the progress of our students than did the state test.

Summary

Providing ELLs with effective instruction requires the appropriate use of assessment. Assessment involves systematic planning and collection of student data from a variety of sources throughout the school year. Periodic summative assessments can provide a summary of what students have learned, but ongoing formative assessments are essential to providing information that drives instruction appropriate to the students' strengths and needs. Norm-referenced tests may be inherently unfair to ELLs because their performance is compared mainly (or exclusively) with the performance of English-proficient students. Criterion-referenced tests may be fairer for ELLs, since these tests report the extent to which students learned the tested content. Both types of test, however, are problematic for ELLs because of unresolved issues about how to test ELLs in a valid and reliable manner. ELLs' lack of proficiency in English means that academic tests given in English cannot provide a fair and accurate measure of the students' true academic ability. ELP tests, while important for tracking progress and planning instruction for ELLs, can likewise never fully measure a student's proficiency because of the complexity of the construct of language proficiency and the multifacetedness of bilingualism.

Because of these unresolved issues, the mandates of ESSA to use ELLs' high-stakes test results for school accountability purposes are problematic. The flexibility ESSA affords states in designing accountability systems that may account for student achievement and growth opens space for more reasonable expectations and, potentially, for better accommodations. It remains to be seen, however, whether these assessments will lead to genuine improvements in large-scale assessments of ELLs. Growth models are experimental, and while they have the potential to provide useful information on and credit for ELLs' growth, there is also great potential for abuse. Given these limitations of standardized and often high-stakes measures, the frequent use of alternative authentic assessments, such as observation, performance assessment, self-assessment, peer assessment, and portfolio assessment, is crucial for obtaining an accurate picture of ELLs' progress. When used consistently over the course of the school year, these assessments provide multiple measures of student performance that document students' growth and thus provide a clearer and more accurate picture of ELLs' language learning and academic progress.

Discussion Questions

1. This chapter lists many of the potentially harmful effects high-stakes testing may have on ELLs. Have you observed any of these effects? Have you experienced any of them first-hand as a student or as a teacher? How can these harmful effects be minimalized?

2. ESSA allows state accountability systems to include both achievement-based indicators and growth-indicators. What are the advantages of such a system? What are some of the specific challenges related to the use and interpretation of growth measures?

3. Why are multiple measures crucial for valid assessment of ELLs? What are some examples of the assessments that should be used through the school year, and how should these assessment results be evaluated?

4. View the video clip of the ELL assessment expert Robert Linquanti, project director for English learner evaluation and accountability support at WestEd. What does Linquanti say about the challenges of assessing ELLs, and how does he describe the important role of formative assessments in the classroom?

5. Review the Six Key Principles for ELL Instruction outlined by the Understanding Language initiative. How can these principles help guide teachers to support ELLs in meeting rigorous grade-level college- and career-readiness academic standards? What do the principles say about assessment?

Research Activities

1. *ELL Student Interview* Interview a current or former ELL who has participated in state-level academic achievement and ELP tests. Ask the student how he or she felt about these tests, and whether or not he or she feels the test provided an accurate measure of his or her ability. Ask what impact the test had on teaching and learning in the classroom.

2. *ELL Teacher Interview* Interview a teacher of ELLs. Ask the teacher about his or her experiences with state-level academic achievement and ELP tests, and

what impact they have had on his or her ELLs. Next, ask what alternative authentic assessments he or she uses with the students, and whether he or she feels these assessments provide more accurate information about the students' knowledge and skills than the high-stakes tests.

3. *ELL Classroom Observation* Observe an ELL classroom that will be participating in a high-stakes test. How is the upcoming test affecting teaching and learning in the classroom? Describe any lesson plans, activities, wall displays, or comments by the teacher or students that suggest a strong focus on the tests. Next, describe any authentic, alternative assessments being used in the classroom. Discuss the impact these may have on ELLs.

4. *Online Research Activity* Review sample test items from Smarter Balanced, from PARCC, or from other state tests (if available). What challenges might these items pose for ELLs at different levels of English proficiency? What accommodations are allowed for ELLs in your state when taking high-stakes tests, and how are these accommodations determined and administered? Review the accommodation policy on your state's education department website, or, if your state is participating in the PARCC consortium or Smarter Balanced, review the accommodation policies outlined on the websites of these state consortia.

Recommended Reading

Brown, H. D. (2018). *Language assessment: Principles and classroom practices* (3rd ed.). New York: Pearson.

Provides clear and detailed principles that are fundamental for evaluating and designing language assessment procedures with many practical examples for assessing ELLs' listening, speaking, reading, and writing abilities in English.

Gottlieb, M. H. (2016). *Assessing English language learners: Bridges to academic achievement* (2nd ed.). Thousand Oaks, CA: Corwin Press.

Written by a leading architect of the WIDA standards, this book provides a useful and practical framework of assessment *as*, *for*, and *of* learning. Teachers will find a wealth of examples and suggestions for ensuring that assessments are beneficial for ELLs and provide the types of information needed to help ELLs attain academic success.

Mahoney, K. (2017). *The assessment of emergent bilinguals: Supporting English language learners*. Bristol, UK: Multilingual Matters.

This highly accessible book makes complex issues of testing and assessment clear for teachers and provides them with practical guidelines for assessing the language and content knowledge of ELLs and making informed instructional decisions.

Seven

Listening and Speaking

For English Language Learners (ELLs) in U.S. schools, developing proficiency in oral English is essential for academic and future professional and personal success.

—WILLIAM M. SAUNDERS AND GISELA O'BRIEN

KEY TERMS

- conversational discourse
- cooperative learning
- corrective feedback
- language progressions
- minimal pairs
- oracy
- productive talk moves
- prompts
- recasts
- silent period
- SOLOM-R
- total physical response
- wait time

GUIDING QUESTIONS

1. What does the research tell us about the relationships between ELLs' oral language development, vocabulary development, literacy development, and educational achievement?
2. How can an understanding of ELLs' listening and speaking strengths and needs inform a teacher's choices of instructional approaches, methods, and strategies?
3. How can state college-and-career-readiness standards and the English language proficiency standards from WIDA, ELPA21, and individual states guide listening and speaking instruction for ELLs?
4. How can teachers help ELLs develop higher levels of oral language proficiency?
5. How can teachers promote oral language use in the classroom as a foundation for ELLs' literacy development and academic achievement in English?

Of the four traditional language skills, listening is by far the one we use most frequently. Think about how much time you spent listening today. Then think about how much time you spent speaking, which typically is second to listening. Right now you are reading, and you might even write a few notes as you read. What you read here could later become the topic for oral discussions. Oral language dominates our day, and even reading and writing tasks provide the impetus for oral conversation.

In the past, language educators considered listening and reading to be passive skills, because students simply received oral or written input. They considered speaking and writing to be active skills, because students had to produce oral and written language. This view no longer holds. Today, as Horwitz (2013) explains:

> Language scholars recognize that listening and reading are by no means passive processes and that both listeners and readers must actively construct the meaning of any language they encounter. Of course, whenever we listen, the words themselves are not the only source of meaning. Gestures, facial expressions, tone of voice, our knowledge of the topic, and the setting and context of the conversation all contribute to our understanding of what other people are saying. (p. 87)

Evidence that listening is an active skill of constructing meaning can be found in the fact that, as political debates and personal arguments attest, even proficient English speakers may hear the same thing but interpret it differently.

What do ELLs need to do to be able to actively construct meaning through oral English? Consider some of the following challenges:

- English speakers do not pronounce individual words separately and distinctly with space between them like the written words on this page. At the most basic level, ELLs have to attend to each phoneme in each word, because the change of one phoneme can change the meaning of an utterance (e.g., *bit/pit*). In normal, everyday speech, however, all the words run together. One friend might ask another, "Did you eat?" using a phrase that sounds more like "Dijaeat?" or "Djeet?"

- English speakers do not always speak in complete sentences. Much of my own research involves audio recording interviews with participants and then making a full transcription of every word the participants say. English speakers often begin a sentence but then start talking about something else without finishing their earlier thought. Oral language is full of sentence fragments, run-on sentences, false starts, hesitations, and embedded clauses, which make it challenging for ELLs to fully comprehend.

- Oral language is invisible (unless someone transcribes it verbatim). Once spoken, an utterance is gone forever (unless someone audio or video records it). ELLs cannot rewind real-life conversations to hear an utterance they missed. They cannot pause and look up a word they hear in the dictionary. If they make a mistake when talking, there is no way to go back, erase it, and try it again. They have to either let it go or try to say it again, if there is still an opportunity to do so.

- Speaking is much more complicated than simply selecting the correct vocabulary words and stringing them together with proper syntax to make sentences. To be comprehensible, an ELL must have adequate pronunciation, a smooth rate and flow of speech, and sufficient vocabulary and grammar, as well as a working understanding of the sociocultural context of the speech event.

- Different types of speech activities are structured by unwritten cultural norms that are known by proficient English speakers but may be elusive to ELLs (e.g., having a friendly conversation, giving a formal presentation, asking the teacher a question, giving opinions in class about a reading, agreeing and disagreeing with another student during a small group activity). Even in everyday conversations, there are norms governing turn taking, adding a point, changing the subject, and ending the conversation. There are also norms governing the use of nonverbal communication, for example, to demonstrate that you are listening and paying attention (making eye contact, nodding your head, saying, "Uh-huh," etc.). Many cross-cultural misunderstandings in oral communication can be explained by differences in pragmatics.

One of the ironies of oral language is that we know it is important and it is the most often used mode of communication, but we tend to spend the least amount of classroom instruction time helping ELLs develop it. This chapter reviews research, theory, policy, and practice on oral language development in K–12 classrooms and helps teachers develop a principled approach to teaching listening and speaking.

What We Know from Research about Oral Language and English Language Learners

This chapter draws on three major reports featuring reviews of the scientific research literature on language and literacy instruction for ELLs that have been conducted by different groups: (1) The Center for Research on Education, Diversity, and Excellence (CREDE) report titled *Educating English Language Learners: A Synthesis of Research Evidence* (Genesee, Lindholm-Leary, Saunders, & Christian, 2006), (2) the National Literacy Panel (NLP) on Language Minority Children and Youth report titled *Developing Literacy in Second Language Learners* (August & Shanahan, 2006a, 2006b; August, McCardle, & Shanahan, 2014), and (3) the National Academies of Sciences, Engineering, and Medicine (2017) report titled *Promoting the Educational Success of Children and Youth Learning English: Promising Futures*. The CREDE and NLP studies received support from the U.S. Department of Education's Institute for Education Science. The National Academies is a private, nongovernmental institutional established by Act of Congress in 1863; it provides independent, objective analysis and advice to the nation to inform public policy decisions. All three reports involved experts in language, literacy, and other academic fields who identified, read, and synthesized relevant academic research meeting rigorous criteria for inclusion. The findings outlined in the CREDE, NLP, and National Academies reports highlight what we currently know—and what we don't—about how to help ELLs in language and literacy learning.

Center for Research on Education, Diversity, and Excellence Report

The lead scholars for the CREDE report, Saunders and O'Brien (2006), reviewed and synthesized the research on oral language development (hereafter referred to as the CREDE reviewers). Their review resulted in the following major findings:

The empirical literature on oral language development in ELLs is small.

The CREDE reviewers found that "there is virtually no U.S. research on how classroom instruction might best promote more academic aspects of oral language development, and there is very little research on oral language proficiency beyond the elementary grades" (p. 19). Our limited understanding means that we have little empirical basis for planning educational interventions that would promote language development. Although educators everywhere recognize the importance of oral language, the report speculates that oral language remains in the shadows of research because researchers have tended to focus on English reading and writing outcomes and general measures of academic achievement, probably because oral language is hard to assess using traditional paper-and-pencil tests. The move to computer-based English proficiency assessments may open up opportunities to analyze student oral language development.

It takes time for ELLs to develop oral English proficiency.

The CREDE reviewers found that ELLs, on average, require several years to develop oral English proficiency and tend to make more rapid progress from lower to middle levels of proficiency (i.e., from Level 1 to Level 3) and slower progress as they move beyond Level 3. They found that by grade 5, "ELLs are performing 3.5 years below native-English speaker norms" (p. 27). They suspect this slowdown is due to the lack of instructional attention to oral language development once students reach the middle levels of English proficiency. Also, the reviewers found, on average, ELLs' English oral language development proceeds at a fairly constant rate that is unrelated to the program they are in. Thus, these findings (1) challenge claims that English-only programs will help ELLs learn English faster than bilingual programs; (2) provide evidence that home language instruction in bilingual classrooms does not delay or impede students' acquisition of English; (3) contradict policies based on the assumption that ELLs can learn English in 1 year; and (4) provide strong evidence that direct, systematic ESL instruction is imperative—especially at higher levels—if students are to avoid a slowdown at the middle levels and continue to make progress toward becoming proficient in English.

ELLs need some English proficiency before interaction with native speakers is beneficial.

The CREDE report challenges the notion that ELLs must interact with "native" or proficient English speakers right away to learn English—a notion that has been used in some cases to justify closing bilingual and ESL programs and placing ELLs in mainstream classrooms. The CREDE reviewers found that interaction in and of itself is insufficient and that ELLs cannot really begin to associate with English speakers until they attain some level of English proficiency. The reviewers describe a study in which a newcomer non-English-speaking ELL failed to benefit from work with English-speaking peers because the class assignments were well beyond her proficiency level, and her peers had no idea how to help her. Nevertheless, the report concludes, interactive activities can be beneficial if they pair ELLs with English speakers and careful consideration is given to the design of the task, the training of the non-ELLs, and the language proficiency of the ELLs.

Use of English outside of school enhances ELLs' oral English development.

The CREDE reviewers caution that this finding comes with three qualifiers: (1) simultaneous development of students' home language does not slow down their development of English oral proficiency; (2) for students at higher levels of English proficiency, their use of English outside of school may not be as critical as their use of English in the school; and (3) the ways in which students use their home language and English at home are interrelated, and their home language and English language development are mediated by a wide range of sociocultural factors. Although using English outside of school seems important, the reviewers are forced to conclude that "it seems quite clear that the relationship among L2 development, L1 maintenance, and language use is quite complex" (p. 34).

Use of home language for beginning-level ELLs contributes to academic development.

The CREDE reviewers describe a study that found that the newcomer elementary school ELLs who received ample home language support and who spoke little English in class during the first half of the year scored higher on an achievement assessment in English than newcomer ELLs who spoke mostly English in class and received little home language support. Like other CREDE report findings, this finding challenges those who advocate for English-only instruction policies and highlights the importance of using bilingual strategies in the classroom.

English oral language proficiency tests fail to capture the full oral language proficiency of bilingual students.

This finding reiterates the point made earlier that this problem with language proficiency tests is due to the complexity of bilingualism and oral language proficiency and to the fact that tests can measure only a very small sample of oral proficiency skills. The CREDE reviewers also found that the notion of "academic language" is problematic because it is often confounded with literacy. They note that more research is needed to clarify what academic oral language proficiency is, independent of literacy and in relation to traditional constructs of literacy. Finally, they note that because of the limitations of these language proficiency tests, decisions about when to place ELLs in mainstream classes should be based on a combination of informed teacher judgments and oral language assessments that are academically oriented and broad in scope.

National Literacy Panel Report

The NLP report found a close relationship between English oral proficiency and reading. Lesaux and Geva (Geva, 2006; Lesaux & Geva, 2006) were the lead scholars for the NLP report reviewing and synthesizing the scientific research in this area (hereafter referred to as the NLP reviewers). Their review resulted in the following major findings:

Oral language skills are more important for reading larger chunks of text for comprehension than for reading at the word level.

The NLP report makes an important distinction between reading larger chunks of text for comprehension and reading at the word level. The reviewers found that students can learn to decode words, including nonsense or "pseudowords," even if they do not know what those words mean.

Oral language skills in English are strongly associated with English reading comprehension.

The NLP reviewers found that the oral language skills needed for reading comprehension include vocabulary knowledge, listening comprehension, syntactic skills, and the ability to handle metalinguistic aspects of language, such as the ability to define words. The more English ELLs can speak and understand, the more they are able to comprehend what they read in English. The reviewers note, however, that the relationship between English oral language proficiency and English reading comprehension is also mediated by several contextual factors, including language use and literacy practices at home, socioeconomic status, and the students' education experiences and the types of instruction they have received. Simply being able to speak English well, however, is not sufficient for students to become strong readers in English. ELLs need to have relevant knowledge about a particular concept, and the oral language skills necessary to talk about it, in order to be able to read about it with comprehension in English. The reviewers found that other sociocultural and instructional factors must also be taken into consideration.

Oral language skills in English are associated with better English writing.

The NLP reviewers found the oral language skills that are related to writing include listening comprehension and vocabulary knowledge. Other aspects of oral language proficiency found to be important for English writing include grammatical skills, decontextualized language skills, and knowledge of cohesion devices (e.g., anaphora, conjunctions, relativization, and temporal reference). These skills are necessary for writers to express ideas that are not limited to the here and now.

English oral language proficiency is not strongly related to English spelling skills.

The NLP reviewers found that students' ability to spell individual words correctly is not related to their vocabulary and syntactic knowledge. Thus, students can memorize the spellings of words without knowing their meaning or how to use them in a sentence. The reviewers warn, however, that this conclusion is tentative because only a small number of studies have addressed this relationship.

Home language literacy skills plus good English oral language skills are strongly associated with good English reading comprehension skills.

The NLP reviewers found that students who can read in their home language and who have developed good oral English proficiency also have an advantage in learning to read in English. In contrast, they found that students with lower levels of oral English proficiency are less able to apply their home language reading skills to reading in English.

ELLs need consistent ESL instruction.

The findings of the NLP report make it clear that "just good teaching" of reading and writing is insufficient for ELLs to develop English literacy skills. For this "good teaching" to be effective, it must be combined with ESL instruction that has a strong focus on helping students develop their English language oral proficiency skills. When such ESL instruction is neglected, ELLs may develop word recognition, spelling, and decoding skills but continue to lag behind their peers in reading comprehension and vocabulary. The NLP report calls for an early, ongoing, and intensive effort to develop English language proficiency, suggesting, as does the CREDE report, that ESL instruction is imperative for ELLs at all levels of proficiency, not just at the beginning levels.

National Academies Report

Although the findings of the National Academies (2017) report are more recent, they are consistent with the findings of the CREDE and NLP reports. The National Academies reviewers note that there are still very few rigorous research studies on the oral language development of ELLs, and thus they caution that their report can offer only tentative conclusions and recommendations.

Conclusion 6-6, however, is clear and somber:

> Evidence suggests that many schools are not providing adequate instruction to English learners (ELs) in acquiring English proficiency, as well as access to academic subjects at their grade level, from the time they first enter school until they reach the secondary grades. Many secondary schools are not able to meet the diverse needs of long-term ELs, including their linguistic, academic, and socioemotional needs. (p. 245)

In an effort to address this concern, the reviewers, in Conclusion 7-2, recommend the following four instructional practices for developing oral English proficiency; each is supported by research evidence.

Provide specialized instruction focused on components of oral language.

This recommendation is based on National Academies reviewers' finding that explicit instruction in vocabulary, phonological awareness, dialoguing, story construction, and story recall was beneficial for ELLs' oral language development. They drew on studies in which "the language components were taught in language-rich environments such as read-alouds of narrative and informational texts" (p. 268). Furthermore, they found that ELLs' oral language development was supported through content instruction that was made more comprehensible through "methods such as using multimedia; children's television; on-screen animations; movements and gestures; dramatization and movement; on-going clarifications of word meanings in multiple contexts before, during, and after reading; and ongoing questioning and discussion about the content presented" (p. 269).

Provide opportunities for interaction with speakers proficient in the learner's second language.

Recall the CREDE finding that ELLs need some English proficiency before interaction with native speakers. This recommendation is consistent with second language acquisition theories that meaningful interaction is essential in learning a new language. The National Academies reviewers note that "speaking is important because it generates feedback, forces syntactic processing, and challenges students to engage at higher proficiency levels" and "generates more input" (p. 269). To be effective, however, such interactive activities, they point out, must be carefully planned, structured, and carried out.

Engage in interactional feedback.

This recommendation underscores the importance of providing corrective feedback for ELLs while they are developing their oral language proficiency. Later, we will explore two types of corrective feedback that research has found to be effective—recasts and prompts.

Dedicate time for instruction focused on oral English proficiency.

This recommendation supports the NLP finding that all ELLs need consistent ESL instruction. It is based on several studies that "suggest that a daily block of time focused on the development of oral English language proficiency can be beneficial" (p. 270).

Using Theory to Guide Decision Making

Our understanding of language teaching and learning helps us with some basic issues related to ELLs' oral language development. Recall that a fundamental goal is to help ELLs develop communicative competence in the oral and written language or languages used at school, and for that development to occur, students must be engaged in language-rich contexts that provide opportunities for interaction as they learn and use listening and speaking for academic purposes. From a cognitive perspective, this interaction provides the means for learners to receive and process comprehensible input and to produce comprehensible output. From a sociocultural perspective, learning, including language learning, takes place through interaction in the students' zone of proximal development (ZPD) with the teacher and more competent peers. From a bilingual perspective, students need to draw on all of the languages in their linguistic repertoire to make meaning.

Theoretical developments in listening and speaking draw our attention to the notion of **oracy,** or the oral skills used in formal education, particularly around reading and writing (Escamilla, Hopewell, & Butvilofsky, 2013). Oracy has three main components: language structures, vocabulary, and dialogue. Escamilla et al. propose that a holistic (bi)literacy program dedicate approximately 25% of literacy instruction to oracy in both Spanish and English.

A principled approach to teaching listening and speaking in K–12 classrooms means that teachers draw on theories of language learning and teaching to make decisions about teaching content to students at different levels of English language proficiency and from diverse sociocultural backgrounds. In this section we apply these theories to brief discussions of the silent period and wait time, teacher talk in the classroom, correcting student speech errors, productive talk moves, and vocabulary development.

Silent Period and Wait Time

Students who are just beginning to learn a new language (i.e., those at Level 1) may not be ready to start speaking when they first enter the classroom. Most language learners therefore go through a **silent period** before they begin to speak.[1] Teachers should not assume that because students do not talk, they are not learning. During the silent period, learners are developing their receptive listening skills as they acquire bits and pieces of the language and process the input for meaning. They are also beginning to figure out how their new language works. Thus, teachers should not force students to talk before they are ready.

For some ELLs, the silent period might be just a few hours. For others, it could be several weeks. Emergent bilingual ELLs born in the United States may not need any silent period because they are typically simultaneous bilinguals with substantial exposure to English before entering school. In contrast, newcomer ELLs without any prior English study or exposure may need a longer silent period. Teachers can encourage student talk by creating supportive classrooms in which teachers scaffold and support students' oral language development. For example, lower-level ELLs may feel comfortable participating in song, chant, or shared reading with the whole class but would feel uncomfortable contributing to a classroom discussion or doing an oral presentation in front of all the other students. Older ELLs often feel self-conscious about their foreign-sounding accents.

When ELLs do feel ready to speak, they may need time to process their thoughts in English before speaking. If a teacher asks them a question, they may need first to mentally translate the question, figure out the answer, and then translate that answer before they can respond to the teacher. Giving students time for this process after asking them a question or requiring them to respond is called **wait time**. Some students may be able to formulate most of what they want to say in English but need a bit of extra time to recall new vocabulary or appropriate forms before speaking. Cultures differ in what is considered an appropriate pause before responding to a question, and so what seems like a very long pause for one cultural group may be very short to another cultural group. Many teachers mistakenly interpret silence as an indication that the student does not understand the question or does not know the answer. This misunderstanding has potentially negative consequences for the ELL, who may be denied opportunities to participate effectively in the classroom interaction.

Teachers must be patient after asking a question. One strategy is simply to wait. Another is to find creative ways to build in wait time. For example, the teacher might ask the class a question for which multiple answers are possible, such as, "Can you give me an example from the text of foods that are healthy for our bodies?" and then go down the line of students and have each give an answer in succession. The ELLs know their turn is coming and will have time to process the question and prepare an answer. Also, hearing other students' answers can help the ELLs confirm their understanding of the question. Another simple strategy is to respond to an ELL who appears unready to answer a question by saying, "Keep thinking, and I'll come back to you in a minute." Chances are, when the teacher comes back, the student will have an answer ready.

Teacher Talk in the Classroom

Teachers typically do most of the talking in the classroom; thus, two important issues need to be addressed. First, teachers should talk less and plan classroom activities that give students regular opportunities to speak (Wright, 2016). The U.S. comedian Gallagher has poignantly observed, "They send us to school to learn to communicate, but all day long the teachers tell us to shut up!" I once took a group of university students to observe a middle school classroom where students sat at their desks arranged in a large circle, dis-

---

[1] Roberts (2014) questions the existence of a silent stage in childhood second language acquisition and suggests that the research evidence to support it is limited.

> **Box 7.1** Adjusting Speech to Make It Comprehensible
>
> - Slow down! Use a slower rate of speech when talking to beginning-level ELLs than you would in normal conversation with proficient speakers, but maintain a steady pace.
> - Speak clearly, but do not over-enunciate to the point where the words sound unnatural.
> - Speak at a normal volume. Shouting does not make English more comprehensible.
> - Use simple sentence structure with beginning-level ELLs (e.g., subject-verb-object). Avoid long, complex sentences with embedded clauses.
> - As students make progress, increase the complexity of the vocabulary and syntax appropriate to their English language proficiency.
> - Emphasize key vocabulary through frequent repetition of these new words throughout the week and across subject areas.
> - Avoid idioms, unless they are explained or were previously taught.
> - Avoid cultural references that may be unfamiliar to students, unless they are explained.
> - Use gestures, facial expressions, realia, and other visuals.
> - Repeat, paraphrase, or use other recast techniques when students do not understand.

cussing the classic book *Animal Farm* by George Orwell. The teacher stood in the middle and directed the discussion. Initially, my students were very impressed with the interactive discussion. Later, however, when they analyzed their video transcript of the lesson, they discovered that the teacher did over 95% of the talking. Only a few of the children spoke and those who did gave only very short answers to the teacher's narrow known-answer questions. Thus, there was actually very little discussion going on in this "classroom discussion."

One effective approach for encouraging more student talk is to use open-ended and higher-order questions and short probes that require students to elaborate. These and other effective strategies for scaffolding student talk will be covered in our later discussion of productive talk moves. Teachers also need to adjust the way they talk with their ELLs to ensure that their speech provides comprehensible input (Box 7.1). Any modifications should take into account the students' level of English language proficiency. For ELLs at the beginning levels teachers should slow down their rate of speech, enunciate clearly, and use a simple sentence structure, avoiding long sentences with complicated syntax. Teachers should also be careful when using idioms and explain the meaning of any that are unfamiliar to ELLs. As students make gains in their English language proficiency, however, they need more complex input in order to make continual progress.

Correcting Student Speech Errors

Teachers need to know how to respond to their students when interacting with them in conversations. A major issue is when and how to provide **corrective feedback**. Errors are a normal part of language learning, but, on one hand, if students are corrected by their teachers every time they open their mouths, they are likely to get frustrated; their affective filters may be raised so high they will never want to talk again in class. On the other hand, if students are never corrected, their development of oral English skills may be impeded.

Teachers should correct only those errors students are ready to learn how to correct. We know from Krashen's (1985) natural order hypothesis that learners acquire some grammatical forms earlier than others, and those that are acquired later may be impervious to direct correction. Thus, it may be a waste of time, for example, to correct errors related to the proper use of -*s* for third-person verbs (e.g., He jump*s*) before a student has a basic vocabulary of verbs and pronouns and an understanding of simple verb conjugation.

A key issue is how corrective feedback should be provided. To keep the affective filter low, students' errors should be corrected in a manner that avoids embarrassment, particularly in front of their peers. But should the correction be explicit or implicit?

According to one aspect of Long's (2018) interaction hypothesis, proficient English speakers should provide corrective feedback when they interact with ELLs. Consider the following two examples of the response Jin receives when he tells his teacher about his trip to the mall:

Example 1

Jin: Teacher! Yesterday I goed to mall with my friend.

Teacher: *No, Jin, don't say "goed." It's* went. *Remember,* go *is an irregular verb. And it's the* mall. *You're forgetting the definite article. Now, try again.*

Example 2

Jin: Teacher! Yesterday I goed to mall with my friend.

Teacher: *You went to the mall with your friend? Cool! I went to the mall last week with my son to buy clothes. What did you buy?*

Example 1 is a direct correction, or what Long refers to as negative feedback. Example 2 is an example of positive feedback. Here the teacher does not correct the student but instead models the correct usage through a positive and reinforcing response, using the correct forms *went* and *the mall,* twice in her response. Such a response in authentic conversations is a form of scaffolding. These indirect forms of corrections are referred to as **recasts**. According to Schmidt's (2012) noticing hypothesis, learners need to notice specific language features in the input in order to acquire them. Of course, there is no guarantee that Jin will notice this modeling in a recast, but if teachers consistently engage their students in conversations and respond to student errors in this manner, they will be providing comprehensible input, and students will likely notice and acquire the correct form unconsciously. Another form of corrective feedback are **prompts**, which may be simple nudges for corrections or reminders of past instruction. For example, if the input in the recasts are going unnoticed by Jin, then direct prompts may be appropriate: "Remember how to say the past tense of 'go'?" or "Not 'I goed,' but 'I . . .'" [pause for student to complete]. Corrective feedback could also be provided through the form of cross-linguistic analysis.

Other error correction issues are related to the students' level of English proficiency, the context of the conversation in which the error occurs, and whether the error leads to misunderstanding or potential embarrassment for the student. There are times when direct correction is appropriate but must be done in an appropriate manner (Box 7.2).

Productive Talk Moves

Productive classroom talk refers to engaging students in discussions "in which they talk, think, and reason together; carefully listen to one another; negotiate meanings; and collaboratively make progress in their thinking" (van der Veen et al., 2017). In a project designed to improve the achievement of ELLs and other culturally and linguistically diverse students, Chapin, O'Connor, and Anderson (2009) found that careful scaffolding of classroom discussions through **productive talk moves** was a key component of suc-

Box 7.2 Corrective Feedback: When and How to Correct Student Speech Errors

When to Correct

- Correct errors of form when students are ready to learn the correct form (e.g., beginning-level ELLs who say "da" for "the" should not be corrected).
- Correct errors when they impede comprehension (e.g., "The stove is in our chicken" [kitchen]).
- Correct errors when they impede communication (e.g., correcting verb tense errors may not be appropriate during a lesson on the metric system).
- Correct errors during ESL or other language-focused instruction when a particular language form has been taught and is being practiced (e.g., to practice the use of the future tense, students are talking about their plans for the weekend; the teacher listens and helps students having difficulty using the correct future tense form).
- Correct errors in the use of a target language form during content-area instruction (e.g., a language objective about using the past tense in combination with a lesson about historical events).
- Correct errors that are unintentionally offensive or that could be embarrassing if the student made the error in front of fluent English speakers (e.g., "I saw a whore [horse] at the farm.").

How to Correct

- Provide implicit corrections through recasts by responding naturally but in a manner that models the correct form (e.g., Student: "My mom, she buy me shirt red." Teacher: "Your mom bought you a red shirt? Very nice! My wife bought me a blue jacket.").
- Provide explicit corrections in a manner that does not embarrass or ridicule the student (e.g., "I think you mean your stove is in your *kitchen*. Is that what you meant?").
- Prompt for corrections with gentle reminders of past instruction (e.g., Student: "At my house we have four pet." Teacher: "Remember how we practiced making plural words? So how would you say you have more than one pet?" Student: "Pets." Teacher: "You got it. Great job!")

cess. In the context of discussions, students were able to develop logical reasoning and learned how to make and support arguments. Although their work centered on mathematics instruction, these same principles and strategies for productive classroom talk have been found to be effective across content areas (Zwiers, 2014). For example, in an experimental study with 460 five-year old students across 21 classrooms, van der Veen et al. (2017) found that their productive talk tools intervention (MODEL2TALK) led to significant improvements in students' oral communicative competence.

Chapin et al. (2009) identify five talk moves that help support students' thinking and learning around targeted instructional concepts (pp. 13–19):

- **Revoicing:** Repeating some or all of what a student said. ("*So you're saying that it's an odd number?*")
  This move is used when it is unclear to the teacher or to other students what a student said. After revoicing, the teacher asks the original speaker to verify that the revoicing was correct.
- **Repeating:** Asking one student to restate another student's reasoning. ("*Can you repeat what he just said in your own words?*")
  This move is similar to revoicing, except that, rather than the teacher, another student responds to what a student said. The original speaker can then confirm whether his intended meaning was stated correctly.

- **Reasoning:** Asking students to apply their own reasoning to someone else's reasoning. ("*Do you agree or disagree? Why?*")
  The teacher refrains from expressing his or her own opinion and uses this move to elicit respectful discussion of a student's ideas. It is important to follow up with "Why?" because requiring students to explain their reason for agreeing or disagreeing with another student's statement helps them develop their thinking.
- **Adding on:** Prompting students for further participation. ("*Would someone like to add something more to this?*")
  This move increases students' engagement in the discussion by asking for further input.
- **Waiting:** Using wait time. ("*Take your time . . . ; we'll wait . . .*")
  This move ensures that students have time to gather their thoughts and prepare to answer.

Zwiers (2014) offers additional discussion functions and starters that can serve as productive talk moves:

- **Clarifying:** "Why isn't that relevant?" "What else do we need to consider?"
- **Analyzing:** "How do all these pieces fit together?" "What pattern is emerging?"
- **Stating an opinion:** "What is your opinion on what she described?"
- **Supporting a point with evidence:** "What evidence would support this point?"

These talk moves are similar to what van der Veen et al. (2017, p. 693) use in their MODEL2TALK intervention, though they include a few additional moves or tools:

- **Challenge or counterexample:** "Does it always work that way?"
- **Metacognitive guidance:** "I don't know/understand what you mean."
- **Conversational ground rules:** "Why is it important that we listen carefully to another?"

Chapin et al. (2009) describe three productive talk formats teachers use to configure classroom interactions for instruction: whole-class discussions, small-group discussions, and partner talk. They emphasize that the use of these formats must be based in principles of establishing and maintaining a respectful, supportive environment; keeping the talk focused on the targeted topic or concept; providing for equitable participation for all students in classroom talk; and explaining expectations for new forms of talk (p. 143). Drawing a parallel to real world conversations in business, institutions, and politics, Zwiers (2014) emphasizes the use of these types of talk moves and formats to help students "see how ideas grow and are built by a group of people," and to challenge them to "think about their own ideas, articulate them, defend them, and modify them in real time" (p. 125).

Vocabulary Development

Although lexical knowledge is only one feature of language, it is one of the more critical features that students of a language must develop. Common sense dictates that the more words ELLs know, the more they can speak and write and understand what they hear and read. One estimate is that ELLs need about 2,000 words to engage in conversations, about 5,000 words to read authentic texts, and over 10,000 words to comprehend complex academic texts (Folse, 2011). To put these numbers into perspective, Biemiller (2010) found that the average English-speaking student enters pre-kindergarten with knowledge of about 3,400 root words, knows about 8,000 word meanings by the end of 2nd grade, and learns about 860 new word meanings each year. By the time they graduate, these students know about 50,000 words (Biemiller, 2011). Thus, ELLs must rapidly develop their English vocabulary knowledge to avoid falling further behind their English-speaking peers. Calderón and Soto (2017) suggest that to catch up, ELLs need to learn between 3,000 and 5,000 words a year.

While developing proficiency in a new language clearly involves increasing vocabulary knowledge, I urge teachers to be cautious and skeptical of the "language gap" or "word gap" research (Hart & Risley, 1995) that has gained much media attention and spawned commercial products and education programs that claim to help "fix" this "gap." This research claims that students from families of low socioeconomic status are exposed to far fewer words than students from families of high socioeconomic status, and that this lower exposure to words leads to low vocabulary knowledge and poor academic achievement. Linguists and other language scholars have pointed to flaws in the conceptualization and methodology of this research, including: its narrow and limited view of language proficiency as vocabulary knowledge; its failure to consider communicative competence and quality of conversations; its failure to account for wide variations in vocabulary knowledge among individuals of high socioeconomic status; its monolingual orientation, which fails to account for lexical knowledge and language skills across a student's entire linguistic repertoire; its failure to account for the rich ways culturally and linguistic diverse students and families communicate and use their languages; and, most important, the way it promotes a deficit view of many culturally and linguistically diverse students and their families. The *Journal of Linguistic Anthropology* published an invited forum edited by Avineri and Johnson (2015) featuring a dozen leading scholars who address these and other critiques of the "language gap" research and its harmful view of students and families.

Educators continue to debate how much vocabulary students can or should be taught directly in a systematic way and how much vocabulary students can acquire naturally or with some guidance within the meaningful contexts of oral interactions and written texts. It is not possible to teach thousands of words directly. Thus, it is imperative for teachers to engage students in the right kinds of oral language activities and to get them engaged in extensive reading, because these are the primary means through which ELLs will naturally acquire the vast number of new vocabulary words in English. The activities outlined in this and subsequent chapters will help facilitate this process.

Some research does suggest, however, that direct, systematic vocabulary instruction leads to higher academic achievement for ELLs (Lara-Alecio et al., 2012; Snow, Lawrence, & White, 2009), and several other researchers in the area of vocabulary development make a strong case for the inclusion of some direct vocabulary instruction. But as Calderon and Soto (2017) point out: "Teaching vocabulary is not an end in itself. It is only a precursor into reading, writing, and conducting rich discussions in every content area" (p. 9).

Vocabulary development should be one of the main components of daily ESL instruction, with further development through sheltered content-area instruction. Vocabulary instruction, however, should not be based on outdated and ineffective methods, such as having students look up and copy dictionary definitions. Rather, as Beck, McKeown, and Kucan (2013) advocate, robust approaches to vocabulary development combine direct explanations of the meanings of words followed by interactive, thought-provoking, and entertaining activities to reinforce these meanings. Similarly, Marzano and Pickering (2005) argue that "teaching specific terms in a specific way is probably the strongest action a teacher can take to ensure that students have the academic background knowledge they need to understand the content they will encounter in school" (p. 1). This statement leaves open the question of which words to directly teach.

Recall Beck et al.'s (2013) framework of three tiers of vocabulary: tier 1—basic words; tier 2—high-utility words that cut across academic content areas, often called *general academic words* or *all-purpose academic words*; and tier 3—content- or domain-specific words. Biemiller (2010) adapted this framework to distinguish tier 1, tier 2, and tier 3 words at the lower primary grades and the upper elementary grades. He bases this distinction on his findings that younger children learn new vocabulary mostly through oral activities, such as teacher read-alouds, whereas older students learn new vocabulary mostly by reading texts on their own. Proponents of direct vocabulary instruction argue that instruction should focus on tier 2 words, because these are the words students will need most to comprehend instruction and texts and to complete academic tasks across content areas. Biemiller (2010) calls these "words worth teaching." Calderón and Soto (2017) suggest that these tiers may vary for ELLs, especially for students at lower levels of English proficiency who may also need direct instruction in tier 1 words. Efforts to create lists of words in each tier have often led to disagreement because categorizing words in this manner is an arbitrary process. Teachers can use existing lists as a guide but should depend on their own judgment to determine which words require direct instruction. Marzano and Pickering (2005) suggest the following six steps for teaching these new vocabulary words to ELLs in a direct-instruction program, which includes requiring students to keep vocabulary notebooks:

1. Provide a description, explanation, or example of the new term (along with non-linguistic representations such as pictures).
2. Ask students to restate the description, explanation, or example in their own words.
3. Ask students to construct a picture, symbol, or graphic representing the term or phrase.
4. Engage students periodically in activities that help them add to their knowledge of the terms in their notebooks.
5. Periodically ask students to discuss the terms with one another.
6. Involve students periodically in games that allow them to play with terms.

Marzano and Pickering note that many of these steps can be facilitated through the use of the students' home languages to maximize their understanding of the new words. Dutro and Kinsela (2010) stress the need for teachers to help ELLs learn to pronounce the new term correctly, provide at least two examples from familiar contexts, and engage students in structured oral or written tasks using the new term. Beck et al. (2013) stress the need for teachers to develop student-friendly explanations of words using everyday language, rather than relying on dictionary definitions. Calderón and Soto (2017) assert that students should practice the new words in five or more sentences with a partner. They also recommend that teachers of older ELLs (grades 2–12) provide dictionary definitions in addition to student-friendly definitions and highlight one trait of each new word (e.g., spelling, cognate, polysemy, grammatical aspect). Biemiller's (2010) suggestions for direct vocabulary instruction also differ for younger and older students but take less time and are carried out mostly within the meaningful context of texts being read to or by students. His suggestions are covered in the next chapter.

Even if teachers do not have a highly structured, systematic, and direct vocabulary instruction program, they can use these same steps during ESL and sheltered content-area instruction to help students learn unknown words within the context of daily classroom interactions and readings. Teachers can watch for and give special attention to the new vocabulary terms their ELLs encounter and need to use. Folse (2006) emphasizes that for students to really learn new vocabulary words, they need multiple encounters with them; thus, as new words are taught, it is important to provide multiple opportunities for students to hear, read, and use these words beyond a single lesson or instructional period. ELLs also need to be taught word-learning strategies so that they can learn new words on their own. Graves (2015) emphasizes the need to foster word consciousness among ELLs across grade levels, which entails creating a word-rich environment in the classroom and developing student interest in learning words and learning about words.

Using Standards to Focus Instruction

We begin this section with a brief review of the Common Core State Standards (CCSS) and the WIDA English language development standards for listening and speaking. Then we examine strategies and activities that focus on listening and on speaking, and those that facilitate meaningful interaction in the classroom. Although our attention in this chapter is on listening and speaking, effective language instruction does not isolate listening, speaking, reading, and writing. Rather, effective content-based language instruction integrates these four domains around content.

Common Core State Standards for Speaking and Listening

The CCSS, which have been adopted by nearly all states in this country, include standards for speaking and listening. The college-and-career-readiness standards in many non–Common Core states are similar to or highly influenced by the CCSS. It is important to note that these speaking and listening standards are geared not to ELLs but to proficient English speakers. This attention to the importance of oral language skills for all students marks a significant shift in English language arts standards, which previously took these skills for granted. The CCSS stress that oral language skills are critical for college and career readiness:

> To build a foundation for college and career readiness, students must have ample opportunities to take part in a variety of rich, structured conversations—as part of a whole class, in small groups, and with a partner. Being productive members of these conversations requires that students contribute accurate, relevant information; respond to and develop what others have said; make comparisons and contrasts; and analyze and synthesize a multitude of ideas in various domains. (ELA Standards, p. 22 © Copyright 2010 National Governors Association Center for Best Practices and Council of Chief State School Officers)

The standards also recognize the role of new technologies, such as digital multimedia texts that often combine words, graphics, hyperlinks, and embedded video and audio, and the need for students to develop the oral skills necessary to communicate effectively through these new technologies.

The CCSS College and Career Readiness Anchor Standards for Speaking and Listening list what students "should understand and be able to do by the end of each grade" in the areas of comprehension and collaboration and the presentation of knowledge and ideas (Box 7.3). These broad standards provide the basis for more specific corresponding listening and speaking standards broken down by grade level. With mainstream teachers in CCSS classrooms now responsible for developing the oral language skills of all their students, ELLs are likely to benefit because teachers will need to have greater awareness of their strengths and weaknesses in listening and speaking in English.

Comprehension and Collaboration

1. Prepare for and participate effectively in a range of conversations and collaborations with diverse partners, building on others' ideas and expressing their own clearly and persuasively.
2. Integrate and evaluate information presented in diverse media and formats, including visually, quantitatively, and orally.
3. Evaluate a speaker's point of view, reasoning, and use of evidence and rhetoric.

Presentation of Knowledge and Ideas

4. Present information, findings, and supporting evidence such that listeners can follow the line of reasoning, and the organization, development, and style are appropriate to task, purpose, and audience.
5. Make strategic use of digital media and visual displays of data to express information and enhance understanding of presentations.
6. Adapt speech to a variety of contexts and communicative tasks, demonstrating command of formal English when indicated or appropriate.

Nonetheless, there is also concern that the listening and speaking demands in the classroom could increase to higher levels that are beyond the reach of many ELLs. The use of English language proficiency (ELP) standards for listening and speaking is needed to prevent this problem by helping teachers differentiate instruction across the content areas for ELLs in ways that are appropriate given an ELL's level of English proficiency. States are expected to have ELP standards that correspond with the CCSS or their own college-and-career-readiness standards. We turn to those next.

English Language Proficiency Standards for Listening and Speaking

Nearly all U.S. states and territories use the ELD standards of the WIDA Consortium (2012a) or the English language proficiency standards shared by members of the English Language Proficiency Assessment of the 21st Century (ELPA21) consortium (CCSSO, 2014). Teachers in states outside of these consortia can still benefit from an understanding of these consortia's standards, in addition to their own state standards. These standards are key to providing differentiated instruction and reasonable expectations for ELLs at different levels of English language proficiency across grade levels and content areas.

The five WIDA ELD standards include (1) communicating for social and instructional purposes, (2) the language of language arts, (3) the language of mathematics, (4) the language of science, and (5) the language of social studies. The four language domains (listening, speaking, reading, and writing) are integrated into four contexts: Interpret, express, co-construct, and adapt expression.

The 10 ELP standards associated with ELPA21 also cut across language and content-area instruction. The first seven standards involve the language needed to engage in specific content-area practices, beginning with a focus on constructing meaning, and then progress to engagement in these practices. These include participating in oral and written exchanges of information, speaking and writing about complex literacy texts and topics, constructing and supporting claims with reasoning and evidence, conducting research and communicating findings, critiquing arguments made by others, and adapting their language choices as appropriate to the task and audience. The last three standards focus on micro-level linguistic features that are important in service of the first seven standards. These include determining the meaning of words and phrases, creating clear and coherent speech and text, and using standard English accurately to communicate in speech and writing.

For nonconsortium states, we consider the examples of California and New York. California has two sets of ELD standards. The first set contains 12 standards that focus on interacting in meaningful ways. They are organized in three clusters: collaborative (engagement in dialogue with others), interpretive (comprehension and analysis of written and spoken texts), and productive (creation of oral presentations and written texts). The second set contains seven standards that focus on learning how English works and are also organized in three clusters: structuring cohesive texts, expanding and enriching ideas, and connecting and condensing ideas. New York's Bilingual Common Core Initiative features New Language Arts Progressions (formerly known as ESL Learning Standards) that are based on the Common Core English language arts and the speaking and listening standards but that focus on the main academic demand of each and Home Language Arts Progressions that align with the language arts standards.

Common to the WIDA, ELPA21, California, and New York English proficiency standards are various forms of **language progressions** across different levels of English proficiency. These progressions outline the expectations for ELLs at each level of English language proficiency in meeting each standard. Based on a "can do" philosophy, these progressions indicate what ELLs *can do* with their developing English language by providing examples of observable language behaviors that ELLs at different levels of proficiency can be expected to demonstrate when completing various classroom tasks. Note that the New York and WIDA progressions outline the types of support or scaffolding students need at each level to meet the expectation. As the level of language proficiency increases, the language demands get higher, and the amount of scaffolding decreases.

Consider the examples in Table 7.1, which are drawn from the WIDA, ELPA21, California, and New York standards and progressions for grade 3 ELLs. Each of these is aligned with CCSS Speaking and Listening Anchor Standard 1, which addresses effective participation in conversations. Each makes clear that ELLs at all levels of English language proficiency are capable of meeting Standard 1 to varying degrees, with appropriate scaffolding and support. To illustrate how these standards and progressions may be put into practice, let's consider an example where student partners are discussing the topic of wedding celebrations across different cultures. Students at Level 1 or 2 can work with their partner to look at photographs of weddings they brought from home and ask each other simple yes-no and wh- questions. This exercise could be further scaffolded by the teacher by providing students with sentence starters (e.g., "*Who is this?*" "This is the bride"; "*What is this?*" "This is her wedding dress."; "*Where did they get married?*" "They got married in Cambodia. The wedding is in the village."). At Level 3, the students could discuss the photographs together in a small group and use a word bank to share information and ask and answer more open-ended questions (e.g., "In Cambodia, weddings are at the bride's house. Where do weddings usually happen in Iraq?"). At Levels 4 and 5, students use the photographs as a support but without the structured models or word banks, because students at these levels are able to construct their own sentences to share information with the whole class. At Level 4, students can engage in sustained dialogue as they ask for and share detailed information about wedding practices (e.g., "In a Cambodian wedding, the groom has to pay for everything. The guests give cash instead of buying wedding gifts."). At Level 5, students can discuss and reflect on the information about wedding practices (e.g., "It is really difficult for Cambodian men to afford the bride price. Sometimes they have to work for several years to save the money needed to get married.").

Using the English language proficiency standards and progressions as a guide, teachers can determine how best to differentiate language and content-area lessons and activities by reflecting on the language functions and supports students at each level of English proficiency would need to accomplish the given tasks. Through this process, teachers establish appropriate expectations for their ELLs at different levels of English. The standards and progressions also provide a guide for determining the type of instruction needed to help ELLs move to the next level of English proficiency.

Promoting Oral Language Development in the Classroom

In this section we discuss classroom activities, strategies, and techniques teachers can use during ESL and sheltered content area instruction to promote students' oral language use and development. Effective teachers use a principled approach to select strategies based on an understanding of language learning. Teachers identify the strengths and needs of ELLs in their classes, with attention to their ELP level, home language literacy, background content-area knowledge, and cultural considerations. They also identify the knowledge and skills students need to participate in and achieve in the activities, lessons, and units that they develop. This information about students and goals enables teachers to select strategies that will enhance the oral language use and development of specific ELLs and differentiate instruction for the range of learners in their classes. The sections that follow offer suggestions for activities that are consistent with the theories and research reviewed above and that successful teachers of ELLs have found to be effective.

Listening

We know from second language learning theory that to learn English, students must receive comprehensible input, and much of that input comes from listening in the context of meaningful interaction. Interactive strategies and activities, such as those described in the following sections, can take place within the students' ZPD, and thus, with proper scaffolding from the teacher or English proficient peers, students can improve their listening skills and reach higher levels of English proficiency.

Total Physical Response
Total physical response (TPR) was developed by Asher (1977, 2009) and is a popular strategy in language learning classrooms throughout the world. Teachers provide a set of commands in the target language to which students respond by taking a specific action. At the initial stages, the teacher models the action as he or she gives the command and thus helps students understand the language in a stress-free manner. For example, a simple TPR lesson for beginning students might entail commands such as, "Stand up," "Sit down," "Pick up your book," "Put the book on the table," and "Put the pencil next to the book." Once students are able to comprehend, they can take the role of the teacher and give the commands and thus develop their speaking ability.

Table 7.1 Progressions in English Language Development and Proficiency Standards for Oral Language (Grade 3)

Level 1 Entering	Level 2 Emerging	Level 3 Developing	Level 4 Expanding	Level 5 Bridging
State reasons for outcomes of experiments on electricity using illustrations or realia and teacher guidance (e.g., "electricity goes"; "electricity stops" when circuit is open or closed).	State reasons for outcomes of experiments on electricity using illustrations or realia, oral sentence starters, and teacher guidance (e.g., "The bulb turned on because . . ."; "The balloons attracted/repelled because . . .").	Explain outcomes of experiments on electricity using illustrations and oral sentence frames.	Explain in detail outcomes of experiments on electricity using illustrations or realia and word/ phrase banks.	Explain in detail outcomes of experiments on electricity using illustrations or realia.

Level 1	Level 2	Level 3	Level 4	Level 5
• Listen to and occasionally participate in short conversations. • Respond to simple yes/no and some wh- questions about familiar topics.	• Participate in short conversations, discussions, and written exchanges. • Take turns. • Respond to simple yes/no and wh- questions about familiar topics.	• Participate in short discussions and written exchanges. • Follow the rules for discussion. • Ask questions to gain information or clarify understanding. • Respond to the comments of others. • Contribute his or her own comments about familiar topics and texts.	• Participate in discussions, conversations, and written exchanges. • Follow the rules for discussion. • Ask and answer questions. • Build on the ideas of others. • Contribute his or her own ideas about a variety of topics and texts.	• Participate in extended discussions, conversations, and written exchanges. • Follow the rules for discussion. • Ask and answer questions. • Build on the ideas of others. • Express his or her own ideas about a variety of topics and texts.

Entering (Beginner)	Emerging (Low Intermediate)	Transitioning (High Intermediate)	Expanding (Advanced)	Commanding (Proficient)
Use pre-taught words and phrases and the previously completed graphic organizers to complete sentence starters that ask questions and link their comments to others' remarks, when following the rules in collaborative conversations in partnership and/or teacher-led small groups.	Use pre-identified words and phrases and the previously completed graphic organizers to complete sentence starters that ask questions and link their comments to others' remarks, when following the rules in collaborative conversations in partnership and/or small groups.	Use a word bank to ask questions and link their comments to others' remarks, when following the rules in collaborative conversations in partnership and/or small groups.	Use the previously completed graphic organizers to ask questions and link their comments to others' remarks, when following the rules in collaborative conversations in partnership and/or small groups.	Use knowledge of the topic, independently, to ask questions and link their comments to others' remarks, when following the rules in collaborative conversations in partnership and/or small groups.

California

Emerging	Expanding	Bridging
Contribute to conversations and express ideas by asking yes-no and wh- questions and responding using short phrases.	Contribute to class, group, and partner discussions, including sustained dialogue, by following turn-taking rules, asking relevant questions, affirming others, and adding relevant information.	Contribute to class, group, and partner discussions, including sustained dialogue, by following turn-taking rules, asking relevant questions, affirming others, adding relevant information, building on responses, and providing useful feedback.

WIDA Consortium, 2012a, p. 67 (courtesy of WIDA Consortium); ELPA 21, Grade 3, Standard 1, p. 70. Retrieved February 2019, from www.elpa21.org/sites/default/files/Final%204_30%20ELPA21%20Standards_1.pdf; EngageNY, 2014, Speaking and Listening (SL), Standard 1, Grade 3, p. 2; California Department of Education, 2014, p. 58.

Many believe TPR is appropriate only for beginning-level ELLs. Asher (1995), however, provides examples of how TPR can be used with intermediate and advanced ELLs to pre-teach new vocabulary words students will encounter in their reading:

> Let's take the vocabulary item "crooked." You can TPR the item with directions in the target language such as, "Luke, make a crooked arm." "Elena, make a straight arm." "Jaime, go to the board and draw a crooked tree." "Maria, run to the board and draw a straight tree." (pp. 2–3)

Today TPR is used by many teachers in its broadest sense to describe any strategy or technique that requires students to physically respond when listening to the target language. Thus, rather than lessons in which teachers merely bark commands at students, students can demonstrate their comprehension by responding with their whole bodies within the context of a variety of academic lessons or tasks. For example:

- Students do a thumbs up or thumbs down to respond to a true-false question related to a unit of study (e.g., "Pigs are reptiles. Thumbs up if this is true; thumbs down if this is false.").
- Students use personal white boards, iPads, or other tablet devices to draw or write a response to an oral question and then hold it up when they are finished (e.g., "Draw and write the name of your favorite snack." "What color is my shirt?" "What is five times eight?" "Draw a cell and label the nucleus.").
- Students point to an illustration or word (or part of a word) in a book that is being read aloud (e.g., "Stacey, show me where the library is in this picture." "Hong, point to the word that means the same as 'hop.'" "Josue, point to the part of the word *unhappy* that means 'not.'").
- Students are called up to the Smart Board or large touchscreen display to manipulate images or text (e.g., "Haiyan, drag the pictures to match them to the correct vocabulary words." "Adegoke, highlight the main idea of this paragraph and underline the supporting details.").
- Students perform a skit or act out a story.

Other language learning activities, strategies, and techniques that could fall under the umbrella of TPR are described elsewhere in this book.

Listening Comprehension Tasks

Listening comprehension tasks require students to listen to a source of spoken language and then complete a task that demonstrates their comprehension. In traditional ESL classrooms, students listen to an audio recording, for example, of a folktale or a conversation between two people and then answer a series of comprehension questions about it. Listening tasks can also focus on particular vocabulary or forms that teachers notice have been problematic for students. Several ESL software programs include listening comprehension exercises and activities. Horwitz (2013) points out, however, that many commercially produced listening materials do not simulate authentic speech, and therefore, may actually be more difficult to understand. She explains:

> Natural listening experiences almost always include a context. People rarely have to understand speech without knowing in advance who is speaking, why the conversation is taking place, and what kind of information is likely to be communi-

cated. Thus, language students are at a distinct disadvantage when their teacher abruptly announces, "I am going to play an audio-file for you" and they have to listen without any background information. (p. 88)

Horwitz notes that in real-life conversations, the speaker conveys the same information in several different ways, creating communicative redundancies. Thus, if listeners did not catch the meaning the first time around, these redundancies can clue them in to what the speaker is talking about.

Videos of authentic speech samples may be a better source for listening comprehension tasks. The video enables students to see the additional visual clues conveying meaning together with the oral language. This combination of seeing and hearing is more authentic, since, other than speaking on the telephone or listening to the radio, most real-life listening tasks are in face-to-face interactions.

For the most authentic speech samples, teachers can also use video clips from popular media, which are now readily available from network TV websites and from social networking video-sharing sites such as YouTube. Popular YouTube stars and channels often produce content that deals with contemporary issues that are culturally relevant and highly entertaining. Teachers need to prescreen any such videos, however, to ensure that the content is appropriate for use with their students. Teachers of older ELLs have found that the high-quality videos of short TED Talks are ideal for creating listening comprehension activities. TED talks are usually interesting and are typically supplemented with multimedia providing additional visual support, and the speakers usually speak very clearly. Audio and video podcasts available from iTunes and other sources also provide an endless supply of authentic high-interest material for listening. Many teachers make use of the podcasts from National Public Radio programs.

Note that these sources can be used to design tasks that address Anchor Standards 2 and 3 of the CCSS for speaking and listening (see Box 7.3). The difficulty of the listening comprehension tasks, however, should be determined by the students' level of English proficiency. For example, for lower-level ELLs, teachers might offer shorter, simpler recordings with speech at a slightly reduced rate than what they provide for advanced ELLs, who should be working with recordings featuring native-speaker interaction. Teachers might ask lower-level ELLs basic questions about recordings that feature interactions between two speakers (e.g., "What are these two friends talking about?"), whereas they might ask advanced ELLs more detailed questions (e.g., "What reasons did Kim give for wanting to join the Marines?"). For longer or more complex tasks, teachers can provide a listening guide, perhaps with places for students to make notes, to support their completion of the task. Teachers can also make use of the wealth of free listening comprehension tasks from Randall's ESL Cyber Listening Lab.

Listening Centers

A listening center is a designated spot in the classroom with a tape, CD, or MP3 player with multiple headphones, where students typically listen to recordings of books and follow along in hard copies. A listening center can also be anywhere in the classroom where a student uses a personal laptop, tablet, or other mobile device. Recordings of children's literature, bestselling novels, and nonfiction books are readily available from publishing companies and school and community libraries. Public libraries throughout the country now make it easy for patrons to check out audio books through the Internet from home. Many language arts curricular programs provide recordings of some of the books in the program. Teachers can make their own audio recordings of books, songs, poems, chants, and articles in newspapers and popular magazines or have strong readers in the class create them for their peers. Teachers can create their own listening comprehension exercises and tasks for students to complete at the centers.

The listening center provides a space in the classroom where students can receive comprehensible input in a low-stress environment. Materials placed in the listening center should reinforce classroom instruction. For example, a teacher might leave a recording of a book or article he or she has read aloud so that students can hear it again. This type of repetition is particularly beneficial for ELLs because they are likely to understand more of the story after each repeated listening.

Many listening centers have replaced old bulky tape recorders and headphones with small, lightweight MP3 players that students can use in class or take home for extra practice. And some teachers have posted audio and video recordings on classroom websites that students and their families can access at home via school provided or personal laptops, tablets, or computers.

A popular and effective resource I used in my classroom was a take-home listening kit. Soon after I began teaching, I realized that few of my ELLs had parents at home who could read aloud to them in English and many parents were also unable to read in their home language. To address this challenge, I took five old tape recorders, long discarded, that I found in a cabinet in our custodian's office and placed each one in a canvas bag along with a picture book and an audio cassette with a recording of the book. Each day, five students would lug the bag home overnight, and with their families listen to the tape and follow along in the book. The next day another five students would check them out. The students loved the kits, which gave them opportunities for listening practice at home with the support of their families. Today, the same activity can easily be done with cheap MP3 players students can fit into their pockets.

Students with computers and Internet access at home can make use of the growing number of digital story books available free online that feature read-alouds of the text. Teachers can also quickly make their own online listening activities for students using free tools that enable teachers (and students) to easily record the audio directly to the web from their computer or mobile device, which is then made instantly available for students on their own mobile devices or computers.

Speaking

According to cognitivist views of second language learning, when students are in situations where they must communicate with others and create comprehensible output, they may become aware of gaps in their developing language and may be pushed to pay more attention to input containing what they need to successfully communicate with others. Sociocultural theories also emphasize the need for students to have opportunities to speak, with scaffolding as needed, in order to learn to speak in a manner that others can understand. The strategies and activities described in the following sections can be used to provide ELLs with opportunities to practice speaking in English within the context of meaningful classroom interactions with their teacher and peers.

Oral Retellings

Oral retellings, commonly used with reading as a comprehension check, are explanations students give in their own words of something they have heard or read. Students might retell a story they read or that was read to them. In a content-area lesson, they might summarize a section of the textbook they read, describe their work on a small group math activity or science experiment, explain a concept the teacher presented orally, or describe an educational video they viewed online. Oral retellings allow teachers to make a quick assessment of an ELL's comprehension and provide opportunities for ELLs to practice using new target words and language structures. Oral retellings can be presented in front of the whole class or in pairs or a small group. The more opportunities the students have to use their new language for the authentic purpose of retelling something they know in a variety of contexts across the curriculum, the more progress they will make in their English language development.

Songs and Chants

Add a rhythm or a tune to a piece of text and it becomes more memorable. Because learning to sing songs in English can be an enjoyable way to learn the language, music is a big part of many classrooms for ELLs of all ages and proficiency levels. Songs can also help students master the proper intonation of words and phrases, and chants (also called jazz chants) or raps can help make learning new vocabulary and language structures easier. YouTube has a plethora of videos of ESL teachers from around the world using songs and chants with their students.[2]

To be most effective, the song should be sung at a moderate pace, and the lyrics should be clearly audible. For added support, the lyrics could be projected on a screen karaoke-style or presented on a poster or student handout; graphics can be used to illustrate key vocabulary. Many ESL curricular programs include recordings of songs with accompanying posters that display the lyrics and include graphics for visual support. Teachers and students can easily create their own posters to go along with popular songs. Adding gestures to the songs provides support for learning new vocabulary. It also allows ELLs at low levels of English proficiency to participate actively before they are ready to sing the words. Singing with gestures is another form of TPR.

Oral Presentations

A simple but effective oral presentation is the traditional show-and-tell. Students show something cool they have brought from home, tell their classmates all about it, and answer questions about it. This activity promotes meaningful interactions. The student showing and telling is highly motivated to speak, and the other students are highly motivated to listen. For ELLs it is also an opportunity to show things from home that can help other students learn about their culture. Although show-and-tell is usually associated with younger students, variations can be used with older ELLs. For example, students could be asked to bring objects and photographs from home to create a personal time capsule and then engage in conversations with their teacher and peers to explain what these items mean to them and why they selected them for the capsule.

Other types of oral presentation provide opportunities for ELLs to use their language skills to complete a project individually or in a small group and then to present their findings or results to the class. The completed projects help support the ELLs' presentations. For example, a poster—whether created on paper or online at sites such as Glogster—will contain images and words students can use to help organize their thoughts and remind them of the needed vocabulary. Students can point to the appropriate parts of the poster as they talk, also facilitating understanding for the ELLs and other students who are listening. PowerPoint, Keynote, Prezi, and other multimedia presentations provide excellent support for ELLs in making oral presentations. VoiceThread makes it easy for students

---

[2] Some educators question the value of using music to learn a new language because singing and speaking use different parts of the brain. This problem can be mitigated, however, by working with the lyrics as a written text before and after singing them.

to create narrated presentations that can be shared and discussed orally online. Note that these types of presentations address Anchor Standards 4, 5, and 6 of the CCSS for speaking and listening (see Box 7.3). Each student's ELP level must be taken into account to ensure that the expectation for the presentation is reasonable. It is important also for teachers to create a supportive environment where students feel safe speaking English in front of the class without fear of being laughed at.

Minimal Pairs

Minimal pairs are words or phrases that differ by only one phoneme, for example, "pen"/"pan," or "he *b*it the boy"/"He *h*it the boy." Working with minimal pairs can help ELLs discriminate between words that initially may sound the same to them. Minimal pairs can also help with pronunciation, particularly when students are having difficulty with phonemes that are not a part of their home language and their errors make it hard for others to understand what they are saying. Jesness (2014) suggests that teachers can make minimal pair practice interactive and meaningful through the use of pictures. For example, a teacher might show a picture of a person making a bed and a person bidding at an auction and ask, "Who is making a bed?" and "Who is making a bid?" or a picture of a child riding a sheep and a sailor on the deck of a ship and ask, "Who is on a sheep?" and "Who is on a ship?" Jesness adds, however, that many students, especially younger students, learn to differentiate English sounds without drills. Drilling these students, then, would be a waste of valuable instruction time. Thus, minimal pair work should be used only on problematic and persistent pronunciation errors, such as those especially those that have the potential to impede meaning in a real conversation.

Strategies for Classroom Interaction

The most important and beneficial listening and speaking that students will do is through interaction with the teacher, their fellow ELLs, and proficient English speakers within the sociocultural contexts of their classroom, school, and neighborhood (Figure 7.1). Interaction is crucial for English language development. The following strategies and activities create opportunities for meaningful interaction in ESL and sheltered content-area instruction contexts as students use their developing oral English skills to accomplish authentic tasks.

Conversational Discourse

Key to meaningful interactions in the classroom that lead to successful English language development are the conversations ELLs engage in with their fellow students and teachers. Zwiers and Soto (2017) define **conversational discourse** as the "use of language for extended, back-and-forth, and purposeful communication" (p. 12) and argues that students need time in class to learn and practice skills for engaging in paired and group conversations to build on each other's ideas and thus construct complex ideas with others. Such conversations, he notes, provide frequent comprehensible input and output, and every turn of the conversation presents a mini-challenge that requires students to pay attention to their partners' words, sentences, and nonverbal cues while determining how to communicate their own ideas in ways that move the conversation forward. Students learn to balance taking control of the conversation at some points with giving up control at other points. This skill involves paying attention to and using paralinguistic cues, such as prosody, gestures, eye contact, intonation, and body language. Students also develop conversation skills, such as clarifying, supporting, and negotiating ideas and evaluating evidence and reasoning. Zwiers suggests that teachers can foster conversational discourse

Figure 7.1 Students' interactions in small groups and with their teacher help further their English language development and strengthen content-area instruction. (Photo by Star Watanaphol.)

and establish a culture of collaborative communication through the use of scaffolds. For example, teachers can create posters or graphic organizers or teach students gestures to represent various conversational skills, such as the productive talk moves described earlier. Teachers can help students learn and practice phrases they can use to start conversations, ask open-ended questions, seek clarification, elicit elaborations and examples, and request evidence that supports their partners' ideas. The following strategies provide opportunities for the development of conversational discourse.

Cooperative Learning

Cooperative learning refers to student collaboration in pairs or in small groups to solve a problem or complete a task or a project. It is most effective when the task is made clear and each student is given a clearly defined role. Although cooperative learning was not created specifically for ELLs, language educators have fully embraced it as an effective strategy for helping ELLs learn both language and academic content. Note that the use of cooperative learning is needed to address Anchor Standard 1 of the CCSS for speaking and listening (see Box 7.3). To be effective, the tasks given must take into account the knowledge and language proficiency of the ELLs. Also, the English proficient students in the group need guidance about how to appropriately interact with and provide scaffolding for their ELL group members

Cooperative learning is a form of scaffolding provided by classroom peers that contributes to the oral language development of ELLs in several ways. The students have to talk and listen to each other to get the job done. ELLs may feel more comfortable (i.e., have a lower affective filter) speaking with their peers in the small group than being called on to speak in front of the whole class. The hands-on learning that is typical of cooperative group work provides context and visual support to make the language used more comprehensible. During the group work, ELLs can practice using key vocabulary and new language structures previously taught in the lesson. For example, if students are working with scales and other materials related to a math unit on weight, they will be able to practice using such new vocabulary words as *scale, weights, pounds, balanced, heavier, lighter, more, less, fewer, weight, ounces, grams, kilograms,* and *pounds* and sentence structures such as, "The _____ is ___ kilograms/pounds heavier than the _____." Finally, cooperative learning makes it possible for ELLs to participate in and complete projects that they might have had difficulty doing on their own.

Cooperative learning also provides a space for students to draw on all of their linguistic resources as they work together to complete specific tasks. Beginning-level ELLs can be placed in groups with classmates at higher levels of English proficiency who speak the same home languages. This grouping makes it possible for the beginning-level ELLs to contribute ideas in their home languages. If groups consist of speakers of the same home language, students can naturally engage in translanguaging as they discuss and work together to fully comprehend and complete the assigned task. This process can be effective, even when the final product or presentation to be shared with the entire class is in English.

Kagan (2009) has outlined structures for organizing cooperative learning groups that can be used for almost any content area at any grade level. I have used many of these structures in my own classrooms, from kindergarten all the way to my courses for graduate students. I describe four of these structures here and explain how they support oral language development.

Think-Pair-Share. The teacher assigns each student a partner and asks a question related to whatever topic the students are studying. Students are given time to think of their answer (and maybe jot down a few notes). Then, at the teacher's signal, they turn and discuss their answers with their partners. The teacher can wander around and eavesdrop on the conversations, providing support as needed. After a few minutes, the teacher may call on pairs of students to report what they talked about. Think-Pair-Share engages students in paired conversations and provides built-in wait time in a low-risk environment. Everyone is talking at once, and the ELLs are talking with only one peer. If their answers are not quite right, their partners may be able to help them clarify misunderstandings. If they are asked to report their answer to the class, they have already had a chance to practice answering with their partners and thus can answer with greater confidence.

Roundtable. The teacher assigns students to small groups of three to six. Each group is given a single sheet of blank paper (or chart paper) and a task that involves brainstorming ideas related to what they are currently learning in class. Each student in the group is given the opportunity to contribute something to the list of ideas, and a recorder writes down the responses on the paper. For example, students might be asked to brainstorm ideas about alternative endings to a story or about why a character acted a particular way. For a simple ESL lesson, lower-level ELLs could be asked to brainstorm a list of items they might find in a kitchen.

Roundtable works well with ELLs because they are working collaboratively with a small group of their peers on a fairly narrow task. They must listen to their peers to make sure they do not repeat something that is already on the list. Their contributions are given equal status by being added to the list along with those of all other group members. Misunderstandings can be clarified by other students in the group. In roundtable, ELLs are likely to pick up new vocabulary and ideas based on the contributions of others in the group.

Concentric Circles. The teacher divides the class into two equal groups. One group makes a circle, with each student facing out. The other group makes a circle around the first circle, with each student paired off with and facing a student in the inner circle. The teacher asks a question or announces a particular topic to discuss or task to complete (e.g., "What is your favorite holiday and why?"). On the teacher's signal, the students in the inner circle give their answers and then the students in the outer circle give theirs. After each student has spoken, the teacher instructs one of the circles to rotate until each student is facing a new partner (e.g., "Outside circle, rotate two students to your left"). The students will then discuss the same question or topic with their new partner. The process repeats until students have rotated to new partners several times.

What makes the use of concentric circles so effective for ELLs is the practice they get listening and speaking in English. In the typical classroom lesson, the teacher talks and calls on one student at a time. Thus, in a 30- to 45-minute lesson, only a small number of students may be given the opportunity to speak, and each student has time to say only a little. With concentric circles, in a fraction of the time, each student can talk about 10 times more. Even better, the repetition of the task with new partners provides beneficial practice—each time the ELL will feel more comfortable and confident, and the conversations will feel more natural. During ESL instruction, concentric circles work particularly well for practicing target language forms over and over in a stress-free situation. It also works well for sheltered-content instruction, such as reviewing material learned and providing repeated opportunities for students to use new vocabulary (e.g., "Tell your partner the three states of matter and give an example of each.").

A variation of concentric circles is shifting lines, which work well in a classroom where it may be difficult to make a circle. The same principle and procedure applies, except students are in two straight lines facing each other. When it is time to change partners, one line shifts to the left, and the student at the front moves to the end of the line.

Numbered Heads Together. Students are assigned to groups of four. Each group is given a number (Group 1, Group 2, . . .) and each student within the group is given a number (Student 1, Student 2, . . .). The teacher asks a question or gives each group a task to complete. When students are finished, the teacher randomly calls out a group number and then a student number (using spinners, dice, slips of paper in a sack, etc.) and asks a question related to the task (e.g., "Group 3, Student 2, What is the third planet from the sun?"). Because any member could be called on to answer the question for the group, each group must make sure that each member is ready to respond. Thus, a great deal of interaction takes place between group members as they prepare. This strategy can be combined with roundtable for groups to report the ideas from their brainstorming. The level of complexity of the tasks and the questions should be based on the proficiency level of the students. In a class with a variety of levels, the teacher can decide the level of difficulty according to which student stands up to answer.

Role Play

Traditional ESL textbooks are full of uninspiring and remarkably unnatural dialogues that are designed to highlight specific language forms for students to learn. Rather than reading these dialogues right out of the book, a better strategy is to put students into role-playing situations where they will need to use the target form. For example, if students are practicing forming and asking questions, they could role play a situation where a student is buying shoes at a shoe store. One could be the salesperson and the other the customer. The customer could make comments and ask questions such as, "I am looking for some running shoes," "Do you have any on sale?" "Do you have size eight?" "These are too tight," and "How much do they cost?" The salesperson would have to respond appropriately. Sometimes the sillier the role plays, the more fun they are and the more likely students are to acquire language subconsciously. Teachers can put different situations on slips of paper and put them in a bag or a hat, and students have to role play whatever they get: "An alien lands in your backyard and wants to know about your planet," or "You are Ellen DeGeneres and you are interviewing Selena Gomez."

Other role plays should try to mirror real-life situations in which the students are likely to find themselves, such as visiting a school counselor, looking for a book at a bookstore, talking to a landlord, or interviewing for a job. For students at Levels 1 and 2, the role plays may need to be kept fairly simple and focus on the use of previously taught vocabulary and language forms (e.g., role play giving directions). The role plays can be more elaborate and open-ended for ELLs at higher levels of English proficiency through information gap activities. Each student could be given a list of information about the person he or she is playing that the other person does not know about. In the bookstore example, the customer might have a list of book topics he or she is interested in, and the bookstore employee has a list of books matching those topics. In sheltered instruction, role plays can be used to practice and understand key concepts along with key vocabulary and new language structures. In math, for example, students could set up a shop and practice making purchases and making change, while in social studies students could role play a political debate between two candidates or participate in a mock trial.

Barrier Games

Students are put into pairs. One student in each pair is the designated artist and is given paper and a pencil. The partner is given a pattern or picture, which he or she places behind some type of barrier where the artist cannot see it. The partner looks at the pattern or picture and then, using English and with hands behind his or her back (to prevent pointing), tells the artist how to draw it. For barrier games to be successful, particularly with ELLs at lower levels of English language proficiency, teachers should pre-teach necessary vocabulary and language structures that can then be practiced through this activity. For more advanced ELLs, the games could involve higher-level content-area vocabulary (e.g., "Draw a cylinder adjacent to a cube in the top right quadrant").

Obstacle Course

In this activity, which is well suited to beginning-level ELLs, the teacher sets up an obstacle course in the classroom or outside on the playground. Students are put into pairs or small groups. One student in each pair or group is blindfolded and must make it through the obstacle course guided only by instructions from his or her partner or teammates, who must speak in English and may not touch the blindfolded student. To be successful, students would need to first learn basic vocabulary and simple phrases related to directions (turn left, go forward, walk backwards, step sideways to the right, stop, etc.).

What Am I?

Students all wear a headband with a card on the front that they cannot see but others can. Alternatively, a card could be taped to each student's back. The card has a picture or the name of some object, animal, or person. Each student has to figure out what is on his or her card by asking questions of other students, such as, "Am I an animal?" "What color am I?" "Do I have wings?" For the game to be successful, the teacher should first make sure the students have learned the vocabulary and language forms necessary to play. For lower-level ELLs, this game could be used to practice basic vocabulary, such as the names of household items, animals, or food. More advanced ELLs can be encouraged to use vocabulary that is associated with a particular unit of content-area study, asking, for example, "Am I surrounded on all sides by water?" ("No.") "Am I surrounded on three sides by water? ("Yes.") "Am I a peninsula?" ("Yes!"). What Am I? is a tried-and-true ESL activity that has been commercialized into the popular game Headbanz.

Acting Out Stories

While oral language development is important for helping students learn to read, reading is also an essential means for developing oral language. Students learn many new words, grammatical forms, and language structures from reading. Acting out stories is a great way for students to internalize new language learned from reading by incorporating it into the oral performance. Student must also communicate with their peers to collaborate in planning, creating props and scenery, and rehearsing for the performance. Acting out stories, however, does not require elaborate costumes, scenery, and props. Beginning-level ELLs can act out simple stories or play the characters with the least amount of dialogue, and more advanced ELLs can act out more elaborate stories or take on the roles with the most dialogue. Alternatively, the students could create and act out a variation or extension of a story. For example, students could act out what would happen if the characters were interacting with each other and the host of a TV talk show as they discuss and debate the central problem of the story.

Class Discussions

With increasing pressure to focus on tested subject areas, teachers often feel there is little time available to simply engage their students in meaningful extended conversations. Nonetheless, class discussions are critically important for ELLs' oral language and academic development. These discussions enable students to demonstrate their knowledge and communicate their thoughts and ideas with their classmates and teachers. Teachers should avoid the traditional but ineffective mode of classroom discussion based on the initiate-response-evaluate (I-R-E) model. Zwiers (2014) calls these "pseudo discussions" because they are teacher centered, they focus on short known-answer questions, they are used to simply transmit knowledge passively, and they do not promote high-level thinking. And they are usually pretty boring. Instead, class discussion should focus on using strategies that cultivate student thinking and provide ample opportunities for students to talk and build off each other's ideas. The teacher facilitates the discussion using the productive talk moves described earlier in this chapter and ensures that the discussion takes place within the students' ZPD, providing scaffolding as necessary.

Class discussion should take place in connection with reading a book together or viewing a video, or as part of a content-area lesson. Within these discussions, students are given opportunities to use key vocabulary and new language structures and forms that help reinforce content-area concepts they have learned. The CCSS place emphasis on the need for students to discuss and answer questions about text read by providing evidence from the text to support their claims. Thus, productive talk moves are key to eliciting such evidence: "How do you know that?" "Where in the text does it say that?" "What evidence from the text can you use to support your argument?" "Show us where in the book the author talks about that." "Rosa, can you give an example from the book that supports what Hyun-Jin is saying?"

Even outside of formal learning tasks, it is important for the class to engage in meaningful discussions about things of interest or concern to the students, many of which are not covered in the official curriculum. I recall having excellent discussions with my students about gangs and crime in their neighborhood that grew out of questions they asked. My primary purpose in having these discussions with my students was not to develop their oral language. But the students were deeply engaged in the discussion, probably much more so than in the more "academically" oriented discussions we had had. Even my squirmy students sat still, listened attentively, and participated in the discussion. The topic was of great relevance to them, and they were learning to see things in whole new ways. Much new language is acquired subconsciously through meaningful interaction; thus, class discussions such as these play a key role in students' oral language development.

Technology for Speaking Practice

Several ESL software programs include opportunities for students to practice speaking. Many programs will record students' voices for them or their teacher to review, and some even produce fancy spectrographs mapping the sound waves of students' speech and comparing them to those of "native" speakers. The use of such software is limited. Students do not need English to talk at computers. The better usages of technology are those that allow ELLs to talk for authentic communication purposes. For example, students can produce podcasts, videos, VoiceThreads, or other narrated presentations online related to things they are learning in class. Knowing their work will be posted online can give students a sense of audience that motivates them to do their best. Voice-over Internet Protocol (VOIP) applications such as Skype, Google Hangouts, and other voice and video chatting programs enable ELLs and proficient English speakers to have meaningful interactions beyond their own classroom. Recordings of these interactions can be reviewed by the teacher and used as formative assessments to drive future instruction tailored to students' strengths and needs. Teachers, however, must carefully structure and monitor these types of activities and lay specific ground rules to ensure that such interactions are safe and appropriate.

Assessing Listening and Speaking

The only way to effectively assess ELLs' oral English proficiency is to talk with them and listen to them talk. The strategies, techniques, and activities described in this chapter provide avenues for observing students' oral language use. In addition, teachers should become skilled at eavesdropping, listening to the students when they are not necessarily engaged in structured academic tasks—when they are coming into the classroom, when they are lined up to go to lunch, when they are eating lunch, when they are out on the playground or in the halls, when they chat with their friends before an assembly starts. Teachers should also engage in conversations with their students in these less structured situations.

In Texas, teachers of ELLs are trained to observe their students' English language use in the classroom in order to make holistic assessments of the students' proficiency. Table 7.2 provides a partial list of activities during which teachers can assess students' listening and speaking ability.

Any time students are listening and speaking, teachers have an opportunity for assessment. But teachers will likely also need to sit down one-on-one with each student and give him or her a task that requires oral language use. One easy and commonly used technique is to show the student an illustration of a scene depicting a lot of activity, such as at a park or a grocery store, and ask the student, for example, "What do you do see?" or "What is going on in this picture?" If the student just points to and names objects, the teacher should use more specific and open-ended prompts, for example, "Why do you think these two children are running to the playground?" or "What do think will happen here?"

Another easy way to elicit oral language in a one-on-one situation is to read a book together and have the student retell the story. Wordless picture books also provide excel-

Table 7.2 Activities for Assessing English Language Learners' Oral Language Proficiency

Listening	Listening and Speaking	Speaking
• Reacting to oral presentations • Responding to text read-aloud • Following directions	• Cooperative group work • Informal, social discourse with peers • Large-group and small-group interactions in academic settings • One-on-one interviews • Individual student conferences	• Oral presentations • Classroom discussions • Articulation of problem-solving strategies

Texas Education Agency, Student Assessment Division, 2005; *Texas Observation Protocols: Training on the Proficiency Level Descriptors* [PowerPoint presentation] (Austin: Texas Education Agency). Copyright © by the Texas Education Agency. All rights reserved.

lent stimuli for students to talk as they use the illustrations to tell a story. Also important is to just chat with students. Ask them about their favorite TV show or YouTube channel, or the music they like to listen to. Ask them what they like to do after school. When students talk about their interests, teachers will likely get a good sample of their oral language ability in English.

Teacher observations can be guided by rubrics. It is tempting to focus on just one aspect of a student's speech, but rubrics make it easy to keep track of the many aspects of oral language. One commonly used rubric is the Student Oral Language Observation Matrix (SOLOM) developed in the 1980s by bilingual educators in California. The revised version of the matrix, **SOLOM-R** (Table 7.3), emphasizes what ELLs can do at each level of proficiency and brings it up-to-date with current research on oral language development. The SOLOM-R helps the teacher focus on five different aspects of a student's oral language proficiency:

1. *Comprehension:* How much does the student understand when he or she is spoken too? How well does he or she follow classroom discussions?
2. *Fluency:* How well is the student able to express his or her ideas? Does the student's speech flow well or are there occasional or frequent pauses leading to halting speech?
3. *Vocabulary:* Does the student have adequate vocabulary to fully describe what he or she is thinking? Does he or she ever use the wrong words?
4. *Pronunciation:* Are others able to understand what the student is saying? Do accent or intonation patterns sometimes lead to miscommunication?
5. *Grammar:* How well is the student able to use correct grammar? Do grammar errors obscure the meaning he or she is trying to convey?

For each of these five areas, students are given a score of 1 to 5, with 1 the lowest and 5 the highest. A student who receives all 1s (total score = 5) would be at the beginning level, and a student with all 5s (total score = 25) would be considered a proficient English speaker. The SOLOM-R provides a description of each level. When assessing a student with the SOLOM-R, the teacher scores each aspect and adds them together to determine the student's overall oral language proficiency.

Now, let's practice using the SOLOM-R to assess a student's oral language proficiency. The following transcript is from an oral presentation by a high school student from Mexico named Bernardo who is describing a bilingual children's picture book he made with his classmate Jesús, using Storybird, a free online program for creating and sharing visual stories. A video of his presentation is available on the companion website. As you watch the video and read the transcript, score his performance with the SOLOM-R.

Table 7.3 Student Oral Language Observation Matrix–Revised (SOLOM-R)

Based on your observation of the student, circle the block in each category that best describes the student's abilities. Add the scores to determine the student's level.

	1	2	3	4	5
Comprehension	Can understand simple words and phrases when spoken slowly accompanied with visual support or gestures.	Can comprehend simple speech when spoken slowly and with frequent repetitions.	Can understand most of what is said at slower-than-normal speed with repetitions.	Can understand nearly everything at normal speed, although occasional repetition may be necessary.	Can understand even rapid speech similar to other proficient speakers.
Fluency	Can produce simple words and phrases to convey meaning, but halting, fragmentary speech can make conversation difficult.	Can express self in simple interactions, but usually hesitant and often forced into silence by language limitations.	Can express self, but with frequent pauses to search for the correct manner of expression.	Can express self with general fluency, with occasional pauses to search for the correct manner of expression.	Can express self fluently and effortlessly similar to other proficient speakers.
Vocabulary	Can use a few words and phrases, but vocabulary knowledge not yet sufficient to express self beyond very basic messages.	Can use small but growing vocabulary, but large gaps in vocabulary knowledge and frequent misuse of words make it quite difficult to express intended meanings.	Can use increasing range of vocabulary, but gaps in vocabulary knowledge and frequent misuse of words make it somewhat difficult to express intended meanings.	Can use extensive vocabulary, but gaps in less familiar domains and occasional misuse of words may require need to rephrase to fully express intended meanings.	Can use extensive vocabulary and idioms similar to other proficient speakers.
Pronunciation	Can say a few words and phrases, but severe pronunciation challenges make speech very difficult for others to understand.	Can express self, but pronunciation challenges necessitate strong concentration on the part of the listeners and frequently lead to misunderstandings.	Can express self, but pronunciation challenges necessitate some concentration on the part of the listeners and occasionally lead to misunderstandings.	Can express self with good pronunciation that seldom leads to misunderstandings, though listeners may detect a nonstandard accent and occasional intonation pattern differences.	Can express self with pronunciation and intonation similar to other proficient speakers.
Grammar	Can say a few words and phrases, but errors in grammar and word order make speech very difficult for others to understand.	Can express self using simple patterns, but frequent errors in grammar and word order in longer utterances frequently obscure intended meanings.	Can express self using longer utterances, though errors of grammar and word order may occasionally obscure intended meanings.	Can express self with only occasional grammatical and/or word-order errors that do not obscure intended meanings.	Can express self with grammatical usage and word order similar to other proficient speakers.

SOLOM-R levels: 1, score 5–11, beginning; 2, score 12–18, intermediate; 3, score 19–24, advanced; 4, score 25, proficient.

Modified by the author from the original SOLOM form (SOLOM, n.d.).

Bernardo's Oral Presentation

> Hi, my name is Bernardo. I make the same book of my, of my friend, Jesús. Uh, it's about one guy who, they could be a superhero. Uh, we made this project for the kids. Uh, it was difficult to find the pictures, to help to write the story. Um, what else? It's uh, it's about one guy to find the witch. And he take to her, to his cousin, and him, to the witch house. And the witch want to, to kill the, the kids. Um, what else? And he trying to, to, to destroy her. Uh, he turn to superhero and he destroyed the monsters, the, destroy the witch. Um, what else? And he fly to his house, to the tía house. And that's it.

After his summary, his teacher and I asked Bernardo some simple questions. In general, he was able to understand the questions, but he had to pause and think before answering in English. His friend Jesús helped him answer some of the questions. When his teacher asked him, "What was most fun about the whole project?" Bernardo responded:

> Like how to make the story. And how to put the pictures. And that was funny because we put some, some, um some words funny like, [pauses, looks around], yeah.

Here is how I scored Bernardo's oral performance. For *comprehension,* I gave him a 3. He was able to understand our questions, which were kept simple and spoken at a slower but natural speed. For *fluency,* I gave him a 3. Although his words flow at a good rate, there are several spots where the flow is interrupted when he struggles a little figuring out what to say next. For *vocabulary,* I gave him a 3. He appears to have adequate vocabulary to describe the story in simple terms, but his description lacks detail. There are spots where he has trouble finding the words to express what he wants to say and has to rephrase his ideas. For example, he has difficulty explaining about the witch kidnapping the cousin and can't find the right words to describe the lightning bolt on the superhero's suit. He also couldn't describe or give examples of the funny words they used in the story. Although his use of "tía" instead of "aunt" could indicate a gap in English vocabulary, even in the English text of their bilingual book, Bernardo and Jesus used "Tía" as the proper noun for the aunt character. For *pronunciation,* I gave Bernardo a 3. I found that I had to concentrate a little to understand what he was saying. Occasional challenges such as pronouncing the word "project" could lead to misunderstanding. I also gave Bernardo a 3 for *grammar.* His errors are frequent, but for the most part they do not obscure the meaning. His story is easy to follow, except for the part about the witch kidnapping the cousin.

According to my ratings, Bernardo's total score is 15, placing him in Level II, Intermediate. How did my scores compare with yours? Perhaps you were harsher on Bernardo than I was and may have given him a 2 in some areas where I gave him a 3. This does not mean you are wrong. Perhaps I am too easy on him. In cases where two raters disagree by 1 point, just award the number in between. Thus, in Bernardo's case, we would give him a score of 2.5.

The exact scores are not as important as how teachers use this information. The evaluation form that appears in Figure 7.2 can be used along with the SOLOM-R. The most important part is the three questions. For question 1, *What are this student's strengths?,* I would say Bernardo has several strengths. His vocabulary is pretty good. He is able to describe nearly everything he wants. His rate of speech shows he is comfortable speaking the language and does not struggle to find each word he wants to say. His pronunciation is good enough that English speakers can understand him if they concentrate a little. And his grammar is sufficiently developed to make his speech comprehensible.

For question 2, *In what areas is this student in need of improvement?,* I would say Bernardo's pronunciation needs to become a little clearer so that it is easier for others to

Student name _____

Grade level _____

Scores

Comprehension _____

Fluency _____

Vocabulary _____

Pronunciation _____

Grammar _____

Total SOLOM-R Score _____   **Proficiency level** _____

1. What are this student's strengths?

2. In what areas is this student in need of improvement?

3. What oral language development strategies, techniques, and activities would be beneficial for this student?

Figure 7.2 Evaluation of the SOLOM-R Oral Language Assessment.

understand him. He needs to improve his grammar so that errors do not prevent listeners from understanding his intended meaning. Because his vocabulary is still limited, he had challenges with fluency, causing his speech at times to be halted.

For question 3, *What oral language development strategies, techniques, and activities would be beneficial for this student?*, I know Bernardo's teacher planned to continue providing him with lots of opportunities in class to use his oral language in authentic ways. For example, Bernardo and his classmates took their completed books to read and share with children at a nearby elementary school. I would not give Bernardo direct pronunciation drills, but I would expose him to more models of fluent English through audio recordings and videos. For grammar, I might focus on practicing the use of past tense. In his presentation, Bernardo was able to use the past tense appropriately in one sentence. This response suggests to me that he is ready to learn more and practice using the past tense more consistently. I also think Bernardo is ready for vocabulary lessons focusing on words to retell narratives (e.g., first, next, and then, after, finally) that he could have used to better describe the sequence of events in his story. What other activities or lessons do you believe would be beneficial to Bernardo? For additional practice with the SOLOM-R, use it to score the video of Jesús's presentation of the same book. A video of Bernardo and Jesús reading their bilingual children's book, *Bruce's Great Adventure,* may be viewed on the companion website. The ELL Language Portraits site provides additional opportunities for SOLOM-R practice.

The oral language progressions from WIDA, ELPA21 and individual state English language proficiency standards can also be used as a rubric for assessing students' oral language development (see Table 7.1). The level of difficulty and the extent to which students needed some form of support to accomplish a particular listening or speaking task can help teachers identify the level at which the student performed. Teachers can also create their own performance indicators for particular academic tasks and their own rubrics tailored to special oral language tasks.

Oral language assessments provide important information about where students are in their oral language development, and, more important, they can be used as formative assessments to help the teacher determine what to do next to help the student continue to make improvements in his or her listening and speaking ability.

Summary

The reviews of the scientific literature by CREDE, NLP, and the National Academies found that typically it takes several years for ELLs to attain English proficiency and that oral language proficiency is essential for reading comprehension; thus, there is a strong need for ongoing ESL instruction focused on oral language development, along with language objectives in content-area lessons. Strategic use of students' home languages can help students develop oral English. Oral language proficiency tests, however, mostly fail to capture the true abilities of ELLs, highlighting the need for ongoing authentic formative assessments. ELLs can learn word-level skills (spelling and decoding) without any comprehension of the words; thus, literacy instruction must include focus on text-level skills, such as comprehension, and must be combined with substantial oral language development instruction. Effective teachers respect the silent period, allow for wait time, adjust their speech to make it comprehensible, maximize opportunities for students to interact, and know when and how to correct student speech errors. The CCSS include standards for speaking and listening for all students. English language proficiency standards and progressions from WIDA, ELPA21, and individual states can be used as formative assessments and can help teachers plan appropriate language and content-area instruction for ELLs. All teachers can create opportunities for students to use their developing English oral language skills in the classroom through meaningful practice and authentic interactions by using vocabulary development strategies, TPR, listening centers, listening comprehension tasks, minimal pair practice, cooperative learning structures, oral presentations, songs and chants, interactive games, acting out stories, role playing, and class discussions facilitated with productive talk moves. Teachers can effectively assess their students' oral language skills simply by talking with them and listening to them talk, and by using rubrics such as the SOLOM-R that draw attention to different aspects of oral language performance.

Discussion Questions

1. If you have learned (or tried to learn) a new language, what struggles did you have with oral language development? What did you find helpful in improving your listening and speaking abilities?

2. Why is oral language development so important for ELLs? How is oral language related to literacy? What happens to ELLs in classrooms that neglect oral language development and focus on teaching word-level decoding skills?

3. Which activities described in this chapter have you observed or used in the classroom? How effective were they? What ideas did you gain from this chapter that you would like to implement in your current or future classroom?

4. Watch the video of two young ELLs engaged in an activity called Chat Show. How does this activity help the students develop their listening and speaking skills? What oral language development strategies and techniques would help students prepare for this activity?

5. Review the Sheltered Instruction Observation Protocol (SIOP) lesson plan titled "Nocturnal vs. Diurnal Animals" provided by the Center for Applied Linguistics. What oral language development strategies, techniques, and activities are integrated into this lesson?

Research Activities

1. *ELL Student Assessment* Using the SOLOM-R, assess the oral language proficiency of an ELL. Use the SOLOM-R evaluation form to identify the student's strengths and areas in need of improvement. Describe appropriate strategies, activities, and techniques from this chapter and other resources that you feel would be effective for improving the student's oral language proficiency. Discuss the findings with the student's teacher, or, if you are a teacher, implement them in your classroom.

2. *ELL Teacher Interview* Interview an ELL teacher about the difficulties faced in helping ELLs develop their oral proficiency skills in English. Ask for a description of particular problems the students encountered with idioms or cultural references that left them confused. What strategies and activities did the teacher find most helpful in improving the students' listening and speaking skills in English?

3. *ELL Classroom Observation* Observe an ELL classroom to determine what strategies, if any, the teacher used to develop students' listening and speaking skills. Keep track of how much time the teacher spends talking and how much time is available for the students to talk. Determine whether there is an appropriate balance between the two, or whether changes are needed to allow more time for ELLs to talk and to make better use of oral language development instructional strategies.

4. *Online Research Activity* Using the ELL Language Portraits site, review and compare the oral language sample videos for two or more students. Assess these students' oral language proficiency using the SOLOM-R embedded in the site. Compare your scores and comments about the students' strengths and areas in need of improvement with the completed forms provided on the site. Describe and discuss any differences.

Recommended Reading

Calderón, M., & Soto, I. (2017). *Vocabulary in context*. Thousand Oaks, CA: Corwin.

Grounded in Calderon's extensive research on vocabulary instruction and development with ELLs, this practical book provides teachers with step-by-step processes for providing vocabulary instruction for ELLs in elementary and secondary schools and during both ELD and content-area instruction.

Newton, J. M., Ferris, D. R., Goh, C. C. M., Grabe, W., Stoller, F. L., & Vanderbilt, L. (2018). *Teaching English to second language learners in academic contexts*. New York: Routledge.

Several leading scholars of second language teaching and learning collaborate to bring teachers a jargon-free practical and principle-based guide to providing effective language instruction. Includes several chapters focused on listening and speaking.

Zwiers, J. & Soto, I. (2017). *Conversational discourse in context*. Thousand Oaks, CA: Corwin.

This helpful book provides teachers with research-based strategies and scaffolds for engaging ELLs in meaningful and extended conversations to develop their oral language and conversational discourse skills. Offers many excellent examples from across grade levels and content areas.

Eight

Reading

The only way to help students improve their reading is to read with them and talk to them about their reading.

—Juli Kendall

KEY TERMS

- balanced approach
- before, during, after
- close reading
- complex texts
- concepts of print
- guided reading
- independent reading
- language experience approach
- narrow reading
- phonics
- read-alouds
- Reader's Workshop
- reading self-assessments
- running record
- shared reading
- text complexity
- word study

GUIDING QUESTIONS

1. What is a balanced approach to literacy instruction?
2. How does reading promote English language development?
3. What does the research tell us about effective reading instruction for ELLs?
4. How can state college-and-career-readiness content standards and English language development standards from WIDA, ELPA21, and individual states guide reading instruction for ELLs?
5. How can an understanding of ELLs' reading strengths and needs inform a teacher's choices of instructional approaches, methods, and strategies?
6. How can teachers assess reading and use assessment results to guide instruction?

Reading is one of the most important skills students learn at school. ELLs face the tremendous challenge of learning to read in a language they are not yet proficient in. They are also expected to learn academic content through reading. Thus, all teachers share in the responsibility of helping ELLs develop proficiency in reading. The National Literacy Panel (NLP) report *Developing Literacy in Second-Language Learners* (August & Shanahan, 2006b) declares:

> Language-minority students who cannot read and write proficiently in English cannot participate fully in American schools, workplaces, or society. They face limited job opportunities and earning power. Nor are the consequences of low literacy attainment in English limited to individual impoverishment. U.S. economic competitiveness depends on workforce quality. Inadequate reading and writing proficiency in English relegates rapidly increasing language-minority populations to the sidelines, limiting the nation's potential for economic competitiveness, innovation, productivity growth, and quality of life. (pp. 1–2)

Everyone agrees that reading is crucial, yet it is one of the most contested areas of the school curriculum.

Literacy instruction for ELLs, like language instruction, is highly controversial and political. We contextualize this chapter within the debates over reading instruction and the need for a balanced approach to literacy instruction for ELLs. This chapter shows teachers how to draw on research, theory, policy, and practice about language to guide their decisions about teaching ELLs to read for enjoyment and academic purposes at school.

Balanced Approach to Literacy Instruction

Since the 1980s the "reading wars" have raged between those favoring a holistic, top-down approach to teaching reading and those favoring a bottom-up, skills-based approach (see, e.g., Wexler, 2018). Those who take a holistic approach recognize that reading is highly complex and multifaceted, and thus they favor instructional programs that begin by immersing students in authentic texts that become familiar, meaningful contexts to support direct reading instruction. Those who take a skills-based approach argue that students must first learn sounds and letters and use them to decode words and then sentences before they can go on to read the extended text of paragraphs and books. Skills-based approaches received support throughout the early 2000s under the No Child Left Behind Reading First grants. Scandal ensued, however, when it was discovered that grant reviewers were personally profiting by directing districts to purchase skills-based programs to which the reviewers had commercial ties. Later, an internal U.S. Department of Education impact study found that Reading First schools failed to show improvement in students' reading comprehension test scores (Institute of Education Sciences, 2008). Yet many schools continue to use these same or similar skills-based programs, which often feature the use of narrow scripts teachers are expected follow with exactness to teach phonemic awareness, phonics, and other discrete reading skills. Such instruction is often problematic for ELLs and other students (Box 8.1).

A **balanced approach** to literacy recognizes the need for some direct instruction in reading skills but emphasizes the importance of providing such instruction in meaningful contexts to ensure that students are able to comprehend and use what they read for authentic purposes. This emphasis on meaning and comprehension makes balanced literacy approaches particularly important for ELLs. A balanced approach recognizes that phonics is just one component of learning to read and that teachers—not scripted curriculum programs—should determine which students need direct instruction on specific phonics skills.

Phonics instruction may need to focus only on the alphabet and sound-spelling correspondences that help facilitate making meaning from text. Students acquire phonics rules subconsciously the more they read and put to use the sequence of letters from known words to figure out new words (Smith, 2006, 2012). Furthermore, phonics must be taught within a meaningful context created by reading accessible books, songs, poems, and chants. Once students are familiar with a text, it can be used for instruction in phonics and other reading skills. Most skills can be taught as mini-lessons—brief but explicit—and should focus only on those letter-sound relationships or other skills that students do not pick up on their own. A balanced literacy approach also includes using the home language to support reading instruction, learning, and assessment in English and the home language.

How Reading Promotes English Language Development

Reading is an excellent source of comprehensible input that enhances English language development. Unlike oral English, to which some ELLs may have limited access, students

Box 8.1 Phonemic Awareness and Phonics Instruction for English Language Learners

Skills-based advocates favor scripted programs that begin with phonemic awareness and phonics drills, and reading materials controlled for students to practice recently learned phonics rules.

Arguments for the Use of Scripted Phonemic Awareness and Phonics Programs

- Students need to be able to hear and distinguish between phonemes before they can learn to read (e.g., between the /t/ and /n/ that distinguish the words *cat* and *can*). Daily phonemic awareness training includes rhyming, initial sound recognition, blending, segmentation, and substitution drills.
- As students become "phonemically aware," they receive phonics instruction to learn how to match phonemes to graphemes (letters) in order to decode (sound out) words. Students are drilled on letter-sound relationships, reading texts with a limited set of words exemplifying new and previously learned letter-sound relationships.

Criticisms of Scripted Phonemic Awareness Training for English Language Learners

- ELLs may not get much out of the drills because they are manipulating the sounds of words they don't know.
- Drills using phonemes that do not exist in their home language leads to frustration.
- Instructional time would be much better spent on more meaningful literacy activities.

Criticisms of Scripted Phonics Programs for All Students

- There are too many phonics rules and too many exceptions to the rules.
- Phonics instruction isolated from authentic texts is not beneficial.
- Lessons are a waste of time for students who have already acquired the target letter sounds naturally.
- Lessons are a waste of time for students who may need to learn more basic letter-sound relationships.
- Lessons are too long and reduce time for activities that lead to more natural acquisition of the target letter-sounds.
- Texts for phonics decoding practice are too contrived and lack the appeal of real children's books that motivate reading.
- Instruction time is better spent teaching phonics and other reading skills within the context of authentic literature.

Criticisms of Using Scripted Phonics Programs with English Language Learners

- Programs take a one-size-fits-all approach to literacy instruction.
- Programs were not developed for ELLs and thus fail to address their unique linguistic and academic needs.
- Programs often force ELLs to decode words they don't yet know the meaning of.
- Students who use these programs often emerge able to decode (word-level skills) but unable to comprehend what they read (text-level skills).
- Use of these programs takes time away from the type of ESL and literacy instruction ELLs need to develop literacy skills in English.

have a virtually unlimited number of opportunities to encounter written English through books, magazines, newspapers, the Internet, and other written sources. Furthermore, ELLs have much greater control over what they read than over what they hear. They can choose the topic and the level of difficulty of the text they read. If they do not understand something, they can go back and read it again. They can take time to figure out the meaning of new words and structures by looking up words in a dictionary, asking a teacher or friend, or figuring out the meaning from the context. Also, they will encounter words, phrases, and structures that are unlikely to occur in spoken English. Correlation studies show that students who read more are faster and better readers, as well as better writers, and also that students who read more have more practical knowledge (Krashen, 2004b).

My own research with refugee ELLs from Southeast Asia, most of whom were students with limited or interrupted formal education, supports these findings (Wright, 2004a). One former ELL I interviewed, Chanty, never attended any school until she arrived in the United States and entered 2nd grade. She was in an ESL program for the first 8 years of her schooling, and much of her ESL instruction focused on grammar, drills, and worksheets. She complained:

> The grammar stuff, it confuses me more. It didn't help me at all. The only time I started to realize what works and what doesn't was in high school, when I started to be interested in books. During the summer, all I did was read books. I read almost half the books in the library. I realized that you have to read so many books to understand how grammar is used . . . . because after reading, you know how to use it, and you just remember it. (p. 11)

Chanty went on to earn a graduate degree in business and is now a successful businesswoman and realtor.

I also found that the some of the refugee ELLs in my study had at least a couple of years of education before the war or received some schooling in the refugee camps. These ELLs could read in their home language and learned to read in English much faster than those who could not. They were also reclassified as proficient English speakers more quickly. This important finding highlights the advantages of home language literacy in developing literacy in English. Those advantages are discussed in the following sections.

What We Know from Research about Reading Instruction for English Language Learners

Recall that the three extensive reviews of the scientific literature on language and literacy instruction for ELLs that have been conducted since 2006: the NLP report (August & Shanahan, 2006a, 2006b; August et al., 2014), the Center for Research on Education, Diversity, and Excellence (CREDE) report (Genesee, Lindholm-Leary, Saunders, & Christian, 2005, 2006), and the National Academies of Sciences, Engineering, and Medicine report (2017). These reports include the following findings related to reading development and instruction:

Literacy instruction approaches for mainstream students are not sufficient for ELLs.

The CREDE report found that despite similarities in English literacy development for proficient speakers and for ELLs, the process for ELLs is more complicated. The National Academies report calls for instruction focused explicitly on developing key aspects of literacy, including comprehension strategy. The NLP report declares that for ELLs to receive the maximum benefit from instruction in phonemic awareness, phonics, fluency, vocabulary, and text comprehension, the instruction should be adapted to their unique needs. The NLP report adds that for ELLs to read and write proficiently in English, instruction in these areas is necessary but not sufficient.

English oral language development is critical for English literacy development beyond word-level skills.

Recall the important distinction the NLP report makes between word-level (i.e., decoding) skills and text-level (i.e., reading comprehension) skills. The CREDE report notes that whereas phonological awareness skills in English are directly related to word-level skills, they are not directly related to reading comprehension. The NLP found that whereas word-level skills in literacy are often taught well enough to allow language minority students to attain levels of performance equal to those of proficient English speakers, text-level skills are not, and therefore language minority students rarely approach the same levels of proficiency in text-level skills achieved by proficient English speakers. ELLs often learn how to decode words but have trouble comprehending what they read because of the lack of attention to their oral English language development. All three reports conclude that students with well-developed oral skills in English achieve greater success in English reading than students with less-developed skills.

Literacy instruction must be combined with high-quality ESL instruction.

The NLP report found that teaching reading skills alone to ELLs is not enough. For ELLs to develop strong English literacy skills, high-quality literacy instruction must be combined with early, ongoing, and extensive oral English development. The National Academies found that the failure of elementary schools to provide instruction that appropriately addresses the linguistic, cultural, socioemotional, and academic needs of ELLs leads to their lack of progress. This lack results in their remaining classified as ELLs as they move on to middle school and high school and can in turn lead to their disengagement.

Oral proficiency and literacy in the first language is an advantage for literacy development in English.

This finding has major implications for bilingual programs and challenges those who claim English-only instruction is superior. According to the NLP report, effective instructional programs provide opportunities for students to develop proficiency in their home language. The review of research revealed that at both the elementary and secondary levels, students instructed in their home language as well as in English performed better, on average, than students instructed only in English on measures of English reading proficiency. Similarly, the CREDE report and the National Academies report found that home language and literacy skills can be transferred to support English literacy development. The National Academies also declares that strong home language and literacy skills supports the development of English language and literacy skills. August (2012), the principal investigator for the NLP report, has outlined what we know from research about transfer between the first and second language (Box 8.2). Goldenberg (2013), in his review of these and more recent rigorous quantitative studies, offers strong evidence that reading instruction in the home language can help ELLs boost their reading skills in English. He also emphasizes that biliteracy achievement itself is a worthy educational goal and an important outcome of bilingual programs.

Individual differences contribute significantly to English literacy development.

No two ELLs are alike, and the NLP and National Academies found that individual differences, such as general language proficiency, age, English oral proficiency, cognitive

Box 8.2 Transfer between the First and Second Language

- Word recognition skills acquired in a first language transfer to the second language.
- There is positive transfer of vocabulary knowledge for words that are cognates.
- Children use spelling knowledge in the first language when they spell in their second language, and errors associated with first language spelling disappear as students become more proficient in their second language.
- There is evidence of cross-language transfer of reading comprehension in bilinguals of all ages, even when the languages have different types of alphabets.
- For comprehension, there is also transfer from students' second language to their first; bilingual students who read strategically in one language also read strategically in their other language. Moreover, the more students use strategies in reading, the higher their reading performance.
- For writing, the studies suggest there are cross-language relationships for writing, but levels of first language and second language proficiency may mediate these relationships.

August, 2012, pp. 56–57.

abilities, previous learning, and the similarities and differences between the home language and English will have an impact on each student's literacy development. This finding underlines the importance of the point made earlier that teachers must know each of their students individually so they can adequately address their unique linguistic and academic needs during literacy instruction.

Most literacy assessments do a poor job of gauging ELL strengths and weaknesses.

The NLP calls into question claims that tests of letter naming and phonological awareness in English are good predictors of English reading performance. The NLP found that in studies related to these tests, researchers did not control for such critical factors as English oral proficiency and home language literacy. Noting that more research is needed, the panel found some limited evidence of the effectiveness of teacher judgment guided by thoughtful reflection on specific criteria to make program placement decisions or select students in need of intensive reading instruction.

Home language experiences can have a positive impact on literacy achievement.

The National Academies found no evidence to indicate that use of two languages in the home—or the use of one language at home and another in school—leads to confusion or puts the development of English at risk. Rather, they found that young students have the capacity to develop high levels of competence in both languages. The NLP found some evidence that students perform better when they read or use material in the language they know best. The NLP also found that reading materials reflective of the students' cultures appears to facilitate comprehension. This evidence provides further support for bilingual approaches that build on the linguistic and cultural funds of knowledge that students bring to school from their homes, and it provides support for the use of multicultural literature. The NLP and National Academies also found research evidence that the parents of ELLs are often able and willing to help their children achieve academic success but concluded that schools typically underestimate and underutilize parents' interest and potential contributions. The panel concludes, however, that there is insufficient evidence to make policy and practice recommendations about home language use. This finding is important because it runs counter to the advice some teachers give to parents to speak and read to their children only in English.

Effective literacy instruction for ELLs provides direct instruction in interactive learning environments.

The CREDE report refers to the direct approach, which emphasizes explicit instruction in skills and strategies, and the interactive approach, which emphasizes learning mediated through interaction with other learners or more competent readers and writers, such as the teacher and other classmates. The NLP and National Academies recommend direct instruction because it ensures that students have the opportunity to master skills that are often embedded and even obscured in complex literacy or academic tasks. But the NLP recommends interaction also because it provides a context in which teachers can modify literacy instruction to accommodate students' individual differences and preferences. Likewise, the National Academies found that literacy skills and effective use of reading strategies should be developed for ELLs through text-based, analytic instruction. In short, these finding support the practice of teaching literacy skills in interactive, meaningful contexts.

Complementing these findings are recommendations from the Institute of Education Sciences, published in a practice guide for educators (Baker et al., 2014). Based on a review of scientific quantitative research studies that met rigorous standards for inclusion in the federal government's What Works Clearinghouse, the guide offers the following recommendations:

1. Teach a set of academic vocabulary words intensively across several days using a variety of instructional activities.
2. Integrate oral and written English language instruction into content-area teaching.
3. Provide regular, structured opportunities to develop written language skills.
4. Provide small-group instructional intervention to students struggling in areas of literacy and English language development. (pp. 3–4)

Although only a small number of studies met their stringent inclusion criteria, the authors of the guide declare the level of evidence "strong" for recommendations 1 and 2, "minimal" for recommendation 3, and "moderate" for recommendation 4.

The National Academies offers its own set of research-based practices for educating ELLs that are consistent with those above and includes the following additional recommendations for reading instruction:

1. Provide explicit instruction in literacy components.
2. Screen for language and literacy challenges and monitor progress.
3. Develop reading and writing abilities of ELLs through text-based, analytic instruction using a cognitive strategies approach.
4. Provide direct and explicit comprehension strategy instruction.
5. Provide opportunities for extended discussion of text meaning and interpretation.
6. Foster student motivation and engagement in literacy learning. (pp. 7–9)

These research findings and recommended practices grounded in mostly quantitative studies are consistent with the findings of qualitative research and with the experiences of ELL educators in terms of practices that have been found to be effective in meeting the needs of the ELL students.[1] The reading instructional strategies and techniques outlined in this chapter are consistent with these recommendations.

---

[1] See, e.g., Beeman & Urow, 2013; Diaz-Rico, 2017; Fountas & Pinnell, 2006; Kendall & Khuon, 2006; Krashen, 2004c; Peregoy & Boyle, 2017.

Common Core State Standards for Reading

The Common Core State Standards (CCSS), which have been adopted by nearly all states, include standards for reading. As with the CCSS for speaking and listening, these standards were designed mainly for English proficient students but apply to all students in Common Core states. The CCSS stress that reading proficiency, certain reading habits, and the successful reading of specific types of texts are critical for college and career readiness:

> To build a foundation for college and career readiness, students must read widely and deeply from among a broad range of high quality, increasingly challenging literary and informational texts. Through extensive reading of stories, dramas, poems, and myths from diverse cultures and different time periods, students gain literary and cultural knowledge as well as familiarity with various text structures and elements. By reading texts in history/social studies, science, and other disciplines, students build a foundation of knowledge in these fields that will also give them the background to be better readers in all content areas. Students can only gain this foundation when the curriculum is intentionally and coherently structured to develop rich content knowledge within and across grades. Students also acquire the habits of reading independently and closely, which are essential to their future success. (© Copyright 2010 National Governors Association Center for Best Practices and Council of Chief State School Officers, p. 10)

The Common Core College and Career Readiness Anchor Standards for reading focus on key ideas and details, craft and structure, integration of knowledge and ideas, and range of reading and level of text complexity (Box 8.3). They provide the basis for more specific corresponding reading standards broken down by grade level.

Major Shifts for English Language Arts and Literacy

Proponents of the CCSS emphasize three major shifts for English language arts and literacy represented in these standards:

1. *Building knowledge through content-rich nonfiction.* The CCSS call for a 50-50 balance between informational reading and literary reading in K–5, with increased focused on informational reading in 6–12 across the content areas (up to 75%), including an increased use of literary nonfiction in English language arts courses.
2. *Reading, writing and speaking grounded in evidence from text, both literary and informational.* The CCSS emphasize the importance of students' being able to answer "text-dependent" questions and to make effective arguments and give detailed information orally and in writing based on texts they have carefully read, rather than relying alone on their prior knowledge or experience.
3. *Regular practice with complex text and its academic language.* The CCSS establishes increasing levels of text complexity, with the goal of preparing students to read and comprehend the types of complex text they will encounter in college and in their careers. This standard includes a focus on developing "academic" vocabulary. (Student Achievement Partners, n.d.; emphasis in original)

Some educators and advocates for ELLs have expressed concern about the de-emphasis on fiction, especially in the primary grades, and the new emphasis on the use of complex nonfiction informational texts. They fear that this shift may make reading instruction much less interesting and comprehensible for ELLs, and since the shift is designed essen-

Box 8.3 Common Core State Standards: College and Career Readiness Anchor Standards for Reading

Key Ideas and Details

1. Read closely to determine what the text says explicitly and to make logical inferences from it; cite specific textual evidence when writing or speaking to support conclusions drawn from the text.
2. Determine central ideas or themes of a text and analyze their development; summarize the key supporting details and ideas.
3. Analyze how and why individuals, events, and ideas develop and interact over the course of a text.

Craft and Structure

4. Interpret words and phrases as they are used in a text, including determining technical, connotative, and figurative meanings, and analyze how specific word choices shape meaning or tone.
5. Analyze the structure of texts, including how specific sentences, paragraphs, and larger portions of the text (e.g., a section, chapter, scene, or stanza) relate to each other and the whole.
6. Assess how point of view or purpose shapes the content and style of a text.

Integration of Knowledge and Ideas

7. Integrate and evaluate content presented in diverse media and formats, including visually and quantitatively, as well as in words.
8. Delineate and evaluate the argument and specific claims in a text, including the validity of the reasoning as well as the relevance and sufficiency of the evidence.
9. Analyze how two or more texts address similar themes or topics in order to build knowledge or to compare the approaches the authors take.

Range of Reading and Level of Text Complexity

10. Read and comprehend complex literary and informational texts independently and proficiently.

tially to raise the bar for all students, they fear also that ELLs will fall even further behind their English proficient peers.

Some ELL experts, however, including those associated with the Understanding Language initiative, are more optimistic about these shifts. Fillmore (2014), for example, argues that ELLs are capable of learning from complex, challenging materials, even before they reach advanced levels of English proficiency, and that they need this type of material to make progress:

> Not only can ELLs handle higher standards and expectations, but that more complex materials are in fact precisely what they have needed, and lack of access to such materials is what has prevented them from attaining full proficiency in English to date. Far too often, educators assume that ELLs must either be given a brief, watered-down oral version of texts that other students are working with, or that they must have their own texts—simplified versions limited to simple sentences and high-frequency vocabulary. If this continues, the promise of the Common Core will be withheld from our ELLs. (p. 624)

Fillmore is not saying that **complex texts** should just be thrown at ELLs to read on their own. Rather, teachers must carefully scaffold and guide the students through multiple readings of the texts, using instructional conversations that "help them discover how meaning is conveyed in the text, to unpack the information stuffed into the words, phrases, clauses and sentences used, and to notice how meaning relates to structures" (p. 20).

To illustrate the kinds of instructional approaches that are likely to help ELLs meet these new CCSS in English language arts and work with complex texts, the Understanding Language (2012) initiative created a sample unit called *Persuasion across Time and Space: Analyzing and Producing Persuasive Texts.* The unit, designed for middle school ELLs at intermediate to advanced levels of English proficiency, includes close readings and analyses of multimodal advertisements; Lincoln's Gettysburg Address; Martin Luther King Jr.'s "I Have a Dream" speech; and speeches by Robert Kennedy, George Wallace, and Barbara Jordan. The approaches and strategies used in this sample unit are consistent with those outlined in this chapter. They provide opportunities to address the reading standards of the CCSS or the reading standards specific to your state.

Text Complexity

The CCSS expectations for students to read increasingly difficult texts has been described as a "staircase" of text complexity, described in the standards as a three-part model:

1. Qualitative dimensions—aspects of text complexity best measured or only measurable by an attentive human reader, such as levels of meaning or purpose; structure; language conventionality and clarity; and knowledge demands.
2. Quantitative dimensions—aspects of text complexity, such as word length or frequency, sentence length, and text cohesion . . . typically measured by computer software.
3. Reader and task considerations—variables specific to particular readers (such as motivation, knowledge, and experiences) and to particular tasks (such as purpose and the complexity of the task assigned and the questions posed) . . . [as determined by] teachers employing their professional judgment, experience, and knowledge of their students and the subject. (© Copyright 2010 National Governors Association Center for Best Practices and Council of Chief State School Officers, app. A, p. 4)

The quantitative dimensions are easily calculated by computerized text analyses. The CCSS uses "Lexile" ranges starting from 450–790 for grades 2 and 3 and extending to 1215–1355 for grade 11 and "college and career ready." Other commonly used measures are the Guided Reading level A–Z system developed by Fountas and Pinnell (2017), and the Developmental Reading Assessment (DRA), which uses a scale of 1–70. The Evaluación del desarrollo la lectura (EDL) is the Spanish-language counterpart of the DRA and is used to assess student's trajectories toward biliteracy. To address the CCSS, some reading curriculum publishers report these various levels for individual books. Thus, you may find a label such as the following on the back cover of a guided-reading book:

Level 2.3 [i.e., grade 2, month 3]
Guided reading level: H
DRA level: 14
Lexile: 520

Care must be used in interpreting quantitative measures of complexity. They are free from human reasoning and thus can be highly misleading. The other two parts of text complexity—qualitative dimensions and considerations of the reader and task—must also be included. Amendum, Conradi, and Hiebert (2017) warn that current models of text complexity lack a theoretical framework and, they argue, the push in the CCSS for students to read more complex texts is not supported by research evidence and may lead to declines in reading outcomes.

Teachers of ELLs must be cautious not to interpret the CCSS requirement for grade-level complex text to mean that students should attempt to read texts only at these levels. That limitation would greatly frustrate students and turn them off reading. Rather, these texts mark the goal for ELLs (and other students) to achieve. Thus, while some use of grade-level complex text may be acceptable with a substantial amount of carefully designed scaffolding as described by Fillmore (2014) and exemplified by the Understanding Language initiative in their sample unit, ELLs will be able eventually to read such complex texts independently only if instruction begins with texts appropriate to their current language and reading proficiency levels. In other words, ELLs can and should move up the staircase of text complexity but starting with the step they are currently on.

Promoting Reading Development for English Language Learners

The research is clear, and it is consistent with the finding of the federal court in *Lau v. Nichols* in 1974: we cannot teach ELLs to read the same way we teach proficient English speakers to read. The instructional strategies and techniques described in this chapter include those commonly used in mainstream classrooms but with suggestions for ways they need to be adjusted (i.e., sheltered or specially designed) to make them appropriate for and effective with ELLs across grade levels and content areas.

ELLs need a balanced approach to literacy instruction that integrates reading, writing, listening, and speaking; that teaches reading skills and strategies within the context of meaningful, authentic communication; and that is differentiated to meet the diverse language and literacy needs of students in the class. Teachers need to understand their ELLs' reading strengths and challenges, and they need to be clear about what they want their students to know and be able to do with reading as a result of their instruction. Teachers need to understand the role of the home language, as well as the role of oral language in English, in reading development in English and other languages.

Reading and learning to read does not take place just during the language arts time or in ESL and English classes. Students read all day in all content areas. Reading from textbooks and other supplementary materials is required for success in most content-area assignments and projects. Thus, for ELLs, all content-area reading is part of their English reading development and all teachers have a responsibility to help ELLs learn to read text associated with the content areas they teach. For students in bilingual, home language arts, and world language programs, all content-area reading in both languages is part of their reading instruction.

This section begins with a brief discussion of developing vocabulary through reading. Next we discuss how teachers can identify ELLs' reading levels, with attention to the complex relationship between English literacy development and English language development. Much of this section is about strategies and techniques that sheltered-content instruction teachers and ESL teachers can use in their classes to facilitate ELLs' development of academic literacies across content areas.

Vocabulary Development through Reading

Reading is one of the primary means by which ELLs acquire new vocabulary words. Students need to know thousands of words in order to comprehend authentic and complex texts, but of course it is impossible to provide direct vocabulary instruction for all un-known words. Fortunately, ELLs can naturally acquire the vast majority of needed vocab-ulary simply by engaging in the types of reading instruction and activities outlined in this chapter. This process can be described as reciprocal causation: "reading comprehension supports vocabulary development" and "vocabulary development supports reading com-prehension" (Lawrence, White, & Snow, 2011, p. 2). Most of the time, students can deter-mine the meaning of unknown words through the context of a sentence or paragraph. They must read enough challenging books that contain unknown words to be exposed to a wide variety of new words.

In many instances, however, context alone may be insufficient or may even lead to misunderstandings of new words. Beck, McKeown, and Kucan (2013) suggest that ef-fectiveness in determining word meanings from context falls along a continuum of four categories of context. To illustrate each of their categories, we'll use the following selec-tion from the picture book *Lima's Red Hot Chilli* written by David Mills and illustrated by Derek Brazell:

> When Lima got home from school she felt hungry.
> "I feel hungry!" she said.
> "Plenty of food in the kitchen!" shouted her mother.
> "But don't eat the red hot chilli!"
> So Lima went to the kitchen for a nibble.
> She found a hairy brown coconut, but it was just . . . too hard.
> The shiny samosas were just . . . too cold. (pp. 1–4)

1. Misdirective contexts: Seem to direct students to the wrong meaning of a word. Ex: *shiny. Shiny* is not typically used to describe fried pastries, and its use in the sentence with *cold* gives no hint about its meaning. The illustration shows Lima making a face and dropping the samosa she has taken from the refrigerator, leav-ing a winding trail of odor. A student might be misdirected to think that *shiny* means "stinky" or something to do with "cold."

2. Nondirective contexts: Seem to be of no assistance in directing the student to any particular meaning of a word. Ex: *nibble.* While the context of hunger and food might be helpful, *nibble* is more abstract. Though it is used mainly as a verb, here it is used as a noun and has no direct reference to any specific food item or type of food. Even the illustrations are of little help in guiding students to a general idea of what a *nibble* is.

3. General contexts: Seem to provide enough information for the student to place the word in a general category. Ex: *coconut.* The context of food, kitchen, and Lima's being hungry and looking for something to eat directs the student to know at least that a *coconut* is some kind of food. The adjectives *hairy, brown,* and *hard* also provide some clues about what a coconut may look like, but only with the illustration can students fully understand the meaning of the word.

4. Directive contexts: Seem likely to lead the student to a specific, correct meaning of a word. Ex: *hungry.* The references to *food, kitchen,* and *eat* and the context of the whole story of Lima looking for something to eat direct students to understand the meaning of the word *hungry.* Also, students' background knowledge of how they feel when they get home from school assists them in learning this word in context.

By understanding these different types of contexts, teachers can analyze texts beforehand to determine which words a student may need little to no assistance learning (general and directive contexts) and which may require extra assistance or warrant direct instruction (misdirective and nondirective contexts).

Any text at or above the students' instructional level will have a range of unknown words; thus, teachers must be selective in determining "words worth teaching" (Biemiller & Boote, 2006). Recall the three tiers of vocabulary: tier 1—basic words, tier 2—general academic words that cut across content areas, and tier 3—content- or domain-specific words. Direct vocabulary instruction advocates argue that instruction should focus on tier 2 words; but ELLs, depending on their proficiency level, may need extra help with all tiers. To select target vocabulary words, Biemiller (2010) recommends that teachers read the text, <u>underline</u> the words they believe students may not know, and then <u>double under-line</u> the words that are absolutely necessary to understand the text. Teachers should then review the words to identify which are tier 1, tier 2, and tier 3 words; determine which words can easily be determined by general and directive contexts; which can be quickly and easily explained during reading; and which may require more direct instruction before or after the reading. Biemiller suggests that 18 to 40 words can be selected, with 6 to 10 of these words selected for focused instruction during each repeated reading for about a week. He recommends the following instructional sequence to teach these vocabulary words within the meaningful context of multiple readings of a text, which his own research found resulted in significant gains in primary-grade students' vocabulary knowledge.

Before First Reading of Text

- Introduce and explain one to three meanings critical for comprehension of the book.
- Read the selection through without stopping.

Immediately after First Reading of Text

- Teach four or five word meanings.
- Reread the text sentences with each target word.
- Briefly explain the word's meaning as it applies to the context of the selection.
- Show students where the sentence is in the selection and point out any related pictures.
- Continue reading the selection.

Subsequent Readings of the Text (throughout the Week)

- Teach four or five new word meanings using the same process as previously.
- Discuss comprehension aspects of the selection.
- Review words taught that day along with the explanations of each word.
- Use printed versions of the words taught to play word games and to do sentence-building activities.

Last Reading of Text (end of Week)

- Review each word taught during the week by using each word in a new sentence not taken from the book.
- Review the explanation of each meaning. (pp. 18–19)[2]

---

[2]Biemiller, A. (2010). *Words worth teaching: Closing the vocabulary gap*. Columbus, OH: McGraw Hill. © Copyright McGraw-Hill Education. Reprinted by permission.

Using many of these same principles, researchers and educators associated with the Strategic Education Research Partnership developed an experimental school-wide direct vocabulary instruction program for middle-school students called Word Generation. Weekly units focus on five target vocabulary words (mostly tier 2). Short texts on issues of high interest to middle-school students featuring the target words are read at the beginning of the week. Students get multiple exposures and meaningful opportunities to use the words throughout the week through 15-minute lessons involving interactive reading, word study lessons, and content-specific activities across their English, mathematics, science, and social studies classes. Activities feature the use of productive talk moves and scaffolds for ELLs. At the end of the week, students write an essay using the target words and take a stand on the issue. Details, materials, and videos of teacher instruction and supporting research are available from the Word Generation website.

Using English Language Development Standards to Guide Reading Instruction

Identifying ELLs' reading levels is important in order to provide appropriate texts and reading instruction. Yet doing so can be challenging, because ELLs enter U.S. schools at different ages with different levels of literacy in their home language and different levels of English language development. In contrast, the frameworks used to identify reading levels in schools are designed for students who already speak English and who are learning to read in the early elementary grades. One commonly used framework identifies four levels of literacy development: emergent, early, early fluency, and fluency. Proficient English-speaking students typically begin at the emergent level in kindergarten and reach the fluency level by 2nd or 3rd grade. The Lexile, DRA, and Fountas and Pinnell systems described earlier are also aligned with specific grade levels, though with some overlap.

For ELLs, these grade-level correspondences may not be relevant, because newcomer ELLs arrive in U.S. schools at all grade levels. Older newcomer ELLs who are literate in their home language will already have knowledge of print and books but nonetheless will need time to transfer this knowledge to English reading. In addition, print conventions may vary between their home language and English, and students need time to learn the differences.

Further complicating these levels of English literacy development are the varying levels of English language development (ELD) among ELLs. ELLs at lower ELD levels are unlikely to surpass the emergent and early levels of English literacy development, regardless of their grade level, because their English is not yet sufficient for them to understand what they read, even if they are able to correctly decode each word in the text.

The ELD standards frameworks from the WIDA and ELPA21 consortia and individual states provide a useful heuristic for considering the language demands of reading and specific literacy tasks at different levels of English language development. Recall that these standards outline progressions across different ELD levels at each grade level. The standards and progressions can give teachers at specific grade levels an understanding of what can be expected of students in the area of reading for social and instructional purposes and across different content areas and an understanding also of what instruction and guidance will be needed to help students move up to the next level. This information is critical for lesson planning and for selecting appropriate books for reading instruction and practice, particularly for guided reading. Consider the ELD standards and progressions in Table 8.1 for reading for grade 2. Note that the level of difficulty of the reading task increases as the level of support decreases for each subsequent proficiency level. Note also that these progressions correspond with CCSS Reading Standard 2.

Selecting Texts

Reading is a great source of comprehensible input that promotes language development, and it is an important vehicle for content-area learning. Also, it provides a strong foundation for writing development. Students need access to a wide range of texts across content areas about different topics in different genres at different levels of complexity, including authentic fiction (children's and youth literature) and nonfiction informational texts. These are the type of books and texts you find in the children's and youth sections of public libraries and bookstores and in magazines and online sources targeting young readers. Teachers should select texts for students to read that support specific instructional purposes, but student choice is also very important.

Reading is an important entry point for addressing goals of multicultural education, such as recognizing and valuing students' home cultures, helping students learn about other cultures, and preparing them to live and work in a diverse society. Students need books that reflect their culture featuring characters they can relate to. Multicultural books need to go beyond surface level features of culture such as food, dress, and holidays. For example, *Lailah's Lunchbox: A Ramadan Story* by Reem Faruqi not only highlights an important Muslim celebration, it tells the story of Lailah, who undertakes the challenge of helping her teacher and her classmates understand her faith and support her month-long fast. Books are needed that lead to discussion of critical issues and social problems that students and their families deal with. Even younger children can be drawn into a discussion of such powerful issues as racism, discrimination, and civil rights by reading books such as *White Socks Only* by Evelyn Coleman, about a young African American girl in the segregated South who runs into trouble when she drinks from a water fountain labeled "White Only"; *The Story of Ruby Bridges* by Robert Coles, about the first African American student to attend a New Orleans elementary school after the Supreme Court's desegregation order; and *The Story of Latino Civil Rights: Fighting for Justice* by Miranda Hunter. Students are more likely to engage in reading when they have books that are reflective of themselves and the worlds they live in.

Structuring Activities

Teachers can use the **before, during, after** (BDA) structure (or into, through, and beyond) to create activities around the reading of any text in any content area. *Before* reading a text, effective teachers help their students activate their prior knowledge, survey or preview the text before reading it, and pre-teach essential vocabulary necessary to comprehend the story. *During* reading, effective teachers model reading strategies, help students learn new vocabulary and grammatical forms, and help readers make connections between the text at hand and other texts they have read or experiences they have had. *After* reading, effective teachers help readers consolidate, elaborate, and deepen their understanding of the text and the connections they have made and provide review and further instruction as needed on new vocabulary words and grammatical forms learned from the text. The use of BDA is included in the following discussion of frameworks and strategies that teachers can use to help their ELLs become proficient readers of English. These same structures, frameworks and strategies apply to home language reading instruction.

Reading *to*, *with*, and *by* English Language Learners

One helpful way of conceptualizing reading instruction in the ELL classroom is to look at reading in three forms: reading *to*, reading *with*, and reading *by* ELLs. All three are

Table 8.1 Progressions in English Language Development and Proficiency Standards for Reading (Grade 2)

Level 1 Entering	Level 2 Emerging	Level 3 Developing	Level 4 Expanding	Level 5 Bridging
Match pictures with information about historical times and people from illustrated texts with a partner.	Identify important information about historical times and people from illustrated texts with a partner.	Sort information about historical times and people from illustrated texts using graphic organizers in small groups.	Sequence information about historical times and people from illustrated texts using graphic organizers in small groups.	Connect information about historical times and people from illustrated texts using graphic organizers (e.g., timelines).

ELPA21

Level 1	Level 2	Level 3	Level 4	Level 5
Use a very limited set of strategies to: • identify a few key words and phrases from read-alouds, simple written texts, and oral presentations.	Use an emerging set of strategies to: • identify some key words and phrases; and • identify the main topic or message/lesson from read-alouds, simple written texts, and oral presentations.	Use a developing set of strategies to: • identify the main topic or message; • answer questions; and • retell some key details from read-alouds, simple written texts, and oral presentations.	Use an increasing range of strategies to: • determine the main idea or message; • identify or answer questions about some key details that support the main idea/message; and • retell a variety of stories from read-alouds, written texts, and oral presentations.	Use a wide range of strategies to: • determine the main idea or message; • tell how key details support the main idea; and • retell a variety of stories from read-alouds, written texts, and oral communications.

Entering (Beginner)	Emerging (Low Intermediate)	Transitioning (High Intermediate)	Expanding (Advanced)	Commanding (Proficient)
Organize pretaught words and phrases on a main-idea-and-details graphic organizer to identify the main idea of a text and its individual paragraphs.	Organize preidentified words and phrases on a main-idea-and-details graphic organizer to identify the main idea of a text and its individual paragraphs.	Organize a bank of phrases and short sentences on a partially completed main-idea-and-details graphic organizer, to identify the main idea of a text and its individual paragraphs.	Organize information, using a glossary, on a main-idea-and-details graphic organizer, to identify the main idea of a text and its individual paragraphs.	Organize information, independently, on a self-created main-idea-and-details graphic organizer, to identify the main idea of a text and its individual paragraphs.

Emerging	Expanding	Bridging
Describe ideas, phenomena (e.g., plant life cycle), and text elements (e.g., main idea, characters, events) based on understanding of a select set of grade-level texts and viewing of multimedia, with substantial support.	Describe ideas, phenomena (e.g., how earthworms eat), and text elements (e.g., setting, events) in greater detail based on understanding of a variety of grade-level texts and viewing of multimedia, with moderate support.	Describe ideas, phenomena (e.g., erosion), and text elements (e.g., central message, character traits) using key details based on understanding of a variety of grade-level texts and viewing of multimedia, with light support.

WIDA Consortium, 2012a, p. 62 (courtesy of WIDA Consortium); ELPA 21, Grade 2, Standard 1, p. 58. Retrieved February 15, 2019, from www.elpa21.org/sites/default/files/Final%204_30%20ELPA21%20Standards_1.pdf; EngageNY, 2014, Reading (R), Standard 2, Grade 2, p. 1; California Department of Education, 2014, p.49.

essential. While these forms are common in elementary school classrooms, they are also just as important at the secondary school level for providing explicit teaching in reading skills as demonstrated through Calderón and Slakk's (2018) successful ExC-ELL (Expediting Comprehension for English Language Learners) model designed for students in grades 6–12.

Read-Alouds

Sessions during which a teacher reads aloud from a book or other text to one or more students are called **read-alouds**. Reading aloud is one of the most important things teachers can do to help ELLs learn to read. If students hear one book read aloud every day from kindergarten through 8th grade, they will experience over 1,600 books—3,200 if the teacher reads two books a day and 4,800 at three a day (Fountas & Pinnell, 2006). For older students, a read-aloud may be a section of a longer text or chapter book.

Read-alouds give students access to text beyond their current level of ability. When parents or teachers read aloud, they are demonstrating the connection between oral and written language while modeling fluent reading and oral production of English. Students are exposed to new content and concepts, a variety of language patterns, and interesting vocabulary—including concepts they may not have been exposed to in their everyday lives and patterns and words they may never hear in ordinary oral interaction. Students are also exposed to a variety of genres and different writing styles. Research has shown that read-alouds stimulate student interests in books (Krashen, 2018). Thus, the more students are read to, the more likely they are to read on their own.

Reading aloud is especially important for ELLs. Some ELLs are fortunate to come from print-rich homes where their parents regularly read aloud to them in their home language or English. However, many ELLs come from homes where parents are unable to read aloud in English to their children; some parents may be unable to read in their home language because of limited educational opportunities in their home countries. Also, many ELLs come from families of low socioeconomic status that have little disposable income for books. Some ELLs rarely see adults or others reading and thus they do not have models of fluent readers who read for enjoyment and information. Students in lower-income neighborhoods have less access to public libraries and typically attend neighborhood schools with the worst school libraries (Krashen, 2014).

Cultural differences may also influence how much parents read aloud to their children at home. As Heath (1982) reveals in her classic study *What No Bedtime Story Means*, mainstream U.S. schools operate on the cultural assumption that children are read to at home. Thus, literacy instruction privileges students from mainstream middle-class homes where reading bedtime stories and other literacy practices closely match the practices of the school. Students whose home literacy practices are different typically face greater challenges in learning to read at school. To make up for these differences, it is imperative that teachers read aloud to their ELLs as much as possible.

Teachers should have a clear purpose for selecting a book to read aloud and should ensure that it is appropriate for the grade and English proficiency level of the students. The book may be selected because it goes along with a current theme, topic, or genre being studied in the classroom, because it addresses a particular topic of concern or interest of the students, or because it contains useful vocabulary and language patterns. Perhaps the teacher selects a high-interest narrative that builds important background for subsequent reading of a more challenging grade-level expository text in a content-area class. Maybe the book is selected just because it is a great book the teacher knows the students will enjoy.

The length of time and type of text selected for a read-aloud will depend on the grade and ELD reading level of the students. Younger and lower-level ELLs need simple and short books with vivid illustrations and only a few lines of text on each page. For older and more advanced students, grade-level chapter books, novels, and articles from magazines, newspapers, or the Internet are more appropriate.

Read-alouds in the classroom should involve the whole group. For a picture book, students should sit on the floor close to the teacher where they can see the pictures and point to words and pictures when appropriate. Sitting together on the floor creates an atmosphere conducive to listening to and enjoying a book as a community of readers. Older students may prefer to sit at their desks, which is fine when there are few illustrations in the book or text. Regardless of the seating arrangement, students should be encouraged to chime in, using gestures, asking questions about the text, and making predictions about what they think is going to happen next. To engage students, teachers can exaggerate the dialogue and use gestures and different voices for different characters. The more interactive and fun it is, the more comprehensible the book or text will be for ELLs. And the more comprehensible it is, the more English they learn from the reading.

A good read-aloud is interactive, and it focuses on the meaning of the text and follows the BDA structure. For example, before reading *The Day Jimmy's Boa Ate the Wash* by Trinka Hakes Noble—a picture book about a class field trip to a farm that ends up in chaos because Jimmy brought his pet boa constrictor—the teacher could have a class discussion about field trips the students have been on and ask whether any of them has ever been to a farm. He could show the students the book, read the title, and discuss the cover illustration, which is sure to elicit conversations about snakes and farm animals. To engage students in the story before reading, the teacher can do a picture walk by showing a few pages and talking with students about the illustrations. He might ask students to make predictions about what they think is going to happen in the story (e.g., "What do you think Jimmy's boa constrictor is going to do at the farm?"). This process establishes the context of the story and sets a purpose for reading. In addition, particularly for ELLs, this "before" discussion is an opportunity to pre-teach unknown vocabulary in a meaningful context. ELLs are likely to know the words *snake* and *clothes* but may not know *boa constrictor* or *the wash*.

Similar procedures can be followed when reading from chapter books with older students or more advanced ELLs. In addition, before reading each chapter, the teacher should lead a brief discussion to review what has happened in the book so far, make predictions about what might come next, pre-teach any key vocabulary, or build background knowledge for any difficult concepts that may be covered in the chapter. Likewise, when teachers read expository texts aloud, for example, from content-area textbooks, they can preview headings, photographs, captions, key words, summaries, and guiding questions.

During the read-aloud, the teacher can make the text more comprehensible and engaging for ELLs by using gestures, pointing to parts of the illustrations that provide hints for the meaning (i.e., pointing to the snake when reading "boa constrictor"), and rephrasing or explaining difficult words or phrases (e.g., "'The wash' means the clothes the farmer's wife just washed and is hanging up to dry"). Decisions about when to use gestures and what words or phrases require rephrasing or explanation are based on the proficiency level of the students. The lower the proficiency level, the greater the amount of gesturing, explaining, and rephrasing required. In a class with a wide range of levels, the teacher should provide the amount needed for the students at the lowest levels.

During the reading, the teacher can think aloud to model how good readers make sense of the text as they are reading, saying, for example, "I wonder why she did that? I'm going to read more to find out," or "It looks as though Sylvia has a problem. Let's read more to see how she solves it." The teacher can make the reading interactive by pausing to allow students to confirm their predictions and to make new ones (e.g., "Were you right that Jimmy's boa would chase the chickens?" "What do you think is going to happen next?"). Care must be taken, however, to ensure that these strategies fit naturally into the flow of the read-aloud and do not distract or take too much time away from the actual reading of the text. The teacher could also pause and allow students to fill in the words, indicating their comprehension.

"After" reading strategies and activities build and check students' comprehension of the book or text and help them extend and deepen their understanding. Too often, many teachers finish the read-aloud and quickly move on to an unrelated activity. Effective teachers make use of the magic moments created by the completion of a good read-aloud. After finishing the book or text, teachers can ask students whether their predictions were correct. They can talk with the students about the parts they liked best and relate the text to others they have read in class, to other content areas, or to out-of-school experiences. These types of discussions are essential for addressing the Common Core reading standards (see Box 8.3), such as making logical inferences from the text and citing specific examples from the text to support conclusions drawn (Standard 1); discussing the theme and summarizing key supporting details and ideas (Standard 2); and analyzing why and how characters, events, or ideas developed and interacted throughout the text (Standard 3). For ELLs at lower ELD levels, teachers can address these standards by asking questions that require only a few words to answer and for more advanced students, open-ended questions that encourage greater elaboration. Discussion and activities should provide ample opportunities for students to use new vocabulary, phrases, and structures learned through the text and to consider how these helped to shape the meaning and tone of the text (Standard 4).

One final but very important tip. After a book has been read aloud, don't put it aside, never to be seen again. Younger students especially love to hear the same books read over and over again. Repeated readings are especially beneficial for ELLs because they need the multiple exposures to new vocabulary and structures, and each reading will lead to greater comprehension. The teacher can also make the book available to students to read during independent reading time, put the book and a recording of it at the listening center, or let the student take the book home to read with the family.

Shared Reading

Shared reading is an example of reading *with* students and has many of the same features as read-alouds. Here, however, the focus is on using texts closer to the students' reading ability and getting them to read along. Shared reading provides teachers with opportunities to teach important concepts of print, demonstrate strategies that good readers use, and involve students as a community of readers.

In the early elementary grades, teachers often have big books, which are oversized versions of books they can use to engage students with the text and illustrations. For students in the upper elementary grades and in secondary schools, any source of enlarged text can be used for shared reading, such as charts (commercial or teacher-made) with poems, chants, and song lyrics; a pocket chart with sentence strips; or text projected on a screen. Secondary school students could be given their own copies of the text.

Shared readings should be done with the whole group. Many texts are appropriate for shared reading. The level of the reading should be slightly higher than the students' current instructional level. For ELLs at the beginning or emergent levels of reading, the text should contain rhyme; rhythm; and repetition of words, phrases, and language patterns. The illustrations should provide maximum support for understanding the text. For more advanced ELLs, the text should more closely resemble grade-level reading materials but contain illustrations or other features to facilitate comprehension. Ideally, the text matches the current theme or topic of study. Also, like read-alouds, shared readings expose students to different genres, including nonfiction, as emphasized in the CCSS. In classes with a wide range of reading and language levels, the teacher can vary the difficulty of the text read on different days. Even books at higher reading levels can be made accessible to lower-level ELLs through the scaffolding provided by the teacher during shared reading.

Shared reading follows the same BDA structure as read-alouds. One big book or enlarged text source can be used for shared reading lessons for a week or more. The first few sessions focus on getting students familiar enough with the text that they can read along; subsequent sessions focus on comprehension and the direct instruction of reading skills and strategies. Biemiller's (2010) vocabulary instruction sequence works particularly well in the context of shared reading.

For students who are just learning to read, the teacher tracks the text by pointing to each word as she reads, using her finger or a pointer stick. As students become familiar with the text, they join in and share in the reading. This is easy for them to do, particularly when the text has rhyme, rhythm, and repetitions. Once students become familiar with the text, teachers can use echo reading, where the teacher reads a line and then students repeat. As students become more competent with the reading, the teacher invites them to come up individually and use their finger or pointer to track the text and lead the class in reading the book. A shared reading text provides a rich and familiar context for ELLs to learn new vocabulary and syntactic structures. Repeated readings help them subconsciously develop understandings of noun-verb agreement, plurals, and other concepts.

For older students at higher English and reading levels, shared reading may include choral reading with emphasis on expressive reading to facilitate comprehension. All students read the text aloud in unison, though there can be variations with different students taking on different parts of the text, which they read alone or with a partner or small group. For example, in reading a poem such as "I Have a Story to Tell You" by Forever Krysia, featuring a dialogue between a fish and the ocean, half the class could read the lines spoken by the fish and the other half the lines spoken by the ocean.[3] Choral reading provides opportunities for students to practice expressive reading, develop new vocabulary and language structures, become aware of complex literary texts, and develop awareness of the ways particular words and phrases are stressed.

Echo reading and choral reading provide scaffolding for ELL readers in a low-risk environment. Students participate as they feel ready. They will not be singled out, because their voices blend in with the voices of other students. Subsequent readings can build comprehensible input though gestures, props, rephrasings, explanations, and so forth. Once students are familiar with the text (perhaps they are simply "reading" it by memory), teachers use the text to teach and model a variety of reading skills and strategies.

For lower-level students who are still learning letters and sounds, the shared reading text can be used, for example, to teach phonics within a meaningful context. The teacher could call on individual students to come point to or mark (using sticky notes, highlighting tape, or other means) certain letters or sounds (e.g., "Phitsamay, can you find the letter *t?*" "Boravy, show me a word that starts with the /d/ sound."). Or specific reading strategies can be taught and modeled. For example, the teacher could cover parts of words and guide students to use picture, phonetic, semantic, or syntactic clues to figure out the words. The words could be revealed and checked to see whether students are correct. Teachers can also use think-alouds or model other effective reading strategies, such as visualizing, questioning, predicting, checking comprehension, re-reading, and making connections.

---

[3] I am grateful to Mayra Salinas, a bilingual San Antonio elementary school teacher, who introduced this technique in one of my courses.

"After" activities can also be extensive and varied. If the teacher's purpose is to focus on vocabulary and syntax, for example, an immediate "after" activity could be to copy selected sentences from the text onto sentence strips and then cut them up so each word is on its own card. Teachers could mix up the words and put them in a pocket chart for the students to put back in the right order. The students would be required to use a range of strategies to put the sentence back together, demonstrating their knowledge of vocabulary and syntax. The possibilities for shared reading activities are far-ranging, with the ultimate purpose to help students learn the strategies and skills they need to become independent readers.

Teachers can make the big books and charts available for students to read during independent reading time. Books read in shared reading often become the most popular books students choose during independent reading. The regular-size versions of the books can be placed on students' desks, put in the classroom library, or even sent home for reading practice. Text from charts can also be reduced to a single page for students to take home and read with their families.

Guided Reading

Guided reading is conducted with small groups of students (three to six) who read at about the same level. Students have their own copies of the same text at their particular instructional level (defined as a text they can read with 90–94% accuracy). Guided reading fulfills the call from the Institute of Education Sciences for intensive small-group reading interventions for ELLs.

The purpose of guided reading is for students to practice reading and using the skills and strategies they have learned through read-alouds and shared readings. The teacher does not read the book to or with the students but instead prepares them to read it on their own. The teacher serves as a coach, providing scaffolding as needed to help students apply their skills to read and make sense of the text. The goal of guided reading is to help students move up to higher reading levels and become independent readers of increasingly difficult texts.

The typical source for guided reading is leveled books that come with reading curricular programs but can also include children's literature or even basal readers if the texts are at the students' instructional level. For beginning-level ELLs at the emergent reading level, the texts should be simple with lots of rhyme, rhythm, and repetition and illustrations that provide support for the meaning of the text. For higher-level ELLs beyond the emergent and early reading levels, the books should contain fewer of these supports and should increasingly resemble grade-level reading material. The text gradient created by Fountas and Pinnell (2017) and other book-leveling systems can offer guides for matching ELLs to appropriate leveled texts. In addition, Appendix B of the CCSS for English language arts provides text samples from a list of books organized by grade level that exemplify the level of complexity and quality that students are expected to engage with at their grade level. Texts at these "exemplar" levels, however, should be used with ELLs only during guided reading if the students have sufficient English and reading proficiency to reasonably engage with the text, and only when they are provided with the scaffolding needed to help them comprehend the texts. Teachers should also view these exemplar texts as the target to aim for as students make progress through guided reading instruction and move up to increasingly complex levels of text.

In guided reading, the teacher follows the BDA structure used in read-alouds and shared readings, beginning with a discussion of the topic to activate prior knowledge and build background knowledge, then moving on to a discussion of the book cover, a picture walk, student predictions, pre-teaching of unknown vocabulary, and so on. The teacher reads the title of the book with the students but does not read any of the text. Next, the teacher directs the students to read the book aloud on their own. While the students are reading, the teacher listens in and provides help where needed, suggesting strategies they can use to figure out and make sense of words and phrases they do not know. Particular care should be taken that the reading does not become a choral reading, with all the students following the lead of the strongest reader in the group. Each student should be reading aloud on his or her own. To prevent choral reading, some teachers have found it useful to stagger when students start reading, directing the first student to read past the first page before inviting the next student to begin.

If the book the students are reading is relatively simple and short, they will likely have time for multiple readings. Once each student has read the book, the teacher can partner up the students to read to each other, and then they can trade partners when they finish. One student, also, could be selected to read with the teacher, who could do a running record of the students' reading. After the readings, the teacher leads the students through postreading activities, such as a discussion of the book that includes comprehension questions. Partner reading—in which partners read alternating sentences aloud to each other—was found to be a very important component of the ExC-ELL model for secondary school ELLs because it provides opportunities for students to practice comprehension strategies, comprehend content, and practice appropriate prosody (e.g., reading with expression, intonation, and flow) (Calderón & Slakk, 2018).

While the students read, teachers identify words, phrases, and structures the students appear to struggle with and use this information to create mini-lessons. For example, suppose students struggled with the word *chew* because they do not know the meaning of the word or the sound made by the consonant cluster *ch*. The teacher could first teach a vocabulary mini-lesson on the word *chew*, explaining and demonstrating its meaning, encouraging a discussion about things one should or should not chew (food, gum, pencils, fingernails, broken glass, etc.), and then return to the book to look at the context of the word *chew*. Next, the teacher could teach a mini-lesson on the /ch/ sound. The students could brainstorm other words that start with *ch* and write these words on paper, white boards, smartboards, or chalkboards or make the words with magnetic letters or other alphabet manipulatives. They could then go back through the story looking for and reading all *ch* words.

Each guided reading session informs the next in terms of the level of books to be read and mini-lessons that need to be provided. Teachers must pay careful attention to the progress of individual students, moving them around and reformulating groups to ensure that students are always engaging with texts at their instructional levels. Because students work in small groups with others of similar proficiency, guided reading also provides an opportunity for teachers to address the Common Core reading standards effectively and efficiently in the areas of key ideas and details, craft and structure, and integration of knowledge and skills (see Box 8.3). Thus, instruction that addresses these standards can be easily differentiated for each guided reading group. Guided reading is also essential for preparing students to meet Standard 10 (independent reading).

Fountas and Pinnell (2017) offer some suggestions for guided reading with ELLs before, during, and after reading. Before reading, teachers should carefully select books and plan a supportive introduction, noting any specific language features (e.g., key vocabulary, idioms, metaphors, or complex syntax) that are key to comprehending the text. For beginning-level ELLS, selected texts should cover familiar topics that are easy to explain, and have strong picture support. Texts that stretch their language knowledge but are not too complex to be beyond comprehension are ideal. The introduction to the text should be used to familiarize student with new vocabulary and language structures, to draw attention to illustrations that can help facilitate comprehension, get them thinking about what the book will be about, and also help them understand the organization of the book. Teachers can point out any complex syntax and have the students practice reading it aloud. During the reading it is important to let students try on their own. Teachers, however, can help as needed with difficult words or point students to contextual cues or other supports but should keep interruptions to a minimum and not try to correct every error. Mainly, teachers should closely observe and identify vocabulary, intonation patterns, word pronunciations, and syntactic structures students may struggle with. After the reading, these observations inform the mini-lessons, which could include work with sight words for beginning-level students or with tier 2 and 3 words for more advanced students. Teachers should also engage students in conversations and other activities that provide opportunities to the use the new vocabulary and language structures from the text.

Close Reading

The Common Core Reading Standard 1 calls for students to "read closely" to determine what a text says explicitly, to make logical inferences from the text, and to draw on evidence from the text in oral and written reports and arguments. Thus, **close reading** refers to the way students engage in their reading of a text to fully understand the information it contains and the inferences that may be drawn from it. Close reading is associated with reading of complex texts and can be done during shared or guided reading lessons. But here the focus is on complex texts that are typically beyond the current level of students— particularly ELLs—and thus close-reading lessons require a great deal of scaffolding and support within the BDA structure. Lapp et al. (2015) suggest that before reading, the teacher selects and analyzes the text complexity, identifies key vocabulary, determines the instruction and supports needed, crafts text-dependent questions, and introduces the text to the students. During reading the teacher guides the students through multiple readings, helps them analyze and annotate the text to answer the questions, and engages students in discussion to build their background knowledge. Students engage in their own independent re-readings of the text and try to find answers to text-dependent questions. They receive guidance and help from the teacher and peers as needed and discuss their findings with each other. Graphic organizers, words walls, and other visuals can be used to facilitate the comprehension process. After the reading, students engage in further projects and respond to oral and written prompts that require use of evidence from the text. As noted earlier, engagement with complex texts in a close-reading lesson must be highly scaffolded for ELLs and should be only supplemental to regular, daily shared and guided reading during which students have opportunities to engage with text at an appropriate level with instruction, scaffolding, and support that moves them to higher levels.

Language Experience Approach

One challenge in helping ELLs learn to read in English, particularly those at the lowest levels of English language development and older newcomers who have not developed literacy skills in their home language, is finding texts that are personally or culturally relevant to the student and have mostly familiar vocabulary and language structures. The language experience approach can help.

The **language experience approach** is inspired by Freire's (1993) critical pedagogy. According to Friere, the student identifies a problem in his or her life, tells a story about that problem, and explores solutions. Alternatively, the student simply tells a story from personal experience. The teacher writes down the story and uses the resulting text for reading instruction with the student. This text is easier for the student to read because it consists of his or her own natural language, experiences, and knowledge. The language experience approach supports students' literacy development by helping them understand "What I say I can write" and "What I write I can read." As students make progress, this concept can be expanded to "What others write I can read." The language experience approach encourages students to see literacy as a vehicle for taking action to improve their lives.

This approach can be varied to accommodate students at different language development and literacy levels, and it can be used for different purposes. For example, students at beginning ELD levels in speaking might bring a picture to scaffold their description of an experience or storytelling, working with a partner or the teacher to learn the vocabulary and language structures they need. Students with more advanced oral English skills but limited reading and writing skills are likely to provide more oral language, which may be difficult for the teacher to write down as they speak. One solution is to make an audio recording that can be transcribed by the teacher or another student. This approach can also be used with shared experiences in content-area classes. For example, a science experiment can be the basis for first talking and then reading and writing about science.

One challenge in using the language experience approach with ELLs is how to handle errors in students' oral language before writing it down. Although there is some debate about the best approach, teachers have found that if they offer corrective feedback, the resulting texts that students read help reinforce correct forms while maintaining the authenticity of the students' own words.

Independent Reading

The purpose of reading *to* and *with* students is to get them to the point where they can successfully engage in **independent reading**, including independent reading of the types of complex literary and information texts emphasized in the Common Core reading standards (see Box 8.3, Standard 10). Thus, students need to be provided time in class every day to read independently. Younger students need about 10 or 15 minutes, older students 20 minutes or more. Many schools use the term *sustained silent reading (SSR)*, though for younger students it is anything but silent, since most students read out loud. Some schools come up with cute alternative names for SSR, such as DEAR time (Drop everything and read), or USSR (uninterrupted sustained silent reading). Others refer to independent reading as *free voluntary reading*, stressing that students should be free to choose what they read.

To be successful, SSR requires an extensive, inviting classroom library where students can find books they are genuinely interested in reading and that are also appropriate to their ELD level in reading. Many teachers have found it helpful to organize their classroom libraries by theme or genre. Books and texts used for read-alouds, shared reading, and guided reading should also be made available. Even magazines and comic books are appropriate. Bilingual books and books in the home languages of the students should also be included. One of the main reasons some students are reluctant readers is that they lack access to interesting books and other reading material; students who have greater access do more reading and are better readers (Krashen, 2004c). Students should be free to choose the material they want to read and to stop reading anything that does not hold their interest. Forcing students to read material that does not interest them is a sure way to kill their enjoyment of reading.

Although students should be given open access to any reading materials in the classroom, they also need to be guided to make appropriate choices. Teachers should monitor the students to make sure they do not always choose books that are too easy or too hard and should also monitor to make sure the students are actually reading. Teachers should always be reading a book of their own choosing. In doing so, they offer the model of an adult who reads for enjoyment—something students may not see at home.

To make SSR enjoyable, some teachers allow students to sit anywhere they like in the classroom—at their desk, under their desk, on their desk, on the floor, on a bean bag chair, on a sofa, on a mat, and so on. Some teachers play soft instrumental music in the background to enhance the reading environment. Lower-level ELLs not yet capable of reading even simple books on their own could listen to a book read aloud by the teacher or another student, listen to a book at the listening center or on a mobile device or a class-room computer.

Krashen (2004b), who cites overwhelming research evidence that the use of SSR in the classroom for students of all ages can transform them into lifelong readers, strongly recommends that SSR be a time simply for enjoyment, with minimal accountability. Teachers should not feel the urge to follow up on SSR time with quizzes, reports, or con-tests in which students earn points and awards for reading. In many schools, however, independent and home reading programs are supplemented with computer-based com-prehension quizzes. One of the most popular programs is Accelerated Reader (Box 8.4), which some literacy experts have criticized (Krashen 2003, Pennington 2010, What Works Clearinghouse, 2016).

Narrow Reading

Narrow reading is a form of independent recreational reading that entails reading sev-eral books on the same subject, by the same author, or in the same genre (Krashen, 2018). Narrow reading can also include reading several books in a series, with recurring char-acters, themes, and plot lines that may or may not build on earlier books in the series (e.g., Captain Underpants, Diary of a Wimpy Kid, Dog Man, Dork Diaries, Harry Potter,

---

Box 8.4 Accelerated Reader

Accelerated Reader (AR), according the publisher's website, is in use in over half the schools in the United States. With AR, students read books and then take online comprehension quiz-zes by computer, or other mobile devices. The program has a system for leveling books, and it includes quizzes for over 190,000 books in its latest database. Students earn points based on the number of books they read and quizzes they pass. Many schools use the points to award prizes. Teachers can track student progress and even print "college and career readi-ness" reports.

The publisher claims that more than 180 research studies support the use of AR. Many teachers and students appear to like it very much. It encourages students to read authentic literature, and teachers have reported that the amount of reading at home and at school has increased dramatically. Many literacy experts, however, are critical of the program's emphasis on extrinsic rewards, pointing out that students frequently appear more interested in the num-ber of points and prizes they earn than in what they are actually reading. The reading compre-hension questions are not difficult, and critics contend that these questions promote only basic recall rather than higher-order thinking. AR includes additional vocabulary quizzes and recorded voice quizzes as a support for ELLs. Students get immediate feedback on their quiz, and they can track their progress by reviewing the books they have read and their quiz scores.

If AR is used, teachers should ensure that it is used only as a supplement to their reading program. Teachers should conduct their own reading assessments and ask students their own comprehension questions and not rely on AR as the only source of information. The use of extrinsic rewards should be limited or eliminated. And teachers should constantly remind students that reading is its own reward and its purpose is not to get points and prizes.

Miss Peregrine's Peculiar Children, Percy Jackson, Red Queen, The Trials of Apollo). Narrow academic reading refers to the narrow reading of academic texts on a topic of high interest to the student. Krashen argues that narrow reading and narrow academic reading are efficient ways to acquire a second language because they maximize comprehensible input and are highly motivating. Students who read several books on the same topic accumulate a great deal of background knowledge, which facilitates comprehension of each new text read on the topic. Similarly, reading books by the same author helps students improve their reading skills by increasing their familiarity with that author's style, favorite expressions, and use of language.

Reader's Workshop

The balanced literacy framework that was originally developed for elementary school has been extended into the secondary schools. While the reading process itself does not change, what does change at the secondary level is the range of genres, the difficulty of the reading material, and the complexity of thinking needed to comprehend texts. Under the Common Core reading standards, students at the secondary level are expected to spend 55% to 70% of their reading time across their courses on informational texts. Additionally, schools are structured differently at the secondary level, and the range of ELLs' reading levels is often greater. Reader's Workshop is used in many secondary schools to meet these challenges.

In Reader's Workshop, the expectation is that all students will read, discover books they love, and, with their teachers and peers, enter the world of literature, become captivated, find satisfaction, and learn (Atwell, 1987). These expectations are demonstrated through the workshop's predictable structure and procedures. Reader's Workshop is offered at least two times a week for one class period and always begins with a 5- to 10-minute mini-lesson based on the teacher's assessment of student needs, interest, and strengths. The mini-lesson also enables teachers to demonstrate to students, for example, how to choose appropriate books, how to use strategies that effective readers use, and how to respond to literature.

Postreading Activities

The purpose of postreading activities—the *after* part of BDA—is to help deepen students' comprehension of the text they just heard or read and to extend their learning beyond the text. Suggestions for postreading activities follow.

Class Discussions

The simplest postreading activity is a discussion involving the whole class or a small group that allows students to engage in meaningful "instructional conversations" (Goldenberg, 2013). Using productive talk moves, a teacher leads a discussion designed to maximize students' comprehension of the text. The teacher can ask comprehension questions and invite students to describe their favorite parts of a story and share their thoughts on the text. These instructional conversations were found to be an essential component of the ExC-ELL model for older ELLs (Calderón & Slakk, 2018) and are critical in addressing the Common Core reading standards (see Box 8.3) to help ELLs across grade levels determine the central ideas and themes; summarize key supporting details and ideas (Standard 2); analyze the characters, events, and ideas in the text (Standard 3); make logical inferences based on evidence from the text (Standard 1); and explore the author's craft, structure of the text, and point of view (Standards 4–6). Through these conversations, teachers help students connect the literature to their daily lives, making what literacy experts call "text-to-self" connections. Teachers also help students make "text-to-text" connections, that is, to relate the book or text to something they read earlier (Standard 9). Interactive class discussions help students expand their comprehension and develop new perspectives. Such classroom discussions may include contributions from students in their home languages.

Reader Response

Reader response goes beyond reading comprehension. To elicit reader response, teachers encourage students to reflect on and extend their understanding of a text. As students think about what they read, they ask authentic questions, make comments and connections, and form opinions. Through reader response, students develop a sense of what is important in the text and thus are able to form judgments about what they are reading. As students interact with other readers by sharing their responses to a text orally (e.g., in literature circles or book clubs) or in writing (e.g., in dialogue journals, reader response logs, or reader's notebooks), they develop new perspectives. Reader response can include personal responses or reactions to characters, setting, plot, and other aspects of a story, open-ended questions, summaries, and reviews. To meet the Common Core Reading Standard 1, students must cite textual evidence to support the conclusions they draw from the text. Reader responses also provides space for students to engage in translanguaging as they draw on all of their linguistic skills across their languages to comprehend and respond to the text.

Graphic Organizers

Graphic organizers help students break down a text into its essential components. Story maps, for example, highlight key developments of the story in sequence. The simplest form of story map is the beginning-middle-end chart, in which students indicate the key plot elements at these points in the story. A problem-solution chart can be used to represent the basic conflict and resolution in the story. Graphic organizers can also be used with expository text structures. Venn diagrams or comparison charts (Fig. 8.1), for example, can be used with texts that feature contrast and comparison; webs or feature charts can

Figure 8.1 Teacher and students work together to create a Venn diagram. (Photo by Star Watanaphol.)

be used with texts that feature description; tree diagrams or outlines can be used with texts that feature enumeration; and flow charts, sequence chains, and cycles can be used with texts that feature chronological or sequential structure or cause and effect. Graphic organizers also provide an opportunity to include text in the home languages of students who are literate in their home language, to further promote comprehension.

Graphic organizers are beneficial for ELLs because they represent the main ideas and other content visually with just a few words. ELLs can demonstrate their comprehension of the text by completing their own graphic organizers in English and their home languages. Graphic organizers also provide an important oral language scaffold for ELLs to talk about and retell stories or summarize expository texts.

Class-Made Books

Students can draw pictures of their favorite parts of a story or of how they might extend the story. For example, after my class read *It Looked Like Spilt Milk* by Charles Shaw, a book about seeing familiar pictures in clouds, my ELLs made their own cloud drawings. They then wrote a sentence for their picture following the structure used in the book ("Sometimes it looked like a face, but it wasn't a face."). We put the drawings and sentences together to make our own class book. Making class books based on the content and language structure of a particular text helps students comprehend the text and gives them practice using new vocabulary and language structures featured in the story. Class-made books can also be bilingual or multilingual, incorporating the home languages of the students in the class. This not only further facilitates comprehension, but also makes class-made books ideal for students to take home and share with their families.

Alternative Endings

Another activity that is fun but also meaningful is to write alternative endings to stories. With lower-level students, creating alternative endings to stories the whole class has read is best done with the whole class together. ELLs with more advanced English proficiency can create alternative endings in small groups or individually. To write an alternative ending, students must understand the story well. Creating alternative endings gives students practice in using new vocabulary and language structures learned in the story, since these will likely be needed in the new endings the students create.

Performed Reading: Reader's Theater

One of the most enjoyable ways to help students comprehend stories they read is to have them act them out, using strategies for promoting oral development. The easiest method is to use simple props representing the characters (e.g., pictures of characters glued to tongue depressors) or just to have students hold up or wear signs with the characters' names on them. Or students could act out the story as a puppet show or put on a live play with costumes, scenery, and props or read from a script in an activity called "Reader's Theater."

Teachers can find scripts on the Internet, but the exercise is most effective when students collaborate to write their own script. By taking a piece of text and transforming it into a different form or genre (in this instance, a script), students must use a wide range of cognitive strategies and higher-order thinking skills that facilitate comprehension. ELLs also benefit from Reader's Theater because it allows them to practice reading with expression and provides extensive practice in using the new vocabulary and language structures learned from the book.

Strategies for Reading across the Curriculum

Students must read complex grade-level texts for a wide range of purposes not only in English language arts but in mathematics, science, and social studies. Teachers can use the following instructional strategies to help all students—particularly ELLs—comprehend content and learn vocabulary through reading in any content area.

Notemaking Guides

For secondary and more advanced ELLs, notemaking guides provide a powerful literacy scaffold as they work to make sense of complex academic texts. The word *notemaking* is used, rather than *notetaking,* to highlight the active process of meaning making involved in this activity. A very simple notemaking guide asks students to write down the purpose for their reading at the top of the form. The rest of the form is divided into two columns. In the left-hand column, students make notes on the important facts, or what the author says, and in the right-hand column, they record their response in the form of questions or comments about what they think as they read and connections they have made. Space may be provided at the bottom of the form for students to write a short summary statement, or a supplemental question may be added there that encourages students to extend their reading beyond the text.

Notemaking guides are easy to create, and they can be adapted for different text types. Cornell Notes is one such form. Teachers can review the notemaking guides to assess how well students understand the main ideas and what connections they are making. Students can use their notemaking guides to support their discussions of expository texts and to consider multiple perspectives on the same text. Notemaking guides also encourage ELLs to use the language associated with specific academic content areas.

Word Study and Interactive Vocabulary Mini-Lessons

Vocabulary is taught implicitly and explicitly through read-alouds, shared reading, guided reading, Reader's Workshop, and performed reading. **Word study** exercises can be integrated into these instructional modes or presented on their own as mini-lessons (Fountas & Pinnell, 2017). The purpose is to help students learn the meaning of new words by talking about how they are used in a sentence, moving them around within a sentence, adding prefixes or suffixes, or manipulating them in graphic organizers, such as word webs, Venn diagrams, and semantic maps, so students can use them successfully in oral and literacy tasks. Other word study activities include work with letter tiles or magnetic letters (or digital versions on tablets or smartboards) to build words, and sorting words by part of speech (e.g., noun, verb, adjective), by semantic categories (e.g., animals, toys, musical instruments), or by their prefixes, suffixes, or base words. For more advanced ELL readers word study may involve work with word analogies (e.g., *clock* is to *wall* as *watch* is to ____), substituting words in sentences with different words, and studying the way certain words are used in context of texts (e.g., *well* in sentences like, "I'm not feeling *well*," "He did *well* on his test," "the steak is *well* done," "*Well,* I don't really know," and "*Well, well, well,* look who just walked in the door"). For ELLs who speak Spanish or other languages that are closely related to English (e.g., French, Portuguese) word study lessons on cognates—words that are similar in form and meaning across languages (e.g., *education/educación*)—can be particularly beneficial (Baker et al., 2014).

Reading Digital Texts

Any text read in an online environment or on an electronic device is a digital text. The Internet has become the prime source of news, information, and social media. eBooks have grown in popularity since the advent of the Kindle in 2007. The increasing use of digital texts in education is inevitable. Many schools across the country have adopted digital versions of textbooks that students can access online, and many schools have invested in dedicated eBook readers, tablets, or other mobile devices that allow students to access eBooks. Publishers of reading curriculum programs are converting their existing titles into eBooks and producing original ones. Some experts, educators, and parents are concerned about the move to eBooks in schools, arguing that reading on a screen is not the same experience as holding and reading a real book, and that the cognitive processes involved may even differ. Some express concern about encouraging young children to stare into small glowing screens more than they already do. There are many unknowns. Research is beginning to explore the effects of using digital media for reading.

Nonetheless, digital texts are here to stay, and students are already consuming and producing them. Despite concerns, digital texts have many advantages over print that open new educational possibilities. Although some digital texts are nothing more than scanned images of printed book pages, many are multimodal, meaning they combine text with images, audio, video, or interactive features. These features can complement and convey meaning and information beyond the written text and thus help deepen students' understanding. Common Core Reading Standard 7 calls on students to integrate and evaluate content presented in these diverse digital media and formats, visually and quantitatively, as well as in words (see Box 8.3).

For ELLs, the multimodal features of eBooks can be very beneficial for their reading comprehension. Consider, for example, *Our Earth* (published by Teacher Created Materials), an informational eBook designed for grade 2 students. Each page features text and vivid color photographs with captions that are presented in an engaging design one would typically find in a printed book. Reading the book on an iPad, a student can tap a paragraph and hear it read aloud in a real human voice, with phrases highlighted as they are read (a feature that can be turned off if desired). Bolded key terms, such as *orbit,* can be tapped to bring up a pop-up glossary window. Another tap will read the word and definition aloud. Students can use highlighters and pens to mark up the text and illustrations, write notes on yellow sticky notes anywhere on the page, bookmark pages, search within the book for specific words or phrases, watch short video clips, and even record themselves reading the book aloud. At the end of the book are interactive word study and comprehension activities, followed by a short assessment. Note that these features mimic many of the scaffolding supports and comprehension activities that teachers provide during guided reading lessons; thus, eBooks can provide these supports to students as needed during independent reading. Care must be taken, however, to ensure that these features *support* rather than *supplant* students' actually reading the words on the pages. Likewise, teachers must ensure that these built-in supports do not supplant their own instruction, even when eBooks are part of a comprehensive reading instruction or intervention curricular program.

Some eBooks provide bilingual support. Students can tap a word and see a translation in their home language. Students reading eBooks on a basic Kindle or via a mobile Kindle app can quickly pull up the definition of any word on the page, and with a couple of clicks or taps, they can look up relevant content words on Wikipedia or search through Google. These features are especially useful for ELLs who encounter unknown cultural references. My first language is English, but even when I read on my Kindle, I frequently look up words that are new to me or that I only vaguely know. I would rarely bother to do this if I were reading a printed version of the text.

Another advantage of eBooks is that thousands of books can be stored on a single device or accessed online. ELLs who come from homes with few books can instantly gain access to interesting texts that they will be motivated to read outside of the classroom on a computer, laptop, tablet, eBook reader, or handheld devices they already own or borrow from the school.

Assessing Reading

To help ELLs improve their reading ability, teachers must use formative assessments to continually monitor their reading. To ensure that students are receiving the appropriate instruction, teachers cannot wait for the results of high-stakes reading tests or other summative assessments at the end of the year. Also, as discussed earlier, high-stakes standardized tests are of questionable validity for ELLs. Teachers should also be wary of slick, quick-and-easy skills-based commercial reading assessments that claim to give accurate measures of students' reading ability in a short time. The following sections describe alternative authentic assessments for ELL reading. Note these same assessments should also be conducted in the home language for students in bilingual programs.

Concepts of Print Checklists

For ELLs of any age at the emergent level of literacy, it is important to assess their development of **concepts of print**, which include understanding the differences between letters and words and words and spaces, knowing where to start reading and how to do a return sweep to continue reading the next line, and understanding the basic features of a book, such as title and front and back cover and even how to hold it properly. Although to literate adults these concepts may appear to be common sense, they must be learned. Children who have parents who read to them at home typically develop these concepts before entering kindergarten. Young ELLs from homes with few books, however, or even older ELLs who lacked opportunities for formal education in their home country may need to develop these concepts at school. ELLs who are literate in their home language will transfer most of these concepts, but they will need to learn about any differences between print conventions in their home language and English. Some languages are read right to left or top to bottom, or both; the front and back covers of books in some languages are the opposite of what they are on English books, with reading proceeding from back to front; some languages are not alphabetic (e.g., Chinese); some alphabetic languages do not follow a strict left-to-right encoding sequence, with symbols written one or more levels above or below the main text line or surrounding another symbol on both sides; some languages do not add space between words. These are just a few examples of differences that may exist between English and other writing systems.

The concepts of print checklist (Figure 8.2) can help teachers identify areas in need of instructional focus. The prompts can be used to elicit the responses needed to complete the checklist, though a simple observation of students during SSR would also suffice.

Running Records

A **running record** (or record of reading) is an excellent tool for in-depth observation of a student's reading performance. A running record is essentially a visual recording of the student's reading word by word. It enables a teacher to identify the reading strategies the student may or may not be using and the types of errors the student makes while reading. These errors reveal what is going on in the student's mind as he or she attempts

Assessing Print Understanding

Student name:

Concepts of Print   ✔ where child answered correctly

1. Holds book correctly .... ☐
2. Recognizes front and back of book .... ☐
3. Identifies title or title page .... ☐
4. Knows where to begin reading .... ☐
5. Differentiates words and spaces .... ☐
6. Differentiates first and last letter .... ☐
7. Realizes that print contains meaning .... ☐
8. Is developing directionality and return sweep .... ☐
9. Recognizes difference between words and letters .... ☐
10. Is developing one-to-one correspondence (word match) .... ☐
11. Knows some lowercase/capital letters .... ☐
12. Identifies some basic punctuation (period) .... ☐

Concepts of Print Prompts

Directions: Choose a simple storybook. Tell the child that you will read the story aloud, but that you need his or her help. Then ask these questions and record the word or actions the child uses to answer.

1. If someone were going to read this book, how would he or she hold it? Show me.
2. Show me the front of the book. The back. *(Give 1/2 point for each.)*
3. Where is the title? Show me with your finger.
4. If someone were to read this story, show me where he or she would begin reading.
5. How many words do you count on this page? *(Use a page with three or four words.)*
6. Look at these words. Find one word and tell me the first and last letter.
7. Show me the part that tells the story. *(Show a page with picture and print.)*
8. Show me where you would begin reading on this page. Then where would you go? *or* Where would someone look if he or she were reading this page? Then where? *(Make sure to cover the return sweep and possibly the page turn.)*
9. How many letters are on this page? *(Use a page with about three words.)* How many words?
10. This page says, "_____" *(Use a simple and repetitive page with only a few words on it, no more than three or four.)* Now you read it and point to each word.
11. Would you show me some capital letters on this page and tell me their names? Now show me some lowercase letters and tell me their name? *(Give 1/2 point for each.)*
12. *(Point to the period.)* Do you know what this is?

Figure 8.2 Concepts of print checklist. (From the Wisconsin Department of Public Instruction, Madison, WI 53702.)

to make meaning from the text. Running records allow a teacher to quickly assess the student's strengths and areas in need of improvement. They can be conducted in both English and in the home languages of ELLs who are literate in the home language, and for students in bilingual education programs.

To administer a running record, the teacher provides the student with a book judged to be at his or her current reading level. As the student reads, the teacher makes a series of specialized marks on a running record recording sheet (Figure 8.3). A check mark indicates each word read correctly, and other special markings are used to indicate words that have been omitted, inserted, or substituted with an incorrect word. Notes are made of inserted and substituted words. Other marks can be used to indicate when students self-correct their errors, when they repeat words or phrases, and when they have to ask the teacher for help. The lines of check marks and other markings correspond with the lines and pages of the book, so the teacher can easily go back and figure out which marks go with each word. Alternatively, a pre-prepared running record could have the text of the book already typed on the form, as in Figure 8.3. A blank piece of paper is also suffi-cient for conducting a running record.

After completing a running record, the teacher asks comprehension questions or asks the student to retell the story. This is a crucial component because it reveals whether the student understood what he or she read or was merely "barking" at the print, that is, reading each word separately and distinctly with pauses in between as if they were a list of isolated words.

Once a running record has been completed, the number of words read correctly (total words minus the errors) is divided by the total number of words. This calculation pro-vides a score that indicates the accuracy of the student's reading. More important, it indicates how appropriate the level of the book is for reading instruction. Books read with 95% accuracy or higher may be too easy for use in guided reading. Books read with 90%–94% accuracy are considered to be at the student's instructional level, or within his or her zone of proximal development (ZPD). That is, the book is sufficiently challenging that, through guidance, the student can gain new reading knowledge and skills by read-ing from this book or others at the same level. Books read with 89% accuracy or less are considered to be at the frustration level and generally are not appropriate for either guided or independent reading. A running record score is a key tool for matching a student to appropriate books. The student's performance and individual errors, however, provide even more valuable feedback.

Consider, for example, the completed running record in Figure 8.4 of an ELL's reading of a passage from *Frog and Toad Are Friends* by Arnold Lobel. An untrained teacher only casually listening to this student, Ly, read might conclude that he just needs more pho-nics instruction. But phonics lessons on initial consonant and basic vowel sounds would be a waste of time for Ly. The running record shows that he has strong phonics knowl-edge and is applying it in specific ways. Notice, for example, that in most instances sub-stituted words all start with the same initial consonant as the correct word. Ly's self-corrections of *spring* and *corner* also illustrate his use of phonics knowledge to figure out unknown words. And *closet* for *closed* was actually very close phonetically, differing in spelling only by the final letter.

Some of the errors also show that Ly is reading for meaning. For example, he first read *horse* for *house* but likely made the change when he realized *horse* did not make sense. There is no horse in the story, but there is an illustration above the text showing Toad's house. The substitution of *yelled* for *shouted* did not change the meaning of the

(*text continues page 229*)

Running Record

Student name:

Grade level:

Book title:

Author:

Book level:

	Errors	Self-corrections

Words read correctly _____ ÷ _____ total words = _____ %.

    Self-corrections: _____

$95\%^+$ = Easy

90%–94% = Instructional

Less than 90% = Frustration

Evaluation

1. What are the student's strengths?

2. What types of errors did the student make? Why might the student have made these errors?

3. Describe specific mini-lessons, strategies, and activities that would be beneficial for this student?

Figure 8.3 Running record and evaluation form.

Running Record Practice

Frog and Toad Spring

	Errors	SC
✓ ✓ ✓ ✓ ✓ Frog ran up the path		
✓ ✓ *horse | house* ⓢⓒ to Toad's house.		❘
✓ *kicked* ✓ ✓ ✓ ✓ He knocked on the front door.	❘	
✓ ✓ ✓ *anger? | an...| * Ⓣ There was no answer.	❘	
✓ ✓ *yelled* ✓ "Toad, Toad," shouted Frog	❘	
✓ ✓ ✓ ✓ *ss|pp|ing|sing? spring* ⓢⓒ "wake up. It is spring!"		❘
Ⓣ ✓ ✓ *vock* //"Blah," said a voice	❘❘	
✓ − ✓ ✓ from inside the house.	❘	
✓ ✓ ✓ ✓ "Toad, Toad," cried Frog.		
(✓ ✓ ✓ *R*❘❘ ✓ "The sun is shining!		
✓ ✓ ✓ *mmm| R|melt*, ✓ The snow is melting. Wake up!"	❘	
✓ ✓ ✓ ✓ ✓ *vock* "I am not here," said the voice.	❘	
✓ *walking in* ✓ ✓ Frog walked into the house.	❘❘	
✓ ✓ ✓ It was dark.		
✓ ✓ Ⓣ ✓ *closet* All the//shutters were closed.	❘❘	
✓ ✓ ✓ ✓ ✓ ✓ "Toad, where are you?" called Frog.		
✓ ✓ ✓ ✓ *vock* "Go away," said the voice	❘	
(✓ ✓ *R|corn|corner* ⓢⓒ from a corner of the room.		❘
✓ ✓ *lie down* ✓ Toad was lying in bed.	❘❘	

91
−15
—
76

76 = 83 %   **Number of Self Corrections** 3

Figure 8.4 Running record of an ELL's reading of "Spring." (From Lobel, A. [1970] pp. 4–6. *Frog and Toad are friends.* New York: HarperCollins.)

(*text continued from page 226*)

text. Neither did errors such as *walking in* for *walked in* and *lie down* for *lying* (in bed). Although these words are not syntactically correct, the correct meaning is still conveyed. Even the omission of *inside* did not alter the meaning. The substitution of *kicked* for *knocked* (notice the similarity in the spelling of these words) was awkward but semantically it is a viable possibility. Thus, despite these errors, it is clear that Ly is reading for meaning.

Some of the errors may be attributed to Ly's ELD level in reading. His knowledge of suffixes and verb tense is not yet fully developed, as revealed by the problems he had reading *melting, walked, lying,* and *closed* with full accuracy. There are also some gaps in his vocabulary. He did not know the words *blah* and *shutters*. Perhaps he was unable to self-correct *closet* with *closed* because when the teacher told him the word *shutters,* he did not know the meaning. If he had known what shutters are, he might have been able to make the semantic connection with *closed* (i.e., shutters can be *open* or *closed*.)

Perhaps Ly does know the word *voice* but simply did not recognize it in print because it is a difficult word to decode. Note however, that he did make use of the letter sounds for *v, o,* and *c* and consistently read the word as *vock* all three times it appeared. Another strategy he used, as revealed by the running record, is repetition. He repeated "The sun is" three times before determining that the next word is *shining.* This repetition shows

Table 8.2 Student Self-Assessment for Independent Reading

4 Outstanding!	3 Wow!	2 So-so	1 Oops!
☐ You read the whole time.	☐ You read most of the time.	☐ You read some of the time.	☐ You wasted precious reading time.
☐ You stayed in one good reading spot the whole time.	☐ You stayed in one good reading spot the whole time.	☐ You changed reading spots.	☐ You moved around a lot.
☐ You have "just right" books. (No pretend game.)	☐ You have "just right" books. (No pretend game.)	☐ You had some "just right" books; you could be a little more careful.	☐ You did not have "just right" books; you were not so careful about book choice.
☐ You are reading way down deep; you are lost in the book.	☐ You talked back to the book you are reading at least once.	☐ You sort of understand what you read.	☐ You played the pretend game.
☐ You respected the readers around you.	☐ You respected the readers around you.	☐ You got through some tricky parts but maybe you just skipped some.	☐ You did not respect the other readers around you; you were off track.
☐ You stopped when it didn't make sense.	☐ You tried certain strategies to get through the tricky spots.		☐ You are not sure if you understand what you read.
☐ You read quietly. Shhh!	☐ You read quietly. Shhh!		
☐ You made predictions.	☐ Your books are making sense or you stop and go back.		
☐ You talked back to the book in your mind and on post-its.			
☐ You had a plan for your reading.			

Originally adapted by Juli Kendal from a classroom photograph appearing in Calkins, 2000, p. 78; also available at http://tinyurl.com/oa852hk

that he was reading for meaning, combining meaning and phonics clues to figure out the correct word. *Corn* was corrected to *corner* in a similar manner.

Ly made 15 errors (self-corrections and repetitions do not count as errors). Thus, he read 76 words correctly out of a total of 91 words, meaning he read this selection with 84% accuracy—well below the frustration level. An analysis of this running record will give the teacher several ideas for the next few reading lessons. First, she knows Ly should be asked to read a slightly less difficult book in the next guided reading session. Second, she may decide that Ly is ready for some word-study lessons on verb tenses and suffixes, particularly because he was able to read some of these correctly but not all of them. Finally, she may decide that Ly could benefit from some phonics mini-lessons on words starting with *kn* and words with the diphthong *oi*. She might also start asking Ly to help open and close the shutters on the classroom windows for the next few days, just to help him learn and remember this new vocabulary word.

Conducting running records take practice, but once teachers get the hang of it, they can do them with ease. As a teacher, I conducted running records almost every day, usually when listening to one of my students read to me during guided reading groups. This formative assessment helped me plan guided reading sessions for the next day. Other times I would conduct very formal running records, particularly on district-identified benchmark books that officially determined students' reading levels. I added these records to the students' reading portfolios as important summative assessments of their progress.

Reading Self-Assessments

Many teachers use **reading self-assessments** for students to keep track of their own use of strategies and to assess their ability to stay on task. See, for example, the rubric shown in Table 8.2 for use with middle school ELLs to self-assess their independent reading. Note that this rubric is not just a self-assessment. It also makes explicit the teacher's expectations for students' behaviors and use of strategies during this important part of the school day.

Summary

Reading is the most important skill students develop in school, yet reading instruction is often the subject of heated political debate. The main source of reading difficulty for ELLs—their beginning levels of oral English—typically gets lost in the debate. Research reviews on literacy instruction for ELLs have identified problems associated with skills-based instructional approaches that lack emphasis on reading for meaning and have brought renewed attention to the need for oral language development and balanced literacy instruction in meaningful contexts.

ELLs in unbalanced literacy programs that focus on skills-based instruction typically are able to decode words successfully but struggle to comprehend the meaning of extended texts. ELLs need balanced literacy instruction that provides greater emphasis on actual reading of authentic texts. The Common Core standards for reading call for engaging students in meaningful literary and informational texts of increasing complexity. Extensive reading of such texts allows students to acquire knowledge and skills, such as new vocabulary and language skills, naturally with scaffolding from their teacher. ELLs' progress through reading levels is affected by age, home language literacy skills, and ELD level in reading, listening, speaking, and writing. ELD standards and progressions help teachers plan reading instruction that is appropriate for students at different levels of English language development. The reading *to*, *with*, and *by* framework helps teachers structure effective instruction and provide scaffolding through the use of interactive read-alouds, shared reading, guided reading, close reading, independent reading, narrow reading, and Reader's Workshop. BDA provides a framework to support students' development of prereading (before), during reading, and postreading (after) strategies that maximize comprehensible input. Word study and interactive vocabulary mini-lessons are also effective ways to maximize students' learning of new vocabulary encountered while reading. To assess students' reading skills and knowledge, teachers can use the print checklist concepts with emergent readers and running records with students at all levels to determine their reading level and analyze miscues (errors) and to plan effective instruction. Self-assessments in reading enable students to monitor their own progress and internalize and meet their teacher's high expectations.

Discussion Questions

1. If you have learned (or tried to learn) a new language, what challenges did you face in learning to read in that language? Did your teachers use any of the reading strategies, approaches, or techniques outlined in this chapter? What role do you feel your home language played in the development of your reading ability in that language? Relate your experience to the challenges ELLs face in learning to read English.

2. The research reports from NLP, CREDE, and the National Academies point out that ELLs who learn to decode may have trouble comprehending what they read. What are some of the sources of this problem? Why is oral language development critical in addressing this issue? How can the framework of reading *to, with,* and *by* ELLs be used to place greater emphasis on meaning and comprehension?

3. In many basal-reading programs, all students are expected to read the same story at the same time and receive the same lessons based on the story. Similarly, the CCSS call for reading instruction in which all students read the same grade-level texts of increasing complexity. How can such approaches be problematic for ELLs? What are some ways you could match ELLs to books more appropriate to their language and literacy levels?

4. View video clip #3, which is part of a reading comprehension and vocabulary lesson taught by the San Francisco 7th grade English teacher Liz Feirst using the Word Generation program. In this clip, Ms. Feirst reads aloud an informational text about violence in the media. What are some of the strategies she uses to engage students in the reading, and to teach, reinforce, and review key vocabulary words? How effective are these strategies and the lesson as a whole? View and discuss the other clips in the lesson to see how she prepared students for the read-aloud and the follow-up oral language activities for students to practice using the new vocabulary.

5. Review Lesson 4 in the model unit *Persuasion across Time and Space*, developed by the Understanding Language Initiative to demonstrate effective instruction for helping ELLs meet the demands of the CCSS in English language arts. This lesson for middle-school ELLs at the intermediate-to-advanced levels of English proficiency involves the reading of the complex historical text "All Together Now," a speech given by Representative Barbara Jordan during the civil rights movement. Discuss the purpose and objectives of the lesson and the strategies and techniques utilized to achieve these objectives. How do these strategies and techniques compare with those in this chapter? How effective do

you feel these are, and how effective do you feel the lesson is as a whole, for helping ELLs meet the CCSS for reading?

Research Activities

1. *ELL Student Assessment* Conduct a running record with an ELL student, using a book that is on about the same level as books he or she is currently reading in class for reading instruction. Determine, according to the results of the running record, whether the book is at the student's instructional level. Complete the evaluation of the student's strengths, errors, and instructional needs.

2. *ELL Teacher Interview* Interview an ELL teacher about the difficulties faced in helping ELL students develop their reading skills in English. Ask about the teacher's views and experiences with helping ELLs meet the expectations of the CCSS or the state's standards for reading. What strategies and activities did the teacher find most helpful in improving the students' reading skills in English?

3. *ELL Classroom Observation* Observe one or more reading lessons for ELLs in a classroom. Record details on the name of the curricular program (if any), the materials used in the lesson, and ways in which the teacher and students interacted with each other and the text. Pay particular attention to the students' actual reading of the text and to evidence of their comprehension (or lack thereof) of the text. Discuss your observations, focusing on what you thought was effective and what could be improved.

4. *Online Research Activity* Using the ELL Language Portraits site, review and compare the reading performance videos of two or more students. Assess these students' reading using the running record forms embedded in the site. Compare your running record, scores, and comments about the students' strengths and areas in need of improvement with the completed forms provided on the site. Describe and discuss any differences.

Recommended Reading

Calderón, M., & Slakk, S. (2018). *Teaching reading to English language learners, grades 6–12: A framework for improving achievement in the content areas* (2nd ed.). Thousand Oaks, CA: Sage.

Paying attention to the often neglected ELLs at the middle and high school levels, the second edition of this popular book highlights Calderón's successful ExC-ELL (Expediting Comprehension for English Language Learners) model and discusses lessons learned in the decade since the first edition was published.

Helman, L. (Ed.) (2017). *Literacy development with English learners: Research-based instruction in grades K–6* (2nd ed.). New York: Guilford.

Provides a detailed synthesis of cutting-edge scholarship on the literacy development of ELLs at all levels of English proficiency. Features case studies, vignettes, samples of student work, and examples of high-quality instruction.

Singer, T. W. (2018). *EL excellence every day: The flip-to-guide for differentiating academic literacy*. Thousand Oaks, CA: Corwin.

Features over 80 effective strategies teachers can quickly flip to for use in differentiating their literacy instruction for ELLs.

Nine

Writing

The only way to help students improve their writing is to read what they write and talk to them about their writing.

—Juli Kendall

KEY TERMS

- analytic scoring
- evidence-based writing
- guided writing
- holistic scoring
- independent writing
- interactive writing
- invented spelling
- journals
- modeled writing
- multi-trait scoring
- personal word book
- primary trait scoring
- process writing
- shared writing
- thematic word chart
- translingual practice
- word wall
- Writer's Workshop

GUIDING QUESTIONS

1. What does the research tell us about effective writing instruction for ELLs?
2. What does a theory of second language writing include?
3. How is writing related to oral language and reading?
4. How can state college-and-career-readiness standards and English language development standards from WIDA, ELPA21, and individual states guide writing instruction for ELLs?
5. How can an assessment of ELLs' writing strengths and needs inform a teacher's choice of instructional approaches, methods, and strategies?

Writing is one of the most important skills students learn in school, and like reading, it is crucial to ELLs' academic success because it is one of the principal means by which ELLs self-reflect and display their knowledge and competence across academic subjects. All teachers share in the responsibility of helping ELLs develop proficiency in writing.

Although all students face the challenge of developing their writing to grade-level expectations, ELLs face the additional challenge of learning to write before they are proficient speakers of English. Another challenge, particularly for newcomers, is that they are learning to adjust socially and culturally to a new country and a new school. Ferris and Hedgcock (2014) point out that ELLs learning to write may need more of everything—procedures, heuristics, content, practice, and feedback—than English-speaking students. They note that, unlike proficient English speakers, ELL writers

- begin with an intact home language and a developing knowledge of spoken and written English as a second language;
- are simultaneously acquiring language and composing skills;
- may or may not be familiar with the Roman alphabet and may thus still be learning English orthographic conventions;
- may produce sentence-level errors influenced by their home language or languages;
- may not have the same topic/schematic knowledge as non-ELL writers because of their home country educational experience;
- may have little or no experience with peer response; and
- may have little or no experience using outside sources, paraphrasing, and quoting.

This chapter helps teachers make principled decisions about teaching writing to the ELLs in their classes, drawing on research, theory, policy, and practice. We first review what we know from current research and theory on writing instruction for ELLs, and then we look at the expectations for student writing under the Common Core State Standards. Next we discuss writing instruction through the framework of writing *to*, *with*, and *by* ELLs. We then consider additional supports teachers can provide as ELLs develop their English writing skills across the content areas. Finally, we describe effective and appropriate ways to assess students' writing.

What We Know from Research on Writing Instruction for English Language Learners

The following findings are from the National Literacy Panel (NLP) report (August & Shanahan, 2006a, 2006b; August et al., 2014), the Center for Research on Education, Diversity, and Excellence (CREDE) report (Genesee, Lindholm-Leary, Saunders, & Christian, 2006), and the National Academies of Sciences, Engineering, and Medicine (2017) report discussed in earlier chapters, and the work of other experts on second language writing.

The writing development process for ELLs is similar to the process for proficient English speakers.

Both ELLs and proficient English speakers must learn the (English) alphabet, spelling, syntax for forming sentences and paragraphs, and conventions for writing specific genres. Both engage in literacy tasks in a variety of social contexts and use writing to interact and develop interpersonal relationships.

ELLs' ability to express themselves in written English is highly dependent on their level of oral English proficiency.

The NLP, CREDE, and National Academies reports found a close relationship between ELLs' oral proficiency in English and their ability to express themselves in written English. This relationship is consistent with research findings on the importance of oral language. With the exception, for example, of older immigrant students who learned to write English in English-as-a-foreign-language classes in their home countries, most ELLs are unlikely to use words in writing they do not know orally, and the language forms they use in writing will typically be limited, at least initially, to the forms they are able to use in conversation. Simply put, ELLs' writing may be only as good as their English speaking ability. Teachers, however, should not delay writing instruction until students are able to speak English well. Beginning-level ELLs benefit from writing instruction that focuses on topics they can talk about. Such instruction supports their English language development.

Students with literacy skills in their home language can transfer many of these skills to English writing.

The NLP, CREDE, and National Academies reports also found a strong relationship between students' writing ability in their home language and their writing ability in English. This relationship is similar to the one found between reading ability in the home language and reading ability in English. As with reading, students' home language writing skills are a major asset because much of their knowledge will transfer to English. For example, a 4th grade student who attended grades K–3 in Mexico will already know how to hold a pencil; how to form letters; how to write words, sentences, and paragraphs; and how writing is used for communication. This student may also be familiar with the conventions of different genres of writing and will simply need to develop enough proficiency in English to use these skills in his or her new language, while learning the conventions, styles, and other features specific to English writing. This transfer of skills is one of the primary reasons bilingual education programs place emphasis on helping ELLs first develop literacy skills in their home language.

Research suggests that letter formation and spelling skills may most easily transfer for those students who are literate in home languages that use the same alphabet as English (e.g., Spanish, French, German, Tagalog). But even if a student has literacy skills in a language with a different alphabetic script, such as Russian, Khmer, Hindi, or Arabic, or a nonalphabetic language, such as Chinese, many other writing skills will still easily transfer to English.

Not all transfer from the first language, however, is positive transfer. The CREDE report found instances of negative cross-language influences that might show up, for example, when a Spanish-speaking ELL applies Spanish phonological and orthographic rules to English spelling. Consider the following sentence a Spanish-speaking ELL wrote in her journal, describing what she did over the weekend:

Dend ay it a sanwich end hotchetoos.

[Then I eat a sandwich and Hot Cheetos.]

This student is using her knowledge of Spanish phonics to write words in English, thus *ay* for *I*, *it* for *eat*, and *end* for *and*. Because the /th/ sound does not exist in Spanish, the student approximates the spelling for *then* by applying Spanish phonics to how she hears and pronounces it, *dend*. The CREDE report emphasizes, however, that this "negative" transfer is actually a good sign because it shows that the student is using an effective strategy, applying her Spanish writing skills to writing in English. Most students quickly figure out what does and what does not transfer. Also, teachers can plan instruction to help students recognize and avoid instances of negative transfer.

English oral language skills have little impact on English word-level writing skills.

Word-level skills such as spelling are not strongly related to oral language skills in English. Thus, ELLs can memorize the spelling of words without knowing their meaning or how to use them in a sentence.

English oral language skills have a strong impact on English text-level writing skills.

English oral language skills have a strong impact on writing when large chunks of text are involved, such as sentences, paragraphs, and complete narratives. Thus, students with well-developed oral language skills in English tend to have better writing skills in English. The oral language skills of listening comprehension and vocabulary knowledge were found to be specifically related to better writing.

As evidence of this finding, consider the responses to the prompt, "What did you do this weekend?" written by two Spanish-speaking students with different levels of oral English proficiency that appear in Figure 9.1. Note that both students are still relying on their knowledge of Spanish writing, and so we see examples of negative transfer in both responses. Student B, however, clearly has better oral English skills. The length and variety of her sentence structures reveal that she has a larger vocabulary and greater knowledge of English syntax to draw on for her writing.

Student A	Student B
I go tu the puga en i go tu mi stesto jos en i go tu mi gamo jos en i go tu mi fen jos en spn the nit en I go tu pore den i go tu mi jos.*	This Friday i do my homework and wend i finchis my mom need help to do the tortillas to send en Mexico. Then wend my fahtre get home wiht my sisteher Mariana my mom med riec with milk and same time my great gran mother she meke os my mom then niting i went to bed and i went to seelp.
	This Saturday in tha mornig i se carates and is april fool day. Then late time my famaly and i went Mall to Buy some. Then the nitgn i read the book and is great then went to seelp.
*I believe this says, "I go to the pulga [flea market] and I go to my sister house and I go to my grandma house and I go to my friend house and spend the night and I go to party then I go to my house."	And This Sunday i was sike and my siste curde me and I was felen good and tehn i tro up. Then at leat my fatrer just came home. My motrer made pinchillo-wit rice. Then at niting y went to seelp.

Figure 9.1 Responses by 2nd grade Spanish-speaking ELLs to the prompt, "What did you do this weekend?"

Age and prior knowledge affect ELLs' writing ability in English.

The demands and expectations for writing increase substantially by grade level. Writing tasks must be appropriate to the age and grade level of students. Notice, however, that "grade-level appropriateness" assumes that students have already progressed through English writing instruction and development in previous grades. Such an assumption cannot be made for newcomer ELLs, who may not have had the opportunity to attend school or develop strong home language writing skills before coming to the United States. Thus, what is appropriate for a 5th grade student born in the United States, for example, may not be appropriate for a 10- or 11-year-old refugee ELL from Burma. Teachers need to differentiate writing instruction for these students, ensuring that it is appropriate to their English proficiency and writing development levels. Writing also requires prior knowledge about topic and genre. Students cannot be expected to write about a topic they know little about in a genre they do not know.

Theoretical Frameworks for Second Language Writing and Translingual Practices

One major challenge in teaching ELLs to write in English is that the field of second language writing is relatively new and we lack a comprehensive theory of second language writing (Silva & Matsuda, 2010). Cumming (2016) notes that each of the various competing theories provides valuable contributions to our understanding of second language writing, and new theories will continue to emerge. But, he argues, a singular theory is unlikely to emerge because "L2 writing is inherently multi-faceted" and involves "multiple issues and orientations that may not even be commensurate with other" (p. 65). Before the 1960s, ESL instruction focused on oral language. The first textbooks on ESL writing did not appear until the 1990s; the first academic journal on the subject, the *Journal of Second Language Writing,* appeared in 1992.

Ferris and Hedgcock (2014) describe how research, theory, and practice in ESL writing has evolved since the late 1960s when the focus was on the application of grammar rules to write well-formed sentences and narrow paragraphs. In 1976, educators and theorists began to focus more and more on the process writers use and the stages of writing they go through, leading to the Writer's Workshop instructional approach (described in a later section). In the late 1980s, greater attention was given to ESL and other second language writing, including writing for academic purposes across content areas. Throughout the 1980s and 1990s the focus on teaching the specialized conventions of academic writing in different content areas continued, and greater attention was given to social interaction in peer response and collaborative writing tasks. The 1990s also brought a critical pedagogy lens to literacy instruction, including the ethical, ideological, political, socioeconomic, and power issues related to literacy instruction and uses in society. Much of this work parallels developments in first language writing, and each focus is aligned with a particular school of thought, though there is considerable overlap among them. Teachers need to understand different theories for both first and second language writing, and the broad range of instructional issues for classroom writing.

At the turn of the 21st century and through the 2010s, sociocultural theories led to views of second language writing through the lens of bilingualism and biliteracy. Thus, research and practice began to look holistically at the ways students draw on their home languages and English as they develop their writing skills (Escamilla, Butvilofsky, & Hopewell, 2017). For example, the term **translingual practice** is used to highlight the ways bilingual students draw on all of their linguistic resources as they produce written texts in English and other languages. Translingual practice is grounded in principles of translanguaging. A translingual approach explores the multidimensional literacy practices of bilinguals (Canagarajah, 2015). As described in a later section, the influence of the literacy practices in one language can lead to writing "errors" in the other. Translingual practice, however, considers the effective ways bilinguals can produce biliterate texts that skillfully interweave words and phrases from one language into the other (also referred to as code meshing), and the ways bilingual writers can produce unique and creative texts in one language that are nonetheless informed by their linguistic knowledge in the other language. Escamilla, Hopewell, and Butvilofsky's (2013) Literacy Squared approach also looks holistically at the writing development of emerging bilinguals. Their research, theory, practice, and professional development is structured around a holistic biliteracy framework that looks at students' two languages side-by-side. They provide tools teachers can use to understand, value, develop, and assess biliterate writing in programs that aim for biliteracy.

Relationship between Reading and Writing

Researchers have found a strong relationship between ELLs' reading ability and their writing ability in English. The more students read at appropriate levels, the more vocabulary and language structures they will acquire. This knowledge, in turn, can be used in their writing. Findings from research also reveal that the more students read, the more they write, and the better they write, the less apprehensive they are about writing (Calderón &

Slakk, 2018). Biliteracy research demonstrates the connection between reading, writing, and oracy across languages (Escamilla et al., 2017).

When young ELLs are exposed to environmental print, such as logos, traffic signs, store names, and product names, and to print in lists, books, letters, brochures, and magazines, they come to understand that people read different kinds of materials for different purposes, that print carries meaning and that it makes sense. This understanding enables young ELLs to write different kinds of texts for different purposes. Storybook reading with young ELLs is essential to support their writing development. The students learn how to handle books, and they learn about story elements and begin to understand the concepts of letter, word, sentence, and directionality. They take this knowledge developed from their reading and apply it to their writing. Students' writing about a text they have read enhances their comprehension of that text, "because it provides [them] with a tool for visibly and permanently recording, connecting, analyzing, personalizing, and manipulating key ideas of the text" (Calerón & Slakk, 2018).

Reading becomes more and more important to students' writing development as they gain greater proficiency in English. Kroll (1993) asserts in the title of her classic article, "Teaching Writing Is Teaching Reading" (and vice versa). She notes three ways in which reading can support ELLs' writing. First, readings can be used as a springboard for a topic to write about. For example, a teacher might read to the class the book *A Chair for My Mother* by Vera B. Williams, which describes a family's effort to save money to buy a comfortable chair for their apartment after losing their furniture in a fire. The students might then be encouraged to write about their own experiences saving money to buy something special. Short newspaper or magazine articles on controversial topics can be effective in motivating older students to write a response and express their own opinions. Second, readings can provide background information and source material for students to write about a specific topic. For example, if students write reports about their home country (or the home country of their parents), they can read related books and articles to find facts and details to include in their writing. Finally, readings can be used as a model of a particular writing feature for students to imitate. For example, if a teacher wants his students to include more dialogue in their stories using quotation marks and using words other than just *said* before or after each quotation, he could read with students a book such as *Arthur and the Lost Diary* by Marc Brown and draw the students' attention to the skillful way in which the author uses dialogue in his stories. Students could practice imitating Brown's style and then integrate it into their own writing to create dialogues. Likewise, in the content areas, reading history reports and science lab reports, for example, provides students with important models to write their own.

Effective teachers understand this strong relationship between reading and writing. Teachers who look at literacy from a bilingual, sociocultural perspective also understand the strong relationship between the home language and English. Effective teachers find creative ways to integrate reading and writing instruction across content areas. They provide meaningful instruction, guidance, and activities for students to use reading to further develop their writing ability.

Stages in English Language Learner Writing Development

Researchers have attempted to identify the stages ELLs may go through in their early writing development, noting that these stages are similar to those proficient-English-speaking writers go through (Peregoy & Boyle, 2017). Samway (2006) lists six stages (Table 9.1). But she urges caution, pointing out that ELLs' writing development is not

Table 9.1 Developmental Stages in Early English Language Learner Writing

Scribble writing (and drawing)	• Scribbles often reflect the orthography of the native language. • Letters are often approximations of standardized letters. • Scribbles for writing and drawing are often differentiated.	
Strings of letters	• There is no sound-symbol correspondence. • Numbers and other symbols are often interspersed. • Spacing between letters is often absent.	
Letters representing whole words or thoughts*	• There is some sound-symbol correspondence. • There are some correctly spelled words, which are usually sight words and high-frequency words that may be displayed in the classroom. • Some spacing appears between words (and sometimes between letters). • There is a simple message, which is often in the form of a label. • Pictures are often as important as the writing. • As first, writers of English tend to capture beginning consonants, then ending consonants, then medial consonants, and finally vowels. • At this stage, students may have difficulty reading their own texts.	
Stylized sentences	• Writing is often patterned (e.g., This is a . . . ; This is a . . .) • Writers may rely on familiar words, often those displayed in the classroom. • Texts become longer and include more conventional spelling. • Students can usually read their own writing.	*I see a hat.* *I see a dog.* *I see a cat.* *I see a man.* *I see a car and a tree and a house.*
Emerging standardized writing	• Messages are longer, often reflecting the writer's eagerness to focus on quantity (frequent use of *and then . . .*) • Punctuation may not be used conventionally. • Spelling may become more unconventional as the writer takes more risks in incorporating less familiar or frequently occurring words. • If L1 uses the same alphabet as English, and the student is literate in L1, some spelling may be based on the sound system of the L1.	*After dad I wend to the truck so we can go to church. Den chur was ofer. So we go to the park ten we go to the house after tha a went to sleep beacouse eat was geatheang dark.*
Standardized writing	• Writing is better organized and more focused. • Word choice is more varied and voice is more apparent. • Spelling is more standardized, except when writers are using unfamiliar vocabulary. • Punctuation is more conventional and varied.	*The gratest memory with my family is when me and my family had a vacation to Galveston. I was so excited to go and to swim in the water. We all packed our close snaks and some food to eat. While my dad was driving I couldn't stop thinking of the fun we are going to through. After we go their we went to a store full of swimig suits sandals water volley balls and a lot of more stuff. Each of us bot swiming suits.*

*There are seven bullet points in this section; but because of space considerations, only one of these types of writing is illustrated.

Samples in the 3rd column were gathered by the author and represent only a single example of what ELL writing may look like at each stage.

Box 9.1 Alternative Approach to Traditional Spelling Tests

The fact that literate individuals can spell tens of thousands of words they have never had on a spelling test provides evidence that students do not learn how to spell through spelling tests.

Spelling tests do not take into account individual students' spelling strengths and needs. All students are given the same list of words, with little attention to their meaning. Many effective teachers have found that they can forgo spelling tests altogether and help students develop their spelling skills in the context of meaningful writing instruction as outlined in this chapter.

If spelling tests must be used, here are some guidelines for alternatives to traditional spelling tests:

- Use formative assessments to identify the words, or types of words, students want and need to learn to spell.
- Use these findings to create different spelling lists for different groups of students.
- Provide word-study mini-lessons throughout the week with each group based on their word lists.
- Test each group of students on their own list of words.

If required to use a school or district prescribed spelling curriculum or list of words:

- Ensure that ELLs know the meaning of each word; provide vocabulary instruction as needed.
- Give a pretest to see which words each student already knows how to spell.
- Require students to practice and do homework only with the words they got wrong.
- Provide word study mini-lessons to small groups using the words the students got wrong.

necessarily linear and varies from student to student, even when they speak the same home language and have had similar amounts of exposure to instruction in English. She notes that quality and quantity may vary from piece to piece and draft to draft for the same writer and that some students may skip stages.

Students' writing often reflects their confidence and engagement as writers. Some students may write only words they already know how to spell. But as they gain more confidence in their writing, they start to take risks by including words they cannot spell correctly yet. To include these words, they approximate the spelling, using their knowledge of sound-symbol correspondence—a process teachers call **invented spelling**, or developmental spelling. Some adults worry that such spelling is a regression in the students' writing ability. Some charge that teachers who allow students to use invented spelling are lazy and are harming students by not demanding standardized spelling and correcting their spelling errors. For this reason, some teachers may be afraid to send student writing home or display it on classroom walls if it contains invented spelling. Those who oppose invented spelling also assume that spelling tests are needed to help students learn how to spell words correctly (Box 9.1).

Opposition to invented spelling shows ignorance of the development of children's writing. As Samway notes, it actually reveals the students' growth as writers. Invented spelling reflects knowledge of phonics but also demonstrates the limitations of phonics to help students determine a word's standardized spelling (e.g., Why isn't *said* spelled *sed?*). Many educators prefer to call invented spelling *temporary* or *transitional spelling,* because it truly is temporary. As students read and write more, and as teachers provide supportive writing instruction and practice, their spelling becomes more standardized (as shown in Table 9.1). And at some stages in the writing process, as we shall see, correcting spelling errors is appropriate.

Common Core State Standards for Writing

The Common Core State Standards (CCSS) include specific standards for writing (Box 9.2). These broad anchor standards, focusing on text types and purposes, production and distribution of writing, research to build and present knowledge, and range of writing, provide the basis for more specific corresponding writing standards broken down by grade level. As noted in previous chapters, these standards were designed for English-proficient students but apply to all students in Common Core states, including ELLs. The CCSS stress that a broad range of writing skills and particular genres of writing are critical for college and career readiness:

> To build a foundation for college and career readiness, students need to learn to use writing as a way of offering and supporting opinions, demonstrating understanding of the subjects they are studying, and conveying real and imagined experiences and events. They learn to appreciate that a key purpose of writing is to communicate clearly to an external, sometimes unfamiliar audience, and they begin to adapt the form and content of their writing to accomplish a particular task and purpose. They develop the capacity to build knowledge on a subject

---

Box 9.2 College and Career Readiness Anchor Standards for Writing

Text Types and Purposes

1. Write arguments to support claims in an analysis of substantive topics or texts, using valid reasoning and relevant and sufficient evidence.
2. Write informative/explanatory texts to examine and convey complex ideas and information clearly and accurately through the effective selection, organization, and analysis of content.
3. Write narratives to develop real or imagined experiences or events using effective technique, well-chosen details, and well-structured event sequences.

Production and Distribution of Writing

4. Produce clear and coherent writing in which the development, organization, and style are appropriate to task, purpose, and audience.
5. Develop and strengthen writing as needed by planning, revising, editing, rewriting, or trying a new approach.
6. Use technology, including the Internet, to produce and publish writing and to interact and collaborate with others.

Research to Build and Present Knowledge

7. Conduct short as well as more sustained research projects based on focused questions, demonstrating understanding of the subject under investigation.
8. Gather relevant information from multiple print and digital sources, assess the credibility and accuracy of each source, and integrate the information while avoiding plagiarism.
9. Draw evidence from literary or informational texts to support analysis, reflection, and research.

Range of Writing

10. Write routinely over extended time frames (time for research, reflection, and revision) and shorter time frames (a single sitting or a day or two) for a range of tasks, purposes, and audiences.

through research projects and to respond analytically to literary and informational sources. To meet these goals, students must devote significant time and effort to writing, producing numerous pieces over short and extended time frames throughout the year. (ELA Standards, p. 18. © Copyright 2010 National Governors Association Center for Best Practices and Council of Chief State School Officers)

These standards represent a significant shift to a focus on writing argumentative and informational texts and producing **evidence-based writing**, that is, writing that features evidence that is grounded in texts the students have read, rather than in their personal views and experiences (e.g., Standards 1, 2, 7, 8, and 9). Evidence-based writing is also referred to as "writing from the source." Some critics are concerned about the de-emphasis of personal narratives and creative writing, along with the disinterest in students' views, experiences, background knowledge, and personal voice in their writing. According to a report in the *Atlantic*, this de-emphasis may reflect the view of the architect of the CCSS, David Coleman, who says

> the new writing standards are meant to reverse a pedagogical pendulum that has swung too far, favoring self-expression and emotion over lucid communication. "As you grow up in this world, you realize people really don't give a s*** about what you feel or what you think," he famously told a group of educators last year in New York. (Tyre, 2012, par. 8)

Ironically, Coleman—named by *Time* magazine in 2013 as one of the 100 most influential people in the world—draws on his own experience to support his bluntly stated argument. Despite his view, there is still space for personal narrative and creative writing in the Common Core (e.g., Standard 3).

Experienced educators value students' work, voices, and emotions in these genres and recognize that these genres are more appealing and can even empower students as they develop as writers. They also provide a foundation for writing the types of informational and argumentative texts that are equally important. For example, Zehr (2017–2018) demonstrates how she combined requirements for analytical and evidence-based writing while also supporting her adolescent immigrant ELLs' social and emotional development. She guided her students through the reading of several books by or about immigrant students like themselves, then helped them draw on these books as sources to reflect on and tell their own personal stories. Zehr observes that through such writing practices:

> My students realize they don't experience the angst of immigration and adolescence alone. They see that many of their peers have also survived trauma or have had similar difficulties adjusting to a new school or a new language and culture. Sharing in this way also can improve their fluency in English and lets them see themselves as writers, which builds their confidence and builds community as well. (pp. 13–14)

As described in a previous chapter, the Understanding Language (2012) initiative created a sample unit called *Persuasion across Time and Space: Analyzing and Producing Persuasive Texts* to illustrate how the CCSS can be put into effective practice with ELLs. In addition to encouraging the close reading of complex texts, the unit is designed to help middle-school ELLs at intermediate to advanced levels of English proficiency write persuasive texts. Thus, the unit includes scaffolded writing activities. The approaches and strategies used in this sample unit are consistent with those outlined in this chapter. They will provide opportunities to address the writing standards of the CCSS or the writing standards specific to your state.

Promoting Writing Development
for English Language Learners in the Classroom

To ensure that ELLs learn to write for social and academic purposes, all teachers need to know their ELLs' strengths and needs in second language writing and have a clear idea of what they want their students to know and be able to do with writing as a result of their instruction. Teachers draw on their understanding of writing development for ELLs and select appropriate strategies to scaffold students' learning, differentiate instruction based on the writing needs of the students in the class, and use classroom-based assessments of writing performance to guide instruction and provide evidence of writing growth.

This section begins with a brief discussion of how to identify ELLs' writing strengths and needs in English. We then review a wide range of instructional strategies teachers can use to promote their ELLs' writing development in any content area and at any grade level.

Using English Language Proficiency
Standards to Guide Writing Instruction

The English language proficiency standards from the WIDA and ELPA21 consortia and individual states provide a useful tool for considering the language demands of writing and specific writing tasks at different levels of English proficiency. Recall that these standards provide progressions across different levels of English proficiency at each grade level. The standards and progressions can give teachers at specific grade levels an understanding of what can be expected of students in the area of writing across different content areas, and also what instruction and guidance will be needed to help students move up to the next level. This information is critical for planning appropriate writing instruction activities and practice, particularly for modeled and guided writing lessons. Consider the English language proficiency standards and progressions in Table 9.2 for grade 6 writing. Note that the level of difficulty of the writing task increases as the level of support decreases for each subsequent proficiency level. Note also that these progressions correspond with the CCSS Writing Standards 1–4.

To meet these standards, teachers need to provide students with ample opportunities for authentic writing. Teachers with ELLs who can or who are learning to write in their home language can build on this strong foundation to guide students' writing development in English. Teachers in WIDA states or states with standards or progressions for Spanish language arts or Spanish language development (or for other home languages) can draw on these tools to determine students' strengths and needs or use rubrics such as those developed by Escamilla et al. (2013) as they track students' progress and help them develop their biliteracy skills.

Writing *to*, *with*, and *by* English Language Learners

Like reading *to, with,* and *by* ELLs, writing *to, with,* and *by* ELLs allows teachers to model and scaffold the writing process to help ELLs become confident and skilled independent writers within a balanced literacy approach. Writing *to* ELLs includes modeled writing, and writing *with* ELLs includes interactive, shared, and guided writing. Writing *by* ELLs includes independent writing, such as journals, and Writer's Workshop.

Modeled Writing

Teachers demonstrate the writing process through **modeled writing**, producing a text in enlarged print on a writing easel, white board, chalk board, or overhead projector or

Table 9.2 Progressions in English Language Development and Proficiency Standards for Writing (Grade 6)

Level 1 Entering	Level 2 Emerging	Level 3 Developing	Level 4 Expanding	Level 5 Bridging
Identify conventions and mechanics in peers' writing (e.g., by highlighting) using models and environmental print.	Identify language to be edited in peers' writing using models and rubrics.	Suggest edits of peers' writing using models and rubrics.	Give reasons for editing peers' writing using models and rubrics.	Explain editing of peers' writing through detailed feedback using models and rubrics.

Level 1	Level 2	Level 3	Level 4	Level 5
With support (including context and visual aids) and nonverbal communication, • communicate simple information about an event or topic; and • use a narrow range of vocabulary and syntactically simple sentences with limited control.	With support (including modeled sentences), • recount a brief sequence of events in order; • introduce an informational topic; • present one or two facts about the topic; • use some commonly occurring linking words (e.g., *next, because, and, also*); and • provide a concluding statement with emerging control.	• Recount a short sequence of events, with a beginning, middle, and end. • Introduce and develop an informational topic with a few facts and details. • Use common transitional words and phrases to connect events, ideas, and opinions (e.g., *after a while, for example, in order to, as a result*). • Provide a conclusion with developing control.	• Recount a more detailed sequence of events or steps in a process, with a beginning, middle, and end. • Introduce and develop an informational topic with facts and details. • Use a variety of transitional words and phrases to connect events, ideas, and opinions (e.g., *however, on the other hand, from that moment on*). • Provide a concluding section with increasingly independent control.	• Recount a complex sequence of events or steps in a process, with a beginning, middle, and end. • Introduce and effectively develop an informational topic with facts and details. • Use a wide variety of transitional words and phrases to show logical relationships between events and ideas. • Provide a concluding section.

Entering (Beginner)	Emerging (Low Intermediate)	Transitioning (High Intermediate)	Expanding (Advanced)	Commanding (Proficient)
Use pre-taught words and phrases to complete cloze paragraphs that clearly introduce, conclude, and support claims by organizing reasons and evidence.	Use pre-identified words and phrases to write two or more paragraphs that clearly introduce, conclude, and support claims by organizing reasons and evidence.	Use a word bank and the previously completed graphic organizers to develop a short essay that clearly introduces, concludes, and supports claims by organizing reasons and evidence.	Use the previously completed graphic organizers and teacher-provided models to develop an essay that clearly introduces, concludes, and supports claims by organizing reasons and evidence.	Use knowledge of the text, independently, to develop a multiple-paragraph essay that clearly introduces, concludes, and supports claims by organizing reasons and evidence.

California

Emerging	Expanding	Bridging
a. Write short literary and informational texts (e.g., an argument for protecting the rainforests) collaboratively (e.g., with peers) and independently.	a. Write longer literary and informational texts (e.g., an argument for protecting the rainforests) collaboratively (e.g., with peers) and independently, using appropriate text organization.	a. Write longer and more detailed literary and informational texts (e.g., an argument for protecting the rainforests) collaboratively (e.g., with peers) and independently, using appropriate text organization and growing understanding of register.
b. Write brief summaries of texts and experiences using complete sentences and key words (e.g., from notes or graphic organizers).	b. Write increasingly concise summaries of texts and experiences using complete sentences and key words (e.g., from notes or graphic organizers).	b. Write clear and coherent summaries of texts and experiences using complete and concise sentences and key words (e.g., from notes or graphic organizers).

WIDA, 2012a, p. 83 (courtesy of WIDA Consortium); ELPA 21, Grade 6, Standard 9, p. 110. Retrieved February 15, 2019 from www.elpa21.org/sites/default/files/Final%204_30%20ELPA21%Standards_1.pdf; EngageNY, 2014, Writing (W), Standard 1, Grade 6, p. 2; California Department of Education, 2014, p. 91.

on a computer projected on a screen so that all the students can see the text as it is being written. This process is particularly important for ELLs because they may lack models of proficient English writing at home. Modeled writing provides the means to address Common Core Writing Standards 2 and 4, as teachers show students how to convey ideas and information clearly and accurately and how to produce clear and coherent writing appropriate to the task, purpose, and audience.

In modeled writing, the teacher controls the pen and composes and writes the text on her own. As she writes, she thinks aloud. Suppose the teacher wants to model how to write a letter to her friend. Some of her comments as she thinks aloud might include the following:

- When I write a letter, I know the first thing I need is the date. I know I need to write that in the middle. First I need to put the month, then the day, then a comma, and then the year. So here at the middle of the top I'm going to write . . .
- Next I need my greeting. I'll skip a line and start writing that here on the left. I'm writing to my friend Phuong, so I'll write "Dear Phuong." I know *Dear* needs to start with a capital *D,* and I also need a capital *P* because *Phuong* is a name. I also remember that I need to put a comma at the end of my greeting.
- Now I'm ready to start my letter. I need to indent so . . .

In addition to talking about conventions and style, the teacher also talks about content. For example:

- I want to tell my friend about a great movie I saw yesterday, so I think first I'll tell her I saw a great movie, and then in the next sentence I'll tell her the name of it.

As she writes she can talk about grammar decisions:

- This is a movie I watched yesterday, so I need to use the past tense. "I saw a great movie yesterday."

The teacher can also discuss decisions about vocabulary and can even model making changes while writing to make better choices:

- I think I need a better word than *great* to describe the movie because I loved it so much. I think I'll use the word *awesome* instead [crosses out *great* and writes *awesome*]. Oh, and now I need to change *a* to *an* because *awesome* begins with a vowel. "I saw an awesome movie yesterday."

And she can also discuss her use of punctuation:

- To make this sentence sound more like how I would say it in an excited way, I'm going to change this period to an exclamation point: "I saw an awesome movie yesterday!"

Modeled writing, as shown here, is an effective tool for teaching new vocabulary to ELLs within this meaningful and authentic context. If necessary, the teacher could draw simple pictures for new vocabulary words to remind students of the meanings.

The text in modeled writing should be kept brief. Teachers should ensure that the complexity and vocabulary of the text is appropriate to the proficiency of their ELLs. They should focus on genres and key skills they want their students to learn and use in their own writing. The topics for modeled writing could be tied into themes or topics being studied in class, or even extensions of read-alouds or shared readings. For example, through modeled writing, the teacher could demonstrate writing a summary of the story or a science report or a persuasive essay. Many elementary school teachers incorporate modeled writing into their daily opening routine by writing morning messages. These typically tell the students about what they are going to be doing in class that day and thus may include a sentence such as, "Today we are going to the library to check out books."

Once modeled writing texts are complete, they should be kept on display in the classroom. Students can refer to them as they write. They also make engaging texts that students will want to read during independent reading time.

Shared Writing

Shared writing is similar to modeled writing, except that in shared writing, the students write *with* the teacher to help compose the text. The teacher controls the pen and acts as the scribe, allowing the students to dictate the text and make decisions about the content, vocabulary, conventions, grammar, and style. Having students help compose the text ensures that it is comprehensible at their current level of English proficiency. The teacher, however, does not just write whatever students say and how they say it, errors and all. Rather, she serves as a guide, sharing ideas and strategies to ensure that the vocabulary is appropriate and the sentence structure is correct as she writes. For example, suppose the class is composing a text describing their field trip to the zoo, and a student suggests adding to a story, "We see monkey play in they house." The teacher could accept this addition, but before or during writing she could prompt the students with corrective feedback to help fix up the sentence:

- "We went to the zoo last week." Do we need to use the present or the past tense? What's the past tense of *see*?
- Was there more than one monkey? OK, so what is the plural form of *monkey*?
- We need a word before "monkeys." We saw [pause to allow the students to say "the"] monkeys.

Like modeled writing, shared writing is an effective tool for teaching new vocabulary and grammar to ELLs within a meaningful context. Here, for example, the teacher can teach the word *cage* and the use of a possessive pronoun to replace *they house* with *their cage*. The teacher could also contribute to the sentence by suggesting "playing around" to replace "play." With such guidance, the student's initial suggestion is further crafted and added to the story as, "We saw the monkeys playing around in their cage." By asking questions like these and providing guidance, the teacher enables students to engage in writing beyond their independent writing level, that is, the teacher is able to scaffold the class's composition of well-written text.

The topics for shared writing, like those for modeled writing, could include current themes and topics, extensions of books from read-alouds and shared readings, or descriptions of shared experiences, such as an assembly or field trip. Shared writing is also an excellent way to introduce and practice a genre in which students will be expected to write independently, and an effective way for a teacher to focus on strategies or skills she notices are lacking in the students' own writing. For example, if it becomes evident from student journals that many are struggling with the future tense, the teacher could guide students in the composition of a text describing an upcoming activity or holiday that requires the use of this tense (e.g., "During spring break, I will go fishing with my dad.").

Shared writing should also incorporate the use of graphic organizers to model the prewriting stage. Graphic organizers can help students see relationships between ideas before they write and also help them generate ideas and vocabulary they will need for the writing. For example, suppose the class wanted to write about their field trip to the park. Together the teacher and students could create a graphic organizer by talking about and

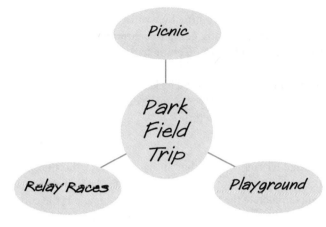

Figure 9.2 Prewriting graphic organizer created during shared writing.

listing the different things they did at the park (Figure 9.2). More details could be added to each of the three main activities. For example, from picnic, the class could add circles for the different things they ate: sandwiches, chips, apples, and cookies. Then, the students could use this graphic organizer as they compose their shared writing text. Creating a graphic organizer also models for students the prewriting process they should use in their own writing. Use of these graphic organizers is essential for addressing Common Core writing standards related to constructing well-structured and organized texts (Standards 2, 3, and 4).

Guided Writing

To address an area of need within students' writing development, teachers can use **guided writing**. Typically guided writing starts with a mini-lesson on some aspect of writing. Students practice the writing principle or strategy they were just taught, under the teacher's supervision, and then share their final written projects.

When I noticed, for example, that my students' writing was overly simple and plain, I created a guided writing activity on adjectives. Our theme for the month was animals. I made a chart with the students, recreated in Figure 9.3. First I had students brainstorm a list of animals and then a list of words we could use to describe these animals (adjectives). Next we brainstormed a list of things these animals could do (verbs) and then the places where they might do these things. As we brainstormed these words, we talked about each one to make sure everyone understood them. Through this process, the students were learning vocabulary in a meaningful context.

Once our chart was completed, I called on a student to choose one animal and put a sticky note by its name (e.g., *monkey*). Next, students chose three adjectives from our list to describe the monkey (e.g., *hairy, playful,* and *wild*), and then a verb (e.g., *swings*), and finally the place (e.g., *jungle*). With all their choices marked, we read our full sentence: "The hairy, playful, wild monkey swings in the jungle." To liven it up, and as an additional support, we sang our new sentence to the tune of "The Farmer in the Dell."

The hairy, playful monkey.
The hairy, playful monkey.
The hairy, playful, wild monkey swings in the jungle.

By now the students were anxious to create other sentences to read and sing, coming up with such jewels as "The yellow, dangerous, slimy snake crawls in the forest" and "The hairy, ugly, smelly dog sleeps in the house."

	Adjective	Animal	Verb	Preposition	Place
	hairy	bird	runs		house
	yellow	dog	swings		jungle
	beautiful	monkey	jumps		cage
	fluffy	cat	eats		zoo
	white	horse	crawls		water
The	dangerous	turtle	sings	in the	field
	ugly	cow	sleeps		farm
	slimy	scorpion	flies		park
	playful	spider	drives		barn
	smelly	snake	bites		forest
	wild	shark	plays		lake

Figure 9.3 Animal adjectives poster.

Once we completed a few sentences together, the students were sent to their desks to write their own sentences from the chart. Everyone, including my reluctant writers, quickly filled up their papers with sentences. When they finished, they read them to each other or to the whole class. We kept our chart up for several weeks for students to read and refer to when doing their own writing. I knew this guided writing activity had been successful when I noticed students were using more adjectives in their journals and other writing.

Interactive Writing

Interactive writing is like shared writing because the students and teacher compose the text together. In interactive writing, however, the students share the pen. It is an excellent technique for young ELLs who are at the beginning stage of writing and learning the alphabet, letter formation, and letter-sound correspondence. It can also be used with older newcomer ELLs at the secondary level, particularly refugees and others who may be students with limited or interrupted formal education who have not had the opportunity to develop home language literacy skills. The teacher begins by guiding the class to form a sentence. It could be a sentence related to a current theme, an extension of a book read-aloud, a morning message, or the beginning of a story or other genre the class will compose together. Suppose, for example, the students are learning about animals that can fly. Using interactive writing, the students will write sentences demonstrating what they know about flying animals. The teacher could ask, "Who can tell me the name of an animal that can fly?" After listening to students' suggestions, the teacher could say, "OK, let's pick one of those animals. How about a bat? Let's make a sentence. *A bat . . .*" Then the students could join in " *. . . can fly.*" The teacher could then ask, "Where does the bat fly?" The students would likely suggest, "in the sky." The teacher could then prompt students to put all the information together in a single sentence: "A bat can fly in the sky."

In preparation for writing this sentence, the teacher draws a line for each word, taking care to make the lines about the length of each word and adding the ending punctuation:

—— ——— ——— ——— —— ——— ———.

The teacher then points to each blank line, prompting the students to read the sentence as if the words were already written. Then, one word at a time, the teacher helps the students say the word slowly, listening for the letters they need. As the students figure out the letters, the teacher asks for volunteers to come up and write the next letter in the word. For example, the teacher might ask, "What letter does *bat* start with?" The teacher can then hand the pen to a student who suggests the letter *b*. If the student is unsure how to write the letter *b*, the teacher can model it for him on a small chalk board or white board or with a sketch app on an iPad or other tablet. Interactive writing is an effective way to teach phonics in a meaningful context because it allows teachers to teach the exact letter-sound correspondences students need to create their message.

When students are at this stage, the teacher should not worry about handwriting. If a student makes a mistake, the teacher can simply cover the error with a sticky note to mask it (some teachers call this a "band-aid"), and then the student can make the correction on top, or, if students are writing on an interactive smart board, their errors can easily be erased, and they can try again. As each word is completed, the students read it aloud and then go back to the beginning of the sentence and read up to the next word they need to add. This process continues until the sentence is complete, at which point they go back and read the entire sentence.

A sentence created this way could be the basis for a classroom book. The teacher could ask one or two students to illustrate the page. After a week or so of interactive writing on flying animals, with illustrations added, the students will have enough to put together into a book that can be used for shared reading, placed in the classroom library for students to read during silent reading time, or checked out by students to take home and read to their families. Interactive writing texts can also be displayed on the walls for students to read and refer to when writing on their own.

When I did interactive writing with my beginning-level writers, I found they got a little bored waiting for a turn to come up and write a letter or word. To solve this problem, I gave each student an individual white board and a marker and eraser. That way they were able to write along and get their own practice writing each letter and word.

As students progress in their writing, they can contribute entire words, and the texts can get longer and more complex.

Journals

Modeled writing, interactive writing, shared writing, and guided writing all provide scaffolding to help ELLs develop as writers and are forms of writing *to* and *with* ELLs. **Independent writing** is writing *by* ELLs. Teachers support independent writing by providing opportunities for students to write, to practice what they have learned, and to move up through the stages of writing development. **Journals** are an outstanding way to support this development. Each student is given an empty notebook and time to write in it every day; students include the date on each entry. Time allotted to journal writing can vary from 10 minutes to 30 minutes a day; older and more proficient writers may be given more time. Journal writing addresses Common Core Writing Standard 10, which calls for a range of writing, including writing completed in a single sitting.

There are two general views about journal writing. One is that students should be free to write about anything they like, and the other is that teachers should assign a topic or use a prompt. A colleague of mine once showed me a journal entry from one of her 2nd grade students, a girl who probably had been writing in her journal daily since kindergarten:

I have nothing left to write about. I'm only 7 years old, and not that much stuff has happened to me yet.

As this young girl reminds us, students may need some guidance to generate topics they can write about. One technique is to do a shared writing activity during which students brainstorm a list of topics they could write about. The list of topics might include my favorite TV show, my favorite cartoon or movie, foods I like or hate, my family, what

I like or don't like about school, something funny that happened to me, a time I was really scared, what I want to be when I grow up, problems in our school or neighborhood, if I were president, and so on. A group of students can quickly fill up a large chart with their ideas. The chart can be posted on the wall so students can refer to it when looking for ideas.

Sometimes further guidance may be necessary. Once, in an effort to get my students to write more, I made a rule that they must write at least five sentences in order to go to recess. No problem, my students figured out:

I like to play.   *I like to jump.*

I like to eat.   *I like to sleep.*

I like to run.

And off to recess they went! They seemed to be stuck at the *stylized sentences writing stage* demonstrated in Table 9.1, but I knew they were capable of doing more and, with a bit more motivation and guidance, could move into the *emerging standardized writing stage.* At our local teacher supply store, I found a little booklet of writing prompt ideas. It had goofy prompts, such as, "If an alien came to your house, what would you do?" and "If you had a million dollars, what would you buy?" I didn't want to stymie my students who were already producing good writing on their own topics, so I decided each day I would put up a prompt on the overhead projector and read it with the students but give them the option of responding to it or writing about something else of their own choosing. It was an instant success; students loved the prompts and were excited to respond to them. The new system helped to break them free from writing isolated lists of sentences. Even when they did not respond to the prompt, they began to write more in the prose style of the emerging standardized writing stage on their own topics. Prompts and sentence starters should also be used to help students write about what they read. Such stimulus-based prompts require students to go back and re-read and analyze the text, and to make references to the text to provide evidence to support their claims (Calderón & Slakk, 2018).

As a general rule, journal writing should not be corrected. This rule does not mean, however, that teachers cannot provide corrective feedback. The most effective way to give this feedback is to make the journals interactive between the student and the teacher. These are also called dialogue journals. In this manner, writing becomes a means for authentic communication between the students and their teacher. The teacher reads the students' entries and then writes back to them in their journal, responding to their writing (Figure 9.4).

I goed to Chke Chz wit my mom
I ply sum vdo game
It Fun

I'm glad you went to Chuck-E-Cheese's with your mom. I bet it was fun. I like to play video games too!

Figure 9.4 Interaction between the student and teacher in a dialogue journal.

Note that the student whose journal entry appears in Figure 9.4 appears to be at the emerging standardized writing stage and is relying on invented spelling. Note also that the teacher does not correct all of the errors directly but instead provides a form of corrective feedback. This process is similar to oral recasts. Embedded in this response are the correct spellings for *Chuck-E-Cheese's, with, played, some, video,* and *games,* as well as a model of the past tense of *go* (*went*), the plural form of *game* (*games*), and the need for the verb *was* before *fun.* Also modeled are proper capitalization and ending punctuation and running prose, with each sentence following the next rather than starting on a new line. Students may not be ready to learn all of these points at once. But the next time this student wants to write about Chuck-E-Cheese's or video games, he is likely to flip back to this page to get the correct spelling from the teacher's response. He may also start capitalizing *I* and use ending punctuation. As he progresses, he will pick up more and more from the teacher's responses.

Newcomer ELLs at the beginning level of English proficiency who are literate in their home language should be allowed to write in their journals in their home language. This is preferable to a blank journal page. As the students' English proficiency develops, teachers will find that the student will begin to write more and more in English. Journals also provide emergent bilinguals at all levels of proficiency opportunities to engage in translingual practice to produce meaningful and engaging bilingual texts. The rubrics associated with the Literacy Squared approach can be used to assess such writing (Escamilla et al., 2013).

One exciting thing about journals is that they are a living record of students' writing development over the course of the school year. I gave students a new journal every month and then labeled their old journals with the name of the month and dropped them into their portfolios. The completed journals were very effective measures of the students' growth, and I showed them to students and parents during conferences: "Here's how Gabriela was writing at the beginning of the year, and here is what her writing looks like now! Notice how much she has improved in . . ."

Besides documenting students' progress in writing development, journals reveal their strengths and areas in need of improvement, allowing teachers to quickly ascertain the strategies and skills they need to focus on in shared and modeled writing, and the types of lessons needed in guided writing. Teachers can also pinpoint skills that only a small number of students need and develop mini-lessons just for these students. Journal writing can be used for formative assessment.

Process Writing and Writer's Workshop

Process writing involves guiding students through the writing process in stages, helping them to focus on ideas first and to take care of corrections related to grammar, spelling, and mechanics toward the end. It aligns with the writing process outlined in Common Core Writing Standard 5 and also addresses Standard 10, which calls for a range of writing, including working on pieces of writing over an extended period. Process writing can also be used for students to write the types of research reports addressed in Standards 7–9. Process writing generally has five stages: prewriting, drafting, revising, editing, and publishing. Recall that these stages were identified in the 1970s when writing research began to focus on how successful writers produce a text from its conceptualization to its final publication. One finding was that successful writers concentrate first on their ideas rather than worrying about having perfect spelling, grammar, and mechanics; otherwise their writing suffers. Process writing works especially well for ELLs. "Correctness" is a challenge for them, but students are still capable of expressing their ideas in writing in less than perfect English. Once the students' ideas are down on paper, teachers can provide instruction and scaffolding to help them improve their writing as they go through the rest of the writing process. Teachers often teach process writing through a collaborative approach called **Writer's Workshop**, which involves the following activities at each stage:

Prewriting. Students get their ideas together, determine the purpose of the writing, and identify who the audience will be (e.g., "My purpose is to tell about my sister's wedding, and my audience is my teacher and the students in the class."). They decide what the main idea will be and what supporting details they want to include. With or without the support of the teacher, they can use the following strategies to prepare to write:

- Talking over their ideas with peers or with the teacher
- Drawing pictures (works well for students at early stages of writing development)
- Brainstorming to create a list of things they can write about or a list of supporting details to include once the main idea has been identified
- Closing their eyes to visualize what they want to write about, concentrating on what they see, hear, smell, feel, and taste
- Using graphic organizers, such as the word web in Figure 9.2
- Creating an outline for organizing the text

Note that many of these prewriting strategies can also be done in the home language, which can provide an effective scaffold for students to formulate their ideas before they write in English. Teachers can also provide some form of shared experiences for students to write about, such as a book that is read aloud, a video watched in class, a science experiment, a field trip, or an assembly.

Drafting. Students focus on getting their ideas down on paper as quickly as possible. The ideas and materials generated during prewriting are an important source at this stage. Those who are unsure where to begin should be encouraged to just start writing. Students should also be taught not to spend time worrying about spelling or grammar. This first draft is evaluated by how consistent the content is with its purpose and its appropriateness for the target audiences.

Revising. After reading over their first draft, students may want to rewrite some sentences and move things around to better organize their arguments or supporting details. They may decide to add more details to support their main idea or feel the need to remove some sentences and details that they determine are off topic and that distract from their main idea and purpose for writing.

At this stage, students often need the help of their peers and the teacher. They meet in peer-response groups to read their drafts aloud and give feedback to one another, or meet individually with the teacher to read their drafts and talk about their writing. They ask questions and receive suggestions for improvement. For example, suppose a student wrote, "I went to the mall. It was fun." The teacher could prompt for more details. "What did you do at the mall? What did you do there that was fun?" After listening to the student's responses, the teacher can say, "Those are great details! Add those to your writing."

Editing. When students have a strong draft with a main idea and supporting details that is well organized, meets its purpose, and that is appropriate for its intended audience, they can then focus on editing for correct spelling, mechanics, and grammar, doing their best to find errors and correct them on their own. If further help is needed, they can get corrections first in peer-response groups and then from the teacher in another teacher conference.

Correcting students' writing at this stage raises two issues: how to correct, and what and how much to correct. First, how to correct: the teacher could merely underline the errors and have the student figure out what's wrong and how to fix them. Or, the teacher could circle each error and give some type of clue by writing in the margin *sp.* for spelling errors, *ten.* for tense errors, or *pun.* for punctuation errors. Or, the teacher could make direct corrections for the student, indicating where the error is and writing in the correction.

Research suggests that direct correction works best for producing accurate revisions (Ferris & Hedgcock, 2014). Students tend to prefer this method because it is easy and fast. But students may learn more when the teacher just underlines the errors and they have to correct them on their own. Both methods are viable. The best choice depends on the goals of a particular assignment. The teacher may want to use a mixture of the two, for example, underlining those errors she believes students are ready to self-correct and providing direct corrections for those errors students are not yet ready to deal with.

To determine what and how much to correct, the second issue, the teacher should focus on (1) errors students are ready to learn how to correct and (2) errors that interfere with meaning. The teacher can also identify points of grammar and mechanics that students are ready to learn and provide instruction on these points through mini-lessons. Although the teacher's goal may be to help students move their writing to the publishing stage, the text does not need to be 100% error free.

Publishing. Once students have edited their work by making their own corrections and corrections from their peers and the teacher, they can either rewrite their final draft in clear handwriting on high-quality white paper, or type it using a computer with word processing software. Students can also add illustrations and a cover.

"Publishing" means making the final draft available to others. One common technique in Writer's Workshop is to read from the Author's Chair: the student sits in the teacher's chair (or another designated chair) to read his or her writing to the class. The class and the teacher can ask the author questions, pointing out the parts they like and, if appropriate, giving constructive feedback to help the student in future writing projects. Published writing can be added to the classroom library or sent home for students to read to their families. Many teachers set up a special wall in the classroom to publish student writing, making it easily accessible for students and classroom visitors to read. Shorter pieces of writing published by students on the same topic can be compiled into a book that can be laminated and bound, then placed in the classroom library or checked out for students to take home and read to their families.

Student writing can also be published on the school's website or a class wiki or blog for the entire world to see (Common Core Writing Standard 6). Making published writing available to a wide audience is an essential step. This is how ELLs develop a sense of audience and gain an understanding of the need for their writing to be well organized and correct so they can convey their intended meaning to their target audience (Common Core Writing Standard 4). It also makes the writing much more authentic than if they simply write something that the teacher grades and returns.

Scaffolding for Independent Writing

Teachers provide scaffolding to support students' independent writing through resources such as word walls, thematic word charts, personal word books, and dictionaries, and by facilitating peer assessment and providing mini-lessons.

Word Walls. A **word wall** is a wall display of words arranged alphabetically under each letter in type large enough for students to read from their desks (Figure 9.5). It should

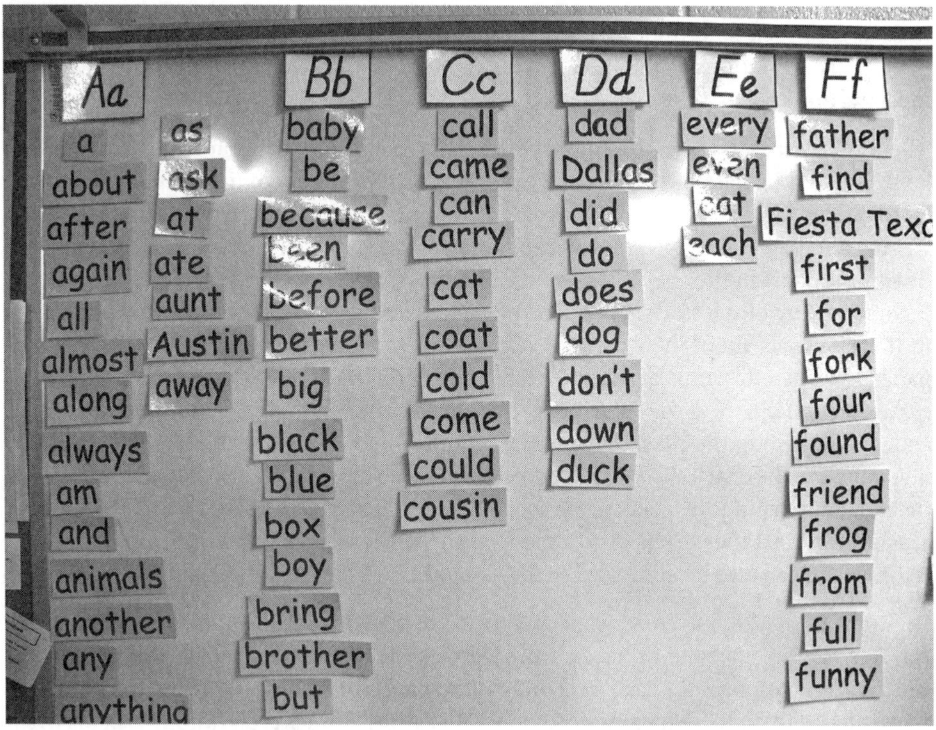

Figure 9.5 Word wall from Mrs. Armstrong's 1st grade class, Scobee Elementary School, Northside Independent School District, San Antonio, Texas. (Photo by author.)

include the words students ask for or use most frequently when they are writing, including, at least initially, high-frequency words. Notice, for example, that the word wall in Figure 9.5 includes "Austin," "Dallas," and "Fiesta Texas" (a local amusement park), all useful words for the students in this classroom who live in San Antonio, Texas. (More examples of word walls can be found on the companion website.)

The word wall should be built up throughout the year. As words are added, students and the teacher discuss their meaning, and students help place the words in the proper location. If the words are affixed to the wall with Velcro or magnets, students can easily remove them and take them to their desk as needed to help with their writing. I used different colors for the word cards to make it easier for students to recognize and remember words they most frequently needed or for higher-level students to help lower-level students:

Stephen: *How do you spell* said?

Vanna: *It's on the word wall, the blue card under* S.

Stephen: *I see it. Thanks!*

Teachers can also develop a range of interactive activities, such as games where students must quickly find and remove a word from the wall, group words by alphabetic or semantic properties, and put words back in their correct locations in alphabetical order. Such activities help students develop their vocabulary skills and ensure that they know how to use the wall to support their writing. Many teachers have found that they can provide additional support by cutting the word wall cards into the shape of the words or making an outline in a bold color around each word following its shape. Some teachers have gone high tech by adding quick response (QR) codes to their word walls for students to scan with their smart phones, iPod Touches, iPads, or other tablets, which link to illustrations, definitions, Wikipedia entries, or other sources that help illustrate the word's meaning and use.

Thematic Word Charts. A **thematic word chart** displays words that relate to the theme being studied in class or to a special occasion, such as an upcoming holiday. Thematic word charts, like word walls, display words that students will likely want to use in their writing and help them learn new vocabulary. To make the word charts fun, students can design the chart in the shape of something representative of the theme. For example, in October, many of my students were very excited about Halloween and wanted to write in their journals about their plans.[1] We made a large picture of a pumpkin out of chart paper. In a shared writing activity, we brainstormed Halloween-related words (*pumpkin, carve, jack-o-lantern, costume, trick-or-treating, candy, fall, autumn, monster, ghost,* etc.) and added them to the chart. During the month, when we read related books, we added new words to the chart. We also added new words when students discovered they needed them during writing. Teachers at the secondary level can create similar word walls for the academic subject they teach (e.g., a math word wall, a science word wall, a history word wall), which can also be enhanced with QR codes.

Personal Word Books. Word walls are great, but they take up a lot of classroom space, and it is just not possible to have all the words all the students need all the time. Thus, another great resource for each student is a **personal word book**. Typically the books are preprinted with high-frequency words and other words students commonly ask for when they write. But the word books include space under each letter section for students to record their own words as they progress through the school year. They may record words that have been added to the word wall or to a temporary thematic word chart. They may come across new vocabulary words in their reading they want to remember and use in their own writing. They may also record new words they learn in ESL or sheltered content-area lessons, and words they have asked a friend or a teacher how to spell. Students who are literate in their home language can make their personal word books bilingual by including translations of words they want to use in their writing. Personal word books are also a great place for students to record words for things they want to write about but that are likely not even in the dictionary, such as the names of movies, TV shows, video games, and video game systems, the names of their favorite food products or their favorite bands and singers, or the names of popular restaurants and other places in the community and surrounding areas.

Personal word books are efficient because they include only words that remind students of the correct spelling of words they know. The definitions are not needed. Thus, the word books can contain a large number of words that students can quickly find when needed. As with word walls, however, students will need instruction, guidance, and practice using their personal word books before they can be an effective support for their independent writing.

Dictionaries. Picture dictionaries (English monolingual and bilingual versions), which are organized by category, are useful for students at the lower and intermediate levels of

---

[1] Care must be taken when using holidays as a theme in your classroom. Some cultural or religious groups may not recognize or celebrate them and parents may prefer that their children not be included in any activities that *celebrate* the holiday. Parents may be OK with students' learning *about* the holiday; thus, make sure that holiday-themed activities have a clear curricular focus, such as teaching vocabulary and writing. The same words, for example, would be a resource for one student who wishes to write about the costume he will wear on Halloween and another who wishes to write in her journal, "I don't go trick-or-treating or carve jack-o-lanterns because in my religion we don't celebrate Halloween."

English proficiency. If they want to write the word *bicycle,* for example, they can just flip to the transportation section, find the picture of the bicycle, and then look to see what it is called in English and how to spell it. The bilingual versions allow students who can read in two languages to make sure they have the word they are looking for. Regular bilingual dictionaries are also a great source for students who are literate in their home language, because they can quickly find the English equivalent of a word they want to write or confirm that a word in English is the word they were looking for. A regular English (monolingual) dictionary, appropriate to the grade level of the student, is effective for students at higher levels of English proficiency who need to check on the precise meaning of a word or its spelling before they use it. Students can also use electronic handheld and online English, bilingual, and multilingual dictionaries, as well as translation tools such as Google Translate or those embedded in programs such as Microsoft Word. A variety of monolingual, bilingual, and picture dictionaries are also easily accessible as mobile apps. For a dictionary to be effective, regardless of the type used, students will need to be taught how to use it as a resource to support their writing.

"Ask Three, Then Me." When students need help with the spelling or definition of a word, they can observe the rule "Ask three, then me." Before approaching the teacher, a student must ask three classmates. If none of them knows how to spell the word, the student may then ask the teacher. Encouraging students to use their peers as resources supports independent writing and frees up the teacher for one-to-one conferences with students and mini-lessons for small groups of students.

Mini-lessons. Mini-lessons are an important source of scaffolding and instructional support for ELL writers and a critical component of Writer's Workshops. The teacher becomes aware of issues that need special attention by reading journal entries and drafts during Writer's Workshop, by conferencing with students, and by conducting formal writing assessments. For example, if a teacher notices four students who were having trouble following capitalization rules consistently, he could pull them together for a quick lesson. The best source for these lessons would be problematic sentences from the students' own writing (with their names removed). The small group can review the rules and then correct the sentences. The teacher then encourages the students to check their own writing for these issues. After a mini-lesson, the teacher monitors the students to see whether they are making improvements and to re-teach those who still need help.

Mini-lessons can also draw upon students' strengths. For example, mini-lessons can focus on cognates—words that are similar in both English and the students' home language—and thus help students quickly learn new vocabulary in English they can incorporate into their writing. Mini-lessons should also be used proactively to teach new concepts and techniques students can incorporate into their writing. For example, for older ELLs who are ready, a mini-lesson could focus on literary devices, such as flashbacks and foreshadowing, or on advanced punctuation, such as colons, semicolons, and dashes. The mini-lesson could involve finding incidents of these in texts with which students are familiar that they can use as models for their own writing.

Writing across the Curriculum

Students should be writing to learn, and therefore they should be writing all day, in all content areas, not just during the writing portion of language arts time. The CCSS also make it clear that literacy skill development is not confined to language arts and that content-area teachers are also teachers of reading and writing. To encourage students to write to learn across the curriculum, many middle and high schools draw on the Collins Writing Program, developed by the literacy expert John Collins (2013). The program uses frequent, usually short, writing assignments to increase students' involvement in lessons, checks on their understanding of concepts, and promotes their thinking about academic content. The program identifies five types of writing:

1. *Capture ideas.* Students write one draft to get a minimum number of ideas down on paper in a set amount of time. Writing is evaluated as complete or incomplete.
2. *Respond correctly.* Students write one draft to demonstrate understanding. Writing is evaluated for correctness of ideas.
3. *Edit for focus correction areas (FCAs).* Students write a draft with attention to up to three targeted writing skills (e.g., topic sentence, conclusion, supporting details, content-specific vocabulary, varied sentence structure, punctuation). Writing is evaluated for content and relative to FCAs.
4. *Peer edit for FCAs.* Like Type 3 writing but critiqued by a peer.
5. *Publish.* Students produce a publishable piece. Writing is evaluated for content and form.[2]

Students can have journals for math, science, social studies, or even art, music, and physical education in which they record notes, describe new concepts they learn, and keep a record of activities they have completed, all examples of Type 1 or Type 2 writing. In math, students write word problems or respond to open-ended math problems. In science, students record observations, write answers to science questions, and write experiment reports. In social studies, students write responses to questions, notes while conducting research, and research reports. In music, students can write the lyrics to songs or even musical notation. Students can incorporate text into their art or write descriptions of their artistic creations. In physical education, students can keep logs about issues related to exercise, nutrition, and health. They also write to keep track of their progress in meeting fitness goals. Each of these activities is an opportunity for students to focus on the language of the specific content area, with attention to content-area vocabulary and genres, and to develop their writing skills in English. When students write regularly for a wide range of purposes across the content areas, they become proficient writers. But to be successful in writing in these different content areas, they must be explicitly taught the specifics of how to write in the styles of those content areas and have opportunities to practice writing in those styles (Calederón & Slakk, 2018).

Writing with Technology

Students today do much of their writing on computers, smart phones, and other mobile devices. These technological developments are forcing teachers to rethink how writing is taught in the classroom. The Internet is also an important source of information for students to draw on to support the types of writing called for in the CCSS. In Reading Standard 7, students are expected to integrate and evaluate content from diverse media and formats, including online information that is presented visually (e.g., images, videos) and quantitatively (e.g., charts, tables, graphs). In Writing Standard 8, students are expected to gather relevant information from multiple print and digital sources, assess their credibility and accuracy, and integrate the information into their writing while avoiding plagiarism. And, as noted earlier, the Internet is an important venue for students to publish their writing and interact with readers of their work (Standard 6).

---

[2]Collins, J. (2013). *Collins Writing Program.* The Writing Site. Retrieved from http://www.collinsed.com/5types.htm, reprinted with permission.

The term *multiliteracies*, introduced by scholars associated with the New London Group (1996), emphasizes that helping students learn simply to decode and produce standardized written text through traditional reading and writing instruction is not sufficient. Students must engage in a wide variety of literacies, including different registers, dialects, and languages. Students must also engage in digital literacies. Written communication in today's multimedia world involves communicating in ways that combine written text with the spoken word, music, images, and video. Many of the digital texts students read or produce are also nonlinear. Consider, for example, a Wikipedia entry or blog posting where hyperlinked words instantly take readers to new entries and original source sites. Or news sites where text-based stories are supplemented by or interwoven with audio and video clips. Consider the next generation of digital textbooks where image slideshows, interactive graphs and tables, and audio and video clips accompany the written text, while hyperlinks connect students instantly to additional sources outside of the book.

Students increasingly are using technology as an efficient means of written communication with others in their everyday lives. Common Core Writing Standard 6 calls for students to use technology and the Internet to interact and collaborate with others through writing. Students in the past may have occasionally written and mailed letters and postcards and perhaps written short notes in class to their friends. Students today, however, write hundreds of e-mail messages, Facebook and Instagram postings, and comments on Internet social networking sites, blogs, and online discussion boards. They spend hours online in chat rooms and in instant messaging programs to "chat" live with others through text. They send hundreds of text messages a week to friends from their smart phones and other handheld devices. Rather than passing notes in class as in the good ol' days, students today get busted for "texting" their friends in class. Teachers should not be afraid to embrace these new technologies in the classroom. They can be highly motivating for ELLs because they reflect the type of writing students want to do and will do in real life. The next section briefly explores some of the ways technology can be used with ELLs as they develop as writers.

Word Processing

On a computer the writing process is less linear than it is on paper because students can easily revise and edit as they write their first draft. When students write on the computer using a word processing program such as Microsoft Word, Pages, or Google Docs, they should be taught to take advantage of the ease of editing the computer offers along with the support of spelling and grammar checkers, dictionaries, thesauruses, and translation tools. Teachers can also give detailed feedback to students using the comment feature, and revisions to drafts made by the teacher and students can be viewed using the track-changes feature. Through Google Docs, the students' files are stored online. Thus, students can start a piece of writing at school and continue working on it at home, in the library, or in any other place that has Internet access through a computer or mobile device. Another advantage is that the documents are accessible to anyone the student allows. Thus, for example, a teacher, paraprofessional, or even a parent could access a student's work in progress, inserting suggestions and comments to help the student revise and further develop the work. Groups of students can also collaborate with one another on a piece of writing or provide peer editing and proofreading. Completed student writing stored in Google Drive or other cloud-based file-sharing programs (e.g., DropBox, OneDrive, iCloud) can be instantly published to the Internet, then easily linked to from a personal or classroom website.

Online Message Boards

Online message boards usually focus on a specific topic, and anyone with knowledge of or interest in that topic can participate by posting information or asking or answering questions. A growing number of message boards are designed for kids, such as the boards on the Nickelodeon website where students are highly motivated to discuss their favorite shows and characters with other fans around the world. There are also boards for students to write their own fan fiction, in which students take the characters from their favorite show, or even across shows, and write their own stories to fill in the gaps, provide backstories or new plot twists, or create alternative endings to the way the show plays out on television. A particularly popular theme in fan fiction is called *shipping* (derived from relation*ship*) where authors pair up characters into new romantic relationships. The site also provides general boards where students can write stories on any topic. When researching this topic by interviewing an expert—my daughter who was 12 years old at the time—I was surprised to learn that she was using the board to write a book documenting her exciting and often awkward first year in middle school and had several fans begging her to write more. Nickelodeon's boards, like many other message boards on sites for kids, are fully moderated by responsible adults (called the "mods" by the kids) who either prevent inappropriate messages from being posted or remove students who post such messages. Teachers can easily set up their own message boards for their classes with control over who can read and post comments, using sites such as Google Groups, Moodle, Ning, and Edmodo.

Key Pals (E-mail and Instant Messaging)

Key pals is essentially the age-old concept of pen pals, but written exchanges between pals occur much faster and more frequently through media such as e-mail and instant messaging. It is essentially having a live conversation through your fingertips, which for an ELL can be a huge advantage. The electronic conversation has features of spoken discourse. Even with instant messaging, there is enough of a delay that the recipient can reread the message a few times to fully comprehend it and still have time to think through the answer carefully, reviewing and revising it as necessary before sending it. In other words, it provides built-in wait time, something rare in oral conversations. In the best of circumstances, ELLs are paired with English speakers who have been trained to be patient and to use their responses to model back the correct spelling and grammar usage their ELL partners have trouble with, rather than to overtly correct their errors. With teacher guidance, support, and monitoring, however, ELLs can also be paired with other ELLs to practice using their new language for authentic communication purposes. The text of the interaction can be saved for students to review and can provide teachers with a rich resource for identifying the needs of the students and planning targeted mini-lessons.

Multimedia Presentations

Multimedia presentation programs, such as PowerPoint and Keynote, along with online tools such as Google Slides and Prezi, are great for ELLs because they allow students to author multimedia texts that incorporate images, animations, sounds, music, and audio or video clips to illustrate what they know or have learned about a particular topic in class or through their own research. Other online tools can facilitate meaningful and authentic multimodal interaction. Voicethread, for example, enables students to narrate their slides, and viewers can post their own text, audio, or video comments right on individual slides. Glogster enables students to present multimedia in the form of an interactive online poster called a *glog,* which others can view and post comments about. Webspiration (the online equivalent of Inspiration and Kidspiration) enables students to create multimedia graphic organizers for use in presentations or as a support for writing. These presentations can be a good alternative to traditionally written reports in English, which ELLs often struggle with. A completed presentation provides an excellent support (scaffolding) for students' oral presentations to the class. Multimedia presentations also provide space for translanguaging where students can incorporate text, audio, and video in more than one language. The online tools enable students to instantly publish their multimedia presentations to the world, giving them a greater sense of authenticity and audience. Some presentations created by ELLs have thousands of views. This sort of response can inspire high-quality and more accurate work.

Blogs, Tweets, and Wikis

A blog (short for web log) is an easy to create web page that bloggers (those who blog) can easily update from any Internet-connected computer, or handheld device. A blog is like a journal in which new entries are added to the top and old ones pushed down the page. Older entries are archived but searchable by date or keywords. Twitter is a "microblogging" service with postings—called *tweets*—limited to 280 characters. These short, highly communicative texts may be of great interest to ELLs because they can read or write them quickly, and they can follow or contribute to twitter feeds on topics of personal interest. Wikis are easy to create websites that can be developed and updated by many students in collaboration. Blogs, tweets, and wikis can include text, hyperlinks, photos, videos, and other multimedia content. Student blogs and classroom-based wikis provide an ideal space for students to share their ideas, their written work, and interesting content they create or find online relevant to things they are learning.

The best feature of blogs, tweets, and wikis is that they are made up of reflections and conversations that are regularly updated. These forms of online communication demand interaction because they engage readers with appealing ideas, questions, and links and ask them to respond. This feature is what makes this technology particularly beneficial for ELLs. For example, many students keep dialogue journals or literature response journals with entries typically read only by the teacher. Why not have the students keep these journals as a blog or wiki, or share their favorite quotations and insights as tweets? Suddenly students' thoughts and ideas are no longer just a school assignment to satisfy the teacher but are open to a much bigger audience. Postings can be read by fellow classmates, other teachers or administrators in the school, family members, or anyone else who is interested, and these readers can write and post their own comments on the student's entries, enabling meaningful written interaction surrounding the work. Because blog postings and wiki contents are permanent (unless deleted by the creator) and searchable, they become in essence an online portfolio of ELLs progress in writing and using English in authentic contexts.

Digital Storytelling

Digital stories are short narratives produced and published using digital tools on a computer, tablet, or other handheld device that incorporate a combination of text, images, narration, music, and video. In the narrowest sense, digital stories are personal narratives produced as videos using video editing software. In a broader sense, a digital story can be

Vinogradova, Linville, & Bickel, pp. 190–191, 2011.

Box 9.3 Stages in the Digital Storytelling Production Process

The following 10 stages can guide ESL students through the digital storytelling production process:

1. Imagining a story to tell in fewer than 5 minutes using words, pictures, and music
2. Participating in the story circle in which everyone tells a story and receives feedback
3. Writing a verbal narrative (150–250 words)
4. Reviewing each other's narratives
5. Collecting still images and thinking about music
6. Storyboarding in PowerPoint
7. Recording the narrative
8. Selecting music and sound effects
9. Producing the digital story using video editing software
10. Presenting digital stories in class

Additional information, resources, and examples can be found at the Center for Digital Storytelling.

any fiction or nonfiction "story" produced in a variety of digital formats. All involve students' going through a process of conceptualizing their story; writing the text or verbal narrative; storyboarding; gathering images, music, and sound effects; and producing and presenting their stories (Box 9.3).

Commonly used tools include iMovie, Voicethread, and Little Bird Tales, which is especially appropriate and easy to use for younger students. There is a wide variety of web-based and app-based tools to support the creation and publication of digital stories. Shelly Terrell has compiled an annotated, online list of more than two dozen apps for digital storytelling.

Digital stories can be a creative and powerful process for ELLs as they engage with the multiliteracies involved in learning the writing and digital skills needed to tell their stories, collaborate with their peers, and develop a sense of community and to share and publish their stories in a manner that gives them a voice (Vinogradova, Linville, & Bickel, 2011). Digital stories can also be easily produced in the home language or bilingually. To demonstrate the power of digital storytelling, view the story titled "Finding Home" produced by a Karen refugee ELL student from Burma named Ta Kwe.

Txtng Language Use

With the increasing use of new technologies, teachers will need to address the writing in these contexts that may differ from "standard" writing taught in our schools. Dey myt Nd ^ ryTN a sentenC lk dis (They might end up writing a sentence like this). This example shows how some students are creating a more efficient writing system adapted to smaller screens and keyboards on handheld devices. You might see some new abbreviations (initialisms) in students' school writing, such as IMHO (in my humble opinion), LOL (laughing out loud), and IOW (in other words), or even emoticons, which are used in text environments the same way paralinguistic clues (e.g., facial expressions, gestures) are used in oral discourse to clarify the intended meaning of uttered words and phrases. As just a few examples, these include :-) for *happy*, :-(for *sad*, :-O for *surprised* or *shocked*, :-@ for *screaming*, and ;-) for *winking*. New abbreviations, emoticons, and other shortcuts appear all the time; standardized images called *emoji* (Japanese for *picture* + *character*) have been incorporated into the universal Unicode and incorporated directly into many smartphones, tablets, and texting programs.

What should teachers do about this trend? First, though some consider what young people are doing to written standard English an abomination, it is important to remember that languages are constantly changing. Consider, for example, the differences between Old, Middle, and Modern English or the deliberate changes Noah Webster and others made to British English to help create standard American English. We may be seeing another phase in a natural progression of language, for language is changed by each generation to better fit into the ways they use it to communicate within their sociocultural contexts. Crystal (2008), in his book *txtng: The Gr8 Deb8*, argues that "the linguistic processes of texting are centuries old" (p. 27). For example, changes in spelling, and even the use of initialisms in written and spoken form for common phrases have been around for many years—soldiers pay school tuition with a GI bill, we get an IT specialist to help with our computers, we eat BLT sandwiches for lunch, when a friend is upset we offer a little TLC, we add a P.S. at the end of letters and e-mails, and we rely on the FBI and CIA to keep us safe. Crystal notes that IOU originated in at least 1618. Omission of vowels and other letters in texting language is also nothing new. After all, what are contractions (e.g., cannot = can't)? And consider the long use of Mr., Mrs., Ms., dept., cm, ft, and kg. Crystal notes that Partridge's *Dictionary of Abbreviations*, published in 1942, long before the texting phenomenon, includes entries such as *difclt* (difficult), *gd* (good), *btwn* (between), and *mtg* (meeting). He observes that nonstandard spellings, such as *gonna, wanna,* and *thru* are over a hundred years old, and some nonstandard spellings have long appeared in the *Oxford English Dictionary,* such as *cos* (1828), *luv* (1829), and *thanx* (1936). He mentions that studies of texting language found that most messages are written in more standard language, and only a tiny part uses the distinct orthography of texting language. He concludes that emerging research provides evidence that "texting does not harm writing ability, and may even help it" (p. 161). Emoticons and emoji images are opening up new ways of conveying meaning in written communication, though the principle is essentially the same as pictographs or ideographs used for centuries.

Nonetheless, teachers should not abandon efforts to teach students standard English. To do so would be irresponsible. Crystal (2008) describes the role teachers need to play in helping students understand when and where texting-like language use is appropriate:

> They need to know when it would be appropriate to text and when it would not be. They need to know when textisms are effective and when they are not. . . . Teenagers have to learn to manage this new behavior, as indeed do we all. For one thing is certain: texting is not going to go away, in the foreseeable future. (p. 163)

Thus, teachers need to recognize and value vernacular varieties of spoken and written English and help students recognize that different forms of writing are appropriate in particular contexts, but that standard English is essential for success in school and in the workplace.

Home-School Writing Connection

Writing can be a deeply personal form of reflection on the world and one's experiences in it. Teachers can open the way for students to engage in reflective writing by allowing them to write on topics of their own choosing in their journals, in Writer's Workshop, and in other writing projects. Students should be encouraged to draw on their funds of knowledge for their writing. The transformative power of having students write about their own lives and experiences is highlighted in the feature film *Freedom Writers,* which tells the story of Erin Gruwell and her inner-city "at-risk" high school students, including many language minority students, at Wilson High School in Long Beach, California. As described on the Freedom Writers Foundation website:

> The Freedom Writers began writing anonymous journal entries about the adversity they faced. They felt free to write about gang violence, abuse, drugs, love, and everything else real teenagers dealt with on a daily basis. The rawness and honesty of their journals was published in a book called, "The Freedom Writers Diary," which became an instant "New York Times" Best Seller.

Their book (Freedom Writers, 1999) provides a vivid example of the power of critical pedagogy and the funds of knowledge orientation. Another powerful means of linking the home, school, and community is having students collaborate with their parents or other family members to produce dual language books in their home language and English. Bilingual volunteers from the community can also provide a valuable resource. For example, 1st grade bilingual students at an elementary school in Muncie, Indiana, collaborated with students in a Spanish course at Ball State University to write, illustrate, and publish bilingual short stories.

Assessing Writing

States use large-scale exams or assessment procedures as summative assessments to determine students' ability in writing. These exams are typically given only to students within selected grade levels. In addition, states are required by the Every Student Succeeds Act (ESSA) to assess the writing proficiency of ELLs annually. In this section, we look briefly at the limitations of these kinds of standardized high-stakes writing exams and then discuss the need for ongoing, formative classroom-based writing assessments.

Standardized High-Stakes Writing Exams

High-stakes standardized exams such as those required by ESSA typically use multiple-choice questions to assess students' writing ability. Although this technique saves time and money for the testing companies who score the tests, effective teachers know that the only real way to assess an ELL's writing ability is to read something he or she has actually written. Fortunately, most states also include writing prompts on their tests to which students must respond and that someone must evaluate.

Another problem with high-stakes writing assessments is that they typically focus on a single genre (e.g., personal narrative, persuasive essay, expository text). Teachers, often under the mandates of their school and district administrators, may feel pressure to teach to the test and spend the majority of the year working only on the genre required on the test. When writing instruction is narrowed to a single genre, students lose out. Rather than learning about the wide range of purposes and uses of writing, students learn that the main purpose of writing is to get a passing score on the writing test. Teachers should also be aware of who is scoring their student's writing on state-level tests. Many testing companies hire temporary employees who have little to no teaching experience and receive minimal training in scoring student writing. These workers are highly incentivized to work as quickly as possible (Glovin & Evans, 2006). Thus, teachers, student, and parents have the right to be skeptical of the test scores.

In real life, people rarely write five-paragraph essays or the types of writing assessed on state tests. Instead they write lists, letters, e-mail messages, text messages, short notes, directions, instructions, and song or rap lyrics. They fill out forms. They post brief updates of what they are doing or thinking about on social networking sites on the Internet, such as Facebook, Instagram, or Twitter, and write brief responses to their friends' posts. They post comments online in reaction to news articles, blog postings, videos, and their friends' photos, or they give feedback to others about products purchased or about the merchants they purchased them from. These more common uses of writing for authentic communication purposes within the lives of students in their sociocultural context typically receive little attention in the classroom. Teachers therefore need to ensure that their students are exposed to a wide variety of writing styles and genres. More important, teachers must help students see writing as a form of personal expression with many uses in real life and provide opportunities for students to write in class for authentic communicative purposes and personal reflection.

Classroom-Based Writing Assessment

Formative writing assessments used throughout the year enable teachers to gauge their students' progress and plan appropriate instruction and opportunities for students to improve their writing. In the opening quotation of this chapter, Juli Kendall points out that the only way for teachers to help ELLs improve their writing is to read what they write and then talk with them about their strengths and areas in need of improvement. In particular, teachers identify those areas in which they believe the student is ready to learn and make improvements. In addition, teachers assess student progress throughout the year by using portfolio assessments, and they encourage students to assess their own work.

The scoring and assessment of student writing can take several forms, including holistic, analytical, and primary trait or multi-trait. In **holistic scoring**, the teacher makes a judgment about the piece of writing as a whole and assigns it a single integrated score or level. Holistic scoring is used in some state English language proficiency assessments of writing. In Texas, for example, proficiency level descriptors for writing in grades 2–12 are used to determine whether ELLs are at the beginning, intermediate, advanced, or advanced-high levels of writing proficiency in English. Holistic scoring puts more emphasis on the students' writing ability than on errors of one type or another. Little information is provided, however, to pinpoint students' strengths and needs.

Analytic scoring with a rubric is more common and helps teachers focus on different aspects of a student's writing. The rubrics consist of separate scales (e.g., 1–4) for each aspect, for example, *composing, style, sentence formation, usage,* and *mechanics* (Table 9.3). Despite this advantage, however, to ensure reliability, teachers who use the analytic rubric must be consistent in how they score student writing. Another caution with such rubrics is to avoid giving students a rigid outline or formula to ensure that their writing gets maximum rubric scores. Once a colleague of mine, in scoring a set of writing exams, discovered that an entire classroom of students produced nearly the same essay in terms of organization, introduction, transitional sentences, and other formulaic chunks of language. With such a "paint-by-number" style of writing, there is little room for creativity and authentic student voice.

Primary trait and multi-trait scoring are commonly used for assessing writing on a specific topic. In **primary trait scoring**, the focus is on a single trait, such as the main idea. In **multi-trait scoring**, several traits can be considered, such as, for an opinion essay, clear opinion (main idea), adequate details to support the opinion, and a strong conclusion. The advantage of primary trait and multi-trait scoring is that they allow the rater to

Table 9.3 Analytic Scoring Rubric for Writing

Domain Score*	Composing	Style	Sentence Formation	Usage	Mechanics
4	Central idea with relevant details in a well-organized text	Well-chosen vocabulary; excellent sentence variety; tone that appeals to readers	Standard word order; no run-on sentences; no sentence fragments; effective transitions	Correct use of inflection (e.g., verb conjugations, plurals, prefixes, suffixes, adverbs, etc.); consistent tense; consistent subject-verb agreement; standard word meaning	Correct use of mechanics (capitalization, punctuation, spelling), and formatting
3	Central idea but with fewer details and some digressions	Acceptable vocabulary choices; some sentence variety; consistent but less appealing tone	Mostly standard word order, some run-on sentences; some sentence fragments; occasional omission of words; errors do not detract from meaning	Mostly correct use of inflections; mostly consistent tense and subject-verb agreement; mostly standard word meaning; errors do not detract from meaning	Mostly correct use of mechanics and formatting; errors do not detract from meaning
2	Lack of a focused central idea, or more than one idea; limited details and many digressions	Basic vocabulary; limited to no sentence variety; inconsistent tone	Some nonstandard word order; several run-on sentences; several sentence fragments; omissions of several words; errors somewhat detract from meaning	Some correct use of inflections; some consistency in tense and subject-verb agreement; several errors in word meaning; errors somewhat detract from meaning	Some correct use of mechanics and formatting; errors somewhat detract from meaning
1	Lack of a central idea; no details, random digressions	Limited vocabulary; choppy sentences; flat tone	Frequent nonstandard word order; mostly run-on sentences or sentence fragments; omissions of many words; errors frequently detract from meaning	Little to no correct use of inflections; frequent tense shifts; little to no subject-verb agreement; many errors in word meaning; errors fully detract from meaning	Little to no correct use of mechanics or formatting; errors fully detract from meaning

*4 = consistent control; 3 = nearly consistent control; 2 = inconsistent control; 1 = little or no control.

Adapted from O'Malley & Pierce, 1996, originally from Virginia Department of Education.

give detailed attention to just one or a few issues at a time. One disadvantage, however, is that it is difficult for raters to focus on a single trait (or set of traits). Also, if the assessment does not consider other factors or traits, it may be too narrow.

The 6+1 Trait Writing model, developed by the Northwest Regional Education Laboratory, is an assessment and instructional framework that combines analytic and multi-trait scoring. The latest version has been aligned with the CCSS. The model is used in schools throughout the country, and teachers of ELLs have found it useful in assessing student writing and identifying the aspects of certain traits on which to focus their instruction to help students improve their writing. Separate rubrics are provided for grades K–2 and grades 3–12.

In classrooms with ELLs who have or who are developing the ability to write in their home languages, teachers can also use the Literacy Squared rubric developed by Escamilla et al. (2013) to assess students' writing in any genre in English and Spanish side by side. Teachers can then use evidence of student writing to inform instruction that taps into students' biliterate potential.

For an example of how a teacher might use an analytical scoring rubric to assess a student's writing, let's look at how Mr. Moreno, a teacher in San Antonio, Texas, evaluated a personal narrative essay by Maria, one of his 5th grade Spanish-speaking ELLs. Maria's writing sample, describing what she did over the spring break, is shown in Figure 9.6. Before looking at Mr. Moreno's scores in the text that follows, read the essay and decide what scores, according to the analytic scoring rubric in Table 9.3, you would give Maria in each of the five areas. Also identify Maria's strengths, the areas in which she is in need of improvement, and instructional strategies that could be used to help her improve her writing.

Spring Brak

I wish this day never fines. On Sunday 12 I went to a cinsiañera on tusday 16 I went to walk about 9 milles from san patrisio to San Fernando. on Sunday 19 I went to chuch and I went to a mexican resturant.

On Sunday 12 I went to a cinsiañero. The party was on San lorenso it began at 10.00 the fud was so good I curent stop eatan they were aibin Sopa de aros, carde gisada and carne asada! I eat som chocalet cake buit candy on top.

On tusday I went to wallk for my dad. I now you are wondering way. my dad was learnig about jesos. wen I was walking my cosend was en front of my so I acsededtly step on hes sou so he fel and then tasde kivn my wo is that meal

On Sunday I went to church the preace is my pren so he awis tas my hu.

The chure that I go to is cald San lorenso I went to See the birgen de guadalupe. Then I went to eat in las palapas.

wen you go to Spring Break you cald do stuf bery fun Taik my gent to church, I went for a walk, I went to a cinsiañera. ¿So wat did you do on Spring Break?

Figure 9.6 Writing sample by Maria (pseudonym), a Spanish-speaking ELL student in Mr. Moreno's 5th grade class.

Mr. Moreno gave Maria the following scores:

Composing	4
Style	3
Sentence formation	3
Usage	2
Mechanics	2

While reflecting on Maria's strengths, the areas in which she is in need of improvement, and instructional strategies that could be used to help her improve her writing, he wrote the following comments:

> Maria is able to express her thoughts. She understands sentence structure. She knows that letters should be capitalized at the beginning of the sentence and that they should end with correct punctuation. She understands the concept of the different parts of the essay which includes the introduction, the body with 3 details, and the conclusion.
>
> Maria needs improvement with her spelling. She applies her prior knowledge of phonics in Spanish as she sounds out words in English, for example *wer* for *were* or *preace* for *priest*. For some words, she is not able to hear all the sounds of the letters and makes up the letters that she thinks go in it, for example *awis* for *always*. Maria learned that for an expository essay you should list the different topics you will write about, but brought that over into a narrative essay, where the author really needs to engage the reader using a story-like style.
>
> Maria would probably best be helped by enlisting the use of a personal word book where she could write the correct spelling for words that she likes to use all the time. In addition, I need to review with Maria the writing strategies for the different types of essays (narrative, expository, persuasive).

How did your scores compare with Mr. Moreno's? Do you agree with his assessment of Maria's strengths, needs, and strategies to help her improve? What more would you add? Might Maria, for example, benefit from some mini-lessons on capitalization and punctuation? It is clear from this sample that she has some knowledge of the rules. With a little more instruction, she can learn about the need to capitalize words at the beginning of sentences and proper nouns (e.g., Mexican, Tuesday, San Lorenzo) and to be more consistent in her use of ending punctuation.

Portfolio Assessment

An assessment of a single piece of student writing will not give a valid and reliable assessment of a student's writing ability. Students' writing development is not linear, and there may appear to be regressions as students take risks and try new genres. Thus, multiple measures are needed, in particular portfolio assessment, based on writing samples collected throughout the year. The portfolio can include journal entries, early drafts and published writing from Writer's Workshop, samples from directed writing lessons, and samples of students' writing in different genres and content areas. It should include samples of unedited writing from throughout the year and samples that highlight the students' strengths and areas in need of improvement. Online or other digital portfolios can include these as well as multimedia texts authored by the students. Some teachers determine what to include in the portfolio, while others work collaboratively with the students to determine which pieces to include. Bilingual programs should include writing samples in two languages.

Each entry should be dated and each should have been assessed separately. By reviewing the writing samples in the portfolio throughout the year, the teachers can undertake formative assessments to see where students are at and what types of instruction and support they need to move to higher levels of writing proficiency. By reviewing student portfolios at the end of the school year, teachers can undertake summative assessments to provide an overall evaluation of the students' writing proficiency.

Peer Assessment and Self-Assessment

Students should be involved in assessing their own writing and that of their peers. They can use the same rubrics the teacher uses or a more "student-friendly" version. Simpler versions are especially appropriate for younger students. Checklists are another form of assessment students can use to evaluate their own writing, particularly during the editing stage of Writer's Workshop. The checklist in Figure 9.7 was developed by a teacher in Chicago. For rubrics and checklists to be effective, however, students must receive instruction, modeling, and practice in using them.

Writing Checklist

Conventions
- My paragraphs are sound.
- Each of my paragraphs has one main idea.
- I have used correct grammar.
- I have used correct punctuation.
- Periods are at the end of my sentences.
- I have quotation marks around dialogue.
- My spelling is correct.
- My handwriting is legible.

Fluency
- My sentences begin in different ways.
- My sentences build upon the ones before.
- My sentences are different lengths.
- The meaning of each of my sentences is clear.
- My sentences flow and use correct grammar.
- There are no run-ons.
- My sentences are complete.

Organization
- My report is sequenced in order.
- My introduction is exciting and inviting.
- My ideas flow and are well connected.
- I have a satisfying conclusion.

Capitalization
- I have capitalized the first word in each sentence.
- I have capitalized people and pet names.
- I have capitalized months and days.
- I have capitalized cities, states, and places.
- I have capitalized titles of books, movies, et cetera.

Word Choice
- Every word seems just right.
- I used a lot of describing words.
- My words paint pictures in the reader's mind.
- I used strong verbs like darted and exclaimed.
- I used synonyms to add variety.

Ideas
- I used a graphic organizer to create and organize ideas.
- My ideas are written in my own words.
- My report is clear and focused.
- I understand my topic.
- My details give the reader important information.
- My ideas relate to one another.
- I have listened to suggestions from the teacher or peers.

Figure 9.7 Self-assessment writing checklist. (Manning, M. S. (2001). Writing checklist. *Write away! A student guide to the writing process* [Online module]).

Summary

Writing is a crucial skill for academic success in school and for effective communication in the sociocultural contexts in which students live. With new technologies, writing is becoming one of the primary means through which individuals in our society interact and communicate with each other. All teachers share in the responsibility for helping ELLs become proficient writers. Research has revealed a strong connection between oral language proficiency, reading proficiency, and writing ability. Thus, teachers can help students become better writers by helping them become better listeners, speakers, and readers, and by helping them use books and other texts as models for their own writing. Research has revealed also that students with home language literacy skills can transfer many of these skills to English writing, but that ELLs' ability to express themselves in written English is highly dependent on their level of oral English proficiency. Thus, teachers should build on the strength of students' writing skills in their home language (or develop them first in the home language, as in bilingual programs), providing extensive oral language development through ESL and sheltered content-area instruction. Bilingual and biliterate students can also draw on all of their linguistic resources to engage in translingual practices as they learn to write and author meaningful texts. The writing *to, with,* and *by* model is a way of framing effective writing instruction through modeling, scaffolding, and ample practice for students to write meaningful text for authentic purposes. Effective formative assessment enables teachers to monitor their students' writing development and plan appropriate instruction.

Discussion Questions

1. If you have learned, or attempted to learn, another language, what challenges did you face in learning to write in the new language? What role did your home language play in the development of your writing ability in that language?

2. What is the relationship between oral language and reading and writing ability? How can oral language development and reading be used to help ELLs improve their writing? And how can writing help students develop their oral language and reading proficiency?

3. Why are modeled writing, interactive writing, shared writing, guided writing, journal writing, and Writer's Workshop important for ELLs? How does the writing *to, with,* and *by* framework provide scaffolding for ELLs to help them become proficient writers of English? Describe any experiences you have with these as a student or teacher.

4. View the video clip of a mini-lesson taught by a teacher as part of Writer's Workshop. The students are working on editing the opinion pieces they wrote, and the teacher is showing students how to work with their partners to edit their writing using a checklist. Make a list and discuss the strategies and techniques the teacher used in the mini-lesson. How effective do you feel this mini-lesson was?

5. Review Lesson 5 in of the model unit *Persuasion across Time and Space* developed by the Understanding Language initiative to demonstrate effective instruction for helping ELLs meet the demands of the CCSS in English language arts. This lesson for middle-school ELLs at the intermediate-to-advanced levels of English proficiency involves analyzing a persuasive speech and then writing their own. Discuss the purpose and objectives of the lesson and the strategies and techniques used to achieve these objectives. How do these strategies and techniques compare with those in this chapter? How effective do you

feel these are, and how effective do you feel the lesson is as a whole, for helping ELLs meet the CCSS for writing?

Research Activities

1. *ELL Student Assessment* Collect one or more samples of an ELL student's writing. Assess the writing using the writing rubric in Table 9.3, the 6+1 Traits writing rubrics, or the criteria your state uses for writing assessments on its English proficiency assessment. Discuss the strengths and areas in need of improvement. Determine instructional strategies to help the student improve his or her writing.

2. *ELL Teacher Interview* Interview an ELL teacher about his or her writing instruction. What are the teacher's views about teaching writing to ELLs? What does he or she see as the role of writing in second language acquisition? How does the teacher see the connections between reading and writing instruction? Does the teacher view writing as an isolated academic subject, or does he or she view writing as an important communicative tool in sociocultural contexts? How does the teacher balance providing effective writing instruction and helping students prepare for state high-stakes writing tests?

3. *ELL Classroom Observation* Observe writing instruction and activities in an ELL classroom. Describe the instructional techniques and strategies, and the skills the teacher emphasizes. How many opportunities do students have to engage in independent writing? What scaffolding or other supports are available for students when writing? How much writing are students doing outside of their regular writing instruction? How effective do you feel the writing instruction for ELLs is in this classroom? What strengths did you observe that you would like to include in your own classroom? What improvements could be made to the teacher's writing instruction?

4. *Online Research Activity* Using the ELL Language Portraits site, review and compare the writing samples of two or more students. Assess these students' writing samples using the rubric and forms embedded in the site. Compare your rubric scores and comments about the students' strengths and areas in need of improvement with the completed forms provided on the site. Describe and discuss any differences.

Recommended Reading

de Oliveira, L. C., & Silva, T. (Eds.). (2016). *Second language writing in elementary classrooms: Instructional issues, content-area writing, and teacher education.* New York: Palgrave Macmillan.

This book features chapters that highlight research in elementary classrooms focused on the writing development of multilingual children, and research in teacher education to prepare elementary teachers to teach L2 writing and address L2 writers' needs

Manchón, R. M., & Matsuda, P. K. (Eds.). (2016). *Handbook of second and foreign language writing.* Boston: De Gruyter Mouton.

This handbook provides both state-of-the-art research and a retrospective critical look at the historical development of the field of second and foreign language writing.

Peregoy, S. F., & Boyle, O. F. (2017). *Reading, writing, and learning in ESL: A resource book for teaching K–12 English learners* (7th ed.). Boston: Pearson.

This detailed book provides a wealth of resources for putting research into effective literacy practices with ELLs and includes extensive chapters on ELLs' writing development.

Ten

Content-Area Instruction

Questions such as, "What do our students know?" and "What can they do?" are particularly important as educators around the world grapple with supporting students still in the process of learning the language of instruction to navigate the language and literacy demands associated with mainstream content area standards.

—GEORGE C. BUNCH

KEY TERMS
- content objectives
- differentiated instruction
- language objectives
- Next Generation Science Standards
- thematic teaching

GUIDING QUESTIONS
1. Why is it important for sheltered instruction to include both content and language objectives?
2. What are the benefits of an integrated, thematic approach to content-area instruction for ELLs?
3. What do the languages of mathematics, science, and social studies include, and who is responsible for teaching them?
4. How can teachers integrate culture into their content-area instruction?
5. How can teachers differentiate their instruction for the ELLs in their classrooms?

ELLs face the challenge of learning to listen, speak, read, and write in English at the same time they are also expected to meet the same grade-level academic content standards as their English-proficient peers. The school system is not set up to allow students to attain proficiency in English before learning academic content, nor should it be. ELLs are capable of learning academic content while developing proficiency in English when instruction is specially designed. In fact, high-quality sheltered content-area instruction further supports and is essential to their English language development.

The strongest program models for ELLs are bilingual programs in which some content areas are taught in the students' home language. Bilingual programs offer the best assurance that ELLs will not fall behind academically while they are learning English, and academic concepts learned in the home language can transfer to English once students have the language skills to talk about and use them. Even in bilingual programs, however, some content areas are taught through sheltered English instruction, the amount of which increases as students move up in grade level. In classrooms where home language instruction is not available or feasible, all content areas are taught in English through sheltered instruction and using bilingual strategies as needed.

In this chapter, we focus on ways in which teachers can provide effective sheltered instruction in the content areas of mathematics, science, and social studies and also discuss the importance of art, music, and physical education instruction for ELLs. An overview of each content area is offered, followed by a brief discussion of the language demands each subject poses for ELLs and ideas for making instruction in these content areas comprehensible for ELLs. We look first at some of the principles of providing effective content-area instruction for ELLs.

Principled Approach to Teaching Content to English Language Learners

The Understanding Language initiative has outlined six key principles for ELL instruction (Box 10.1). Some of these principles have been addressed in previous chapters, and others are addressed here. The principles calling for rigorous, standards-aligned, grade-level-appropriate instruction specially designed for ELLs through deliberate and appropriate scaffolds may be addressed through sheltered content-area instruction. The Sheltered Instruction Observation Protocol (SIOP) model provides a valuable tool for helping educators plan, deliver, and evaluate effective sheltered instruction (Echevarria, Vogt, & Short, 2017). The SIOP includes 30 observable items organized into eight key components of effective sheltered instruction and contains a rubric for evaluating each item on a scale of 0 to 4. The creators of the SIOP also provide lesson plan templates to help teachers design lessons based on these key components. Many of the principles, ideas, strategies, and techniques described in this chapter are reflected in the SIOP.

Differentiated Instruction for English Language Learners in Content-Area Classes

All students differ in prior knowledge, academic proficiency, learning styles, and sociocultural background. Thus, one-size-fits-all instruction is problematic, especially for the diverse group of students under the ELL label. When classrooms have a wide range of

---

Box 10.1 Understanding Language Initiative: Key Principles for English Language Learner Instruction

The Common Core State Standards (CCSS) in English Language Arts and Mathematics as well as the Next Generation Science Standards (NGSS) require that English Language Learners (ELLs) meet rigorous, grade level academic standards. The following principles are meant to guide teachers, coaches, ELL specialists, curriculum leaders, school principals, and district administrators as they work to develop CCSS-aligned instruction for ELLs. These principles are applicable to any type of instruction regardless of grade, proficiency level, or program type. Finally, no single principle should be considered more important than any other. All principles should be incorporated into the planning and delivery of every lesson or unit of instruction.

1. Instruction focuses on providing ELLs with opportunities to engage in discipline-specific practices which are designed to build conceptual understanding and language competence in tandem.
2. Instruction leverages ELLs' home language(s), cultural assets, and prior knowledge.
3. Standards-aligned instruction for ELLs is rigorous, grade-level appropriate, and provides deliberate and appropriate scaffolds.
4. Instruction moves ELLs forward by taking into account their English proficiency level(s) and prior schooling experiences.
5. Instruction fosters ELLs' autonomy by equipping them with the strategies necessary to comprehend and use language in a variety of academic settings.
6. Diagnostic tools and formative assessment practices are employed to measure students' content knowledge, academic language competence, and participation in disciplinary practices.

Understanding Language. (2013). *Key principles for ELL instruction.* Retrieved from https://ell.stanford.edu/sites/default/files/Key%20Principles%20for%20ELL%20Instruction%20with%20references_0.pdf, reprinted with permission.

diversity in their students' language and academic proficiency, teachers should not provide all students with the exact same curricular materials, lessons, and instruction. Recall that the U.S. Supreme Court ruled in *Lau v. Nichols* that this sink-or-swim approach is unconstitutional because it fails to address the unique language and academic needs of ELLs.

Teachers need to tailor instruction to the unique language and academic needs of each student, that is, they need to provide **differentiated instruction**. This approach, of course, requires more work, but it is the hallmark of teachers who are true professionals. Anyone can give the same books, worksheets, homework, and tests to a group of students, praising those who do well and blaming those who fail. Effective teachers, however, know their students, and by using authentic formative assessments can continually determine their language and academic needs relative to the instructional goals. Teachers use this information to differentiate instruction so that their ELLs can achieve academically and continue to develop the English they need for academic success. This chapter illustrates ways that teachers can differentiate instruction for ELLs.

Language and Content-Area Objectives

Recall that sheltered instruction lessons include both **language objectives** and **content objectives**, reflecting the fact that the content-area instruction is also language instruction for ELLs. Thus, sheltered content-area instruction supports, but does not replace, ESL instruction. When teaching content areas to ELLs, teachers must focus on helping all students understand the concepts and helping ELLs learn the language necessary to communicate with others in accomplishing academic tasks related to the content-area concept.

For an example of how language and content-area objectives can be combined, consider a science lesson on the water cycle. Students will collaborate in small groups to create posters illustrating the water cycle and prepare an oral presentation to the class using their completed poster. The content and language objectives for this lesson might look something like this:

Content Objectives

Students will be able to
- Identify and describe the stages of the water cycle
- Create a poster illustrating the stages of the water cycle in sequence

Language Objectives

Students will be able to
- Use oral and written English and key vocabulary with members of the group to *identify* the stages in the cycle, *describe* each stage, and *explain* the importance of these stages
- Use oral and written English to collaborate with other students to *plan* and *develop* a water-cycle poster
- Make an oral presentation to the class in which the group *identifies, describes,* and *explains* the stages of the water cycle *using sequencing language*

Note that the content-area objectives are the same for all students in the class. Note also that the language objectives direct attention to the language of the content area, that is, the key vocabulary, genres, and registers that all students need to learn. The language objectives, however, will need to be differentiated according to students' English language proficiency and literacy levels.

More specifically, in this lesson all students need to learn new content-specific (tier 3) vocabulary, such as *precipitation, condensation,* and *evaporation,* and general academic (tier 2) vocabulary, such as *cycle* and *process.* Key vocabulary about the water cycle also includes tier 1 words, such as *cloud, water, rain, storm, sun, sunshine, heat, rise, fall, puddle, lake, ocean*—common words already known by proficient English speakers that may be unknown by some of the ELLs. Further, all students need to be able to use the language of science to *identify, describe,* and *explain* the stages of the water cycle orally and in writing, and the formal language necessary for an oral presentation. English speakers will have the oral English they need to interact with others in their group, but ELLs may vary in their ability to use English to, for example, agree, disagree, give opinions, or make suggestions. ELLs also may vary in their ability to comprehend and use sequencing language in a discussion of the various stages.

Adding language objectives to a science lesson is one way to provide differentiated instruction, because it adds a focus beyond that provided for non-ELLs. But the expected level of performance of each ELL related to the language objectives may not be the same. Each student's level of English proficiency must also be taken into consideration. A newly arrived ELL, for example, would have great difficulty serving as the group's spokesperson with responsibility to describe in detail the intricacies of the water cycle, even if he or she has the same knowledge and understanding as the non-ELLs. Students at this proficiency level could, however, label and read the names of the different stages on their group's poster, and then a student with higher language proficiency could provide detailed descriptions.

Using English Language Proficiency Standards to Guide Content-Area Instruction

As discussed in the preceding chapters, the English language proficiency (ELP) standards of the WIDA and ELPA21 consortia, along with those of individual states, are used to guide both English language development instruction and academic content-area instruction. WIDA includes specific standards (nos. 2–5) focused on the language ELLs need to communicate the information, ideas, and concepts necessary for academic success in the content areas of language arts, mathematics, science, and social studies. Standards 1–7 of the ELP standards used by states in the ELPA21 consortium focus on the language ELLs need in order to engage in content-specific practices associated with English language arts, mathematics, and science. Non-consortium states such as California, New York, and Texas likewise have designed their ELP standards to cut across the different content areas. For example, California's English language development standards indicate the following "critical principles for developing language and cognition in academic contexts":

> While advancing along the continuum of English language development levels, English learners at all levels engage in intellectually challenging literacy, disciplinary, and disciplinary literacy tasks. They use language in meaningful and relevant ways appropriate to grade level, content area, topic, purpose, audience, and text type in English language arts, mathematics, science, social studies, and the arts. Specifically, they use language to gain and exchange information and ideas in three communicative modes (collaborative, interpretive, and productive), and they apply knowledge of language to academic tasks via three cross-mode language processes (structuring cohesive texts, expanding and enriching ideas, and connecting and condensing ideas) using various linguistic resources. (California Department of Education, 2014, p. 36).

These ELP standards and progressions provide an important and useful tool for differentiating content-area instruction for ELLs based on their level of English proficiency. Recall that the various ELP standards and progressions provide descriptions and examples of observable language behaviors ELLs at different levels of English proficiency can be expected to demonstrate as they engage in classroom tasks.

Strategies for Modifying Textbooks and Instructional Materials

Grade-level content-area curricular materials were not developed with ELLs in mind, and therefore modifications may be required to make grade-level content-area instructional materials accessible. Strategies for modifying text in textbooks include outlining, using graphic organizers, rewriting the text in simplified English, and reading it aloud with students, pausing to paraphrase, explain, or provide examples to help ELLs understand the meaning. Reiss (2012) suggests that teachers give instruction in and practice using textbook aids: the table of contents, the index, chapter titles and section headings, outlines and questions, chapter summaries and review sections, glossaries, text boxes and highlighted areas, text organizers, and graphics and other visuals. There is a growing trend among publishers of content-area textbooks and curricular programs to address the needs of ELLs. For example, some teacher's guides include suggestions for modifying content and activities to make them more comprehensible for ELLs. Some publishers also provide separate supplemental materials in simplified English or in other languages. Caution and professional judgment, however, must be exercised with these resources. Some ELL educators have found them to be superficial, oversimplified, and forced. In most instances, more substantial modifications and adaptations will be needed—guided by ELP standards and progressions—to make the content accessible and comprehensible for ELLs at different levels of English proficiency.

Thematic Teaching and Lesson Planning

The number-one complaint among classroom teachers is that there is not enough time to teach everything. This problem has been exacerbated by pressure to raise test scores. Teachers have been pressured to provide narrow teaching-to-the-test instruction, often using curricular programs and test prep materials mandated by the school or district. To ensure coverage of all content areas, teachers can use **thematic teaching**, selecting a theme that can be explored through all content areas. For younger children the theme might be a topic, such as Butterflies or Ocean Life. For older students, themes can be more abstract and broad, such as Change or Inequality. Thematic teaching allows easy crossover among content areas. A science lesson on weather, for example, could incorporate elements of mathematics, art, and writing by having students record the temperature every day for a week, draw pictures illustrating the weather for each day, and write about which day they felt had the best weather.

Thematic teaching, however, does more than save time. It provides and builds on students' background knowledge and thus facilitates comprehensible input. If students learn new vocabulary and concepts about the weather through science instruction, they will understand more when they talk about and read about the weather in other content areas. Teachers can use a template to plan thematic lessons, filling in simple ideas for lessons in each content area (Figure 10.1). For example, for the theme of Immigration, under reading, we might put, "Read *How Many Days to America* by Eve Bunting and Beth Peck"; under writing, "Write stories about families' immigration"; under math, "Make a bar graph showing from what countries students' families emigrated," and so forth. Once

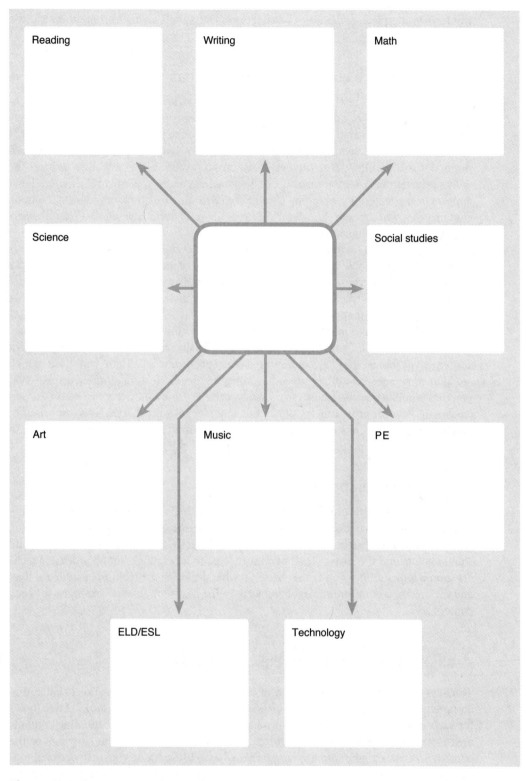

Figure 10.1 Thematic lesson planning form.

this form is complete, each idea can be developed into a full sheltered content-area lesson or activity.

Use of Literature across the Content Areas

Although grade-level textbooks are typically written at a level inaccessible to ELLs, teachers can find other books dealing with the same concepts at more accessible levels. They can read these books aloud to the class or use them for shared reading and guided reading to reinforce and further develop content-area knowledge. Works of both fiction and nonfiction with content-area themes are appropriate. For a social studies unit on the early settlement of America, for example, the teacher could supplement the material that appears in the textbook by reading aloud *Sarah Morton's Day* by Kate Waters. The book contains vivid photographs and descriptions of life in Plymouth Plantation from the perspective of a young Pilgrim girl.

With older ELLs, teachers may be tempted to use content-area textbooks from lower grade levels. They should be cautious, however, about using them. Although these books may be beneficial because they provide content similar to the more challenging grade-level textbooks but written at a more accessible level, their use may suggest to ELLs that they are less capable than their grade-level peers.

Some educational publishers, recognizing the need for supplemental textbooks, particularly for older ELLs, have begun publishing books that are designed to help ELLs learn academic vocabulary and key content-area concepts in English. These textbooks, which are aligned to specific content areas but not grade levels, feature simplified text, vivid graphics and illustrations labeled with new vocabulary and questions and exercises, and teacher's guides for providing lessons in the language of content areas. It is important to note that these textbooks are not designed to replace grade-level textbooks but rather to provide a scaffold to prepare students to use grade-level texts.

Multicultural Perspectives

Integrating ELLs' cultures into instruction is easily achieved in language arts by reading relevant books. Instruction in mathematics, science, social studies, physical education, and the arts can also incorporate multicultural perspectives and contributions and should go beyond the surface level of culture (e.g., food, clothing, and holidays). Teachers should look for books and other materials that deal with the realities of students' lives and the diverse communities in which they live. The next section offers examples for each content area.

Sheltered Instruction in the Content Areas

Teachers can shelter their instruction to make mathematics, science, and social studies comprehensible to the ELLs in their classes. The following discussion looks at five topics for each area, that teachers should consider when sheltering and differentiating content-area instruction for linguistically and culturally diverse learners: the language of the content area, making instruction comprehensible to ELLs, modifying instructional materials, using literature, and integrating students' cultures. Charts showing the sample performance indicators from the Teachers of English to Speakers of Other Languages (TESOL) standards for mathematics, science, and social studies are also included. These are followed by a brief discussion of the importance of art, music, and physical education for ELLs.

Mathematics

Mathematics is one of the main subjects covered on state high-stakes tests, and therefore, along with language arts, it tends to get the most attention in the classroom. Unfortunately, teachers may feel pressure to push through math instruction at a rapid pace to cover all concepts that may appear on the test. Math learning is cumulative, and basic concepts must be mastered before students can learn more advanced concepts. It is therefore imperative that ELLs receive comprehensible math instruction to avoid falling far behind their grade-level peers.

The Common Core standards for mathematics are designed to bring about three major shifts in math education. First, they significantly narrow the scope of math concepts taught, especially in the elementary grades, so that more time can be given to helping students gain a solid foundation for more demanding math concepts, procedures, and applications in the secondary grades. Second, they emphasize coherence across and within grades, so that each new standard is an extension of previous learning. Third, they emphasize rigor within the major topics so that students develop conceptual understanding, procedural skills, and the ability to apply skills in problem-solving situations. Although these new standards may be beneficial for students who begin school in kindergarten in the United States, they could make it harder to address the needs of newcomer ELLs, especially students with interrupted formal education who arrive in upper grade levels and are unlikely to have the foundations assumed by the standards. Thus, the principles of providing differentiated instruction remain important. (See the companion website for a video clip of the mathematics education professor Judit Moschkovich discussing ELLs and the Common Core standards for mathematics.)

Language of Mathematics

A major misperception about math is that it is easy for ELLs because it is mostly numbers. Research shows, however, that math tests have high language demands that pose significant difficulties for ELLs (Avalos, Medina, & Secada, 2018). Some of my own research has documented the tremendous challenges math can pose for newcomer ELLs. For example, I analyzed the vocabulary and syntax demands of a state math exam which proved to be far more complex than the vocabulary and syntax of the simplified math worksheets used by their teacher for classroom math instruction (Wright & Li, 2006, 2008). Moschkovich (2018) notes the need to move beyond a simple view of mathematical language as low-level language skills consisting of single vocabulary words. She argues for an expanded view of academic literacy in mathematics that includes mathematical proficiency, mathematical practices, and mathematical discourses.

Educators and researchers have analyzed the language of math and found that it has a unique vocabulary and syntax and unique semantic properties and text features (Avalos et al., 2018; Kersaint, Thompson, & Petkova, 2013). Words such as *divisor, denominator,* and *quotient* are rarely used outside of math, and many common words, such as *table, column,* and *face,* have specific meanings in math contexts. Imagine the confusion an ELL might feel when the teacher says, "Look at the table to find the answers."[1] There are also terms that have different meanings within math, such as *square* (i.e., *square* shape, the *square* of four [4^2], and the *square* root of four [$\sqrt{4}$]). ELLs may also be confused by homonyms of math terms, such as *sum* (*some*) and *plane* (*plain*). Another challenge is the use of multiple words for the same mathematical idea (i.e., *addition, add, plus, sum*). The math register also has a unique set of complex phrases, such as *least common multiple* and *negative exponent.*

---

[1] Kersaint et al., 2013, notes that the two meanings of the English word *table* suggested here are two separate words in Spanish: *mesa* (dinner table) and *tabla* (math table).

The syntax of math can be very confusing for ELLs. Often there is no one-to-one correspondence between words and the symbols they represent. For example, "x is less than twenty-two" takes more words to say than symbols to write "$x < 22$." Also, word order may differ from the way numbers and symbols appear in a numeric sentence. For example, $(x + y)^2$ would be read, "The square of the sum of x and y." Mathematical texts are dense and conceptually packed. They require left-to-right as well as up-and-down eye movement and must be read more slowly than natural-language texts and often several times. Furthermore, the texts are often crowded with symbols and notation that convey precise mathematical meanings and content (Avalos et al., 2018). Mathematical information is often presented in tables, charts, graphs, and other visual representations. Math texts are often written in the passive voice (e.g., "If a weight is placed on a scale . . ."), which is less common in spoken discourse (Kersaint et al., 2013).

Word problems can be particularly challenging because they contain complex syntax and difficult—and usually irrelevant—vocabulary. In my own research, for example, new-comer ELLs had difficulty comprehending a simple word problem in which they were told a farmer grew a certain number of *watermelons*, but then were asked "how many *melons* did he sell?" Even when the teacher taught them the word *watermelon,* the students did not make the connection with the word *melons.* Thus, solving word problems correctly requires vocabulary knowledge and English reading-comprehension skills. ELLs who are highly skilled in math will have difficulty demonstrating those skills until they attain enough proficiency to handle the linguistic demands of math instruction and assessment in English. Avalos et al. (2018) found that ELLs encounter two principal difficulties when approaching word problems: "the mental time and effort necessary to process semantic structures, syntax, and vocabulary between languages, and the potential ambiguity of mathematics word problems" (p. 56).

Another challenge for newcomer ELLs is that they may have learned math symbols and algorithms for problem solving in their home country that differ from those taught in the United States. For example, in several Asian countries the decimal is used to separate place value and the comma is used for number values less than 1, the exact opposite of how they are used in the United States (e.g., 5,300,200.10 would be written 5.300.200,10). And algorithms for long division differ substantially in other countries. Most other countries emphasize mental math; thus, ELLs with strong math skills from their home country find it tedious and wasteful when required to "show your work." Other cultural differences may affect math instruction for ELLs. For examples, most ELLs come from countries that use the metric system and may find the illogical measurement system used in the United States baffling. Learning about money can also be confusing. Not all countries use decimals in their money systems (e.g., in Japan 1 Yen is the smallest currency); in some countries the size of the bill or coin corresponds with its value, while in the United States all bills are the same size (and color) and nickels and half-dollars are bigger than dimes and dollar coins, respectively, yet lesser in value. And our love for fractions in the United States is not shared in other countries where more emphasis is placed on decimals.[2]

Despite the language challenges, Moschkovich (2018) emphasizes that even while ELLs are learning English, they "can participate in discussions where they grapple with important mathematical content." She argues that talking is central to learning mathematics with understanding. Talking to learn math can be in developing English, everyday English, a mixture of both English and the home language (translanguaging), or in more formal academic registers.

---

[2] One award-winning U.S. mathematician, Dennis DeTurck, argues that the United States should de-emphasize fractions, in a short 2-minute lecture at the University of Pennsylvania titled, "Down with Fractions!."

Figure 10.2 Calendar wall, Scobee Elementary School, Northside Independent School District, San Antonio, Texas. (Photo by author.)

Making Mathematics Instruction Comprehensible for English Language Learners

To help students learn the vocabulary and language structures of math, teachers can make illustrated math word charts to go along with math units, such as geometric shapes or measurement words. Better yet, they can make these word charts with the students during shared or modeled writing. Note the wide variety of charts and visuals in the photograph in Figure 10.2 of an elementary school classroom, including a number line, a 100 chart, a calendar, coins, a clock, a list of ordinal numbers, a chart of skip counting by 2s, 5s, and 10s, math facts, and clue words for word problems signaling the correct operation. Charts like these provide visual support and offer opportunities for daily practice of these concepts (See the companion website for examples.)

ELLs can get hands-on practice with pattern blocks, sorting manipulatives, counting manipulatives, base-10 blocks for teaching place value and regrouping, pie-slice manipulatives for learning fractions, clocks, play money, rulers, protractors, compasses, three-dimensional shapes, measuring spoons and cups, balance scales, and weights. These and other manipulatives help ELLs understand concepts that they might not fully grasp if they were only to hear them explained or see them in print (Figure 10.3). They also allow ELLs to demonstrate what they know without having to rely only on words, spoken or written.

Teachers can also make math comprehensible for ELLs using bilingual strategies and technology designed to enhance or support math instruction. For example, several software programs use the computer's multimedia capabilities to help students understand and practice math concepts, often in the context of games and other entertaining activities. Students can also use multimedia programs to create their own presentations that demonstrate their understanding of math, and they can use spreadsheet software to create their own charts and graphs.

Modifying Mathematics Instructional Materials

Teachers can use role playing to help ELLs understand new vocabulary and unfamiliar concepts in word problems. In a unit on money and how to make change, for example, the math textbook might offer the following word problem:

> Michael's mother pays him $20 for mowing the front lawn. Michael goes to the store and buys a toy train for $8, and a music CD for $10. He also wants to buy a video game for $15, but he realizes he does not have enough money. If he pays the cashier with a $20 bill, how much change should he get in return after his purchase?

Figure 10.3 Wall charts, number charts, and manipulatives all help ELLs understand and engage with the language of mathematics. (Photo by Star Watanaphol.)

To solve this problem, ELLs must be able to read and comprehend English well. Some of the contextual information may be unknown to them, such as mowing the lawn (many may not have lawns or lawn mowers). The words *cashier* and *purchase* may be unknown. Also, the irrelevant information about the cost of the video game is confusing. ELLs may have difficulty pulling out the needed numbers and figuring out the required mathematical operations to set up and solve the program.

To modify this and other word problems, the teacher could have students role play similar situations, using, in this instance, a toy cash register, play money, and several items marked with different prices. Once the teacher has helped students learn the vocabulary and language needed for this activity, they could take on the roles of customer and cashier and practice counting out their money and making change. After role playing, students could be guided in writing word problems to record the situations they acted out (e.g., Reggie has a $10 bill. He bought a magazine for $3 and a candy bar for $2. How much change should he receive?). Eventually, the students would be able to answer other word problems without the hands-on manipulatives and role playing. Note how the same math concepts are being covered; but modified and scaffolded in this way, the content becomes more accessible to ELLs.

Using Literature to Support Mathematics Instruction

Many books are available, both fiction and nonfiction, with mathematical themes. My students loved Barbara Barbieri McGrath's *M&M's Brand Counting Book*. Despite its blatant advertising of unhealthy candy to impressionable young children, the book provides an entertaining way to explore number concepts and easily leads into extension activities involving the use of yummy manipulatives. *The Doorbell Rang* by Pat Hutchins tells the story of a family's batch of cookies that gets further and further divided as more and more friends come over and the cookies must be evenly shared. Cindy Neuschwander has written a series of books appropriate for upper elementary and lower secondary students in which solving math problems is central to the plot; titles include *Sir Cumference and the First Round Table: A Math Adventure; Mummy Math: An Adventure in Geometry;* and *Patterns in Peru: An Adventure in Patterning.* For students in the secondary grades, *What's Your Angle, Pythagoras? A Math Adventure* by Julie Ellis and Phyllis Hornung provides a fictionalized account of Pythagoras discovering his theorem that can help readers understand the relevant math. Daniel Kenney and Emily Boever have authored a series of humorous chapter books for grades 3 and higher titled *The Math Inspectors.* The books follow the adventures of a detective agency run by kids who use math to solve local mysteries.

Integrating Students' Cultures into Mathematics Instruction

Integrating students' cultures into math instruction is not simply a matter of writing word problems with ethnic names that deal with supposedly "cultural" content. While word problems should have a diversity of names, care must be taken to avoid introducing offensive stereotypes.

A better and more effective approach is to help students connect math to their own lives in their families, their communities, and the world. For example, an elementary school in Livermore, California, undertook a project through a collaborative online project called Connecting Math to Our Lives.[3] The students started by learning about biographies and practiced writing some on their own. They then went to their school library, where they examined and categorized the biographies by race, class, disability, and gender, using percentages, fractions, and bar graphs. After sorting, classifying, recording, and using math to summarize and analyze their data, the students found that the vast majority of the biographies were about dead white men. The project did not end there. The findings inspired the students to ask questions that led to discussions about equity and representation. Their work extended to collaboration with another school, whose students also analyzed their library's biography collection. Later, the two groups worked together to analyze the biography collection of the main branch of the San Francisco Public Library, where they found imbalances similar to the ones at their own school libraries. Students from both schools met with the public librarians to present their findings and their concerns about the collection. Note that the students also used oral and written language for expository and persuasive purposes in this authentic task.

Math instruction can also include discussions of the multicultural history of math and in particular the contributions of Indian and Arabic mathematicians. The 10 digits of our number system (0 1 2 3 4 5 6 7 8 9), for example, are called Hindu-Arabic numbers, a reflection of their origin. Explanations and charts illustrating the history and origins of our number system can be found on the Internet by googling "Hindu-Arabic numeral system." Also, *algebra* is an Arabic word (*al-gebra;* originally *al-jebr*), first used in writing by the mathematician Muhammad ben Musa al-Khwarizmi in the 9th century CE. Students may be surprised to learn that the *al-* prefix in Arabic is a definite-article prefix roughly equivalent to *the* in English. Presenting this history to students may be particularly engaging for students of Indian and Middle Eastern heritage and help all students counter confusing messages they receive about other parts of the world.

Science

Science has always been a popular subject for sheltered instruction because its tangible concepts and processes facilitate hands-on learning, and thus make it fairly easy to shelter for ELLs. Furthermore, students are naturally curious about how things work in the world. The science experiments on the children's television show *ZOOM* and other chil-

---

[3] See Cummins, Brown, & Sayers, 2007, for more details.

dren's television shows with a science theme, such as *SciGirls* and *Sid the Science Kid,* are very popular. Popular shows such as *Myth Busters* and YouTube channels such as Vsauce owe their success to the scientific wonder of children and adults alike. Science fiction shows and movies captivate viewers of all ages.

One unfortunate result of the heavy federal testing requirements of the Every Student Succeeds Act (ESSA) is that it focuses on math and reading. Thus, science tends to receive less attention, especially in schools in high-poverty areas with large numbers of ELLs. In the past, many teachers felt pressure to teach to the test, and science was all but eliminated at the elementary school level. But federal policy does require that students be tested in science three times between 3rd grade and high school. When these science tests were first developed and administered, many schools realized the cost of their having neglected science instruction for several years. This concern, along with growing attention to the need for more students and workers with expertise in the STEM fields (science, technology, engineering, and mathematics) has set the stage for science to make a comeback as an important content area.

Next Generation Science Standards

Central to the science comeback are the **Next Generation Science Standards** (NGSS), developed in partnership by a group of states, the National Research Council, the National Science Teachers Association, the American Association for the Advancement of Science, and Achieve, a nonprofit education reform organization that has coordinated the effort (NGSS Lead States, 2013). Just over half the states (26) participated as "lead states," giving guidance in the development and feedback on earlier drafts but without any commitment to adopt them once completed. The NGSS were released in April 2013. At the time of this writing, 19 states and the District of Columbia have officially adopted the NGSS. Many more states will likely adopt the NGSS over the next few years, or at least will align their own state science standards with them.

The NGSS are grounded in the *Framework for K-12 Science Education*, developed by the National Research Council (2012) of the National Academy of Sciences. The NGSS are considered to be college-and-career-readiness standards and thus are fully aligned with the requirements of ESSA. The developers of the NGSS stress that these standards are not a science curriculum but rather are student performance expectations that indicate what students should know and be able to do at the end of each grade level.

Lee et al. (2018) find that instructional shifts in science education driven by the NGSS promote language learning with ELLs. These shifts include:

- Focus on explaining phenomena and designing solutions to problems.
- Three-dimensional learning, featuring the following dimensions:
  - Scientific and engineering practices;
  - Cross-cutting concepts that unify the study of science and engineering through common applications across fields;
  - Core ideas in four disciplinary areas: physical sciences; life sciences; earth and space sciences; and engineering, technology, and applications of science.
- Learning progressions. (pp. 38–39)[4]

Lee et al. (2018) also note recent shifts in language instruction that are conducive to promoting science learning. These shifts include a focus on using language for authentic communication purposes, recognition of different academic registers of language, a focus

---

[4]Lee, O., Grapin, S., & Haas, A. (2018). How the NGSS science instructional shifts and language instructional shifts support each other for English learners: Talk in the science classroom. In A. L. Bailey, C. A. Maher, & L. C. Wilkinson (Eds.), *Language, literacy, and learning in the STEM disciplines: How language counts for English learners* (pp. 35–52). New York: Routledge, reprinted with permission.

on the importance of interaction, and the recognition that ELLs can meaningfully participate in content-area lessons and discussions with less-than-perfect English. Lee et al. (2018) describe how these corresponding shifts benefit ELLs in science instruction:

> In the science classroom, learners are mutually engaged in making sense of the natural and designed world. They develop a shared repertoire of resources (e.g., science notebooks) and practices (e.g., developing models) for advancing the goals of the community. As learners build on each other's ideas and co-construct scientific understanding, they also engage in the types of purposeful interactions that promote language learning. Through participation in such interactions with the teacher and more experienced peers, learners are apprenticed into the practices of the community and supported in developing the language as well as other meaning-making resources needed to carry out those practices and express their emerging ideas and understandings. In short, as students use language to do science in socially mediated activity, they develop their science and language proficiency in tandem. (pp. 37–38).[4]

(See the companion website for a video clip of Okhee Lee, a science and ELL expert who contributed to the development of the NGSS.)

Language of Science

The language of science can be confusing for ELLs because, like the language of math, it uses many words from everyday life that have different meanings. ELLs may know that they eat off a *plate,* but in studying earth science, they will encounter *plate tectonics.* They may know words such as *cell* (as in *cell phone*), *tissue* (something to use when you sneeze), and *organ* (a musical instrument at church), but in the life sciences these words have very different meanings. In addition, students will need to learn many new vocabulary words for each topic they encounter in science.

Just as important as specialized science vocabulary is the way language is used to learn and talk about science (i.e., the Discourse of science). Students learn to ask questions and form hypotheses just as scientists do. Students make predictions and come up with explanations. They design experiments, collect data, identify and manipulate variables, record results, and draw conclusions. In moving through the scientific process, students collaborate with others in a group. They also communicate their findings in the genre of science reports; even oral reports of scientific findings are expected to use specific language forms. Each of these is representative of different language functions that are often unique to science. Thus, to be successful in science, ELLs must learn how to talk the talk of science.

Even non-ELLs must learn new concepts and content-specific (tier 3) vocabulary in science instruction. ELLs are at a disadvantage, however, because not only are they still developing their proficiency in English, they may also have less experience with the genre and register expected in their science assignments. One particular challenge in science is the writing of lab and other science reports—a specific genre requiring a unique discourse style and textual structure. Schleppegrell (2002) explains:

> This means that ESL students need to learn to adopt the register features that give their work the authoritativeness and the textual structures that realize the meaning expected in standard academic English. Academic registers have evolved the way they have because they are functional for their purposes, and if students do not draw on appropriate register features, they fail to achieve the purposes of the text. (p. 140)

The Common Core standards for English language arts include reading and writing standards for literacy in science and technical subjects for secondary school students in three grade-level bands: 6–8, 9–10, and 11–12. These standards apply the more general K–12 College and Career Readiness Anchor Standards for reading and writing to the reading and writing of science texts. These standards emphasize that reading is critical to building knowledge in science and technical subjects:

> College and career ready reading in these fields requires an appreciation of the norms and conventions of each discipline, such as the kinds of evidence used in . . . science; an understanding of domain-specific words and phrases; an attention to precise details; and the capacity to evaluate intricate arguments, synthesize complex information, and follow detailed descriptions of . . . concepts. . . . When reading scientific and technical texts, students need to be able to gain knowledge from challenging texts that often make extensive use of elaborate diagrams and data to convey information and illustrate concepts. (ELA Standards, p. 60. © Copyright 2010 National Governors Association Center for Best Practices and Council of Chief State School Officers)

Meeting these standards does not require, however, that students develop fluent English before they can fully engage the language of science. As Lee, Quinn, and Valdés (2013) have argued:

> When supported appropriately, most ELLs are capable of learning subjects such as science through their emerging language and of comprehending and carrying out sophisticated language functions (e.g., arguing from evidence, providing explanations) using less-than-perfect English. They *can do* a number of things using whatever level of English they have and can participate in science and engineering practices. By engaging in such practices, moreover, they grow in both their understanding of science and their language proficiency (i.e., capacity to do more with language). (p. 5)

Lee, Quinn, and Valdés were all involved in the development of the NGSS, including addressing the needs of ELLs as outlined in Appendix D of the standards. The idea of ELLs being able to use "less-than-perfect English" to master the science standards is important. The second author, Quinn, is an award-winning theoretical physicist. She notes that she works with a wide range of renowned international scientists, many of whom speak "less-than-perfect English" (personal communication, April 10, 2013).

Making Science Instruction Comprehensible for English Language Learners

Inquiry-based (or discovery) science is an effective means for helping ELLs successfully learn science concepts and develop English language skills. Inquiry-based science investigations are an important part of addressing the NGSS. Discovery science includes the processes that are at the heart of science instruction: observing, using space-time relationships, using numbers, measuring, classifying, communicating, predicting, inferring, interpreting results, formulating hypotheses, controlling variables, defining operations, and experimenting. Hands-on activities provide rich language opportunities for students to explore real experiences using purposeful language in a meaningful context.

Lee et al. (2018) found that science instruction in the classroom forms a community of practice that "can be a rich environment for both science and oral language learning with English learners, as they *use language to do science* in socially mediated activity" (p. 35). Teachers, however, need to ensure that their science classroom is a community of practice conducive to science and language learning. Langman and Bayley (2007) tracked the progress of a newcomer ELL, Manuel, in a middle school science classroom in a large urban South Texas school district. They found that Manuel had very few opportunities to develop his English language skills in the science classroom. Part of the problem, they found, stemmed from the teacher's false assumption that simply hearing English all day would be sufficient for him to learn English. An in-depth analysis of audio and video recordings made throughout the semester revealed, however, that Manuel had few opportunities to practice sustained English while focusing on scientific tasks. Of particular concern was that even though the science teacher had received some SIOP training and acknowledged the need to provide specialized assistance for her ELLs, she was unclear about how to provide that assistance. Some of her attempts to help Manuel were actually counterproductive in facilitating his English language development. Lacking in this teacher's classroom were clearly articulated language objectives, meaningful hands-on activities that were specially designed to ensure participation of ELLs at all levels of English proficiency, and a system for monitoring and assessing Manuel's progress in meeting these objectives.

Consider the following example of an inquiry-based science lesson called Mystery Powders, which enables students to learn new vocabulary and provides opportunities for students to engage in sustained English use within a community of practice.[5] Students are organized into cooperative learning groups of four. Each group is given a bag containing a different white powder (e.g., baking soda, flour, powdered milk, cleaning powder), a magnifying glass, a cup of water, a spoon, waxed paper, and a recording sheet (Figure 10.4). The students' task is to figure out what their powder is by using their senses of sight, smell, and touch. (They may not use their sense of taste, because some of the powders may be inappropriate to eat.) They then make a hypothesis about what their powder is and what will happen when it is mixed with water. Next they conduct their experiment and record their results. They then make a decision, based on the results, about whether they want to keep or revise their hypothesis. Each student in the group is given a specific role:

Student 1: Pick up and set up materials.
Student 2: Lead group in observations and conducting the experiment.
Student 3: Record results on the sheet.
Student 4: Report findings to the class.

In this lesson, the main language objective is that students will interact with each other in English using the language of science to communicate the information, ideas and concepts necessary to complete the assignment (e.g., *asking* questions, *discussing* results, *recording* observations, *reporting* findings). The main content objective is that students will use the scientific process to identify their mystery powder. This lesson addresses the following dimensions of the NGSS:

- Practices: planning and carrying out investigations, analyzing and interpreting data, and engaging in argument from evidence
- Disciplinary Core Ideas: structure and properties of matter, chemical reactions
- Crosscutting Concepts: patterns, cause and effect, energy and matter

The lesson addresses the following NGSS physical sciences standards:

- Standard 2-PS1-1. Plan and conduct an investigation to describe and classify different kinds of materials by their observable properties.
- Standard 2-PS1-2. Analyze data obtained from testing different materials to determine which materials have properties best suited for an intended purpose.

---

[5] This is a simplified version of an activity popular among science teachers. I learned about it from Dr. Marilyn Thompson, a statistics professor and former high-school science teacher. I created the forms in Figures 10.4 and 10.5 that accompany this lesson.

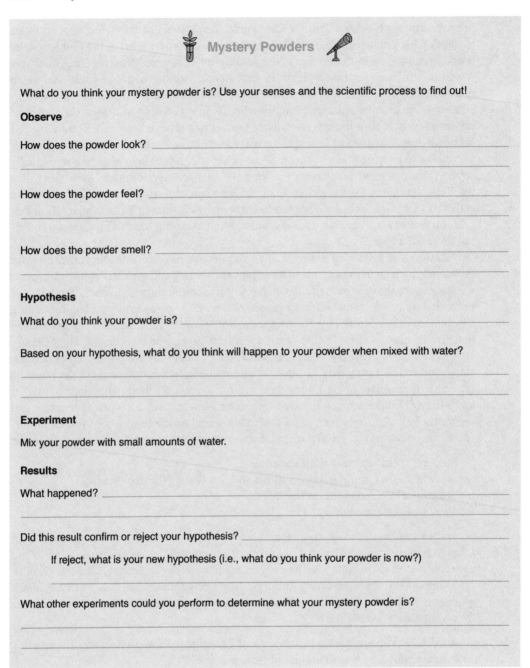

Mystery Powders

What do you think your mystery powder is? Use your senses and the scientific process to find out!

Observe

How does the powder look? _____

_____

How does the powder feel? _____

_____

How does the powder smell? _____

_____

Hypothesis

What do you think your powder is? _____

Based on your hypothesis, what do you think will happen to your powder when mixed with water?

_____

_____

Experiment

Mix your powder with small amounts of water.

Results

What happened? _____

_____

Did this result confirm or reject your hypothesis? _____

　　　If reject, what is your new hypothesis (i.e., what do you think your powder is now?)

_____

What other experiments could you perform to determine what your mystery powder is?

_____

_____

Figure 10.4 Mystery Powder recording sheet.

To meet the content and language objectives for this lesson, students will need vocabulary to describe how powders might look, smell, and feel. One way to provide it is to create a vocabulary chart with the students (through modeled or shared writing or as a separate ESL lesson) before they conduct the experiment (Figure 10.5). To be more effective, the teacher could bring in items (realia) for students to see, feel, and smell that illustrate the meanings of these words. Once the chart is completed and students begin the science project, the teacher monitors each group, helping students refer to the chart as

Sight	Smell	Touch
It looks . . .	**It smells . . .**	**It feels . . .**
white	good	hard
brown	bad	soft
dirty	sweet	powdery
off-white	sour	fine
tan	bitter	coarse
bright		rough
hard	**Like . . .**	dry
soft	(name of	wet
powdery	food or	smooth
shiny	powder)	sticky
sandy		
fine	**Or . . .**	**Like . . .**
coarse	it has	small rocks
rough	no odor	crystals
dry		
wet		(name of
smooth		food or
messy		powder)
dusty		
Like . . .		
crystals		
small rocks		
snow		

Figure 10.5 Vocabulary helper for Mystery Powder science lesson.

necessary to find the words to discuss and record their observations of their mystery powder. Students can use the completed recording sheet when making an oral report of their findings to their class, and the teacher can use it to assess the students' performance.

Modifying Science Instructional Materials

Mainstream science textbooks pose considerable challenges for ELLs. Cervetti and Pearson (2018) note that challenging features of science textbooks include high density of information, technical language, and complex sentences. They also found that students often have to infer logical connections between ideas presented in the text that are not explicitly stated. Dobb (2004)—paraphrasing Rosenthal (1995)—describes well the struggles ELLs may face when reading science textbooks:

> The factual and direct style of scientific writing can be dull, impersonal, and decidedly harder to understand than narrative fiction. The English classroom, where the most direct teaching of language occurs, rarely exposes the EL to expository writing with complex content. In the textbook, content is often unfamiliar, and new vocabulary is introduced rapidly and constantly. Details are usually presented before general ideas and concepts. Dense passages require rereading. There is infrequent repetition or restatement of information.

When faced with fact-packed textbooks and the necessity to slow down and reread material, even the most motivated EL complains of fatigue and frustration. Students with strong academic preparation in their primary language may need two or three times as long to read the textbook as they would to read the same material in their stronger language. Without careful instruction, their engagement with the text and comprehension tend to be low. Frequently, they miss the major science concepts and find little positive reinforcement in their attempts to keep up. (pp. 27–28)[6]

One of the best ways to give ELLs access to the concepts of science is to get the concepts off the pages of the textbook. Students will learn a concept if they experience and discover it rather than just read about it. No teacher, however, can realistically turn every concept in the textbook into a hands-on, inquiry-based lesson. Other options are to provide students, especially those at the intermediate and advanced levels, with instruction in the structure and supports in the textbook. Outlines and graphic organizers can help them identify the main ideas and information structure of the text. Teachers can also rewrite parts of the text in simplified English and use supplemental science textbooks, designed for ELLs.

Using Literature to Support Science Instruction

Nonfiction books that address scientific themes are readily available. A thematic unit on the solar system, for example, could incorporate books by Seymour Simon, such as *Our Solar System,* and others by the same author on the sun, the moon, the individual planets, stars, and comets, meteors, and asteroids. Older students with higher levels of English proficiency would benefit from supplemental books such as Kenneth C. Davis's *Don't Know Much about Space* and *Don't Know Much about the Solar System,* written and illustrated in a much livelier manner than the typical grade-level textbook. On the fiction side, there are dozens of titles in the Magic School Bus series, from simple picture books to longer chapter books, on a wide variety of scientific topics. Students' interest in science could also be piqued by reading science fiction. Students can also make their own science books to develop and practice their written English language skills and to demonstrate their knowledge of science.

Integrating Students' Cultures into Science Instruction

The National Science Teachers Association (2000) emphasizes the importance of valuing the contributions and uniqueness of culturally and linguistically diverse students. To tap into the strengths students bring into the classroom, the association calls for the provision of multicultural science instruction. Their position statement on multicultural science includes the following declarations:

- Children from all cultures are to have equitable access to quality science education experiences that enhance success and provide the knowledge and opportunities required for them to become successful participants in our democratic society;
- Curricular content must incorporate the contributions of many cultures to our knowledge of science;
- Science teachers are knowledgeable about and use culturally-related ways of learning and instructional practices;
- Instructional strategies selected for use with all children must recognize and respect differences students bring based on their cultures.

---

[6]Dobb, F. (2004). *Essential elements of effective science instruction for English learners* (2nd ed.) [Electronic version]. Los Angeles: California Science Project.

Helping students understand the contributions of many cultures to our science knowledge can be easily addressed through reading books about the origins of science in other cultures. For example, books by George Beshore include *Science in Ancient China,* which discusses rockets, water wheels, the compass, and other inventions, and *Science in Early Islamic Culture,* which discusses advances in medicine and surgery by Middle Eastern scientists in ancient times.

A key component of multicultural science should be for students to engage in scientific inquiry about issues that affect them, their families, and their communities. Students in the agricultural community of Oxnard, California, for example, learned about the strawberry fields surrounding their school, where many of the ELLs' parents worked as agricultural laborers (Cummins, Brown, & Sayers, 2007). Through Project Fresa ("strawberry" in Spanish), the students realized they knew very little about strawberries and generated a list of questions about how they are planted, grown, and harvested. Students' parents became sources of expert knowledge on the topic, and children were able to learn from the funds of knowledge within their communities. The students' inquiries, however, went well beyond science. They began asking questions about the business aspects of strawberry farming, including the low pay and poor working conditions of the laborers. Thus, what started as a scientific inquiry was extended to a powerful social studies inquiry. The International Education and Research Network (iEarn) provides opportunities for similar types of collaborative scientific inquiry projects on an international scale. One recent project titled *Water Is Life* brought together 22 schools from the United States and nine other countries to collaborate on an action research project and to take local community action in relation to the United Nations Sustainable Development Goals on the sustainability and health of the world's water.

Social Studies

Social studies, unfortunately, tends to receive less attention in the school curriculum at the elementary school level. With ESSA, and NCLB before it, focusing school testing accountability on reading and math, nontested subjects are often neglected. But social studies is a critically important content area, especially for ELLs. The National Council for Social Studies (NCSS) has conducted political advocacy and public awareness campaigns to promote social studies education in schools to prevent the further erosion of this essential content area.

The NCSS advocacy campaign is carried out under the theme "Today's Social Studies . . . Creating Effective Citizens." An advocacy toolkit prepared by the NCSS explains that social studies is much more than looking at maps and memorizing dates: "Today's social studies provides students with the knowledge, thinking skills and experiences that will allow them to grow into effective citizens." Social studies teaches students "to understand cultures—systems of beliefs, knowledge, values, and traditions—so they can relate to people in our nation and throughout the world." The ultimate outcome is to "prepare people to take their place as effective, participating members of our democracy."

Social studies is a broad label covering several disciplines. NCSS defines it as "the integrated study of the social sciences and humanities to promote civic competence." These disciplines include anthropology, archaeology, economics, geography, history, law, philosophy, political science, psychology, religion, sociology, and appropriate content from the humanities, mathematics, and natural sciences. The NCSS declares that through these disciplines, social studies teaches about culture; time, continuity, and change; people, places, and environment; individual development and identity; individuals, groups, and institutions; power, authority, and governance; production, distribution, and consumption; science, technology, and society; global connections; and civic ideals and practices. This is what makes social studies so important to a complete education.

Language of Social Studies

The language of social studies poses unique challenges to ELLs. Unlike the language of science, which for the most part describes tangible or readily observable processes, social studies deals largely with abstractions (de Oliveira & Obenchain, 2018). Concepts such as *government, law, democracy, freedom, rights, justice, poverty, immigration,* and *elections* cannot be illustrated with simple drawings, and they frequently defy simple explanations. Terms such as the *American Revolution, slavery, westward expansion,* and *the Trail of Tears* are abstractions of very complex events, chains of events, or intricate webs of related events (Martin, 2002).[7] These abstractions enable us to talk about complex social and historical phenomena as if they were a tangible thing (e.g., "The American Revolution led to America's independence from England"). But these abstractions carry a heavy semantic load and require substantial background to understand and substantial language skills to use properly within the discourse of social studies.

For example, for an ELL unfamiliar with the abstraction *American Revolution,* this term would have to be "unpacked," by explaining the following facts and events:

America was originally a colony of England.
Many Americans felt England was treating them unfairly.
They wanted to be independent from England.
They fought a war against England from 1775 to 1783.
This war was called the American Revolution.
America won the war and became an independent nation.

The American Revolution was, of course, much more complex than these few sentences suggest, but even within this simple unpacking are more abstract terms that may need further unpacking: *colony, fairly, independent, war, nation,* and *revolution.* de Oliveira and Obenchain (2018) note also that many terms used in social studies education are culturally contextualized and thus have very specific meanings within the United States. Thus, such culturally embedded examples will be more familiar to English speakers born in the United States. They use the example of *democracy,* which has some shared characteristics (e.g., rule by the people), but the way democracy is understood, enacted upon, and organized institutionally is different in the United States than it is in other democratic countries, such as Mexico and Japan.

Another linguistic challenge in social studies involves how time is marked and how sequence is distinguished from setting in time. Students writing about something they experienced in the past would need to know words such as *first, then, next,* and *finally* and how to use them appropriately to mark the sequence of events in their story. Setting in time, in contrast, combines a series of events into one "chunk" that historians may conventionalize under names such as the Middle Ages, the Renaissance, or the Cold War (Martin, 2002). Such chunking of time enables us to talk about periods ranging from a single day (e.g., Black Friday) to millions of years (e.g., the Jurassic Period) as if they were singular events. Understanding and using named time chunks appropriately in spoken and written discourse can be very difficult for ELLs, particularly those who may be en-

---

[7] Note that the abstraction *slavery* is free from agency. In this form, it is simply something that exists. *Enslavement,* in contrast, suggests agency—some people were enslaving other people. Thus, this term carries a heavier moral indictment than the first term. Think about how other abstractions used in social and political discourse may also mask responsibility or misrepresent a socially complex issue.

countering such concepts for the first time. Thus, teaching key vocabulary to ELLs in social studies is more involved than it is in other areas.

As with science, the Common Core standards for English language arts include specific reading and writing standards for literacy in history/social studies for secondary school students. These standards declare:

> Reading is critical to building knowledge in history/social studies. . . . College and career ready reading in these fields requires an appreciation of the norms and conventions of [the] discipline, such as the kinds of evidence used in history . . . ; an understanding of domain-specific words and phrases; an attention to precise details; and the capacity to evaluate intricate arguments, synthesize complex information, and follow detailed descriptions of events and concepts. In history/social studies, for example, students need to be able to analyze, evaluate, and differentiate primary and secondary sources. . . . Students must be able to read complex informational texts in these fields with independence and confidence because the vast majority of reading in college and workforce training programs will be sophisticated nonfiction. (ELA Standards, p. 60. © Copyright 2010 National Governors Association Center for Best Practices and Council of Chief State School Officers)

As with science, however, students can actively engage in important social studies discussions and academic tasks with "less-than-perfect English." Bunch (2014), in a study with linguistically diverse students in a 7th grade social studies classroom, found that students were able to accomplish academic tasks in small groups drawing on their range of linguistic resources that many would dismiss as "nonacademic language." Bunch calls this the "language of ideas," which he distinguishes from the "language of display," wherein students used more "academic-like" language when discussing their groups' findings with the teacher and the class as a whole. His findings challenge the problematic construct of "academic language."

Making Social Studies Instruction Comprehensible for English Language Learners

One of the first ways to make social studies instruction comprehensible to ELLs is to find out what students already know about the particular topic or concept to be taught. A three-column K-W-L chart can be very useful here. Students brainstorm and list what they *know* in the first column, then what they *want to know* in the second column. Later they will fill in what they *learned*. Filling out the columns on the K-W-L chart also gives teachers of ELLs a way to find out what vocabulary knowledge they already have on the topic. For a unit on transportation, for example, ELLs might show that they know the words *car, boat, airplane,* and *street* but not *ship, ferry, tanker, pickup truck, semi-truck, highway,* or *freeway.*

The language of social studies focuses on abstract concepts, but the field itself offers a wide variety of visuals that can help make instruction more comprehensible. Portraits of historical people, photographs of historical places, and drawings, photographs, or video clips of historical and contemporary events can go a long way in helping students comprehend concepts, and they can have a lasting effect. When I think about the civil rights movement, for example, my mind goes back to the disturbing images of "White Only" signs and the inspiring audio and video recordings of Martin Luther King Jr. speaking before massive cheering crowds. Appropriate images to support social studies instruction can be found though a quick search using Google images. Social studies also relies heavily on visuals such as charts, graphs, maps, globes, and historical political cartoons. Authentic historical items, or replicas, such as uniforms, period clothing, coins, stamps, documents, flags, and artifacts from different cultures can also create a great deal of interest among students and help make instruction more comprehensible. Examples of these and other realia can be found on the companion website. Role playing can be a very effective form for making social studies concepts comprehensible. For example, students can get a better grasp of democracy and the electoral process if they hold an election in class. When working as a bilingual paraprofessional in a high school social studies class, I helped the ELLs make a video about their rights under the U.S. Constitution. The students acted out various scenes in which their rights were being violated. When students experience concepts, they are much more likely to comprehend and remember them.

Social studies also enables students to explore current events and the history behind them and understand the ways these events affect them, their families, and their communities. Including current events in the social studies curriculum can be as simple as clipping articles from newspapers, magazines, and the Internet to use as read-alouds, shared readings, or guided readings and facilitating a discussion with the students about the events. *Time* magazine's *Time for Kids* and *Scholastic News* are excellent commercial resources designed for younger students, and are available in both print and online digital versions. The online versions are enhanced with audio and video options and thus provide additional support for ELLs. Other excellent and free resources for teaching older ELLs about current events, such as Breaking News English, are available on the Internet.

Online educational games are another rich resource that can help make learning social studies engaging and comprehensible. For example, iCivics is a nonprofit organization founded by former U.S. Supreme Court Justice Sandra Day O'Connor, which offers free lessons, materials, and online games to help engage students in meaningful civic learning. Current Supreme Court Justice Sonia Sotomayor, who serves on the board, directed an effort to make one of the most popular games—Do I Have a Right?—more accessible to all students. This includes an English-language voice-over option, a Spanish version of the game (¿Tengo Algún Derecho?), and accompanying materials in both English and Spanish.

Modifying Social Studies Instructional Materials

The abstract language of social studies can make social studies textbooks especially challenging for ELLs. To make the text more accessible, teachers can simply read it aloud, using before-during-and-after strategies and stopping to look at and discuss the illustrations, tables, charts, graphs, captions, boxes, and so on. Lower-level ELLs could also be paired with a reading buddy when reading the text. Another strategy is for the teacher or a student with strong reading ability to make an audio recording of the text for ELLs to listen to as they follow along in the text. Among the advantages of this strategy for ELLs is that they learn pronunciation of unfamiliar words and make new associations between words they know orally but may not recognize in writing because the spelling of the words differs from the way they are pronounced (Reiss, 2012).

Teachers also can use graphic organizers with students to break down the text to its most basic structure and content. For example, here is some text from a 5th grade social studies textbook, describing how farmers in the middle colonies made a living:

> Farmers raised livestock such as cattle and pigs. They grew vegetables, fruits, and other crops in the fertile soil. Farmers grew many different grains, such as wheat, corn, and barley. In fact, they grew so much grain used to make bread that the middle colonies became known as the "breadbasket" of the thirteen colonies.[8]

---

[8] *Houghton Mifflin Social Studies, 5th Grade*, 2005, p. 197. Houghton Mifflin Company, Boston.

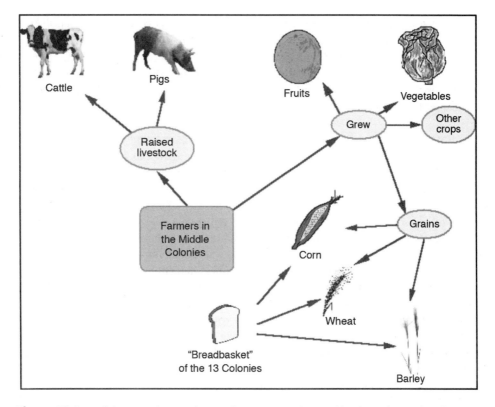

Figure 10.6 Modification of text with a graphic organizer. (Created by the author with Kidspiration software).

From this text, the teacher, along with the students, could create a graphic organizer like the one in Figure 10.6. Note how that organizer presents the same information but in fewer words and with visual organization and support to facilitate comprehension. Students who may have struggled with the meanings of the words *livestock, cattle,* and *grains* in the text can easily determine their meaning with the support of illustrations added to the graphic organizer.

Some teachers have found the "ten important sentences" strategy to be useful in helping students focus on the main ideas and basic essence of a social studies text. The teacher and students identify the 10 most important sentences in the text, which are copied onto the board or on a chart, then read by the class and discussed. This strategy can also be used with fiction and other genres.

Some textbook companies recognize that not all students will be reading at grade level and thus may have trouble accessing the core grade-level social studies textbook. Houghton Mifflin, for example, has a series of supplemental, leveled social studies readers for grades K–6. These readers can be integrated into shared and guided readings lessons and made available for students during independent reading.

Using Literature to Support Social Studies Instruction
Books can easily be found to support whatever content is covered in the main social studies textbook. But teachers should also consider using external literature to fill in gaps or cover topics given only slight mention in a textbook. For example, the internment of Japanese Americans during World War II is a topic rarely explored in-depth in mainstream textbooks. Younger students can learn about this great injustice in U.S. history

through fiction books, such as *Baseball Saved Us* by Ken Mochizuki, *So Far from the Sea* by Eve Bunting, and *Flowers from Mariko* by Rick Noguchi and Deneen Jenks, or non-fiction books, such as *The Children of Topaz: The Story of the Japanese American Internment Camp* by Michael O. Tunnell and George W. Chilcoat. Books appropriate for older students include *I Am an American: A True Story of Japanese Internment* by Jerry Stanley and *Farewell to Manzanar* by Jeanne Wakatsuki Houston and James D. Houston.

Integrating Students' Cultures into Social Studies Instruction

In recent years, publishers of social studies and history textbooks have made efforts to better represent the ethnic and cultural diversity of the United States. Often, however, what makes it into textbooks that may be reflective of the cultures of ELLs is limited and relegated to sidebars and boxes. For example, when my colleague Sovicheth Boun and I conducted a national study of Southeast Asian American college students, many of the participants complained that during their years in K–12 schools, the only place their countries' history or culture was ever mentioned was in chapters on the Vietnam War in history textbooks, and these depictions were all one-sided (Boun & Wright, 2013).

The easiest way to incorporate students' cultures into social studies is to make them a focus of study. If the ethnic and cultural groups represented by the students in your class, school, and community are not represented in your social studies texts, you can create your own units. Be careful, however, not to make assumptions about what the students already know. For example, one of my former colleagues suggested that there was no need for me to teach my Cambodian American students about Cambodian history and culture, yet few of my students understood the tragedy of the Cambodian genocide and what had caused their families to flee as refugees and ultimately resettle in the United States. Because of the trauma of their experiences, the students' parents did not talk about them much, making it all the more important to include that history in social studies instruction.

I also created my own material for a unit on community workers to make it more relevant for my Cambodian American students. I was unsatisfied with the books, visuals, and other materials provided in our somewhat dated curricular program because all the community workers were depicted as white, and so I headed out into the local community with a digital camera. Within a one-mile radius of the school, I took photos of several Cambodian Americans who worked in the community, including a doctor, a teacher, a police officer, a librarian, a social worker, a business person, and a shop owner, and photographs of African American and Latino community workers, including a firefighter, a bus driver, and a crossing guard. I used the photos to create a bulletin board display and a book. The students enjoyed learning about community workers with these materials, because they were an accurate depiction of workers in their community, some of whom they even recognized.

Students' own communities also offer an excellent resource for learning about cultures other than their own. The school where I taught was in the inner city, where in the prior year nearly a hundred youths died in a major gang war between Cambodian and Mexican gangs. Every one of my students and their families was affected in one way or another by the gang violence and ethnic tensions in the community. And because our bilingual program further separated some Cambodian and Mexican students from each other, I felt it was important to teach my Cambodian students about Mexican Americans. Many students thought *Mexican* was a bad word and equated it solely with gang members, since this was the only context in which they heard the word used within their immediate families. Students would say, for example, "A Mexican shot my uncle" or "Some Mexicans chased my brother after school and beat him up." My young students, a few of whom declared outright, "I hate Mexicans," were shocked to find out that some of their favorite teachers, staff members, and even their beloved principal were Mexican American. We had some social studies lessons where these individuals came and talked with the students about their culture. We read multicultural literature together, including *Bread, Bread, Bread* by Ann Morris (a book about different kinds of bread eaten around the world), which was followed by a visit from the PTA president, who came in and taught us how to make tortillas like the ones in the book. Through such activities, my students gained a broader, more accurate, and much more positive view of their fellow community members.

Art, Music, and Physical Education

Art, music, and physical education (PE) have been receiving short shrift in schools where instruction focuses narrowly on preparing ELLs and other students for state high-stakes tests. Like social studies, because these content areas are not on the test, they tend to get deemphasized or even eliminated altogether. This trend is of great concern to educators because these content areas are as crucial as all the other areas to a well-rounded education.

A strong argument for including the arts in a well-rounded education comes from the Consortium of National Arts Education Associations (see MENC, 2018), which reminds us, "The arts are inseparable from the very meaning of the term education." The consortium established the National Standards for Arts Education, covering the areas of dance, music, theater, and the visual arts, and issued a summary statement that includes a list of reasons for this assertion (Box 10.2).

The implication of this statement is that to deny ELLs and other students arts instruction is to deny them the opportunity to become educated. Note the emphasis on the arts as a means of reflection, high-order thinking, expression, and communication, and the role of the arts in developing skills valued in the workplace. These and other points made in the statement show why it is imperative for teachers of ELLs to resist the pressure to exclude the arts from the classroom.

An equal emphasis should be put on PE, an essential component of a complete education for all children. According to the Centers for Disease Control (2018), the rate of childhood obesity in the United States is too high and poses serious problems that put children and adolescents at risk for poor health. In 2018 the prevalence of obesity was 18.5% and affected about 13.7 million children and adolescents. Rates were higher for children from families of low socioeconomic status and disproportionately affected Hispanic and black students. Key to resolving this crisis is to encourage students to adopt and maintain healthier patterns of eating and exercise.

Despite wide recognition of the obesity crisis, more and more schools are reducing their PE programs. Some elementary schools no longer have PE teachers or a schoolwide program, relying instead on classroom teachers to provide their own PE instruction. But because of the overemphasis on preparation for high-stakes tests, many teachers have found little time left in the day for the "luxury" of PE. Even schools with full-time PE teachers have felt the pressure to reduce the amount of time for PE instruction, and some have the coaches regularly drilling students with test preparation materials. Many schools have even eliminated recess to make more classroom time for test preparation.

The place of PE in the curriculum is defined in the National Standards for K–12 Physical Education, established by the Society of Health and Physical Educators (SHAPE America) (2013). The document declares that PE has academic standing equal to other subject areas. The standards describe a physically literate individual as one who achieves

Box 10.2 Importance of Arts Education

The National Standards for Arts Education includes the following statement on the importance of arts education:

> Knowing and practicing the arts disciplines are fundamental to the healthy development of children's minds and spirits. That is why, in any civilization—ours included—the arts are inseparable from the very meaning of the term education. We know from long experience that no one can claim to be truly educated who lacks basic knowledge and skills in the arts. There are many reasons for this assertion:
>
> - The arts are worth studying simply because of what they are. Their impact cannot be denied. Throughout history, all the arts have served to connect our imaginations with the deepest questions of human existence: Who am I? What must I do? Where am I going? Studying responses to those questions through time and across cultures—as well as acquiring the tools and knowledge to create one's own responses—is essential not only to understanding life but to living it fully.
> - The arts are used to achieve a multitude of human purposes: to present issues and ideas, to teach or persuade, to entertain, to decorate or please. Becoming literate in the arts helps students understand and do these things better.
> - The arts are integral to every person's daily life. Our personal, social, economic, and cultural environments are shaped by the arts at every turn—from the design of the child's breakfast placemat, to the songs on the commuter's car radio, to the family's night-time TV drama, to the teenager's Saturday dance, to the enduring influences of the classics.
> - The arts offer unique sources of enjoyment and refreshment for the imagination. They explore relationships between ideas and objects and serve as links between thought and action. Their continuing gift is to help us see and grasp life in new ways.
> - There is ample evidence that the arts help students develop the attitudes, characteristics, and intellectual skills required to participate effectively in today's society and economy. The arts teach self-discipline, reinforce self-esteem, and foster the thinking skills and creativity so valued in the workplace. They teach the importance of teamwork and co-operation. They demonstrate the direct connection between study, hard work, and high levels of achievement.

NAfME (National Association of Music Educators). (2018). *Summary statement: What students should know and be able to do in the arts*. Retrieved from: https://nafme.org/my-classroom/journals-magazines/nafme-online-publications/summary-statement -what-students-should-know-and-be-able-to-do-in-the-arts-2/.

and maintains a health-enhancing level of physical activity and fitness; who values physical activity for such reasons as health, enjoyment, challenge, self-expression, and social interaction; who is able to demonstrate competency in a variety of motor skills and movement patterns; and who exhibits responsible personal and social behavior that respects self and others. Thus, PE instruction is not just about participation; rather, like other academic content areas, it focuses on helping students gain important knowledge and skills necessary for success in life.

Because art, music, and PE typically carry less of a language demand than math, science, and social studies, ELLs can often participate in them more easily and quickly and excel in them from the beginning. Artistic, musical, and physical talents easily transcend language barriers. Thus, students who developed these talents before beginning school in the United States bring in strengths that can be built on immediately. As with the other content areas, however, there are specific ways of using language associated with art, music, and PE, as well as content, concepts, and theories beyond the surface-level activities of these subjects that require higher levels of English proficiency to comprehend. Teachers can make instruction in these content areas more comprehensible for ELLs with the support of literature and the use of other strategies similar to those suggested for math, science, and social studies. For more details on the language demands and teaching of these important content areas, see the supplemental readings (art; music; physical education) on the companion website.

Assessing the Content Areas

When assessing students' work in content areas, teachers must ensure that the assessment is a valid measure of the students' knowledge of the content and not a measure of their language proficiency. For example, giving students a math test consisting only of word problems on measurement may be more of a test of the students' English reading comprehension skills than of their math knowledge and skills. In this instance, a better approach for ELLs who are at early levels of English language development would be to give them objects and measurement tools, with a simplified answer sheet to record their answers.

Performance assessments and other forms of alternative assessment should mirror the activities students do when learning in each content area. For example, in science, students' understanding of different cycles (e.g., water cycle, animal life cycles, cell division) can be assessed by asking students to arrange pictures depicting each stage in the cycle in the correct sequence. In social studies, maps students make of their neighborhood can be assessed using a rubric with items such as, "map includes: house, school, street, library, park"; "map includes a key"; "map includes a scale"; and "map includes a compass rose." In art, if students are making masks from different cultures, they could use a checklist for self-assessment or peer assessment to evaluate their final projects (e.g., "My mask is original, not a copy of the teacher's model"; "My mask is based on masks from a particular culture"; "I used a variety of materials to create my mask"). In music, the teacher could use an observational checklist to monitor and assess a student's performance (e.g., "Student is able to do the movements that go with the song"; "Student is able to sing all the words to the song"). In PE, students could self-assess by keeping a log of their exercise, heart rates, calories burned, and other physical activities in class and at home. They could also keep a food journal to track and analyze the nutritional value of what they eat. These and other types of performance assessments can remove the language barriers and allow students to show what they know and can do.

The language objectives associated with each content area should also be assessed using the formal and informal assessments described in earlier chapters. Teachers should use ongoing alternative and authentic assessments along with formal assessments to ensure that they have multiple measures of their students' knowledge and skills.

Summary

To be successful in school, and in life, ELLs must be given access to the core curriculum that equals that of their English-speaking peers. To ensure that ELLs receive that access, instruction in the content areas must be comprehensible, if not through home language instruction, then through sheltered instruction using bilingual strategies as needed. The SIOP is one popular model that can help teachers plan, deliver, and evaluate effective sheltered content-area instruction. One key to effective content-area lessons for ELLs is the inclusion of both content and language objectives. The language objectives should address the challenges posed by the unique language of each content area, including the unique vocabulary, language structures, discourse styles, and genres. Objectives should be appropriate to students' levels of language proficiency and content knowledge.

Because of the wide range of abilities among ELLs (and other students), it is imperative that teachers differentiate their instruction. The English language proficiency standards and progressions from WIDA, ELPA21, and individual states provide a useful tool for determining how academic tasks in different content areas can be differentiated for students at different levels of English proficiency. Textbooks and other content-area instructional materials are designed for English-proficient students and therefore must be modified and adapted to make them accessible to ELLs. Thematic teaching ties together the different content areas by building background knowledge, making it possible for skills developed in one content area to facilitate comprehension and further learning in other areas. Teachers can find books outside the core textbook that may be more appropriate to the academic and English proficiency levels of some students and that may inspire discussions and activities that further reinforce core content-area concepts while promoting English language development. Integrating different cultures into content-area instruction, particularly those of the ELLs, can make lessons more meaningful and motivating. Ongoing formal and informal authentic assessments in the content areas offer multiple measures and therefore a valid depiction of ELLs' academic achievement. The results of these assessments help teachers plan further content-area instruction tailored to students' unique linguistic and academic needs.

Discussion Questions

1. Why is it important for content-area lessons for ELLs to have both content and language objectives? What would the consequences be if lessons consistently had one but not the other?

2. Why do ELLs need effective instruction in every content area? What are some of the harmful effects of providing ELLs with instruction only in the content areas that are on a state's high-stakes tests? Despite the pressure to prepare students for high-stakes tests and to raise test scores, what are some ways teachers can ensure that they are providing effective instruction for their students in all the content areas and not just the tested ones? Give examples from your personal experiences or observations.

3. What are some of the challenges content-area instruction and textbooks pose to ELLs? If English is not your first language, describe some of your experiences with the challenges you faced in learning academic content and using grade-level textbooks. Discuss different strategies for sheltering instruction and modifying textbooks to make instruction and materials more accessible for ELLs.

4. On the ¡Colorín colorado! website, view the video and related materials of a social studies lesson for high school ELLs centered on the reading of a letter Captain John Smith wrote to Queen Anne in 1616 about Pocahontas. What strategies did the teacher use to support her students' English language development in this lesson? How effectively does this lesson address specific academic content standards?

5. Review the sheltered instruction 9th-grade history lesson plan designed for beginning-level ELLs. What strategies and techniques are used to make this lesson comprehensible for ELLs? How do these compare with the principles and strategies outlined in this and previous chapters? How effective do you feel this lesson will be for beginning-level ELLs? What else might you add to make this lesson more effective?

Research Activities

1. *ELL Student Interview* Interview a current or former ELL student and ask which content areas were the most challenging for him or her in school. Ask what strategies and techniques the teacher used (if any) that were helpful in making the content areas more accessible.

2. *ELL Teacher Interview* Interview an ELL classroom teacher and ask about the challenges of teaching different content areas to ELLs and what strategies and techniques he or she uses to shelter content-area instruction to make it more comprehensible for ELLs.

3. *ELL Classroom Observation* Observe a content-area lesson and evaluate it using the SIOP. Present and discuss the results in class, including what changes could be made, if any, to improve the lesson and make it more comprehensible for ELLs.

4. *Online Research Activity* Review Appendix D of the NGSS, titled "'All Standards, All Students': Making the Next Generation Science Standards Accessible to All Students" and the accompanying case study, "English Language Learners and the Next Generation Science Standards," focusing on a 2nd grade earth science lesson. Describe, discuss, and evaluate the strategies and techniques recommended in the appendix and used in the case study to help ELLs meet the NGSS.

Recommended Reading

Bailey, A. L., Maher, C. A., & Wilkinson, L. C. (Eds.). (2018). *Language, literacy, and learning in the STEM disciplines: How language counts for English learners*. New York: Routledge.

The contributors to this edited volume are among the leading scholars in the areas of math and science for ELLs. They synthesize the research on language challenges inherent in learning mathematics and science and provide the latest ideas for improving STEM literacy.

de Oliveira, L. C., & Obenchain, K. M. (Eds.). (2018). *Teaching history and social studies to English language learners*. New York: Palgrave Macmillan.

This edited collection focuses on instructional effectiveness in working with ELLs, drawing on the National Council for Social Studies C3 Framework and Curriculum Standards, the Common Core State Standards for English Language Arts, and content from history, geography, and civics.

Hansen-Thomas, H., & Langman, J. (2020). *Engaging English learners in mathematics classrooms: Teaching through talking*. Philadelphia: Caslon.

This highly accessible book helps teachers understand the language of math and the unique challenges the math register may pose for ELLs and provides specific strategies and techniques for scaffolding math instruction through effective talk.

Eleven

Translanguaging, Effective Instruction, and Advocacy for English Language Learners

When you explain it in Khmer, it's so easy!

—Nitha, a newcomer ELL from Cambodia

KEY TERMS
- action research
- advocacy
- cognates
- concurrent translation
- dual language books
- parental engagement
- preview-review
- primary language support
- translanguaging strategies

GUIDING QUESTIONS
1. What are translanguaging strategies, and how can they be used effectively to enhance English language development and sheltered English content-area learning in culturally sustaining ways?
2. What are the characteristics of effective programs for ELLs?
3. What are some strategies for advocating for ELLs and promoting parental engagement?
4. How can teachers conduct action research to inform effective teaching and learning in ELL classrooms?

Throughout this book we have considered the challenges millions of students across the country face learning and learning through a new language. Imagine what it would be like for you. Perhaps you do not need to imagine because this was your own experience. How difficult would it be to pay attention, follow directions, complete class work, and, in short, learn? Effective bilingual education programs are best suited to addressing these challenges through instruction in both the home language and English. But most ELLs are in classrooms where English is the medium of instruction. This does not mean that non-bilingual classrooms should be strictly English-only.

When bilingual education cannot be provided, children still should have the right to attend a school that shows full respect for their home language and encourages its use. Recall that effective programs for ELLs have a language-as-a-resource orientation (Ruiz, 1984), adopt pluralist discourses (de Jong, 2011), and engage in culturally sustaining pedagogies (Paris & Alim, 2017). Thus, regardless of program type, the home language of ELLs is valued as a resource as students learn English and academic content. Even teachers who do not speak the students' home languages can facilitate such support through the use of translanguaging strategies. *Translanguaging pedagogy* was discussed in earlier chapters. Here we dig deeper by reviewing research supporting home language use in the classroom and consider a variety of ways teachers can incorporate effective translanguaging strategies.

The Teachers of English to Speakers of Other Languages (TESOL) International Association has defined a set of six principles for the exemplary teaching of ELLs (TESOL International Association Writing Team, 2018). These principles, shown in Box 11.1, and

Teachers of English to Speakers of Other Languages (TESOL) International Association has defined core principles for the exemplary teaching of ELLs. Each principle is followed by specific practices aligned with the principle. TESOL emphasizes that these principles must be implemented as a whole. Below is a sample of the practices.

1. Know your learners.
    1a. Teachers gain information about their learners.
    1b. Teachers embrace and leverage the resources that learners bring to the classroom to enhance learning.
2. Create conditions for language learning.
    2b. Teachers demonstrate expectations of success for all learners.
    2c. Teachers plan instruction to enhance and support student motivation for language learning.
3. Design high-quality lessons for language development.
    3a. Teachers prepare lessons with clear outcomes and convey them to their students.
    3b. Teachers provide and enhance input through varied approaches, techniques, and modalities.
4. Adapt lesson delivery as needed.
    4a. Teachers check student comprehension frequently and adjust instruction according to learner responses.
    4b. Teachers adjust their talk, the task, or the materials according to learner responses.
5. Monitor and assess student language development.
    5a. Teachers monitor student errors.
    5b. Teachers provide ongoing effective feedback strategically.
6. Engage and collaborate within a community of practice.
    6a. Teachers are fully engaged in their profession.
    6b. Teachers collaborate with one another to co-plan and co-teach.

TESOL's 6 Principles for Exemplary Teaching of English Learners website provides details on each principle, along with specific classrooms activities, vignettes, and other resources to help teachers put them into practice.

their associated practices are consistent with those that have been addressed throughout this book. This chapter presents and discusses a list of characteristics shared by effective ELL programs that extend and go beyond TESOL's six principles. These include important considerations related to addressing students' language and academic development, valuing students' home languages and cultures, assessing students' progress, engaging students' families, and advocating for ELLs. We conclude with a discussion of the role all teachers can play as action researchers within their own classrooms or collaboratively across programs and grade levels and throughout the school.

Support for a Translanguaging Pedagogy

Recall that translanguaging refers to the ways bilingual and multilingual students draw on all of their linguistic resources to make meaning as they communicate and engage in tasks in the classroom and beyond (García, 2009a). This includes, but goes beyond, the natural and creative ways bilinguals use both languages at the word, sentence, paragraph, or conversation level—traditionally referred to as code-switching. Translanguaging also includes the ways bilinguals may engage in part of a task in one language and another part in their other language, such as reading or listening to a text in their home language then discussing or writing about it in English. In other learning tasks, bilinguals may use both languages simultaneously in perfectly natural ways. In classrooms, **translanguaging strategies** can be used to help students learn academic content while supporting their English language and bilingual development. García and Li Wei (2015) describe this as "translanguaging to learn" and "translanguaging to teach." García, Johnson, and Seltzer (2016) provide a detailed framework for a translanguaging pedagogy for instruction and assessment that strategically and purposefully leverages the natural flow of students' bilingualism. It includes strategies that teachers can use with emerging bilinguals in English-medium classrooms to draw on all of the languages in students' linguistic repertoires within the context of standards-aligned instruction.

The term *primary language support* has long been used to refer to the use of a student's home language to support sheltered-content and English as a second language (ESL) instruction. It is different from home language *instruction,* which refers to the teaching of entire lessons in the home language of students, as in bilingual education programs. An important rationale for primary (or home) language support is to make instruction in English as comprehensible as possible for ELLs so they can learn the content and acquire more English. Thus, strategic use of students' home languages is especially important in sheltered English immersion and other nonbilingual program models. Translanguaging strategies should be an essential part of any program model for ELLs and can be provided even if the teacher can speak only English, and in classrooms where students speak many different languages.

Translanguaging is central to culturally sustaining pedagogies (Paris & Alim, 2017). Bucholtz and Lee (2017) assert that "a pedagogy that truly sustains culture is one that sustains cultural practices too often excluded from classroom learning and leverages these as resources both for achieving institutional access and for challenging structural inequality" (p. 45). Translanguaging is one of these cultural practices. Thus, as Valdés (2017) observes, a translanguaging pedagogy is a compelling example of a culturally sustaining pedagogy.

The power of ELLs' home languages as a resource is widely recognized across the field. Principle 1 of TESOL's six principles for exemplary teaching of ELLs states that teachers must embrace and leverage the resources ELLs bring to the classroom. Knowledge of their home language or languages is one of the greatest resources ELLs bring. Item 19 of the Sheltered Instruction Observation Protocol (SIOP) calls for ample opportunities for students to clarify key concepts in their home language as needed with an aide, peer, or home language text (Echevarria, Vogt, & Short, 2017). The Common Core State Standards Initiative emphasizes the need for ELLs to be allowed to draw on their home languages to meet the standards. The Next Generation Science Standards include the use of the home language as a key support for helping ELLs meet the standards (Lee, Grapin, & Haas, 2018). Even those opposed to bilingual education, and even the text of the English for the Children laws that have restricted bilingual education, recognize the need for some use of home languages in the classroom.

Research has consistently revealed ways that the home languages of ELLs are effectively leveraged in the classroom. For example, Gort (2012) studied the writing development of Spanish-speaking ELLs in 1st grade and found that the students drew on both languages for clarification and problem solving during the writing process. Hopewell (2011) conducted a mixed-methods study on the reading comprehension skills of 4th grade Spanish-speaking ELLs and found that there were greater opportunities for teaching and learning when students were able to draw on and use both English and Spanish when engaged in English reading-comprehension tasks than when they were restricted to using only English. Sayer's (2013) ethnographic study of translanguaging in a 2nd grade bilingual classroom documented the success of the teacher in establishing a flexible bilingual environment in which students were able to move fluidly between English and Spanish and between the standard and vernacular varieties (e.g., Spanglish or "TexMex"). He found this environment helped students make sense of content and language learning and helped to legitimize the students' identities as bilingual Mexican Americans. Escamilla, Hopewell, and Butvilofsky (2013) provide longitudinal evidence of emergent bilingual students' trajectories toward biliteracy in reading and writing. Their holistic biliteracy framework shows teachers how to use two languages for instructional purposes. García and Kleyn (2016) present several ethnographic case studies from New York classrooms where translanguaging is used effectively in lesson designs and in spontaneous moves by teachers and students during specific teaching moments. Research on vocabulary development has documented the promise of word study lessons on cognates, that is, words that are similar in English and the home language (National Academies, 2017).

Some of my own research has looked at the benefits of translanguaging. In one study (Wright, 2006b), I worked with two newcomer non-English-speaking 5th grade students from a rural area of Cambodia, Nitha and Bora, at a Texas intermediate school. Their classroom teachers, their ESL teachers, and other teachers did not speak Khmer but allowed the girls to use a bilingual Khmer-English picture dictionary, to write notes and translations in Khmer on their school papers, and to work together and help each other in Khmer. They had excellent Khmer literacy skills and could do basic computations, but their mathematics skills were far below what was expected of 5th grade students in Texas (Wright & Li, 2006, 2008). Our weekly sessions focused on word problems and the math concepts they struggled to grasp in class. They were able to solve word problems easily and grasp the new concepts quickly once they were explained in Khmer. I vividly recall one occasion where their teacher had been trying hard to help them learn the concept of fractions, but they just were not getting it. When I met with the girls, I explained and modeled the basic concepts of fractions, and both girls let out an audible, "Ohhhhhh!" They both quickly started completing their fractions problems, getting all the answers right. About halfway through the worksheet, Nitha smiled and said, "When you explain it in Khmer, it's so easy!" Their teacher reported that Nitha and Bora were able to do work independently after receiving support in their home language.

As natural and effective as translanguaging can be, language learning classrooms cannot be a translanguaging free-for-all zone. Translanguaging must be strategic and conducive to meeting the language learning goals of the classroom. This includes ensuring that ELLs make progress in their English language development and ultimately attain proficiency in English, and ensuring that students in bilingual programs attain high levels of literacy and proficiency in both target languages. Thus, before we look at effective translanguaging strategies, we should acknowledge that some uses of the home language may be less effective in helping ELLs learn English.

For example, in **concurrent translation** (also called direct translation), a teacher repeats everything she says or reads in English in the other language or has a bilingual paraprofessional translate for her sentence by sentence or line by line. When students know a translation is coming they have no need to attend to the English, and thus they acquire little English. Ulanoff and Pucci (1999) conducted an experimental study in 3rd grade bilingual (Spanish-English) classrooms using a pretest/post-test design with a vocabulary test based on words from the picture book *The Napping House* by Audrey Wood and Don Wood. Students in all three classes were given the pretest, and then the class-rooms were randomly assigned to one of three groups. Group 1, the control group, received instruction only in English; Group 2 received concurrent translation; and Group 3 received translanguaging support in the form of preview-review. After administering the post-test, Ulanoff and Pucci found that the students in Group 3 (preview-review) knew more new vocabulary words in English than did the students in the other two groups. They also found that those in Group 2 (concurrent translation) learned even fewer English vocabulary words than those in Group 1, who received instruction all in English.

Another ineffective method is to substitute text written in English with oral translation into the home language, such as when well-meaning teachers or paraprofessionals translate an English book aloud as if it were written in the students' home language, or when they point to instructions written in English and translate them aloud into a student's home language. In these instances, there is no correspondence between the written text and the oral language. All students hear is the translation, and they do not engage with the text in English. Thus, the instructional construct is changed from reading in English to listening comprehension in the home language. Students are unlikely to acquire any English, since no English is presented for them to comprehend.

Translanguaging Strategies

Providing effective translanguaging strategies is easiest when the teacher or a classroom paraprofessional can speak the home language of the students. But even when neither can and even when there are multiple languages within the same classroom, teachers can still make use of effective translanguaging strategies.

The following questions can be used as a guide to determine whether a translanguaging strategy or technique is effective in facilitating language learning or academic content:

1. Does the strategy allow ELLs to quickly grasp a concept that was previously inaccessible when taught or explained only in English?
2. Does the strategy prepare ELLs to attend to instruction or print in English and receive greater amounts of comprehensible input?
3. Does the strategy lower the affective filter of ELLs and thus allow greater amounts of comprehensible input?
4. Does the strategy enable greater interaction between ELLs and others in the classroom for social and academic purposes?
5. Does the strategy enable the teacher to assess the ELLs' understanding of content taught in English?

Each of the following strategies addresses one or more of these questions.

Use Preview-Review

Researchers have found **preview-review** to be a highly effective translanguaging strategy (Freeman & Freeman, 2000, 2008; Ulanoff & Pucci, 1999). Preview-review (sometimes called preview-view-review) takes just a few minutes before and after a lesson or read-aloud and maximizes students' comprehension in English. If the teacher cannot speak the students' home language or languages, preview-review may be provided by a bilingual paraprofessional or classroom volunteer.

Preview involves having a brief discussion with students in their home language to activate prior knowledge or build background knowledge related to the book to be read or lesson to be taught. For example, if a teacher is doing a unit on plants, he or she asks students in their home language everything they know about plants and guides the discussion to cover the key ideas that will be taught in English. For a read-aloud, the teacher activates prior knowledge about the topic of the book and builds background knowledge by discussing the cover and doing a picture walk to help students understand the characters and settings and allow them to make predictions about what they think will happen. Teachers can also use the students' home language with other prereading strategies.

After this preview, the teacher presents the lesson or reads the book in English, using appropriate sheltered instruction strategies and techniques. Next, the teacher or paraprofessional briefly reviews with the students in their home language the key ideas in the lesson or asks comprehension questions about the book read. This discussion and students' answers will reveal how much of the instruction or read-aloud in English the students were able to understand. If there are any minor misunderstandings, they can be resolved immediately. If it becomes clear that the students understood little, the teacher knows that re-teaching will be necessary with appropriate adjustments to facilitate greater comprehension. In contrast to concurrent translation, which diverts students' attention from the English input, previewing in the home language prepares the students to pay attention to the English and thus maximizes comprehensible input. Reviewing then provides a check to determine how much of the English input students were able to comprehend.

Give Quick Explanations during Whole-Class or Small-Group Instruction

One of the easiest translanguaging strategies is to give quick explanations in the home language during a lesson taught in English to the whole class or a small group. Quick explanation should be given when it becomes clear that some ELLs are not getting it, or when the concept is too difficult to explain or demonstrate in English only. For example, during a social studies lesson on the U.S. government, it may be difficult for a teacher to convey the meaning of the word *freedom*. Abstract concepts are difficult to explain by the techniques that work for concrete nouns and verbs, such as gesturing, pointing to objects, or drawing pictures. Many Spanish-speaking ELLs, however, would quickly understand if the teacher simply said that *freedom* is *libertad* in Spanish. Once students have the concept, the teacher can go on and develop it further in English.

Some teachers in classrooms with both ELLs and monolingual English-speaking students are hesitant to use or allow translanguaging in a whole class setting because it can interrupt instruction and the monolingual English speakers will not understand the explanations. Although this may be a legitimate concern, many explanations take just a few seconds, and there is no research evidence that monolingual English speakers are harmed by hearing a few words spoken in another language. On the contrary, it may be beneficial for them to learn a few words in the language or languages of their classmates. Chances are they are already learning some from their bilingual friends at school. For concepts that may require more extensive explanation, such as a math lesson on probability, the teacher or a bilingual paraprofessional can work with a group of ELLs who need the support while the other students work on their own.

Give Quick Explanations for Individual Students

As students work independently, teachers and bilingual paraprofessionals look for and provide assistance to students who appear to need help. If the student is an ELL, a simple explanation in the home language may be all the student needs to complete the work. If students are having trouble understanding written directions, the teacher or bilingual professional should ask the student to read the directions aloud or read them aloud to the student, in English, while tracking the text and then ask the student what he or she thinks the instructions say to do. The teacher or paraprofessional should provide an explanation in the home language based on the student's response rather than provide a word-for-word translation of the directions.

Pull Students Aside to Re-teach Concepts

If it becomes apparent during independent working time that some of the ELLs are having difficulty, the teacher or paraprofessional can pull a group of students aside and re-teach the concepts in the home language.

Read Aloud Books in the Home Language
That Reinforce Concepts Taught in English

In thematic teaching, teachers identify books that can be used across the curriculum relevant to a selected theme. Some of these books could be in the home languages of the ELLs and could be read aloud to students during appropriate times. For example, in connection with a lesson on plant growth, the teacher could read aloud to her Spanish-speaking ELLs the book *¡Tiempo de calabazas! (It's Pumpkin Time!)* by Zoe Hall and Shari Halpern, which describes how pumpkins grow. This book would help activate students' prior knowledge on the topic or help them build background knowledge so they are more likely to receive greater comprehensible input.

Accept Students' Contributions in Their
Home Languages During Class Discussions

Teachers who speak the home languages of their ELLs can allow them to contribute to class discussions in their home language. For example, if the teacher is reading a book about pets, an ELL may wish to share something about her puppy. The teacher would allow her to speak in the home language and then would repeat back in English what she said. The repeating back should not be a translation but an acknowledgment that conveys the same information the student shared. For example, "Oh, how cute! Your puppy likes to jump on you and lick your face when you come home from school." This type of response fits the flow of the discussion, acknowledges the student's contribution to the discussion, makes her comments accessible to all students in the class, and models back to her in English the information she shared. The student feels included, and the teacher knows the student was able to follow and comprehend the discussion in English because she was able to contribute to the discussion in an appropriate way.

If the teacher does not speak the home language of the student, and if no paraprofessional is available, it may be possible to have another student in class who is bilingual translate for the ELL. Teachers do need to be careful not to rely too heavily on other students as translators, though allowing one student to translate for another on occasion is a wonderful way to acknowledge and value that student's bilingual skills.

Label the Classroom in English and the Students' Home Languages

An effective language and literacy strategy is to label classroom objects (e.g., *chair, clock, computer, desk, door, pencil sharpener*) with bilingual or multilingual word cards. This exercise is particularly effective if the students help make the labels. Words the teacher does not know can be obtained from a bilingual parent or volunteer or from a dictionary. An online translation tool can also be used, but results should be checked with students to make sure they are correct before posting them. These labels help students learn the names of classroom objects in English and send students the message that their home languages are valued as a resource for learning in the classroom (Freeman & Freeman, 2011). They can also help monolingual English-speaking students in the class learn vocabulary in the home languages of the ELLs.

Create Instructional Wall Displays in Home Languages

Effective teachers use the classroom walls to display and celebrate student work and to display instructional resources, such as charts and posters. Teachers can easily modify these displays to add the students' home languages. Many commercially made charts, posters, and other displays are available in Spanish. For example, if the students are learning about weather, the teacher could display two identical weather posters—one in English and one in Spanish—or simply add Spanish text to the English version by creating labels on a computer and gluing them to the poster next to the corresponding English texts. For languages other than Spanish, gluing on labels may be the only option, but it is not hard to do. If the teacher does not speak the home language or languages of the ELLs in the class, the project could be given to a bilingual paraprofessional or volunteer or to more advanced students in the class with bilingual skills. When referring to these displays during instruction, the teacher could call on ELLs to read aloud the texts in their home language before discussing the displays in English. (See the companion website for more examples of bilingual charts and displays.)

Engage Students in Cognate Word Study Lessons

Cognate word study lessons are very beneficial in helping Spanish-speaking ELLs quickly acquire English vocabulary and improve their English reading comprehension. **Cognates** are words in the two languages that come from the same root, such as *education* (in English) and *educación* (in Spanish). Many tier 2 general academic words such as *process* (*proceso*) and tier 3 content-specific words such as *metamorphosis* (*metamorfosis*) are cognates, and thus students can quickly learn them in English since they vary only slightly in spelling and pronunciation from words they already know. Cognates, however, can be misleading because two words that appear to be similar may differ slightly in meaning (partial cognates) or may be unrelated altogether (false cognates). Cognate word study should also include instruction about partial and false cognates.

Some partial cognates are specific in one language but general in another. For example, the English words *casserole* and *parents* have specific meanings, whereas the Spanish words from the same roots, *cacerola* (saucepan) and *parientes* (relatives), are more general. In some cognate pairs, the meaning of the English word may have a more negative connotation than the Spanish word, as in *disgrace* and *desgracia* (misfortune), and vice versa, as in *to be interested* and *ser interesado* (have an ulterior motive). Some words may have related meanings but are nonetheless different, such as *library* and *librería* (bookstore). False cognates may appear to be similar but have unrelated meanings, such as *exit* and *éxito* (success).[1]

Many great stories illustrate the danger of false cognates. One true story involves an American Mormon missionary in Mexico. On her first Sunday at church in Mexico, the bishop called on her to come to the pulpit to introduce herself to the congregation. The missionary was a bit flustered because she had studied Spanish for only two months prior to her arrival. She wanted to begin by saying, "I'm embarrassed, and it's the bishop's fault," so she said in Spanish, "*Yo estoy embarazada y es la culpa del bishop.*" The congregation burst into laughter, and the bishop's face turned bright red. Only later did she learn she had announced to the congregation, "I'm pregnant, and it's the bishop's fault!"

Despite the potential dangers, with proper instruction, cognates can be very useful. Even if teachers do not speak Spanish, they can use cognates to prepare word-study lessons. Just as cognates are easy words for Spanish-speaking students to learn in English, so too are they easy words for English-speaking teachers to learn in Spanish. Cognate

---

[1] All examples of cognates are from Crandall, 1981.

word study can be further facilitated by the creation of a cognate word wall in the class-room. Some teachers also create word walls for partial cognates and false cognates.

Use the Home Language to Support Writing in English

Writing is really hard, and one of the hardest parts for students is just figuring out what to write about and how to organize their thoughts. The prewriting activities discussed in an earlier chapter may be easier for ELLs to do first in their home language with the support of a bilingual teacher or paraprofessional who can talk with them and help them brainstorm ideas. If the ELLs can write in their home language, they could use it to create graphic organizers, such as word webs, or create outlines. In some instances, it may even be appropriate to allow students to write their first draft in their home language. The teacher or paraprofessional can provide assistance as needed with vocabulary when the students begin to write in English. Even if the teacher or paraprofessional does not speak the home language of the ELLs, he or she can still allow them to use their home language in prewriting activities and initial drafts.

Provide Bilingual Dictionaries and Mobile Translation Apps

Bilingual dictionaries can be an important resource for ELLs who are literate in their home language. Schools should have a collection of dictionaries for students who do not already have their own. Simply having the dictionaries, however, is not enough. Teachers will need to show students how to use them and encourage their use when appropriate. The dictionary is also a resource for teachers who do not speak the students' home lan-guage. Teachers can simply look up words in English and point to the translation for the students. For example, a teacher who is reading with a small group of students notices that one of her Korean ELLs does not know the meaning of the word *uncle*, which ap-pears in the book. The teacher could quickly look up the word *uncle* in the student's dictionary and point to the translation. The teacher does not need to know how to read Korean, or any other non-English language for that matter, to look up words in a bilin-gual dictionary.

Bilingual picture dictionaries are also an excellent resource. Many are organized by topic (body parts, family members, food, clothing, classroom, doctor's office, etc.) and provide illustrations with numbered objects. The numbers correspond to a list of vocab-ulary words below the picture in the two languages. The popular *Oxford Picture Dictio-naries,* published by Oxford University Press, are available in 13 bilingual editions: Ara-bic, Brazilian Portuguese, Cambodian (Khmer), Chinese, Farsi, Haitian, Japanese, Korean, Polish, Russian, Spanish, Thai, and Vietnamese. Teachers who are familiar with these dictionaries can coordinate them with classroom themes and lessons.

Electronic bilingual and multilingual dictionaries and mobile apps such as Google Translate offer another easy resource. These handheld devices and apps contain thousands of words. The user types a word or phrase to bring up the translation. Some models and apps provide a spoken pronunciation of the word. The dictionaries and apps are available for many languages. Google Translate, for example, includes more than 100 languages. During oral conversations, an ELL may hear a word he or she does not know the mean-ing of and would like to look up. But if the student also does not know how the word is spelled, the teacher or another student in the conversation, with the ELL's permission, could type in the word for the student to get the translation. Some models and apps (in-cluding Google Translate for more than 30 languages) have built-in voice recognition. Students (or teachers) can simply say a word or phrase in one language, and the device will display and speak the translation. The Google Translate app also has a feature for more than 30 languages that uses the mobile device's camera. Students can point the camera at a book page or other source of text written in one language and the app will render the translation in the selected target language (though with often very limited and inaccurate results).

The roles of bilingual dictionaries and translation apps in the language classroom are a subject of debate, with some educators concerned that students will rely on them rather than using other vocabulary-learning strategies, such as figuring out the meaning of words based on context or even using an English-only dictionary. Educators seem to agree, however, that some bilingual dictionary and translation app use, particularly for ELLs at the lower levels of English proficiency, is beneficial. As with any scaffold, to be effective, the scaffold of bilingual dictionary or app use should be slowly reduced. As students' proficiency in English grows, they will rely less on them. I believe, however, that even ELLs who are more advanced should be allowed to access bilingual dictionaries and translation apps when needed, particularly when they are writing, because these resources can help them find the precise words in English to express thoughts that are still in their home language.

Accept Initial Writing in Students' Home Language as They Transition to English Writing

Newly arrived ELLs with low levels of English proficiency are unlikely to be able to write much in English. If these students have literacy skills in their home language, teachers should consider allowing them initially to write in their journals in their home language. Even if the teacher cannot read what is written, at least the students are writing. As a teacher, I would much rather have writing in a student's home language than a blank page. Teachers may be able to find a colleague or friend who can read the language and tell them what it says. But eventually teachers will notice that the students will begin to write in English when they feel ready. Most likely, by the end of the school year, the journal entries will be entirely in English.

Read-Aloud Home Language Versions of Books Used in Class

Some English-language books teachers use for read-alouds are available in other languages, particularly Spanish. Teachers or paraprofessionals can read the home language version aloud to ELLs before the English version is read to the whole class. If the teacher does not speak the home language but has a recording of the book in the home language (recorded commercially or by a paraprofessional or volunteer), she could make the book and audio recording available at the listening center. The home language version can also be sent home for students to read with their families. When students have a chance to read or listen to the home language version, they gain familiarity with the book's characters, setting, plot, and concepts. Then, when the teacher reads the same book aloud in English, these students will be able to understand much more because of their background knowledge of the book. Thus, comprehensible input is maximized. Teachers should take care not to read the home language and English versions back to back, because this process would be too much like the ineffective concurrent translation method discussed earlier.

Provide Home Language and Dual Language Books for At-Home Reading Programs

Teachers encourage their students to read at home and encourage parents to read with their children. Many ELLs, however, come from low-income homes with few books. Also, many parents of ELLs do not read English well, if at all, and thus have difficulty reading aloud to their children English books brought home from school. To address these issues, teachers can obtain a collection of books in the home languages of their ELLs and create a classroom lending library of books children can check out to read at home. Reading is reading. Reading or being read to at home in the home language promotes literacy development and allows parents to participate in their children's education. Along with the linguistic and literacy skills that can transfer from the home language to English is the enjoyment of reading, the development of life-long readers, and a model of parents as fluent readers.

In **dual language books** the text of the two languages may appear one above the other, side by side, or on opposite pages. These books can be very useful because teachers, students, and students' family members can read either the English or the home language text or both in the same book. Recordings can be sent home along with the book in both languages, or better yet, the teacher could send home a digital audio recorder for a family member to record the book in the home language. Having the two languages side-by-side does not necessarily recreate the problem of concurrent translation in print, because the students do attend to the English language text, and the home language text provides support to make the English text comprehensible.

Home and dual language books are easy to find. Many school libraries and most public libraries have non-English collections. Spanish-language books, including dual language books, can be ordered through book clubs, such as Scholastic's Club Leo en Español, or purchased from a bookstore. Children's books in languages other than Spanish and English can be ordered online through booksellers such as Amazon or companies that specialize in world language books for schools. A simple Google search for "children's books" and the name of the language you are looking for will usually return a surprising number of relevant resources.

Students can also create their own dual language books. A good example is a project by students at Thornwood Public School, an elementary school near Toronto, Canada. The students created dual language books in 17 languages with assistance from family, friends, teachers, and older ESL students in the school. These dual language books are featured on their website. Thornwood's efforts illustrate the possibilities for using translanguaging strategies, even in schools that are highly multilingual and where teachers do not know all the languages spoken by their students. (See Cummins et al., 2005, for more details on this project.)

Send Home Letters in the Students' Home Languages

Many effective teachers send home monthly or weekly letters to parents describing what students are learning in class, suggesting ways parents can help, and reporting other classroom news. For ELLs, these letters could be sent in their home language, preferably with English on one side and the home language on the other. Some parents may not be able to read in their home language but can find someone who can either read the home language version to them or orally translate the English for them. Many schools and districts employ bilingual liaisons and translators who can assist with these translations. Some curriculum programs also provide parent letters in the back of the teachers' guide in several languages that teachers can simply copy and send home.

Allow Students to Help Each Other

Students who are advanced or proficient in both English and their home language are an excellent source of support for ELLs from the same language background. Teachers need only to facilitate their help in an appropriate and effective manner. When newcomer ELLs arrive, teachers can assign them a buddy who speaks the same language to help orient the new student to the classroom and school routines. The teacher can make seating arrangements so that lower-level ELLs are seated near a bilingual student who can provide quick clarifications and assistance when needed. When students work in centers, teachers can arrange for lower-level ELLs to partner with higher-level ELLs or fluent bilingual students who can help guide them through the required tasks. Teachers must be careful, however, to establish clear guidelines to ensure that the buddy's own learning is not disrupted and the lower-level ELL does not become overly dependent.

Use Computer Software and Internet Resources

Many educational software programs come with built-in home language support, typically in Spanish but occasionally in other languages as well. This support could range from running the program completely in another language to translations and explanations to help students interact with the program in English. Microsoft Office Suite programs (e.g., Word, PowerPoint, Excel, Outlook) have built-in translation tools that offer translations of single words, phrases, sentences, and even an entire document into several languages. The Google Translate website offers the same free tools as its mobile app for more than a hundred different languages. Also, online bilingual dictionaries are available in more than a hundred different languages.

These translation tools are generally effective for translating single words and common simple phrases. Students and teachers must use caution, however, when using them to translate entire sentences, paragraphs, and documents. Translation is a fine art that requires an expert human touch. Computers can only approximate this task. Translation tools are notorious for producing translations riddled with errors. They are intended to give users just a rough idea of what a text is about. Under no circumstances should a teacher use these tools to translate letters or other communications with parents or to create classroom materials without having them first checked and corrected by a knowledgeable translator.

Seek Bilingual Parents or Community Volunteers

A powerful translanguaging strategy is to seek out bilingual parents or community volunteers. Assistance for just an hour or so a week can go a long way, as my experience with the two newcomer Cambodian students shows. Teachers should plan ahead to maximize the use of the volunteer's time, keeping, for example, a running list of concerns or questions and classwork the students had difficulty completing. Teachers should also provide instructional materials the volunteers can use to re-teach difficult concepts in the home language and set up a system that allows the volunteers to report back on the students' progress.

Effective Programs and Advocacy for English Language Learners

Providing Effective English Language Learner Programs

Although strong forms of bilingual education, such as those described in an earlier chapter, hold the most promise for helping students achieve academically and develop and maintain their bilingual and biliteracy skills, the best, most appropriate, and most feasible program for an individual school or classroom is determined by such factors as the sociocultural context of the school and background of the students and the unique needs of the ELL population to be served. All effective program models, however, share the characteristics described in the following sections.

Effective Programs Ensure That English Language Learners Attain Proficiency in English

TESOL Principles 2 and 3 call for teachers to create conditions for language learning and to design high-quality lessons for language development. ELLs have the right to develop English language proficiency to the highest levels possible (Corson, 2001). They need English to succeed in school and in life in the United States. ELL programs must therefore provide systematic and direct ESL instruction that is (1) tailored to the linguistic needs of the ELLs, (2) designed to help them improve their English language proficiency each year, and (3) designed to help them be redesignated as "fluent English proficient." Language and literacy instruction goes beyond the cognitive processes of individual students and their acquisition of discrete skills (Street, 1984; Wiley, 2005). Effective teachers understand the crucial role they play in helping their students obtain communicative competence in English for a wide range of social and academic purposes. Effective programs recognize that attaining proficiency in English can take several years and thus are longitudinal, spanning several grade levels.

Effective Programs Ensure That English Language Learners Are Given Equal Access to the Core Curriculum

TESOL Principle 4 calls for teachers to adapt lesson delivery as needed. ELLs have the right to learn the same academic content as English-proficient students. But academic instruction must go beyond the memorization of facts and acquisition of knowledge and skills as outlined in state college-and-career-readiness standards. Critical pedagogy (Freire, 1993; Wink, 2000) emphasizes that teaching and learning amount to more than the simple transfer of knowledge and skills from teacher to student, deposited in their heads the way money is deposited in a bank. Rather, education must be transformative, enabling ELLs to learn and use relevant content knowledge to challenge the unequal power relations in society that have adversely affected them, their families, and their communities. Effective programs empower students with the linguistic and cultural capital necessary to succeed in school and to pursue opportunities for higher education and careers that can lift them out of lives of poverty and oppression. Equal access to the core curriculum may be provided by teaching content areas in the home language or teaching content areas through the use of sheltered instruction or using a combination of the two. Avoiding one-size-fits-all approaches and curricular materials, effective programs provide differentiated instruction tailored to the linguistic and educational needs of each student.

Effective Programs Value Students' Home Languages and Translanguaging Practices

Effective programs that use the home language of the ELLs as a resource for teaching and learning have a "language-as-resource" orientation (Ruiz, 1984). Also, in recognition of the devastating consequences of home language loss (Fillmore, 1991; Wright, 2004a), effective programs support students' bilingual language development as they develop proficiency in English. The highest-quality programs help students become fully bilingual and biliterate in English and their home language. Effective programs also recognize that students do not speak their two languages as isolated, separate entities; rather, they value the ability of bilingual students to draw on their multiple linguistic resources as they translanguage for effective communication and learning purposes.

Effective Programs Value Students' Home Cultures

ELLs should not be expected to give up their home cultures to become "Americanized." Schools should not be viewed as assimilation factories. Diversity is the reality of the

United States. Critical pedagogy emphasizes the need to value students' home cultures as a strength on which to build. Effective programs engage in culturally sustaining pedagogies that develop and sustain ELLs' biculturalism so they can function well in their home and community environments, as well as in the wider U.S. society. These programs also recognize and are sensitive to the fact that students' identity development is a dynamic, ongoing process. They help students understand and appreciate the United States as the multicultural society it is and prepare students to be effective citizens of the community, nation, and world.

Effective Programs Make Use of Multiple Ongoing Authentic Assessments

TESOL Principle 5 calls on teachers to monitor and assess student language development. Effective programs recognize the problems, limitations, and potential harm of high-stakes standardized testing for ELLs. They use authentic alternative language and content-area assessments throughout the year to obtain valid measures of students' progress. The results of these formative assessments, combined with their understanding of linguistics and second language development, help teachers make professional judgments as they plan instruction tailored to the unique language and educational needs of each student.

Effective Programs Have Teachers Who Are Fully Credentialed and Certified to Work with English Language Learners

Many outstanding new and veteran teachers who are not certified to work with ELLs may nonetheless have ELLs placed in their classrooms. These teachers have a responsibility to do everything they can to meet the needs of their ELLs as they pursue appropriate training and additional certification.

Effective Programs Have Teachers Who Are Advocates for English Language Learners and Their Families

In effective programs, teachers go beyond just providing comprehensible instruction for their students. These teachers know their ELLs and understand the challenges they and their families face within the sociocultural contexts in which they live. They understand how imbalances in power relations in society may disadvantage students' families and silence their voices. Critical pedagogy requires teachers to take action when injustices occur. Teachers need to advocate for their students within their schools and districts to ensure that they receive the services and resources to which they are entitled. Teachers are often in the best position to judge the impact of various policies and programs on their ELLs and their families, and they have a responsibility to inform and work with parents and to speak out and fight for changes when such policies and programs are failing or having harmful effects. Specific strategies for advocacy are outlined in the next section.

Effective Programs Provide Ongoing Professional Development Opportunities for Teachers and Administrators

TESOL Principle 6 calls for teachers to engage and collaborate within a community of practice. Teachers and administrators, like other professionals, must keep current with their field and must have opportunities to reflect on their practice and network with others in their field. Thus, effective programs provide ongoing opportunities for professional development for teachers and administrators of ELLs. In addition to school or district training, educators in effective programs join professional organizations, attend professional conferences, and read the professional literature. Through such activity, ELL educators are able to further develop the teaching and learning in their classrooms and schools and are better able to advocate for their students.

Effective Programs Promote Active Parental Engagement

Effective programs recognize and overcome linguistic, cultural, and other kinds of barriers preventing the full participation of ELL parents. As primary stakeholders, parents of ELLs must be included in decision-making processes that affect students and therefore must be provided with accommodations to facilitate their active engagement.

Advocating for English Language Learners

ELLs and their families, many of whom are from lower-socioeconomic homes and communities, typically are among the least empowered individuals in our society. When policies at the school have a negative impact on ELLs or their families, there may be several factors which discourage the parents from speaking out. First, they may be unfamiliar with the educational system and may not fully understand how changes may affect their children. Second, if they do not speak English and no one at their child's school can speak their language, they will find it difficult or impossible to speak out. Third, even if parents understand the changes and can communicate with the school, they may be hesitant to do so because their culture emphasizes respect for teachers and the school. Finally, many parents of ELLs work full-time and some may even work two or more jobs to support their families, making it difficult for them to find time to go to the school to express their concerns. For these and other reasons, it is important for teachers to engage in **advocacy** efforts to bring about positive changes and equitable treatment for their ELLs. The sections that follow offer a few ideas for doing so.

Take Advantage of the Positive Aspects of Federal and State Policies for English Language Learners

The problems associated with federal and state policies for ELLs, particularly as they relate to mandates for high-stakes testing and accountability, have been discussed at length throughout this book. These policies, however, have at least raised awareness that schools are responsible for meeting the needs of ELLs. Education for ELLs has had an unfortunate history of underfunding, and teachers have found it difficult to get the resources they need for their ELLs.

As a teacher of ELLs, you can take advantage of federal education programs by going to your administrators and districts. Ask how federal Title III and state funds for ELLs are being used in your school and district. Provide a list of needed resources. Does your school lack ESL curricular programs? Search for one you like, give the details to your administrator, and recommend it for purchase. Are there supplemental materials, software programs, mobile apps, or other technologies you think would help your students? Put a list together, write out the rationale, and explain to your administrator how such materials would help your ELLs make progress in meeting language proficiency and content-area standards. Do you have an idea for an after-school program that would benefit the students and their families? Approach your administrator and ask him or her to help you get funding from the district, apply for an external grant, or set up a GoFundMe page to fund the program.

Trained and certified teachers of ELLs often become the "go-to" person at their campuses for colleagues with questions about how best to meet the needs of ELLs. Take advantage of these opportunities to assist your colleagues, and you will be able to make a difference for the ELLs in your own classroom and throughout your school.

Keep Data to Show the Progress of English Language Learners in Learning English and Academic Content

Collect data from multiple authentic alternative assessments for your ELLs and synthesize the information in ways that can be shared with parents, school and district administrators, and the public. This process is particularly important when the results of invalid high-stakes tests create a false depiction of the quality of teaching and learning in your classroom or school. Teachers whose ELLs obtain low scores on statewide high-stakes tests can turn around and provide strong evidence of the students' growth. Consider the examples that follow from a 3rd grade classroom consisting mostly of ELLs. Each pair of examples illustrates a different point about how students' progress can be demonstrated. We'll use the example of Trinh, a newcomer student from Vietnam who failed the state test despite making tremendous progress after only a year in the United States. The teacher's follow-up comments illustrate how the results of authentic assessments can be synthesized and summarized for the entire class.

Progress in acquiring English can be demonstrated through oral language assessments such as the SOLOM-R, observational checklists, and audio recordings taken throughout the year.

- "Trinh was classified as level 1 [beginning] at the beginning of the year. She's now at a level 3. Here's an audio clip of how she sounded at the beginning of the year. Notice she was able to speak in only one- or two-word utterances because of limitations in her vocabulary and syntax knowledge. Now listen to this audio clip recorded last week."
- "Ninety-one percent of my students moved up at least one English language proficiency level. Four of my students this year were reclassified as fluent English proficient."

Progress in reading can be demonstrated through running records taken throughout the year, through logs of books read, and through literature response projects.

- "Trinh started the school year reading books at the kindergarten level; now she's reading end-of-2nd-grade books with 90% accuracy. Her book log shows she read over 150 books this year. Note how she began with simple picture books, and now she has started to read grade-level chapter books. Here's a story map she made of a book she read last week, so you can see that she is comprehending what she reads."
- "Eighty-nine percent of my students moved up at least one grade in their reading ability; 60% have moved up two grade levels in their reading. Together as a class we have read over 2,000 books."

Progress in writing can be demonstrated through journals, papers published through Writer's Workshop, and other written projects across the content areas.

- "At the beginning of the year, Trinh had difficulty just writing a single sentence in English. Take a look at her journal from the first month of school. Notice how she wrote just a few words in English to label her drawings. I let her write in Vietnamese at the beginning until she gained more confidence in writing in English. Now look at her journal from December. Note how she was able to write one-paragraph stories all in English. Here's her journal from this month. You'll see now she is writing longer stories with several paragraphs. Here are some of her published papers from Writer's Workshop."
- "At the beginning of the school year, most of my students were getting 1s and 2s on their writing as assessed with our grade-level writing rubric. Now 86% of the students are getting 3s and 4s on their writing."

Progress in the content areas can also be demonstrated through authentic assessments, such as those collected in a math portfolio.

- "Here's Trinh's math portfolio. Note that at the beginning of the year, she could solve only 20 addition problems and 13 subtraction problems in 3 minutes. By January you can see she solved 100 such problems in 3 minutes. Here are the results from a performance-based assessment we did on measurement. Trinh was given a set of objects and measuring tools. She was able to measure and compare all of the items correctly.
- "Ninety-three percent of my students have mastered basic arithmetic, as determined by our 3-minute math-fact tests. On the rubric we used for the performance test at the end of measurement unit, all but three students got 4/4."

The results of these assessments paint a much more accurate and telling picture of the quality of teaching and learning in this teacher's classroom than high-stakes tests. They also provide a clear picture of the students' progress since the beginning of the school year—something high-stakes tests cannot do.

Work for Changes to Current Policies That Are Potentially Harmful to Your Students

Teachers often feel helpless to change bad education and language policies that have adverse effects on their students, on their classrooms and schools, and even on themselves. Teachers who feel it is wrong to force ELLs to take high-stakes tests in English before they reach a level of proficiency in their new language sufficient to comprehend it—and hold teachers accountable for the results even if they are likely invalid—nonetheless feel they have no choice but to go along with the system. Teachers do need to comply with what is required in their state and school. But they also have a professional responsibility to try to minimize the harm as much as they legally can within the confines of their own classroom. Outside of school hours, however, teachers are private citizens who have the full right to advocate for change. If policies are harming your students, speak up! Gather evidence from your classroom that documents harm being done. Take this evidence to school and district administrators. Talk to parents. Organize colleagues and parents to testify at district and state school board meetings. Write letters to the editor of the local newspaper. Write letters to local and state policymakers. Invite them to your school and classroom. Join local and national networks of educators working for change. Blog, tweet, post comments on Facebook, create YouTube videos, and use other forms of social media to document and share what you see firsthand in your classroom and school.

Your rights as a citizen are not surrendered when you become a teacher. Just be sure you understand state laws about what activities are allowed on campus and what must be done off school grounds. Teachers are often afraid that such political advocacy may get them in trouble. It is possible you may step on some toes and make some administrators unhappy. But the reality is, in most states, teachers have a legal right to due process, meaning it is very difficult to fire a teacher (unlike administrators, who are very easy to fire). I once heard an inspiring speech by a nationally board certified teacher who worked in an inner-city school in Arizona with many disadvantaged students. An audience member—another teacher—asked whether she was afraid of getting in trouble for her political advocacy work. She laughed and said, "What's the worst they could do to me? Assign me to the district's poorest, most overcrowded, and lowest-performing school where nearly all of the students are ELLs? Well, guess what? I'm already there, the kids are great, and I love it!"

Serve on Key School, District, and State Committees

Most schools and districts have several committees that make important decisions—or at least important recommendations to decision makers—that can affect ELLs. These committees address policies, programs, standards, assessments, curriculum adoption, reclassification of students, and other issues. It is imperative that teachers who advocate for their ELLs serve on these committees as well as on those at the state level that also consider issues that can affect ELLs.

Join Professional Organizations

Teachers can join one or more of the many professional organizations that bring together teachers, administrators, community leaders, researchers, and scholars who wish to find ways to ensure that ELLs receive high-quality education. These include associations for ESL and bilingual educators, as well as those for specific content areas (reading, math, science, music) and school administrators who also address ELL concerns. Membership in these organizations typically includes discounts to national conferences; subscriptions to magazines, newsletters, and journals published by the organization; access to resources on the Internet; and numerous opportunities for professional development, networking, leadership development, and support for advocacy. Many national organizations also have state affiliates and even local affiliates.

Read Professional Literature

Effective teachers stay current with their field by regularly reading the professional literature, which includes academic and professional journals, magazines, newsletters, and current books. These publications allow teachers to keep abreast of the latest research in the field, learn about current issues, learn about advocacy efforts, and obtain ideas for improving the teaching and learning in their classrooms.

Connect through Professional Websites, Listservs, Blogs, and Twitter Feeds

Keeping connected to and staying abreast of the field does not mean that you have to pay for print publications. Websites, listservs, blogs, and Twitter feeds offer the means for ELL educators to share and discuss ideas, news, and information. Listservs are e-mail distribution and discussion lists, and messages are sent to all subscribing members. They can generate a few e-mails a month or up to dozens a day. Some listservs are public and can be joined by anyone, some are limited to members of a specific organization or group within an organization, and some are by invitation only. Blogs can serve the same function, without cluttering up e-mail inboxes, by providing a space online for users to react and respond to news and information. Twitter is a form of micro blogging, and its short messages can include images and links to detailed blog postings and other online content. Interested readers can subscribe to specific Twitter feeds, which they can read online or easily access by smart phone or tablet. Many professional organizations, special interest groups, education agencies, and individual scholars maintain websites, Facebook pages, listservs, blogs, and Twitter accounts. Sites such as Instagram and Pinterest also support communities of ELL education practice.

Increasing Opportunities for Parental Engagement

Schools can and must increase **parental engagement** at the school. Some teachers may have the false impression that the parents of many of their ELLs are not involved in their children's education because they have no interaction with the parents or because the parents do not help their children with homework. This lack of interaction, however, may be due simply to language barriers or parents' work schedules, or to parents feeling un-welcome at the school. Parents of ELLs typically lack sufficient English to provide exten-sive help with homework. Despite these misconceptions and misunderstandings, parents of ELLs are usually highly involved in their children's education in ways teachers cannot see. Parents may see their duties as ensuring that their children get to school on time, have the materials they need for school, and have a place to do their homework. They likely admonish their children to listen to, respect, and obey their teachers.

Parents, like their children, can and should learn about the culture of U.S. schools, including the importance of and expectations for parental engagement. Teachers and other school personnel can help parents become aware of these issues in a culturally sen-sitive way. They can also increase parental engagement through programs and activities that make it easy for the parents to get involved. Many schools have found the following suggestions effective.

Create Family Literacy Programs

Parents of many ELLs speak little or no English, and some may even lack literacy in their home language. If your school or district does not already have a family literacy program, work on getting one started. ESL and home-language literacy classes for parents can be held during the school day or after school. Academic courses can be offered for parents without a high school diploma to earn a GED, which can open the way to better jobs or a college education. Family literacy programs can also focus on providing parents with the knowledge and skills needed to help their children with school assignments.

Hold Parent and Family Night Events throughout the School Year

Schools should also find as many ways as possible to get parents on campus, and not just for the traditional back-to-school night, open house, or parent-teacher conferences. Events can be planned throughout the year, such as Reading Night, Math Night, Social Studies Night, Science Night, or Technology Night. Parent forums can be held with guest speakers who discuss issues of concern to parents. Parent-teacher organization meetings, science fairs, school carnivals, music concerts, multicultural celebrations, and award pro-grams are other ways to bring the parents to the school. Parents should also be involved in helping organize such events.

Recommend Parents to Serve on Key School and District Committees

As the primary stakeholders in policy decisions affecting their children, parents should be given opportunities to be members of committees that set and implement policies, programs, and curricula for ELLs and other students. Get to know the parents of your ELLs well so you can have names ready to recommend when such opportunities arise. If committees exist without parent representation, insist that parents be added.

Take or Send Parents to Local and National Conferences

Some national organizations, such as the National Association for Bilingual Education and its state affiliates, include parent institutes and conference sessions designed for par-ents. Registration fees for parents are reduced to an affordable level. Schools or districts should provide support for parents to attend these professional meetings to learn about policies, programs, and other initiatives that may affect their children and their schools, learn strategies and techniques for helping their children at home, learn how to advocate for their children and schools, and network with other parents and educators. School districts, county or regional education offices, and even state education offices also occa-sionally host conferences, workshops, and institutes for parents. Teachers of ELLs should find out about these opportunities, recruit parents to go, and contact organizers to make sure the parents' language needs will be accommodated.

Accommodate Parents' Language Needs

Under Title VI of the Civil Right Acts, schools are required to communicate with parents in a language they can understand. Executive Order 13166, "Improving Access to Services for Persons with Limited English Proficiency," requires federal agencies and recipients of federal funds—including school districts and schools—to provide meaningful access to services for those who are not proficient in English.

The easiest way to accommodate the language needs of parents is to hire administrators, teachers, secretaries, community liaisons, and paraprofessionals who can speak the languages spoken by parents. School districts can hire personnel to translate important district documents and letters sent to parents. Individual schools can hire community liaisons who can do the same for school documents sent home. At my former elementary school, announcements were sent home regularly in English, Spanish, and Khmer. Translation for Spanish and Khmer was also provided at parent meetings. Our principal spoke Spanish, and Khmer translation was provided by the Khmer-speaking community liaison or by one of the Khmer bilingual teachers. Some schools purchase professional translation equipment with headphones that parents can wear to hear a translation provided by a school staff member. When schools or school districts do not have the personnel who speak a needed language, state departments of education should be asked for assistance.

Action Research

Although we have a large body of research that offers an excellent foundation, there is much we still need to learn about second language learning, providing effective language and content-area instruction for ELLs, and assessing ELLs' language and content-area knowledge and progress in a valid and reliable manner. Researchers (including me) will continue to design studies aimed at answering some of the pressing questions in our field. In conducting such research, we have to gain access to schools, classrooms, and students and obtain the necessary permissions. We refer to your schools and classrooms as "research sites." If you ever have the opportunity to participate in a research study— either as a participant or as a co-researcher—with an outside researcher in your school or classroom, I encourage you to go for it. Research with real students and teachers, in real schools and classrooms, is crucially needed. Participation in such studies usually has direct or indirect benefits. Before agreeing, however, make sure you fully understand the purposes of the research, who is sponsoring it, and what safeguards have been put into place to protect your anonymity and that of your school and your students. Also be sure that the methods used in the study pose little or no risk to you or your students. You should be asked to sign a consent form that provides this information and makes clear that you have the right to withdraw from the study at any time without any repercussions.

Although studies conducted by outside researchers are critically important, other kinds of research efforts also can inform effective practice. As teachers or administrators, you have unrestricted access to rich "research sites." You also have the benefit of understanding the local context and knowing the "research participants"—your students—in ways an outside researcher never can, simply because you work with them several hours a day throughout the school year. Thus, you should see yourself not only as a teacher but also as a researcher.

An important trend in education is for teachers and administrators to conduct **action research** in their own schools and classrooms. Action research can be a tool for teacher self-evaluation and critical reflection as teachers systematically collect and analyze data from their own classrooms and use the results to improving teaching and learning.

Action research is important also because not all classrooms are the same. You may read a great research study in an academic journal about a particular strategy or technique that was found to be effective, but in a setting and with students very different from your own. Through action research, you can test whether that strategy or technique works in your classroom. Action research can be viewed as a tool for answering the question, "What works here, in my own classroom, with my own students?"

Here are just a few simple examples. Say you are wondering whether the spelling basal you are using is really helping your ELLs become better spellers. You could design a simple study in which you compare the list of words given on spelling tests with the words students are actually using in their journals, Writer's Workshop texts, or written work in other content areas. Results that reveal a mismatch between words being tested and words students are actually using as they write would be evidence that you need to provide more meaningful spelling instruction. A similar action research project could be done with words on the word wall or in students' personal word books. As another example, say you wanted to find out whether students who read more at home have higher vocabulary knowledge than students who read less at home. You could collect data by having students keep reading logs and then develop a simple measure of vocabulary. If your results show that students who read more at home do have better vocabularies, your next action research project might be to determine which strategies are most effective for increasing the amount of at-home reading students do. As a final example, say you are considering whether to try to increase students' comprehension of science lessons by using a translanguaging strategy such as preview-review. You could compare students' comprehension (as measured through classroom-based assessments) on lessons that begin with preview-review to those that do not. If you find that preview-review is effective, you will feel confident about providing it for future lessons.

Many excellent books are available that educators can use to guide their action research. Grabe and Stoller (2013) offer a flexible 12-step framework for conducting action research that may be applied to any content-area investigation (Box 11.2).

Box 11.2 Action Research

Twelve steps for conducting action research in the classroom:

1. Establish a purpose and decide on a topic.
2. Pose a specific question (narrowing the focus of enquiry).
3. Anticipate the outcome(s).
4. Specify the type(s) of data to collect.
5. Determine ways to collect data in an ethical manner.
6. Consider issues related to time.
7. Collect data systematically.
8. Examine and analyze data.
9. Reflect on results.
10. Generate practical solutions.
11. Experiment with and monitor solutions.
12. Share insights with colleagues.

Grabe, W., & Stoller, F. L. (2013). *Teaching and researching reading* (2nd ed.) (p. 167). New York: Routledge, reprinted with permission.

Summary

Pedagogically sound translanguaging strategies enable ELL and other bilingual students to draw on all of their linguistic resources to engage in learning language and academic content. Researchers have documented evidence of the effectiveness of translanguaging as an instructional strategy for ELLs. The SIOP Model, the Common Core State Standards, and the Next Generation Science Standards all include use of home languages as a key component in giving ELLs equal access to high-quality standards-based instruction. Translanguaging sends a strong message to ELLs that even in an English-medium classroom, their home language is valued and is a viable resource for learning. This message creates a culturally sustaining environment for ELLs that affirms their identity and that is conducive to effective language and content-area teaching and learning. Effective programs for ELLs ensure that students attain proficiency in English and are given equal access to the core curriculum. These programs value students' home languages and cultures and make use of multiple ongoing authentic assessments that drive instruction tailored to the unique linguistic and academic needs of students. Effective programs have teachers who are fully credentialed and certified to work with ELLs and who are true advocates for students and their families. Schools with effective programs provide ongoing professional development opportunities for teachers and administrators and promote active parental engagement. To advocate for their ELLs, effective teachers take advantage of the positive aspects of federal and state policies for ELLs to obtain needed resources and create effective programs. They keep data to show the progress of ELLs in learning English and academic content, which can be used to counter invalid results from standardized high-stakes tests, and work to change policies that are potentially harmful to their students. They serve on key school, district, and state committees, become active members of professional organizations, and stay current in the field by reading professional literature. To promote active parent engagement, effective programs create family literacy programs, hold parent and family night events throughout the school year, get parents on key school and district committees, send parents to local and national conferences, and accommodate parents' language needs to enable their full participation. Finally, teachers in effective programs undertake action research projects to determine the best ways to educate their ELLs.

Discussion Questions

1. Why should teachers be advocates for their ELLs? And why is parental engagement so important? Discuss any experiences you have had in advocating for students and promoting parental engagement.
2. Describe any experiences you have had with the translanguaging strategies discussed in this chapter. How effective were these strategies?
3. The press has reported cases of principals or teachers who outlaw any use of ELLs' home languages in the classroom or school. Describe any instances you may have heard about or seen personally. Why is outlawing these languages a mistake? What do these educators misunderstand about the role home languages can play in helping ELLs learn English and academic content through English?
4. View the video clip of an ELL classroom in Minnesota featured on the ¡Colorín Colorado! website. What characteristics of effective programs for ELLs were evident in this video?
5. On TESOL's 6 Principles for Exemplary Teaching of English Learners website, choose one of the principles to explore in more depth by reviewing the corre-

sponding classroom activities, vignettes, and other resources associated with that principle. Describe how you would put this principle into practice in your own classroom.

Research Activities

1. *ELL Student Interview* Interview a current or former ELL student about his or her experiences with translanguaging at school. Did any teachers or paraprofessionals speak his or her language? Was the student allowed to speak to other students in the home language in the classroom? What specific translanguaging strategies, if any, did the student's teachers use? Did the student find these strategies helpful?

2. *ELL Teacher Interview* Interview a teacher about the ways in which he or she strives to provide effective instruction for ELLs. Ask about each of the characteristics of effective ELL programs outlined in this chapter. How well is this teacher's school doing in relation to these characteristics? What changes, if any, does the teacher, or do you, feel need to be made?

3. *ELL Classroom Observation* Translanguaging Strategy Inventory: Visit an ELL classroom or do an evaluation of your classroom if you are already teaching. How many of the following evidences of translanguaging can you find in the classroom? Discuss your findings with the classroom teacher or with a colleague.
   - ☐ Bilingual/multilingual classroom labels (wall, door, desk, chair, clock, etc.)
   - ☐ Bulletin boards and other wall displays that include students' home languages
   - ☐ Bilingual dictionaries
   - ☐ Books and other instructional materials in the students' home languages
   - ☐ Bilingual computer software or use of online bilingual resources on the Internet
   - ☐ Mobile apps with bilingual support
   - ☐ Student writing in home languages
   - ☐ Preview-review
   - ☐ Assistance in home languages provided by the teacher
   - ☐ Acceptance by the teacher of home language comments and answers during classroom discussions
   - ☐ Assistance provided by students for each other in their home language
   - ☐ Student use of home languages when working in pairs and small groups
   - ☐ Bilingual paraprofessional or classroom volunteers
   - ☐ Cognate word study lessons
   - ☐ Other _____

4. *Online Research Activity* Pick two or three languages spoken by ELLs in a school with which you are familiar. Do an Internet search and make a list of resources that could be used to provide translanguaging support (e.g., posters, dictionaries, bilingual charts, online translation tools). Discuss your list with school administrators and teachers.

5. *Action Research Project* Conduct an action research project, following the steps outlined in Box 11.2. If you are currently teaching, conduct the study in your classroom; otherwise pick an appropriate classroom for the research. Be sure to develop a research question relevant to the needs of the ELLs in the classroom.

Recommended Reading

García, O., Johnson, S. I., & Seltzer, K. (2016). *The translanguaging classroom: Leveraging student bilingualism for learning*. Philadelphia: Caslon.

This book provides clear guidance for teachers on how translanguaging can be used strategically and purposefully as an instructional and assessment framework to support bilingual students.

García, O., & Kleyn, T. (Eds.). (2016). *Translanguaging with multilingual students: Learning from classroom moments*. New York: Routledge.

This book brings together a group of teachers and educators and highlights six empirically grounded ethnographic case studies that describe how translanguaging is used in lesson designs and in the spontaneous moves made by teachers and students during specific teaching moments.

TESOL International Association Writing Team. (2018). *The 6 principles for exemplary teaching of English learners*. Annapolis Junction, MD: TESOL Press.

This book, written by a team of leading ELL researchers and educators, highlights each of the six principles identified by TESOL International for teaching ELLs, with vivid examples, guidelines, and other resources to help teachers put them into effective practice in their own classrooms.

Glossary

academic language proficiency. Refers to the level of language proficiency students need to successfully comprehend and perform grade-level academic tasks. This term is problematic, however, because the level of proficiency needed varies widely and depends on the tasks and the language demands.

accommodations. In testing ELLs, refers to modifications in the testing environment or testing procedures, or modifications to the test instrument itself, that are intended to make up for a student's lack of proficiency in the language of the test (e.g., providing extra time, oral interpretation of test directions or items, or home-language versions of the test).

action research. A form of teacher self-evaluation and critical reflection that involves their collecting and analyzing data from their own classrooms and using the results to improve teaching and learning.

additive bilingualism. A situation in which a second language is eventually added to a student's home language without replacing it.

advocacy. Going beyond daily teaching responsibilities to support causes and work for changes to ensure the equitable treatment of ELLs within the school, district, state, and country and to ensure that their unique linguistic, academic, and cultural needs are being fully addressed.

affective filter. Refers to factors such as fear, anxiety, shyness, and lack of motivation that can block comprehensible input and thus prevent second language acquisition. Lowering the affective filter allows learners to receive more comprehensible input and thus enables them to acquire more of the second language.

analytic scoring. A form of assessment that focuses on several aspects of a student's performance, normally guided by a rubric that includes separate analytic scales. For example, a rubric to assess student writing may contain separate analytic scales for composing, style, sentence formation, usage, and mechanics.

assessment. The process of collecting and analyzing a wide variety of data from students that provides evidence of their learning and growth over an extended period.

assimilationist discourses. Discourses that devalue ELLs' home languages and cultures, seeing them as problems to overcome (also called *monolingual discourses*).

balanced approach. An approach to literacy instruction that recognizes the need for some direct instruction in reading skills but emphasizes the importance of providing such instruction in meaningful contexts to ensure that students are able to comprehend and use what they read for authentic purposes.

before, during, after (BDA). In literacy instruction, refers to strategies used before, during, and after reading a text to maximize students' comprehension. Also referred to as *into, through,* and *beyond.*

bias. In testing, refers to the unfair advantages or disadvantages that may be given to certain students that can affect their performance. For example, a test given in English will be biased in favor of proficient English speakers and biased against students who lack proficiency in English.

Bilingual Education Act. Added in 1968 as Title VII of the Elementary and Secondary Education Act (ESEA). Before passage of the No Child Left Behind (NCLB) Act, it provided federal support for bilingual and other programs for ELLs and their families through competitive grants.

bilingual immersion. Describes programs that target language minority students who are English dominant and native English speakers who desire to become bilingual. Students are initially instructed 90%–100% in the non-English target language for the first 2 years of the program. Instruction evens out gradually to 50% instruction in English and 50% in the non-English language as students move up in grade level.

bilingual strategies. Refers to the use of translanguaging and other strategies for providing support for English language learners in their home language during language and academic content-area instruction.

close reading. Refers to the way students engage in the reading of a text, particularly a complex text, to fully comprehend the information it contains and the inferences that may be drawn from it.

cognates. Words that are similar in two languages because they come from the same root (e.g., *education* in English and *educación* in Spanish).

cognitive approaches. Approaches to language learning and teaching focused on the cognitive processes in the brain of the learner.

Common Core State Standards (CCSS). "Next generation" college-and-career-readiness standards in English language arts and mathematics developed by a coalition of states that have been adopted by nearly all states.

communicative competence. The ability to use a language to communicate effectively and appropriately with other speakers of the language. Includes grammatical, discourse, sociolinguistic, and strategic competence.

communicative language teaching (CLT). Language teaching approaches, methods, strategies, and techniques that focus on helping students develop communicative competence.

complex texts. Texts that may be above a students' independent reading level but that can be made comprehensible through careful scaffolding. Complex texts vary in terms of genre and typically have one or more of the following features: high lexical density, complex syntax, implicit meaning, figurative language, archaic language, literary devices, and others.

comprehensible input. Oral or written language that is slightly above a second language learner's current level of proficiency in the second language and thus provides linguistic input that leads to second language acquisition. Represented by the formula $i + 1$, where i is the current level of proficiency, and $+1$ is input slightly above this level.

comprehensible output. Oral or written language produced by a second language speaker that is comprehensible to the individual or individuals with whom he or she is communicating. Second language learners' need to produce comprehensible output pushes them to pay attention to gaps in their proficiency and thus may prompt them to notice more in the input and motivate them to learn the language they need to express their intended meanings.

comprehensive support and improvement (CSI). An intervention plan for schools that have one or more chronically low-performing subgroups on state tests or other achievement measures, as required by the Every Student Succeeds Act (ESSA). Districts must establish CSI plans for the lowest 5% of all schools, and for high schools with less than a 67% graduation rate.

concepts of print. Refers to such reading-related issues as understanding the differences between letters and words and words and spaces; knowing where to start reading and how to do a return sweep to continue reading the next line; and understanding the basic features of a book, such as the title and the front and back covers, and even how to hold the book properly.

concurrent translation. Providing line-by-line translation of teacher instruction or texts into the students' home language. Considered a poor use of the home language because it removes the need for students to attend to the second language and thus interferes with second language acquisition.

consequential validity. Validity concerns focused on the consequences associated with the interpretation and use of test scores. Emphasizes that decisions with high-stakes consequences for students, teachers, and schools should not be based on invalid interpretations of student test scores.

content-based instruction (CBI). An approach to second language instruction in which content-area subjects and topics are used as the basis of instruction.

content objectives. Lesson plan objectives that specify what students should know and be able to do by the end of a lesson related to the targeted academic content.

conversational discourse. Refers to the ways speakers use language for extended, back-and-forth, and purposeful communication.

cooperative learning. A process in which small groups of students collaborate and interact to accomplish a specific learning task or activity.

corrective feedback. Refers to various forms of feedback to language learners designed to help them recognize and correct errors in their language production.

criterion-referenced test. Test designed to measure the degree to which students have mastered tested content.

critical language testing. Language testing that takes into consideration a close examination of the uses and consequences of tests in education and society.

culturally sustaining pedagogies. Pedagogies that aim to address issues of power and social inequities through positive social transformation by sustaining linguistic, literate, and cultural pluralism in classrooms and schools.

developmental bilingual education (DBE). A form of bilingual education for ELLs who initially receive about 90% of content-area instruction in their home language and 10% of content-area instruction through sheltered instruction. Home language instruction decreases slowly as sheltered English instruction increases, as students move up in grade level. Instruction continues in both languages until the end of the program, even after students attain proficiency in English, to ensure that they attain strong bilingual and biliteracy skills. Also referred to as *maintenance late-exit bilingual education*.

differentiated instruction. Instruction that is tailored to the unique language and academic needs of each student.

discourse/Discourse. As defined and distinguished by Gee (2012), discourse (with a lowercase *d*) refers to language in use or connected stretches of language that make sense, such as conversations, stories, reports, arguments, and essays. Discourse (with a capital *D*) is made up of distinctive ways of speaking/listening and also often writing/reading, coupled with distinctive ways of acting, interacting, valuing, feeling, dressing, thinking, and believing with other people and with various objects, tools, and technologies to enact specific socially recognizable identities engaged in specific socially recognizable activities.

dual language books. Books printed in two languages in which one language appears above the other or the two languages are written side by side on one page or on opposite pages.

dual language education. Refers to bilingual education programs that develop bilingualism, biliteracy, grade-level academic achievement, and sociocultural development for all students. Also called *dual immersion.* Includes both one-way and two-way immersion programs.

dual language learner. Commonly used to refer to young children up to 8 years old who have at least one parent who speaks a language other than English at home.

dynamic assessment. A sociocultural view that emphasizes that teaching and learning are an inherent part of all assessment.

dynamic bilingualism. A view of bilingualism that rejects the notion of a bilingual as two monolinguals in one and recognizes that bilinguals draw on all of their linguistic repertoires in complex and dynamic ways for authentic social and academic purposes.

Elementary and Secondary Education Act (ESEA). The main body of federal education policy and law and the source for education funding to state and local education agencies. Passed in 1965 and binding on all states and entities that accept federal education funding.

emergent bilingual. An alternative label for ELLs that draws attention to the other language or languages in their linguistic repertoires, situates these learners in a continuum of bilingual development, and emphasizes that a fundamental goal of programs for these learners should be to help them attain high levels of proficiency in both their home language and English.

English as a second language (ESL). An academic subject, course, or program designed to teach English to students who are not yet proficient in the language.

English for the Children initiatives. Referendums put to voters in four states with large ELL populations that would place severe restrictions on bilingual education programs. In 1998, California voters approved Proposition 227; in 2000, Arizona voters approved Proposition 203; and in 2002, Massachusetts voters approved Question 2. An attempt to pass a similar initiative in Colorado (Amendment 31) failed.

English language development (ELD). An alternative label for English as a second language (ESL) programs and instruction, commonly used at the elementary school level.

English language learner (ELL). A label for students who are non-native speakers of English and are in the process of attaining proficiency in English. Sometimes shortened to English learner (EL).

Equal Educational Opportunities Act (EEOA) of 1974. A federal law that declares, "No state shall deny educational opportunities to an individual on account of his or her race, color, sex, or national origin." Includes the mandate that educational agencies take appropriate actions to help ELLs overcome language barriers that impede their equal participation in education programs.

ESEA Flexibility. An initiative of the Obama administration to grant relief from certain federal mandates under the No Child Left Behind Act, such as the adequate yearly progress requirements and accountability provisions of Title I, in exchange for state-negotiated accountability programs aligned with the administration's criteria, including the creation or adoption of new college-and-career-readiness standards and assessments.

evaluation. The use of assessment data to make judgments about the progress of students' learning, the effectiveness of teacher instruction, or the quality of educational programs.

Every Student Succeeds Act (ESSA) of 2015. The most recent reauthorization of the Elementary and Secondary Education Act (ESEA). Provides federal education funding and sets official federal education policy with specific requirements related to instruction, assessment, accountability, and other educational issues.

evidence-based writing. Student writing that features evidence grounded in texts the students have read.

formative assessment. The use of ongoing assessments that help to identify a student's strengths and needs and thus inform subsequent instruction, building on these strengths while addressing these needs.

genre. In systemic functional linguistics theory, a goal-directed activity to achieve a particular cultural purpose, such as the creation of a particular kind of text (either spoken or written) through deliberate lexical and grammatical choices that make it the kind of text that it is (e.g., an e-mail message, a speech, a lab report, a short story).

growth models. Refers to a variety of experimental measures that attempt to show student growth, based on results of standardized tests.

guided reading. A form of literacy instruction in which small groups of students who read at about the same level are matched to texts at their appropriate instructional level, and the teacher provides support as the students attempt to read the texts on their own.

guided writing. A form of literacy instruction designed to address an area of need within students' writing development. Typically, guided writing lessons start with a mini-lesson on some aspect of writing; students practice the writing principle or strategy they were just taught under the teacher's supervision and then share their final written projects.

heritage language. In the United States, refers to a non-English language to which one has a family tie. Both ELLs and students who are proficient in English and may have little to no proficiency in their heritage language, as is common for second- and third-generation immigrant students, may be designated heritage language students.

heritage language program. A program for language minority students to develop or maintain their heritage language; includes bilingual programs for

ELLs, foreign language classes targeting native speakers in K–12 and post-secondary education, and community-based after-school or weekend programs.

heteroglossic perspective. Views bilingualism as the norm and treats the languages of bilinguals as co-existing.

holistic scoring. A form of assessment in which a student's performance (e.g., a writing sample) is given a single score that represents a judgment of the performance as a whole.

home language instruction. The teaching of literacy or content-area instruction in the home language of ELLs.

independent reading. Reading that students are able to do on their own with little or no support.

independent writing. Writing that students are able to do on their own with little or no support.

interactive writing. Writing instruction for ELLs who are at the beginning stage of writing, in which the teacher and the students compose a short sentence or paragraph. The teacher helps the students construct the sentence or sentences in enlarged text (e.g., on chart paper) by guiding individual students as they come up to add individual letters or words and helping them make relevant sound-symbol correspondences.

invented spelling. Also called *developmental spelling*, transitional spelling, or temporary spelling; refers to a temporary stage emergent writers may go through as they rely on their knowledge of sound-symbol correspondences to write words as the words sound to them.

journals. Notebooks in which students write regularly to practice and develop their writing skills.

language-as-problem orientation. A point of view in which the home language of ELLs is viewed as a problem to be overcome as students learn English and academic content through English.

language-as-resource orientation. A point of view in which the home language of ELLs is viewed as a strength to be developed and built on to help the students learn English and academic content.

language experience approach. A literacy instruction approach in which students dictate stories based on their own experiences, and teachers transcribe the students' dictations into texts and then use those texts for reading instruction.

language majority student. Describes a student who is a native speaker of the standard language variety spoken by the dominant group of a given society. In the United States, the term covers students who speak standard English.

language minority student. Describes a student who is not a native speaker of the language spoken by the dominant group of a given society. In the United States, the term covers all students who speak languages other than standard English. Sometimes rendered as language *minoritized* student to emphasize the unequal power structures in society that create dominant and minoritized groups.

language objectives. Lesson plan objectives that specify what students should know and be able to do by the end of the lesson related to language learning and the use of language needed to complete the accompanying content objectives.

language progressions. Statements that outline the language expectations for ELLs at each level of English language proficiency associated with specific standards and academic tasks.

language socialization. The process by which individuals acquire the knowledge and practices that enable them to participate effectively in a language community.

Lau Remedies. Regulations issued by the U.S. Department of Education Office of Civil Rights following the U.S. Supreme Court decision *Lau v. Nichols* (1974), outlining requirements for school districts and schools to address the needs of ELLs.

lexicon. The vocabulary of a language.

Look Act. Legislation passed in 2017 by the Massachusetts State Legislature—Bill H.4032. "An Act relative to language opportunity for our kids (LOOK)." Essentially reverses Question 2 by undoing restrictions on bilingual education programs and allows school districts flexibility in providing language acquisition programs for ELLs. The Act also established the state's Seal of Biliteracy.

minimal pairs. Words that differ by a single phoneme (e.g., *sand/hand, bit/bet, rag/rat*), typically used to help students distinguish specific sounds that change the meanings of words and help students improve their pronunciation.

modeled writing. Writing instruction in which the teacher constructs a text in enlarged print (e.g., on chart paper), demonstrating a variety of writing strategies and techniques students are expected to learn and use in their own writing.

monoglossic perspective. Views monolingualism as the norm and treats the languages of bilinguals as two separate distinct systems, as if students are two monolinguals in one (double monolingualism).

morphology. The study of the structure of words. The central unit of study is the morpheme, the smallest unit of meaning or grammatical function.

multilingual learner. A term used to capture the broad range of students who are bi/multilingual or who are learning, and learning through, more than one language.

multiple measures. Different forms of formal and informal formative and summative assessments used together to provide accurate measures of what a student knows and can do.

multi-tiered systems of support (MTSS). An umbrella term that encompasses response to intervention (RTI) and other positive behavioral interventions and supports.

multi-trait scoring. Refers to scoring a piece of student writing by considering several traits, for example, clear opinion (main idea), adequate details to support the opinion, and a strong conclusion.

narrow reading. A form of independent recreational reading that entails reading several books on the same subject, by the same author, or in the same genre.

newcomer program. For beginning-level ELLs who have been in the United States for only 1 or 2 years. Such programs typically provide intensive English instruction and may include some home language instruction and ample primary language support.

next-generation assessments. Assessments that are designed to measure required college-and-career-readiness standards and corresponding English language proficiency standards. Most of these assessments are delivered by computer or mobile devices and include technology-enhanced questions that go beyond traditional paper-and-pencil multiple-choice tests. Some also use computer-adaptive testing techniques.

Next Generation Science Standards (NGSS). "Next generation" science standards developed by national science and science education associations in cooperation with more than half of the states.

No Child Left Behind Act (NCLB) of 2001. A reauthorization of the Elementary and Secondary Education Act that was in effect until the passage of Every Student Succeeds Act in 2015. Introduced a heavy emphasis on accountability through standards and high-stakes testing.

norm-referenced test. A test designed to compare a student's score to those of other students. Test results are usually reported as percentile rankings (e.g., a student at the 71st percentile rank scored higher than 71% of the students in the test's norming population, that is, a group of students who have already taken the test).

one-way immersion. A dual language bilingual education program that typically serves only speakers of the same home language. Programs serving all ELLs are more accurately called *development bilingual education*. Programs serving all English speakers are more accurately called *bilingual immersion programs*.

oracy. The ability to express one's self well in speech. Also can denote the oral skills used in formal education, particularly around reading and writing. Oracy has three main components: language structures, vocabulary, and dialogue.

parental engagement. The direct involvement and active engagement of parents in the education of their children.

performance assessment. A form of assessment in which students are evaluated on their ability to perform a specific academic task or set of related tasks (e.g., use oral language to role play interactions at the market, write an essay, conduct a science experiment, measure and compare a set of objects using a scale).

personal word book. A book provided for each student that contains a list of high-frequency words and other words students commonly ask for when they write, and space under each letter section for students to record their own words as they progress through the school year.

phonics. A component of reading instruction in which students learn the phonetic value (i.e., sounds) of individual letters and combinations of letters.

phonology. The study of the sound systems of languages.

pluralist discourses. Discourses that recognize ELLs' home languages and cultures as rich resources for helping them learn English and academic content and that strive to help them develop high levels of proficiency and literacy in both languages (also called *multilingual discourses*).

portfolio assessment. Assessment of student work collected throughout the school year and organized in a portfolio. Enables the assessment of students' progress and growth based on authentic samples of student work.

pragmatics. The study of language in use, that is, how individuals produce and interpret language in social interaction in specific contexts.

preview-review. A form of primary language support in which a lesson or a read-aloud conducted in English is previewed, and then reviewed, in the home language of the ELLs.

primary language support (PLS). Using a student's home language during English as a second language (ESL) or sheltered English content-area instruction to make the English instruction more comprehensible.

primary trait scoring. Refers to scoring a piece of student writing by focusing on a specific trait, for example, the ability to craft a thesis statement in a persuasive essay.

process writing. A form of writing instruction in which students are guided through five stages: prewriting, drafting, revising, editing, and publishing. Often taught through a collaborative approach called Writer's Workshop.

productive talk moves. A range of strategies that teachers use to scaffold effective classroom discussions.

prompts. Refers to a variety of ways a speaker can directly or indirectly provide feedback in a manner that prompts his or her conversation partner to correct an error.

Proposition 58 ("English proficiency. Multilingual Education"). A California voter initiative passed in 2016 that essentially reversed Proposition 227's restrictions on bilingual education. It declares that schools must ensure that students become proficient in English, authorizes dual-language immersion programs, calls for parental and community input on language acquisition programs, and recognizes the rights of parents to select available programs that best meet their children's needs.

Race to the Top (RTTT). A grant program, part of the Obama administration's American Recovery and Reinvestment Act of 2009, that provided more than $4 billion in competitive grants for states to begin education reform efforts aligned with specific criteria, including the creation or adoption of new college- and career-readiness standards and assessments.

read-alouds. Sessions during which a teacher, parent, or other proficient reader reads aloud from a book or other text to one or more students.

Reader's Workshop. A structure for reading instruction often used in secondary schools that enables teachers to tailor instruction to students' strengths, interests, and needs.

reading self-assessments. Tools or procedures used by students to assess their own reading performance.

recasts. Refers to a variety of ways a speaker can indirectly provide corrective feedback for a conversation partner by repeating the partner's utterance in a positive and reinforcing manner that models correct usage.

redesignation. The reclassification of a student from ELL status to fluent English proficient status, based on the results of an English proficiency test and other criteria established by a school district or state.

register. Variation in the use of language based on the context in which the language is used.

reliability. The consistency with which a test or assessment measures what it is measuring.

response to intervention (RTI). A model for school improvement and for identifying students in need of special education involving three tiers of instructional support and interventions.

running record. A reading assessment tool that provides a visual record of a student's reading performance word by word on a specific text.

scaffolding. Support or assistance provided to a student within his or her zone of proximal development (ZPD) by a more knowledgeable teacher or peer to help the student learn a new concept or develop new skills.

semantics. The study of the meaning of words, phrases, and sentences.

sequential bilingualism. The development of proficiency in a second language after proficiency has been developed in the first language.

shared reading. Reading instruction in which the teacher reads a big book or other source of enlarged text with the students, modeling a variety of reading strategies and using the text (once the students are familiar with it) to teach reading skills.

shared writing. Writing instruction in which the teacher, in collaboration with the students, constructs an enlarged text (e.g., on chart paper). Students suggest sentences and revisions, and the teacher models the use of a variety of writing strategies that students are expected to use in their own writing.

sheltered English immersion (SEI). A program model for ELLs that combines English as a second language (ESL), sheltered content-area instruction, and bilingual strategies. Sometimes called *structured English immersion.*

sheltered instruction. Grade-level content-area instruction provided in English in a manner that makes it comprehensible to ELLs while supporting their English language development.

Sheltered Instruction Observation Protocol (SIOP). An instructional model and tool for planning, implementing, and evaluating sheltered English content-area instruction developed by Echevarria, Vogt, and Short (2017).

silent period. A period of time many new learners of a second language go through before they feel comfortable speaking in the new language.

simultaneous bilingualism. The development of proficiency in two languages at the same time.

sociocultural perspectives. Perspectives on language learning and teaching that focus on the sociocultural context surrounding the learner that facilitates the learning process.

SOLOM-R (Student Oral Language Observation Matrix-Revised). An assessment of students' oral language proficiency using an analytic scoring rubric that focuses on the aspects of comprehension, fluency, vocabulary, pronunciation, and grammar. The original version, developed by bilingual teachers in Southern California in the 1980s, has been revised for this book by the author to reflect current understanding of oral language development and to focus on what ELLs can do at each level.

special education. Specially designed instruction to meet the unique needs of a child with a disability, guided by regulations in the Individuals with Disabilities Education Act.

specially designed academic instruction in English (SDAIE). Another term for sheltered instruction, preferred in California and other states because it places emphasis on the fact that such instruction is academically rigorous but specially designed to match the linguistic needs of the student.

standard error of measurement (SEM). A statistical measure that indicates a range of trustworthiness of an individual student's standardized test score. For example, the actual score of a student who earned a score of 50 on a test with an SEM of 3 would be between 47 and 53 (e.g., 50 +/− 3).

submersion. The process of placing ELLs in a mainstream classroom where they receive no English as a second language (ESL), sheltered-content instruction, or primary language support. Also called "*sink or swim.*"

subtractive bilingualism. A situation in which a second language eventually replaces a student's home language.

summative assessment. Assessments that provide a summary of what students know and can do. Typically given at the end of a unit or at the end of a school year.

superdiversity. A term used to describe diversity across and within immigrant and ethnic groups; includes a range of factors beyond language and ethnicity (e.g., race, education level, country of origin, migration history, socioeconomic status).

syntax. The study of the rules governing the relationships between words and the ways they are combined to form phrases and sentences.

targeted support and improvement (TSI). An intervention plan that school districts must implement in cases where one or more subgroups of students are consistently underperforming on state tests and other achievement measures, as required under the Every Student Succeeds Act.

teaching for transfer. Teaching that recognizes and values the vast store of knowledge students have in their home language and that enables them to effectively draw on this knowledge when learning or learning through their new language.

testing. The administration of tests, singular instruments designed to systematically measure a sample of a student's ability at one particular time.

text complexity. A combination of qualitative and quantitative measures to determine the level of reading difficulty of a book or other text.

thematic teaching. Teaching a series of content-area lessons across different content areas, focusing on a unifying topic or theme.

thematic word chart. A list of key vocabulary related to a theme currently under study.

total physical response (TPR). A language teaching approach in which students physically respond to language input (e.g., commands) to internalize the meaning and demonstrate their comprehension of the language.

transitional bilingual education (TBE). A program model for ELLs in which home language content-area instruction is provided for the first few years of the program, in addition to sheltered English content-area instruction and English as a second language (ESL). The amount of home language instruction decreases as sheltered English immersion (SEI) increases. Students are transitioned to mainstream classrooms after just a few years in the program.

translanguaging. In its original conceptualization, refers to the practice in which bilinguals receive information in one language and then use or apply it in the other language. In its expanded sense, refers to the natural and normal ways bilinguals use their languages in their everyday lives to make sense of their bilingual worlds. In teaching, refers to pedagogical practices that use bilingualism as a resource rather than ignore it or perceive it as a problem.

translanguaging pedagogy. Education that effectively leverages the translanguaging practices of multilingual learners and teachers in bilingual and English-medium classrooms.

translingual practice. A term used to highlight the ways bilingual students draw on all of their linguistic resources as they produce written texts in English or a mixture of two languages.

translanguaging strategies. Strategies that allow students to draw on the languages and dialects that make up their linguistic repertoire. Students and teachers can leverage these linguistic resources to support student comprehension of complex content and texts, and to engage in academic tasks.

two-way immersion. A dual language bilingual education program that serves both English speakers and ELLs from the same language background. Variations emphasize the amount of time devoted to each language. In a 50/50 model, half of the instruction is in English and half is in the other target language across several grade levels. In a 90/10 model, instruction begins in kindergarten and 1st grade with 90% of instruction in the home language, and 10% in English. As students move up in grade level, the amount of home language instruction decreases, and the amount of English instruction increases until both make up 50% of instruction time.

universal design. An approach to test design that seeks to maximize accessibility for all targeted test takers.

validity. The accuracy of a test or assessment in measuring what it purports to measure.

value-added measurements (VAMs). The use of high-stakes test results to calculate student academic growth over time. VAMs are often (mis)used in teacher evaluation systems.

wait time. The period of time after a question has been posed during which students can think and formulate answers in their head before being required to answer aloud. Particularly important for ELLs who may need extra time to process input and formulate output in their second language.

word study. Short mini-lessons focusing on the morphological or semantic properties of words and related sets of words.

word wall. An enlarged list of words organized alpha-betically and displayed on a classroom wall to support students' vocabulary and literacy development.

Writer's Workshop. An instructional approach to writing in which students work independently and at their own pace as they move through the five stages of process writing with teacher and peer guidance and support.

zone of proximal development (ZPD). Refers to a metaphorical space between what an individual can do on his or her own and what he or she can do with support from a teacher or other more knowledgeable person.

Youth and Children's Literature

Beshore, G. W. (1998a). *Science in ancient China*. New York: Franklin Watts.

Beshore, G. W. (1998b). *Science in early Islamic culture*. New York: Franklin Watts.

Brown, M. (1998). *Arthur and the lost diary*. Boston: Little, Brown.

Bunting, E. (1998). *So far from the sea*. Boston: Clarion.

Bunting, E., & Peck, B. (1990). *How many days to America? A Thanksgiving story*. New York: Houghton Mifflin.

Coleman, E. (1999.) *White socks only*. Morton Grove, IL: Albert Whitman.

Coles, R. (2004). *The story of Ruby Bridges*. New York: Scholastic.

Davis, K. C. (2001a). *Don't know much about space*. New York: HarperCollins.

Davis, K. C. (2001b). *Don't know much about the solar system*. New York: HarperCollins.

Ellis, J., & Hornung, P. (2004). *What's your angle, Pythagoras? A math adventure*. Watertown, MA: Charlesbridge.

Faruqi, R. (2015). *Lailah's lunchbox: A Ramadan story*. Thomaston, ME: Tilbury House.

Hall, Z., & Halpern, S. (2002). *¡Tiempo de calabazas!* [It's pumpkin time!]. New York: Scholastic.

Houston, J. W., & Houston, J. D. (2002). *Farewell to Manzanar*. New York: Houghton Mifflin.

Hunter, M. (2005). *The story of Latino civil rights: Fighting for justice*. Broomhall, PA: Mason Crest.

Hutchins, P. (1989). *The doorbell rang*. New York: HarperTrophy.

Lobel, A. (1970). *Frog and toad are friends*. New York: HarperCollins.

McGrath, B. B. (1994). *The M&M's brand counting book*. Watertown, MA: Charlesbridge.

Mills, D., & Brazell, D. (1999). *Lima's red hot chilli*. London: Mantra.

Mochizuki, K. (1993). *Baseball saved us*. New York: Lee & Low.

Morris, A. (1993). *Bread, bread, bread*. New York: HarperTrophy.

Noble, T. H. (1992). *The day Jimmy's boa ate the wash*. New York: Puffin.

Neuschwander, C., & Geehan, W. (1999). *Sir Cumference and the first Round Table: A math adventure*. Watertown, MA: Charlesbridge.

Neuschwander, C., & Langdo, B. (2005). *Mummy math: An adventure in geometry*. New York: Holt.

Neuschwander, C., & Langdo, B. (2007). *Patterns in Peru: An adventure in patterning*. New York: Holt.

Noguchi, R., & Jenks, D. (2001). *Flowers from Mariko*. New York: Lee & Low.

Shaw, C. (1992). *It looked like spilt milk*. New York: HarperTrophy.

Simon, S. (2007). *Our solar system* (revised ed.). New York: Collins.

Stanley, J. (1994). *I am an American: A true story of Japanese internment*. New York: Crown.

Tunnell, M. O., & Chilcoat, G. W. (1996). *The children of Topaz: The story of the Japanese American internment camp*. New York: Holiday House.

Waters, K. (1989). *Sarah Morton's day: A day in the life of a pilgrim girl*. New York: Scholastic.

Williams, V. B. (2007). *A chair for my mother* (25th anniversary ed.). New York: HarperTrophy.

Wood, A., & Wood, D. (1989). *The napping house*. San Diego, CA: Harcourt Brace.

References

Abedi, J. (2017). Utilizing accommodations in assessment. In E. G. Shohamy, I. Or, & S. May (Eds.), *Language testing and assessment, Encyclopedia of language and education* (3rd ed., pp. 303–322). Cham, Switzerland: Springer International.

Abedi, J., & Ewers, N. (2013). *Accommodations for English language learners and students with disabilities: A research-based decision algorithm*. Santa Cruz, CA: Smarter Balanced Assessment Consortium.

Adger, C. T., Snow, C. E., & Christian, D. (Eds.). (2018). *What teachers need to know about language* (2nd ed.). Washington, DC: Center for Applied Linguistics.

Alim, H. S. (2015). Hip Hop Nation language: Localization and globalization. In J. Bloomquist, L. J. Green, & S. L. Lanehart (Eds.), *The Oxford Handbook of African American Language*. Oxford, UK: Oxford University Press.

Alim, H. S., Rickford, J. R., & Ball, A. F. (Eds.). (2016). *Raciolinguistics: How language shapes our ideas about race*. Oxford, UK: Oxford University Press.

Alvear, S. (2015). Reading achievement among English language learners: Evidence of two-way bilingual immersion advantages. *Houston Education Research Consortium—Research Brief, 3*(2), 1–4.

Amendum, S. J., Conradi, K., & Hiebert, E. H. (2018). Does text complexity matter in the elementary grades? A research synthesis of text difficulty and elementary students' reading fluency and comprehension. *Educational Psychology Review, 30,* 121–151. doi:10.1007/s10648-017-9398-2

American Education Research Association, American Psychological Association, & National Council on Measurement in Education. (2014). *Standards for educational and psychological testing* (2nd ed). Washington, DC: American Education Research Association.

American Institutes for Research. (2012). *National evaluation of Title III implementation: Report on state and local implementation*. Washington, DC: Author.

American Institutes for Research & WestEd. (2006, January 24). *Effects of the implementation of Proposition 227 on the education of English learners, K–12: Findings from a fiveyear evaluation*. Washington, DC, & San Francisco, CA: Authors.

Amrein, A. L., & Berliner, D. C. (2002). High-stakes testing, uncertainty, and student learning. *Education Policy Analysis Archives, 10*(18). Retrieved from https://epaa.asu.edu/ojs/article/viewFile/297/423

Asher, J. J. (1977). *Learning another language through actions: The complete teacher's guidebook*. Los Gatos, CA: Sky Oaks Productions.

Asher, J. J. (1995). A conversation with Dr. James J. Asher . . . TPR and education. [Electronic version.] *Ideas for Excellence: The Newsletter for ESL/Bilingual Education, 3*(4), 1–4.

Asher, J. J. (2009). *Learning another language through actions* (7th ed.). Los Gatos, CA: Sky Oaks Productions.

Atkinson, D. (Ed.). (2011). *Alternative approaches to second language acquisition*. New York: Routledge.

Atwell, N. (1987). *In the middle: Writing, reading, and learning with adolescents*. Portsmouth, NH: Boyton/Cook.

August, D. (2012). How does first language literacy development relate to second language literacy development? In E. Hamayan & R. Freeman (Eds.), *English language learners at school: A guide for administrators* (2nd ed.) (pp. 56–57). Philadelphia: Caslon.

August, D., McCardle, P., & Shanahan, T. (2014). Developing literacy in English language learners: Findings from a review of the experimental research. *School Psychology Review, 43*(4), 490–498.

August, D., & Shanahan, T. (Eds.). (2006a). *Developing literacy in secondlanguage learners: Report of the National Literacy Panel on languageminority children and youth*. Mahwah, NJ: Lawrence Erlbaum.

August, D., & Shanahan, T. (Eds.). (2006b). Executive summary. *Developing literacy in second-language learners: Report of the National Literacy Panel on language-minority children and youth*. Retrieved from http://www.cal.org/projects/archive/nlpreports/Executive_Summary.pdf

Avalos, M. A., Medina, E., & Secada, W. G. (2018). Reading mathematical problems: Exploring how language counts for middle school students with varying mathematics proficiency. In A. L. Bailey, C. A. Maher, & L. C. Wilkinson (Eds.), *Language, literacy, and learning in the STEM disciplines: How language counts for English learners* (pp. 56–78). New York: Routledge.

Avineri, N., & Johnson, E. J. (2015). Bridging the "language gap" [Invited Forum]. *Journal of Linguistic Anthropology, 25*(1), 66–86.

Bailey, A. L., & Huang, B. H. (2011). Do current English language development/proficiency standards reflect the English needed for success in school? *Language Testing, 28*(3), 343–365.

Bailey, A. L., Maher, C. A., & Wilkinson, L. C. (Eds.). (2018). *Language, literacy, and learning in the STEM disciplines: How language counts for English learners*. New York: Routledge.

Bailey, F., Burkett, B., & Freeman, D. (2008). The mediating role of language in teaching and learning: A classroom perspective. In B. Spolsky & F. M. Hult (Eds.), *The handbook of educational linguistics* (pp. 606–625). Malden, MA: Blackwell.

Baker, C., & Wright, W. E. (2017). *Foundations for bilingual education and bilingualism* (6th ed.). Bristol, UK: Multilingual Matters.

Baker, S., Lesaux, N., Jayanthi, M., Dimino, J., Proctor, C. P., Morris, J., . . . Newman-Gonchar, R. (2014). *Teaching academic content and literacy to English learners in elementary and middle school (NCEE 2014-4012)*. Washington, DC: U.S. Department of Education.

Banks, J. (2018). *An introduction to multicultural education* (6th ed.). Boston: Allyn & Bacon.

Beck, I. L., McKeown, M. G., & Kucan, L. (2013). *Bringing words to life: Robust vocabulary instruction* (2nd ed.). New York: Guilford.

Beeman, K., & Urow, C. (2013). *Teaching for biliteracy: Strengthening bridges between languages*. Philadelphia: Caslon.

Berliner, D. C. (2013). Effects of inequality and poverty vs. teachers and schooling on America's youth. *Teachers College Record, 115*(12), 1–26.

Bhabha, H. K. (2004). *The location of culture*. New York: Routledge.

Biemiller, A. (2010). *Words worth teaching: Closing the vocabulary gap*. Columbus, OH: McGraw Hill.

Biemiller, A. (2011). Vocabulary: What words should we teach? *Better: Evidenced-Based Education, 3*(2), 10–11.

Biemiller, A., & Boote, C. (2006). An effective method for building meaning vocabulary in primary grades. *Journal of Educational Psychology, 98*(1), 44–62. doi:10.1037/0022 -0663.98.1.44

Blanton, C. K. (2007). *The strange career of bilingual education in Texas, 1836–1981*. College Station: Texas A&M University Press.

Boun, S., & Wright, W. E. (2013). K–12 schooling experiences of Southeast Asian American students. In R. Endo & X. L. Rong (Eds.), *Educating Asian Americans: Achievement, schooling, and identities* (pp. 75–101). Charlotte, NC: Information Age.

Bracey, G. W. (2007). *What's the value of growth measures?* Jamaica Plain, MA: FairTest: National Center for Fair and Open Testing.

Brisk, M. E., & Parra, M. O. (2018). Mainstream classrooms as engaging spaces for emergent bilinguals: SFL theory, catalyst for change. In R. Harmon (Ed.), *Bilingual learners and social equity: Critical approaches to systemic functional linguistics* (pp. 127–151). Dordrecht, The Netherlands: Springer.

Brown v. Board of Education of Topeka, 347 U.S. 483 (1954).

Brown, H. D. (2018). *Language assessment: Principles and classroom practices* (3rd ed.). New York: Pearson.

Bucholtz, M., & Lee, J. S. (2017). Language and culture as sustenance. In D. Paris & H. S. Alim (Eds.), *Culturally sustaining pedagogies: Teaching for learning and justice in a changing world* (pp. 43–59). New York: Teachers College Press.

Bunch, G. C. (2014). The language of ideas and the language of display: Reconceptualizing "academic language" in linguistically diverse classrooms. *International Multilingual Research Journal, 8,* 70–86.

Burr, E., Haas, E., & Ferriere, K. (2015). *Identifying and supporting English learner students with learning disabilities: Key issues in the literature and state practice*. Washington, DC: U.S. Department of Education, Institute of Education Sciences, National Center for Education Evaluation and Regional Assistance, Regional Educational Laboratory West. Retrieved from https://ies.ed.gov/ncee/edlabs/regions/west /pdf/REL_2015086.pdf

Byram, M. (1997). *Teaching and assessing intercultural communicative competence*. Clevedon, UK: Multilingual Matters.

Calderón, M. (2013). *CCSS and effective instruction for ELs: A whole school approach*. Paper presented at the Common Core State Standards and English Learners [Online Webinar]. Washington, DC: NCELA.

Calderón, M., & Slakk, S. (2018). *Teaching reading to English language learners, grades 6–12: A framework for improving achievement in the content areas* (2nd ed.). Thousand Oaks, CA: Sage.

Calderón, M., & Soto, I. (2017). *Vocabulary in context*. Thousand Oaks, CA: Corwin.

California Department of Education. (2014). *California English language development standards: Kindergarten through grade 12* [Electronic version]. Retrieved from https://www.cde.ca.gov/sp/el/er/documents/eldstnds publication14.pdf

Calkins, L. (2000). *The art of teaching reading*. Boston: Pearson/Allyn & Bacon.

Canagarajah, S. (2015). Clarifying the relationship between translingual practice and L2 writing: Addressing learner identities. *Applied Linguistics Review, 6*(4), 415–440.

Canale, M., & Swain, M. (1980). Theoretical bases of communicative approaches to second language teaching and testing. *Applied Linguistics, 1*(1), 1–47.

Capps, R., Fix, M., Murray, J., Ost, J., Passel, J. S., & Herwantoro, S. (2006). *The new demography of America's schools: Immigration and the No Child Left Behind Act* [Electronic version].Washington, DC: Urban Institute.

Carreira, M., & Chik, C. H. (2018). Making the case for heritage language instruction: A guide to meeting the needs of learners in the classroom and beyond. In S. Bauckus & S. Kresin (Eds.), *Connecting languages and cultures: A heritage language festscrift in honor of Olga Kagan* (pp. 3–26). Bloomington: Slavica Publishers – Indiana University.

Castagno, A., & McCarty, T. L. (2018). *The anthropology of education policy: Ethnographic inquiries into policy as sociocultural processes*. New York: Routledge.

Castañeda v. Pickard, 648 F.2d 989 (5th Cir. 1981).

Centers for Disease Control and Prevention. (2018). Childhood obesity facts. Retrieved from https://www.cdc .gov/obesity/data/childhood.html

Cervantes-Soon, C. G., Dorner, L., Palmer, D., Heiman, D., Schwerdtfeger, R., & Choi, J. (2017). Combating inequalities in two-way language immersion programs: Toward critical consciousness in bilingual education spaces. *Review of Research in Education, 41*, 403–427. doi:10.3102/0091732 X17690120

Cervetti, G. N., & Pearson, D. P. (2018). Reading and understanding science texts. In A. L. Bailey, C. A. Maher, & L. C. Wilkinson (Eds.), *Language, literacy, and learning in the STEM disciplines: How language counts for English learners* (pp. 79–100). New York: Routledge.

Chamot, A. U. (2009). *CALLA handbook: Implementing the Cognitive Academic Language Learning Approach* (2nd ed.). Boston: Pearson.

Chapin, S. H., O'Connor, C., & Anderson, N. C. (2009). *Classroom discussions: Using math talk to help students learn* (2nd ed.). Sausalito, CA: Math Solutions.

Chik, C., & Wright, W. E. (2017). Overcoming the obstacles: Vietnamese and Khmer Heritage Language Programs in California. In O. Kagan, M. Carreira, & C. Chik (Eds.), *A handbook on heritage language education: From innovation to program building* (pp. 222–236). New York: Routledge.

Christiansen, M. H., & Chater, N. (2017). Towards an integrated science of language. *Nature Human Behavior, 1*(Article #0163), 1–4.

Cohan, A., & Honigsfeld, A. (2017). Students with interrupted formal education (SIFEs): Actionable practices. *NABE Journal of Research and Practice, 8*(1), 166–175.

Collins, J. (2013). *Collins Writing Program*. The Writing Site. Retrieved from http://www.collinsed.com/5types.htm

Combs, M. C., Evans, C., Fletcher, T., Parra, E., & Jiménez, A. (2005). Bilingualism for the children: Implementing a dual-language program in an English-only state. *Educational Policy, 19*(5), 701–728.

Common Core State Standards Initiative. (2010). *Common core state standards for English language arts and literacy in history/social studies, science, and technical subjects*. Retrieved from http://www.corestandards.org/assets /CCSSI_ELA%20Standards.pdf

Cook, G., Linquanti, R., Chinen, M., & Jung, H. (2012). *Exploring approaches to setting English language proficiency performance criteria and monitoring English learner progress. National evaluation of Title III implementation supplemental report*. Washington, DC: U.S. Department of Education.

Corson, D. (1999). *Language policy in schools: A resource for teachers and administrators*. Mahwah, NJ: Lawrence Erlbaum.

Corson, D. (2001). *Language diversity and education*. Mahwah, NJ: Lawrence Erlbaum.

Council of Chief State School Officers (CCSSO). (2012). *Framework for English Language Proficiency Development Standards corresponding to the Common Core State Standards and Next Generation Science Standards*. Washington, DC: Author.

Council of Chief State School Officers (CCSSO). (2014). English language proficiency (ELP) standards. Retrieved from http://www.elpa21.org/sites/default/files/Final%20 4_30%20ELPA21%20Standards_1.pdf

Coxhead, A. (2000). A new academic word list. *TESOL Quarterly, 34*(2), 213–238.

Crandall, J. A. (1981). *Teaching the Spanish-speaking child: A practical guide*. Washington, DC: Center for Applied Linguistics.

Crawford, J. (2012). *Good news and bad news: Educating English learners in the age of Obama*. Paper presented at the National Association for Bilingual Education, Dallas, TX.

Crawford, J. (2015). *Educating English learners: Language diversity in the classroom* (5th ed., Kindle version). Portland, OR: DiversityLearningK12.

Crawford, J., & Krashen, S. (2015). *English learners in American classrooms: 101 questions, 101 answers* (Updated ed.). Portland, OR: DiversityLearningK12.

Crawford, J., & Reyes, S. A. (2015). *The trouble with SIOP.* Portland, OR: Institute for Language and Education Policy

Crystal, D. (2001). *A dictionary of language* (2nd ed.). Chicago: University of Chicago Press.

Crystal, D. (2008). *txtng: The gr8 db8.* New York: Oxford University Press.

Crystal, D. (2010). *The Cambridge encyclopedia of language* (3rd ed.). Cambridge, UK: Cambridge University Press.

Cumming, A. (2016). Theoretical orientations to L2 writing. In R. M. Manchón & P. K. Matsuda (Eds.), *Handbook of second and foreign language writing* (pp. 65–90). Boston: De Gruyter Mouton.

Cummins, J. (2008). BICS and CALP: Empirical and theoretical status of the distinction. In B. Street & N. Hornberger (Eds.), *Encyclopedia of language and education: Vol. 2. Literacy* (2nd ed.), pp. 71–83. New York: Springer.

Cummins, J. (2012). How long does it take for an English language learner to become proficient in a second language? In E. Hamayan & R. Freeman (Eds.), *English language learners at school: A guide for administrators* (2nd ed.) (pp. 37–39). Philadelphia: Caslon.

Cummins, J. (2017). Teaching for transfer in multilingual school contexts. In O. García, A. Lin, & S. May (Eds.), Bilingual and multilingual education. Encyclopedia of language and education (3rd ed., pp. 103–115). New York: Springer.

Cummins, J., Bismilla, V., Chow, P., Cohen, S., Giampapa, F., Leoni, L., Sandhu, P., & Sastri, P. (2005). Affirming identity in multilingual classrooms. *Educational Leadership, 63*(1), 38–43.

Cummins, J., Brown, K., & Sayers, D. (2007). *Literacy, technology, and diversity: Teaching for success in changing times.* Boston: Pearson/Allyn & Bacon.

Custodio, B. K., & O'Loughlin, J. B. (2017). *Students with interrupted formal education: Bridging where they are and what they need.* Thousand Oaks, CA: Corwin.

Davis, J. L. (2010). Danevang, Texas. In *The handbook of Texas.* Retrieved from https://tshaonline.org/handbook/online/articles/hnd04

D'Brot, J. (2017). *Considerations for including growth in ESSA accountability systems.* Washington, DC: Council of Chief State School Officers.

de Cohen, C. C., Deterding, N., & Clewell, B. C. (2005). *Who's left behind? Immigrant children in high and low LEP schools.* Washington, DC: Urban Institute.

de Jong, E. J. (2011). *Foundations for multilingualism in education: From principles to practice.* Philadelphia: Caslon.

de Jong, E. J., Gort, M., & Cobb, C. D. (2005). Bilingual education within the context of English-only policies: Three districts' response to Question 2 in Massachusetts. *Educational Policy, 19*(4), 595–620.

Del Valle, S. (2003). *Language rights and the law in the United States: Finding our voices.* Clevedon, UK: Multilingual Matters.

de Oliveira, L. C., & Avalos, M. A. (2018). Critical SFL praxis among teacher candidates: Using systemic functional linguistics in K–12 teacher education. In R. Harmon (Ed.), *Bilingual learners and social equity: Critical approaches to systemic functional linguistics* (pp. 109–123). Dordrecht, The Netherlands: Springer.

de Oliveira, L. C., & Obenchain, K. M. (2018). Introduction. In L. C. de Oliveira & K. M. Obenchain (Eds.), *Teaching history and social studies to English language learners: Preparing pre- and in-service teachers* (pp. 1–6). New York: Palgrave Macmillan.

de Oliveira, L. C., & Obenchain, K. M. (Eds.). (2018). *Teaching history and social studies to English language learners: Preparing pre- and in-service teachers.* New York: Palgrave Macmillan.

de Oliveira, L. C., & Silva, T. (Eds.). (2016). *Second language writing in elementary classrooms: Instructional issues, content-area writing, and teacher education.* New York: Palgrave Macmillan.

Diaz-Rico, L. T. (2017). *The crosscultural, language, and academic development handbook: A complete K–12 reference guide* (6th ed.). Boston: Pearson/Allyn & Bacon.

DiCerbo, P. A., Anstrom, K. A., Baker, L. L., & Rivera, C. (2014). A Review of the Literature on Teaching Academic English to English Language Learners. *Review of Educational Research, 84*(3), 446–482. doi:10.3102/0034654314532695

Dobb, F. (2004). *Essential elements of effective science instruction for English learners* (2nd ed.) [Electronic version]. Los Angeles: California Science Project.

Dor, D. (2015). *The instruction of imagination: Language as a social communication technology.* Oxford, UK: Oxford University Press.

Doran, L. (2017). Growth accountability measures continue ascendency under ESSA. Retrieved from InsideSources: http://www.insidesources.com/growth-accountability-measures-essa/

Dove, M. G., & Honigsfeld, A. (2017). *Co-teaching for English learners: A guide to collaborative planning, instruction, assessment, and reflection* Thousand Oaks, CA: Corwin.

Dual Language Schools.org, 2019.

Duran, C. S. (2017). *Language and literacy in refugee families.* London, UK: Palgrave Macmillan.

Dutro, S., & Kinsella, K. (2010). English language development: Issues and implementation in grades 6–12. In *Improving education for English learners: Research-based approaches.* Sacramento, CA: California Department of Education.

Echevarria, J., & Graves, A. (2014). *Sheltered content instruction: Teaching English language learners with diverse abilities* (5th ed.). Boston: Pearson/Allyn & Bacon.

Echevarria, J., Short, D., & Powers, K. (2006). School reform and standards-based education: An instructional model for English language learners. *Journal of Educational Research, 99*(4), 195–211.

Echevarria, J., Vogt, M., & Short, D. J. (2017). *Making content comprehensible for English learners: The SIOP model* (5th ed.). Boston: Pearson.

Economic Policy Institute. (2010). *Problems with the use of student test scores to evaluate teachers.* Washington, DC: Author.

Educational Testing Service. (2012). *Coming together to raise achievement: New assessments for the Common Core State Standards.* Princeton, NJ: Center for K–12 Assessment & Performance Management at ETS.

Edwards, J. (2013). Foundations of bilingualism and multilingualism. In T. K. Bhatia & W. C. Ritchie (Eds.), *Handbook of bilingualism* (2nd ed.) (pp. 5–25). Malden, MA: Blackwell.

EngageNY. (2013). *NYS Bilingual Common Core Initiative: Theoretical foundations.* Retrieved from http://www.engageny.org/sites/default/files/resource/attachments/nysbcci-theoretical-foundations.pdf

Escamilla, K., Butvilofsky, S., & Hopewell, S. (2017). What gets lost when English-only writing assessment is used to assess writing proficiency in Spanish-English emerging bilingual learners? *International Multilingual Research Journal,* 1–16. doi:10.1080/19313152.2016.1273740

Escamilla, K., Hopewell, S., & Butvilofsky, S. (2013). *Biliteracy from the start: Literacy squared in action.* Philadelphia: Caslon.

Espinoza-Herold, M., & González-Carriedo, R. (2017). *Issues in Latino education: Race, school culture, and the politics of American success.* New York: Routledge.

Everett, D. L. (2008). *Don't sleep, there are snakes: Life and language in the Amazonian jungle.* New York: Random House.

Everett, D. L. (2017). *How language began: The story of humanity's greatest invention.* New York: Liveright.

Fagan, J. F., & Holland, C. R. (2002). Equal opportunity and racial differences in IQ. *Intelligence, 30*(4), 361–387.

Faltis, C., & Ramírez-Marín, F. (2015). Secondary bilingual education: Cutting the Gordian knot. In W. E. Wright,

S. Boun, & O. García (Eds.), *Handbook of bilingual and multilingual education* (pp. 334–351). Malden, MA: Wiley-Blackwell.

Farrington v. Tokushige, 273 U.S. 284 (1927).

Faulkner-Bond, M., Waring, S., Forte, E., Crenshaw, R. L., Tindle, K., & Beklnap, B. (2012). *Language instruction educational programs (LIEPs): A review of the foundational literature.* Washington, DC: U.S. Department of Education.

Ferris, D. R., & Hedgcock, J. (2014). *Teaching L2 composition: Purpose, process, practice* (3rd ed.). New York: Routledge.

Field, R. (2008). Identity, community and power in bilingual education. In J. Cummins & N. H. Hornberger (Eds.), *Encyclopedia of language and education: Vol. 5: Bilingual Education* (2nd ed.), pp. 77–89. New York: Springer.

Field, R., & Menken, K. (2015). What might the process of language education policy development look like at the district and school levels relative to Common Core State Standards? In G. Valdés, K. Menken, & M. Castro (Eds.), *Common Core, English language learners, and equity: A guide for all educators.* Philadelphia: Caslon.

Fillmore, L. W. (1991). When learning a second language means losing the first. *Early Childhood Research Quarterly, 6*(3), 323–346.

Fillmore, L. W. (2013). *English learners and the Common Core: A fighting chance to learn.* Paper presented at the Common Core State Standards and English Learners (Webinar). Washington, DC: National Clearinghouse for English Language Acquisition.

Fillmore, L. W. (2014). English language learners at the crossroads of educational reform. *TESOL Quarterly, 48*(3), 624–632. doi:10.1002/tesq.174

Fillmore, L. W., & Snow, C. E. (2018). What teachers need to know about language. In C. T. Adger, C. E. Snow, & D. Christian (Eds.), *What teachers need to know about language* (2nd ed., pp. 1–51). Washington, DC: Center for Applied Linguistics.

Finegan, E. (2012). *Language: Its structure and use* (6th ed.). Boston: Wadsworth/Cengage Learning.

Fish, J. M. (Ed.). (2002). *Race and intelligence: Separating science from myth.* Mahwah, NJ: Lawrence Erlbaum.

Flores v. Arizona, 172 F. Supp. 2d 1225 (D. Ariz. 2000).

Flores, N., & Beardsmore, H. B. (2015). Programs and structures in bilingual and multilingual education. In W. E. Wright, S. Boun, & O. García (Eds.), *Handbook of bilingual and multilingual education* (pp. 205–222). Malden, MA: Wiley-Blackwell.

Folse, K. S. (2006). *The art of teaching speaking: Research and pedagogy for the ESL/EFL classroom* (4th ed.). Ann Arbor: University of Michigan Press.

Folse, K. S. (2011). Applying L2 lexical research findings in ESL teaching. *TESOL Quarterly, 45*(2), 362–369. doi:10 .5054/tq.2010.254529

Fountas, I. C., & Pinnell, G. S. (2006). *Teaching for comprehending and fluency: Thinking, talking, and writing about reading, K–8.* Portsmouth, NH: Heinemann.

Fountas, I. C., & Pinnell, G. S. (2017). *Guided reading: Responsive teaching across the grades.* Portsmouth, NH: Heinemann.

Fox, J. (2017). Using portfolios for assessment/alternative assessment. In E. G. Shohamy, I. Or, & S. May (Eds.), *Language testing and assessment, Encyclopedia of language and education* (3rd ed., pp. 135–147). Cham, Switzerland: Springer International.

Francis, D. J., Rivera, M., Lesaux, N., Kieffer, M., & Rivera, H. (2006). *Practical guidelines for the education of English language learners: Researched-based recommendations for the use of accommodations in large-scale assessments.* Portsmouth, NH: Center on Instruction.

Frank, S. L., Bod, R., & Christiansen, M. H. (2012). How hierarchical is language use? *Proceedings of the Royal Society B, 279*(1747), 4522–4531. doi:10.1098/rspb.2012 .1741

Freedom Writers. (1999). *The Freedom Writers diary: How a teacher and 150 teens used writing to change themselves and the world around them.* With E. Gruwell. New York: Doubleday.

Freeman, D. E., & Freeman, Y. S. (2011). *Between worlds: Access to second language acquisition* (3rd ed.). Portsmouth, NH: Heinemann.

Freeman, D. E., & Freeman, Y. S. (2014). *Essential linguistics: What you need to know to teach reading, ESL, spelling, phonics, and grammar* (2nd ed.). Portsmouth, NH: Heinemann.

Freeman, Y. S., & Freeman, D. E. (2000). Preview, view, review: An important strategy in multilingual classrooms. *NABE News, 24*(2), 20–21.

Freeman, Y. S., & Freeman, D. E. (2008). English language learners: Who are they? How can teachers support them? In Y. S. Freeman, D. E. Freeman, & R. Ramirez (Eds.), *Diverse learners in the mainstream classroom: Strategies for supporting all students across content areas* (pp. 31–58). Portsmouth, NH: Heinemann.

Freire, J. A., Valdez, V. E., & Delvan, M. G. (2017). The (dis) inclusion of Latina/o interests from Utah's dual language education boom. *Journal of Latinos and Education, 16*(4), 276–289.

Freire, P. (1993). *Pedagogy of the oppressed* (20th Anniversary ed.). New York: Continuum.

Funk, A. (2012). *The languages of New York State: A CUNY-NYSIEB guide for educators.* Retrieved from http:// www.nysieb.ws.gc.cuny.edu/files/2012/07/NYSLanguage Profiles.pdf

Gandara, P., & Hopkins, M. (Eds.). (2010). *Forbidden language: English learners and restrictive language policies.* New York: Teachers College Press.

García, E. E., & Markos, A. M. (2015). Early childhood education and dual language learners. In W. E. Wright, S. Boun, & O. García (Eds.), *The handbook of bilingual and multilingual education* (pp. 301–318). Malden, MA: Wiley Blackwell.

García, O. (2009a). *Bilingual education in the 21st century: A global perspective.* Malden, MA: Wiley-Blackwell.

García, O. (2009b). Emergent bilinguals and TESOL: What's in a name? *TESOL Quarterly, 43*(2), 322–326.

García, O. (2017). Translanguaging in schools: Subiendo y bajando, bajando y subiendo as afterword. *Journal of Language, Identity & Education, 16*(4), 256–263. doi:10 .1080/15348458. 2017.1329657

García, O., Johnson, S. I., & Seltzer, K. (2016). *The translanguaging classroom: Leveraging student bilingualism for learning.* Philadelphia: Caslon.

García, O., & Kleyn, T. (Eds.). (2016). *Translanguaging with multilingual students: Learning from classroom moments.* New York: Routledge.

García, O., & Lin, A. (2017). Translanguaging in bilingual education. In O. García, A. Lin, & S. May (Eds.), *Encyclopedia of language and education: Vol. 5. Bilingual and multilingual education* (3rd ed.), pp. 117–130. Cham, Switzerland: Springer International.

García, O., & Li Wei (2014). *Translanguaging: Language, bilingualism, and education.* New York: Palgrave Macmillan.

García, O., & Li Wei. (2015). Translanguaging, bilingualism, and bilingual education. In W. E. Wright, S. Boun, & O. García (Eds.), *Handbook of bilingual and multilingual education* (pp. 223–240). Malden, MA: John Wiley & Sons.

Gardner, H. (2011). *Frames of mind: The theory of multiple intelligences* (3rd ed.). New York: Basic.

Gass, S. M. (2018). *Input, interaction, and the second language learner* (Routledge Linguistics Classics ed.). New York: Routledge.

Gee, J. P. (2012). *Social linguistics and literacies: Ideology in discourses* (4th ed.). New York: Routledge.

Gee, J. P. (2014). Decontexualized language: A problem, not a solution. *International Multilingual Research Journal, 8*(1), 9–23. doi 10.1080/19313152.2014.852424

Genesee, F., Lindholm-Leary, K., Saunders, W. M., & Christian, D. (2005). English language learners in U.S. schools: An overview of research findings. *Journal of Education for Students Placed at Risk, 10*(4), 363–385.

Genesee, F., LindholmLeary, K., Saunders, W. M., & Christian, D. (2006). *Educating English language learners: A synthesis of research evidence.* New York: Cambridge University Press.

Geva, E. (2006). Second-language oral proficiency and second-language literacy. In D. August & T. Shanahan (Eds.), *Developing literacy in second-language learners: Report of the National Literacy Panel on Language-Minority Children and Youth* (pp. 123–152). Mahwah, NJ: Lawrence Erlbaum.

Gewertz, C. (2018). In the testing arena, a wait-and-see attitude as states eye ESSA's offer of new leeway. *Education Week, 37*(5), 21–22.

Gibbons, P. (2014). *Scaffolding language, scaffolding learning: Teaching English language learners in the mainstream classroom* (2nd ed.). Portsmouth, NH: Heinemann.

Glovin, D., & Evans, D. (2006, December). How test companies fail your kids. *Bloomberg Markets*, 126–142.

Goldenberg, C. (2013). Unlocking the research on English learners. *American Educator, 37*(2), 4–38.

Goldschmidt, P. (2018). *Handbook for developing and monitoring the English language proficiency indicator and English learner progress.* Washington, DC: Council of Chief State School Officers. Retrieved from https://ccsso.org/sites/default/files/2018-03/Guide%20to%20Monitoring%20and%20Evaluating%20EL%20Indicator%20Final%202018%2003%2004.pdf

Gollnick, D. M., & Chin, P. C. (2016). *Multicultural education in a pluralistic society* (10th ed.). Upper Saddle River, NJ: Merrill Prentice Hall.

Gomez v. Illinois State Board of Education, 811 F.2d1030 (7th Cir. 1987).

Gómez, L., Freeman, D. E., & Freeman, Y. S. (2005). Dual language education: A promising 50–50 model. *Bilingual Research Journal, 29*(1), 145–164.

González, N., Moll, L. C., & Amanti, C. (Eds.). (2005). *Funds of knowledge: Theorizing practices in households, communities, and classrooms.* Mahwah, NJ: Lawrence Erlbaum.

Gort, M. (2012). Code-switching patterns in writing-related talk of young emergent bilinguals. *Journal of Literacy Research, 44*(1), 45–75.

Gottlieb, M. H. (2016). *Assessing English language learners: Bridges from language proficiency to academic achievement* (2nd ed.). Thousand Oaks, CA: Corwin.

Gottlieb, M. H., & Nguyen, D. (2007). *Assessment and accountability in language education programs.* Philadelphia: Caslon.

Gould, S. J. (1981). *The mismeasure of man.* New York: Norton.

Grabe, W., & Stoller, F. L. (2013). *Teaching and researching reading* (2nd ed.). New York: Routledge.

Graves, M. F. (2015). Building a vocabulary program that really could make a significant contribution to students becoming college and career ready. In D. P. Pearson & E. H. Hiebert (Eds.), *Research-based practices for teaching Common Core literacy* (pp. 123–142). New York: Teachers College Press.

Haas, E., Huang, M., Tran, L., & Yu, A. (2016). *The achievement progress of English learner students in Nevada.* Washington, DC: U.S. Department of Education, Institute of Educational Sciences, National Center for Education Evaluation and Regional Assistance, Regional Educational Laboratory West.

Hakuta, K. (1986). *The mirror of language: The debate on bilingualism.* New York: Basic.

Hakuta, K. (2011). Educating language minority students and affirming their equal rights: Research and practical perspectives. *Educational Researcher, 40*(4), 163–174. doi:10.3102/0013189X11404943

Hakuta, K., Butler, Y. G., & Witt, D. (2000). *How long does it take English learners to attain proficiency?* Santa Barbara: University of California Linguistic Minority Research Institute.

Haladyna, T. (2002). *Essentials of standardized testing.* Boston: Pearson/Allyn & Bacon.

Halliday, M. A. K., & Matthiessen, C. M. I. M. (2004). *An introduction to functional grammar* (3rd ed.). New York: Oxford University Press.

Hamayan, E. (2012). What is the role of culture in language learning? In E. Hamayan & R. F. Field (Eds.), *English language learners at school: A guide for administrators* (2nd ed., pp. 47–49). Philadelphia: Caslon.

Hamayan, E., Marler, B., SánchezLópez, C., & Damico, J. (2013). *Special education considerations for English language learners: Delivering a continuum of services* (2nd ed.). Philadelphia: Caslon.

Haney, W. (2002). Revealing illusions of educational progress: Texas high-stakes tests and minority student performance. In Z. F. Beykont (Ed.), *The power of culture: Teaching across language difference.* Boston: Harvard Education.

Hansen-Thomas, H., & Langman, J. (forthcoming). *Engaging English learners in mathematics classrooms: Teaching through talking.* Philadelphia: Caslon.

Harold, B. (2018). Tenn. struggles to clean up huge online testing mess. *Education Week, 37*(30), 8–9.

Harris, D. (2011). *Value-added measures in education: What every educator needs to know.* Cambridge, MA: Harvard Education.

Hart, B., & Risley, T. (1995). *Meaningful differences in the everyday experiences of young American children.* Baltimore, MD: Paul H. Brookes.

Hartlep, N. (2017). Special issue editor's introduction: 50 years of model minority stereotype research. *Journal of Southeast Asian American Education and Advancement, 12*(2), 1–8.

Hartshorne, J. K., Tenenbaum, J. B., & Pinker, S. (2018). A critical period for second language acquisition: Evidence from 2/3 million English speakers. *Cognition* (online first). doi:10.1016/j.cognition.2018.04.007

Haycock, K. (2006). No more invisible kids. *Educational Leadership, 64*(1), 38–42.

Heath, S. B. (1982). What no bedtime story means: Narrative skills at home and school. *Language in Society, 11*(1), 49–76.

Heath, S. B. (1983). *Ways with words: Language, life, and work in communities and classrooms.* New York: Cambridge University Press.

Heineke, A. J. (2017). *Restrictive language policy in practice: English learners in Arizona.* Bristol, UK: Multilingual Matters.

Helman, L. (Ed.) (2017). *Literacy development with English learners: Research-based instruction in grades K–6* (2nd ed.). New York: Guilford.

Herrera, S. G., Cabral, R. M., & Murry, K. G. (2013). *Assessment accommodations for classroom teachers of culturally and linguistically diverse students* (2nd ed.). Boston: Pearson/Allyn & Bacon.

Herrnstein, R. J., & Murray, C. A. (1994). *The bell curve: Intelligence and class structure in American life.* New York: Free Press.

Hill, E. G. (2004). *A look at the progress of English learner students.* Sacramento, CA: Legislative Analyst's Office.

Hopewell, S. (2011). Leveraging bilingualism to accelerate English reading comprehension. *International Journal of Bilingual Education and Bilingualism, 14*(5), 603–620.

Horwitz, E. K. (2013). *Becoming a language teacher: A practical guide to second language learning and teaching* (2nd ed.). Boston: Pearson/Allyn & Bacon.

Hout, M. (2002). Test scores, education, and poverty. In J. M. Fish (Ed.), *Race and intelligence: Separating science from myth* (pp. 329–354). Mahwah, NJ: Lawrence Erlbaum.

Howard, E. R., Lindholm-Leary, K. J., Rogers, D., Olague, N., Medina, J., Kennedy, B., Sugarman, J., & Christian, D. (2018). *Guiding principles for dual language education* (3rd ed.). Washington, DC: Center for Applied Linguistics.

Huffman, T. (2018). *Tribal strengths and native education: Voices from the reservation classroom.* Amherst: University of Massachusetts Press.

Hymes, D. (1972). On communicative competence. In J. B. Pride & J. Holmes (Eds.), *Sociolinguistics.* Harmondsworth, UK: Penguin.

Institute of Education Sciences. (2008). *Reading First impact study: Interim report.* Washington, DC: U.S. Department of Education. Retrieved from http://ies.ed.gov/ncee/pdf/20084016.pdf

Jaumont, F. (2017). *The bilingual revolution: The future of education is in two languages.* Brooklyn, NY: TBR Books.

Jencks, C., & Phillips, M. (Eds.). (1998). *The black-white test score gap*. Washington, DC: Brookings Institution Press.

Jensen, A. R. (1995). The differences are real. In R. Jacoby & N. Glauberman (Eds.), *The bell curve debate: History, documents, opinions* (pp. 617–629). New York: Times Books.

Jensen, A. R. (1998). *The g factor: The science of mental ability*. Westport, CT: Praeger.

Jesness, J. (2014). *Teaching English language learners K–12: A quick-start for the new teacher* (Reissue edition). New York: Skyhorse.

Kagan, S. (2009). *Kagan Cooperative Learning*. San Clemente, CA: Kagan Cooperative Learning.

Kane, M. T. (2017). *Measurement error and bias in value-added models* (Research Report ETS RR-17-25). Princeton, NJ: Educational Testing Service.

Kendall, J., & Khuon, O. (2006). *Writing sense: Integrated reading and writing lessons for English language learners*. Portland, ME: Stenhouse.

Kern, R., & Kramsch, C. (2014). Communicative grammar and communicative competence. In C. A. Chapell (Ed.), *The encyclopedia of applied linguistics* (pp. 1–6). Boston: Wiley-Blackwell. doi:10.1002/9781405198431.wbeal1433

Kersaint, G., Thompson, D. R., & Petkova, M. (2013). *Teaching mathematics to English language learners* (2nd ed.). New York: Routledge.

Kloss, H. (1998). *The American bilingual tradition*. Washington, DC, and McHenry, IL: Center for Applied Linguistics and Delta Systems. (Original work published 1977.)

Krashen, S. D. (1985). *The input hypothesis: Issues and implications*. London: Longman.

Krashen, S. D. (1998). Comprehensible output. *System, 26*, 175–182.

Krashen, S. (2003). The (lack of) experimental evidence of Accelerated Reader. *Journal of Children's Literature, 29*(2), 16–30.

Krashen, S. D. (2004a, November). *Applying the comprehension hypothesis: Some suggestions*. Paper presented at the 13th International Symposium and Book Fair on Language Teaching (English Teachers Association of the Republic of China), Taipei, Taiwan. Retrieved from http://www.sdkrashen.com/content/articles/eta_paper.pdf

Krashen, S. D. (2004b, April). *Free voluntary reading: New research, applications, and controversies*. Paper presented at the RELC conference, Singapore. Retrieved from http://www.sdkrashen.com/content/articles/singapore.pdf

Krashen, S. D. (2004c). *The power of reading: Insights from the research* (2nd ed.). Portsmouth, NH: Heinemann.

Krashen, S. D. (2012). *How much testing?* Retrieved from http://dianeravitch.net/2012/07/25/stephen-krashen-how-much-testing/

Krashen, S. D. (2014). *Why invest in libraries*. Retrieved from http://skrashen.blogspot.com/2014/02/why-invest-in-libraries.html

Krashen, S. D. (2017). The case for comprehensible input. *Language Magazine*. Retrieved from https://www.languagemagazine.com/2017/07/17/case-for-comprehension/

Krashen, S. (2018). The conduit hypothesis: How reading leads to academic language competence. *Language Magazine*. Retrieved from http://www.sdkrashen.com/content/articles/2018_the_conduit_hypothesis.pdf

Krashen, S. D., & Terrell, T. (1983). *The natural approach: Language acquisition in the classroom*. San Francisco, CA: Alemany.

Kroll, B. (1993). Teaching writing is teaching reading: Training the new teacher of ESL composition. In J. G. Carson & I. Leki (Eds.), *Reading in the composition classroom: Second language perspectives* (pp. 61–84). Boston: Heinle and Heinle.

LaCelle-Peterson, M., & Rivera, C. (1994). Is it real for all kids? A framework for equitable assessment policies for English language learners. *Harvard Educational Review, 64*(1), 55–75.

Langman, J. (2008). Language socialization. In J. M. González (Ed.), *Encyclopedia of bilingual education* (pp. 489–493). Thousand Oaks, CA: Sage.

Langman, J., & Bayley, R. (2007). Untutored acquisition in content classrooms. In Z. Hua, P. Seedhouse, Li Wei, & V. Cook (Eds.), *Language learning and teaching as social interaction* (pp. 218–234). New York: Palgrave Macmillan.

Lapp, D., Moss, B., Grant, M., & Johnson, K. (2015). *A close look at close reading: Teaching students to analyze complex texts*. Alexandria, VA: ASCD.

Lara-Alecio, R., Tong, F., Irby, B. J., Guerrero, C., Huerta, M., & Fan, Y. (2012). The effect of instructional intervention on middle school English learners' science and English reading achievement. *Journal of Research in Science Teaching, 49*(8), 987–1011. doi:10.1002/tea.21031

Lau v. Nichols, 414 U.S. 563 (1974).

Lauen, D. L., & Gaddis, S. M. (2012). Shining a light or fumbling in the dark? The effects of NCLB's subgroup-specific accountability on student achievement. *Educational Evaluation and Policy Analysis, 34*(2), 185–208. doi:10.3102/0162373711429989

Lawrence, J. F., White, C., & Snow, C. E. (2011). *Improving reading across subject areas with Word Generation* (CREATE Brief). Washington, DC: Center for Research on the Educational Achievement and Teaching of English Language Learners.

Lee, J. S., & Wright, W. E. (2014). The Rediscovery of heritage and community language education in the United States. *Review of Research in Education, 38*, 137–165.

Lee, O., Grapin, S., & Haas, A. (2018). How the NGSS science instructional shifts and language instructional shifts support each other for English learners: Talk in the science classroom. In A. L. Bailey, C. A. Maher, & L. C. Wilkinson (Eds.), *Language, literacy, and learning in the STEM disciplines: How language counts for English learners* (pp. 35–52). New York: Routledge.

Lee, O., Quinn, H., & Valdes, G. (2013). Science and language for English language learners in relation to Next Generation Science Standards and with implications for Common Core State Standards for English language arts and mathematics. *Educational Researcher, 42*(4), 223–233. doi:10.3102/0013189X13480524

Lesaux, N., & Geva, E. (2006). Synthesis: Development of literacy in language-minority students. In D. August & T. Shanahan (Eds.), *Developing literacy in second-language learners: Report of the National Literacy Panel on Language-Minority Children and Youth* (pp. 53–74). Mahwah, NJ: Lawrence Erlbaum.

Lightbown, P. M., & Spada, N. (2013). *How languages are learned* (4th ed.). New York: Oxford University Press.

Lin, A., & He, P. (2017). Translanguaging as dynamic activity flows in CLIL classrooms. *Journal of Language, Identity & Education, 16*(4), 228–244. doi:10.1080/15348458.2017.1328283

Lindholm-Leary, K., & Hernández, A. (2011). Achievement and language proficiency of Latino students in dual language programmes: Native English speakers, fluent English/previous ELLs, and current ELLs. *Journal of Multilingual and Multicultural Development, 32*(6), 531–545. doi:10.1080/01434632.2011.611596

Link, H., Gallo, S., & Wortham, S. E. F. (2017). The production of schoolchildren as enlightenment subjects. *American Education Research Journal, 54*(5), 834–867.

Long, M. H. (2018). Interaction in L2 classrooms. In J. I. Liontas & M. DelliCarpini (Eds.), *The TESOL encyclopedia of English language teaching*. Hoboken, NJ: John Wiley & Sons. doi:10.1002/9781118784235.eelt0233

Lyster, R., & Genesee, F. (2012). Immersion education. In C. A. Chapelle (Ed.), *The Encyclopedia of Applied Linguistics*. Malden, MA: Wiley-Blackwell.

MacDonald, R., Boals, T., Castro, M., Cook, H. G., Lundberg, T., & White, P. A. (2015). *Formative language assessment for English learners: A four step process*. Portsmouth, NH: Heinemann.

MacSwan, J., & Rolstad, K. (2003). Linguistic diversity, schooling, and social class: Rethinking our conception of language proficiency in language minority education. In C. B. Paulston & R. Tucker (Eds.), *Sociolinguistics: Essential reading* (pp. 329–341). Oxford, UK: Blackwell.

MacSwan, J., Rolstad, K., & Glass, G. V. (2002). Do some schoolage children have no language? Some problems of construct validity in the PreLas Español. *Bilingual Research Journal, 26*(2), 213–238.

Mahoney, K. (2017). *The assessment of emergent bilinguals: Supporting English language learners.* Bristol, UK: Multilingual Matters.

Mahoney, K., Thompson, M., & MacSwan, J. (2005). *The condition of English language learners in Arizona: 2005.* Retrieved from http://www.terpconnect.umd.edu /~macswan/EPSL-0509-110-AEPI.pdf

Manchón, R. M., & Matsuda, P. K. (Eds.). (2016). *Handbook of second and foreign language writing.* Boston: De Gruyter Mouton.

Manning, M. S. (2001). Writing checklist. *Write away! A student guide to the writing process* [Online module]. Retrieved from http://cuip.uchicago.edu/%7Emmanning /2001/chklist.htm

Martin, J. R. (2002). Writing history: Construing time and value in discourses of the past. In M. J. Schleppegrell & M. C. Colombi (Eds.), *Developing advanced literacy in first and second languages: Meaning with power* (pp. 87–118). Mahwah, NJ: Lawrence Erlbaum.

Marzano, R. J., & Pickering, D. J. (2005). *Building academic vocabulary: Teacher's manual.* Alexandria, VA: Association for Supervision and Curriculum Development.

Massachusetts Language Opportunity Coalition. (2017). *LOOK Act.* Retrieved from https://languageopportunity .org/look-act/

Massachusetts State Department of Education. (1990). The condition of transitional bilingual education programs. *Annual report FY89.* Boston, MA: Author.

Maxwell, L. (2012). *Ed. dept. releases guide for states on English-language proficiency.* Retrieved from http://blogs .edweek.org/edweek/learning-the-language/2012/02/ed _dept_releases_guide_for_sta.html

McIntyre, E., Kyle, D., Chen, C.-T., Munoz, M., & Beldon, S. (2010). Teacher learning and ELL reading achievement in sheltered instruction classrooms: Linking professional development to student development. *Literacy Research and Instruction, 49*(4), 334–351.

McKinney, C., & Norton, B. (2008). Identity in language and literacy education. In B. Spolsky & F. M. Hult (Eds.), *The handbook of educational linguistics* (pp. 192–205). Malden, MA: Blackwell.

Menken, K. (2008). *English learners left behind: Standardized testing as language policy.* Clevedon, UK: Multilingual Matters.

Menken, K., & García, O. (2010). *Negotiating language policies in schools: Educators as policymakers.* New York: Routledge.

Mensh, E., & Mensh, H. (1991). *The IQ mythology: Class, race, gender, and inequality.* Carbondale: Southern Illinois University Press.

Messick, S. (1995). Standards of validity and the validity of standards in performance assessment. *Educational Measurement: Issues and Practices, 14*(4), 5–8.

Meyer v. Nebraska, 262 U.S. 390 (1923).

Migration Policy Institute (2016). Largest U.S. immigrant groups over time, 1960–present. Retrieved from https:// www.migrationpolicy.org/programs/data-hub/charts /largest-immigrant-groups-over-time

Mitchell, R., Myles, F., & Marsden, E. (2013). *Second language learning theories* (3rd ed.). New York: Routledge.

Moll, L. C. (Ed.). (2013). *L. S. Vygotsky and education.* New York: Routledge.

Morita-Mullaney, T. (2017). Borrowing legitimacy as English Learner (EL) Leaders: Indiana's 14-year history with English language proficiency standards. *Language Testing, 34*(2), 241–270. doi:10.1177/0265532216653430

Moschkovich, J. (2018). Talking to learn mathematics with understanding. In A. L. Bailey, C. A. Maher, & L. C. Wilkinson (Eds.), *Language, literacy, and learning in the STEM disciplines: How language counts for English learners* (pp. 13–34). New York: Routledge.

NAfME (National Association of Music Educators). (2018). *Summary statement: What students should know and be able to do in the arts.* Retrieved from: https://nafme.org/my -classroom/journals-magazines/nafme-online-publications /summary-statement-what-students-should-know-and-be -able-to-do-in-the-arts-2/

National Academies of Sciences, Engineering, and Medicine. (2017). *Promoting the educational success of children and youth learning English: Promising futures.* R. Takanishi & S. Le Menestrel (Eds.). Washington, DC: National Academies Press.

National Board for Professional Teaching Standards. (1998). *English as a new language standards for teachers of students age 3–18+.* Arlington, VA: Author.

National Center for Educational Statistics. (2016). Table 219.46. Public high school 4-year adjusted cohort graduation rate (ACGR), by selected student characteristics and state: 2010–11 through 2014–15. Retrieved from https://nces.ed.gov/programs/digest/d16/tables/dt16 _219.46.asp

National Center for Educational Statistics. (2017a). English language learners in public schools. Retrieved from https:// nces.ed.gov/programs/coe/pdf/coe_cgf.pdf

National Center for Educational Statistics. (2017b). *English language learner (ELL) students enrolled in public elementary and secondary schools, by state: Selected years, fall 2000 through fall 2015.* Retrieved from https://nces.ed.gov /programs/digest/d17/tables/dt17_204.20.asp

National Center for Educational Statistics. (2018). *English learners in public schools.* Retrieved from https://nces.ed .gov/programs/coe/indicator_cgf.asp

National Clearinghouse for English Language Acquisition (NCELA). (2018). Title III State Profiles. Retrieved from https://ncela.ed.gov/t3sis/index.php

National Council for Social Studies (NCSS). (n.d.). *Toolkit: Today's social studies . . . creating effective citizens.* Retrieved from https://www.socialstudies.org/advocacy/toolkit

National Education Association. (1966). *The invisible minority . . . pero no vencibles: Report of the NEA-Tucson Survey on the Teaching of Spanish to the Spanish-speaking.* Washington, DC: Department of Rural Education, National Education Association.

National Governors Association Center for Best Practices, & Council of Chief State School Officers. (2010). *Common Core State Standards.* Washington, DC: Author.

National Research Council. (2012). *A framework for K–12 science education: Practices, cross-cutting concepts, and core ideas.* Washington, DC: National Academies Press.

National Science Teachers Association (NSTA). (2000, July). *Multi-cultural science education.* NSTA Position Statement. Retrieved from http://www.nsta.org/about/positions/multi cultural.aspx

New London Group. (1996). A pedagogy of multiliteracies: Designing social futures. *Harvard Educational Review, 66*(1), 60–92.

Newton, J. M., Ferris, D. R., Goh, C. C. M., Grabe, W., Stoller, F. L., & Vanderbilt, L. (2018). *Teaching English to second language learners in academic contexts.* New York: Routledge.

NGSS Lead States. (2013). *Next Generation Science Standards: For states, by states.* Washington, DC: National Academies Press. Retrieved from http://www.nextgenscience.org/

Nichols, S., & Berliner, D. C. (2007). *Collateral damage: How high-stakes testing corrupts America's schools.* Cambridge, MA: Harvard Education Press.

Nisbett, R. E. (1998). Race, genetics, and IQ. In C. Jencks & M. Phillips (Eds.), *The black-white test score gap* (pp. 86–102). Washington, DC: Brookings Institution Press.

Norton, B. (2013). Identity and language learning: Extending the conversation (2nd ed.). Bristol, UK: Multilingual Matters.

Ochs, E., & Schieffelin, B. (1984). Language acquisition and socialization: Three developmental stories and their implications. In R. Schweder & R. LeVine (Eds.), *Culture theory: Essays in mind, self, and emotion* (pp. 276–320). New York: Cambridge University Press.

Ochs, E., & Schieffelin, B. (2017). Language socialization: An historical overview. In P. A. Duff & S. May (Eds.), *Language* socialization: *Encyclopedia of language and education* (3rd ed., pp. 3–16). Dordrecht, The Netherlands: Springer.

Office for Civil Rights. (2010). *Letter to AZ Superintendent of Public Instruction Tom Horne regarding OCR Case Number 09064006*. Retrieved from http://www.edweek.org/media/azella.pdf

Office of English Language Acquisition (OELA). (2012). *The biennial report to Congress on the implementation of the Title III State Formula Grant Program: School years 2006–2008*. Washington, DC: U.S. Department of Education.

Office of English Language Acquisition (OELA). (2017). Profiles of English learners. Retrieved from https://ncela.ed.gov/files/fast_facts/05-19-2017/ProfilesOfELs_Fast Facts.pdf

Office of English Language Acquisition (OELA). (2018a). Profiles of English learners. Retrieved from https://ncela.ed.gov/files/fast_facts/Profiles_of_ELs_4.12.18_MM_Final_Edit.pdf

Office of English Language Acquisition (OELA). (2018b). Languages spoken by English learners. Retrieved from https://ncela.ed.gov/files/fast_facts/FastFacts-Languages-Spoken-by-ELs-2018.pdf

Ohanian, S. (2002). *What happened to recess and why are our children struggling in kindergarten?* New York: McGraw Hill.

O'Malley, J. M., & Pierce, L. V. (1996). *Authentic assessment for English language learners: Practical approaches for teachers*. Reading, MA: Addison Wesley.

Ovando, C., & Combs, M. C. (2018). *Bilingual and ESL classrooms: Teaching in multicultural contexts* (6th ed.). New York: Rowman & Littlefield.

Palmer, D. K., Zuñiga, C. E., & Henderson, K. (2015). A dual language revolution in the United States? On the bumpy road from compensatory to enrichment education for bilingual children in Texas. In W. E. Wright, S. Boun, and O. García (Eds.), *Handbook of bilingual and multilingual education* (pp. 447–458). Malden, MA: Wiley-Blackwell.

Paris, D., & Alim, H. S. (Eds.). (2017). *Culturally sustaining pedagogies: Teaching and learning for justice in a changing world*. New York: Teachers College Press.

Park, M., Zong, J., & Batalova, J. (2018). *Growing superdiversity among young U.S. dual language learners and its implications*. Washington, DC: Migration Policy Institute. Retrieved from https://www.migrationpolicy.org/research/growing-superdiversity-among-young-us-dual-language-learners-and-its-implications

Pennington, M. (2010). *The 18 reasons not to use Accelerated Reader*. Retrieved from https://blog.penningtonpublishing.com/reading/the-18-reasons-not-to-use-accelerated-reader/

Peregoy, S. F., & Boyle, O. F. (2017). *Reading, writing, and learning in ESL: A resource book for teaching K–12 English learners* (7th ed.). Boston: Pearson/Allyn & Bacon.

Peske, H. G., & Haycock, K. (2006). *Teaching inequality: How poor and minority students are shortchanged on teacher quality*. Washington, DC: Education Trust.

Philips, S. U. (1983). *The invisible culture: Communication in classroom and community on the Warm Springs Indian reservation*. Prospect Heights, IL: Waveland.

Pienemann, M. (2015). An outline of processability theory and its relationship to other approaches to SLA. *Language Learning, 65*(1), 123–151. doi:10.1111/lang.12095

Poehner, M. E., Davin, K. J., & Lantolf, J. P. (2017). Dynamic assessment. In E. G. Shohamy, I. Or, & S. May (Eds.), *Language testing and assessment, Encyclopedia of language and education* (3rd ed., pp. 243–256). Cham, Switzerland: Springer International.

Pompa, D., & Hakuta, K. (2012). Critical policy levers for effective implementation of Common Core State Standards for ELLs. Retrieved from http://ell.stanford.edu/publication/critical-policy-levers-effective-implementation-common-core-state-standards-ells

Popham, W. J. (2017). *Classroom assessment: What teachers need to know* (8th ed.). Boston: Pearson.

Portes, A., & Rumbaut, R. G. (2014). *Immigrant America: A portrait* (4th ed.). Berkeley: University of California Press.

Poza, L., & Valdés, G. (2017). Assessing English language proficiency in the United States. In E. G. Shohamy, I. Or, & S. May (Eds.), *Language testing and assessment, Encyclopedia*

of language and education (3rd ed., pp. 427–440). Cham, Switzerland: Springer International.

Pray, L. (2003). An analysis of language assessments used in the referral and placement of language minority students into special education. *Dissertation Abstracts International, 64*(3), 766.

Pu, C. (2008). Chinese American children's bilingual and biliteracy development in heritage language and public schools. *Dissertation Abstracts International, 69*(7), 766.

Ramirez, J. D. (1992). Executive summary. *Bilingual Research Journal, 16*, 1–62.

Ravitch, D. (2013a). *Big business supports the Common Core*. Retrieved from http://dianeravitch.net/2013/02/13/15153/

Ravitch, D. (2013b). *Why I cannot support the Common Core Standards*. Retrieved from http://dianeravitch.net/2013/02/26/why-i-cannot-support-the-common-core-standards/

Reardon, S. F. (2011). The widening academic achievement gap between the rich and the poor: New evidence and possible explanations. In G. J. Duncan & R. J. Murnane (Eds.), *Whither opportunity?* (pp. 91–116). New York: Russell Sage Foundation.

Reiss, J. (2012). *102 content strategies for English language learners: Teaching academic success in grades 3–12* (2nd ed.). Boston: Pearson.

Richards, J. C., & Rodgers, T. S. (2014). *Approaches and methods in language teaching* (3rd ed.). New York: Cambridge University Press.

Rickford, J. R. (2005). Using the vernacular to teach the standard. In J. D. Ramirez, T. G. Wiley, G. de Klerk, E. Lee, & W. E. Wright (Eds.), *Ebonics: The urban education debate* (2nd ed.) (pp. 18–40). Clevedon, UK: Multilingual Matters.

Rivera, C., & Collum, E. (Eds.). (2006). *State assessment policy and practice for English language learners*. Mahwah, NJ: Lawrence Erlbaum.

Roberts, T. (2014). No so silent after all: Examination and analysis of the silent stage in childhood second language acquisition. *Early Childhood Research Quarterly, 29*, 22–40.

Rolstad, K. (2004). Rethinking academic language in second language instruction. In J. A. Cohen, K. T. McAlister, K. Rolstad, & J. MacSwan (Eds.), *ISB4: Proceedings of the 4th International Symposium on Bilingualism* (pp. 1993–1999). Somerville, MA: Cascadilla.

Rolstad, K. (2017). Second language instructional competence. *International Journal of Bilingual Education and Bilingualism, 20*(5), 497–509. oi:10.1080/13670050.2015.1057101

Rosenthal, J. W. (1995). *Teaching science to language minority students: Theory and practice*. Clevedon, Great Britain: Multilingual Matters.

Ruiz, R. (1984). Orientations in language planning. *NABE Journal: Journal of the National Association for Bilingual Education, 8*(2), 15–34.

Rumberger, R. W., Gándara, P., & Merino, B. (2006). Where California's English learners attend school and why it matters. *UC Linguistic Minority Research Institute Newsletter, 15*(2), 1–2.

Sacks, P. (1999). *Standardized minds. The high price of America's testing culture and what we can do to change it*. Cambridge, MA: Perseus.

Samway, K. D. (2006). *When English language learners write: Connecting research to practice, K–8*. Portsmouth, NH: Heinemann.

Saunders, W. M., & O'Brien, G. (2006). Oral language. In F. Genesee, K. Lindholm-Leary, W. M. Saunders, & D. Christian (Eds.), *Educating English language learners: A synthesis of research evidence* (pp. 14–63). New York: Cambridge University Press.

Savile-Troike, M., & Barto, K. (2017). *Introducing second language acquisition* (3rd ed.). Cambridge, UK: Cambridge University Press.

Sawchuk, S. (2010). *NEA's delegates vote "no confidence" in Race to The Top*. Retrieved from http://blogs.edweek.org/edweek/teacherbeat/2010/07/neas_delegates_vote_no_confide_2.html#comments

Sayer, P. (2008). Demystifying language mixing: Spanglish in school. *Journal of Latinos and Education, 7*(2), 94–112.

Sayer, P. (2013). Translanguaging, TexMex, and bilingual pedagogy: Emergent bilinguals learning through the vernacular. *TESOL Quarterly, 47*(1), 63–88.

Schieffelin, B. B., Woolard, K. A., & Kroskrity, P. V. (1998). *Language ideologies: Practice and theory* (Vol. 16). New York: Oxford University Press.

Schleppegrell, M. J. (2002). Challenges of the science register for ESL students: Errors and meaning-making. In M. J. Schleppegrell & M. C. Colombi (Eds.), *Developing advanced literacy in first and second languages: Meaning with power* (pp. 119–142). Mahwah, NJ: Lawrence Erlbaum.

Schmidt, R. (2012). Attention, awareness, and individual differences in language learning. In W. M. Chan, K. N. Chin, S. Bhatt, & I. Walker (Eds.), *Perspectives on individual characteristics and foreign language education* (pp. 27–50). Boston: de Gruyter.

Shin, S. J. (2013). *Bilingualism in schools and society: Language, identity, and policy.* New York: Routledge.

Shohamy, E. G. (2001). *The power of tests: A critical perspective on the uses of language tests.* New York: Longman.

Shohamy, E. G. (2011). Assessing multilingual competencies: Adopting construct valid assessment policies. *Modern Language Journal, 95*(3), 418–429.

Shohamy, E. G. (2017). Critical language testing. In E. G. Shohamy, I. Or, & S. May (Eds.), *Language testing and assessment, encyclopedia of language and education* (pp. 441–454). Cham, Switzerland: Springer International.

Shohamy, E. G., & Menken, K. (2015). Language assessment: Past to present misuses and future possibilities. In W. E. Wright, S. Boun, & O. García (Eds.), *Handbook of bilingual and multilingual education* (pp. 253–269). Malden, MA: John Wiley & Sons.

Short, D., & Boyson, B. (2012). *Helping newcomer students succeed in secondary schools and beyond.* Washington, DC: Center for Applied Linguistics.

Short, D., Fidelman, C. G., & Louguit, M. (2012). Developing academic language in English language learners through sheltered instruction. *TESOL Quarterly, 46*(2), 334–361.

Shyong, F. (2018, February 26). For Asian Americans, the 2018 Winter Olympics brought unexpected joy and familiar anger. *Los Angeles Times.* Retrieved from http://www.latimes.com/local/lanow/la-me-asians-olympics-column-20180226-story.html

Silva, T., & Matsuda, P. K. (Eds.). (2010). *Practicing theory in second language writing.* Anderson, SC: Parlor.

Simons, G. F., & Fennig, C. D. (Eds.). (2018). *Ethnologue: Languages of the world* (21st ed.). Dallas, TX: SIL International.

Singer, T. W. (2018). *EL excellence every day: The flip-to-guide for differentiating academic literacy.* Thousand Oaks, CA: Corwin.

Smith, F. (2006). *Reading without nonsense* (4th ed.). New York: Teachers College Press.

Smith, F. (2012). *Understanding reading* (6th ed.). New York: Routledge.

Society of Health and Physical Educators (SHAPE America). (2013). National Standards for K–12 Physical Education. Retrieved from https://www.shapeamerica.org/standards/pe/

Steele, J. L., Slater, R. O., Zamarro, G., Miller, T., Li, J., Burkhauser, S., & Bacon, M. (2017). Effects of dual-language immersion programs on student achievement: Evidence from lottery data. *American Education Research Journal, 54*(1S), 282S–306S.

Strauss, V. (2013). *Former education commissioner blasts Common Core process.* Retrieved from http://www.washingtonpost.com/blogs/answer-sheet/wp/2013/02/13/former-education-commissioner-blasts-common-core-process/

Street, B. (1984). *Literacy in theory and practice.* Cambridge, UK: Cambridge University Press.

Student Achievement Partners. (n.d.). *Common Core shifts.* Retrieved from http://www.achievethecore.org/downloads/E0702_Description_of_the_Common_Core_Shifts.pdf

Student Oral Language Observation Matrix (SOLOM). (n.d.). Retrieved from http://www.cal.org/twi/EvalToolkit/appendix/solom.pdf

Sugarman, J. (2017). *Beyond teaching English: Supporting high school completion by immigrant and refugee students.* Washington, DC: Migration Policy Institute.

Swain, M. (2005). The output hypothesis: Theory and research. In E. Hinkel (Ed.), *Handbook of research in second language teaching and learning* (pp. 471–483). New York: Routledge.

Swain, M., & Suzuki, W. (2008). Interaction, output, and communicative language learning. In B. Spolsky & F. M. Hult (Eds.), *The handbook of educational linguistics* (pp. 557–570). Malden, MA: Blackwell.

Teachers of English to Speakers of Other Languages (TESOL). (2006). *PreK–12 English language proficiency standards.* Alexandria, VA: TESOL Press.

Teachers of English to Speakers of Other Languages (TESOL). (2016). *English learners and ESSA: What educators need to know.* Alexandria, VA: TESOL Press. Retrieved from http://www.tesol.org/docs/default-source/ppt/tesol-essa-resource-kit-final0d938542f2fd6d058c49ff00004ecf9b.pdf?sfvrsn=0

Terman, L. M. (1916). *The measurement of intelligence.* Boston: Houghton Mifflin.

TESOL International Association Writing Team. (2018). *The 6 principles for exemplary teaching of English learners.* Annapolis Junction, MD: TESOL Press.

Texas Education Agency. Student Assessment Division. (2005). *Texas Observation Protocols: Training on the Proficiency Level Descriptors* [PowerPoint presentation]. Austin: Texas Education Agency.

Thomas, W. P., & Collier, V. P. (2002). *A national study of school effectiveness for language minority students' long term academic achievement.* Santa Cruz, CA: Center for Research on Education, Diversity, and Excellence.

Thomas, W. P., & Collier, V. P. (2013). *Dual language education for a transformed world.* Albuquerque, NM: Fuente.

Thorpe, H. (2017). *The newcomers: Finding refuge, friendship, and hope in an American classroom.* New York: Scribner.

Tyre, P. (2012, September 19). The writing revolution. *The Atlantic.* Retrieved from https://www.theatlantic.com/magazine/archive/2012/10/the-writing-revolution/309090/

Ulanoff, S. H., & Pucci, S. L. (1999). Learning words from books: The effects of read aloud on second language vocabulary acquisition. *Bilingual Research Journal, 23*(4), 319–332.

Umansky, I. M., & Reardon, S. F. (2014). Reclassification patterns among Latino English learner students in bilingual, dual immersion, and English immersion classrooms. *American Educational Research Journal, 51*(5), 879–912. doi:10.3102/0002831214545110

Understanding Language. (2012). *Persuasion across time and space: Analyzing and producing persuasive texts.* Retrieved from http://ell.stanford.edu/sites/default/files/ela_archives/understanding_language_materials_Jan2013.pdf

Understanding Language. (2013). *Key principles for ELL instruction.* Retrieved from https://ell.stanford.edu/sites/default/files/Key%20Principles%20for%20ELL%20Instruction%20with%20references_0.pdf

U.S. Census Bureau. (2015). Census Bureau reports at least 350 languages spoken in U.S. homes. Washington, DC: Author. Retrieved from www.census.gov/newsroom/press-releases/2015/ch15-185.html

U.S. Census Bureau. (2016). Quick facts: United States. Retrieved from https://www.census.gov/quickfacts/fact/table/US/PST045217

U.S. Commission on Civil Rights. (2018). *Public education funding inequity in an era of increasing concentration of poverty and resegregation.* Washington, DC: Author.

U.S. Department of Education. (2003). *Non-regulatory guidance on the Title III State Formula Grant Program. Part II: Standards, assessments, and accountability.* Washington, DC: Office of English Language Acquisition, Language Enhancement, and Academic Achievement for Limited English Proficient Students.

U.S. Department of Education. (2009a, March 7). Education Department to distribute $44 billion in stimulus funds [Press release]. Retrieved from http://www.ed.gov/print/news/pressreleases/2009/03/03072009.html

U.S. Department of Education. (2009b, July 24). President Obama, U.S. Secretary of Education Duncan announce national competition to advance school reform [Press release]. Retrieved from https://www.ed.gov/news/press-releases/resident-obama-us-secretary-education-duncan-announce-national-competition-adva

U.S. Department of Education. (2012). *ESEA Flexibility.* Washington, DC: Author.

U.S. Department of Education. (2016a). *English learner tool kit for state and local education agencies.* Washington, DC: Office of English Language Acquisition. Retrieved from https://www2.ed.gov/about/offices/list/oela/english-learner-toolkit/eltoolkit.pdf

U.S. Department of Education. (2016b). *Nonregulatory guidance: English learners and Title III of the Elementary and Secondary Education Act (ESEA), as amended by the Every Student Succeeds Act (ESSA)* Retrieved from https://www2.ed.gov/policy/elsec/leg/essa/essatitleiiiguidenglishlearners92016.pdf

Valdés, G. (1997). Dual-language immersion programs: A cautionary note regarding the education of language-minority students. *Harvard Educational Review, 67*(3), 391–429.

Valdés, G. (2014). Heritage language students: Profiles and possibilities. In T. G. Wiley, J. K. Peyton, D. Christian, S. C. K. Moore, & N. Liu (Eds.), *Handbook of heritage, community, and Native American languages in the United States: Research, policy, and educational practice* (pp. 27–35). New York: Routledge; Washington, DC: Center for Applied Linguistics.

Valdés, G. (2017). Foreword. In O. García, S. I. Johnson, & K. Seltzer, *The translanguaging classroom: Leverage student bilingualism for learning* (pp. v–vii). Philadelphia: Caslon.

Valdés, G., & Figueroa, R. A. (1994). *Bilingualism and testing: A special case of bias.* Norwood, NJ: Ablex.

Valdés, G., Menken, K., & Castro, M. (2015). *Common Core, Bilingual and English language learners: A Resource for educators.* Philadelphia: Caslon.

Valdés, G., Poza, L., & Brooks, M. D. (2015). Language acquisition in bilingual education. In W. E. Wright, S. Boun, & O. García (Eds.), *Handbook of bilingual and multilingual education* (pp. 56–74). Malden, MA: Wiley-Blackwell.

Valentino, R. A., & Reardon, S. F. (2014). *Effectiveness of four instructional programs designed to serve English language learners: Variation by ethnicity and initial English proficiency.* Retrieved from https://cepa.stanford.edu/sites/default/files/Valentino_Reardon_EL%20Programs_14_0319.pdf

van der Veen, C., van der Wilt, F., van Kruistum, C., van Oers, B., & Michaels, S. (2017). MODEL2TALK: An intervention to promote productive classroom talk. *The Reading Teacher, 70*(6), 689–7000.

VanPatten, B. (2003). *From input to output: A teacher's guide to second language acquisition.* Boston: McGraw Hill.

VanPatten, B. (2017). *While we're on the topic: BVP on language, acquisition, and classroom practice.* Alexandria, VA: American Council on the Teaching of Foreign Languages.

VanPatten, B., & Jegerski, J. (Eds.). (2010). *Research in second language processing and parsing.* Amsterdam, The Netherlands: John Benjamins.

Vinogradova, P., Linville, H. A., & Bickel, B. (2011). "Listen to my story and you will know me": Digital stories as student-centered collaborative projects. *TESOL Journal, 2*(2), 173–202. doi:10.5054/tj.2011.250380

von Raumer, K. (1858). Wolfgang Ratich. *American Journal of Education, 5*(13), 229–256.

Vygotsky, L. S. (1978). *Mind in society: The development of higher mental processes.* Cambridge, MA: Harvard University Press.

Walqui, A. (2015). What do educators need to know about language as they make decisions about Common Core State Standards implementation? In G. Valdés, K. Menken, & M. Castro (Eds.), *Common Core, English language learners, and equity: A guide for all educators.* Philadelphia: Caslon.

Walqui, A., & van Lier, L. (2010). *Scaffolding the academic success of adolescent English language learners: A pedagogy of promise.* San Francisco, CA: WestEd.

Weber, N. (2000, August). *Sink or swim? A look into an English immersion class.* Retrieved from http://ldt.stanford.edu/~ninaweb/Sink%20or%20swim.pdf

Weiss, J. (2011). *The innovation mismatch: "Smart capital" and education innovation.* Retrieved from http://blogs.hbr.org/innovations-in-education/2011/03/the-innovation-mismatch-smart.html

Wexler, N. (2018, May 19). Why Johnny still can't read—And what to do about it. *Forbes,* 1–2. Retrieved from https://www.forbes.com/sites/nataliewexler/2018/05/19/why-johnny-still-cant-read-and-what-to-do-about-it/#23e809572e22

What Works Clearinghouse. (2016). *WWC intervention report: accelerated reader.* Retrieved from https://ies.ed.gov/ncee/wwc/Docs/InterventionReports/wwc_accelerated reader_061416.pdf

WIDA Consortium. (2012a). *2012 Amplification of the English Language Development Standards: Kindergarten–grade 12.* Madison: Board of Regents of the University of Wisconsin System.

WIDA Consortium. (2012b). *English language learner can do booklet, grades prekindergarten–kindergarten.* Madison: Board of Regents of the University of Wisconsin System.

Wiley, T. G. (2005). *Literacy and language diversity in the United States* (2nd ed.). Washington, DC: Center for Applied Linguistics.

Wiley, T. G. (2012). A brief history and assessment of language rights in the United States. In J. W. Tollefson (Ed.), *Language policies in education: Critical issues* (2nd ed.) (pp. 61–90). New York: Routledge.

Wiley, T. G. (2014). The problem of defining heritage and community languages and their speakers: On the utility and limitations of definitional constructs. In T. G. Wiley, J. K. Peyton, D. Christian, S. K. C. Moore, & N. Liu (Eds.), *Handbook of heritage and community languages in the United States: Research, educational practice, and policy* (pp. 19–26). New York: Routledge; Washington, DC: Center for Applied Linguistics.

Wiley, T. G., & Rolstad, K. (2014). The Common Core State Standards and the great divide. *International Multilingual Research Journal, 8*(1), 38–55. doi:10.1080/19313152.2014.852428

Wiley, T. G., & Wright, W. E. (2004). Against the undertow: The politics of language instruction in the United States. *Educational Policy, 18*(1), 142–168.

Wink, J. (2000). *Critical pedagogy: Notes from the real world* (2nd ed.). New York: Addison Wesley Longman.

Wisconsin Literacy Education and Reading Network Source. (n.d.). Assessing print understanding. Retrieved from wilearns.state.wi.us/apps/PDF/print_prompts.pdf

Wolfe, T. (2016). *The kingdom of speech.* New York: Little, Brown.

Wright, W. E. (1998). The education of Cambodian American students in the Long Beach Unified School District: A language and educational policy analysis. *Dissertation Abstracts International, 37*(2), 409.

Wright, W. E. (2004a). What English-only really means: A study of the implementation of California language policy with Cambodian American students. *International Journal of Bilingual Education and Bilingualism, 7*(1), 1–23.

Wright, W. E. (2004b). Intersection of language and assessment policies for English language learners in Arizona. *Dissertation Abstracts International, 65*(2), 389.

Wright, W. E. (2005). The political spectacle of Arizona's Proposition 203. *Educational Policy, 19*(5), 662–700. doi:610.1177/0895904805278066

Wright, W. E. (2006a). A catch-22 for language learners. *Educational Leadership, 64*(3), 22–27.

Wright, W. E. (2006b). Meeting the needs of newcomer non-Spanishspeaking ELLs: A case study of two Cambodian students in a suburban intermediate school. In M. Cowart & P. Dam (Eds.), *Cultural and linguistic issues for English language learners* (pp. 108–141). Arlington, VA: CANH NAM; San Marcos: Texas Woman's University.

Wright, W. E. (2007). Heritage language programs in the era of English-only and No Child Left Behind. *Heritage Language Journal, 5*(1), 1–26.

Wright, W. E. (2008). No Child Left Behind Act of 2001, Title I. In J. M. González (Ed.), *Encyclopedia of bilingual education* (pp. 607–612). Thousand Oaks, CA: Sage.

Wright, W. E. (2014). Khmer. In T. G. Wiley, J. K. Peyton, D. Christian, S. K. C. Moore, & N. Liu (Eds.), *Handbook of heritage and community languages in the United States: Research, educational practice, and policy* (pp. 284–296). New York: Routledge; Washington, DC: Center for Applied Linguistics.

Wright, W. E. (2016). Let them talk! *Educational Leadership, 73*(5), 24–31.

Wright, W. E., & Baker, C. (2017). Key Concepts in Bilingual Education. In O. García, A. Lin, & S. May (Eds.), *Encyclopedia of Language and Education: Vol. 5. Bilingual and Multilingual Education* (3rd ed.), pp. 65–80. Cham, Switzerland: Springer International.

Wright, W. E., & Choi, D. (2005). *Voices from the classroom: A state-wide survey of experienced third grade English language learner teachers on the impact of language and highstakes testing policies in Arizona.* Tempe: Educational Policy Studies Laboratory, Arizona State University. Retrieved from h https://files.eric.ed.gov/fulltext/ED508521.pdf

Wright, W. E., & Li, X. (2006). Catching up in math? The case of newly arrived Cambodian students in a Texas intermediate school. *TABE Journal, 9*(1). Retrieved from https://www.tabe.org/site/handlers/filedownload.ashx?moduleinstanceid=189&dataid=224&FileName=TABE_Journal%20Vol%209%202006.pdf

Wright, W. E., & Li, X. (2008). High-stakes math tests: How No Child Left Behind leaves newcomer English language learners behind. *Language Policy, 7*(3), 237–266.

Wright, W. E., & Pu, C. (2005). *Academic achievement of English language learners in post Proposition 203 Arizona.* Tempe: Language Policy Research Unit, Educational Policy Studies Laboratory, Arizona State University.

Zehler, A. M., & Sapru, S. (2008). Learning to read in Khmer. In K. Koda & A. M. Zehler (Eds.), *Learning to read across languages: Crosslinguistic relationships in first and second-language literacy development* (pp. 188–200). New York: Routledge; Washington, DC: Center for Applied Linguistics.

Zehr, M. A. (2010a). Groups say ELLs got short shrift in Race to the Top. *Education Week, 30*(6).

Zehr, M. A. (2010b). Ariz. ELL programs found to violate civil-rights law. *Education Week, 30*(3), 10–11.

Zehr, M. A. (2017–2018). Celebrating the voices of immigrant students. *American Educator, Winter,* 13–15.

Zong, J., & Batalova, J. (2017). *Sub-Saharan African immigrants in the United States.* Washington, DC: Migration Policy Institute. Retrieved from https://www.migrationpolicy.org/article/sub-saharan-african-immigrants-united-states#Educational_and_Professional_Attainment

Zong, J., Batalova, J., & Hallock, J. (2018). Frequently requested statistics on immigrants and immigration in the United States. *Migration Information Source,* (February 8). Retrieved from https://www.migrationpolicy.org/article/frequently-requested-statistics-immigrants-and-immigration-united-states#Children

Zwiers, J. (2014). *Building academic language: Meeting the Common Core Standards across disciplines, grades 5–12* (2nd ed.). San Francisco, CA: Jossey-Bass.

Zwiers, J., & Crawford, M. (2011). *Academic conversations: Classroom talk that fosters critical thinking and content understandings.* Portland, ME: Stenhouse.

Zwiers, J., & Soto, I. (2017). *Conversational discourse in context.* Thousand Oaks, CA: Corwin.

Index

A

Academic achievement of ELLs, 13–17
Academic language
    demands of, 45–47, 46b
    functions of, 43
    proficiency in, 42–43, 43b
    in reading, 200
    vs. second language instructional competence, 45
Academic purposes, language for, 42–47, 43b, 45b, 46b
Academic socialization vs. academic language
        proficiency, 42–43
Academic writing, 237
Accelerated Reader (AR), 218, 218b
ACCESS 2.0, 85, 142, 145
Accommodations, 56, 135–137, 138t–139t
Additional language, English as, 58, 94
Additive bilingualism, 23
Adequate yearly progress (AYP), 76
Advocacy, 316–319
    effective programs and, 315
    and federal and state policies for ELLs, 316
    need for, 316
    political, 318
    for social studies, 291
African American slaves, linguistic restriction of, 72
African American students, graduation rates for, 15
African American Vernacular English, 40–41, 58
Alaska Native students, graduation rates for, 15
Arizona Proposition 203, 86
Arts education, 297–299, 298b
Asian American model-minority myth, 15
Assessing Comprehension and Communication in
        English State-to-State for English Language
        Learners (ACCESS for ELLs), 85
Assessment(s), 125–155
    accommodations in, 135–137, 138t–139t
    alternative authentic, 147–152
    basics of, 126–134
    bias in, 132–134, 133f
    bilingual, 137
    challenges with online testing for, 144–146
    consequential validity in, 146–147
    content-area testing for, 135–141, 299
    criterion-referenced tests for, 128
    critical language testing for, 146–147
    critical look at requirements for, 134–147
    domains of, 130
    dynamic, 127
    effective programs and, 315
    vs. evaluation, 127

Every Student Succeeds Act and challenges of,
        137–141, 139f
    formative, 127
    growth models and, 138–141
    Joint Standards on, 134–135
    language proficiency testing for, 141–146, 142b
    of listening and speaking, 186–190, 187t, 188t, 190f
    "next-generation," 144
    norm-referenced tests for, 127–128
    performance, 149, 150t
    portfolio, 151–152, 268–269
    of reading, 198, 224–230
    reliability of, 129–130
    self-, 149–151, 151f, 269, 269f
    standard error of measurement for, 129–130
    summative, 127
    technology-enhanced items in, 144–145
    vs. testing, 126–127
    universal design of, 135
    validity of, 130–132, 132b
    value-added measures and, 140–141
    of writing, 264–269, 266t, 267f, 269f
Assimilation, 21, 73
Assimilationist discourses, 3
Authentic assessments, alternative, 147–152
Authentic speech, 177–178

B

Balanced approach to literacy instruction, 194, 195b
Bias, 132–134, 133f
Bilingual(s) and bilingualism
    additive, 23
    defined, 41
    dynamic, 5, 24
    emergent, 5–6, 58, 143–144
    historical perspective on, 70–74, 71b, 71f–73f
    need for, 24–25, 25b
    vs. not English-proficient, 5–6
    promotion on individual and societal levels of,
        23–25, 24b, 25b
    and second language acquisition, 60–61
    sequential, 5
    simultaneous, 5
    subtractive, 23, 24, 24b
    and translanguaging, 41–42
    what teachers need to know about, 41–42
    and writing, 237
Bilingual assessments, 137
Bilingual Common Core Initiative, 96
Bilingual dictionaries, 310–311

Page numbers followed by b, f, or t refer to boxes,
figures, or tables, respectively.

Bilingual education
  developmental (maintenance, late-exit), 104–105, 105f, 106b, 120t
  one-way dual language, 104–105, 105f, 106b, 120t
Bilingual education *(continued)*
  strong forms of, 118, 120t
  transitional (early-exit), 102–104, 103f, 103t, 104b, 120t
  weak forms of, 118, 120t
Bilingual Education Act (1968), 70, 74–75, 81
Bilingual immersion programs, 109–110, 110f, 111b, 120t
Bilingual parents, 313
Bilingual program models, 102–112
  bilingual immersion programs as, 109–110, 110f, 111b, 120t
  for content-area instruction, 272
  developmental bilingual education as, 104–105, 105f, 106b, 120t
  dual language programs as, 105–109, 107b, 107t, 109b, 120t
  heritage language programs as, 110–112, 112b, 120t
  and Title VII funds, 75
  transitional bilingual education as, 102–104, 103f, 103t, 104b, 120t
Bilingual strategies
  in instructional program, 95t, 98–99
  for mathematics, 281
Bilingual students
  English language proficiency of, 159–160
  help from, 312–313
Bilingual teachers, collaboration with, 121
Biliteracy and writing, 237
Books
  alternative endings to, 221
  class-made, 221, 250
  complexity of, 200, 201–203
  digital, 222–224
  dual language, 311–312
  home language, 308, 311–312
  with mathematical themes, 282–283
  multicultural, 207
  read-aloud, 308, 311
  selection of, 207
  strategies for modifying, 276
  to support science instruction, 290
The Bridge, 61
Brown v. Board of Education (1954), 87
Building background in sheltered instruction, 97

C
California
  English language proficiency standards for, 172–173, 175t
California Department of Education (CDE), 96
California Proposition 58, 86
California Proposition 227, 86
CALLA (cognitive academic language learning approach), 43–44
Can Do descriptors, 13, 14t
Castañeda standard, 88
Castañeda v. Pickard (1981), 87–88, 89b
CCSS. *See* Common Core State Standards (CCSS)
CCSSO (Council of Chief State School Officers), 82, 85, 96
CDE (California Department of Education), 96
Center for Research on Education, Diversity, and Excellence (CREDE) report, 158–160, 196–199

Center for Research on Evaluation, Standards and Student Testing (CRESST), 85
Certification, effective programs and, 315
Chants, 179
Checklist
  for observation, 148–149
  for writing, 269, 269f
Chinese schools, 112
Chomsky, Noam, 50, 51, 52, 53
Citizenship, English proficiency as requirement for, 73
Civil Rights Act, 89b, 321
Class discussions, 185–186
  contributions in home language in, 308
  postreading, 219–220
Classroom, labeling of, 308
Classroom-based writing assessment, 265–269, 266t, 267f, 269f
Classroom book, 221, 250
Classroom interaction, strategies for, 180–186, 181f
Close reading, 216
Cognates, 36, 309–310
Collaboration among ESL, bilingual, sheltered English immersion, and mainstream teachers, 121
Common Core en Español, 84, 96–97
Common Core State Standards (CCSS)
  for content-area instruction, 273b
  and Every Student Succeeds Act, 77
  on language for academic tasks, 46b, 47
  language standards for all students in, 5, 31–32, 32b
  for mathematics, 279
  for reading, 200–203, 201b
  for social studies, 293
  for speaking and listening, 170–171, 171b
  and translanguaging, 304
  for writing, 241–242, 241b, 285–286
Common Core State Standards (CCSS) Consortia, 84–85
Communicative competence, 38–39, 58, 63
Communicative language teaching (CLT), 58, 63–64
Community language(s), 6
Community language programs, 110–112, 112b, 120t
Complex texts, 200, 201–203
Composing in analytic scoring rubric for writing, 266t
Comprehension in Student Oral Language Observation Matrix–Revised, 187, 188t
Comprehensive support and improvement (CSI), 80
"Compulsory ignorance" laws, 72
Computer software in translanguaging, 313
Concepts of print, 224
Concepts of print checklists, 224, 225f
Concurrent translation, 305–306
Consequential validity, 146–147
Construct-irrelevant variance, 131, 134
Content-area instruction, 272–301
  in art, music, and physical education, 297–299, 298b
  assessment of, 299
  bilingual programs for, 272
  differentiated for ELLs, 273–274
  home language, 96–97
  in instructional program, 95t, 96–98
  and language and content objectives, 274–275
  in mathematics, 279–283, 281f, 282f
  multicultural perspectives in, 278
  in science, 283–291, 288f, 289f
  sheltered, 97–98, 272, 278–299
  in social studies, 291–297, 295f
  strategies for modifying textbooks and instructional materials for, 276

thematic teaching and lesson planning for, 276–278, 277f

use of literature in, 278

using English language proficiency standards to guide, 275–276

Content-area learning, keeping data on progress in, 318

Content-area testing, 135–141

accommodations for ELLs in, 135–137, 138t–139t

Every Student Succeeds Act and challenges of, 137–141, 139f

Content-based instruction (CBI), 58, 64

Content teachers as language teachers, 61–62

Conventions in writing self-assessment, 269f

Conversational discourse, 180–181

Conversational ground rules, 167

Conversational language proficiency, 42–43

Cooperative learning, 64, 65, 181–183

Core curriculum, equal access to, 314

Correction

of student speech errors, 164–165, 166b

of writing, 254

Corrective feedback, 164–165, 166n

Council of Chief State School Officers (CCSSO), 82, 85, 96

Court decisions, important, 87–88, 89b

Credentialing, effective programs and, 315

Criterion-referenced test, 128

Critical language testing, 146

Critical pedagogy, 65

Culturally and linguistically diverse students, 6

Culturally sustaining pedagogies (CSP), 22

Culture(s)

of ELLs, 18–22, 20t

integrated into science instruction, 290–291

and mathematics, 280, 283

and social studies instruction, 296–297

Curriculum

reading across, 222

writing across, 257–258

D

Demographic trends in ELLs, 6–10, 7f, 7t, 8b, 9f

Developing Literacy in Second Language Learners (NLP report), 160–161

Developmental bilingual education (DBE), 104–105, 105f, 106b, 120t

Differentiated instruction in content classes, 273–274

Discourse, social practice and, 39–40

Discourse competence, 38

Drop-out rates, 15

Dual language, 105–106

Dual language books, 311–312

Dual language immersion (dual language programs), 105–109, 107b, 107t, 109b, 120t

vs. bilingual immersion programs, 110

Dual language learner, 6

Dynamic assessment, 127

Dynamic bilingualism, 5, 24

E

Early-exit programs, 102–104, 103f, 103t, 104b, 120t

Ebonics, 40–41, 58

Economically disadvantaged, improving academic achievement of, 77–80

Educating English Language Learners: A Synthesis of Research Evidence (CREDE report), 158–160

Educational achievement of ELLs, 13–17

Educational opportunities, equal access to, 2–3

Educational Testing Service (ETS), 85

EEOA (Equal Educational Opportunities Act, 1974), 87, 89b

Effective ELL programs, 313–316

EL (English learner), 4

ELD. *See* English language development (ELD)

Elementary and Secondary Education Act (ESEA, 1965), 74

and Every Student Succeeds Act (ESSA, 2015), 3, 77–82, 85

and No Child Left Behind Act (2002), 75–76

Obama administration and, 76–77

requirements for language proficiency of, 143–144

and Title VII Bilingual Education Act (1968), 74–75

Elementary and Secondary Education Act (ESEA) Flexibility (2011), 76–77, 82, 83b, 85

Emergent bilinguals, 5–6, 58, 143–144

English

nonstandard varieties of, 5, 40–41

as official language, 70

outside of school, 159

as privileged, 109

standard American, 32b, 40

English as an additional language (EAL), 58, 94

English as a new language (ENL), 58, 94

English as a second language (ESL), 94

defined, 94

and English language arts, 101

in-class, 95t

in instructional program, 94–96, 95t

at intermediate and advanced levels, 95–96

pull-in (push-in), 114–115

pull-out, 95t

purpose of, 94–95

self-contained classrooms for, 115–116, 116b, 118, 119b, 120t

as separate content area, 95

vs. sheltered instruction, 99–100, 100t

sociocultural perspective on, 58

English as a second language (ESL) instruction

in-class, 114–115

and literacy instruction, 197

need for consistent, 161

pull-out, 113–114, 114b

English as a second language (ESL) programs, 120t

English as a second language (ESL) teachers, 2

collaboration with, 121

English as a second language (ESL) withdrawal classes, 113–114, 114b

English for speakers of other languages (ESOL), 94

English for the Children initiatives, 86, 115

English immersion, sheltered (structured), 115–116, 116b, 118, 119b, 120t

English language arts, ESL and, 101

English language development (ELD)

defined, 94

reading and, 194–196

English language development (ELD) standards, 44, 45b

English language learners (ELLs), 1–26

culture and identity of, 18–22, 20b

defined, 1, 3–4

diversity of, 1–2, 10–23, 10t

educational achievement of, 13–17

effective programs for, 313–316

foreign-born, 10t, 19, 20b

English language learners (ELLs) *(continued)*
gifted and talented, 10t
highly schooled newcomer, 10t
historical and demographic trends in, 6–10, 7f, 7t,
8b, 9f
home languages of, 11–13, 11t, 12b
indigenous, 10t
keeping data on progress of, 317–318
learning more about your, 25–26
levels of English language proficiency of, 13, 14t
long-term, 10t
native U.S.-born, 10t, 19, 20b
newcomer, 10t
reclassified, 10t
refugee, 10t, 15
socioeconomic status of, 13
Spanish-speaking, 11–12, 11t, 12b
special education considerations for, 2, 10t, 17–18,
18t
transnational, 10t
use of term, 58
English language proficiency (ELP)
of bilingual students, 159–160
of ELLs, 13, 14t
as requirement for naturalization and citizenship, 73
screening test for, 3
English Language Proficiency Assessment for the 21st
Century (ELPA21) Consortium, 4
on academic language proficiency, 44
Common Core State Standards and, 83b, 85
and complexity of language proficiency construct,
142
on content-area instruction, 275–276
on literacy development, 206, 208t
online testing by, 144, 145
standards for listening and speaking, 171–173, 174t
and Title I, 79
and writing instruction, 243, 244t
English language proficiency (ELP) standards, 76
to focus on oral language instruction, 170–173,
171t, 174t–175t
to guide content-area instruction, 275–276
to guide reading instruction, 206, 208t–209t
to guide writing instruction, 243, 244t–245t
English learner (EL), 4
English Learner Tool Kit, 81
English-medium program models, 112–118
in-class ESL instruction as, 114–115
newcomer program as, 116–117, 117b, 120t
pull-out ESL instruction as, 113–114, 114b
sheltered (structured) English immersion as,
115–116, 116b, 118, 119b, 120t
submersion (sink or swim) as, 117–118, 119b, 120t
"English Proficiency. Multilingual Education," 86
ENL (English as a new language), 58, 94
e-portfolios, 152
Equal access to educational opportunities, 2–3
Equal Educational Opportunities Act (EEOA, 1974),
87, 89b
ESEA. *See* Elementary and Secondary Education Act
(ESEA, 1965)
ESL. *See* English as a second language (ESL)
ESOL (English for speakers of other languages), 94
ESSA. *See* Every Student Succeeds Act (ESSA, 2015)
ETS (Educational Testing Service), 85
Evaluation, 127. *See also* Assessment
Every Student Succeeds Act (ESSA, 2015), 3, 77–82
and accommodations, 135–136

challenges of measuring achievement and growth
with, 137–141, 139f
and high-stakes writing exams, 264
and instructional models and programs, 92, 93b
and science instruction, 284
Title III (language instruction for English learners
and immigrant students) of, 80–82
Title I (improving academic achievement of the
economically disadvantaged) of, 77–80

F
Family literacy programs, 320
Family night events, 320
Farrington v. Tokushige (1927), 87
FCAs (focus correction areas), 258
Federal policy, 74–82
and advocacy, 316
Elementary and Secondary Education Act (ESEA)
as, 74
Every Student Succeeds Act as, 77–82
No Child Left Behind Act as, 75–76
Obama administration and, 76–77
Title VII Bilingual Education Act as, 74–75
Feedback
corrective, 164–165, 166n
interactional, 162
First language
transferring from, 57, 197, 198b
use of term, 58
First language acquisition, 51
Flores v. Arizona (2000), 88
Fluency
in Student Oral Language Observation Matrix–
Revised (SOLOM-R), 187, 188t
in writing self-assessment, 269f
Fluent English proficient, 3–4, 314
Focus correction areas (FCAs), 258
Foreign-born ELLs, 10t, 19, 20b
Formative assessment, 127
Freire, Paulo, 65
Funds of knowledge, 17

G
Gates Foundation, 83b
General academic words, 169
General contexts and vocabulary development, 204
Genre, 39
Gifted and talented ELLs, 10t
Gómez and Gómez Dual Language Enrichment
Model, 107
Gomez v. Illinois State Board of Education (1987),
88
Graduation rates, 15
Grammar, 34–35
in Student Oral Language Observation Matrix–
Revised (SOLOM-R), 187, 188t
Graphic organizers
for reading, 220–221, 220f
for social studies, 294–295, 295f
for writing, 247–248, 248f
Growth models, 138–141
Guided reading, 214–216
Guided writing, 248–249, 249f

H
Heritage language, 6
Heritage language programs, 110–112, 112b, 120t
Heritage language speaker, 6

Heteroglossic perspective, 94
Highly schooled newcomer ELLs, 10t
High-stakes standardized writing exams, 264–265
Historical trends in English language learners, 6–10,
    7f, 7t, 8b, 9f
Holistic biliteracy framework, 61
Holistic scoring, 265
Home and New Language Arts Progressions, 96
Home cultures, effective programs and, 314–315
Home language(s)
    books in, 308, 311–312
    contributions to class discussions in, 308
    effective programs and, 314
    of ELLs, 11–13, 11t, 12b
    initial writing in, 311
    instructional wall displays in, 309
    journal writing in, 252
    labeling of classroom in, 308
    letters to parents in, 312
    literacy skills in, 161, 234–235
    loss of, 23, 24, 24b
    read-aloud books in, 308, 311
    to support writing, 310
    tests in, 136, 138t–139t
    use for beginning-level ELLs of, 159
Home language experiences and literacy development,
    198
Home language instruction, 95t, 96, 304
    content-area, 96–97
    literacy, 96
Home language survey, 3, 141

I
Identity of ELLs, 18–22, 20t
Immersion
    one-way, 106
    sheltered (structured) English, 115–116, 116b, 118,
        119b, 120t
    two-way (dual language), 105–109, 107b, 107t,
        109b, 120t
Immersion programs, 110–112, 112b, 120t
    bilingual, 109–110, 110f, 111b, 120t
Immigrants, 6–8, 7f, 19, 20b, 21, 70
    language instruction for, 80–82
Improving the Academic Achievement of the
        Economically Disadvantaged, 77–80
In-class ESL instruction, 95t, 114–115
Independent reading, 217–218, 218b
Independent writing, 250–252, 251f
    scaffolding for, 254–257, 255f
Indigenous ELLs, 10t
In-school heritage language programs, 111
Instructional materials
    for mathematics, 281–282
    strategies for modifying, 276
Instructional program(s), 92–124
    bilingual strategies in, 98–99
    collaboration among ESL, bilingual, sheltered
        English immersion, and mainstream teachers in,
        121
    content-area instruction in, 95t, 96–98
    determining most appropriate, 121–123, 122b
    ESL and English language arts in, 101
    ESL in, 94–96, 95t
    ESL vs. sheltered instruction in, 99–100, 100t
    essential components of, 94–101, 95t
    Every Student Succeeds Act on, 92, 93b
    evolving perspectives on, 94

Instructional program models, 101–118
    bilingual, 102–112
    English-medium, 112–118
    typology of, 118, 119b, 120t
Instructional wall displays in home languages, 309
Interaction, in sheltered instruction, 97
Intercultural communicative competence, 38
The Invisible Minority...pero no vencibles, 74

J
Joint Standards for educational testing, 134–135
Journal writing, 250–252, 251f

K
Khmer Emerging Education Program (Project KEEP),
    112
Knowledge of language, 30–31, 32b, 33–42
Korean schools, 112

L
Labeling of classroom, 308
Language, 29–49
    for academic purposes, 42–47, 43b, 45b, 46b
    bilingualism in, 41–42
    Common Core State Standards for, 31–32, 32b
    communicative competence in, 38–39
    defined, 30
    examples of issues related to, 29–30
    knowledge of, 30–31, 32b, 33–42
    lexicon of, 37
    morphology of, 33–34
    phonology of, 33
    pragmatics of, 36–37
    register and genre in, 39
    semantics of, 35–36
    social practice and discourse in, 39–40
    spelling of, 37–38
    syntax of, 34–35
    translanguaging in, 41–42
    variations of, 40–41
Language acquisition
    five stages of, 63
    vs. language learning, 53
Language acquisition device (LAD), 51
Language and education policy, 69–91
    Elementary and Secondary Education Act (ESEA)
        and, 74
    Every Student Succeeds Act and, 77–82
    evolution of federal, 74–82
    historical perspective on, 70–74, 71b, 71f–73f
    at local level, 88–89
    No Child Left Behind Act and, 75–76
    Obama administration and, 76–77
    state-led initiatives and consortia on, 82–85
    state policies for ELLs as, 85–87
    Title VII Bilingual Education Act and, 74–75
Language arts, language for academic success in, 43b
Language-as-problem orientation, 3, 60, 103
Language-as-resource orientation, 3, 23–24
Language bias, 132–134, 133f
Language demands, 45–47, 46b
Language experience approach to reading, 216–217
Language functions, receptive vs. productive, 46b
Language instruction education programs, 80
Language Instruction for English Learners and
        Immigrant Students, 80–82
Language Instruction for Limited English Proficient
        and Immigrant Students, 75–76

Language learning and teaching, 50–68
  advantages of older students and adults in, 5b
  advantages of young children in, 5b
  behaviorist perspective on, 51
  beyond approaches and methods for, 65–66
  bilingual and multilingual pluralist perspectives on, 60–61
  language socialization research on, 60
  sociocultural perspectives on, 57–61
  sociolinguistic contributions to, 58
  traditional teaching approaches and methods for, 62–65
  zone of proximal development and scaffolding in, 58–60
Language majority student, 6
Language minority student, 6
Language objectives
  in content-area instruction, 274–275
  in sheltered instruction, 98, 100
Language practices, 39
Language proficiency
  academic, 42–47, 43b, 45b, 46b
  cognitive academic, 42
  complexity of, 142–143
  conversational, 42–43
  time to develop, 42, 43b
Language proficiency testing, 141–146, 142b
  challenges with ESSA requirements for, 143–144
  challenges with online, 144–146
  complexity of, 142–143
  washback effect of, 141
Language programs, heritage (community, world for native speakers), 110–112, 112b, 120t
Language progression, 172–173, 174t–175t
Language restrictions, 72–74
Language socialization research, 60
Languaging, 39
Late-exit bilingual education, 104–105, 105f, 106b, 120t
Latinx students
  graduation rates for, 15
  as non-nons, 141, 142b
Lau Remedies, 87
Lau v. Nichols (1974), 86, 87, 89b, 203, 274
Learning disabilities vs. language difficulties, 17–18
Legislation, important, 87–88, 89b
Lesson planning, 276–278, 277f
Lexicon, 37
Linguistic restrictionism, 72–74
Linguistics bias, 132–134, 133f
Linguistic simplification, 136, 138t–139t
Listening, 156–192
  assessing, 186–190, 187t, 188t, 190f
  Can Do descriptors for, 14t
  listening centers for, 177–178
  listening comprehension tasks for, 176–177
  promoting development in classroom of, 173–178
  research on, 158–162
  strategies for classroom interaction for, 180–186, 181f
  total physical response for, 173–176
  using standards to focus instruction in, 170–173, 171t, 174t–175t
  using theory to guide decision making on, 162–170
Literacy development. See also Reading
  home language experiences and, 198
  individual differences in, 197–198

levels of, 206, 208t–209t
  oral language development and, 197
  oral proficiency and literacy in first language and, 197, 198b
  promotion of, 203–224
Literacy instruction. See also Reading
  balanced approach to, 194, 195b
  for ELLs vs. mainstream students, 196–197
  English oral language development and, 197
  and ESL instruction, 197
  home language, 96
  research on, 196–199
Literacy programs, family, 320
Literacy Squared approach, 237, 267
Local level, language policy at, 88–89
Long-term ELLs, 10t

M
Mainstream teachers, collaboration with, 121
Maintenance bilingual education, 104–105, 105f, 106b, 120t
Massachusetts Question 2, 86
Mathematics, 279–283
  culture and, 280, 283
  integrating students' cultures into, 283
  language for academic success in, 43b
  language of, 279–280
  made comprehensible for ELLs, 281, 281f, 282f
  modified instructional materials for, 281–282
  using literature to support, 282–283
Meyer v. Nebraska (1923), 87
Minoritization, 6
Minority students, academic achievement of, 15–17
Misdirective contexts and vocabulary development, 204
Monitor hypothesis, 53
Monitor model of second language acquisition, 53–55
Monoglossic perspective, 94
Monolingual forms of education, 118, 120t
Multicultural books, 207
Multicultural education, 22
Multicultural perspectives on content-area instruction, 278
Multicultural science, 290–291
Multilingual learner, 6
  and second language acquisition, 60–61
Multiliteracies, 259
Multiple measures of assessment, 152–153
Multi-tiered systems of support (MTSS), 18
Music education, 297–299

N
National Assessment of Education Process (NAEP), 15
National Center for Fair and Open Testing, 128
National Council for Social Studies (NCSS), 291
National Council on Measurement in Education, 134
National Governors Association, 82, 83b
National Literacy Panel (NLP) report, 160–161, 196–199
National Standards for Arts Education, 298b
National Teacher Professional Development grants, 81
Native Americans
  bilingual immersion programs for, 110
  coercive assimilation policies targeting, 73
  graduation rates for, 15

Native language, use of term, 58
Native speakers, 5
    opportunities for interaction with, 162
    world language programs for, 110–112, 112b, 120t
Native U.S.-born ELLs, 10t, 19, 20b
Naturalization, English proficiency as requirement
        for, 73
NCLB. *See* No Child Left Behind (NCLB, 2002)
NCSS (National Council for Social Studies), 291
Negative transfer, 57
Newcomer centers, 116–117, 117b, 120t
Newcomer ELLs, 10t
Newcomer programs, 116–117, 117b, 120t
New language, English as, 58, 94
New York
    content-area instruction in, 275
    English language proficiency standards for,
        172–173, 175t
New York Bilingual Common Core Initiative, 84
"Next-generation assessments," 144–146
Next Generation Science Standards (NGSS), 47, 273b,
        284–285, 404
NLP (National Literacy Panel) report, 160–161,
        196–199
No Child Left Behind (NCLB, 2002), 4, 75–76
    challenges of measuring achievement and growth
        with, 137–141, 139f
    failure to meet achievement targets of, 15
Nonstandard varieties of English, 5, 40–41
Norm-referenced test, 127–128

O

Observation for assessment, 148–149
One-way dual immersion, 110–112, 112b, 120t
One-way dual language bilingual education, 104–105,
        105f, 106b, 120t
One-way immersion, 106
Online testing, 144–146
Open-ended questions, 164
Oracy. *See also* Oral language
    defined, 162
Oral language, 156–192
    assessing, 186–190, 187t, 188t, 190f
    challenges of, 157
    keeping data on progress in, 317
    listening comprehension tasks for, 176–177
    and literacy instruction, 197
    oral retellings for, 178–179
    productive talk moves in, 165–167
    promoting development in classroom of, 173–186
    and reading comprehension, 160
    research on, 158–162
    and spelling, 160
    strategies for classroom interaction for, 180–186,
        181f
    teacher talk in classroom and, 163–164, 164b
    technology for speaking practice for, 186
    total physical response for, 173–176
    using standards to focus instruction in, 170–173,
        171t, 174t–175t
    using theory to guide decision making on,
        162–170
    vocabulary development in, 167–170
    and writing, 160, 234, 235, 236f
Oral presentations, 179–180
Oral retellings, 178–179
Organization in writing self-assessment, 269f

P

Paralinguistic clues, 262
Parent(s)
    accommodating language needs of, 321
    bilingual, 313
    educational level of, 13
    letters in home languages to, 312
Parental engagement
    effective programs and, 316
    increasing opportunities for, 319–321
Partnership for the Assessment of Readiness for
        College and Careers (PARCC), 83b, 84–85, 144,
        145
Part/whole relationships, 36
PE (physical education), 297–299
Peer assessment, 149–151, 269
Performance assessment, 149, 150t
*Persuasion across Time and Space: Analyzing and
        Producing Persuasive Texts* (Understanding
        Language initiative), 202, 242
Phonemes, 33
Phonemic awareness, 194, 195b
Phonics, 194, 195b
Phonology, 33
Physical education (PE), 297–299
Pluralist discourses, 3, 24
    and second language acquisition, 60–61
Policy(ies), 69–91
    Elementary and Secondary Education Act (ESEA)
        and, 74
    Every Student Succeeds Act (ESSA) and, 77–82
    evolution of federal, 74–82
    historical perspective on, 70–74, 71b, 71f–73f
    important court decisions and legislation and,
        87–88, 89b
    at local level, 88–89
    No Child Left Behind Act and, 75–76
    state, 85–87
    state-led initiatives and consortia on, 82–85
    Title VII Bilingual Education Act and, 74–75
    working for changes in, 318
Political advocacy, 318
Portfolio assessment, 151–152, 268–269
Poverty, 13, 15–17
Power relationships among social identity groups, 22
Practice in sheltered instruction, 97
Pragmatics, 36–37
Preparation in sheltered instruction, 97
Preview-view-review for translanguaging, 306–307
Primary home language other than English
        (PHLOTE), 141
Primary language, use of term, 58
Primary language loss, 23, 24, 24b
Primary language support, 304
Productive language functions, 46b
Productive talk moves, 165–167
Program models, 101–118
    bilingual, 102–112
    English-medium, 112–118
    typology of, 118, 119b, 120t
Progress, keeping data on, 317–318
Project KEEP (Khmer Emerging Education Program),
        112
*Promoting the Educational Success of Children and
        Youth Learning English: Promising Futures*
        (National Academies of Sciences, Engineering,
        and Medicine report), 161–162

Proposition 58 (California), 86
Proposition 203 (Arizona), 86
Proposition 227 (California), 86
Pull-in ESL instruction, 114–115
Pull-out ESL instruction, 95t, 113–114, 114b
Push-in ESL instruction, 114–115

Q
Question(s), 36
    multiple-choice, 264
    open-ended and higher-order, 164
Question 2 (Massachusetts), 86

R
Race to the Top (RTTT, 2009), 76, 82, 83b
Raciolinguistics, 41
Read-aloud books, 210–212
    in home language, 308, 311
Reading, 193–232
    to, with, and by ELLs, 207–219
    across curriculum, 222
    assessment of, 198, 224–230
    balanced approach to, 194, 195b
    CAN DO descriptors for, 14t
    close, 216
    Common Core Standards for, 200–203, 201b
    concepts of print checklists for, 224, 225f
    effective instruction in, 199
    graphic organizers for, 220–221, 220f
    guided, 214–216
    independent (sustained silent, free voluntary),
        217–218, 218b
    keeping data on progress in, 317
    language experience approach to, 216–217
    overview of, 193–194
    phonemic awareness and phonics instruction for,
        194, 195b
    Reader's Workshop for, 219
    running records of, 224–228, 227f, 228f
    self-assessments of, 229t, 230
    shared, 212–214
    text complexity for, 200, 201–203
    text selection for, 207
    using English language development standards to
        guide, 206, 208t–209t
    vocabulary development through, 203–206
    what we know from research on, 196–199, 198b
    word study for, 222
    and writing, 237–238
Reading comprehension, oral language skills and, 160,
    161
Receptive language functions, 46b
Reclassified ELLs, 10t
Redesignation, 3–4
Refugee ELLs, 10t, 15
Register, 39
Research, action, 321–322, 322b
Response to intervention (RTI), 18, 18b
Retellings, oral, 178–179
RTI (response to intervention), 18, 18b
RTTT (Race to the Top, 2009), 76, 82, 83b
Rubrics for performance assessment, 149, 150t
Running records of reading, 224–228, 227f, 228f

S
Scaffolding, 58–60
    for independent writing, 254–257, 255f
School accountability programs, 79–80

Science, 283–291
    discourse of, 285
    Every Student Succeeds Act and, 284
    inquiry-based (discovery), 286–289, 288f, 289f
    integrating students' cultures in, 290–291
    language for academic success in, 43b
    language of, 285–286
    made comprehensible, 286–289, 288f, 289f
    modifying instructional materials for, 289–290
    Next Generation Science Standards for, 47, 273b,
        284–285
    using literature to support, 290
Scoring
    analytic, 265, 266t, 267–268, 267f
    holistic, 265
    primary trait vs. multi-trait, 265–267
Screening test for English language proficiency, 3
SDAIE (specially designed academic instruction in
    English), 64, 97, 115–116, 116b, 118, 119b, 120t
Second language acquisition (SLA), 51–66
    advantages of older students and adults in, 52b
    advantages of young children in, 52b
    with all teachers as language teachers, 61–62
    audiolingual method for, 62–63
    behaviorist perspective on, 51
    beyond approaches and methods for, 65–66
    bilingual and multilingual pluralist perspectives
        on, 60–61
    cognitive approaches to, 52–57, 52b, 53b
    communicative language teaching for, 63–64
    comprehensible output hypothesis of, 55–56
    content-based instruction for, 64
    critical pedagogy for, 65
    critical period hypothesis of, 52b
    five stages of, 63
    grammar-translation method for, 62
    innatist perspective on, 51
    input processing model of, 56–57
    interaction hypothesis of, 55
    language socialization research on, 60
    monitor model of, 53–55
    natural approach for, 63
    new vs., 53b
    noticing hypothesis of, 56
    processability theory of, 56
    sociocultural perspectives on, 57–61
    sociolinguistic contributions to, 58
    theories of, 51–61
    traditional teaching approaches and methods for,
        62–65
    transfer from first language in, 57
Second language instructional competence (SLIC),
    45
SEI (sheltered English immersion), 115–116, 116b,
    118, 119b, 120t, 121
Self-assessments
    of listening and speaking, 149–151, 151f
    of reading, 229t, 230
    of writing, 269, 269f
Self-contained ESL classrooms, 115–116, 116b, 118,
    119b, 120t
Semantics, 35–36
Sequential bilingualism, 5
Sheltered classrooms, 115–116, 116b, 118, 119b, 120t
Sheltered content-area instruction, 97–98, 272,
    278–299
Sheltered English immersion (SEI), 115–116, 116b,
    118, 119b, 120t, 121

Sheltered instruction
  content-based, 64
  criticism of, 97–98
  defined, 97
  vs. ESL, 99–100, 100t
  ESL vs., 99–100, 100t
  essential components of, 95t
  key components of, 97
  language objections in, 98, 100
  training for, 98
  variations in implementing, 98
Sheltered Instruction Observation Protocol (SIOP),
    97–98, 273, 304
Silent period, 162–163
Simultaneous bilingualism, 5
SLA. *See* Second language acquisition (SLA)
Social identity groups, power relationships among, 22
Socialization
  vs. academic language proficiency, 42–43
  teacher as agent of, 31
Social practice and discourse, 39–40
Social studies, 291–297
  defined, 291
  integrating students' cultures into, 296–297
  language for academic success in, 43b
  language of, 292–293
  made comprehensible, 293––294
  modifying of instructional materials for, 294–295,
    295f
  using literature to support, 295–296
Sociocultural perspectives on second language
    acquisition, 57–61
SOLOM-R (Student Oral Language Observation
    Matrix–Revised), 187–190, 188t, 190f
Spanglish, 58, 305
Spanish-English bilingual education, 70
Spanish language arts standards, 96
Spanish-speaking ELLs, 11–12, 11t, 12b
Speaking, 156–192
  Can Do descriptors for, 14t
  challenges of, 157
  correcting student errors in, 164–165, 166b
  oral presentations for, 179–180
  oral retellings for, 178–179
  productive talk moves for, 165–167
  promoting development in classroom of, 178–180
  research on, 158–162
  teacher talk in classroom and, 163–164, 164b
  using standards to focus instruction in, 170–173,
    171t, 174t–175t
  using theory to guide decision making on, 162–170
  vocabulary development in, 167–170
Special education considerations for English language
    learners, 2, 10t, 17–18, 18t
Specially designed academic instruction in English
    (SDAIE), 64, 97, 115–116, 116b, 118, 119b, 120t
Speech errors, correcting, 164–165, 166b
Spelling, 37–38
  alternative approaches to testing of, 240, 240b
  invented (developmental, temporary, transitional),
    240
  literacy skills in home language and, 235
  nonstandard, 263
  oral language proficiency and, 160
State-led initiatives and consortia, 82–85
State policies, 85–87
  and advocacy, 316
Strategic Education Research Partnership, 206

Strategies in sheltered instruction, 97
Structured English immersion, 115–116, 116b, 118,
    119b, 120t
Student Oral Language Observation Matrix–Revised
    (SOLOM-R), 187–190, 188t, 190f
Students with interrupted formal education, 10t
Submersion, 117–118, 119b, 120t
Subtractive bilingualism, 23, 24, 24b
Summative assessment, 127
Superdiversity, 12
Sustained silent reading (SSR), 217–218, 218b

T
Targeted support and improvement (TSI) plans, 80
TBE (transitional bilingual education), 102–104, 103f,
    103t, 104b, 120t
Teacher(s)
  as agent of socialization, 31
  classroom talking by, 163–164, 164b
  collaboration among, 121
  as educator, 31
  of English language learners, 2–3
  as evaluator, 31
  knowledge about language needed by, 33–38
  professional development opportunities for,
    315–316
  reasons to know about language for, 30–31
Teachers of English to Speakers of Other Language
    (TESOL), 45b, 278, 302–303, 303b, 304, 314
Teaching for transfer, 57
Temporary spelling, 240
TESOL (Teachers of English to Speakers of Other
    Language), 45b, 278, 302–303, 303b, 304, 314
Test(s) and testing. *See also* Assessment
  accommodations in, 135–137, 138t–139t
  vs. assessment, 126–127
  critical look and requirements for, 134–147
  defined, 126
  Joint Standards for, 134–135
  language proficiency, 141–146, 142b
Test score pollution, 131
Textbook modification
  for mathematics, 281–282
  for science, 289–290
  strategies for, 276
Text complexity, 200, 201–203
Text selection, 207
Thematic teaching, 276–278, 277f
Thematic word charts, 256
Think-Pair-Share, 182
"Third space," 21–22
Title I
  of Every Student Succeeds Act, 77–80
  of No Child Left Behind, 75–76
Title III Language Instruction for Limited English
    Proficient and Immigrant Students, 75–76
Title III of Every Student Succeeds Act, 80–82
Title VI Civil Rights Act, 89b
Title VII Bilingual Education Act (1968), 74–75
Transfer from first language to second language, 57,
    197, 198b
Transitional bilingual education (TBE), 102–104, 103f,
    103t, 104b, 120t
Translanguaging, 303–313
  benefits of, 305
  bilingualism and, 41–42, 303–304
  bilingual parents or community volunteers for, 313
  cognate word study lessons for, 309–310

Translanguaging *(continued)*
  computer software and INTERNET resources for, 313
  concurrent translation in, 305–306
  as culturally sustaining pedagogy, 304
  defined, 41–42, 303–304
  in dual language programs, 107–108
  effective programs and, 314
  heteroglossic perspective and, 94
  home language and dual language books for, 311–312
  home languages during class discussions for, 308
  home language to support writing for, 310
  initial writing in home language for, 311
  instructional wall displays for, 309
  labeling of classroom for, 308
  letters sent home in home languages for, 312
  pulling students aside to re-teach concepts for, 308
  purposes of, 99
  quick explanations during whole-class or small-group instruction for, 307
  quick explanations for individual students for, 307–308
  read-aloud books in home language for, 308, 311
  research on, 304–305
  strategies for, 61, 304, 306–313
  support for, 303–306
Translation, 134
  concurrent (direct), 305–306
  mobile apps for, 310–311
Translingual practice, 237
Transnational ELLs, 10t
Tree diagrams, 221
TSI (targeted support and improvement) plans, 80
Two-way immersion, 105–109, 107b, 107t, 109b, 120t

U
Understanding Language initiative, 201–202, 242, 273, 273b
Undocumented immigrants, 8
Uninterrupted sustained silent reading (USSR), 217–218, 218b
Universal design, 135
U.S.-born ELLs, 10t, 19, 20b
USSR. *See* uninterrupted sustained silent reading

V
Validity, 130–132
Value-added measures, 140–141
Vernaculars, 305
Vocabulary
  acquisition and use of, 32b
  interactive mini-lessons on, 222
  of mathematics, 279–280
  of science, 284, 288–289, 289f
  of social studies, 292
  in Student Oral Language Observation Matrix-Revised (SOLOM-R), 187, 188t
  tiers of, 44, 169, 205
Vocabulary development
  through listening and speaking, 167–170
  through reading, 203–206
Volunteers, community, 313

W
Washback effect of language proficiency testing, 141
Whole language, 64–65
WIDA Consortium, 4
  CAN DO descriptors of, 13, 14t
  Common Core State Standards and, 83b, 85
  on content-area instruction, 275–276
  English language development standards of, 44, 45b, 171–173, 174t
  language proficiency testing standards of, 142
  Spanish language development standards of, 96
  and Title I, 79
Word problems, in mathematics, 280
Word Study, 222
Word walls, 254–256, 255f
World language programs for native speakers, 110–112, 112b, 120t
Writing, 233–271
  academic, 237
  across curriculum, 257–258
  age and, 236
  assessment of, 264–269, 266t, 267f, 269f
  Can Do descriptors for, 14t
  checklist for, 269, 269f
  Common Core State Standards for, 241–242, 241b
  correction of, 254
  dictionaries for, 256–257
  drafting of, 253
  editing of, 253–254, 258
  emerging standardized, 239t, 251–252
  evidence-based, 242
  focus correction areas for, 258
  graphic organizers for, 247–248, 248f
  guided, 248–249, 249f
  in home language, 311
  home language to support, 310
  home–school connection in, 263–264
  independent, 250–252, 251f
  interactive, 249–250
  journal, 250–252, 251f
  keeping data on progress in, 317
  prior knowledge and, 236
  in letters representing words or thoughts, 239t
  literacy skills in home language and, 234–235
  and multiliteracies, 259
  oral language skills and, 160, 234, 235, 236f
  overview of, 233–234
  promoting development of, 243–257
  range of, 241b
  reading and, 237–238
  scaffolding for independent, 254–257, 254f
  shared, 247–248, 248f
  and spelling, 235, 240, 240b
  stages in development of, 238–240, 239t, 240b
  standardized, 239t
  translingual practice and, 237
  using English language proficiency standards to guide, 243, 244t–245t
  what we know from research on, 234–236, 236f
  word walls for, 254–256, 255f
  Writer's Workshop for, 237, 252–254

Z
Zone of proximal development (ZPD), 58–60

Companion Website

http://wright3ed.caslonpublishing.com/

The Companion Website includes the resources indicated in the book by colored text, *plus* hundreds of additional tools and resources for students, professors, and independent users.

Free registration with new book
Registration fee for users with second-hand books

1. Go to the URL http://wright3ed.caslonpublishing.com/
2. Click "Register Now."
3. Click "I Agree" to the terms.
4. Click "Yes" if you have an access code (included with purchase of a new book).
5. Click "No" and purchase an access code (if you have a used book).
6. Enter your 25-digit registration code, 5 digits in each block and click "Continue."
7. Enter your first and last name, unique username, and email address.
8. Enter your password and confirm.
9. Select "Professor/Assistant," "Student," or "Independent Learner."
10. Click "Continue."

Professor Registration

Please register before the class begins, and register each new class you teach.

- Select your university from the drop-down list.
  - If your university is not listed—add the university.
- Add your course information.
- Click "Done."

Student Registration

- Select your university from the list.
  - If the university is not listed—notify the instructor.
- Select the course from the list.
  - If the course is not listed—notify the instructor.
- Click "Done."

Independent Learner Registration

Use *only* if professor is *not* using Companion Website as part of a course.